The South Africa Reader

THE SOUTH

AFRICA

READER

HISTORY, CULTURE, POLITICS

Clifton Crais and Thomas V. McClendon, editors

DUKE UNIVERSITY PRESS   *Durham and London*   2014

© 2014 Duke University Press
All rights reserved
Printed in the United States of America on acid-free paper ∞
Typeset in Monotype Dante by BW&A Books, Inc.

Library of Congress Cataloging-in-Publication Data
The South Africa reader : history, culture, politics /
Clifton Crais and Thomas V. McClendon, eds.
pages cm— (World readers)
Includes bibliographical references and index.
ISBN 978-0-8223-5514-4 (cloth : alk. paper)
ISBN 978-0-8223-5529-8 (pbk. : alk. paper)
1. South Africa—History. 2. South Africa—Civilization.
3. South Africa—Politics and government.
I. Crais, Clifton C.
II. McClendon, Thomas V., 1954–
III. Series: World readers.
DT1719.S675 2013
968—dc23
2013018961

Dedicated to Nelson Mandela and to all those who died
in the struggle for freedom in South Africa.

Contents

A Note on Style

Throughout this volume we have tried to remain true to the tenor and meaning of the original texts. Very often we have had to substantially abridge texts, for which we offer our apologies. South Africa's linguistic history and racially divisive past has produced a combustible politics over the words that people have used to describe themselves and others. Generally, we have preserved language that today is offensive but that remains a part of the country's difficult history. In some instances we have standardized spelling and usage to avoid confusion. Where further explanation seemed absolutely necessary, we have confined this information between unobtrusive brackets, or in the occasional note. A short glossary serves as an additional guide to navigating South Africa's past and present.

Acknowledgments

We have had a great deal of help in completing this book. We are grateful to our respective institutions, Emory University and Southwestern University, and their Departments of History for material and intellectual support. Thomas McClendon received additional support from the United Methodist Board of Higher Education.

Many archivists and librarians have made our effort possible and have been a pleasure to work with. These include the staffs of the Campbell Collections of the University of KwaZulu-Natal, the Free State Archives, the Iziko Social History and Art Collections, Museum Africa, the Parliament of South Africa, and the UWC (University of the Western Cape) Robben Island Mayibuye Archives. We also appreciate the able assistance of the staff of the Woodruff Library at Emory and the Smith Library Center at Southwestern.

Several Emory graduate students have tirelessly contributed to this project. We wish to acknowledge Jessica Reuther, Kara Moskowitz, and Jane Hooper. The outstanding work of Aby Parsons and Molly McCullers was especially central to our successful completion of the book. A draft of the book was piloted in an undergraduate course at Emory University, where students offered very helpful observations.

We appreciate the generosity of many colleagues who helped us track down sources and citations. We are also grateful to the authors of some of the selections who helped us obtain permission to use their material, in some cases waiving their own share of royalties. In many cases, however, literary publishers were unwilling to work with an academic publisher, resulting in the absence of some texts we wished to include; we have included the titles of these works in the section "Suggestions for Further Reading." We are especially grateful to Patricia Hayes for contributing her thoughtful essay on the work of Santu Mofokeng, and to the photographer for allowing us to use his work. Our thanks also to Tanya Buckingham and Isaac Dorsch at the University of Wisconsin Cartography Lab for creating the maps.

Duke University Press has been an outstanding publisher to work with. We have had unstinting support from the editors of the World Readers Series, Valerie Millholland, and Gisela Fosado. The press's graduate interns,

Vanessa Doriott Anderson and Lorien Olive, have been invaluable in helping us secure permissions. We also gained important critical insights into the project from the comments of the anonymous reviewers.

Finally, we are grateful to our spouses, Pamela Scully and Nancy McClendon, and families for encouraging and supporting our work.

Abbreviations

ANC	African National Congress
AZAPO	Azanian People's Organisation
COSAS	Congress of South African Students
COSATU	Congress of South African Trade Unions
DA	Democratic Alliance
FRELIMO	Frente de Libertação de Moçambique (Front for the Liberation of Mozambique)
ICU	Industrial and Commercial Workers' Union
IFP	Inkatha Freedom Party
MK	Umkhonto we Sizwe (Spear of the Nation)
NP	National Party
NUSAS	National Union of South African Students
PAC	Pan Africanist Congress
SACP	South African Communist Party
SADF	South African Defence Force
SASO	South African Students' Organisation
SWAPO	South West Africa People's Organisation
TAC	Treatment Action Campaign
TRC	Truth and Reconciliation Commission
UDF	United Democratic Front

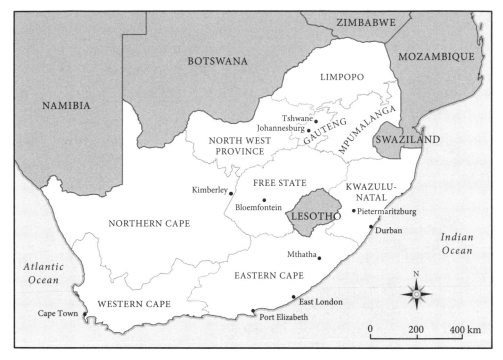

Contemporary South Africa. University of Wisconsin Cartography Lab.

Introduction

Few events in recent history have captured the world's imagination as South Africa's first democratic elections in 1994. Over the course of three days in late April, nearly twenty million people voted, most for the first time in their lives. In cities and in small villages, lines a mile long snaked to polling stations as people waited patiently to cast their votes and begin creating a democracy at Africa's southern tip. On a bright day in Pretoria a few weeks later, the newly elected president, Nelson Mandela, spoke to millions of South Africans and to the world. "We are moved by a sense of joy and exhilaration when the grass turns green and the flowers bloom," he began, recalling the country's earlier international pariah status and the deep trauma its people experienced:

> That spiritual and physical oneness we all share with this common homeland explains the depth of the pain we all carried in our hearts as we saw our country tear itself apart in a terrible conflict, and as we saw it spurned, outlawed and isolated by the peoples of the world, precisely because it has become the universal base of the pernicious ideology and practice of racism and racial oppression. We, the people of South Africa, feel fulfilled that humanity has taken us back into its bosom, that we, who were outlaws not so long ago, have today been given the rare privilege to be host to the nations of the world on our own soil. . . . We enter into a covenant that we shall build the society in which all South Africans, both black and white, will be able to walk tall, without any fear in their hearts, assured of their inalienable right to human dignity—a rainbow nation at peace with itself and the world. . . . Let freedom reign.[1]

A mere five years earlier, the country had teetered on the edge of political collapse: internationally isolated, its economy in shambles, Nelson Mandela languishing in prison, many urban townships occupied by the military amid extraordinary violence with thousands dead and more than thirty thousand arrested for political offenses, and the entire country under a state of emergency. Many believed that South Africa was inexorably heading toward civil war and bloody revolution. In the space of just a few months, however, the government unbanned the outlawed African National Congress (ANC) and other organizations and released Mandela from prison after more than twenty-seven years in captivity. Negotiations followed. Violence continued, indeed some of the worst the country ever experienced occurred in the four years leading to the elections. But somehow South Africa dismantled more than fifty years of racial laws known as apartheid ("apartness") and took tentative steps toward creating a democratic society.[2]

Two decades after the 1994 elections, much has changed. The country remains Africa's economic powerhouse, producing more electricity than the rest of the continent south of the Sahara Desert. The transition from apartheid, particularly the creation of the Truth and Reconciliation Commission in 1995, has become a model for politicians and international transitional-justice experts seeking peaceful transitions from societies that have experienced civil wars and dictatorial regimes.[3] Accepted into the broader international community, South Africa's leaders play important roles in regional and international politics. South Africa's culture, scenic beauty, and rich history attract millions of tourists annually. The works of the country's artists, writers, and musicians have garnered increasing international attention. In 2010 South Africa successfully hosted the soccer World Cup.

South Africa enjoys political stability. In addition to the ruling ANC, there is a spirited opposition party. Except for the world economic recession in 2008–9, the country has enjoyed solid annual increases in GDP. South Africa's currency remains relatively stable. The country, however, has persistently high levels of poverty and inequality. Indeed, South Africa may be the most unequal society in the world.[4] While a notable black elite rapidly emerged after 1994, whites still maintain a very high level of income compared to the vast majority of South Africans, who face stubbornly high rates of unemployment and shortages of housing and access to adequate education and medical care, in addition to a severe HIV/AIDS crisis. Nearly six million people are HIV positive, approximately 12 percent of South Africa's population of forty-eight million. The official unemployment rate is at least 25 percent. There are very high levels of sexual violence, with upward of five hundred thousand women raped yearly. Racial and ethnic relations remain tense, and the politics of identity volatile. Xenophobia has led to outbreaks of bloodshed, notably the deaths of more than sixty people in May 2008. There have been many worrisome incidents of corruption and theft of public resources, including charges of corruption as well as rape against the country's current president, Jacob Zuma. Many of the world's most pressing problems—from poverty and inequality to gender and race relations—reside in one of its most beautiful lands.[5]

South Africa, with its fraught, contentious society and a public culture of near constant spectacle and debate, has long captured the fascination of foreigners. It is home to exotic flora and fauna. The Western Cape alone contains more than eight thousand species of plants. Some of our earliest ancestors lived in South Africa; scientists continue to unearth important material from archaeological sites across the country. South Africa's natural history powerfully shaped the study of evolution and human ancestry, influencing thinkers such as Carl Linnaeus, Georges Cuvier, and Charles Darwin. In the seventeenth century, Europeans settled in a region with a Mediterranean climate around what is today Cape Town because of its strategic location as the maritime gateway between the Atlantic and Indian Oceans. There Europeans established a slaveholding society. The discovery in the nineteenth century of what was then the world's largest supply of diamonds and gold attracted investors and brought immigrants and laborers from countries such as England, Russia, and India, as well as from across the wider region of southern Africa.

It is South Africa's extraordinarily complex modern history of inequality and race relations and the political movements this history has spawned that has engrossed the attentions of the country's own peoples and riveted the outside world. Beginning in the 1950s, the National Party government instituted a massive experiment in social engineering that came to be known as apartheid. Every level of society came to be ordered around race and ethnicity, from sexuality, housing, and education to the very territorial organization of the country. The government destroyed entire neighborhoods, forcing black residents into new townships, such as Soweto (which means Southwest Townships). Tens of millions of people found themselves caught in a web of legislation that controlled where they could live, work, and be educated. Beginning in the 1960s, the government forcibly removed more than three million people to one of the so-called homelands (Bantustans), invariably impoverished areas of the country designated on the basis of tribal affiliation. Apartheid defined blacks as "temporary sojourners" in "white" South Africa, though whites were never more than 20 percent of the population.[6]

"Petty apartheid" concerned racially discriminatory laws that gave whites privileged access to housing, beaches, schools, and public facilities such as toilets, as well as to certain jobs. People whom the government defined as black or Bantu suffered the worst. Other groups, such as Indians and Coloureds (people of mixed-race descent), also endured discrimination. Petty apartheid bears similarity to racial legislation found in many other areas of the world, particularly the southern United States in the era of Jim Crow. Grand apartheid or "separate development" meant something else altogether, a set of policies aimed at depriving black people of citizenship within the republic and the creation of ten separate Bantustans. These were meant to become ostensibly self-governing, independent states. The policy failed miserably, though, at massive human cost.

Apartheid grew out of an earlier era of discriminatory legislation rooted in white settlement and imperial conquest. For much of its modern history, many South Africans were also colonial subjects within the British Empire. This complicated history—of disenfranchised racially persecuted citizens, exploited workers, colonized peoples, and a small group of highly privileged elites—spawned kaleidoscopic political movements: anticolonial revolts, passive-resistance campaigns, labor struggles, nationalist movements, and armed resistance, to name just a few. Scholars, politicians, and the general public continue debating the meaning and content of the antiapartheid struggle, since it contained aspects of decolonization and nationalism, the quest for civil rights, and the demands of exploited workers.[7]

South Africa is remarkably diverse, its modern history one of trauma and resilience. In Johannesburg or Cape Town one can hear the nation's eleven spoken languages; meet millionaires while many people beg in the street; pray at a church, mosque, or Hindu shrine; or seek the help of a traditional healer (*sangoma*). The very definition of what it means to be South African is debated in newspapers, on television, and on the street. South Africans are fiercely nationalistic, but the lineaments of their history remain enormously contested. There is very little consensus on the most basic aspects of a past that they share but that tears them apart.[8]

The South Africa Reader brings together in a single volume a wealth of materials that offer entry into the past and present of this complex, conflicted, cacophonous society. Taken as a whole, the selections eschew any single argument. Instead, they show the remarkable diversity of South Africa and the ways its people have shaped the country's development. The selections offer the reader the opportunity to listen in, as it were, to people debating their present and past and imagining what the future might be.

In political terms, South Africa is a young country, barely a century old. Its origins lie in the fiercest and costliest colonial conflict of the imperial age, the South African (Anglo-Boer) War of 1899–1902. In 1910, what had been two British colonies, two Boer republics, and a number of recently conquered African territories became the Union of South Africa; in 1961 it became the Republic of South Africa. Even the territorial limits of South Africa were subject to debate. At different points in the twentieth century, politicians discussed incorporating Bechuanaland (Botswana), Basutoland (Lesotho), Southern Rhodesia (Zimbabwe), and South-West Africa (Namibia) into the union. Any of these developments would have profoundly altered the course of modern South African history.

Acknowledging the country's diversity is essential for developing a deeper appreciation of its history, culture, and politics. Large areas of South Africa were similar to other parts of British colonial Africa. There officials governed African communities, whose people spoke one of a number of Bantu languages, through a system of "indirect rule" and customary law administered by chiefs and headmen. These conquered territories became native reserves and, in the apartheid era under the policies of separate development, the Bantustans. Ethnicities such as Xhosa, Zulu, Pedi, and Tswana, as well as contemporary debates over the role of "traditional rulers," are a direct result of this history.[9]

The Western Cape could not be more different. In the precolonial era, this region was settled by Khoesan-speaking peoples who lived by herding cattle and sheep or by hunting and gathering. Europeans typically referred to these groups as either the Hottentots or the Bushmen, derogatory terms that also failed to appreciate the rich histories of both groups. The salubrious environment and strategic position of Cape Town led to the formation of a small colony founded by the Dutch East India Company in the middle years of the seventeenth century. Colonial agriculture controlled by settlers, or *boers* (farmers), would come to depend on imported slaves, many of them from diverse areas across the Indian Ocean and as far away as Indonesia. The colony's labor force would also include subjugated Khoesan peoples. Out of this mixture of people would emerge new ethnicities, particularly the Afrikaners (defined as white) and the Coloureds (at times referred to as "Brown Afrikaners"), who spoke a Dutch patois later known as Afrikaans.[10]

Beginning in the late 1700s and accelerating in the nineteenth century, South Africa fell within the orbit of British imperialism. In the interior, the discovery of diamonds in 1867 and the world's largest supply of gold in the 1880s led to a rapid industrial revolution as well as to conflict among Africans, Britons, and Boers. The transformation of South Africa's economy from one dependent largely on agricultural produce to the mining of precious minerals and secondary manufacturing had profound implications for the country's history: the rise of industrial cities like Johannesburg, the making of a massive black working class, and the emergence of vibrant cultural styles, to name just a few.

One can write the history of twentieth-century South Africa through its racially discriminatory laws that controlled everything from race and sexuality to employment. But South Africa was always more than oppressive legislation. It was an exuberant society of township culture, religious change, and political life with consequences for the rest of the continent and the world. The themes explored in the selections allow readers to enter into discussion and debate on South Africa's obstreperous past and contentious present—of oppressed and oppressor, white and black, women and men, histories shaped by forces inside and outside the country. *The South Africa Reader* does not attempt to offer a totalizing view of the country, nor a mere grab bag of original texts. It seeks rather to show the interaction of peoples and the intersection of forces that, combined, have shaped South Africa's development.

This anthology comes at an important moment. Municipal elections in May 2011 saw a small but significant decline in support for the ruling ANC and a surprising increase for the Democratic Alliance, a party historically associated with white liberals. South Africans have begun expressing increasing discontent with the ANC, the organization long associated with the struggle against oppression and with bringing democracy to the country. The ANC's "tripartite" alliance with trade unions and the Communist Party remains tenuous. More generally, the tumultuous years of struggle, repression, and democratic change have begun the transition from present politics to recent history. South Africans are beginning to develop new perspectives on their modern past. And they are continuing historic conversations with themselves and others about South Africa's place in the world. *The South Africa Reader* is produced to join in with these ongoing conversations.

The book contains eight parts, beginning with African stories of the past. Throughout *The South Africa Reader*, the politics of the past and the emergence of various groups are central themes, whether the recalled memory of a once indentured worker in the nineteenth century, the complaints of a *trekboer* (migratory cattle rancher) heading into South Africa's interior, or a widow's testimony before the Truth and Reconciliation Commission. Parts II and III examine South Africa's history from the seventeenth century to the development of slavery and the expansion of European empire, in addition to the emergence of new forms of identity and ways of understanding the world. Parts IV and V take up South Africa's economic and political revolutions, the rapid emergence of a labor-hungry industrial economy, and the consolidation of white domination. The final three parts are dedicated to South Africa after 1948, when the National Party took control of the state and began introducing its policies of apartheid. These parts chart the often violent confrontations between the government and black South Africans, but they continue themes introduced in earlier parts, such as religion, the politics of ethnicity, and the creation of vibrant cultural styles. Part VIII, exploring the tentative creation of a postapartheid society, is intended to provoke discussion about the "new" South Africa.

South Africa is a terminological nightmare. Many of the selections deploy terms and contain ideas that readers will find offensive. The words people have used to describe themselves and others have had the most profound consequences. Many historical terms today are repugnant, such as *Kaffir* and *Hottentot*, and have been abandoned in contemporary official usage. *Kaffir*, for example, began as a term to refer to the Xhosa people and became a generalized epithet applied to all Africans. Other terms remain fraught and publicly contested. South Africans argue over the terms *white* and *black*. When an Afrikaner identity first arose is still debated, although the Afrikaans language was codified along with the formation of a political party in the late nineteenth century. *Boer*, which means "farmer," has recently become tinged with racist overtones. *Coloured* emerged as a formal category after the ending of slavery in the context of British attempts to describe people of mixed racial descent involving the Khoesan, Europeans, and Asian and African slaves. There continues to be wide disagreement as to whether this term should be cast into the historical dustbin, an unfortunate relic of South Africa's racist past, or whether it can be reclaimed for a different future. These debates form part of wider and ongoing conversations that South Africans have about who they are and how they see themselves in the modern world.

Notes

1. "Statement of Nelson Mandela at his Inauguration as President," May 10, 1994, accessed April 10, 2013, www.anc.org.za/show.php?id=3132.
2. For an overview of the transition see Allister Sparks, *Tomorrow Is Another Country: The Inside Story of South Africa's Road to Change* (Chicago: University of Chicago Press, 1996).
3. See Catherine M. Cole, *Performing South Africa's Truth Commission* (Bloomington: Indiana University Press, 2009).
4. Clifton Crais, *Poverty, War, and Violence in South Africa* (New York: Cambridge University Press, 2011).
5. For a scholarly introduction to South Africa's history, see Carolyn Hamilton, Bernard K. Mbenga, and Robert Ross, eds., *The Cambridge History of South Africa*, vol. 1 (New York: Cambridge University Press, 2010); and Robert Ross, Anne Kelk Mager, and Bill Nasson, eds., *The Cambridge History of South Africa*, vol. 2 (New York: Cambridge University Press, 2011).

6. Nancy L. Clark and William H. Worger, *South Africa: The Rise and Fall of Apartheid* (New York: Pearson Longman, 2004).

7. Tom Lodge, *Black Politics in South Africa since 1945* (London: Longman Group, 1983).

8. See, for example, Adam Ashforth, *Witchcraft, Violence, and Democracy in South Africa* (Chicago: University of Chicago Press, 2005).

9. Clifton Crais, *The Politics of Evil: Magic, State Power and the Political Imagination in South Africa* (New York: Cambridge University Press, 2009); and Thomas V. McClendon, *White Chief, Black Lords: Shepstone and the Colonial State in Natal, South Africa, 1845–1878* (Rochester, N.Y.: University of Rochester Press, 2010).

10. On South Africa's connection to the Indian Ocean World, see Kerry Ward, *Networks of Empire: Forced Migration in the Dutch East India Company* (New York: Cambridge University Press, 2012). See also Richard Elphick and Hermann Giliomee, eds., *The Shaping of South African Society, 1652–1840* (Middletown, Conn.: Wesleyan University Press, 1989).

I

African Worlds, African Voices

Determining when South African history "began" has long been a controversial subject in the country's public culture. Until about fifty years ago, nearly all white South Africans rejected the idea that indigenous peoples had a history. They believed that South African history began with European settlement in the seventeenth century. The popular term *Bushman*, typically used by colonists to describe hunter-gatherers, suggested a people without culture or history, people who lived in nature. One definition for *Hottentot*, another racial epithet referring to pastoralist peoples of the Cape, means to "become or live as a person without civilization or culture." The words defining people profoundly shaped South Africa's history. They remain important to how people understand themselves and others, and the terms have broader ramifications, ranging from the organization of museum displays to land rights and the outcomes of elections.

Before about two thousand years ago, people in southern Africa lived in small communities and survived by hunting and gathering. They spoke what is today known as Khoesan, a family of languages that foreigners found distinctive because of its "clicks." Linguists speculate that human language may have begun in southern Africa, and that Khoesan is humanity's most ancient extant tongue. Hunter-gatherers left exquisite rock paintings depicting the world around them as well as magical creatures and trance dancing. In some areas, rock painting continued well into the nineteenth century. These paintings eventually became a way of telling the history of colonial conquest and settlement.

Much of our knowledge of the distant past rests on the work of archaeologists. They have documented the development and spread of cattle and sheep rearing from what is today Botswana. By about two thousand years ago, herding had spread into the southwestern Cape. The communities that herding supported are associated with the Khoekhoe, though people typically had multiple ways of referring to themselves and others. Herders shared with hunter-gatherers the same general language and cosmology. In the colonial era, independent hunting and herding communities disappeared as the result of violence and disease; most of their descendants were absorbed into the Coloured population.

In the eastern and generally less arid parts of South Africa, people lived by farming sorghums and millets and herding cattle. The spread of these forms of livelihood is associated with peoples who spoke Bantu languages. Many also practiced iron making, so that archaeologists use the terms *early* and *late* Iron Age to depict these technological developments. Farming had spread south of the Limpopo River by the third century of the Common Era, roughly eighteen hundred years ago. By about 1300 CE, farmers reached the southernmost limits of agriculture, due to rainfall patterns, in the area near the contemporary city of East London. People living in these communities typically traced descent through the male line and organized political life around hereditary chiefs.

Colonial rule, and particularly apartheid, rested on the assumption that people existed as discrete racial and tribal groups. One was black or white, a Zulu or an Afrikaner. In fact, the South African past is marked by heterogeneity and cultural diversity. Most societies, for example, were multilinguistic. Communities frequently had people from various backgrounds, including outsiders. The Xhosa language owes its clicks to interaction with the neighboring Khoesan herders and hunter-gatherers. Bantu-speaking men often married Khoesan women. As agriculturalists, they recognized hunter-gatherers as the "original people" and depended on their ritual knowledge for ensuring plentiful rains.

In a country so profoundly shaped by race and ethnicity, the politics and history of identity remain fraught topics. South Africans have yet to develop ways of discussing their pasts that do not rest on racial and ethnic stereotypes. There is the temptation to see ancient histories in contemporary ethnic identities and political institutions, smoothing away or in some cases erasing far more complicated histories. South African society remains rife with racial and ethnic tension. Claims to the past using group identities had, and continue to have, material consequences, including the distribution of state resources.

The selections that follow invite the reader into this difficult and contested terrain. The readings are not statements of how things "were." In each case, the powerful invention of ethnicity that unfolded across South Africa during the nineteenth and early twentieth centuries, which we cover in part III of the *Reader*, shaped the author's understanding of the world. They are cultural texts about identity and worldviews. In these stories we learn of Khoesan beliefs and colonial oppression; Nguni ideas about God, ancestors, and the early history of the Zulu Kingdom; and African intellectuals interpreting South Africa's rich oral traditions for a new generation.

"A Story Is Like the Wind" and
"The Sun Is Thrown into the Sky"

//Kabbo

Little is known about //Kabbo, which means "dream" in the Khoesan language. He was likely born in the late 1810s on the flat arid lands of the Northern Cape near the small city of Upington. Wild game was depleted and his family was starving, so //Kabbo turned his hunter's prowess to a white settler's sheep. Arrested with other so-called Bushmen rustlers, //Kabbo spent part of his sentence at Breakwater Station prison in Cape Town, an area now developed into the trendy Waterfront district. Released in 1871, //Kabbo moved to The Hill, the home of Wilhelm Bleek in the Cape Town suburb of Mowbray. A remarkable German linguist, Bleek served as the curator of a rich ethnographic collection in the South African Public Library. Over the course of more than two decades, Bleek and his sister-in-law, Lucy Lloyd, interviewed, translated, and transcribed the stories and collected the pictorial representations of people often represented as the Bushmen or the San (//Xam). The archive they produced is the single most important source of information on the San, most of whose communities were subjugated over the course of the eighteenth century. Many San were simply hunted down and shot. Others, particularly children, became laborers on white farms. Only a few semi-independent San existed by the late nineteenth century, including //Kabbo's people in the Northern Cape.

In "A Story Is Like the Wind," //Kabbo recounts his capture and prison experience and his longing for home. He describes the beginning of the world in "The Sun Is Thrown into the Sky." These are among South Africa's earliest recorded African stories.

A Story Is Like the Wind

My wife was there, I was there, my son was there; my son's wife was there, carrying a little child on her back; my daughter was there, also carrying a little child; and my daughter's husband was there. We were like this in number. . . . The . . . African policemen took us when we were like this, while we were not numerous. . . .

I was eating a springbok [a small antelope] when [the policeman] took me; he bound my arms. My son and I, together with my daughter's husband, were put into the wagon while the wagon stood still. We went away, bound, to the magistrate. We who were in the wagon ran along swiftly upon the road while our wives walked along upon their feet. We ran, leaving them; we altogether ran, leaving them behind.

We went to talk with the magistrate. . . . We had to put our legs into the stocks; another white man laid a piece of wood upon our legs. We slept, stretched out in the stocks. The day broke, while our legs were in the stocks. Early, we took our legs out of the stocks to eat meat; then we again put our legs into the stocks; we sat, while our legs were in the stocks. We lay down, we slept, while our legs were inside the stocks. . . .

The magistrate came to take our legs out of the stocks, because he wished that we might sit comfortably while we ate; for it was his sheep that we were eating. The Korannas [also prisoners] came to join us. They also came to put their legs into the stocks; they slept while their legs were in the stocks. . . . We left that place and went to Victoria [Victoria West, seat of the local magistracy]. On the way, we ate sheep. Our wives ate their sheep on the way too, as they came with us to Victoria. We came to Victoria to roll stones, as we worked on the road. We lifted stones with our chests. We rolled great stones. We carried earth with a big handbarrow that needed many Bushmen to lift it. We loaded the wagon with earth and we pushed it. Other people—Bushmen people—walked along with us. We were pushing the wagon's wheels; we were pushing. We poured the earth down and we pushed it back. . . .

We again had our arms bound to the wagon chain; we walked along to Beaufort, fastened to the wagon, under the hot sun. Our arms were set free on the road. We got tobacco from the magistrate; we smoked it in a pipe of sheep's bones as we went along. We came into Beaufort jail. The rain fell upon us while we were there. Early the next morning, our arms were made fast and we were bound again. We splashed into the water; we splashed, passing through the water in the riverbed. We walked upon the road. We walked, following behind the wagon until, still bound, we came to the Breakwater [a prison in Cape Town]. . . .

I sit waiting for the moon to turn back for me, so that I may return to my place; so that I may listen to all the people's stories when I visit them, . . . stories from their own place and other places too. These are the stories which they tell while the sun grows warm. I want to return to my place so

Koranna Hottentots preparing to move. Aquatint by Samuel Daniell. Courtesy of Free State Archives Photographic Collection, VA4136.

that I may sit in the warm sun listening to the stories which come from a distance. . . . I shall get hold of a story from yonder, because the stories float out from a distance, while the sun is a little warm. I feel that I must visit there, so that I can talk with my fellow men. . . . My fellow men are those who listen to stories which float along from afar; they listen to stories from other places. But I am here; I do not obtain stories because I do not visit, I do not hear the stories which float along. I feel that the people of another place are here; they do not possess my stories. They do not talk my language. . . .

I am waiting for the moon to turn back for me, so that I may set my feet forward on the path. I only await the moon; then, I will tell my Master that this is the time when I should be sitting among my fellow men, those who walking meet their like. I ought to visit; I ought to talk with my fellow men; for I work here together with women; I do not talk with them, for they merely send me to work.

I must first sit a little, cooling my arms so that the fatigue may go out of them. I must merely sit and listen, watching for a story that I want to hear, waiting for it to float into my ear. Those are the people's stories to which I will listen with all my ears, while I sit silent. I must wait, listening behind me along the road, where my name floats; my three names (Jantje, /Uhi-ddoro and //Kabbo) float behind me along the road to my place. I will go and sit down there and, listening, I will turn my ears backwards to where my feet's heels have stepped, and wait for a story to travel to me along the road. For a story is like the wind. It is wont to float along to another place. In this way, our names pass through to the people of that place, even though they do not perceive our bodies going along. For our names are those which, floating, reach a different place. . . .

[//Kabbo] only awaits the return of the moon. He waits for the moon to go around, so that he may return home, so that he may examine the water pits, those at which he drank. He will work, putting the old hut in order, gathering his children together, so that they may work, putting the water in order for him; for he went away, leaving the place, while strangers were those who walked there. . . .

And so I must sit waiting for the Sundays to pass that I remain here, on which I continue to teach you. I will not wait again for another moon; for this moon is the one about which I told you. . . . I desire that it should do as I have said and return for me. For I have sat waiting for the promised boots, that I must put on to walk in, which are strong for the road. For the sun will go along above me, burning strongly. And the earth will become hot, while I am still only halfway. I must go together with the warm sun, while the ground is hot. For a little road it is not; it is a great road and it is long. I should reach my place when the trees are dry. . . . I shall walk there, letting the flowers become dry while I still follow the path. . . .

The Sun Is Thrown into the Sky

The First Bushmen, the men of the Early Race[,] . . . were those who first inhabited the earth. Their children were the ones who worked with the Sun. The people who came later say that it was those children who made the Sun ascend, for their mothers had told them that they should throw the Sun-person up into the sky, so that he might warm the earth for them; so that they might sit in the Sun and feel its warmth. Until that time, the Sun was a man who lived on earth. In the beginning, he gave forth brightness only in the space around his own dwelling. The rest of the country remained very cloudy, as it looks now when the Sun is behind thick clouds. The sky was dark and black. The shining came from one of the Sun's armpits, as he lay asleep with his arm lifted up. When he put down his arm, darkness fell everywhere; when he lifted his arm up again, it was as if day had come. In the day, the Sun's light used to be white, but at night, it was red, like a fire.

The children of the Early Race gently approached the Sun-armpit to lift him up while he lay sleeping. Their mothers had spoken to them and told them to do this. An old woman was the one who had instructed them. She herself had no young male children, so she spoke to the children's mothers. For she saw that these were clever children, who would understand nicely what to do when they went to that old man, Sun-armpit. The old woman spoke to the children through their mothers, telling them to tell their children that they should throw the Sun-armpit up into the sky, so that the Bushman rice [a gathered food source] might become dry for them. So that while the Sun moved along across the whole sky, it would make all places bright. This is what the mothers said:

"O children! You must wait till the Sun-armpit lies down to sleep. Then, you must gently approach him while he lies asleep. Take hold of him all together, and lift him up so that you can throw him into the sky."

This is what the old woman had told the mothers to say to their children. The children came and the children went away again. The old woman said:

"You must sit down and wait. You must look to see whether the Sun's eyes are still open or whether he sleeps. You must go and sit down and wait for him to fall asleep."

And so the children sat down and waited, as they had been told to do. The Sun lay down; he lifted up his elbow. His armpit shone upon the ground as he lay sleeping. The children took hold of him and threw him up into the sky the way they had been instructed to do. The old woman had said:

"O children going yonder! You must talk to the Sun when you throw him up. You must tell him that he must altogether become the Sun, so that he can go forward as the proper Sun—the Sun which is hot, which stays hot in the sky as he moves along high above us; so that as his heat shines down, the Bushman rice can become dry."

This was the old woman's message to the children, the old woman whose head was white. And so, when the time was right, the children arose and stealthily approached the Sun. They all took hold of him together and lifted him up while he was still hot and threw him up into the sky.

Then the children returned to their mothers. One of them said: "I and my younger brothers and their friends and their friends' brothers all took hold of him. I told them: 'You must grasp him firmly—grasp the old man firmly, and throw him up.'"

Another youth spoke and said: "O my grandmother! We threw the Sun up, we told him that he should properly become the Sun, which is hot, for we are cold. We said: 'O my grandfather Sun-armpit! Remain in your place in the sky. Become the sun that is hot, so that the Bushman rice may dry for us. Make the whole earth light, give heat, so that the whole earth may become warm in the summer. Shine properly, taking away the darkness; you must come, so that the darkness will go away.'"

And so it is thus. The Sun comes, and the darkness goes away; the Sun sets [and] the darkness returns and the Moon comes out. The day breaks, the Sun comes out again and the darkness goes away as the Sun moves across the sky. At night, the Moon comes out to brighten the darkness; the darkness departs. The Moon shines, making bright the darkness as it goes along. The Moon sets; the Sun follows it, driving away the darkness. The Sun takes away the Moon. As the Moon stands in the sky, the Sun pierces it with the Sun's knife, and the Moon decays away because of what the Sun does with its stabbing rays. Therefore, the Moon pleads with the Sun, saying: "O Sun! Leave for my children at least the backbone!"

And so the Sun does this. It promises to leave the Moon's backbone for the Moon's children. And so the Moon goes painfully away. Painfully, he returns home, moving along the sky. The Sun desists from cutting him further. For the sake of the Moon's children, he leaves the Moon's backbone behind. Because of this, the Moon again goes on to become another Moon, which is whole again. He lives again, even though it seemed as if he had died. He becomes a new Moon. He again puts on a stomach; he becomes large. . . . He feels that he is a shoe, therefore he walks in the night. . . .

The Sun is here and all the earth is bright. The Sun is here, and the people walk about while the place is light. They perceive the bushes, they see the other people, and the meat which they are eating, and the springbok. They hunt the springbok in summer, and also the ostrich, while the Sun shines down on them. They shoot the springbok, they steal up on the gemsbok and the kudu, while the Sun makes the whole place bright for them. They also visit each other, while the Sun shines upon the path. They travel in summer, hunt in summer, spy the springbok in summer; they go round to head off the springbok and lie down in a little house of bushes, while the springbok come.

On God and Ancestors

Ndukwana ka Mbenwana

James Stuart (1868–1942) was born in the British colony of Natal. As a young man, he became fluent in Zulu and served in the Native Affairs Department as an interpreter before becoming a magistrate and later assistant secretary for native affairs. In the 1890s and early 1900s, Stuart interviewed large numbers of elderly Zulu informants about their memories and traditions concerning the early history of the Zulu Kingdom and surrounding areas. He recorded their words as accurately as possible and his notes have been preserved. (Italics are from The James Stuart Archive *and indicate material originally written down in Zulu.)*

*Ndukwana ka Mbenwana, interviewed repeatedly between 1897 and 1903, was an employee of James Stuart and was one of his most productive informants. Ndukwana was born in the Zulu Kingdom in the 1830s. In the following document, from an interview in 1900, Ndukwana discusses some of the central religious concepts among Zulu-speaking (and by extension other southern African) peoples, including terms for the creator god and the importance of ancestral spirits (*amadhlozi*). God, Mvelinqangi, created all things but was a remote figure, not one with whom people were in communication (unlike Jesus and the God of Christianity). Ancestral spirits, on the other hand, were an active presence in people's lives. Instances of misfortune or illness led people to consult diviners, who specified appropriate propitiation for the ancestors, often in the form of sacrificing an animal. Ndukwana further instructs us that ancestors, including the ancestors of departed kings, sometimes appeared in homesteads (kraals, or family compounds) in the form of snakes. In the last part of the excerpt, Ndukwana relates a story of a fight between two large snakes, identified as the founding Zulu king, Shaka, and his brother and assassin, Dingane. The snake fight relates the historical event of Dingane's murder of Shaka in 1828.*

We say *that all things were created (datshulwa) by Mvelinqangi* ["first to appear," a Zulu term for the deity]. We however do not know for certain. *Mvelinqangi is a personality. No one knows where he lives.* It is merely an *expression (isiga), this, of saying, "Mvelinqangi created all things"*—a common saying or proverb. *All* say he *did the creating.* There is nothing understood among the

Zulus about *Mvelinqangi* living in the sky, on or in the earth, or anywhere. Nothing is declared of him but that he created all things. It is not known who created him. Only today (recently) do we hear of an *inkosi* [lord], that he lives in heaven, and that his name is Jesus. There was no definiteness about our knowledge of *Mvelinqangi*. We never used to apply the word *Nkulunkulu* [another Zulu term for God] to the creator; that has been imported by missionaries and *kolwas* [African Christians].

We believe in the existence of *amadhlozi*; we *accept* them. *People before us believed in the existence of amadhlozi*. We become assured of the existence of *amadhlozi* in this way. Some person may suddenly be overtaken by a serious illness, *and he would become unconscious*. His friends or relations would then go off to *izinyanga* [doctors, diviners]. He (the *innyanga*) [doctor, diviner] would say, *"The idhlozi wants something to eat."* *Indeed*, says Ndukwana, *that is how we see that the idhlozi* [ancestral spirit] *exists*, for soon after people had left to consult the doctor, the invalid would be found to have come to again. The doctors *(those consulted)* would say who the *idhlozi* was. The consulters would come back and find the sick person sitting up and eating food. Some doctors would say, *"They want such-and-such a beast,"* specifying as they spoke the precise colour of the beast in the kraal. This is the evidence which creates or brings about conviction as to the existence of *amadhlozi*. When consulters return from the doctor they *address the idhlozi; they give praise to it with a beast* etc. A person getting a sudden and alarming seizure would be splashed with water on his eyes, also on and about the head; if such treatment was not successful in restoring him, men would go and consult a doctor. It frequently occurs that after the consulters have been away such time as would admit of their reaching the doctor, the invalid would *recover consciousness* and *sit up*, which events would coincide in time with the naming of the *idhlozi* by the doctor. The naming might be particular, or somewhat indefinite. The actual name might be given, or the *idhlozi* might be said to be simply the sick man's "father" or "mother" or "grandfather" or "grandmother" etc.

The *idhlozi* is what *gives a man his vital force (hambisa's umuntu)*. The reality of the existence of *amadhlozi* is perceived when a sudden severe illness overtakes a person. . . .

These snakes are known among us; they visit the kraals, and people will know by sight who such-and-such a snake is. That is to say, *amadhlozi* are these snakes—not every snake but particular ones. The *mhlwazi* snake, *a snake of the veld* [grassland]—*if you keep a look-out you may see it*—is an *idhlozi* snake. It does not bite, though it looks as if it would do so. An *idhlozi* does not bite a man; if it came along and a person sat still it might even pass right over his foot. *The large snakes are easily seen.* These are the departed *kings*. One sees them accompanied by other snakes, of a smaller description and which are understood by natives to be *izinceku* or servants of the large one. . . .

People believe that when a person dies a snake at once appears which is the deceased's *idhlozi*. The body may be buried but the snake remains. The great *amadhlozi* were always known by sight. Tshaka's [Shaka, the founding Zulu king] *idhlozi* for instance was known; people would say, *"That is Tshaka!".* . .

A remarkable incident in connection with *the great amadhlozi* occurred during [the Zulu king] Mpande's reign, of which Ndukwana speaks from personal knowledge. Two *snakes* came to Nodwengu and there fought. These two snakes were "Tshaka" and "Dingana" [Dingane, Shaka's brother, assassin, and successor, who ruled immediately before Mpande], i.e. those kings' *amadhlozi*. "Tshaka" was *overcome* by "Dingana." Mpande then said the men of Nodwengu were to *arm and kill "uDingana,"* for, it was said, *"Here is the evil-doer who killed the king."* The snake was accordingly hunted by the regiments all about the *fence*, its retreat cut off here then there, until at last it was killed. It was not killed with sticks, straight or knobbed, but with assegais [spears], for no one would dare to use a stick, no one dared approach it too closely, not for fear of being bitten, but out of respect. These great snakes were *treated with great respect.* "Dingana" (snake) was then taken away to a spot below the present wagon-drift on the White Umfolozi and there burnt. . . . [I]n spite of this killing and burning of "Dingana," "Dingana" still exists in the same form as before, i.e. as an *idhlozi*. "Do *amadhlozi* ever die?" he asks doubtingly. "Tshaka" was not actually killed; though *overcome* by "Dingana," the snake got away. People saw that Dingana yet again was bent on killing the *king*. . . . Cattle were provided, *addressing of the amadhlozi* was done, and they were *praised*, and cattle slaughtered and consumed.

The Black People and Whence They Came

Magema M. Fuze

Magema Fuze, born circa 1840, was a kholwa *(African Christian) and close associate of Natal's liberal Anglican bishop John William Colenso. As a boy, Fuze learned to read and write under the tutelage of Colenso's Zulu confidant, William Ngidi, and went on to work in Colenso's missionary endeavors as a printer. Fuze wrote* The Black People and Whence They Came *in the early years of the twentieth century and published it in 1922. It was the first book-length work in Zulu by an indigenous author.*

Fuze's book includes an account of the birth of Shaka and his role as the founding king of the Zulu Kingdom. Like many traditional accounts, including those given by Stuart's informants, Fuze's version emphasizes that Shaka rose from obscurity and became a powerful conquering king. More recent interpretations suggest that the early Zulu Kingdom was more defensive than expansionist. Scholars also argue that various black and white oral and written traditions have intertwined since the time of Shaka to emphasize either his creative political and military abilities to bring diverse peoples together under one state or his destructive nature as a devastating conqueror. Fuze's narrative contains both these strains, but it stresses Shaka's creativity and military prowess. Fuze sees Shaka as a warrior king whose exploits brought people together into a new, stronger nation and so casts him as an ancestor of modern African nationalism.

The advent of Shaka was as follows. His father, Senzangakhona, used to herd cattle along with the other boys of his age, and it was the custom in those times for all boys of the same age-group [*intanga*] to come together to be circumcised in the several localities to which they belonged. And there was a place where Senzangakhona used to stay with the boys of his locality [*isigodi*], to which food was sent from their homes; and there was a clump of bushes where they used to stay and where they ate their meals.

One day there passed by a man of the Langeni clan . . . searching for food [*thekela*, or to visit neighbors for food in time of scarcity]. The Prince

[Senzangakhona] and his small group of boys were eating at the time. The man was hungry, and when the Prince saw that he was hungry, he called him, and when he came forward, he saluted the Prince. He [Senzangakhona] then asked him where he came from and where was his home, and the man told him that he was one of Mbhengi of Nguga whereupon he gave instructions for him to be given food, and so he was given food, and he ate until he was satisfied. . . .

When [Mbhengi] had finished his meal, the man took the path and went home. On arrival there he soon made the matter known to the girls and to everybody, telling them that he had met the Prince [*umNtwana*, or royal child] of the Zulu chief by whom he was saved from starvation. . . .

When the girls heard all this, they became enamoured of that Prince. . . . And then their princess [*inkosazana*, or the chief's daughter], Nandi, said to that man, "What about our going with you, for you to show us that Prince of the Zulu people who is so good?" The man agreed. And those girls . . . then went with that man and eventually arrived at that clump of bushes. And then the man went and sat down near the bushes where the Prince and his boy companions were sitting. They saw the girls, and they [the girls] were summoned. . . . Then they were asked where they came from and whither they were going. Their princess, Nandi, replied and said she had come to see the son of the chief. She was then questioned as to why she wished to see him. She said she had come to see him because she loved him, and she wanted him to make love [*soma*, or premarital, nonpenetrative sex] to her. All the girls were then invited to come forward, which they did, and stood in a line. And then the Prince saw Nandi, the princess of Mbhengi of Nguga. And indeed they came together right there, as desired by the princess. And what do you know? It was right there that the princess got pregnant.

For a time it was concealed that the princess was pregnant, but eventually it became apparent. . . . Messages were sent to those in high places in the Zulu clan. And then it was that Mudli . . . began asking his brother, Senzangakhona, whether he knew anything of this matter [in which it was alleged] that Nandi, the princess and daughter of Mbhengi of Nguga, was pregnant by him? It seems that Senzangakhona at first tried to deny it, for shame and for fear of his brother, but finally admitted it.

And so it came about that the days passed until eventually Nandi gave birth to a son, Shaka, at her home in the Langeni clan. The child stayed in the home of its mother, where it was well treated and nourished until it grew up.

When the child had grown up to the age when he was able to herd cattle with the son of the Langeni chief, he [Shaka] was in the habit of tormenting him when they were playing with toy cattle made out of stones. . . .

When the mother of Nandi heard this, she also became worried, hearing all the people in the home speaking critically of her daughter's child, saying that he had bad habits, and she realised that they would eventually kill him. And so she left, taking her daughter's child and departing with him for her former home where she was born, in the Mthethwa country under Dingiswayo, and placed him there in the care of the old woman who was her mother.

And it was there that Shaka lived and grew up to become a young man, a warrior under Dingiswayo for whom he used to fight valorously. His heroism resounded throughout the country, and the fame of his heroism reached the ears of his father in the Zulu country. And so his father came, wanting to see his son who was a hero.

Senzangakhona spent several days with the Mthethwa, and there was much rejoicing because of the visit of the Zulu chief. But the main business which was done there among the Mthethwa during those days, was to find doctors to medicinally influence [*thonya*, or to not bewitch] the father, that he might be overshadowed by the son [overcome by Shaka's shadow or influence or *isithunzi*], so that he [Shaka] should enter into the chieftainship. . . .

And it was about to happen that the son also followed behind him, leaving the Mthethwa and returning to the Zulu country. And as soon as Shaka left for the Zulu country, Dingiswayo also left home on a visit to Zwide, the chief of the Ndwandwe. . . . It was on this occasion that Zwide put him to death (1818). And from there began the series of evil events that brought about the many wars that have never ceased.

Shortly after Shaka's arrival at home, an alarming report was received to the effect that his "father" Dingiswayo was no longer alive. . . . And it was shortly after his arrival at home that he killed his brother, Nomkwayimba. At the time the chief was sick, and as soon as he heard that "your son Shaka has arrived and killed his brother Nomkwayimba," he was so shocked at that report that he died immediately (1818).

Shaka, being angered by the murder of his "father" Dingiswayo, marshalled the Zulu and the Mthethwa and the Hlubi people to arms. It came to resemble the funeral hunt or ceremonial war [*ihlambo*, or the washing of spears] for his father, Senzangakhona. The army sallied forth and made for the Ndwandwe country. But Zwide was very strong, and more fearsome than the other chiefs; therefore Shaka, whilst making an advance movement, wanted to draw the Ndwandwe army downwards [southwards, for

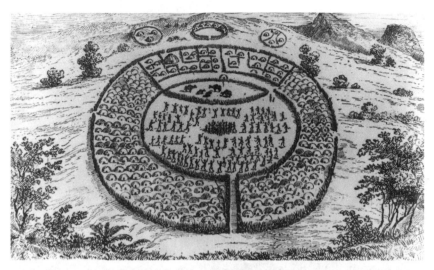

Dingane's capital, Umgungundhlovu, at the time Piet Retief was killed, 1838. Artist unknown. Courtesy of Campbell Collections of the University of KwaZulu-Natal, D05/025.

the Ndwandwe lived to the north], and as he was doing all these movements, he was devising a plan to draw Zwide into the Zulu country. . . .

[The Ndwandwe army] advanced towards Mahlabatini where the Zulu country was situated. As for Shaka, he wanted to draw it towards the Mhlathuze river, so that it should fight at Nkandla and Nsuze, where the country is extremely broken. He had proclaimed to all the homesteads in the Zulu country that the foodstuffs should be removed, and that the homesteads should be abandoned and destroyed by fire. . . .

There the two armies attacked one another, and there was the smell of war, and the dust rose up high. Well! Seeing that the Ndwandwe were so strong, what was the outcome? The Zulus were so enraged that their anger could only be quenched with water [Zulu saying], and they were fighting a fight of death. For in fact, before the clash, Shaka had given the order that the bundles of spears were to be abandoned, and that each man was to carry a short stabbing spear together with only one spear for throwing as the army was about to engage. No-one carried three or more spears as was formerly the custom. . . .

The army fought with great intensity until darkness fell, and it was dreadful. For several days it fought with terrible fury. The horror continued until Shaka realized that he had mauled Zwide's forces considerably, and that they were hungry through not being able to get food anywhere, their

The Zulu king Shaka
kaSenzangakhona.
Artist unknown.
Courtesy of Campbell
Collections of the
University of KwaZulu-
Natal, D37/007.

own supplies which they carried with them being quite exhausted; and he thereupon devised another plan, and dispatched several companies to go to the capital occupied by Zwide himself; and when they saw that the capital was no longer far away, they were to chant the Ndwandwe national war song so that there should be no alarm, and then enter the capital and seize Zwide. . . .

And so those companies that were sent to Zwide's capital did what they were sent to do. Indeed, as they approached the Ndwandwe capital they chanted the Ndwandwe national war song, to announce that they had destroyed the Zulus. And it was then that the women of the place came out with shouts of praise and victory. And so the enemy was able to approach to very close quarters. "What! It's Zulu kaMdlamfe!" [Senzangakhona's Zulus]. To their horror they heard shouts of *"Ngadla!"* [I have stabbed]. "Alas for my father's cow!" [their response]. And before they realized what had happened, there were many who had already fallen. When Zwide heard this, he jumped up and broke through the far end of the enclosure and fled. . . .

Hau! [an exclamation of surprise or awe]. And the Zulu army continued with its work of destruction.

And so the Ndwandwe nation came to be completely scattered. Many collected their belongings and made their way north. . . .

But as for Shaka, he could not put down his shield but continued to attack other clans, wishing to subject them to his rule. It was thus that there arose Shaka's praise: "Isidlu-kula-dlwedlwe [long-armed robber who robs with violence] who destroys with his shield ever ready on his knees." . . .

And so Shaka ruled and became a king, as foretold by his grandfather, Ndaba, that it would be a Zulu kingship. . . . He wished to fulfill this prophecy, and so attacked all those who opposed him, but those who submitted, he left and ruled through them. . . .

And such were Shaka's upheavals in South Africa. He arrived unexpectedly, and he arrived when Zulu power was not great in Zululand, being less than many other powers which were greater than it. He came and raised up the power of his people so that it became stronger than all the others that had been strong, and they who had been above his father and grandfather he humbled and lowered. It was a most astonishing feat. And yet it was the great announcement foretold by his great-grandfather, Ndaba, that he alone would be a great king, for from his progeny would unexpectedly appear the one who would rule the whole of South Africa.

Mhudi

Solomon T. Plaatje

Solomon Tshekisho Plaatje (1876–1932), a founding member of the African National Congress and the author of sub-Saharan Africa's first novel written by an African, was one of the most important African intellectuals and nationalists in the early twentieth century. He was born on a farm in the Orange Free State near the diamond-rush city of Kimberley, and Plaatje's parents were devout Lutherans with roots in the Barolong peoples. Plaatje received most of his education at a mission station, which in the nineteenth century was one of the only avenues by which Africans could gain schooling. He developed a command of English and what was known then as Cape Dutch (later standardized as Afrikaans) in addition to a number of African languages. In the 1890s Plaatje moved to Kimberley, where he joined the educated African community and worked as a clerk in the city post office. Plaatje served as a translator during the South African War (1899–1902), living in Mafeking during the famous siege when the Boer forces surrounded the small town.

Following the war, Plaatje became increasingly involved in African politics and culture. He edited Koranta ea Becoana *(Bechuana Gazette), a newspaper published in the Setswana language. In 1910 Plaatje became the first secretary of the South African Native National Congress (later the African National Congress). He wrote his most famous work,* Native Life in South Africa, *to protest the Natives Land Act of 1913, which prohibited black ownership or rental of land outside the native reserves (see part V).*

Throughout his life, Plaatje maintained a deep interest in African culture and history. He traced his descent back to what he believed were the early Barolong kings. Plaatje was especially interested in the Setswana language, and he collected and published a small volume of proverbs and folktales. He wrote much of the novel Mhudi: An Epic of South African Native Life a Hundred Years Ago *during various visits to London, and he completed the manuscript in 1920. In the novel, which was published in 1932, the protagonist, Mhudi, imagines the history of the Barolong people in the early part of the nineteenth century, a particularly turbulent time when European intrusion into areas further into the interior and upheavals in the area that gave rise to the Zulu Kingdom led to widespread movement and con-*

flict. For many years scholars referred to these events as the mfecane, *but research now points to multiple causes of political consolidation and warfare in the early nineteenth century, including colonial intrusion and the expanding world trade in commodities such as ivory. The selection focuses on Barolong life and the wars associated with the Ndebele king Mzilikazi, who had once served under Shaka.*

Two centuries ago the Bechuana [Tswana] tribes inhabited the extensive areas between Central Transvaal and the Kalahari Desert. . . . In this domain they led their patriarchal life under their several chiefs who owed no allegiance to any king or emperor. They raised their native corn [sorghum] which satisfied their simple wants and, when not engaged in hunting or in pastoral duties, the peasants whiled away their days in tanning skins or sewing magnificent fur rugs. They also smelted iron and manufactured useful implements which today would be pronounced very crude by their semi-westernized descendants.

Cattle breeding was the rich man's calling and hunting a national enterprise. Their cattle which carried enormous horns ran almost wild and multiplied as prolifically as the wild animals of the day. Work was of a perfunctory nature, for mother earth yielded her bounties and the maiden soil provided ample sustenance for man and beast.

But woman's work was never out of season. In the summer she cleared the cornfields of weeds and subsequently helped to winnow and garner the crops. In winter times she cut the grass and helped to renovate her dwelling. In addition to the inevitable cooking, basket-making, weaving and all the art-painting for mural decorations were done by women. Childless marriages were as rare as freaks so, early and late in summer and winter, during years of drought and of plenty, every mother had to nourish her growing brood, besides fattening and beautifying her daughters for the competition of eligible swains.

Fulfilling these multifarious duties of the household was not regarded as a drudgery by any means; on the contrary, the women looked upon marriage as an art; the daughter of a well-to-do peasant, surrounded by all the luxuries of her mother's home, would be the object of commiseration if she were a long time finding a man. And the simple women of the tribes accepted wifehood and transacted their onerous duties with the same satisfaction and pride as an English artist would the job of conducting an orchestra.

Kunana, near the present boundary between Cape Colony and Western Transvaal, was the capital city of the Barolong, the original stock of the several tribes, who also followed the humdrum yet interesting life of the other Bechuana Natives. They planted their stations in different directions over scores of miles; and it was often easier to kill wild animals nearer [to] home than go to the cattle-post for meat. Very often the big game ran thalala-motse (when wild animals continued their frolics straight through a Native village) when there would be systematic slaughter of antelopes and orgies of wild-beef eating. . . .

These peasants were content to live their monotonous lives, and thought naught of their oversea kinsmen who were making history on the planta-tions and harbours of Virginia and Mississippi at that time; nor did they know or care about the relations of the Hottentots and the Boers at Cape Town nearer home. The topography of the Cape Peninsula would have had no interest for them; and had anyone mentioned the beauty spots of the Cape and the glory of the silver-trees on their own subcontinent, they would have felt disappointed on hearing that they bore no edible fruit.

To them the limit of the world was Monomotapa (Portuguese East Africa)—a whiteman's country—which they had no ambition to see. Of monetary wealth they had none except their flocks and herds. A little bartering was done with neighbouring tribes in exchange for other com-modities, and none could be so mean as to make a charge for supplying a fellow-tribesman with the necessaries of life. When the rainy season was good everyone had too much [more than enough] corn, and in years of drought the majority went short of porridge. Strange to relate, these sim-ple folk were perfectly happy without money and without silver watches. Abject poverty was practically unknown; they had no orphanages because there were no nameless babies. When a man had a couple of karosses (ani-mal hide cloaks) to make he invited the neighbours to spend the day with him cutting, fitting in and sewing together the sixty grey jackal pelts into two rungs, and there would be intervals of feasting throughout the day. On such an occasion, someone would announce a field day at another place where there was a dwelling to thatch; here too the guests might receive an invitation from a peasant who had a stockade to erect a third homestead on a subsequent day; and great would be the expectation of the fat bullock to be slaughtered by the good man, to say nothing of the good things to be prepared by the kind hostess. Thus a month's job would be accomplished in a day.

But the anomaly of this community life was that, while the many seams in a rich man's kaross carried all kinds of knittings—good, bad and indifferent —the wife of a poor man, who could not afford such a feast, was often gowned in flawless furs. It being the skilled handiwork of her own husband, the nicety of its seams seldom failed to evoke the admiration of experts.

Upon these peaceful regions over one hundred years ago there descended one Mzilikazi, king of a ferocious tribe called the Matabele, a powerful usurper of determined character who by his sword proclaimed himself ruler over all the land.

Mzilikazi's tribe originally was a branch of the Zulu nation which Chaka [Shaka] once ruled with an iron rod. Irritated by the stern rule of that monarch, Mzilikazi led out his own people who thereupon broke away from Chaka's rule and turned their faces westward.

Sweeping through the northern areas of . . . Natal, they advanced along both banks of the Vaal River, driving terror into man and beast with whom they came in contact. They continued their march very much like a swarm of locusts; scattering the Swazis, terrifying the Basuto and the Bapedi on their outposts, they drove them back to the mountains at the point of the assegai [spear]; and, trekking through the heart of the Transvaal, they eventually invaded Bechuanaland where they reduced the Natives to submission. . . .

The town of the Barolong having been mercilessly sacked, their cattle-posts and homesteads flattened to the ground and the surviving occupants scattered in all directions, all their belongings having fallen into the hands of Mzilikazi's victorious army, the king, on learning of their success, ordered the warriors to remain on the Malmani River with their booty until he had prepared a feast for their reception. The Feast of Welcome and an elaborate programme having been decided upon, the king sent messengers to the Ngwaketsi, Bakwena, Bakgatla and other Bechuana tribes, inviting their chiefs to attend a Matabele festival, or send representatives to Inzwinyani if they could not attend in person.

This army of destruction was led by Langa, second living son of Mzilikazi—an impetuous youth, very jealous of the dignity pertaining to his station. Despite his extreme youth, he had several times vowed to wage war against his people if, on the death of his father, they attempted to pass him over in favour of his elder half brother of another house. This lightning raid on Kunana was his first military exploit. His army was composed mainly of young men supplemented by a few of the senior divisions.

By daybreak on the day of the feast there was a significant stir among the Matabele people. The call had sounded the previous afternoon from hill-top to hill-top, so cowmen left their herds in charge of small boys, villagers left the women behind and, travelling all night, hastened towards the capital, where they were that day expecting to count the booty and divide the trophies of victory. By the first streak of dawn, thousands of men began to assemble at the great rallying place, the circular stockade in the centre of the city, surrounded by the king's headquarters. . . .

When Mzilikazi emerged from his dwelling, surrounded by his body-guard and accompanied by his chiefs, arrayed in their brilliant tiger-skins [leopard skins], the effect of the recent victory was manifest by the satisfaction on every face. The appearance of the royal party was hailed with tumultuous shouts. The rattle of the assegais on the shields rivalled even the rattle of a heavy hailstorm. The court jesters sang and leaped, bedecked in all manner of fantastic head-dresses, till the cat-tails round their loins literally whirled in the air.

The king, with more than usual dignity, acknowledged the royal salute of "Bayete" from thousands of leather-lunged Matabele. Having seated himself upon his wooden throne, which was decorated for the occasion with lion and leopard skins, King Mzilikazi surveyed the excited mass of humanity before him. With so many thousands in attendance, it was no uncommon thing for a joyous festival of the kind to end with a death sentence on any who might upset the uncertain temper of Mzilikazi the Terrible; therefore men grasped their shields and gripped their spears and stood erect, lest a faulty pose should irritate the eye and rouse the ire of the Great One. The crowd stood breathless and at high tension, while court jesters and mbongis (oral bards) were lauding the greatness of Mzilikazi and reciting the prowess and deeds of valour associated with his ancestry.

Whistles blew, drums began to sound and hundreds of men chanted a song of victory, while thousands of warriors stamped a rhythmical mark-time in harmony with the tom-toms. The excitement grew, while the soldiers broke into their familiar war dance.

The infection was not limited to the men. Long files of Matabele women were descending the hills along the tortuous footpaths heading into the capital from every direction. They carried on their heads earthen pots full of beer for the entertainment of the conquering heroes, singing at the same time praises of the victors. Nearly every one of the files of singing women was headed by a group of syncopating cymbalists, ringing or beating time with their iron cymbals in a rhythm with their steps, as they wound their way down towards the level valley bottom, across which the city lay. The women of the city were busy in between their huts, outside the frenzied crowd of warriors. Their business was to cook and prepare the eatables for the festival which was to follow the great indaba (assembly); yet they also caught the infection. Beside the numerous fireplaces in the courtyards, groups of shimmying girls sang the praises of Langa, high-born son of the Great One, and warbled national ditties to the glory of Matabele arms. Some minded the boiling flesh-pots and joined the chorus of singers, while others tinkled little rattles in harmony with the shimmy.

They had heard that such an enormous booty of horned cattle had never before been captured in the history of human warfare. No one, much less a woman, cared to know the cause of the raid, for the end had amply justified the means. They knew, and for them the knowledge was enough, that Prince Langa had raided the Barolong cattle-posts, killed the owners and captured every beast. Hence their joy was too great to consider the relatives of their own young fighters who fell at the point of the spears of the Barolong defenders.

The members of a constantly warring nation like the Matabele had been drilled from childhood to face the most devastating situation without the tremor of an eyelid. Today, especially, the booty more than counterbalanced the loss of the good Matabele blood spilled in the enterprise. With this magnificent addition to the national wealth and the national food supply, it should be impossible in future for the sister, wife or mother of a spearman to run short of beef; so the women of the city were in high glee.

They danced and sang:

Come, let us sing!
   Mzilikazi has a son.
Come, let us sing!
   Langa is the name of his son.
Come, let us dance!
   Langa has a spear!
Come, let us prance!
   His sword is a sharp pointed spear.
Go forth and summon the girls of Soduza
   To the dance;
Go call the maidens to the Puza,
   And the dance;
For Mzilikazi has a son!
Langa, the Fighter, is his son!

. . . Suddenly King Mzilikazi gave a signal, and the dancing and the singing in the inner circle ceased; far away in the distant outskirts of the city was to be heard a swelling chant mingled with the rumble of tom-toms; ever louder and louder droned the barbaric music—the victorious army of Langa was returning; the victorious army from Kunana laden with the spoils of victory. As they entered the great enclosure, the home regiments squeezed aside and prepared a way for Langa and his regiments to approach the king. The newcomers had their own mbongis who loudly proclaimed the latest success that the youthful army had scored for the Matabele arms.

II

Colonial Settlement, Slavery, and Peonage

In 1652 the European employees of the Dutch East India Company who formed a small refreshment station for ships at the southern tip of Africa, now Cape Town, had no intention of conquering African communities or creating an expansive colony of white settlement that exploited the labor of slaves and indentured Khoesan inhabitants. Within a few years, however, the Dutch East India Company had released some employees to become independent farmers and had begun importing slaves. In less than a century, Europeans had expanded four hundred miles into the interior, subjugating the Khoesan and settling areas in the dry north and, in the east, near the Fish River, which bordered Xhosa-speaking peoples.

Enslaved people came mostly from Madagascar, India, and East Asia. Their labor produced wine, wheat, and other products that helped sustain European maritime commerce in the Atlantic and Indian Oceans. In the drier interior lands, *trekboere* (migratory cattle farmers) plundered Khoesan communities, forcing people into indentures and using their skills to help raise sheep and cattle for butchers in Cape Town. By the time the Cape fell to the British in the final years of the eighteenth century, a full-fledged colonial society had emerged, composed of company officials, colonists, slaves from Asia and Africa, indentured Khoesan laborers, and peoples of mixed-race descent. Some people of mixed ancestry moved into white society. Others migrated out of the Cape Colony where they became known first as Basters and then Griquas. In the nineteenth century, the term *Coloureds* emerged to refer to people who acknowledged mixed-racial heritage. They typically spoke Cape Dutch, which later became the Afrikaans language, and worshiped in the Calvinist faith, though there is a small population of Muslims whose history is tied to slaves and exiles to the Cape from what is today Indonesia. Today, Coloureds number about four million people, or just under 9 percent of South Africa's population.

Though *Coloured* was deployed in popular usage and in racially discriminatory laws for more than a century, many people today refuse the term, preferring instead to claim a pure, indigenous Khoesan ancestry. Identity politics remain contentious, particularly in the Western Cape, where many people fear the dominance of "blacks" (in this sense, people from Bantu-speaking African communities), as supposedly seen in the ruling African National Congress (ANC). In South Africa's first democratic elections, Coloureds in the Western Cape voted largely for the National Party, the very party responsible for their racial oppression under apartheid. A majority later supported the ANC. However, the current opposition party, the Democratic Alliance, received decisive Coloured support in the 2011 countrywide municipal elections amid various racial slurs by ANC officials, one of whom complained of an "over supply of Coloureds" in the Western Cape Province.[1]

The legacies of this early colonial past thus remain controversial and fraught. The slave past is pervasive across the Western Cape, yet remains largely unacknowledged by its descendants. Many white South Africans jealously guard their racial purity, despite historical evidence to the contrary, especially for those descended from the early settlers. Ultimately, two of South Africa's ethnic groups emerged from this history who largely shared the same culture, even as race would come to divide them: the Coloureds and the Afrikaners. Today, the two groups make up about 15 percent of South Africa's total population of nearly fifty million people.

The selections that follow speak to this discordant past and underscore the ways that diverse peoples understood their colonial world. The colonial society that emerged would profoundly shape the course of South Africa's modern history. Colonial settler accounts rationalize the necessity of slavery and the violent domination of slaves and indigenes and bemoan the meddlesome intervention of missionaries and British officials imbued with abolitionist sensibilities. Slaves and debt peons recount the violence of their masters, imagine a time when they had lived freely, and rejoice in the ending of forced labor. The South African frontier was famously violent, with colonists who formed bands called commandos literally hunting down and exterminating Khoesan communities, killing adults and capturing children to use as farm labor. The Cape's incorporation into the British Empire around 1800 radically altered society, particularly by ending peonage and slavery and introducing the ideal that no person is above the law. A new ethnic element was introduced as British officials encouraged the settlement of thousands of British subjects in the eastern portions of the colony beginning in 1820, partly to serve as a buffer between Africans and Afrikaners. In the 1830s frontier politics led to the migration of thousands of Afrikaners out of the Cape Colony and deeper into the South African interior, in what has come to be known as the Great Trek, a central part of Afrikaner nationalist mythology.

Note

1. "Manyi: 'Over-supply' of Coloureds in Western Cape," *Mail and Guardian*, February 24, 2011, accessed April 12, 2013, http://mg.co.za/article/2011-02-24-coloureds-overconcentrated-in-wcape-says-manyi.

An African Woman at the Cape: Krotoa

(c. 1642–74)   *Relationships of choice transforming*

Julia C. Wells   *into relationships of colonial control*

The woman known as Krotoa, or Eva, emerges primarily from the journals of the first governor of the Cape Colony, Jan van Riebeeck, collected in the editor H. B. Thom's Journal of Jan Van Riebeeck *(1952–58). Krotoa lived with van Riebeeck's family as a servant before becoming a valued interpreter. In the early years of the settlement, the Dutch relied on trade with the Khoekhoe to obtain cattle and sheep in exchange for tobacco, copper, beads, and alcohol. People like Krotoa, who could negotiate both worlds, were highly valued. Krotoa's life as an intermediary and as the wife of the Danish surgeon Pieter van Meerhof form part of an early period of relatively peaceful interactions between Africans and Europeans. European-Khoekhoe relations declined steadily in the years following the First Khoekhoe War of 1659. A second war broke out in 1673, leading to the swift collapse of the Khoekhoe in the region around Cape Town and increasing intolerance. Banished a number of times to Robben Island, Krotoa died, destitute, in the winter of 1674. Three centuries later, the issue of the relationship of her descendants to prominent white Afrikaner families such as Paul Kruger emerged into public discussion and, with it, the legacies of South Africa's early colonial history.*

Quite possibly, Eva, born Krotoa, is the most written about African woman in South African historiography. Her name fills the journals of the Dutch East India Company almost from the very start of their little feeding-station at the Cape of Good Hope in 1652. She is known as a Khoena [Khoe] girl taken into Dutch commander Jan Van Riebeeck's household from the age of about twelve, who later became a key interpreter for the Dutch, was baptised, married a Danish surgeon, Pieter Van Meerhoff, but then died as a drunken prostitute after his death. Yet her persona remains an enigma. . . .

Virtually all of the representations of Eva construct her as a helpless victim of vicious culture clashes. Today's racial consciousness, laced with assumptions of inevitable African / European hostility, is often read back into

37

the historical record. Frustratingly large gaps in that record leave room for a wide range of interpretations, depending heavily on the subjectivities of the historian. Virtually all previous writers, however, have judged Eva primarily by the tragic circumstances of her death, while minimizing the considerable achievements of her earlier years. . . .

Circumstantial evidence supports the possibility that Krotoa lived with her "uncle" Autshumato (called Harry by the Dutch) at the time of the Dutch landing. The records confirm that she was separated from her sister in infancy, as well as the fact that Eva showed consistent hostility to the Goringhaiqua clan and to her own mother, who lived with them. In contrast, her fate and fortunes were closely tied with those of Autshumato, for whom she clearly expressed deep concern and compassion on several occasions.

The implications are quite important, as Autshumato's Goringhaicona people were sedentary, non-pastoral hunter-gatherers who collected shellfish in the vicinity of Table Bay. For years before the Dutch came to settle, Autshumato served as a postal agent for passing ships from a number of countries, having been taken to Java by the English in 1631. He and his followers camped at Table Bay and greeted van Riebeeck when he landed. They then lived adjacent to the Dutch tents during the construction of the first fort and became the first Africans proletarianized [became workers] by the Dutch colonial presence. Thus, if Krotoa lived with Autshumato when the Dutch first arrived, her going into service with them might have been a relatively smooth transition, as many Goringhaicona readily did odd-jobs for the Dutch in return for food, tobacco or drink. Her mother's people, the Goringhaiqua, by contrast, were pastoralists only rarely seen by the Dutch during their first year.

Possibly the Dutch needed more than casual help when, only a few months after arriving, the first baby was born to the chaplain / sick-healer, Willem Barentssen Wijlant, and his wife. Two days after the birth, both the new father and Mrs van Riebeeck came down with a virulent disease which had been spreading rapidly through the settlement, leaving a few casualties. Extra assistance with the new baby could thus have become particularly urgent. The sick-comforter, Wijlant, routinely led short excursions out of the fort to try to barter with Khoena. Like van Riebeeck, he was an evangelical Calvinist, eager to find converts among the local people. In view of his religious zeal, and possibly the need of his wife for assistance with the new baby, he might have initiated negotiations to obtain the services of a young Khoena girl. They probably turned to Autshumato first, since he already had a long history of working for Europeans. Perhaps he selected Krotoa because of her status as ward, separated from her biological parents.

Although Krotoa was certainly too young to have exercised much free will about where she lived and worked, her service in the commander's household could have been viewed as an honour and a form of apprenticeship by the Khoena. Contemporary evidence from the journal describes a young African girl raised in the home of a non-related but prestigious chief and hence honoured as highly as if she were his daughter. The German officer Ludwig Alberti described similar customs among the amaXhosa [Xhosa], nearly a century and a half later. Clearly, the people among whom Krotoa lived differentiated between low and high ranking Dutch, greeting ships' captains or the commander as long-lost friends, throwing their arms around their necks in warm embrace. From the Khoena point of view, the presence of a young girl in the home of a neighbouring "chief" might be seen not only as an honour but as a token of friendship and a useful way to gather intelligence. . . .

Over the next few years, Eva developed a persona in the records, not simply as "Van Riebeeck's favourite maid," but as a highly valued interpreter.[1] For her, it was a period of relative isolation from her people and of significant acculturation among the Dutch. Living with the van Riebeeck family, she took advantage of her position to learn Dutch fluently, "almost as well as a Dutch girl."[2] Her induction into the Dutch language and way of life may also have been facilitated by van Riebeeck's two nieces, of relatively comparable ages to Eva. One of these, Elizabeth van Opdorp, years later took in Eva's children while she was incarcerated on Robben Island.

Eva's standing with the Dutch, however, went beyond her enthusiastic embrace of the Dutch language and culture. Despite clear efforts to present a picture of respectability and decorum regarding Eva, van Riebeeck reveals a high level of personal concern for her. The journal conveys a muted sense of a father daughter relationship; stresses Eva's closeness to van Riebeeck's wife, Maria; and highlights efforts to convert Eva to Christianity. . . .

Although the evidence is entirely circumstantial, a case can be made that van Riebeeck had an intimate relationship with Eva at some point. The most compelling evidence comes from the larger picture, taken as a totality. The trust and reliance that van Riebeeck invested in Eva clearly transcended the boundaries of a conventional master-servant relationship. He invited her to important meetings, explained important decisions to her, consulted her privately about vital issues, gave her freedom to come and go and made her an active sales agent. Perhaps most revealing is the sharp contrast between van Riebeeck's attitude towards Eva and that of his successor, Zacharius Wagenaar. The new commander treated Eva with outright churlishness and hostility, hardly appropriate behaviour towards one who had proved herself so invaluable. By comparison, van Riebeeck had been gentle, considerate, tolerant, indulgent and trusting of Eva in a highly subjective way.

. . . [H]er words and views commanded extraordinary respect and authority, as revealed in comments [in the journal] such as "this was also observed by Eva," "Eva said the same," "we must attend Eva's last parting advice" and "this Eva had often told us." She provided not only information but also moral judgments on its validity. For example, she claimed the Goringhaiqua could not be trusted because their promises did not come from the heart.

Further, the interest van Riebeeck took in her clearly suggests affection. When she was away from the fort, he followed her movements carefully, apparently being supplied with a steady stream of intelligence by others. At times, references to her subjective feelings slipped in—she gave a "half-suppressed sigh," felt "much dejected," became depressed and was wilful, "we could not think of detaining her against her will; for nothing could be properly done with her." The journal-writer often conveyed Eva's words verbatim while generally summarizing other interpreters. In two places, van Riebeeck admitted to confidential, if not secret, information about her that he did not record in the journal. . . .

Eva's successful career as an interpreter rested not only on her good language skills and her closeness to the Commander but also on her unique ability to acquire information about the Khoena of interest to the Dutch. Previous studies have tended to assume that she simply "knew" about political developments in the hinterland because she was Khoena herself. But much of what she shared with the Dutch went beyond what could have been known or understood by the twelve-year-old girl who first entered their service. . . .

Eva's reputation as a Dutch collaborator is even more unmistakable during the course of a serious hostage crisis . . . [six years after she entered service]. By mid-1658, the Dutch had started importing slaves, only to find that they quickly absconded into the interior. Van Riebeeck clearly found Eva far more sympathetic to his wish to have local Khoena participate in returning the run-aways than his chief male interpreter, a Goringhaiqua named Doman. After spending a year in Java, Doman returned highly suspicious of colonial intentions. The journal records how, in a private conversation between van Riebeeck and Eva, she poured out her heart about the intense rivalry between herself and Doman. She accused him of telling the Khoena too much about the Dutch, to which he replied: "I am Hottentoosman, and not Dutchman, but you, Eva, *soubat* (curry favour with) the Commander." She further alleged that it was Doman's people, the Goringhaiqua, who had the slaves and were likely to sell them into the interior in exchange for dagga [marijuana].

The Dutch then gave Eva all the credit (or blame) for proposing they take two sons of the Goringhaiqua chief, Gogosoa, as hostages, until all the slaves were returned. Considering the level of restraint the Dutch had exercised to date against using force with their Khoena adversaries, this implied a significant revision of policy. Malherbe suspects that the Dutch set up Eva as a scapegoat, since the tactic of hostage-taking was in no way unfamiliar to them. In fact, the free burger [citizen] (and husband of Elizabeth Van Opdorp) Jan Reijnertz had held Gogosoa hostage just a month previously to secure the return of some stolen cattle. If hostage-taking was already a common strategy, it is more likely that Eva only suggested names of effective candidates. Whatever her level of complicity, Doman and his people presumed her guilty of openly assisting the Dutch. Fearing for her life, van Riebeeck ordered her not to leave the fort.

However, tensions soon spiraled out of hand. The hostages languished in the fort for over a week, and only a few missing slaves reappeared. The hostages themselves argued that they should be joined by further hostages from all the local Khoena chiefdoms. So the Dutch took more, including Eva's uncle, Autshumato, and seized all of his cattle. In the process, the Dutch killed one of his followers, the first Khoena death at their hands. Within two days, all parties concluded a peace treaty which freed the hostages and secured the return of the slaves. Significantly, it also contained clauses stating that the Goringhaiqua now gave up all claims to the Cape peninsula. So what had started out as a tussle over runaway slaves ended up with a Khoena cession of land to the Dutch, the imprisonment of Autshumato, the confiscation of his cattle and a Khoena death—and both sides blamed Eva!

It was a messy affair, which reportedly left Eva "depressed" and no doubt urgently raised the issue of where her loyalties lay. She promptly visited Autshumato, who had been sent to Robben Island as a prisoner for his role in stealing company livestock five years earlier. But nothing she said or did could undo his sorry fate. Van Riebeeck compared her to Esther, pleading for her uncle, Mordecai. Doman's accusations of her traitorous behaviour escalated, with the journal reporting him as saying: "'See! There comes the Hollander's advocate again, she is coming to deceive her own countrymen with a parcel of lies, and to betray to the last,' and other expressions to make her odious." If ever Eva needed friends and allies it was now, since her thorough identification with Dutch interests at this stage could have sealed her off from Khoena confidence altogether. Instead, the reverse happened as Eva embarked on a bold new strategy to shore up her position.

Ironically, the depression in the livestock trade during the crisis created an opportunity for Eva to redeem herself. Few Khoena came near the fort for fear of being taken hostage. Within a few days of the treaty, Eva and Doman, now acting in concert, requested permission "to pay a visit to their friends" in order "to make them known to us." It was the first time that Eva acted as a trade agent in her own right, although the male interpreters frequently did so. Since one of the hostages had been a Cochoqua named Boubou, it is possible that Eva surmised that she could expect a warm reception from his people. After all, the great Cochoqua co-chief, Oedasoa, had gone to the trouble of taking Eva's sister as a wife after kidnapping her from another chief.

Armed with brass, iron, beads, tobacco, bread and brandy for "her mother and friends," Eva set out. Her immediate change of apparel from Dutch clothes into Khoena skins shocked the Dutch, who liked to view her as having become one of them. No doubt it signified her strong wish to identify more fully with her own people and to seek their acceptance. She received a mixed reception. The Goringhaiqua apparently perceived her as an irredeemable sell-out. Even her own mother refused to have anything to do with her. In contrast, Chief Oedasoa and her sister, "who had not seen her since infancy," warmly welcomed her. This contact not only launched Eva on the most active stage of her career but also turned the tide in northern trade for the Dutch. Her activities as intermediary between the Dutch and the Cochoqua proved pivotal. . . .

Eva also continued to serve Dutch trading interests somewhat independently of the Cochoqua. Early in 1659 she provided the Dutch with elaborate descriptions of the Namaqua, an even more powerful chiefdom to the north of the Cochoqua, and, it would emerge later, their sworn enemies. On the basis of her accounts, van Riebeeck authorized a northward expedition of exploration by free burger volunteers in early February. Eva suggested which inland people would provide the best guides for the journey and insisted that the Namaqua could link the Dutch with the powerful inland Chobona, and eventually the Monomotapa and the Vigiti Magna River. This intelligence from Eva demonstrates her immersion in the Dutch beliefs and aspirations of the day. They trusted heavily in a map, now known to be largely mythical, drawn up by Huygens van Linschoten and published in Amsterdam in 1623, which portrayed a northward-flowing river named

Vigiti Magna, upon which sat the kingdom of the Monomotapa, believed to be rich in gold, ivory and pearls. . . .

In addition to her [Eva's] growing Khoena loyalties, van Riebeeck might well have been shaken in his relationship with her by the active entry into her life of Pieter Van Meerhoff, who arrived in the Cape in March 1659.

Surprisingly little serious attention has been given by scholars to the nature of the relationship between Pieter and Eva. Recent writers, such as Coetzee and Abrahams presume that this relationship reflected only macropatterns of colonial exploitation of the powerful over the weak. They see the marriage as just one step along the road to Eva's eventual tragic demise and her miserable alienation from the Khoena. Pieter comes across as simply one more cog in the relentlessly grinding colonial machine. They fail to notice that Pieter emerges from the pages of the journal as a vividly flamboyant personality. A few historians have noted his distinctive flair, but never analyzed or discussed it in the context of his relationship with Eva. . . .

The relationship was a durable one, lasting nine years and producing three children. The couple remained unmarried for four years, then married in 1664 and remained together until Pieter's death in 1667. Eva's subsequent inability to cope with life surfaced following his death, suggesting that his loss had a devastating impact on her, perhaps triggering a full mental breakdown. Further circumstantial evidence, however, suggests that the pair also shared considerably in advancing the trading interests of the Dutch and Khoena—an enterprise for which they were, together, ideally suited. Given the broad outlines of their relationship, one can just as easily project theirs as a romantic liaison of choice.

Hailing from Copenhagen, Pieter first enlisted in the Dutch East India Company as a soldier and was subsequently appointed under-surgeon, the rank he held upon his arrival in the Cape in 1659. . . .

The chances are that Pieter and Eva struck up an intimate relationship soon after his arrival in 1659, since by 1663 they had two children. This implies that the relationship started . . . at a time when Eva was at the peak of her intermediary role. If Pieter acted opportunistically, it was to share in Eva's power and prestige, not her weakness. . . .

Once the rebellion ended, Pieter flung himself wholeheartedly into the pursuit of the Namaqua and greater riches, a quest initiated by Eva even before his arrival. He alone volunteered to travel on all six northern exploration expeditions over the next four years. . . . Their dedication to expanding trade, perhaps for personal gain, became a common thread in their relationship. . . .

The deterioration and eventual abandonment of the Namaqua quest in many ways embodies the shifting climate which also marginalized the unique chemistry of Pieter and Eva working together as a team. As it became clearer that the Monomotapa empire [in Zimbabwe] was not at hand and that the great river to the north could not provide access to wealthy trading partners, the enthusiasm for sensitive and friendly contacts with the indigenous people faded. The whole spirit of Dutch / Khoena contact shifted to cruder pragmatism, laced increasingly with racism and militarism. Eva's relationships with the key men in her life changed dramatically, one by one. . . .

In this context, the formality of marriage made sense. It certainly gave Eva greater status in Wagenaar's eyes and removed the possibility of his treating her as an ordinary servant. It also signalled their capitulation to living as socially acceptable members of Dutch society and an end to their in-betweenness. Their bid for conformity worked well. Along with a proper Christian marriage, the couple received a wedding banquet, a promotion for Pieter and a special marriage gift for Eva, the same as for all company employees. About one year later, Pieter was again promoted, this time to the position of Superintendent of Robben Island, moving there with a pregnant Eva and their two children. This appointment lasted two years before Pieter was given command of a prestigious expedition to Madagascar and Mauritius, key new spheres of influence for the Dutch. Clearly his superiors still appreciated his inter-cultural skills, as his instructions admonished him to treat the natives there well, not like the other Dutch. However, without the invaluable coaching from Eva and her kin, he misjudged his new native contacts, who killed him while trying to negotiate on the beach of Antongil Bay in Mauritius in 1666.

By the beginning of 1667, Eva had effectively lost all the influential men in her life. The loss of Pieter triggered a dramatic downhill slide that ended only with her dishonourable death on 29 July 1674. During those years the Dutch commanders accused her of abandoning her children, of rowdy drunken behaviour, of promiscuity and producing several more children. They incarcerated her on Robben Island several times, allowing her back on promises of improved behaviour, but claimed she never reformed. Despite her disgraceful demise, the Dutch community gave her a Christian burial and a few years later laid down strict terms for the adoption of her two surviving children fathered by Pieter.

What killed Eva off was not simply her inability to adapt to Dutch society, as some believe, but rather the dynamic within colonialism which so soon made bridging, trans-cultural people like her and Pieter redundant. This became all the more painful to her after she had tasted the extraordinary power and influence that she could exercise as a woman trusted by both sides in the initial colonial encounter. Eva died her slow and miserable death in a world in which the illusion of harmony had already evaporated. The cause into which she had thrown her life no longer existed. Van Riebeeck's restraint in dealing with the Khoena and his personal indulgence towards her left when he did; Oedasoa decided to tolerate the Dutch at arm's length, disgruntled that they could not be made to bend to his will; and Pieter died seeking a new frontier. When the dream shattered, so did Eva.

Notes

1. David Gordon, "From Rituals of Rapture to Dependence: The Political Economy of Khoikhoi Narcotic Consumption c. 1487–1870," *South African Historical Journal* 35, no. 1 (November 1966): 66.
2. "Memorandum Left by Van Riebeeck for His Successor, Zacharius Wagenaar, 5 May 1662," in Donald Moodie, ed., *The Record* (Cape Town: A. A. Balkema, 1959).

The Necessity of Slavery

W. S. van Ryneveld

The first slaves arrived at the Cape just six years after the colony's founding. Slavery grew with the rise of settler agriculture, particularly in the eighteenth century, as slavery was expanding throughout the Atlantic world. In 1775 about one-half of the colonial population of just over twenty-two thousand was enslaved. Before the British abolition of the slave trade in 1807, the Cape had imported more than sixty thousand slaves. Approximately one-quarter came from Africa; the remainder came from India, Madagascar, and Indonesia.

A distinctive feature of South African history is the fact that the British took over a slave-based colonial society at the very moment when the antislavery movement was gaining force in England. Following the first British occupation of the Cape in 1795, officials began inquiring into the status of Cape slavery and, possibly, abolishing the importation of slaves into Cape Town. In 1797 Governor George Macartney (1737–1806), who earlier had ruled over Madras and had been appointed as Britain's first envoy to China, produced a questionnaire for W. S. van Ryneveld (1765–1812), then a member of the Cape's Council of Policy, which consisted of Dutch East India Company officials. Van Ryneveld's reply points to the importance of slavery in Cape colonial society.

We know very well, that here, both within and without the Colony, no sufficient number of white people can be obtained to perform in culture [agriculture] the labour of the slaves; and, on the other hand, experience shows us every day that the procreation of slaves, in proportion to number, is very trifling, and even not worth mentioning; and that, moreover, a very considerable number of slaves is lost by continual disorders, especially by bile and putrid fevers, to which they are very subject.

The political state of this Colony, I think, is actually of that nature that, however injurious slavery of itself may be to the morals and industry of the inhabitants, still the keeping of slaves has now become, as it is styled, a necessary evil; and, at least, a sudden interdiction to the importation of slaves would occasion a general injury, as long as such a number of hands as is

Boers returning from hunting with slave. Illustration by Samuel Daniell. © British Library Board (062461). Used with permission.

requisite for the culture cannot be obtained from another part, at a rate that may be thought proportionate to the produce arising from the lands. . . . It is very true that at present there may be found some white or free persons apt for that purpose; yet apart from the number of these persons not being sufficient in any degree to supply the number of slaves wanted, the high hire and expensive maintenance of such free labourers would still render the employing of them impracticable. . . .

. . . The treatment of the slaves here is in general on a quite different and much milder footing than it is in the said colonies [the West Indies], owing not only to the laws properly guarding in this respect, but also to the high price of the slaves themselves being a continual incitement to care, for such masters as are influenced more by selfishness than by any principle of humanity. . . .

It is true, slavery is hard of itself. I have at the moment that I write the present memorial a feeling of all its weight, that ought to make an impression on the mind of every reasonable being; yet, besides it not being my task to treat of slavery by itself, a subject on which so many books have already, particularly in the present century, been published, I cannot but observe that slavery in this Colony has now become a necessary evil, which cannot be removed without sacrificing the Colony, and perhaps the poor slaves themselves that are in it. . . .

I perfectly acknowledge . . . that if there were no slaves at the Cape[,] the [white] peasants would then be more industrious and useful to the State, and that the facility of procuring slaves renders the inhabitants of this country lazy, haughty and brutal.

Every kind of vice and a perfect corruption of morals is owing to that. But how to help it? If slavery had been interdicted at the first settling of this Colony, then the inhabitants would doubtless have become more industrious and useful to each other; they would be obliged to associate in a narrower compass of land, and the Colony would never have so exceedingly extended beyond its ability and beyond the exigence of its population.

Yet, the business is done. Slavery exists and is now even indispensable. It is absolutely necessary because there are no other hands to till this extensive country, and therefore it will be the work, not of years, but as it were of centuries to remove by attentive and proper regulation this evil established with the first settling of the Colony.

Should the slaves be now declared free, that would immediately render both the country and these poor creatures themselves miserable; not only all tillage would then be at an end, but also the number of freemen, instead of their being (as now) useful members of, would then really become a charge to, society. And should the importation of slaves be interdicted, on a sudden, without any means being provided towards supplying other hands for the tillage, then the Colony would thereby be caused to languish (the procreation of slaves being so inconsiderable in comparison with their mortality) and especially the culture of grain would thereby be reduced to decay.

A Rebel Slave

Galant

Slavery persisted in the Western Cape for nearly two centuries. Unlike Brazil and the Caribbean, where slaves often formed an overwhelming majority of the population, the Cape never experienced a major slave revolt. Far to the east, peons rose against their masters in the massive Hottentot (Khoe) Rebellion of 1799–1802. In the western areas of the Cape, however, resistance typically involved flight into the interior or individual acts, such as theft. One exception was the small revolt of thirteen slaves and Khoesan laborers in the district of Worcester during the summer of 1825. Led by Galant, a twenty-six-year-old slave, the men murdered three colonists before attempting to flee into the interior. After they were captured and tried, the state executed Galant and two accomplices, their heads severed from their bodies and "stuck upon iron spikes affixed to separate poles in the Bokkeveld, there to remain till consumed by time and the birds of the air."[1]

The Galant Rebellion came at a time when British colonial authorities were attempting to reform slavery at the Cape. The British had abolished the slave trade in 1807, and over the next decades attempted to reform Cape slavery through various "ameliorative" legislation, which culminated in the ending of slavery across the British Empire in 1834. In 1823 Governor Lord Charles Somerset issued a proclamation allowing slaves to marry, limiting the hours they could work, and restricting the violence that masters could inflict on their human chattel. Galant's testimony—a rare instance in which we can listen to the voice of a slave—sheds light on the conditions of servitude as well as on the impact of British abolitionism.

During the last harvest at my master's place when I and the other people, namely Isaac, Achilles, Antony, and Platje, were together, we spoke of the ill-treatment of our master towards us, and that he did not give us victuals and clothes. On that occasion one Campher who lives at a little distance from my master's place was present, who said to us that when our master should beat us . . . we should then seize and kill him. . . .

After the harvest was got in, my master rode to Mr. Jan Plessis on a visit, taking with him the Hottentots [Khoe] Isaak Thys and Isaac Rooy and myself. We conversed with the people there also about our ill usage, when the Hottentot Jochim and Adonis spoke to us of the ill treatment they experienced from their master, on which we agreed to murder our masters and go from the one place to the other where we should be joined by the people there. When we came home in the evening we found Mr. Barend van der Merwe at my master's place with his slave Abel, with whom I also spoke, and who agreed to kill his master likewise. The next morning he and his master went away, but returned shortly afterwards for one of the reins that he had let fall, on which he departed again and remained away. The third day, which was on a Tuesday, he came to me in my hut in the evening and told me that he had spoken with his master's people and that they were all ready. . . .

When we came to the place of Barend van der Merwe, . . . and while Mr. Barend was speaking with Klaas, I went with Abel round the corner of the house and into the kitchen. I remained at the middle door and Abel went into the room to get the guns, and came out with two that were loaded and two bandoliers with shot and horns with powder, of which he gave me one, and as soon as we went out of the kitchen door Abel fired the first shot at his master while he stood talking to the Hottentots Isaac and Hendrik whom he had found behind the house, but which missed him, on which B. van der Merwe made his escape into the house, but ran out again through the kitchen door and got up the hill along the quince hedge. . . . The wife of Barend van der Merwe likewise made her escape, we did not do her any harm. . . .

Before we came to my master's place, we first rode to the place of Jan Dalree to see whether Master Campher and the Hottentot Platje were there, but not finding them at home we proceeded to my master's place, where having arrived we turned our horses loose and waited till daybreak to murder the master. When it was day my master came out of the house and went to the kraal, on which, I, Abel, Isaac Thys, and Klaas rushed into the house in order to get possession of the guns and ran to the rack where they hung and took them away. My mistress then came towards us and laid hold of the guns, but let one of them fall, and as she held the other fast and would not give it up, the people called out to me to fire at her, and while I was about to fire the gun on one side in order to frighten her, during which she was struggling with the people to keep the gun, she suddenly turned round, through which she received the shot, and in consequence let the gun fall out of her hands. I then took up the gun and brought it out, and while I was standing at the front door, the other people came up to me, when we ran away together. When we got to the kraal we heard from the Hottentot

Valentyn that Master Rensburg had mounted a horse and ridden off; Isaac Thys and Abel thereupon got before him, so that he was obliged to return. As my master was going from the kraal to the house, Abel gave him a shot which grazed him, and when master got into the house Abel gave him a second shot through the window which passed close by his eyes, and thereupon when he opened the front door I shot him dead.

After that, Abel came in through the back door and fired at Master Rensburg on the firehearth, who together with the schoolmaster Verlee laid hold of the muzzle of the gun, with which they struggled to the kitchen door, when I gave Verlee a shot in the arm, with which he walked to the middle door and then fell. We then went into the house, where we found a pistol near the table and another in a pot in the kitchen, and powder and ball on a table in the bedroom; after we found the pistols Klaas discovered that Verlee the Schoolmaster still lived, on which Abel gave him a second shot through the head, and as he was not yet dead, Isaac Rooy gave him a third shot with a pistol. . . .

We meant to murder all the masters that did not treat their people well, to lay waste the country if we were strong enough, and then to escape to Caffreland [Kaffirland]; and if the Commando [armed group of colonists] should be too strong, to remain at the places of the murdered people. . . .

[M]y mistress [master's wife] said to my wife, a Hottentot named Betje, that a Newspaper was come from the Cape which she dare not break open, but that a time would be prescribed when it might be opened. [Here Galant is referring to the Somerset proclamation that ameliorated slavery, as well as to the extension of British rule in the rural districts of the Cape.] When the Newspaper was opened my mistress said that it stood therein that there was another great nation that was unknown; that there were orders come to make the Slaves free, and that if it was not done the other nation would then come to fight against the Farmers. My mistress afterwards further told me that it was also said in the Newspapers that the Slaves must be free, but if the Farmers would not allow it then it would not take place, to which I did not say anything. Another Newspaper came afterwards, when my wife Betje told me that her mistress had said if we would go to the King for the money and bring it to her on the table, that then we might be free. I desired her to keep it quiet, which she did. Some time after, another Newspaper came, when my wife told me that her Mistress had said that the first Englishman who came to make the slaves free should be shot, as well as the slaves; upon which I again advised her to be silent, for that if our master should hear of it he would punish us, and that she must not tell it to anybody else; but I desired her to ask the Mistress why the slaves were to be free, as she spoke so often about it. She told me afterwards that she had asked her, and that her Mistress had said it was because there came too many white children among the black Negroes, and therefore that they must be free. I then desired her again not to tell it to anyone, and not to talk so much about it. Another Newspaper then came, when she informed me that her Mistress had said that the Farmers were too hardly off, and that they were obliged to put up with too much from the Blacks. My wife came to me one day to the land weeping, and on my asking her the reason she said that while she was in the kitchen she had asked for a piece of bread, and that her master was so angry that he said he would shoot her and all the people in a lump, and leave us to be devoured by the crows and vultures. I again told her to be quiet, for that I could not well believe her although she was my wife, as she could not read or write no more than myself.

Once that Barend van der Merwe was at my master's place on his return from Worcester where he had been to fetch the slave Goliath who had made a complaint, I was in the stable preparing forage for the horses. It was dark, so that nobody could see me in the stable. My master called Barend van der Merwe out and came with him into the stable without seeing me, when I heard my master ask him whether he had had his slave flogged, to which he answered no, for that the black people had more to say with the Magistrate of late than the Christians; further saying but he shall nevertheless not remain without a flogging, for when I come home he shall have one. I also heard Barend van der Merwe say to my master on that occasion I wish that the Secretaries or Commissioners had died rather than that they should have come here, for that since that time they had been obliged to pay so much for the *Opgaaf* [taxes] and also for the Slaves. My master gave for answer I wish that the first Commissioner who put his foot on the wharf from on board had broken his neck, for that it was from that time one was obliged to pay so much for the Slaves, which they were not worth. My master likewise said to Barend van der Merwe that he must keep himself armed in order to shoot the first Commissioner or Englishman who should come to the Country to make the Slaves free, together with the Slaves all in one heap. . . .

The first time I complained at Tulbagh of my master was that I one morning went into the kitchen and asked my wife Betje, who was Cook, how it came that our victuals were so bad, as we had nothing else than soup, to which she answered she could not dress better victuals than her mistress gave her. While I was speaking to her in this manner, my master, who was in the fore part of the house, asked who was talking there. I answered it was I, on which my master got up and went into the room and brought out a *Sjambok* [ox or animal-hide whip] and an ox thong with which he bound my arms, and in this manner hoisted me up to the beam, when he broke a stick to pieces on my body and said that we must eat what he gave us even if he gave us ordure [excrement]. When I went to complain to the *Landdrost* [magistrate], he was not at home, on which my master had me made fast to a pole by the undersheriff and flogged. This took place not a year before the last ploughing time. After I had received my punishment my master took me home, and when I came into the house he tied me to a ladder and flogged me again, but of that I did not complain. . . .

On that occasion my master beat to pieces a jacket that cost me eight rixdollars, and I asked him for the money to pay the tailor that I bought it from, and of that I complained. When I was at Worcester my master sent his brother Isaac van der Merwe to fetch me home, when the *Landdrost* said that as my jacket was beaten to pieces and he had heard what I had to say I should not get a Flogging. The *Landdrost* likewise asked Master Isaac in my presence if he had not seen the newspaper in which it was forbidden to flog a slave with a *sjambok*. Master Isaac answered yes I have read it, on which the *Landdrost* asked him if his brother then did not know of it and had not read it, to which he likewise answered yes; the *Landdrost* then said that if they wanted to flog a Negro they must make use of a quince switch as thick as the undersheriff's ratan, or a thong, and give as many strokes as they deserved, from twenty-five to thirty-nine. . . . I heard the *Landdrost* say to my master that he must be cautious how he acted with me, for that my complaints were too great and that if I complained to the Gentlemen (Court) and that the business went farther, he might possibly lose me; for that he the *Landdrost* had done it only to satisfy my master. . . .

I have still further to speak about my child that is dead, his name was David, and his mother is the Hottentot Betje. My master said she must leave that child, which was twelve months old and began to creep about, at home, as it was too troublesome, because the mother had to cook and also to take care of the cattle. Once on coming home she found the child made fast to a tree and when she laid hold of it, it screamed out; she then examined the child's body, and found that it had been cruelly beaten. She asked old Frein, the wife of Achilles, how the child came so sore, and she said that her Mistress had ordered her to bind the child to the tree; she asked likewise how the child became so beaten, but she said she did not know and that she (Betje) must go herself and ask the Mistress how it happened, which Betje accordingly did, and the mistress said that master had done it out of malice. Betje then took the child away, and after that the sores were nearly healed, which was about a month and fifteen days afterwards, and the child began again to creep about and had gone to its mother at the water; my master took an ox thong which he doubled and flogged the child with, after which he brought it home. When Betje came from the water, my master beat the child again. The water was far from the house and Betje had gone there to wash the meat that was to be dressed. Master beat the child so long till that it was silent, and the same evening of that day the child died. I was not at home, for I was out to collect fifty-eight oxen belonging to my master. I was out twenty-six days at the Carroo [Karoo; arid scrubland] for the cattle. When I came home my wife Betje told me all those circumstances, on which I said I would go and complain of it, but she answered that master had asked her pardon and said that he had done it in a passion, in consequence of which I did not complain.

Note

1. "The Trial of Galant and Others," in *Records of the Cape Colony from February 1793 to April 1831* (London: Printed for the Government of Cape Colony, 1897–1905), 340.

Unconfessed

Yvette Christiansë

Until the final years of apartheid, slavery and its legacy rarely entered public discussion. Major changes in museum and public history followed the elections of 1994, including new displays at the former Dutch East India Company Slave Lodge in Cape Town. Controversies erupted in the city following the discovery of a slave burial ground at a building excavation site. The location of the slave past within public memory remains fraught, however, particularly with respect to the issue of mixed-race descent. The dismantling of racially discriminatory legislation produced enormous anxiety over definition among those people who under apartheid had been defined as Coloured. In the Western Cape especially, people began asserting Khoesan ancestry while denying slave or mixed-race descent.

Yvette Christiansë left apartheid South Africa at the age of eighteen, moving to Swaziland, Australia, and, finally, the United States, where she is a professor at Fordham University in New York City. Unconfessed, *her first novel, centers on the life of the slave woman Sila van den Kaap ("of the Cape"), based on court records from the nineteenth century. The novel is part of a broader literary trend concerned with the history of slavery pioneered by the Afrikaans and English writer André Brink, who wrote* A Chain of Voices *in the late 1970s using the records of the Galant Rebellion. Other literary writers who have explored slavery include Zoë Wicomb, whose* You Can't Get Lost in Cape Town *and other works move between the slave past and the politics of history and identity in contemporary South Africa. A distinctive feature of* Unconfessed *is its central concern with gender and the predicaments of women in South Africa.*

I miss those who were family to me on *Oumiesies'* [old missus's] farm. I have been thinking about them. I wish you had been with me then, all of you children. They would have looked after you. If I counted everyone I call family, we would fill a village of our own.

Now. Let me see if I can still remember. The number of lives that *Oumiesies* said she could do with as she wanted was fifteen before she sent some to [Master] Theron in the hope of peace between them.

There was Philip from Malabar. His name was Philip but he was not brother to Philipina who was, is, Alima's daughter and Spaasie's sister. You know how it is. They just give us names that lie around and sometimes the names make us brothers and sisters. Philip spoke a language that none of us understood. He had a mark over his left eyebrow, like this, and he was gentle with the animals. His job was the garden around the house and the fields. He was the only one from that place, Malabar.

Amerant came from Batavia. She worked in the house. Perhaps it was because they had no one else from their lands that she and Philip kept close together. Some days I would hear them talking, each in his or her own tongue, laughing. Amerant. She had two children who were sold away from her before she came to *Oumiesies*. It was Philip who brought some life back to her. She pleased *Oumiesies* greatly. But who knows what goes on in the hearts of witmens [white men]? *Oumiesies* was so pleased that, one day, when she had us all sewing, she said, Amerant, tomorrow you will go to Master Theron's farm. Amerant said, *Oumiesies*? What does *Oumiesies* want me to do there? *Oumiesies* said, you will be housemaid there. Amerant asked, and when must I come back? *Oumiesies* did not even look up from the stitching. She said, give me the green thread, you will stay there. Amerant began crying. *Oumiesies* was cross. She said, you will not cry. If you cry I will send for Master's Theron's *mandoor* [slave foreman] and he will give you something to cry about.

Philip's eyes went dull the day he asked if he could go with Amerant. *Oumiesies* said she needed him, but that he could drive the wagon when she went to see Theron. So, he saw Amerant sometimes, but not enough. He worked *Oumiesies*' fields in sadness. Then, after a long time, when *Oumiesies* saw how sad he was, she said she would read that big black book and find out what her god had to tell her. Her god must have liked Philip and Amerant because *Oumiesies* said to go to Master Theron. But that god does not see what goes on on Theron's farm because Theron sold them. *Oumiesies* was cross. She sent her *advocaat* [lawyer] to tell him that Amerant and Philip must be sent back or he must pay her. The *advocaat* came and said there was no money. So *Oumiesies* said Theron had to find Amerant and Philip and send them back to her. But we did not see them again. Maybe they are still together. I do not know. *Oumiesies* was angry. She said, never again. But it was too late for Amerant and Philip. And it was not true anyway.

Now. Who else? Oh. Yes. It would have been better if *Oumiesies* had sent Petro away. He also worked in the field. His anger made him unpleasant. Philip kept him in line. Petro was afraid that Philip might curse him in that language, you see.

And then there were those of us who are called Mozbiekers [from Mozambique]. We all came in ships and we never got that rolling world out of our ears because, on some days, one of us would stumble and the others knew the ocean was sending us a message.

Spaasie you know about. And Roosje, who was Mozbieker like me and Alima, but did not want to talk about it. She said it made a person mad with anger that had nowhere to go but across a room, or a table. Spaasie said no, anger came from not knowing there was something else.

Spaasie taught me many things—how to cook, how to make quince wine. Spaasie and Philipina, daughters of Alima, who was with *Oumiesies* for many years until she was old and then *Oumiesies*, who, good as she could be to us, could not be trusted and sent her and Philipina to Theron.

There were others who made that long journey in the ships. There were Mars, Anthony, and Isac. Mars and Anthony worked in the fields too, but Mars also kept the cattle. Isac was *Oumiesies'* favorite, after Alima and Johannes. Isac was clever. Sometimes we laughed and said he walked like a woman. Mars was sad and quiet, but Anthony was angry all the time, like Petro. Mars said that Anthony saw no difference between himself and the cattle. We all learned to find happiness, however it came. We tried with him, but happiness walked on the other side of his valley. He wanted to fight his way out of the place into which he had been brought. Who could blame him? But what could he do? So, he was always angry and he and Petro were always fighting. *Oumiesies* told Isac he must whip them if they fought. Isac swore at them for this. One morning Mars had a broken nose. Petro had a broken finger. *Oumiesies* took a *sjambok* [whip] and hit them both herself. I want to say more about Anthony, but there is nothing more to say. He longed for an army to lead against the *witmens*. I did not dislike him. We were close in years. I kept myself away from him. A woman's heart would break over such an unhappy man. I heard he was taken up by a man named Van der Riet but that may not be so.

Mars was older than me. Once, he asked me to lie with him. I said no. He asked Amerant. Philip wanted to hit him. He apologized. Then he wanted Philipina, but she said she would never go with a man. I do not know what happened to Mars.

Isac was gentle. He alone could reach Anthony. He put his arm around Anthony's shoulders and the anger would settle. Some nights, I know this, he lay with Anthony. Then, Anthony would be quieter but not happier. Ja [Yes], Isac. A good man. He understood things and even *Oumiesies* asked him what should be done with this, or that, when to plant this, when to take care of that. When she called him valuable, he said he liked Isac better and she just laughed. I heard he went to Cape Town and is now one of those men who prays five times a day [a Muslim]. I heard he went to Stellenbosch and is working for two winemakers. I heard he died when a horse kicked him in the head. Someone said he got his freedom and started walking back to where he was born. I do not know. You tell me which is true. Maybe one, maybe none.

Spaasie and Roosje's children you know of. Galate, Roosje's eldest, liked to chew on a stem of grass. Galate is the smell of grass and hay. Her brother Cesar needed caring. Spaasie cared for him and Galate because Roosje's care was filled with sadness and anger. She was too busy keeping anger on the horizon and her children reminded her of things she wanted to forget.

How much is too much?

I have told you about Spaasie's children. Galant her eldest, the same age as Roosje's girl, Galate. Roosje was angry when I asked why their names were so close. Spaasie said, Theron named them. Her face told me not to ask any more questions when Johannes walked out of the kitchen. If Galant was on this island, he would be in the same hut as Matroos, Soldaat, Keizer, and Vigiland. But you could trust his brother Arend, to find honey when no one else could. On a Sunday afternoon, while we rested, he searched for honey. He would sit near water and wait for the bees, then follow them. Quick on his feet, sharp eyes, charming to bees. Frederik was the next for Spaasie. He kept to her like a shadow, like Sariel, his sister, who was the baby of Spaasie's babies.

You would have liked them. We were all together on *Oumiesies'* farm and that was the year eighteen and six. . . .

All this talk of *Oumiesies'* farm. Last night I dreamed of it again.

The big change began one day when Theron visited with his wife and children. Spaasie said, you watch, he brings the children when he wants money. Roosje said, then he is a fool who never learns.

I carried the tray with tea and *koek* [cake] for the children, and Spaasie brought the cups and plates. So, we were in the room when *Oumiesies* was saying no. She did not stop when we came in, even though Theron and his wife tried to tell her to be quiet. In my house, *Oumiesies* said, you tell me what to do in my own house? Theron's wife told me and Spaasie to get out. *Oumiesies* said, I am mistress of this house until the day I die. You do not come into my house and tell my people what to do. Then she told us to leave everything on the table and go.

Well, you know we did not go far. We leaned at the door. Theron argued again for money. When his mother said no again, his wife said they needed extra hands to work on their land, young hands. *Oumiesies* said no. She asked them where Amerant and Philip were. She wanted to know where Philipina was. Theron said it was not his fault that he had debts. And his wife said, *Moeder* [mother], you have so much and you are one person, we are two with four children. We could not hear what *Oumiesies* said to that, but we heard Theron shout that what she said was not true. And his wife cried, Jesus in heaven protect me from hearing such things. She said, my husband is a good husband. Then we did hear *Oumiesies*. She said, he knows, the Lord knows, I know it, everyone who has eyes in their head can see your husband's bastards.

Spaasie pulled me away and said, go, take the children to the far field, stay there until I send for you. My heart was shaking when I took all the children. Sariel was on my back. We went into the far field and waited. I watched the path. The shadows grew long, longer, and then it was dark. Then the children were not happy. I had to make up a game and then I had to tell them to just sit still. It was late when the lamp swayed at the edge of the field. Johannes came with Spaasie. They said nothing until we were all back in our hut and Sariel was asleep.

Johannes said, Spaasie, you and Roosje must get *Oumiesies* to baptize you and your children. He said many people like us had been baptized and there was one woman in Cape Town who had children from her master, but made sure that she and they were baptized. When the master died and his family tried to sell them, she went to the fiscal [Dutch East India Company employee, prosecutor], who told the master's family that they could not sell those who had been baptized. Spaasie said, I know, I know. Johannes said, Sila, you must help them. You must speak to *Oumiesies* and make sure that all the children are baptized. I said yes.

The next day I tried to speak to *Oumiesies*, but she was too cross. She looked at me and then at Frederik, who was next to me. She would not talk to me all that day and told Spaasie to keep the children out of her rooms. But that night, when Isac brought the Bible to her for *boekevat* [prayers], she called all of us, even Anthony and Petro. She read about a man with many sores. She read until her voice trembled.

When she stopped, she looked at Spaasie and Roosje. She said, I want to know, once and for all. Johannes turned his face away, but Spaasie touched his shoulder. She said, *Oumiesies* knows I have done nothing wrong. *Oumiesies* said, spit it out! Spaasie said, ja. Roosje nodded too. *Oumiesies* went red in the face, then pale, then red again.

She looked at me. And you? Her eyes were hard. You tell them here in front of everyone. In front of this book!

Me? I did not have any children.

Oumiesies lifted the big book in the air. She said, you will tell me in the presence of god, have you lain with my son?

Spaasie said, *Oumiesies*, we have all kept him away from her.

Oumiesies threw the book down on the table and shouted at me. Me! Why did she not go and shout at that son of hers? She said, what kind of women are you to let such things happen? I said, *hai*! *Oumiesies* must know I never did this. I was cross. I said, *Oumiesies* must go ask her son.

She turned her face away. But I remembered what Johannes asked me to do. So I said outright, just like that, can *Oumiesies* help us children? She looked at me. She said what are you talking about? I said, can the children be baptized? For a long time she said nothing. Then she took cake and gave some to Sariel and the other children. She said, I will see about Spaasie and Roosje and their children. And then she sent us away.

Spaasie and Roosje were happy with me. Johannes said, you are not afraid. But my mouth was sour. What kind of heart did *Oumiesies* have? I thought of Amerant and Philip, and of Alima and Philipina. That old woman could do what she liked with us. I told Spaasie and Roosje. They said, do not worry, we will make sure that *Oumiesies* takes care of you too. But I had seen something in *Oumiesies'* eyes, something for which I did not have words. It made me cold inside. And that night I dreamed of so many tiny white snakes crawling all over the world.

A week later, Theron came back to shout at *Oumiesies*. Isac was in the room with *Oumiesies*, helping her with her accounts. He told us everything, how Theron shouted that the priest had been to him and some of *Oumiesies'* neighbors too, and the priest had asked him to come and speak to his mother to ask her what she was thinking. Why did she ask a priest to baptize slave children? He said he would tell anyone that she was a madwoman and would lose everything. Isac told us how *Oumiesies* told her son that she had promised her god that she would set things right. Theron said he would wash his hands of her. Isac said that when Theron rode off *Oumiesies* was shaking and went into her room. There was no *boekevat* [prayers] that night. Or the next. And never again.

A few days after Theron stamped out of the house, Johannes came back from the town with many things on the wagon and news that made him come quickly to the kitchen where I was sewing with Roosje. I remember. Spaasie was making bread. We laughed when we saw Johannes hop-hopping and asked if he had been drinking *arak* [anise spirits]. He said, Spaasie, give me a cup of *Oumiesies'* fresh *melk* [milk], today is a day for celebration. He said, good things will begin for us, the English have become rulers again.

There is a governor who does not like the settlers, and there is talk that they will end all slavery. He said there is someone who will watch out for us.

Spaasie said, speak up, old man. Who is this who is going to care for us?

Many people, Johannes said.

Where are these people? we asked.

Far away, in the English country. We laughed even more. Johannes would not listen. He said there was talk of people who did not like slavery and they were pushing the English *kgosi* [king] to make a law that would protect us. Johannes said that the governor was already very cross with the settlers and wanted them to answer when they mistreated slaves. If Theron beats any of us again, we can go to the governor.

You should have heard us laugh. Roosje said, Ja? And how do we get to the governor? I said, we can ride in *Oumiesies'* carriage like ladies.

We were all still laughing when the kitchen door was kicked in. It was Theron. He pointed at us and said he was going to punish us all. He called *Oumiesies* and when she came he said to her, the British are taking away our land and now they are trying to take our right to be our own masters. It was as Johannes said. *Oumiesies* and Theron and all their people had to make a list of who we were. That is what made Theron very angry.

You see, this is what it was, the governor sent a message to all masters and mistresses and said all of those that they called slaves had to be registered. The governor said in that message that the king of England and those who help him now desired that we be written into a book. Spaasie said this was good. Roosje asked for what. Spaasie said it meant someone wanted to know where we were and that could only be good. Roosje asked if she thought the world would one day wake up and fix itself up.

We all laughed, except for *Oumiesies'* son. I heard him fight with his mother when he told her not to put all of us down on paper and she told him he had too much of his weak father in him. She said he lied on paper about who was and was not on his farm. We should have listened to that, more than we have listened to our own laughter.

But, too late for that. And that is why I tell you, *listen*, Baro. Listen. This is my family in this world of demons. This is your family too. Together we hold the demons from swallowing us up completely. Do you understand me? This is our family. Johannes, he who said I danced like a slender branch in a gentle breeze.

Poor Johannes with that broken body of his.

You see. Johannes looked at the world and wanted it to be different, but also knew what was what. When Spaasie wanted us to remember where we

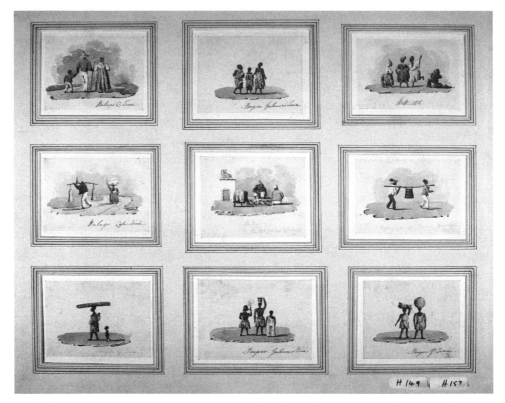

Malay life in Cape Town. Watercolor by Henry Clifford de Meillon. Courtesy of Iziko Social History & Art Collections, H 149–157.

came from, he said, you Mozbiekers make it hard for yourselves. You do not know when to stop. You hit your heads on the wall because you do not like the wall where it is, but wall has no thought. Wall is wall. And these people who call themselves masters and madams have walls inside them. Teach this girl how to live here, now, not like a bird born with two heads, one to look behind, one to look forward. There is no behind. This is behind. And there is no forward. This is forward. Teach her this and you will take the pain away.

Roosje agreed with him, but liked to tease him. When he said there is no behind, she hit herself and said, hey, Johannes, here's behind, here's a good *gat* [asshole], that's all the behind I have. He did not like this, but he laughed. And Spaasie was cross, but she said nothing. She let them laugh at her. Sometimes, if Johannes was really cross about the words she wanted me to remember, if he shouted, give this up, she would tell him quietly,

Johannes that is your leg speaking to you. Then he would go away, limping that limp and she would be upset with herself.

Alima once said, Sila, be careful of pain. It is a chain they fix to you. It is a chain they want you to pull around your own heart. Be careful. *Heesh* [leave it alone]. That woman knew things.

I wanted Johannes to like me. I liked to dance for him, even when I knew about him and Alima. I learned that I could just like a man. This is important for us. In the business of men and women we are on the top of a long slope and we get kicked down. No time to say, hey, wait. So I learned to have a special place in my heart for Johannes, and it made me happy when he smiled and clapped to keep time as I danced.

These are all family. And you must know that we all share the same parent. We have that parent's eyes. Look. Next time you go past Lys or Mina or Rachel—yes, even Mina because she too is family—look into their eyes and you will see your own and your mother's. We are the offspring of that Cape of Good Hope, and that Cape of Good Hope is the place that fathers one branch of what the minister's wife calls a family tree, while another is mothered. And, let me tell you, that place makes us who we are but it will deny us. I know this as sure as I stand here and look upon that town today. It is those wives of those fathers that you must watch with the most careful eye. They are jealous and they tell themselves lies. They stare over our heads and clutch their pretty, well-pressed children to their sides, staring and waiting for the man of the house to come home.

But then, there are mothers. And then there are mothers.

Bobotie Recipe

Clifton Crais

Bobotie is South Africa's national dish. Its origins lie in the Western Cape and the development of slavery in the second half of the seventeenth century. It is a quintessentially creole dish combining African, European, and Indonesian foods. From Khoekhoe pastoralists came beef and lamb. From Europe came the tradition of making egg and milk custards, meatloaf, and ground meat with rich toppings similar to British shepherd's pie or Greek moussaka. And from Indonesia came curries and spices such as cumin, coriander, dried peppercorns, turmeric, and, crucially, rice. The word Bobotie likely is related to the traditional Javanese rice-based dish called bobotok. Bobotie began among the urban slave population in Cape Town, whose descendants came to be known as the Cape Malay community, but the dish became common throughout farming communities in the Western Cape and beyond. It is invariably served over a bed of yellow rice along with chutney and sliced banana.

Serves four to six people

Ingredients

FOR THE FILLING

    2 pounds ground sirloin or lamb. You may also mix the two meats. (Traditionally bobotie was prepared using leftover meat.)

    1 large onion, finely diced

    2 tablespoons vegetable oil or butter

    2 thick slices of stale white bread without the crust

    Juice of half a lemon (you can add more if you like less sweetness), or a tablespoon of red wine vinegar

    10–12 dried apricots, finely diced

    1/4 cup sultanas (golden raisins)

    3 tablespoons slivered almonds, roasted in a dry frying pan

    1 tablespoon curry powder

    1 teaspoon ground turmeric

    1 teaspoon fresh ginger, grated

3 cloves garlic, chopped
3 bay leaves
3 lemon leaves (if available)
1 cup milk
Salt and pepper to taste

FOR THE TOPPING
 1 cup milk
 2 eggs
 1/2 teaspoon salt

Directions

Preheat oven to 180 degrees Fahrenheit. Sauté onion in the oil (or butter) on a medium heat until golden. Add meat, chopped garlic, grated ginger, curry powder, and turmeric. Brown meat on medium heat. While the onion is cooking, soak bread in milk. Set aside. When the meat has browned, add the soaked bread, sultanas, almonds, diced apricots, and lemon juice. Add salt and pepper. Mix thoroughly, ensuring the soaked bread breaks apart. Remove from heat and place mixture in a heavy, buttered casserole dish. Roll up the bay and lemon leaves and bury them into the mixture. Cover with foil. Cook for ninety minutes.

 To prepare the topping, whisk two eggs with one cup milk. Add salt. Remove casserole from the oven. Carefully pour the topping mixture over the meat. Return to the oven and bake, uncovered, for a further fifteen to twenty minutes or until the topping has cooked and is lightly browned. Serve with yellow rice.

The Subjugation of the Eastern Cape Khoekhoe

John Barrow

South Africa's frontier was among the most violent of anywhere in the colonial world. European settlement expanded rapidly over the course of the eighteenth century, particularly in the more arid regions of the Cape east of Swellendam. Colonists, known as trekboere *(migratory cattle farmers), survived by herding sheep and cattle, which entered the maritime trade as brined meat to support sailors traveling between Europe and the East Indies. The Dutch East India Company struggled to control its expanding colony, particularly relationships between settlers and Africans. The* Strafkommando *(punitive group of armed citizens), an institution originally created in 1715 to replace Dutch East India Company soldiers protecting against Khoesan raids, evolved into a predatory force by which colonists plundered Khoesan herds and destroyed communities.*

By the mid-1770s Khoesan communities west of the Gamtoos River had been subjugated. In the next two decades, ferocious genocidal violence unfolded along the frontier. In 1799 Khoesan who were reduced to peonage, as well as those still precariously living independently, rose up in rebellion against Dutch settlers. The war followed the first British occupation of the Cape (1795–1803) and the attempt by the British colonial government to extend control over the trekboere. The war's end marked the eclipse of the Eastern Cape Khoekhoe and the entrenchment of unfree labor and the continuation of extraordinarily high levels of violence on white farms. Sir John Barrow (1764–1848), the private secretary to the British governor, traveled into the interior and produced a detailed report that condemned the Boers as violent, degenerate colonists but lauded enlightened British rule. In the excerpt, Barrow describes the condition of the Khoekhoe and quotes from Klaas Stuurman, one of the last independent Khoekhoe leaders in the Cape.

It has been observed, with too much truth, that if a black should only strike a white, he runs the charge of being tortured and torn in pieces. . . . But if a white man murders a black belonging to himself, he puts him into the ground, and nothing more is said about it. . . . Such is the distribution of justice between a man compelled to be a slave, and one born to be free. . . . "We lived very contentedly," said [Klaas Stuurman], "before these Dutch plunderers molested us; and why should we not do so again, if left to ourselves? Has not the *Groot Baas* (the Great Master) given plenty of grass-roots, and berries, and grasshoppers for our use; and till the Dutch destroyed them, abundance of wild animals to hunt? And will they not return and multiply when these destroyers are gone"?

. . . Twenty years ago . . . the country beyond the Gamtoos river . . . abounded with kraals or villages of Hottentots, out of which the inhabitants came to meet them by hundreds in a group. Some of these villages might still have been expected to remain in this remote and not very populous part of the colony. Not one, however, was to be found. There is not in the whole extensive district of Graaf-Reinet a single horde of independent Hottentots; and perhaps not a score of individuals who are not actually in the service of the Dutch. These weak people, the most helpless, and in their present condition perhaps the most wretched, of the human race, duped out of their possessions, their country, and finally out of their liberty, have entailed upon their miserable offspring a state of existence to which that of slavery might bear the comparison of happiness. It is a condition, however, not likely to continue to a very remote posterity. The name of Hottentot will be forgotten or remembered only as that of a deceased person of little note. Their numbers of late years have rapidly declined. . . . [T]heir extreme poverty, scantiness of food, and continual dejection of mind, arising from the cruel treatment they receive from an inhuman and unfeeling [colonial] peasantry, who have discovered themselves to be removed to too great a distance from the seat of their former government to be awed by its authority, have exercised, in the most wonton and barbarous manner, an absolute power over these poor wretched reduced to the necessity of depending upon them for a morsel of bread. There is scarcely an instance of cruelty said to have been committed against the slave of the West-India [West Indies] islands, that could not find a parallel from the Dutch farmers of the remote parts of the colony towards the Hottentots in their service. Beatings and cutting them with thongs of the hide of the sea-cow [hippopotamus] or rhinoceros, is a gentle punishment, though these sort of whips which they call *sjamboks* are most horrid instruments, tough, pliant, and heavy almost as lead. Firing small shot in the legs and thighs of a Hottentot is a punishment not unknown. . . . Instant death is not unfrequently the consequence of punishing these poor wretches in a moment of rage. This is of little consequence to the farmer; for though they are to all intents and

purposes his slaves, yet they are not transferable property. It is this circumstance which, in his mind, makes their lives less valuable and their treatment more inhuman. . . .

By resolution of the old government, as unjust as it was inhuman, a peasant was allowed to claim as his property, till the age of five-and-twenty, all
the children of the Hottentots in his service to whom he had given in their
infancy a morsel of meat. At the expiration of this period the odds are ten
to one that the slave is not emancipated. . . . Should he be fortunate enough
to escape at the end of the period, the best part of his life is spent in a profit-
less servitude, and he is turned adrift in the decline of life . . . without any
earthly thing he can call his own, except the sheep's skin upon his back.

The condition of those who engage themselves from year to year is little
better than that of the other. If they have already families, they erect for
them little straw-huts near the farmhouse. Their children are encouraged to
run about the house of the peasant, where they receive their morsel of food.
This is deemed sufficient to establish their claim to the young Hottentots;
and should the parents, at the end of the term for which they are engaged,
express a desire to quit the service, the farmer will suffer them to go, perhaps turn them away, and detain their children.

The Treatment of Indentured Laborers

R. J. van der Riet

Peonage (the inboek *system) was pervasive across the Cape. It allowed farmers to indenture workers up to the age of twenty-five, though in reality many spent their entire lives in servitude. Violence permeated colonial labor relations. While the Dutch East India Company had attempted to curb settler violence, greater control began emerging only in the British era, most notoriously in the so-called Black Circuit court of 1812, in which officials encouraged laborers to file complaints against their masters. This document, written in 1810 by the senior official in the Stellenbosch district, sheds light on the violence of rural master-servant relations and farmers' belief in the necessity of forced labor.*

Many Europeans [i.e., visitors] and those who do not know the natives at first-hand, or have never employed them, cannot understand how lazy and stubborn a nation they are. They are by nature untrustworthy, slothful and drowsy, with very few exceptions.

And if the masters can get no work from the children of Hottentots, by obligation, in return for the care and trouble taken in their upbringing, or have no prospect of keeping such Hottentot children in service, . . . then many of the masters will soon perish from concern and worry. They will not be able to make a living anywhere for a Hottentot with children cannot obtain employment. This I have seen so often in the course of my professional duties. The farmers in the interior assert, and do so with right, that the children of this nation are more of a liability than the services of their mothers can be an asset. . . . The trouble and expense is made tolerable [only] by the prospect of the services yet to be received. Should these services be abolished, would not the obligation fall away which motivated the farmer in the interior to bring up the children of this nation? These services having been abolished, the prospect falls away and therefore, this nation, instead of being done a service, would be done a disservice by regarding them as a free people who should enjoy ideal freedom, which would in practice make them unhappy. . . .

I have already dealt with the trades . . . and so I pass on to . . . the way in which the natural freedom which inspires useful conduct might be deadened by a period of 25 years' service. This would certainly be a valid argument, or appear to be, but experience has taught me that, for the greatest part, Hottentots who have grown up outside service wander about and become thieves. As they have never been encouraged to work in their youth, they are completely incompetent and incapable of doing so in their more advanced years, and the idea that they are free is more a burden to them than a real sentiment.

That nobody has the right to force a free people into bondage, as you assert . . . is correct but superficial, for that flower could bear bitter fruit. What would become of us and of the whole colony if the natives were to feel that they should be free, were to know their power, and then to join together to regain their natural freedom as the original possessors of this country? In effect, nothing but a second St Domingo [Haiti]. Is a policy not therefore required which will ensure that, although this nation is not in effect a nation of slaves, they might still be instilled with a certain sense of service and that the dangerous and idealistic feeling of freedom might be weakened, or at least kept within certain limits?

In my position, it has often been my experience that there are female Hottentots who leave their children, even those who were born among their own nation, and are never even heard to ask after them. What is now to be done with such unfortunate creatures (*schepselen*), who are without a father or mother? Should they beg for food along the road, or should they work? No farmer will take such a child in, except with the assurance that he can demand the labour of the child for a certain number of years. And to prevent such miserable people from perishing from hunger and worry, it has become customary for *Landdrosts* [magistrates] and *Heemraden* [magistracy councilors] to bestow such a Hottentot child or children until his twenty-fifth year on one of the inhabitants who takes pity on him. This is done on condition that when the father or mother comes to ask for that child, as often happens once the children are able to work, fair compensation must be made to the inhabitant with whom the child was indentured, according to the judgment of the College [of Heemraden] for the trouble and care which he has taken.

In my experience, it has also often happened that the father and mother of Hottentot children themselves come voluntarily to give their children to the inhabitants until their twenty-fifth year, as they do not think themselves able to support their child or children.

Protesting the Vagrancy Ordinance

Various

Six years before the abolition of slavery in the British Empire, the Cape's new rulers ended the system of peonage (inboek). Ordinance 50 (1828) outlawed the inboek system, prohibited the indentureship of children without the express permission of their parents, and permitted Khoesan to own land. White farmers detested the new law, which they believed would increase vagrancy and theft and make it impossible for them to discipline their workers. Missionaries generally applauded its passing, believing that the newly found freedoms would aid their efforts at spreading Christianity and creating peasant communities at the various mission stations in the colony. One such community emerged at the Kat River along the colonial border, where former peons built a number of churches and farmed their own land.

In 1834 and just at the moment of abolition in the British Empire, mostly British colonists in the Eastern Cape led an effort to enact a vagrancy law. That winter, the residents of Kat River met to protest the proposed legislation, where they recounted their personal and collective histories of peonage. The document that follows is a transcript of that meeting; it is one of the few times we can hear former peons talking about their pasts and describing their experiences of freedom. Ultimately the law did not pass, though in 1856 the colonial government enacted the Masters and Servants Act, followed by legislation such as the Vagrancy Act of 1879; versions of both laws remained in force into the 1970s. As a result of increasing persecutions by local farmers, many Kat River peasants rebelled in the Eighth Frontier War (1850–53).

Mr. Magerman rose and spoke as follows—In Mr. Fischer's time I was "ingebocked" for ten years, when I was so young (here showing his height them) to my "Baas" David Van der Merwe in the Camdeboo. My Baas promised then to bring me up and instruct me as his own children—but I had to be among the dogs in the ashes. I was many a time . . . flogged . . . so that when I ran from the fire hearth the ashes were strewed and the coals after me, and the dogs alarmed would pursue me.

I got no instruction and no clothes—I know nothing. My Mother was obliged from bad treatment to run away and leave me—and my Father soon

Khoekhoe mounted gunman from Kat River Settlement. From the Collection of the Parliament of South Africa, 19358 (xvii).

after—and when he would attempt to get a sight of me, the dogs were sent after him. . . . I got so little to eat from my Baas. [I had] to steal to support life—yes my friends I [became a] "Schelm" [*skelm*; rascal]. I was tied hand and foot and beat. . . . I had to run away from my Baas through the wolves and [lions], to my Mother in the neighbourhood of the Cape. Yes I had to leave all my cattle and my Father's cattle in my Baas's hand. I became a paarde-wagten [groom responsible for horses] and after I had taken long charge of the horses, I thought I would ask my Master for some wages—he told me to [bring] the horses together which I did. He told me to point out to him what horse I would like. I pointed to a young Mare, but my Master did not answer one word—no my friends, what means that if you ask a thing, and the person gives no answer (a person here answers him "unwillingness")—yes—I stopped some time longer but seeing I was to receive nothing I ran away again, and found my Father in Graaff Reinet and now [I am with] my Mother and my young brother here there is he (pointing to a young lad in the Meeting)—I never thought I would have seen him again. . . .

Today we sit in the shade and you know if you go out of the Sun into the shade, and go back into the Sun again then you feel the Sun still more. Also if this Law passes then will we feel it more than ever—for then we must stand the heat of the Sun and the "Baas" above all. I was always naked before but now that I have come here I appear to be something like human being (showing his red jacket)—my friends I desire to remain here, and not run away any more therefore I hope the Law will not pass. . . .

Mr. Andries Stoffel rose and said that this was the first day and the first place that he was allowed to speak on behalf of his Nation.—I thank God—I thank the King and his council—I thank the Governor (Cole)—I thank Dr. Philip, and I thank Mr. Stockenstrom. I am a little confused today. Two men that have already addressed the meeting have mentioned about the Cape and the Kat River, these words have aroused me, for never had any man required from the Sout River to the Kat, whither we Hottontots were born in such poverty or misery as we were long in. It was over the Zwartkops River that the Hottontots were first consulted about their grievances for the Majesty Commissioners, and after their return to His Majesty the 50th Ordinance came out, then did we first taste freedom that other men eat so sweet. We rejoice at the very word freedom and Free labour even before it is mingled with water + ground it is 20 times sweeter than forced labour. . . . I was born at the Bushmans river among that sheep and cattle, but we soon lost all our property and our land and water. Where is there now a Hottontots Kraal on their own ground? I was obliged to leave the service of the Farmer, and my 130 sheep + 30 cattle to this day in his hand. I ran away to these English only with my dog. The 50 ordinance is a Wonder (here the speaker's feelings overcome him for a moment). . . .

Mr. Andrius Pretorius—My friends, this is the first day that we have en joined to meet by law to consider the state of our Nation. Our fathers occupied the land from the Sout River to the Great Kat River. He sees the land but he cannot possess it. Our fathers had abundance of cattle and sheep, and then there were no vagrants, for they could support themselves. They became weak and lost their property and were obliged to enter into the service of the Farmers. There they became vagrants on account of hard treatment and bad pay. . . . Let the Boer hire the settler for that or the Settler the Boer, and let him see what he will make of it. The [government] have indeed given us freedom but we can still get no money and so that we must become vagrants. . . .

Mr. Winvogel Smit seconded the resolution by saying that when he was very young he saw his Father going with bow and arrows. He saw his Mother tied to a window and branded by a Boer, and after she got [loose] she had to flee through the wilderness among the wild beasts, and I had alone to take care of the Boer's sheep, but today am I here where I see one of my own Nation sitting and writing in the Chair, and the children reporting behind, for which I thank God.

Manifesto

Piet Retief

Between 1836 and the mid-1840s between six thousand and fifteen thousand Boers (roughly 10 percent of the Cape's white population) migrated into South Africa's interior, where they would establish the Natalia Republic (1839), the South African Republic (1852), and the Orange Free State (1854). These migrations collectively came to be known as the Afrikaner Great Trek. In the latter nineteenth century and especially in the twentieth century, the Great Trek became a foundational part of Afrikaner nationalism, most visibly in the reenactment of the trek in 1938 and the construction of the Voortrekker Monument in Pretoria during the late 1930s.

Afrikaner nationalists portrayed the Great Trek as a singular, heroic migration of a chosen Christian people into the barbarous interior. For the nationalists, the Great Trek represented the birth of the Afrikaner nation after fleeing British oppression. Ordinance 50 and the ending of slavery challenged the personalized and often violent rule of master and servant. British rulers preferred the state's prison to the master's whip. Neither the abolition of peonage nor slavery, however, produced the revolution in class relations in the Cape that many Boers feared. For many reasons, Europeans had been moving across the Cape's border for decades. Land in the Cape Colony had become increasingly scarce from the late eighteenth century, which encouraged young farmers to eye land further in the interior. The Great Trek thus represented both a decisive turning point in Boer history and a continuation of expansive colonial frontiers of trade and settlement.

Piet Retief (1780–1838) was a quintessential frontier farmer who lived in the area near Grahamstown, the seat of the Eastern Cape government and of British colonial settlement. He lived largely by livestock farming and land speculation. Like many other farmers, Retief lost much of his cattle and property in the colonial conflicts with the neighboring Xhosa peoples, and he experienced firsthand the British policies that ended peonage and slavery. Retief emerged as a trekker leader, leading parties of migrants into the Natal region where, along with sixty trekkers, he was murdered on the order of the Zulu king Dingane after seeking the cession of Natal.

Klaas Smit's river wagon broke down crossing the drift. Painting by Thomas Baines. Courtesy of Museum Africa, Johannesburg, MA 1052.

Numerous reports having been circulated throughout the colony, evidently with the intention of exciting in the minds of our countrymen a feeling of prejudice [against] those who have resolved to emigrate from a colony where they have experienced, for so many years past, a series of the most vexatious and severe losses; and, as we desire to stand high in the estimation of our brethren, and are anxious that they and the world at large should believe us incapable of severing that sacred tie which binds a Christian to his native soil, without the most sufficient reasons; we are induced to record the following summary of our motives for taking so important a step, and also our intentions respecting our proceedings towards the native tribes which we may meet with beyond the boundary:

1. We despair of saving the colony from those evils which threaten it by the turbulent and dishonest conduct of vagrants, who are allowed to infest the country in every part; nor do we see any prospect of peace or happiness for our children in any country thus distracted by internal commotions.

2. We complain of the severe losses which we have been forced to sustain by the emancipation of our slaves, and the vexatious laws which have been enacted respecting them.

3. We complain of the continual system of plunder which we have ever endured from the Caffres [Xhosa] and other coloured classes, and par-

ticularly by the last invasion of the colony [the war of 1834–35], which has desolated the frontier districts and ruined most of the inhabitants.

4. We complain of the unjustifiable odium which has been cast upon us by interested and dishonest persons, under the cloak of religion, whose testimony is believed in England, to the exclusion of all evidence in our favour; and we can foresee, as the result of this prejudice, nothing but the total ruin of the country.

5. We are resolved, wherever we go, that we will uphold the just principle of liberty; but, whilst we will take care that no one shall be held in a state of slavery, it is our determination to maintain such regulations as may suppress crime, and preserve proper relations between master and servant.

6. We solemnly declare that we quit this colony with a desire to lead a more quiet life than we have heretofore done. We will not molest any people, nor deprive them of the smallest property; but, if attacked, we shall consider ourselves fully justified in defending our persons and effects, to the utmost of our ability, against every enemy.

7. We make known that when we shall have framed a code of laws for our future guidance, copies shall be forwarded to the colony for general information; but we take this opportunity of stating that it is our firm resolve to make provision for the summary punishment of any traitors who may be found amongst us.

8. We propose, in the course of our journey, and on arriving at the country in which we shall permanently reside, to make known to the native tribes our intentions, and our desire to live in peace and friendly intercourse with them.

9. We quit this colony under the full assurance that the English Government has nothing more to require of us, and will allow us to govern ourselves without its interference in future.

10. We are now quitting the fruitful land of our birth, in which we have suffered enormous losses and continual vexation, and are entering a wild and dangerous territory; but we go with a firm reliance on an all-seeing, just, and merciful Being, whom it will be our endeavour to fear and humbly to obey.

The History of the Afrikaans People

C. P. Bezuidenhout

Afrikaner nationalism emerged with a distinctly theological vision. Intellectuals such as C. P. Bezuidenhout saw in the Afrikaners a people chosen by God. In his polemic from 1882, Bezuidenhout transcribed history as biblical experience. In a metaphor reminiscent of African American rhetoric in the United States, the British become latter-day Egyptian tyrants, the Great Trek a new Exodus, and Piet Retief the Afrikaners' Moses. At the center of this theological vision is a belief that Afrikaners were preordained by God to colonize South Africa, and the idea that humanity was composed of unassimilable races.

In the selection, Bezuidenhout begins with what came to be known as the Slagtersnek Rebellion of 1815–16, which unfolded along the Cape Colony's eastern frontier. Most Boers bristled at the attempts by the British to extend formal control over the region, including changes to the land-tenure system and especially the use of courts to curb violence. In 1815 a Khoekhoe laborer laid a complaint against his employer, Cornelius Frederik Bezuidenhout, which led to a cascade of events that culminated in charges and ultimately to the beginnings of a conspiracy by frontier farmers to overthrow British rule. The British later botched the execution of five prisoners, to the great outrage of local Boers.

The remainder of the selection depicts the history of the early trekkers, their relations with the Zulu Kingdom, and especially their trials and tribulations in what became the Orange Free State. The author depicts the British as dastardly and Africans as savage and untrustworthy, idioms that would endure within Afrikaner nationalist ideology, in addition to their use in legitimating Boer control over African land. Silent in this mythic history is a more complex past that included unprovoked Boer predations on African communities.

The author of this history is an Afrikaner, born of Afrikaans parents, patriots from time immemorial, descendants and shoots of the vine, brought here from Holland over the seas. He is heartily interested in the welfare, the growth and salvation of his people. . . . It is surprising to know how the Afrikaans people were used to spread salvation and blessings to so many

Europeans; to remove thousands of obstructions to open up riches and trea-
sure, of gold and precious stones; and this they had done with danger to
their lives and at the cost of rivers of blood and tears; surprising I say, to
know of all of this and observe as well that despite this the Afrikaans people
are suppressed, misjudged and persecuted by the so-called civilized English
Government. . . .

Wander in spirit through the history of our people from Cape Town as
far as Natal and you will find them on mountains and rocks in the midst of
roaring lions and savage barbarians; as cedars of God. Their paean became
reflected in the echo of the forest and valley; everywhere they were found it
was clear to see in them that they were a planting of the Lord. . . .

Not for too long did the vine brought over from Egypt and planted in
Canaan grow before passers-by began plucking from it; the wild boar came
out of the wood to waste the vine; the wild beast of the field came to devour
its leaves and shoots. . . .

What the passers-by were for ancient Israel, the British Government has
been for our people from early times and still today; how has the vine of our
people not been plucked from, and how do passers-by still pluck from it to
this very day! . . .

We begin our first historical account by making mention of the diaboli-
cal deed executed on Slagtersnek by the British Government.

When I was a youth this event was told to me by several people who
were contemporaries and witnesses of the hellish deed. After England had
made itself master of Africa by means of cunning and violence[,] the indigenous peoples of Africa began living among the farmers, being incited by
missionaries in various ways to tell all kinds of lies to the British officials to
the detriment of our beloved forefathers because they possessed the same
savage quality of the boar in the wood and the wild beasts of the fields,
like the Canaanite and Amorite in Canaan. English officials were gullible
enough to believe lies and follow chimeras. . . . When I am going to tell you
how our people were provoked and suppressed your blood will boil in your
veins. I was solemnly informed by grey-beards of that time how our forefathers were suppressed and their rights restricted. It so happened that close
to Slagtersnek, Kat River, and its environs, the Hottentots had tied children
of white people in front of bees' nests, broken anthills on some and in this
way tortured them. Was it to be wondered at that our forefathers no longer
wanted to bear the English yoke; that they had exposed their lives to danger
for their freedom? . . . Faber and [C. F.] Bezuidenhout were in a small laager
[defensive formation of wagons in a circle], Faber went out to find a way
through the bush to escape from the hellish tyranny, [and] Bezuidenhout

had a son of less than 14 years of age, named Gert Frederijk. Then, unexpectedly a mixed army, red, yellow and black, stormed them, but Bezuidenhout with his son and wife defended themselves with everything in their power. The Dragoons and English shot furiously at them, they hit Bezuidenhout; his back being wounded he sat against a wagon wheel. His wife, the heroine, stood beside him and loaded the muskets for him. His son sat under the wagon[;] he rested the musket on a spoke because an 8 pounder was too heavy for him to hold as a child. He fired together with his father against the superior power of the enemy, and however carefully this has been kept a secret, they killed a number of them. The wife had received some 30 bullets through her clothing but was not wounded. . . .

Now Faber, another Bezuidenhout, and three others were arrested and sentenced to death. . . . The bloodhound was insatiable in its bloodthirstiness, and that was the cause of the gallows breaking down when they were half dead. . . . There is a large crowd assembled together—two parties. On the one side a beloved group of friends weep and lament, about to give their dear true friends and fathers a last farewell kiss on their lips. On the other side triumph is trumpeted: see how the criminals make haste with hellish haste to take the lives of their prey before acquittal arrives. When they had been hanging for some moments, the gallows broke; our beloved ones regained consciousness. . . . Our beloved ones lurched around half moribund; prayed for pardon and grace; women and children crawled in the dust, fell to the ground at the feet of the heartless judge, wetting the feet of the Commander in Chief with hot tears. A voice of crying and lamentation reverberated through the air, but in vain; they had once more to ascend [the steps] and die this cruel death. . . .

In 1834 some of our ancestors trekked from the Cape Colony after they had received good reports from the Commission that they had sent out to Natal; however, some time after that they returned following unsatisfactory rumours, and came through unscathed; but in 1836 a large number of our forefathers had decided to now leave the country forever, due to the injustice they had to suffer under the British Government; they trekked across the Great River [Orange River] towards the site of the Moroko; shortly thereafter an even larger party also crossed the Great River from the Graaff Reinet district, of which Gert Maritz was the leader, later again another party from Uitenhage, under the leadership of Jakob Uijs, Karel Landman and others. They trekked north along the Vaal River, where they came into contact with Mozielakatze [Mzilikazi; king of the Ndebele people]. The kaffirs then unexpectedly attacked our forefathers while they were gathered together in small encampments; and at first 28 and afterwards 25 were cru-

Defying the Law. Artist unknown. Courtesy of Free State
Archives Photographic Collection, VA3720.

elly murdered. Some of them escaped through God's dispensation to warn
those who were still trekking on. They then formed a small laager. The
enemy stormed them with savage cries. It became a battle for life and death,
but they were victorious in the name of the Lord. . . .

In the vicinity of the town named Weenen, Dingaan [the Zulu king] perpetrated the last cruel murders by an unexpected attack on small groups
of our beloved voortrekkers [Boers who migrated into the interior] in this
land; it was an indescribable scene: mutilated and smashed men, women
and children, scattered on the ground! . . .

Now the other voortrekkers planned to take revenge on Dingaan for the
blood of their dear relations. They tried this, but without much success,
since they were too few in number, but when Andries Pretorius and his
men joined them they advanced against them with a mounted Commando
of 46 men. Then Karel Landman joined them with his men. On daybreak on
the 16th December 1838 they advanced on Dingaan. . . . They destroyed and
subjugated the entire empire of Dingaan. . . . After the glorious victory that
God gave to our loved ones, they discovered the skeletons of the 60 heroes
[referring to Retief and his party] and then experienced grief once more. . . .

[Afrikaners] arrived between the Orange River and Riet River, some bought farms or tracts of land; others rented grazing land from the tribes to whom the land belonged. How altogether differently did our respected voortrekkers act! Were they descendants of Great Britain, they would promptly have sent police upon police, soldier upon soldier and soon deprived the Korannas of their land and their freedom!

Our noble voortrekkers did not do this, they knew and served a just sovereign and they knew that an oppressor was a thief and a thief a murderer, therefore those that could not find land to buy rented such for a fixed period and paid for it; when the landowners established their own Government, it happened that a Barolong made inroads upon the rights of the farmers, for which the field cornet [local official who acted as policeman and militia leader] gave him a hiding and allowed him to leave. He then complained to the Koranna chief, Adam Kok; he had a subpoena served on the field cornet. What a cheek the Griqua had! . . . When the field cornet failed to appear he sent an armed force and was brave enough to start shooting at our beloved voortrekkers, those men of spirit; the result was that the Korannas had to flee in order not to be punished. When mister Englishman got to know about this he felt himself obliged to promptly (because the Griquas and Boers were too weak to take up weapons against him to defend their right) seize Adam Kok's land; then he would once more have robbed the Boers of their freedom. The Government then proclaimed the entire land between the Great and Vaal Rivers on the 3rd February 1848 [British declaration of the Orange River Sovereignty]! What do you say now, dear readers, of our historical account? Behold there an uncivilized act by the most civilized Government! Behold there the act of a barbarian, performed by the pious Statesmen of England. . . . Our ancestors were compelled to take up arms to fight for life, justice and freedom. . . . Sir Harry Smith and [Henry] Warden advanced upon them with an army of 1900 men; on our side 400 men; hazardous, yes, dear readers? 400 against 1900. Our forefathers built their hope upon the just God who did not leave them shamed. On the 29th August 1848, the English together with Griquas and Kaffirs and still other accomplices attacked our beloved voortrekkers, but they discovered their mistake as we commonly say, and God neither willed it nor were the 400 men of whom only five were put out of combat, totally destroyed. . . .

Although our heroes of old defeated the English at Boomplaats, they held on to the land. Most of our ancestors then trekked across the Vaal River under General Andries Pretorius. The British Government became despondent as a result of various problems, and then returned the Free State. . . . The Act of Freedom of Convention [Orange River Convention] was signed

on the 23rd February 1854 by all the officials from both sides and was rati-
fied by the Queen. Now the Free State farmers were a free people. Thereafter they elected the Right Honourable J. H. Brand, formerly Advocate in
the Colony. Now the Free State had a competent man at its head and now
the vine flourished with prosperity. Adam Kok saw that it would not be
best to live among Afrikaans farmers indefinitely. He sold the land and the
rights belonging to it as legitimate property belonging to the Free State government for an amount of £4000 sterling. Not long after these events the
Basothos once again started showing their brutality in the old fashion by
provoking the inhabitants and stealing from them. However much the Free
State President attempted in every way possible to argue with them, it was
to no avail. The Free State was compelled to use other methods. In May 1865
the war broke out. This continued for a little more than a year, after which
peace was declared, the Basotho having lost many men and livestock; for
damages they had to cede a certain territory to the Free State.

Thereafter peace reigned but it was of short duration, for before long
they murdered Krijno and Bosch. They refused to hand over the murderers and were so brutal that they challenged the Boers. Jan Brand knew well
how he had to approach and proceed in the matter, and our Afrikaners
brought them to book. It was clear that, while not obstructed on their path
by the British in the Free State, the boar from the Caledon wood would
certainly have to be destroyed. They consequently paid dearly in goods and
blood. It was indeed wonderful to see how sometimes a few on our side
defeated thousands and with the exception of Thababizico [Thaba Bosiu] all
their strongholds were overrun and if mister Englishman did not intervene
Moshesh [Moshoeshoe] with Thababizico and all would soon have been
lost. But as soon as the blacks suffered defeat there appeared the foreman of
the old lady, should anyone touch a kaffir beware! Promptly mister Englishman would arrive! But this is nothing new; this is the way and the manner
in which England has gone about things, from the time when they set foot
on African soil.

Biltong Recipe

Clifton Crais

The semiarid environment found in much of South Africa is ideal for the curing of meat. Hunter-gatherers and Khoekhoe pastoralists used the dry air and herbs to preserve strips of beef and game, especially animals such as kudu, gemsbok, and springbok, hanging the meat in their reed huts. European settlers brought to South Africa their own traditions of curing meat. Biltong (rump strips) emerged out of South Africa's early colonial history, including commerce from the Indian Ocean. The Dutch introduced the use of wine vinegar and especially the addition of black pepper and coriander imported from East Asia. Biltong is today ubiquitous; in many respects biltong is the country's most famous food product. In the eighteenth and nineteenth centuries, biltong would become an important source of food in the interior, similar to jerky in North and South America. Vast herds of animals once roamed large areas of South Africa. In some areas hundreds of thousands of antelope tramped through valleys in annual migrations. Men with horses and guns reduced these herds to dried meat.

There are as many varieties of biltong as there are opinions on how best to prepare it: kudu or beef, thick or thin, spices, drying, and so on. Typically, biltong recipes, including the one here, include vinegar, sugar, salt, coriander, and coarse ground black pepper. Other recipes include spices such as aniseed, garlic salt, allspice, and red pepper. Changing the amount of marinating, curing, and airing, as well as the thickness of the meat, alters taste and tenderness.

Ingredients

4 pounds venison or beef, such as London Broil, or ostrich
3 cups course salt
2 cups brown sugar
Coarsely ground black pepper
Coarsely ground roasted coriander seeds (you may add additional
   spices, such as red pepper or paprika)
1 1/2 cups of brown vinegar or red-wine vinegar

2 teaspoons baking soda (bicarbonate of soda)

1/4 teaspoon saltpeter (optional; some health experts warn against the use of nitrates)

String

Large metal paperclips

Directions

Remove fat. Cut meat into strips no thicker than 1/4 inch. Cut with the grain. Place meat strips into a bowl. Add vinegar and soak for one hour. In a separate bowl, mix the sugar, black pepper, ground roasted coriander seeds and other spices, baking soda, and saltpeter (optional). Remove the meat strips. Place the thickest strips at the bottom of an enamel container. Cover with a thin layer of salt and then a layer of spices. Repeat until you have filled the container with strips of meat. Add a final layer of salt and spices. Cover container. Cure for twelve hours. Remove strips of meat from container and dip them quickly in hot water. Pat dry. Sprinkle with additional spices as desired. Hang the strips of meat so they do not touch, in a well-ventilated area away from direct sunlight, to ensure proper air circulation. Traditionally an S-shaped hook was run though one end of the meat strips and the meat was hung from wires. You may use metal paperclips and string as a substitute. Direct a fan on the meat to assist drying and to avoid flies. Depending on temperature and humidity, the meat should be dried in approximately thirty-six hours.

Biltong is best eaten as a snack.

III

Frontiers

The early decades of the nineteenth century found South Africa in a state of near-constant turmoil. The Great Trek extended early colonial social relations further into the interior, including the predatory violence pioneered by Boer commandos. Conquest generated considerable instability across the Orange River involving trekkers, Griqua (people of mixed-race descent who had earlier migrated from the Cape Colony), and numerous African communities. Out of this turmoil emerged African polities, including the Basotho Kingdom of Moshoeshoe, which is located in what is today Lesotho; various Griqua captaincies; and, in the 1850s, the Boer republics of the Orange Free State and the South African Republic.

In the hinterland of what is today Durban on the Indian Ocean coast, the militaristic Zulu Kingdom emerged in a region of instability and political innovation fueled by the international ivory trade, significantly reshaping, in contest with its rivals to the north and west, the wider region's political map. Despite good relations with British merchants settled on the coast, in the 1830s the Zulu Kingdom came into conflict with land-hungry trekkers from the Cape Colony. The British intervened in the 1840s, leading to the creation of the colony of Natal. British farmers eventually took up sugar production, using large numbers of Indian indentured servants who were brought to South Africa in the 1860s. Many other Indians followed as voluntary immigrants.

The Cape itself had now come into the full orbit of the British Empire: land- and labor-hungry British colonists settled along the eastern frontier, and officials with their new policies and belief in the rule of law spread across the colony. The Eastern Cape frontier remained a place of extraordinary violence. Frontier wars had first broken out in the late 1700s. Colonial conflict continued into the next century, culminating in the great war of 1850–53—at the time one of the most brutal and costly wars anywhere in the empire—and the conquest of Xhosa-speaking peoples living west of the Kei River. The terrible suffering of war, combined with drought and a devastating cattle epizootic, led to the millenarian cattle-killing movement and its attendant mass starvation, one of the most dramatic and remembered moments in South African history.

Britain's African empire began in South Africa; colonial policies devised in the Eastern Cape and in Natal spread across large areas of the continent. Conflict was just part of the story, however. More missionaries came to South Africa than any part of the empire, beginning what would become a religious revolution. Mission stations dotted the landscape, the great majority located in so-called tribal areas. Missionaries (many became colonial officials) played an important role in translating Africa's oral cultures into the written word. The dictionaries, grammars, and ethnographic works they produced powerfully shaped the modern invention of South Africa's major ethnic groups.

The encounter with Christianity often began around issues such as rain, the ancestors, and the definition of God, as well as land and crops. Black South Africans created a unique vision of Christianity, fusing new beliefs with older ways of seeing the world. Mission stations became social laboratories, leading to the creation of a new generation of African intellectuals, professionals, and political leaders schooled in British history, parliamentary traditions, and ideas of free speech. The foundation of South Africa's national anthem, "Nkosi Sikelel' iAfrika" (Lord, bless Africa) began as a hymn in a small Methodist mission station and was adapted to music composed by a Welshman.

The readings included in this part highlight the turmoil of this period of empire and colonial expansion and emphasize the "long conversation" that unfolded within the colonial encounter, particularly between Africans and missionaries. By the end of the nineteenth century, South Africa's political map had been completely redrawn. Kingdoms had emerged, colonies founded, and the British Empire had spread deeper into the interior. From these developments emerged politicized ethnic identities and a powerful historical myth of an "empty land" that would underpin Afrikaner claims to territory in the Orange Free State and the South African Republic. The highly charged politics of the 1980s around land alienation and ethnicity drew on this fraught past.

Just as profoundly, fundamental cultural changes were also unfolding. People adopted new religions. New identities emerged. Novel forms of communication, such as writing and the telegraph, spread. And unresolved tensions—particularly between the British and the Boers of the new republics—festered and occasionally broke into open conflict.

Among the Xhosa in 1800

Johannes Theodorus van der Kemp

*Doctor, soldier, courtier to the Prince of Orange, philosopher, and theologian, Jo-
hannes Theodorus van der Kemp (1747–1811) became the first head of the London
Missionary Society in South Africa. In 1799 he traveled east from Cape Town to
evangelize among the Xhosa and particularly among the followers of Chief Ngqika
(Gika). The Eastern Cape would become South Africa's most missionized area,
leading to remarkable religious change and to the creation of institutions, such as
schools, central to the rise of an African nationalist elite. Van der Kemp's writings
shaped subsequent discussions among missionaries and African converts on such
issues as the word for God and African belief systems.*

*Most early missionaries like van der Kemp used African intermediaries, in this
case Khoekhoe converts who understood the Xhosa language. The eccentric missionary attracted few followers. Ngqika at first believed that van der Kemp was a British
agent and considered having him murdered. Ngqika subsequently granted the missionary a tract of land. He also expected van der Kemp to use his access to God to
bring plentiful rain to his drought-stricken lands.*

Satan roared like a lion. It would not be prudent to mention the particulars
of his assaults; but it was resolved that I should be killed as a conspirator
against the king [Ngqika] of this country, and the Colonists; and I was forbidden any longer to instruct the Heathens. But the Lord directed me, and
assured me of his assistance by means of Psalm xxxiv. 14–23; and as he had
encouraged me yesterday by Ezek. ii. 6. I continued by his grace to instruct
and catechize my people, notwithstanding some of the children were kept
back by their parents and masters. Sarah expressed her cleaving to Christ,
and the two other Hottentot women belonging to her family signified that
they wished to have an interest in him. . . .

The king came to me, asking what law he must follow to obtain rain
for his country? I said that God had sufficient reasons to keep his rain back
from this country. Asking what these reasons were? I answered, that the
evils committed in his country were more than sufficient to account for it.

Hottentot woman being baptized. Artist unknown. Courtesy of Free State Archives
Photographic Collection, VA3719.

He said, he knew not of any crimes committed under his dominion, and
if I knew of them, I should mention them. I then represented to him the
plunderings and excesses of some of his Captains against the Christians, to
which he made no reply. . . .

A deputation from Gika came to me, requesting, in his name, that as
his magicians could make no rain, I should give rain to the country. . . . I
answered that I could not accept the king's present, nor procure rain, as this
depended entirely upon God's pleasure; but that I could, and would pray for
it. Taking a walk, and reflecting on what I had said, I considered that the
Lord would certainly give rain, if I could pray for it in the name of Jesus,
and I perceived at the same time some desire for the Glory of God. I then returned to Gika's Caffrees [kaffirs], and said, "Jesus Christus, intakha Thiko,
Inkoessi zal izoulou. Dia khou theta au le: lo khou nika invoula, mina
kossliwe." (Jesus Christ, the son of God, is Lord of Heaven. I will speak to
him, and he will give rain; I cannot.) One of the Colonists then present said,
with a visible displeasure, that I might talk this as well to the wolves, as to
these barbarians. At night we came into Quakoubi, where we found the rest
of our people, and also the family of Sarah. This country was quite different
from what it was last year. It had lost all its pleasant verdure. The Caffrees
had set the dry grass on fire, by which also my house was burnt down to the
ground, and most of the inhabitants had left it for want of food. I found the
cattle which Gika had sent to me, and I told our people what had happened.
They looked upon me as a fool, and said, that if I did not like to keep the

cows, that they would take care that the king should never get them back. I then prayed for rain in subordination to the glory of God.

In the morning it pleased the Lord to give us a plentiful rain, which continued all the day, with thunder in the afternoon. . . .

The rain continued very heavy. The Caffrees of this country all knew what had been transacted between Gika and me with respect to the rain. Some of our thoughtless people asked them, "who it was that had procured this rain?" with a view to divert themselves with their superstitious prejudices, supposing that they would mention me as the cause of it; but one of the Caffrees gave them this answer, "Tinkhanna has talked to the Lord (Inkoessi) [Inkosi] on high, and he has given us rain!" Upon this the very man, who had made the observation, which I mentioned the 30th of October, now said, "You will see that this ignorant and obstinate nation, by such events, will be induced to embrace the Christian religion!" I did not speak, but I kept all these things, and pondered them in my heart.

The Problem of God

Robert Moffat

Robert Moffat (1795–1883) and his wife, Mary, left the Cape for South Africa's interior in 1820, settling at Kuruman near the Vaal River among Setswana-speaking peoples. He continued missionizing in South Africa for another fifty years. Moffat's daughter, born and raised in South Africa, would marry the missionary-explorer David Livingstone. Like many missionaries at the time, Moffat was keenly interested in producing dictionaries and grammars of local African languages so that he could translate the Bible. (Moffat lugged a heavy iron hand printing press from Cape Town to Kuruman.) He was concerned with understanding African beliefs, particularly concerning God, which he considered important to his strategy of converting people to Christianity.

Missionary writings had a powerful impact on the formation of modern ethnicities, such as the Tswana. Before the late nineteenth century, people in this region spoke Setswana but lived in diverse communities centered on the political office of local chiefs. Like other peoples at the time, they defined themselves in various ways. Identity tended to be localized. Out of the missionary encounter and colonial conquest emerged the idea that people lived in discrete tribes in which a shared language and geography composed an ethnic or tribal identity. The various tribes that today make up South Africa—Zulu, Xhosa, Tswana, and so on—took shape only in the 1800s.

[W]ith respect to the national atheism of the Kaffirs[,] . . . they have no word in their language to express the idea of the Deity; the individuals just mentioned, calling him "Thiko," which is a corruption of the name by which God is called in the language of the Hottentots, literally signifying, one that induces pain. . . .

Among the Bechuana [Tswana] tribes, the name adopted by the missionaries is *Morimo*. This has the advantage of the names used by the Kaffirs and Hottentots, being more definite, as its derivation at once determines its meaning. *Mo* is a personal prefix, and *rimo* is from *gorimo*[,] "above." From the same root *legorimo*, "heaven," and its plural *magorimo*, are derived. The

genius of the Sechuana [Setswana] language warrants us to expect a correspondence between the name and the thing designated; but in this instance
the order is reversed. Morimo, to those who know anything about it, had
been represented by rain-makers and sorcerers as a malevolent *selo*, or thing,
which the nations in the north described as existing in a hole, and which,
like the fairies in the Highlands of Scotland, sometimes came out and inflicted diseases on men and cattle, and even caused death. This Morimo
served the purpose of a bugbear, by which the rain-maker might constrain
the chiefs to yield to his suggestions, when he wished for a slaughter-ox,
without which he pretended he could not make rain.

As to the eternity of this existence, they appear never to have exercised
one thought. Morimo is never called *man*. As the pronouns agree with the
noun, those which Morimo governs cannot, without the greatest violence
to the language, be applied to *Mogorimo*, "a heavenly one," which refers to a
human being. This power is, in the mouth of a rain-maker, what a disease
would be in the lips of a quack, just as strong or weak as he is pleased to
call it. I never once heard that Morimo did good, or was supposed capable
of doing so. More modern inquiries among the natives might lead to the
supposition that he is as powerful to do good as he is to do evil; and that
he has great an inclination for the one as for the other. It will, however, be
found that this view of his attributes is the result of twenty-five years' missionary labor; the influences of which, in that as well as in other respects,
extend hundreds of miles beyond the immediate sphere of the missionary.
It is highly probable, however, that, as we proceed farther into the interior,
we shall find the natives possessing more correct views on these subjects.

According to native testimony, Morimo, as well as man, with all the different species of animals, came out of a cave or hole in the Bakone country,
to the north, where, say they, their footmarks are still to be seen in the
indurated rock, which was at that time sand. In one of Mr. Hamilton's early
journals, he records that a native had informed him that the footmarks of
Morimo were distinguished by being without toes. Once I heard a man of
influence telling his story on the subject. I of course could not say that I
believed the wondrous tale, but very mildly hinted that he might be mis-
informed; on which he became indignant, and swore by his ancestors and
his king, that he had visited the spot, and paid a tax to see the wonder; and
that, consequently his testimony was indubitable. I very soon cooled his
rage, by telling him, that as I should likely one day visit those regions, I
should certainly think myself very fortunate if I could get him as a guide
to that wonderful source of animated nature. Smiling, he said, "Ha, and I
shall show you the footsteps of the very first man." This is the sum-total of

the knowledge which the Bechuanas possessed of the origin of what they call Morimo, prior to the period when they were visited by missionaries. Thus their foolish hearts are darkened; and verily this is a darkness which may be felt. Such a people are living in what Job calls "a land of darkness and the shadow of death," spiritually buried, and without knowledge, life, or light. . . .

Even the rain-maker when asked by the missionary why he could thus honour the little malicious thing which they called Morimo, that only came out of a hole to inflict pain[,] taking advantage of our Christian views as to the meaning of the word, would promptly reply, "Do not you say Morimo is the governor of the heavens, and that he only can make rain? Why then should we not honour him?" This showed his skill in the appropriation of our principles to serve his own purposes. He also exhibited considerable cunning in this transfer; for, should rain not come at his call, he could bring in the Morimo of the teachers for some part, if not the whole, of the blame. Thus, when hail injured their crops, or rain fell in the cold and unseasonable part of the year, they would use the vilest epithets, and curse both the missionaries and their Morimo. When we assured them that God was in the heavens, and that He did whatever He pleased, they blamed us for giving Him a high position beyond their reach; for they viewed their Morimo as a noxious reptile. "Would that I could catch it, I would transfix it with my spear," exclaimed S., a chief, whose judgment on other subjects would command attention. . . .

One of the most convincing proofs that the minds of the people are covered by the profoundest darkness, is, that after the missionary has endeavoured for hours to impart to them a knowledge of the Divine Being, they not unfrequently address to him the question, "What is it you wish to tell me?" And if any thing were wanting to confirm this conviction, surely this fact will be sufficient, that even where he has succeeded in conveying to the vacant mind of the savage, ideas which he considers as paramount to all others, he is told that, certainly these fables are very wonderful, but not more so than their own.

Visit to a Mission Community in Natal

John William Colenso

In 1853 John William Colenso (1814–83) became the Anglican bishop of Natal, a British colony neighboring the Zulu Kingdom. Like many ministers of the early Victorian era, Colenso was strongly influenced by the evangelical movement and saw his role in Natal as one of spreading the gospel to the indigenous population as well as serving the needs of the white Anglican population. Colenso traveled to Natal in 1854 to learn about African communities firsthand, to form alliances, and to make plans for his work there.

Like the fictional missionary Mr. Brown in Chinua Achebe's novel Things Fall Apart, *Colenso believed that in order to teach Africans about Christian beliefs, he had to become proficient in the Zulu language and to understand and respect indigenous religious concepts in order to engage in meaningful dialogue. In the excerpt, Colenso recounts his meetings with the mission community of* kholwa *(African Christians) at Edendale, near the colonial capital of Pietermaritzburg. He takes careful note of the signs of agricultural and industrial progress, and then he engages leading African men in a discussion of religious concepts. Colenso's description offers a glimpse into the lives of South Africa's early Christian converts whose descendants would play an important role in the country's politics.*

Monday, Feb. 13.—By and by, we crossed the river, the first I have had to ford in South Africa; and at length reached the cultivated lands of the Mission. On our way we passed a field, where three Kaffirs were ploughing: one led the horse, another walked behind and whipped it, the third very cleverly turned up a regular furrow. There was no white man by; the work was going on entirely by themselves. Large crops of mealies [corn, maize] waved around us, as we drew near to the station. Natives of all ages were sitting in groups, as we passed along, at the doors of their little houses, or *huts*,—for their habitations at present scarcely deserve a better name, as their removal to this site is recent, and they have been too much occupied in paying for the land they have purchased, to have bestowed much labour upon the im-

provement of their abodes. At the door of the Mission-house we received a
hearty welcome from the excellent missionary and his wife.

Mr. Allison was formerly stationed in the Bechuana [Tswana] country,
and afterwards at Indaleni, in this colony, in connexion with the Wesley-
ans [Methodists]. Having separated from that body for some reason, he has
purchased this station, comprising 6,000 acres of good land, very pleasantly
situated in the bosom of some fine hills, which also belong to it; and here he
devotes himself to improve the condition of the 500 or 600 Kaffirs who constitute his people. The peculiarity of Mr. Allison's position is this, that the
land is not bought for himself, but for his natives, and paid for by their labour. It cost £1,300 to purchase it, for which Mr. Allison became responsible.
The property was then divided into 100 shares at £16 each, namely, £10 for
a suburban lot of about an acre, and £6 for a town lot of about a rood, (these
being, of course, both cultivable pieces of ground,) with as much of Kaffir
ground for mealies as they please, and the right of grazing over the unen-
closed portion. Almost all the purchasers have now paid for their shares,
and some of them have bought several. There were about 420 Christians on
the estate, (many of whom had been for years with Mr. Allison, before he removed to this station some three years ago, to which fact it is probably that
the remarkable success of his experiment is in some measure owing,) and
160 heathens, who were allowed to purchase allotments, and live among the
rest, but were required, of course, to abandon their grosser native habits. . . .

Mr. Allison then took us to look at a new watermill, which he had just
erected, for grinding mealie-corn into meal. Of this he was deservedly proud:
he had erected it entirely by the help of the Kaffirs on the premises, except
that an Englishman cut the stones for him. It was now wholly managed by
two Kaffirs, one of whom, Daniel, was a cheerful, intelligent-looking fellow,
of (perhaps) twenty-five years of age, who had been with Mr. Allison twelve
years, and whose first attempts at *book-keeping* I inspected, commencing at
Feb. 1, 1854. There were entries of the sale of the meal,—6d. [pence] to Sally
1s. [shilling] to Johannes, &c., and very neat they were. Daniel was dressed
like any decent Englishman, in trousers, jacket, and good black hat, and, as
Mr. Allison assured me, he "had the feelings of an English gentleman, and
during twelve years had never been known to commit an immoral action."
The other miller, Kombas, was still a heathen, but a well-conducted, hope-
ful, person. In fact, "his conduct," Mr. A. said, "was exemplary." This man
had a great genius for mechanics, had made a wooden gunlock, and was
particularly fond of drawing. I carried away with me several of his draw-
ings, and among them one sheet of paper, which he had filled with figures

of common things around him, expressly for my own use, and at my own desire, while I was talking with his *umFundise* (teacher). . . .

We now went to the chapel, the bell having been rung to call the people in for service. A most gratifying sight it was, to walk up through the large assemblage of black people, all seated on the ground—the front rows consisting of well-dressed men, all Christians, and the back of heathens, but still in decent costume. There were present also, I remarked, many young mothers with their infant children, who formed a very interesting portion of the assembly. When all was hushed, Mr. A. gave out a hymn in Kaffir,—one, I believe, of a Wesleyan collection. It was sung to the tune of Shirland, and very harmoniously. The sound of the women's voices, as they rose with a swell in one part of it, was very touching, and is still lingering in my memory. . . .

Our next scene was a private interview with the twelve chief men of the station, who came into the dining-room and seated themselves, some on chairs, some on the floor, ready to converse on any subject whatever. They formed a very interesting group, with much variety of intelligence in their black faces. One, who sat at their head, was certainly a very plain man in countenance, but there was an earnest seriousness in his face, which drew at once your attention, and assured your affection, to him. This man, Johannes, was (Mr. A. told me) "a very wise man. Whenever he spoke every mouth was closed, and his judgment, which was never given hastily, was sure to guide the rest." He had been one of Dingaan's [Dingane's] soldiers, and described to me the bloody proceedings of that king. Another was a young chief, a very handsome, noble-looking fellow. A third was a half-caste, of slave origin, with a face that might have been easily mistaken for a white man's. This was a thoroughly good man, who had a cottage in the town, where he sheltered for a time any miserable of his own race he met with, and tried to teach them the Truths of God. A fourth, named Job, Mr. A. called his "philosopher." He "had deep thoughts upon many subjects," and made some curious remarks in the course of our conversation. Having observed the time and labour spent in constructing the water-mill, Job said, "Well! I always thought that Noah was very slow in his building of the Ark, but now I understand it all." . . .

I found, as I had been led to expect by Mr. Allison, that his people were unanimous in their disapproval of the word for God, now commonly in use among the Missionaries—*uTixo* [Thixo],—which, they said, "had no meaning whatever for the Kaffirs. They used it because they found it in their Bibles; but it was not a word of their language at all." "The proper word for

God was *iTongo*, which meant with them a Power of Universal Influence—a Being under whom all around were placed." "For instance," said one, "if we were going on an expedition, we should, in ordinary circumstances, have trusted to our household gods, which we call *amaHlose* [*amadlozi*; ancestors]; but if some unusual danger of the desert threatened us, or if a violent storm terrified us, we should throw these away, and trust in iTongo. All the Kaffir tribes, whether on the frontier or to the north, would understand iTongo; but the latter would have no idea whatever of what was meant by uTixo, though the former are now used to it through the Missionaries."

I may here mention, before I pass on, that, having received this important information, I resolved to direct my inquiries especially to this point, whenever opportunity should be afforded me, in my intercourse with the Kaffirs of the district. The conclusion to which I have come . . . is, that these Kaffirs were undoubtedly right in condemning the word uTixo, as one utterly without meaning in the Kaffir tongue, besides containing an odious click, indicated by the letter x, which is not to be pronounced as the English x, but by thrusting the tongue against the teeth at the side of the mouth, and suddenly withdrawing it. The origin of this word is very uncertain; but it is said to be the name of a species of mantis, which is called "the Hottentot's god." At all events, it would seem that Dr. Vanderkemp, who first laboured among the Hottentots some sixty years ago, adopted this word in his teaching as the name of God; and the Wesleyan and other Missionaries have carried it from west to east, first among the British Kaffirs, and now among the tribes of Natal. . . .

The true words for the Deity in the Kaffir language—at least in all this part of Africa—are *umKulunkulu*, literally, The Great-Great One = The Almighty, and *umVelinqange*—literally, The First Comer-Out = The First Essence, or, rather, Existence. . . . The amount of unnecessary hindrance to the reception of the Gospel, which must be caused by forcing upon them an entirely new name for the Supreme Being, without distinctly connecting it with their own two names, will be obvious to any thoughtful mind. It must make a kind of chasm between their old life and the new one to which they are invited; and it must be long before they can become able, as it were, to bridge over the gulf, and make out for themselves, that this strange name, which is preached to them, is only the white man's name for the same Great Being, of whom they have heard their fathers and mothers speak in their childhood. . . .

They spoke of *witchcraft*—that "for one suspected of it there was no rest, no escape. The curse would follow him when he leaves his tribe—and not only him, but every member of his family,—till all were exterminated."

It should be observed, however, that the English word *witchcraft* very imperfectly expresses the offence of the *umTakati* [*umthakathi*], which word is used to denote generally a *criminal* of the grosser kind—more especially one, who is supposed to have attempted or actually caused the death of another, oftentimes his chief, by poisoning. It appears certain that the Kaffirs are acquainted with the powers of many noxious herbs, of which Europeans know nothing: and, although a cruel chief may often abuse the skill of the *inYanga* (medicine-man, or witch-doctor) of the tribe, to point out some unfortunate being as the cause of sickness or death in his own family, or among his people, in order that he may "eat him up" and take possession of his cattle, yet it can hardly be doubted, from all that I have heard, that the persons thus accused are not unfrequently really guilty of some grave offence or other, and deservedly punished. . . .

At last I asked them, "What message should I take to England for them?" One of them said, "Tell the good people of England that we have innumerable friends, wandering like lost sheep, and that we shall be very grateful, if they will send herders and watchers to save them." Hereupon Johannes gravely shook his head, and intimated that this message did not quite satisfy him. All evidently deferred to him, while, in a very dignified manner, he delivered himself of the following:

> When you come to your friends at home, please to convey our salutations to the righteous people there. We praise them for their act in sending a person out to this country to teach our people. While yet we were in darkness, many prayed for us. God made a passage over the sea. They stretched forth their hand to us, and we have received blessings through them. Jehovah heard them, and on account of their prayers there are now those in this land who know his name. Now, today, let them not be weary. There are more sheep yet: let them not tire; let them put up more prayers, more and mightier, than the former, for the multitude still left.

Nkosi Sikelel' iAfrika (God Bless Africa)

Enoch Sontonga and Samuel E. Mqhayi

Versions of this hymn are sung across much of southern Africa, in various languages. "Nkosi Sikelel' iAfrika" was first composed in the final years of the nineteenth century by Enoch Sontonga, a Methodist mission-school teacher working in Johannesburg. The South African Native National Congress (later renamed African National Congress) performed the song at its inaugural meeting in Bloemfontein in 1912. The organization formally adopted the hymn in 1925. In 1927 the famous Xhosa poet Samuel E. Mqhayi added several verses. A version of the hymn, combined with the former anthem "The Call of South Africa," became South Africa's national anthem in 1997.

"Nkosi Sikelel' iAfrika" combines African praise singing styles within the musical structure of a Methodist hymn. At the center of the song is the idea of redemption and blessing. The hymn originally appealed to the nascent black elite but soon became a mainstay across South Africa's religious communities and, increasingly, became the most powerful political expression of shared suffering and oppression for the majority of South Africa's peoples.

Nkosi, sikelel' iAfrika
Malupakam' upondo lwayo;
Yiva imitandazo yetu.
(Lord, bless Africa
May her horn rise high up;
Hear Thou our prayers and bless us.)

Chorus
Yihla Moya, yihla Moya
Yihla Moya Oyingcwele
(Descend O Spirit
Descend, O Holy Spirit)
Sikelela iNkosi zetu;
Zimkumbule umDali wazo;

Zimoyike zezimhlouele,
Azisikelele.
(Bless our chiefs;
May they remember their Creator;
Fear Him and revere Him,
That He may bless them.)

Sikelel' amadol' esizwe,
Sikelela kwa nomlisela
Ulitwal' ilizwe ngomonde,
Uwusikilele.
(Bless the public men,
Bless also the youth
That they may carry the land with patience,
and that Thou mayst bless them.)

Sikelel' amakosikazi;
Nawo onk'amanenekazi;
Pakamisa wonk'umtinjana
Uwusikilele.
(Bless the wives;
And also all young women;
Lift up all the young girls
And bless them.)

Sikelela abafundisi
Bemvaba zonke zelilizwe;
Ubatwese ngoMoya Wako
Ubasikelele.
(Bless the ministers
Of all the churches of this land;
Endue them with Thy Spirit
And bless them.)

Sikelel' ulimo nemfuyo;
Gzota zonk'indlala nezifo;
Zalisa ilizwe nempilo
Ulisikelele.
(Bless agriculture and stock raising;
Banish all famine and diseases;
Fill the land with good health and bless it.)

Sikelel' amalinga etu
Awomanyana nokuzaka,
Awemfundo nemvisiswano
Uwasikele.
(Bless our efforts of union and self-uplift,
Of education and mutual understanding
And bless them.)

Nkosi Sikelel, Afrika;
Cima bonk' ubugwenza bayo
Nezigqito, Nezono zayo
Uwazikelele.
(Lord, bless Africa
Blot out all its wickedness
And its transgressions and sins,
And bless us.)

Dingane's Killing of Retief

F. Owen

*On December 16 each year, South Africa celebrates the Day of Reconciliation to cele-
brate and promote the end of racial division promised by the postapartheid order
that began in 1994. Under apartheid, the holiday was known as the Day of the Vow,
or Dingane's Day. It commemorated a decisive victory by Boer trekker forces over
the army of the Zulu king Dingane kaSenzangakhona at the Ncome River (which the
Boers came to call Blood River) in northern Natal, on December 16, 1838. Afrikaner
nationalists, the descendants of the Boers, later attributed this victory to divine
intervention.*

*The battle of Blood (Ncome) River flowed from the settlement of a group of trek-
kers in Natal beginning in late 1837. The trekker leader Piet Retief corresponded with
Dingane, seeking cession of the area (which became Natal) southwest of the Thukela
River. Dingane, aware of the recent Boer defeat to Mzilikazi's forces on the highveld,
decided to attempt to drive out the Boer settlers by launching a surprise attack.
Dingane invited Retief and a group of his followers to the Zulu capital. There, after
leading the Boers to believe that he was willing to make the sought-after transfer of
land, Dingane ordered the Boer party seized and executed on February 6, 1838. The
following is an excerpt from the diary of Reverend F. Owen, a missionary who was
a resident at Dingane's capital.*

Dingaan [Dingane] sent for me at sunset to write a letter to Mr. Retief, who
with a party of Boers is now on his way to the Zulu capital. The letter was
characteristic of the chief. He said that his heart was now content, because
he had got his cattle again [Retief's party had recaptured some cattle for
Dingane from a rival chief]. He requested that the chief of the Boers would
send to all his people and order them to come up to the capital with him,
but without their horses. He promised to gather together all his army to
sing and dance. He said he would give orders that cattle should be slain for
them in every place through which they passed on the road, and he promised to give them a country. I asked him how they could come without their
horses. He said, "Tell them that they must bring their horses, and dance

upon them, in the middle of the town, that it might be known which could dance best, the Zulus or the 'Abalungu' [*abelungu*]" (the general name given to white people). The Dutch will be too wise to expose themselves in this manner. . . .

Large parties of Zulus in their war-dress were yesterday evening entering the town. This morning, when we were at family prayer, the unusual sound of muskets was heard from the west. This proved to be the arrival of the Boers, who presently entered the town on horseback, with their guns in their hands. An immense concourse of Zulus were present to receive them. The deputation, in number about sixty, brought with them the cattle which they had recovered from Sikonyela. The Boers immediately showed Dingaan the way in which they danced on horseback, by making a sham charge at one another, making the air resound with their guns. This was something which the Zulu chief had never witnessed. In their turn, the Zulus exhibited their skill in dancing. About noon I paid a visit to Mr. Retief, who with his party, after the amusement was over, were sitting under the trees fronting the gate of the town. The answer which he gave Dingaan, when he demanded the guns and horses, was to show the messenger his grey hairs, and bid him tell his master that he was not dealing with a child. . . .

A dreadful day in the annals of the mission. I shudder to give an account of it. This morning, as I was sitting in the shade of my wagon, reading the Testament, the usual messenger came, with hurry and anxiety depicted in his looks. I was sure that he was about to pronounce something serious. And what was his commission? While it showed consideration and kindness in the Zulu monarch towards me, it disclosed a horrid instance of perfidy— too horrid to describe—towards the unhappy men who for a few days have been his guests, and are now no more. He sent to tell me not to be frightened, as he was going to kill the Boers. This news came like a thunderstroke to myself and to every successive member of my family as they heard it. The reason assigned for this treacherous act was that they were going to kill him; that they had come here, and that he had now learnt all their plans. The messenger was anxious for my answer; but what could I say? I was fearful on the one hand of seeming to justify the treachery: and on the other of exposing myself and my family to probable danger if I appeared to take their part. Moreover, I could not but feel that it was my duty to apprise the Boers of the intended massacre; while certain death would have ensued, I apprehended, if I had been detected in giving them this information. However, I was released from this dilemma by beholding an awful spectacle. My attention was directed to the blood-stained hill nearly opposite my hut, and on the other side of my wagon, which hides it from view, where all the executions at this fearful spot take place, and which was destined now to add sixty more bleeding carcasses to the number of those which have already cried to heaven for vengeance. "There!" said some one, "they are killing the Boers now!" I turned my eyes, and, behold! an immense multitude on the hill. About nine or ten Zulus to each Boer were dragging their helpless, un-armed victims to the fatal spot—where those eyes which awaked this morning to see the cheerful light of day for the last time, are now closed in death.

Mpande Seeks an Alliance with the Boers in Natal

Volksraad of the Republic of Natalia

After the Boer defeat of the Zulu forces at Blood (Ncome) River, the Zulu Kingdom was fractured as rivals began to challenge the Zulu king Dingane's authority. In September 1839 Mpande kaSenzangakhona, Dingane's brother, led his followers across the Thukela River to seek an alliance with the Boers. Earlier in the year, the Boer settlers had constituted themselves as the Republic of Natalia, with a capital at the new settlement of Pietermaritzburg. In October Mpande ("Panda") met with the republic's legislature, the Volksraad, to further that alliance. In return for Mpande's agreement to cede Natal, the Boers recognized Mpande's claim on the Zulu throne. Their military alliance defeated Dingane, who fled and was killed by Swazi forces.

Because of the strategic importance of the harbor at Port Natal, where British traders had been settled under Zulu protection since the 1820s, Britain annexed Natal just five years after Mpande's meeting with the Volksraad. But the territorial arrangements and mutual recognition worked out there remained in effect, with Britain stepping into the jurisdictional shoes of the defunct Boer republic. Mpande ruled the Zulu Kingdom until his death in 1872, when he was succeeded by his son Cetshwayo kaMpande.

Minutes of the Volksraad

15th October, 1839
[Panda, who had come within the limits of Natal, was interrogated before the council.]

What did you come here for, and why did you cross the Tugela [Thukela]?

To escape from Dingaan, and to seek for protection amongst you.

Why did you escape from Dingaan?

Because I heard that Dingaan wanted to proceed further into the interior, and because I did not wish to join him; and also because he would

106

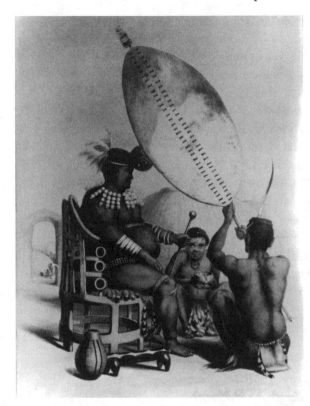

The Zulu king Mpande kaSenzangakhona, seated on his chair in the great kraal of Nondengu, being shaded by a shield bearer and attended by a snuff bearer. Artist unknown. Courtesy of Campbell Collections of the University of KwaZulu-Natal, D37/010.

certainly cause me to be murdered, should he ascertain my unwillingness to join him.

Give us a statement of all the particulars.

I was informed that Dingaan had sent four regiments to Sapusa, in
order to encroach on the country of that chief; but he was defeated by
that chief with the loss of many head of cattle, and Dingaan then sent
for two other regiments.

Did these regiments go thither?

Yes, they complied with that order; and when they reached the place,
they heard that Dingaan, together with his cattle, women, children,
&c., had already proceeded onward. They then returned. I asked them
for the reasons why they returned. They answered that they had not
found Dingaan, as he had proceeded onward. Dingaan then sent to me
to ascertain why I and my people had not proceeded, and whether we
intended to join the white people. After that I received another mes-

sage, ordering me to join Dingaan, and thank him that he had not made us suffer for our disobedience. I then told my captains that they might go if they chose. Some went. On their way they again met some messengers with cattle, who came to call me. I clearly saw from all this that Dingaan cherished hostile views against me. At last Umsela, the chief captain of Dingaan, came in person, and said to my people, "Why don't you rise and proceed onward, or do you wait for Panda? If you wait for him, I can tell you that in a short time one of Dingaan's commandos will surround him. Don't you clearly see that he has turned his face towards the whites?" Umsela having said this, part of my people joined him, but the greatest part turned back and said to me, "Will you sit here and wait until the commando surprises us?" I said, We will go. I have heard of there being white people at the Tugela; I will immediately send a message thither. At last I arrived at the Tugela with the half of Dingaan's people, where I met Mr. De Lange.

Who was the chief of the Zulu country before Chaka [Shaka]?

His father, Senzagakona.

What were you under his orders?

One of the great captains, which I was until the death of Chaka.

Did you often go on commando?

Yes; but not once under Dingaan.

Why did you not wish to go with Dingaan?

Because I have heard that the white people wish to live in peace with us: and why should I allow myself to be murdered by a villain, or take to flight with him?

Where have you lived?

In the country near the Ganzela.

What is the reason that you did not become king instead of Dingaan?

Chaka had sent me on a commando against a chief called Sotshangana; and when I returned I was told that Dingaan had put himself on the throne in my absence, and had murdered my father [the king, who was actually his brother], Chaka, and all the royal family.

Has not Dingaan endeavoured to murder you when you returned?

No; but Hlela and Dambuza, the great captains, wished to kill me, but Dingaan would not allow it, pretending that I had not influence enough, and could do no harm.

When you sent a message to the Tugela, you were already effecting your escape?

Yes.

Where did you meet Mr. De Lange?

On this side of the Tugela.

If you had not met the whites at the river, would you, notwithstanding, have continued your way?

Yes; as I was proceeding, I would not have stopped.

Do you not know that according to treaty no Zulu is allowed to come to this side of the Tugela?

Yes; but what is a man not capable of when his life is in danger.

Panda; this day you must be sincere.

Yes; for that reason I came hither in person to speak to you, gentlemen. I shall lay my heart open to you.

If Dingaan had acted like you, war would have been at an end.

Therefore you see that I come personally and deal with you in a more upright manner than Dingaan. I wish to be your friend and act according to your wishes.

What do you now expect of us?

As the gentlemen now give me liberty to speak, I would request of you the piece of ground between the Umhlali and Umvoti.

Why won't you live on the other side of the Tugela?

Because I am afraid of Dingaan, as I have divided the people.

Don't you know, then, that Dingaan may not murder any people?

Yes; but he will not care about that.

Do you consider yourself strong enough to wage war against Dingaan?

Not at the present moment; but if the people receive information of the peace, they will certainly come to me in crowds.

Do you know how the people are inclined?

Yes; I have also sent out spies, but as Dingaan's commando was in the bushes, they have not been able to do anything.

Do you know how many captains will join you, when they hear of the peace between you and us?

Of three I have already heard. They are on the other side of Dingaan, and cannot therefore come at present.

How many regiments has Dingaan wherewith he wages war?

This I cannot say with certainty, as many have been killed in the battle with Sapusa. He probably has many yet.

Have many of Dingaan's people been killed?

Yes; as well of his people as of those of Sapusa.

Have you received intelligence, or do you know with certainty where Dingaan now is?

No; I do not at the present moment know where he is, I cannot say with certainty. I have heard that he (Sapusa) had killed more than half of Dingaan's people in the last conflict.

Can't you send out spies, whom you as well as we may trust?

Yes, this I will do immediately; perhaps as soon as I get to my camp. Perhaps the spies I have sent out have returned. I shall lose no time; for my heart is now full of joy, as I see that you deal with me in so good and kind a manner.

You know that we will no longer allow Dingaan to kill women, and children. You must therefore send us a report as soon as possible, so that we may take steps accordingly.

Yes; that I will do: and as the gentlemen are so kind towards me, they must open their hearts very wide for me—yes, as wide as my arm. [He lifted his arm on high.]

Statement of the Prophetess Nonkosi, 23rd October 1857

Nonkosi

In the mid-1850s prophecies began circulating throughout the Xhosa-speaking peoples of the Eastern Cape. The most important prophets were two girls, Nongqawuse and Nonkosi. They said that if the people slaughtered their cattle and stopped planting crops, the dead would arise and prosperity would return to the land. Cattle would appear and storage bins would overflow with grain. The world would begin anew. In response, Africans slaughtered approximately four hundred thousand cattle. The cattle-killing movement occurred immediately following the devastating Eighth Frontier War that saw the defeat of African communities west of the Kei River and formal conquest by the British Empire. Moreover, a disease that afflicted African herds followed on the heels of war, destroying vast numbers of the cattle, which people depended on for a vital source of food (mainly in the form of milk) as well as for sacrifices that connected them to their ancestors. Most people adhered to the prophecies. Mass starvation followed in what has come to be known as the cattle-killing of 1856–57. Approximately forty thousand people died.

My name is "Nonkosi." My father and mother are dead, as also all my relations. My mother died of sickness, but my father and other relatives died of famine. My father died last moon; he used to have many cattle and was a witch-doctor in his practise. He was more frequently called upon by "Umhala" [Mhala] than any other Chief. . . . I was playing at a vlei [marsh] near the Impongo, and bathing, when a man who called himself "Umlanjeni" [Mlanjeni, an earlier prophet] showed himself out of the water. I became afraid. The next day I went again to see him; he then spoke to me saying that he had come here to raise the dead, and that this was to be told by me to all the Chiefs. "Umlanjeni" took a liking to another girl who was with me at the time, saying I was reserved and did not answer his questions satisfactorily. He however afterwards said that this girl he had taken a fancy to, lived too far off, and that he wished to have communications with me as

The Sotho king Moshoeshoe. Artist unknown. Courtesy of Free State Archives Photographic Collection, VA4183.

before. "Umlanjeni" told me that he had been to Moshesh [Moshoeshoe, the king of the Sotho] to put the country right, and had left some corn there. He showed me 6 cows in the water, their heads appearing above the surface of the water. . . .

"Umlanjeni," who sometimes came out of the water, and sat on the ground with me. He told me that he came from a country underneath the vlei and said that there were a great many things there which *we* did not possess. One day, without knowing that I had moved from where I was standing at the side of the vlei, I found myself in this country of which "Umlanjeni" spoke to me. There were a great many Kraals [cattle enclosures] with cattle, sheep, goats and pigs. Their huts were round, and very smoothly plastered, and they were filled with corn, bread and sugar. The first Kraal I came to was "Umlanjeni's"; he said that he would not give me anything to eat, as their food would kill any person from the country above so long as all the cattle were not killed,—that one little girl had already died who eat it. In leaving this place I ascended a perpendicular hole, and was carried by "Umlanjeni." When I reached the top I found that the water was spread over this place. I asked "Umlanjeni" why it was that the water did not flow down this hole. He said it was not water but a sort of door belonging to *their* country.

Heart of Redness

Zakes Mda

The cattle-killing movement of 1856–57 would come to be the defining moment in the history of the Xhosa-speaking peoples, and the most controversial. The movement has remained a part of South African public memory as a moment of "national suicide" and has entered the country's political vocabulary to describe disorder, insecurity, chicanery, and nativism. Many black South Africans see in the cattle killing European trickery, believing that the English plotted in getting Africans to destroy their grain and cattle and thus making conquest all the easier.

Zakes Mda was born in the Eastern Cape, the son of a prominent political activist. Mda's novel Heart of Redness moves between the present (circa 2000) and the cattle-killing years. The novel's central tension centers on the conflict between believers and unbelievers, which Mda sees in the twenty-first century as a tension between tradition and modernity and between community-centered and business-centered economic development. The events in this selection concern the Xhosa prophet Mlanjeni and the war that preceded the cattle killing.

Mlanjeni, the Man of the River. He was only eighteen. Yet his head was not full of beautiful maidens. It did not throb with stick fights and *umtshotsho* [young men's] dances. Instead he brooded over the evil that pervaded the world, that lurked even in the house of his own father, Kala. As a result he refused to eat his mother's cooking, for he said it was poisoned. He decided to fast because food enervated him. Women had an enfeebling power on him. So he kept himself celibate.

In order to stay clean he eschewed the company of other human beings, and spent his time immersed to the neck in a pool on the Keiskamma River. There he lived on the eggs of ants and on water grass.

"That son of Kala has something to him," said Xikixa to his twins. "He is a child, but he already talks of big things."

"I have heard his father talking with him about his behavior," said Twin-Twin. "Yet he will not listen."

"Kala is right," said the patriarch. "What does a boy who has not even been to circumcision school know about witchcraft and disease?"

When the time came, Mlanjeni went to the circumcision school. Both Twin and Twin-Twin were among the *amakhankatha*—the men who taught the initiates how to be men. Xikixa was the *ingcibi*—the doctor who cut the foreskin. They saw that Mlanjeni was very thin and weak. They did not think he would survive the rigors of the mountain. But he did, and went on to become the new prophet of the amaXhosa [Xhosa] people.

And the amaXhosa people believed in him, for it was clear that he had contact with the spirit world and was charged by the ancestors with the task of saving humankind from itself.

As his teachings unfolded, people knew that indeed he was the next great prophet after Nxele, the man who had revealed the truths of the world thirty years before. And both of them spoke against *ubuthi*, the evil charms that were poisoning the nation, and against witchcraft.

Whereas Nxele had preached about Mdalidephu, the god of the black man; Thixo, the god of the white man; and Thixo's son, Tayi, who was killed by the white people, Mlanjeni worshipped the sun.

Nxele used to talk of the great day that was coming, when the dead would arise and witches would be cast into damnation in the belly of the earth. But his career was stopped short by the British, who locked him up on Robben Island. Before he surrendered he promised that he would come back again. Alas, he drowned trying to escape from the island.

"Can it be that Mlanjeni is the reincarnation of Nxele?" Twin wondered. "After all, the amaXhosa nation is still awaiting the return of Nxele."

As Mlanjeni was praying to the sun, it scorched the earth. There was famine in the land. Cattle were dying. And those that still lived, you could count their ribs. As the Man of the River was waning away from his fasting, men and women of the land were waning away from starvation. And he told them that it was because of ubuthi.

"Leave ubuthi alone," he preached. "As long as there is witchcraft among you, there will be disease. People and animals will die. Cast away ubuthi! You do not need ubuthi to invite good fortune or to protect yourselves! Cast it away, and all come to me to be cleansed!"

"This sickly boy is Nxele himself. Nxele has returned as he promised he would," said Twin.

"No, he is not Nxele," responded Twin-Twin. "Mlanjeni is a prophet in his own right."

This difference of opinion developed into a serious disagreement between the twins, to the extent that they took up sticks to fight each other.

Women screamed and called the patriarch. When Xikixa arrived, he was happy. His sons had never disagreed on anything before, let alone fought each other. Now, for the very first time, they were not seeing things with the same eye. A spat over prophets.

"I was becoming worried about you two," he said, taking the sticks away from them. "Now you are becoming human beings."

People came to the homestead of Mlanjeni's father to be cleansed by the wonder child. They came from all over kwaXhosa [Xhosa land], even from beyond the borders of the lands that had been conquered by the British. Those who had poisonous roots and evil charms disposed of them and were cleansed. But still, some people held tight to their ubuthi, and lied that they had got rid of it.

Mlanjeni set up two antiwitchcraft poles outside his father's house. Those suspected of witchcraft were required to walk between them. The innocent walked through. Terrible things happened to those who had ubuthi even as they approached the sacred poles.

From early dawn, hundreds of people gathered outside the house. Among them were Xikixa, his wives, his other children from the junior houses, Twin-Twin and his wives and children, and Twin. People had come because word had spread up to the foothills of the Maluti Mountains that Mlanjeni cured the sick, and made the lame to walk, the dumb to speak, and the blind to see.

He was a man of great power. He lit his pipe on the sun, and when he danced drops of sweat from his body caused the rain to fall.

The Man of the River appeared at the door of his hut, and after one word from him people saw the star of the morning coming down from the sky and placing itself on his forehead. Another word from him and the earth shook and the mountains trembled. He disappeared into the hut again. And people began to sing a thunderous song that echoed in the faraway hills. They sang until the sun rose from behind the mountains and moved to the center of the sky.

Mlanjeni emerged again, raised his spear to the heavens, and touched the sun. The sun came down to touch his head, and went through his body until it was bright like the sun itself. People prostrated themselves, shouting, "Mlanjeni! Mlanjeni is our true Lord! The Man of the River is the conqueror of death!"

One by one they began to walk between the poles. The clean were unscathed. The unclean were struck by weakness and fear as they approached the poles. Then they writhed on the spot, unable to move. The people shouted, "Out! Get out, witchcraft!" until the victims staggered through the poles to Mlanjeni, who gave them some twigs that would protect them from further evil and keep them pure.

Twin-Twin's wife from the senior house stood up and slowly walked towards the poles. It was as though she was in a trance. As she moved between the poles she froze. She was paralyzed. Mlanjeni began to dance a frenzied dance around the poles, and the crowd chanted, "She is fixed! She is fixed! She is a witch!"

Twin-Twin rushed to his wife, who was writhing on the ground in agony. He was shouting, "No! No! My wife is not a witch! There must be a mistake!"

A group of zealots grabbed him and dragged him to the donga [ravine] below Kala's homestead. There they flogged him with whips. They beat him until he was almost unconscious. Then they went back to the Man of the River expecting his praise.

"Twin-Twin is a wizard. That is why he was defending his wife who was clearly identified as a witch by the poles," said Mlanjeni feebly. "But you had no right to beat him up. I have said it before, no person should ever be harmed for being a witch. Witchcraft is not in the nature of men and women. They are not born with it. It is an affliction that I can cure."

Twin-Twin's weals opened up and became wounds. After many months the wounds healed and became scars. But occasionally they itched and reminded him of his flagellation. At the time he did not know that his progeny was destined to carry the burden of the scars.

For a long time he was angry at the injustice of it all. He was not a wizard, and was sure that his wife was not a witch. Yet his own father and twin brother were blaming him for stupidly defending the honor of a woman who had been declared a witch by none other than the great prophet himself. And now both Xikixa and Twin were ostracizing his senior wife.

It did not escape Twin-Twin that this was the second time he had quarreled with his twin brother, and on both occasions the prophet was the cause.

But he continued to defend Mlanjeni. When the British decided to hunt the prophet down—claiming they did not approve of his witch-hunting and witch-curing activities—he was just as furious as the rest of the men of kwaXhosa.

Twin-Twin suppressed the bitterness in his heart and went with Twin, his father, and a group of mounted men to meet the white man who called himself the Great White Chief of the Xhosas, Sir Harry Smith [the governor of the Cape Colony]. He watched in humiliation as the Great White Chief commanded the elders and even the chiefs to kiss his staff and his boots. And they did. And so did he.

The Great White Chief was running wild all over the lands of the ama-Xhosa, doing whatever he liked in the name of Queen Victoria of England. He even deposed Sandile, the king of the amaXhosa-ka-Ngqika. This caused all the chiefs, even those who were Sandile's rivals, to rally around the deposed king.

The Great White Chief was relentless in his pursuit of Mlanjeni. He suspected that the prophet was plotting something sinister against the Great Queen and her Empire. He instructed his magistrates to summon him to their offices, where disciplinary measures would be taken. When the prophet refused to hand himself over, the Great White Chief felt personally insulted. One of his most zealous magistrates sent a soldier called John Dalton with a detachment of policemen to Kala's homestead to arrest the Man of the River. But Mlanjeni was nowhere to be found. Queen Victoria's men did not know that he had buried himself under the sacred waters of the Keiskamma River.

The Great White Chief read conspiracy and uprising in this whole sorry affair. He summoned all the kings and chiefs of the amaKhosa [amaXhosa] people for the usual boot-kissing ritual. He vowed that he would restore law and order throughout British Kaffraria and Xhosaland. But some of the most important kings and chiefs did not attend the ceremony. A further insult to the Empire.

Twin-Twin observed the ceremony from a distance. He reported to the men of his village how the white man who had styled himself the father of the amaXhosa had ranted and raved and threatened to raze the whole amaXhosa nation to the ground.

The people had had enough of the Great White Chief. Mounted men, led by Xikixa, went to the Keiskamma River to consult with the prophet. Mlanjeni ordered that all dun and yellow cattle be slaughtered, for they were an abomination. He doctored the military men for war so that the guns of the British would shoot hot water instead of bullets. The Great War of Mlanjeni had begun.

It was an ugly and tedious war that lasted for three years, during which the Khoikhoi [Khoekhoe] people of the Kat River Valley abandoned their traditional alliance with the British and fought on the side of the amaXhosa. Twin and Twin-Twin fought in the war. And so did Xikixa, who was still strong enough to carry a shield and a spear. The Great White Chief was frustrated. He was heard on many occasions talking of his intention to exterminate all amaXhosa.

"Extermination is now the only word and principle that guides us. I loved these people and considered them my children. But now I say exterminate the savage beasts!" he told his field commanders. Some of them were seen marching to war with the word "Extermination!" emblazoned on their hats.

Twin and Twin-Twin fought under General Maqoma in the Amathole Mountains. It was by and large a guerrilla war. They ambushed the British soldiers when they least expected it. The great size of the mountain range made things very difficult for the Imperial forces, and gave the amaXhosa armies many opportunities to destroy the enemy soldiers.

It was at one such ambush that Twin and Twin-Twin—accompanied by a small band of guerrilla fighters—chanced upon a British camp hidden in a gorge. A small group of British soldiers were cutting off the ears of a dead umXhosa soldier.

"What are they doing that for? Are they wizards?" asked Twin-Twin. "Or is it their way of removing *iqungu*?"

Iqungu was the vengeful force generated by war medicines. A soldier who died in war could have his iqungu attack the slayer, bloating and swelling up his body until he died. The amaXhosa believed that the British soldiers had their own iqungu. Therefore, they mutilated the bodies of slain British soldiers to render their iqungu powerless. This was considered savagery of the worst kind by the British, whenever they came across their dead comrades with ripped stomachs on the Amathole slopes.

"It is not for iqungu," explained Twin, who seemed to know more about the ways of the British from listening to fireside gossip. "It is just the witchcraft of the white man. They take those ears to their country. That's what they call souvenirs."

The twins saw that the leader of the soldiers was a man they had met before. John Dalton. He had been one of the soldiers accompanying the Great White Chief during the boot-kissing ceremony. He had been introduced then as an important man in the entourage of soldiers. He spoke isiXhosa, so he was the interpreter. It was the same John Dalton who had been sent with a detachment of policemen to hunt down the Man of the River.

Then, to the horror of the men watching, the soldiers cut off the dead man's head and put it in a pot of boiling water.

"They are cannibals too," hissed Twin-Twin.

The British soldiers sat around and smoked their pipes and laughed at their own jokes. Occasionally one of the soldiers stirred the boiling pot, and the stench of rotten meat floated up to the twins' group. The guerrillas could not stand it any longer. With bloodcurdling screams they sprang from their hiding place and attacked the men of Queen Victoria. One British soldier was killed, two were captured, and the rest escaped.

"It is our father!" screamed Twin. "They were going to eat our father!"

It was indeed the headless body of Xikixa.

"We were not going to eat your father," said John Dalton, prisoner of war, in his perfect isiXhosa. "We are civilized men, we don't eat people."

"Liar!" screamed Twin-Twin. "Why would you cook anything that you are not going to eat?"

"To remove the flesh from the skull," explained Dalton patiently. He did not seem to be afraid. He seemed too sure of himself. "These heads are either going to be souvenirs, or will be used for scientific inquiry."

Souvenirs. Scientific inquiry. It did not make sense. It was nothing but the witchcraft of the white man.

While they were debating the best method of killing their captives, a painful and merciless method that would at least avenge the decapitated patriarch, the British soldiers returned with reinforcements from a nearby camp. Only Twin and Twin-Twin were able to escape. The rest of their party was killed.

It gnawed the souls of the twins that their father met his end in the boiling cauldrons of the British, and they were never able to give him a decent burial in accordance with the rites and rituals of his people. How would he commune with his fellow ancestors without a head? How would a headless ancestor be able to act as an effective emissary of their pleas to Qamata [the deity]?

In the meantime, the Great White Chief was getting ever more desperate. He was unable to win the war outright. The British firepower was stronger, but the guerrilla tactics of the amaXhosa soldiers were creating havoc. General Maqoma and the Khoikhoi chief, Hans Brander, were giving the Imperial armies a hard time. Mutinies became the order of the day. Queen Victoria's men refused to go to the Amathole Mountains to be slaughtered like cattle by the savage amaXhosa. The Great White Chief was recalled to his country in disgrace, and was replaced by Sir George Cathcart, who proceeded to the eastern frontier to attend to the war with great enthusiasm.

People were disappointed with Mlanjeni's prophecies. None of them were coming true. The Imperial bullets did not turn into water. Instead, amaXhosa men were being killed every day.

But when the amaXhosa were about to give up, the Khoikhoi kept them fighting. At least they had muskets, although they were running out of ammunition. General Maqoma and Chief Brander destroyed more than two hundred farmhouses and captured five thousand cattle from the colonists.

Khoikhoi women sold their bodies to the British soldiers in order to smuggle canisters of gunpowder to their fighting men. Twin and his friends made snide remarks behind these women's backs. They slept with British soldiers, the men remarked. They seemed to forget that it was for the gunpowder that was saving the amaXhosa nation from utter defeat that the women were prostituting themselves.

It was with one of these Khoikhoi women, Quxu, that Twin fell in love. The amaXhosa guerrillas called her Qukezwa. He had seen her leading a group of Khoikhoi women who smuggled gunpowder under their hide skirts, and heard that she was the daughter of an important Khoikhoi chief.

The next time Twin saw Qukezwa it was at the crossroads. She was standing in front of a pile of stones, oblivious of him. She added another stone to the pile, and carefully placed green herbs on top of it. All the while she was chanting softly, "Father of fathers, oh Tsiqwa! You are our father. Let the clouds burst and the streams flow. Please give life to our flocks, and to us. I am weak, oh Tsiqwa, from thirst and hunger! Give me fields of fruit, that your children may be fed. For you are the father of fathers. O Tsiqwa! Let us sing your praises. In return give us your blessings. Father of fathers! You are our Lord, O Tsiqwa!"

She then quietly walked away. She seemed to remember something, and went back to the pile of stones.

"And, O Tsiqwa," she pleaded, "give us strength to win this war! To drive those who have come to desecrate our sacred grounds into the sea!"

Twin was struck with wonder.

"Who is this Tsiqwa you are addressing?" he asked softly. "I do not see anyone."

She was startled. But then composed herself when she saw a smiling umXhosa soldier standing in front of her.

"Tsiqwa is the one who tells his stories in heaven. He created the Khoikhoi and all the world. Even the rocks that lie under water on the riverbed. And all the springs with their snakes that live in them. That is why we never kill the snake of the spring. If we did, the spring would dry out."

Twin was captivated by her wisdom. He did not let on that her words were beyond him, and she felt at ease in his presence. Soon they were chatting like old friends. And in the days that followed he made a point of speaking with her whenever she brought smuggled gunpowder to the caves where the guerrilla fighters were hiding. He was in love. He ignored the mocking laughter of his comrades-in-arms who called her a whore.

From this daughter of joy he learned more about Tsiqwa. Together they sang the song of Heitsi Eibib, the earliest prophet of the Khoikhoi. The song told the story of how Heitsi Eibib brought his people to the Great River. But they could not cross, for the river was overflowing. And the people said to Heitsi Eibib, "Our enemies are upon us, they will surely kill us."

Heitsi Eibib prayed, "O Tsiqwa! Father of fathers. Open yourself that I may pass through, and close yourself afterwards."

As soon as he had uttered these words the Great River opened, and his people crossed. But when the enemies tried to pass through the opening, when they were right in the middle, the Great River closed upon them, and they all perished in its waters.

Whenever they sang this song, Twin wished the same thing could happen to the British.

Sometimes Qukezwa took her beau to the crossroads where there were piles of stones. At different crossroads there were different piles of stones. The lovers added one more stone each time they visited. They also placed green twigs of aromatic herbs such as *buchu* on the stones. She explained, "To place a stone on this grave of Heitsi Eibib is to be one with the source of your soul."

"How can one man have so many graves?" Twin asked.

"Because he was a prophet and a savior," she said. "He was the son of Tsiqwa. He lived and died for all the Khoikhoi, irrespective of clan."

Twin was sad that no one had ever died for the amaXhosa people in the same way that Heitsi Eibib had died for the Khoikhoi.

At night she taught him about the stars. Up in the heavens where Tsiqwa told his stories she showed him the bright stars which she called the Seven Sisters.

"They are the seven daughters of Tsiqwa, the Creator. The Seven Sisters are the star mothers from which all the human race has descended," she explained.

There was no doubt in Twin's mind that he wanted to marry this daughter of the stars. Twin-Twin tried to talk him out of it. He reminded his brother that there were amaXhosa maidens who had never opened their thighs for British soldiers. "What do you see in this *lawukazi*?" he cried.

But Twin was immovable in his resolve to marry Qukezwa.

"At least wait until the war is over," pleaded Twin-Twin. He hoped that time would cure his brother's infatuation.

But Twin would not wait. He married her. And for him she danced the dance of the new rain. And of the new moon.

In the meantime, the war was raging. And Sir George Cathcart would stop at nothing to win it. If he could not defeat the amaXhosa people in the field of battle, he was going to starve them into submission. He ordered his soldiers to go on a rampage and burn amaXhosa fields and kill amaXhosa cattle wherever they came across them, instead of spending their time hunting down guerrillas in the crevices of the Amathole Mountains. When the troops found unarmed women working in the fields, they killed them too.

The great fear of starvation finally defeated General Maqoma's forces, and the amaXhosa surrendered to the British. They turned against Mlanjeni, the Man of the River, because his charms had failed. But other nations continued to believe in him. Messengers from the distant nations of the Basotho, the abaThembu, the amaMpondo and the amaMpondomise visited him, asking for war charms and for the great secret of catching witches.

Six months after the war ended, the great prophet died of tuberculosis.

Although the twins' wealth remained intact—they had hidden most of their herds in the Amathole Mountains—they were disillusioned with prophets. They were devastated by the death of their father, who had ended up as stew in a British pot.

Mlanjeni's war, however, had given Twin a beautiful yellow-colored wife, and Twin-Twin the scars of history.

IV

All That Glitters

Until the second half of the nineteenth century, South Africa was of little world economic importance beyond its strategic position in the maritime trade that connects the Atlantic and Indian Oceans. In parts of the Eastern Cape, settlers raised merino sheep for export to English woolen manufacturers. Western Cape farmers produced mostly low-quality wine and brandy, as well as wheat, primarily for local consumption. A once thriving trade in ivory had long declined with the disappearance of South Africa's elephant herds. The manufacturing sector remained especially small, restricted to artisanal work. South Africa remained a mostly agrarian economy with an undeveloped export market.

The discovery of diamonds in the mid-1860s and the beginning of large-scale gold mining some two decades later, in what would become Johannesburg, profoundly altered the course of South African history. At the time, South African mines contained the world's largest deposit of both minerals. Overnight South Africa became a central part of the world economy, particularly since most major currencies were pegged to the price of gold. The region quickly became Africa's industrial behemoth, attracting capital investment from Europe and the United States and drawing workers from around the world. Miners, speculators, and entrepreneurs flooded to the diggings. A massive migrant-labor system developed, whereby African workers from South Africa, Lesotho, Portuguese East Africa (Mozambique), and as far afield as Northern Rhodesia (Zambia) labored for part of the year before returning to their rural homes. By the early twentieth century, African communities throughout southern Africa depended on the wages of male mine workers. Cities emerged where there had been farms: Kimberley, at the heart of the diamond-mining industry, and Johannesburg, South Africa's City of Gold, today one of the continent's largest urban areas. The mining industry rapidly accelerated the building of railways, dockyards, and roads, and it provided opportunities for both white and black entrepreneurs. In many parts of the world, the shift toward an industrial economy unfolded over a century or more. South Africa's industrial revolution took place in fewer than three decades.

Mining in South Africa was uniquely capital and labor intensive. Miners had to dig deeper into the earth once surface areas had been exhausted; gold mining now takes place more than ten thousand feet below the surface. Within just a few years, miners in Kimberley created the world's largest constructed hole. On the Witwatersrand (the "Rand") the amount of gold per ton of ore could be pitifully small. Especially in the 1890s, its extraction required an expensive process that required vast amounts of cyanide. The resulting high fixed costs of gold mining and other concerns, such as controlling the supply of diamonds, led to consolidation of ownership after a brief period of feverish prospecting. Out of this tumultuous era emerged South Africa's most famous companies, such as De Beers Consolidated and the Anglo-American Corporation, in addition to fabulously wealthy and politically powerful capitalists, such as Cecil Rhodes.

South Africa's mineral revolution took place in the heyday of British imperial expansion and at the peak of pseudo-scientific racism in Europe and in the Americas. How the industry came to be organized profoundly affected class, ethnic, gender, and race relations and also led to the political consolidation of the region under white and British imperial domination. The location of the mineral reserves far in the interior created a number of fundamental economic and political challenges for the rising class of industrialists and their financial backers. In 1867 prospectors discovered diamonds in what was then Griqualand West, hundreds of miles from Cape Town, and in 1885 gold was found still further in the interior of the Boer South African Republic (Transvaal), which was headed by Paul Kruger. Both areas had depended on farming and herding and lacked infrastructure to support industrial production. As the diamond mines expanded in Griqualand West in the 1870s, white miners demanded greater control over black workers. In 1880 the Cape Colony formally annexed the territory, expanding British imperialism deeper into the interior and thwarting the designs of politicians in the neighboring Boer republic, the Orange Free State. The remaining independent African societies also soon came under colonial domination, most famously following the defeat of the Zulu Kingdom in 1879. The South African Republic presented an altogether more formidable set of problems.

The greater Southern African region had come within the orbit of the British Empire earlier in the nineteenth century. British rule had profoundly reshaped social relations in the Cape, leading in part to the Great Trek. British relations with the Boer republics had remained tense since their formation earlier in the century. In the late 1870s, the British annexed the South

African Republic (Transvaal), which led to violent skirmishes and a tense settlement that restored its sovereignty a few years later. The gold revolution, however, powerfully connected South Africa to the British Empire and the center of world finance, the city of London. Many Boers bristled at the movement into the South African Republic of tens of thousands of white miners and entrepreneurs, whom they called *uitlanders* (foreigners), and at the smug imperialism of industrialists such as Rhodes who envisioned a British Empire stretching from Cape Town to Cairo. Tensions broke into war in 1899, which lasted until 1902. The South African (or Anglo-Boer) War, which pitted the British Empire and its South African colonies against the Boer republics and resulted in the region's political consolidation as the Union of South Africa in 1910, became a defining moment in South Africa's modern history.

The readings included in this part attempt to give readers a sense of the remarkably rapid pace of change during this tumultuous period, from the industrial revolution to the making of a black working class, from the defeat of African societies to Africa's bloodiest colonial war. From this cauldron emerged many of the defining features of modern South Africa.

The Story of the Diamond Fields

Anthony Trollope

In 1877 the English novelist Anthony Trollope (1815–82) toured South Africa and published an account of his journey the following year. Trollope's travels occurred just as the emerging mineral revolution and the consequent acceleration of imperial conquest were gathering steam in South Africa, which would soon help to fuel a wider scramble for Africa by the European powers. Trollope wrote that he determined to set off for South Africa just after Sir Theophilus Shepstone annexed the Boer republic of the Transvaal for Britain. This event was associated with a wider, but aborted, plan for confederation of the various South African colonies and Boer republics under British authority. The larger goals of the British imperialists crafting this plan were to subdue independent African kingdoms in order to bring greater security to the nascent Boer republics and to thereby create conditions for the free flow of African labor to the diamond mines of Griqualand West, which would be annexed to the Cape Colony. Though the confederation plan did not come to fruition, its aims were realized two decades later, after the opening of the Witwatersrand gold mines propelled Britain to full-scale conquest of the Boer republics in the South African War of 1899–1902.

In the excerpt, Trollope introduces the development and operation of the diamond mines near Kimberley. He quickly acquaints us with the massive scale of the mining operations and the presence of large numbers of African men doing most of the manual labor. Although Trollope is predisposed to see these men as "ants" and as half-clothed savages, he is also a sharp-eyed observer and journalist who details the conditions associated with diamond mining. He also discusses the problem of diamond theft in the mines. This led a few years later to the creation of closed compounds, which facilitated very tight control of workers and helped keep a lid on wages.

The industrial scale of activity on the new diamond mines, and later the gold mines of the Witwatersrand, led to the development of two new cities in South Africa: Kimberley and, more spectacularly, Johannesburg. Here, nearly a decade before the founding of Johannesburg, Trollope describes the diamond-mining boomtown of Kimberley. As a typical liberal Victorian who believed that slavery was wrong but

*that whites must continue to be masters over blacks, in order to "civilize" them,
Trollope firmly argues for the colonial belief in the civilizing value of labor for subject populations. He also notes the gun trade at Kimberley, thriving on the desire of
African migrant workers to convert wages, earned in a few months at the mines, into
firearms to bring back to their rural homes across southern Africa. This trade had
precipitated, a few years earlier, the crisis in Natal discussed in "The Trial of Langalibalele," the next entry in this part. Finally, Trollope also forecasts the declining
value of diamonds as they are pulled from the ground at an accelerating rate. It was
this tendency that led to the rapid consolidation of mining claims in the 1880s, which
culminated in a monopoly for Rhodes's De Beers, still the world's largest miner and
marketer of diamonds.*

The first known finding of a diamond in South Africa was as recent as
1867;—so that the entire business which has well nigh deluged the world of
luxury with precious stones and has added so many difficulties to the task of
British rule in South Africa is only now,—in 1877,—ten years old. . . .

And this diamond was found by accident and could not for a time obtain
any credence. . . .

It was in 1870 that the question seems to have got itself so settled that
some portion of the speculative energy of the world was enabled to fix itself
on the new Diamond Fields. In that year various white men set themselves
seriously to work in searching the banks of the Vaal up and down between
Hebron and Klipdrift,—or Barkly as it is now called, and many small parcels
of stones were bought from Natives who had been instigated to search by
what they had already heard. The operations of those times are now called
the "river diggings" in distinction to the "dry diggings," which are works of
much greater magnitude carried on in a much more scientific manner away
from the river,—and which certainly are in all respects "dry" enough. . . .

The commencement of diamond-digging as a settled industry was in
1872. It was then that dry-digging was commenced, which consists of the
regulated removal of ground found to be diamondiferous and of the washing and examination of every fraction of the soil. The district which we as
yet know to be so specially gifted extends up and down the Vaal river from
the confluence of the Modder to Hebron, about 75 miles, and includes a
small district on the east side of the river. Here, within 12 miles of the river,
and within a circle of which the diameter is about 2 1/2 miles, are contained
all the mines,—or dry diggings,—from which have come the real wealth of
the country. . . .

It is of the dry diggings that the future student of the Diamond Fields
of South Africa will have to take chief account. . . . Of these dry diggings

The diamond diggings, 1872, *Illustrated London News*, 31 August 1872.

there are now four, Du Toit's Pan, Bultfontein, Old De Beers,—and Coles-berg Kopje or the great Kimberley mine, which though last in the Field has thrown all the other diamond mines of the world into the shade. . . .

The New Rush, the Colesberg Kopje,—pronounced Coppy,—and the Kimberley mine are one and the same place. It is now within the town of Kimberley,—which has in fact got itself built around the hill to supply the wants of the mining population. Kimberley has in this way become the capital and seat of Government for the Province. As the mine is one of the most remarkable spots on the face of the earth I will endeavour to explain it with some minuteness, and I will annex a plan of it which as I go on I will endeavour also to explain.

The Colesberg hill is in fact hardly a hill at all,—what little summit may once have entitled it to the name having been cut off. On reaching the spot by one of the streets from the square you see no hill but are called upon to rise over a mound, which is circular and looks to be no more than the debris of the mine though it is in fact the remainder of the slight natural ascent. It is but a few feet high and on getting to the top you look down into a huge hole. This is the Kimberley mine. You immediately feel that it is the largest and most complete hole ever made by human agency. . . .

Here everything is so gathered together and collected that it is not at first easy to understand that the hole should contain the operations of a large number of separate speculators. It is so completely one that you are driven at first to think that it must be the property of one firm,—or at any rate be entrusted to the management of one director. It is very far from being so. In the pit beneath your feet, hard as it is at first to your imagination to separate it into various enterprises, the persons making or marring their fortunes have as little connection with each other as have the different banking firms in Lombard Street. There too the neighbourhood is very close, and common precautions have to be taken as to roadways, fires, and general convenience.

You are told that the pit has a surface area of 9 acres. . . .

You stand upon the marge and there, suddenly, beneath your feet lies the entirety of the Kimberley mine, so open, so manifest, and so uncovered that if your eyes were good enough you might examine the separate operations of each of the three or four thousand human beings who are at work there. It looks to be so steep down that there can be no way to the bottom other than the aerial contrivances which I will presently endeavour to explain. It is as though you were looking into a vast bowl, the sides of which are smooth as should be the sides of a bowl, while round the bottom are various marvellous incrustations among which ants are working with all the usual energy of the ant-tribe. And these incrustations are not simply at the bottom, but come up the curves and slopes of the bowl irregularly, half-way up perhaps in one place, while on another side they are confined quite to the lower deep. The pit is 230 feet deep, nearly circular, though after awhile the eye becomes aware of the fact that it is oblong. . . .

When the world below is busy there are about 3,500 Kaffirs at work,—some small proportion upon the reef which has to be got into order so that it shall neither tumble in, nor impede the work, nor overlay the diamondiferous soil as it still does in some places; but by far the greatest number are employed in digging. Their task is to pick up the earth and shovel it into the buckets and iron receptacles. Much of it is loosened for them by blasting which is done after the Kaffirs have left the mine at 6 o'clock. You look down and see the swarm of black ants busy at every hole and corner with their picks moving and shovelling the loose blue soil. . . .

But though there are but 408 claims there are subdivisions in regard to property very much more minute. There are shares held by individuals as small as one-sixteenth of a claim. The total property is in fact divided into 514 portions, the amount of which of course varies extremely. Every master miner pays 10s. [shillings] a month to the Government for the privilege of working whether he own a claim or only a portion of a claim. In working this the number of men employed differs very much from time to time. When I was there the mine was very full, and there were probably almost

4,000 men in it and as many more employed above on the stuff. When the "blue" [diamondiferous earth] has come up and been deposited in the great wooden boxes at the top it is then lowered by its own weight into carts, and carried off to the "ground" of the proprietor. Every diamond digger is obliged to have a space of ground somewhere round the town,—as near his whim as he can get it,—to which his stuff is carted and then laid out to crumble and decompose. This may occupy weeks, but the time depends on what may be the fall of rain. If there be no rain, it must be watered,—at a very considerable expense. It is then brought to the washing, and is first put into a round puddling trough where it is broken up and converted into mud by stationary rakes which work upon the stuff as the trough goes round. The stones of course fall to the bottom, and as diamonds are the heaviest of stones they fall with the others. The mud is examined and thrown away,— and then the stones are washed, and rewashed, and sifted, and examined. The greater number of diamonds are found during this operation;—but the large gems and those therefore of by far the greatest value are generally discovered while the stuff is being knocked about and put into the buckets in the mine.

It need hardly be said that in such an operation as I have described the greatest care is necessary to prevent stealing and that no care will prevent it. The Kaffirs are the great thieves,—to such an extent of super excellence that white superintendence is spoken of as being the only safeguard. The honesty of the white man may perhaps be indifferent, but such as it is it has to be used at every point to prevent, as far as it may be prevented, the systematized stealing in which the Kaffirs take an individual and national pride. The Kaffirs are not only most willing but most astute thieves, feeling a glory in their theft and thinking that every stone stolen from a white man is a duty done to their Chief and their tribe. I think it may be taken as certain that no Kaffir would feel the slightest pang of conscience at stealing a diamond, or that any disgrace would be held to attach to him among other Kaffirs for such a performance. They come to the Fields instructed by their Chiefs to steal diamonds and they obey the orders like loyal subjects. Many of the Kaffir Chiefs are said to have large quantities of diamonds which have been brought to them by their men returning from the diggings,—but most of those which are stolen no doubt find their way into the hands of illicit dealers. I have been told that the thefts perpetrated by the Kaffirs amount to 25 per cent on the total amount found;—but this I do not believe.

The opportunities for stealing are of hourly occurrence and are of such a nature as to make prevention impossible. These men are sharpsighted as birds and know and see a diamond much quicker than a white man. They will pick up stones with their toes and secrete them even under the eyes of those who are watching them. I was told that a man will so hide a diamond in his mouth that no examination will force him to disclose it. They are punished when discovered with lashes and imprisonment,—in accordance with the law on the matter. No employer is now allowed to flog his man at his own pleasure. And the white men who buy diamonds from Kaffirs are also punished when convicted, by fine and imprisonment for the simple offence of buying from a Kaffir; but with flogging also if convicted of having instigated a Kaffir to steal. Nevertheless a lucrative business of this nature is carried on, and the Kaffirs know well where to dispose of their plunder though of course but for a small proportion of its value.

Ten shillings a week and their food were the regular wages here as elsewhere. This I found to be very fluctuating, but the money paid had rarely gone lower for any considerable number of men than the above-named rate. The lowest amount paid has been 7s. 6d. a week. Sometimes it had been as high as 20s. and even 30s. a week. A good deal of the work is supplied by contract, certain middlemen undertaking to provide men with all expenses paid at £1 a week. When mealies [corn] have become dear from drought,— there being no grass for oxen on the route,—no money can be made in this way. Such was the case when I was in Griqualand West. It is stated by Mr. Oats, an engineer, in his evidence given to the Committee on the Griqualand West Annexation Bill, in June 1877—that the annual amount of wages paid at Kimberley had varied from £600,000 to £1,600,000 a year. Nearly the whole of this had gone into the hands of the Kaffirs.

Perhaps the most interesting sight at the mine is the escaping of the men from their labour at six o'clock. Then, at the sound of some welcomed gong, they begin to swarm up the sides close at each other's heels apparently altogether indifferent as to whether there be a path or no. They come as flies come up a wall, only capering as flies never caper,—and shouting as they come. In endless strings, as ants follow each other, they move, passing along ways which seem to offer no hold to a human foot. Then it is that one can best observe their costume in which a jacket is never absent but of which a pair of trowsers rarely forms a portion. A soldier's red jacket or a soldier's blue jacket has more charms than any other vestment. They seem always to be good humoured, always well-behaved,—but then they are always thieves. And yet how grand a thing it is that so large a number of these men should have been brought in so short a space of time to the habit of receiving wages and to the capacity of bargaining as to the wages for which they will work. I shall not, however, think it so grand a thing if anyone addresses them as the free and independent electors of Kimberley before they have got trowsers to cover their nakedness. I must add also that a visitor to Kimberley should if possible take an opportunity of looking down upon the mine by moonlight. It is a weird and wonderful sight, and may almost be called sublime in its peculiar strangeness. . . .

Of the adult male population two-thirds are of coloured races,—Kaffirs for the most part,—and one-third is European. At present both the one and the other are a shifting people;—but the Kaffirs shift much the quickest. Each man remains generally only six or eight months on the Fields and then returns home to his tribe. This mode of life, however, is already somewhat on the decrease, and as the love of making money grows, and as tribal reverence for the Chieftains dies out, the men will learn to remain more constantly at their work. Unless the diamonds come to an end all together,— which one cannot but always feel to be possible,—the place will become a large town with a settled Kaffir population which will fall gradually into civilized ways of life. There is no other place in South Africa where this has been done, or for many years can be done to the same extent. I mention this here because it seems to be so essentially necessary to remember that South Africa is a land not of white but of black men, and that the progress to be most desired is that which will quickest induce the Kaffir to put off his savagery and live after the manner of his white brethren. . . .

The work of civilizing as it has been carried out by simple philanthropy or by religion is terribly slow. One is tempted sometimes to say that nothing is done by religion and very little by philanthropy. But love of money works very fast. In Griqualand West, especially in the Diamond Fields, and above all at Kimberley, it is not only out in the wilds, by the river sides, on the veld, and in their own kraals, that the black men outnumber the white; but in the streets of the city also and in the work shops of the mine. And here they are brought together not by the spasmodic energy of missionaries or by the unalluring attraction of schools but by the certainty of earning wages. The seeker after diamonds is determined to have them because the making of his fortune depends upon them; and the Kaffir himself is determined to come to Kimberley because he has learned the loveliness of 10s. a week paid regularly into his hand every Saturday night.

Who can doubt but that work is the great civilizer of the world,—work and the growing desire for those good things which work only will bring? If there be one who does he should come here to see how those dusky troops of labourers, who ten years since were living in the wildest state of unalloyed savagery, whose only occupation was the slaughter of each other in tribal wars, each of whom was the slave of his Chief, who were subject to the dominion of most brutalizing and cruel superstitions, have already put themselves on the path towards civilization. They are thieves no doubt;— that is they steal diamonds though not often other things. They are not Christians. They do not yet care much about breeches. They do not go to school. But they are orderly. They come to work at six in the morning and go away at six in the evening. They have an hour in the middle of the day, and know that they have to work during the other hours. They take their meals regularly and, what is the best of all, they are learning to spend their money instead of carrying it back to their Chiefs. . . .

Because of this I regard Kimberley as one of the most interesting places on the face of the earth. I know no other spot on which the work of civilizing a Savage is being carried on with so signal a success. The Savages whom we have encountered in our great task of populating the world have for the most part eluded our grasp by perishing while we have been considering how we might best deal with them. Here, in South Africa, a healthy nation remains and assures us by its prolific tendency that when protected from self-destruction by our fostering care it will spread and increase beneath our hands. But what was to be done with these people? Having found that they do not mean to die, by what means might we instruct them how to live? Teach them to sing hymns, and all will be well. That is one receipt. Turn them into slaves, and make them work. That is another receipt. Divide the land with them, and let them live after their own fashions;—only subject to some little control from us. That was a third. The hymns have done nothing. The slavery was of course impossible. And that division of land has been, perhaps not equally futile, but insufficient for the growing needs of the people;—insufficient also for our own needs. Though we abuse the Kaffir we want his service, and we want more than our share of his land. But that which no effort of intelligence could produce has been brought about by circumstances. The Diamond Fields have been discovered and now there are ten thousand of these people receiving regular wages and quite capable of rushing to a magistrate for protection if they be paid a shilling short on Saturday night. . . .

I cannot say that Kimberley is in other respects an alluring town; perhaps as little so as any town that I have ever visited. . . .

And the meat was bad, the butter uneatable, vegetables a rarity, supplied indeed at the table at which I sat but supplied at a great cost. Milk and potatoes were luxuries so costly that one sinned almost in using them. A man walking about with his pocket full of diamonds would not perhaps care for this; but even at Kimberley there are those who have fixed incomes,—an unfortunate Deputy Governor or the like,—to whom sugar at 2s. 6d. [pence] a pound and other equally necessary articles in the same proportion, must detract much from the honour and glory of the position. . . . For the understanding of this it must be known that almost everything consumed at Kimberley has to be carried up from the coast, five hundred miles, by ox-wagons, and that the oxen have to feed themselves on the grasses along the road. When there has been a period of drought there are no grasses, and when there are no grasses the oxen will die instead of making progress. Periods of drought are by no means uncommon in South Africa. When I was at Kimberley there had been a period of drought for many months. There had, indeed, been no rain to speak of for more than a year. As one consequence of this the grocers were charging 2s. 6d. a pound for brown sugar. Even the chance of such a state of things militates very much against the comfort of a residence. . . .

The diamond dealers whom I saw were the honest men, who keep their heads well above water, and live in the odour of diamond sanctity, dealing only with licensed diggers and loving the law. But there are diamond dealers who buy from the Kaffirs,—or from intermediate rogues who instigate the Kaffirs to steal. These are regarded as the curse of the place, and, as may be understood, their existence is most injurious to the interests of all who traffic honestly in this article. The law is very severe on them, imprisoning them, and subjecting them to lashes if in any case it can be proved that a delinquent has instigated a Kaffir to steal. . . .

Next to diamond dealing the selling of guns used to be the great trade in Kimberley, the purchasers being Kaffirs who thus disposed of their surplus wages. But when I was there the trade seemed to have come to an end, the Kaffirs, I trust, having found that they could do better with their money than buy guns,—which they seldom use with much precision when they have them. There was once a whole street devoted to this dealing in guns, but the gun shops had been converted to other purposes when I was there. Great complaint had been made against the Government of Griqualand West for permitting the unreserved sale of guns to the Kaffirs, and attempts have been made by the two Republics—of the Transvaal and the Orange Free State—to stop the return of men when so armed. . . . But yet the Kaffirs are very numerous and the white men are comparatively but a handful; I would have a Kaffir as free to shoot a buck as a white man. And yet I feel that the Kaffir must be kept in subjection. The evil, if it be an evil, has now been done, for guns are very numerous among the Kaffirs.

There can hardly be a doubt that Kimberley and the diamond fields have been of great service to the black men who obtain work. No doubt they are thieves,—as regards the diamonds,—but their thievery will gradually be got under by the usual processes. . . . And there can be as little doubt that the finding of diamonds has in a commercial point of view been the salvation of South Africa. The Orange Free State . . . has been so strengthened by the trade thus created as to be now capable of a successful and permanent existence. . . . As regards the Cape Colony generally, if quite the same thing need not be said, it must be acknowledged that its present comparative success is due almost entirely to the diamonds,—or rather to the commercial prosperity caused by the consumption in which diamond finders and their satellites have been enabled to indulge. The Custom duties of the Cape Colony in 1869, before the diamond industry existed, were less than £300,000. In 1875 that sum had been very much more than doubled. And it must be remembered that this rapid increase did not come from any great increase of numbers. The diamond-digging brought in a few white men no doubt, but only a few in comparison with the increase in revenue. There are but 8,000 Europeans in the diamond fields altogether. Had they all been new comers this would have been no great increase to a population which now exceeds 700,000 persons. The sudden influx of national wealth has come from the capability for consumption created by the new industry. White men looking for diamonds can drink champagne. Black men looking for diamonds can buy clothes and guns and food. It is not the wealth found which directly enriches the nation, but the trade created by the finding. It was the same with the gold in Australia. Of the national benefit arising from the diamonds there can be no doubt. Whether they have been equally beneficial to those who have searched for them and found them may be a matter of question. . . .

If the diamonds still be there in twenty years' time,—as to which I altogether decline to give my opinion,—a railway will have been carried on to Kimberley, and planks will have been carried up, and perhaps bricks from some more favoured locality, and possibly paving stones, so that the town shall be made to look less rowdy and less abominable. And pipes will be laid on from the Vaal river, and there will be water carts. And with the dust the flies will go into abeyance. And trees will have been planted. And fresh butter will be made. And there will be a library and men will have books. And houses will have become pleasant, so that a merchant may love to sit at home in his own verandah,—which he will then afford to have broad and cool and floored. And as the nice things come the nasty habits will sink. . . . Some mode of checking the Kaffir thieves will perhaps have been found,— and the industry will have sunk into the usual grooves. Nothing, however, will tend so much to this as the lessening of the value of diamonds. The stone is at present so precious that a man's mind cannot bear to think that one should escape him.

The Trial of Langalibalele

British Parliamentary Papers

In 1873 Langalibalele kaMthimkhulu (1818–89), the inkosi (chief) of one of the larg-est chiefdoms in Natal, came into conflict with colonial authorities over the alleged failure of young men in his district to register the firearms they had purchased while engaged in migrant labor on the Kimberley diamond mines. The colony's secretary for native affairs, Sir Theophilus Shepstone, summoned him to the capital, but Lan-galibalele feared that he was being lured into a trap and so delayed complying. An African messenger, Mahoyiza, sent to Langalibalele by Shepstone, was allegedly stripped (he was made to take off his coats, for fear that he was armed) and insulted by Langalibalele's men. As a result, Lieutenant Governor Sir Benjamin Pine and Shepstone sent an armed force to arrest the chief, who retreated into neighboring Ba-sutoland. A skirmish in the mountainous border area led to the deaths of five of the colonial forces. Pine and Shepstone deposed Langalibalele, disbanded his chiefdom, and brought him in chains to the colonial capital, Pietermaritzburg.

There, in January 1874, a farcical trial ensued, appropriately held under a circus tent. The following document is an excerpt from the trial transcript. Pine presided and the prosecutor was John Shepstone, the brother of Theophilus, who was also a member of the court. The court included a range of colonial officials and compli-ant chiefs. The latter were there to help substantiate officials' claim that the trial was conducted under "native" law. In fact, the charges and trial accorded neither with customary procedure nor with colonial law, and the chief was not permitted to have legal representation. The court convicted him and sent him into exile in the Cape Colony. However, the liberal Anglican bishop John Colenso's efforts on behalf of Langalibalele made the proceedings into an imperial scandal and the sentence was reduced. The affair illustrates the growing white pressure on African leaders and communities, and concerns about African resistance, which led to broader imperial conquest over the next quarter century in the context of the mineral revolution.

The Court again met on Friday, the 23rd January, 1874, at 11 A.M. . . .

His Excellency [the lieutenant governor] said: At the last meeting I stated that we intended to allow counsel to appear for the prisoner, and we selected Mr. Escombe for that purpose. Mr. Escombe, on being informed that this Court was of a peculiar nature and jurisdiction, and that he must confine himself within certain limits, could not accept the duty, and I think properly. He said that, as an English counsel, he must ever be at full liberty to say or do what he liked, or he could not take up the case at all, and, therefore, he had declined; but looking at the peculiar character of this Court, and its being so directly contrary to Kaffir usage, custom, and law, to allow counsel, I made up my mind that it would not be desirable to allow, or ask anyone else to say anything, or act for the prisoner; he could only say something in extenuation of the guilt of the prisoner, because he had admitted it, and this Court is willing to take the most lenient view it can of the prisoner's conduct, and there is no necessity to urge that course; we shall be as merciful as circumstances will admit of. The native chiefs are aware that it is competent for them to put any question to assist the prisoner, if they feel so disposed. . . .

The Secretary for Native Affairs explained, that at the commencement of last year he had become aware that the Magistrate of Weenen county, and Langalibalele, were not acting cordially together. He said, several instances of that sort were brought to my notice by the Magistrate, and after a time he requested that I would send for Langalibalele. . . .

The Secretary for Native Affairs continued: I may mention that messengers came from Langalibalele twice. . . . On each of these occasions I fully explained to the messengers the contents of this message, because I saw there was a disinclination to render obedience. On the 29th October also, the day before your Excellency started from Pietermaritzburg, two men, named Bomba and Makalika, arrived in town, pretending to have been sent from the prisoner, and took the opportunity of explaining to them also the whole state of the case, and requesting them to go at once to Langalibalele, and tell him if he would only meet your Excellency, and explain his conduct no harm whatever would happen; but, if he did not, very serious consequences must, from the nature of things, happen.

His Excellency asked Langalibalele if, having heard what the Secretary for Native Affairs had said, he had any questions to ask him.

Prisoner replied: I have nothing to say; I am simply awaiting the decision which your Excellency may arrive at, and when that is given I should wish a note or pass in order that I may send about and collect my children (tribe).

His Excellency told the prisoner he was most anxious he should put any questions he wished to the Secretary for Native Affairs, or make any statement he desired.

Prisoner, in reply, called himself an Umtagati [evildoer], admitted that he had sinned, and had nothing to say; he confessed his guilt.

His Excellency asked the native chiefs, members of the Court, if they wished to ask any questions or say anything, especially anything in favour of the accused.

Zatshuke expressed his surprise at what Langalibalele had said just now, when asking for a pass, before he knew what his sentence would be, especially after admitting his guilt at the same moment. That conduct barred them from saying anything in prisoner's favour. . . .

His Excellency: I understand the principal dispute between the Magistrate and Langalibalele arose with reference to the registration of guns; that the Government did not object to the natives having firearms they had lawfully bought, but insisted, and properly so, upon the fulfilment of the law regarding registration, and that, as I understand it, was resisted.

The Secretary for Native Affairs said a large number of Diamond Fields tickets [mine workers' employment documents] had been found by the forces in the Location [native reserve], and he had seen a large number of guns, many of which had never been registered in this Colony.

Mr. Hawkins: They were ordered by Mr. Mellersh to bring in the guns, were they not?

The Secretary for Native Affairs: That was a particular case of five guns; at first they refused, but ultimately took in these five guns on further pressure being brought to bear upon them. The broader question between the Magistrate and prisoner was that of registration generally.

His Excellency: Do you think the conduct of Langalibalele has been, in any large degree, influenced by fear of the consequences if he came in?

The Secretary for Native Affairs: I suppose it must have been influenced by fear to some extent, but I have no idea what grounds he had for fear.

His Excellency: You have had large experience, and have virtually been governing the natives for a long time: have you ever known a chief who has come to explain his conduct to be badly treated?

The Secretary for Native Affairs: We have always been careful to avoid anything of the kind, because it would so easily set matters wrong; anything having the appearance of bad faith, or entrapping any native, has never been done. . . .

His Excellency: I believe the chiefs of this Colony are aware of the consequences of not obeying a summons from this Government to come in and explain their conduct—they are aware that it is a very grave offence.

The Secretary for Native Affairs: They all know that to refuse obedience is an act of contumacy [rebellion]. . . .

His Excellency requested Mahoiza to describe to what extent he had been stripped.

Mahoiza said: When they delivered the message that I was to be stripped, because they thought I had a gun hidden away in my possession, as Mr. John Shepstone had at the arrest of Matyana [Matshana, another chief whom the secretary for native affairs had deposed], I opened my coat, and said, "You can search me and see if I have." While I was making these remarks they came up and took off my clothes. They intended to strip me altogether, but I said I had no other dress to wear, and I was allowed to retain my trousers and boots. They took off my coat, waistcoat, shirt, and gaiters.

His Excellency inquired: Did they offer to allow you to put on your clothes again when they found out you had no gun?

Mahoiza: I suggested that I should be allowed to put on my clothes again, but they would not consent. They said, "Let us take him to the Chief as he is," and in this guise I went before the Chief. Anyone acting under fear would never treat a messenger from the Supreme Power in that way.

Mr. Hawkins asked: Did they give you any beer?

Mahoiza replied: About a quart of beer was handed round, according to Kaffir custom; but when I said I was hungry, Langalibalele said, "What will you eat? The cattle are all gone."

His Excellency (to prisoner): Have you anything further to say? I shall be glad to hear anything you have to say.

Prisoner replied: I have nothing more to say beyond thanking Mr. John Shepstone for what he said on my behalf. It is quite true that I acted under fear, and was urged on by other people—Mabuhle and others, the official witnesses, to do what I did.

His Excellency said: Tell Langalibalele I have heard his case with all the care I have been able to bestow upon it, and it has been tried according to the usages and customs of Kaffir law; but we have endeavoured to temper that law with the principles of humanity in which we have been brought up, and under which we are accustomed to act, that I have now heard all he has to say on the whole case, and I shall reserve my judgment until next week, when he will receive the judgment of myself and the Court in this case. . . .

The Coming of the Anglo-Zulu War

Cetshwayo kaMpande

Cetshwayo kaMpande (ca. 1826–84) ascended to the Zulu kingship in 1873 after the death of his father, Mpande kaSenzangakhona (see part III). Though the Zulu Kingdom was independent, it depended on good relations with the neighboring colony of Natal. In 1877 Sir Theophilus Shepstone annexed the Boer republic of the Transvaal to Britain in pursuit of an imperial scheme to confederate the white colonies and republics of South Africa under British authority. Though a British commission proposed a reasonable settlement of a long-simmering boundary dispute between the Transvaal and the Zulu Kingdom, the British high commissioner Sir Bartle Frere decided to provoke war in order to crush the independence of the Zulu Kingdom. Frere and other British imperialists believed that the continued independence of African kingdoms, such as the Zulu and Pedi, stood in the way of their goal for the region: a British confederation that would promote the free flow of labor and goods to and from Kimberley's diamond mines and preserve British control over South Africa's strategic coast, the gateway to Britain's most important colony, India. In late 1878 Frere delivered an ultimatum that required Cetshwayo to disband his army, along with other unacceptable demands. In January 1879 the British invaded the kingdom. A notorious defeat at the hands of Zulu forces at Isandlwana led British political and military authorities to embrace a full-scale war to decisively defeat Cetshwayo's army. Nine months later, the king was captured and exiled to Cape Town.

In 1881 Cetshwayo wrote a long letter to the governor of the Cape Colony, Sir Hercules Robinson. The king recounted the events leading to the Anglo-Zulu War of 1879, including the boundary dispute, and demanded a hearing. In 1882 he was permitted to travel to London, where the colonial secretary Lord Kimberley agreed to restore him to a vastly reduced portion of his kingdom. There, rivals who had been placed in positions of power by the British again attacked him and, displaced from his seat of power, he died in 1884.

I am writing to you, Sir Hercules Robinson, Governor of this land, to ask why my case is kept quiet even now, seeing that the Boers have sued for peace and their affair is quieted. I think now is the right time to hear and

Cetshwayo kaMpande.
Photographer un-
known. Courtesy of
Campbell Collections
of the University
of KwaZulu-Natal,
D37/013.

learn about the grounds on which the arguments for killing me (i.e. destroying my country and taking me captive) were based. . . .

As soon as I heard of my father's death, I sent men with an ox to report to
Mr. Shepstone and to the Assembly of Natal—to whom Mpande belonged—
about the death of the King. I thought it fit, on my father's death, that you
the English nation should be present and witness the settlement of the Zulu
country under my rule, seeing that this house, King, and country of this
land are not with-out or outside the English nation, but within the English
nation. . . .

After this the Boers came into my country in the north with many men,
as if they came to war with us, surrounded the Zulu kraals, and beat the
inmates, telling them to leave their homes, as they (the Boers) were going to
live there. . . . When the Boers did this the Zulus got alarmed, specially because on going away the Boers said they were coming in force on the mor-

row, and it will be good for the Zulus to be found gathered and together; for these reasons the Zulus armed themselves and kept themselves in readiness. . . . This is what was called in Natal "Cetywayo has armed himself, and is about to fight." . . .

After this Mr. Shepstone went up country, saying that he would settle about these lands, viz., begin by Transvaal, then Usikukuku's, then Swaziland, then return by Zululand, and settle the question for me about the boundary of Zululand that was claimed by the Boers, and finally settle about the country claimed by the Boers. When Mr. Shepstone arrived at Newcastle he sent Nkabane to me while staying at Mbonambi. This messenger came to me . . . and said that he was sent by Mr. Shepstone to say, "I am now passing on, and am about to go and arrange matters with the Boers. Tell my child (Cetwayo [Cetshwayo]) that I do not know how matters will turn out, as the Boers seem about to be troublesome. I will tell him (Cetwayo) about the result when I have talked with the Boers." . . .

After this I sent up to Mr. Shepstone, who was at Pretoria [capital of the Transvaal] . . . to say to Mr. Shepstone, "Where are you now, as I have not heard from you for so long? How is it that everything is so quiet, and I do not hear about you? I, your son, feel anxious about you, and wish to hear all about you and your proceedings." Mr. Shepstone then sent back and said, "I am still talking with the Boers; but I do not know about the result of the conference yet. I am sure, though, that they wish to be insubordinate and inattentive, but the soldiers overawe them." He continued and said, "I will . . . return by Zululand and settle everything about the country for you." . . . He continued and said, "I am soon coming to Zululand. You are noisy, as I hear that you have built a kraal, and have called it Kwamaizekanye. Are you calling me then, and saying, 'Well, you may come then?'"

The Zulus then got surprised, and said, "How is it that Mr. Shepstone is sending such a message to you? About what have you quarrelled? You have only sent men to learn if anything has happened to him, and to know about his proceedings, and how comes he to talk thus?"

. . . I was then very much surprised, and said to my chiefs, "How can Mr. Shepstone talk thus?" I did not, however, say anything to Mr. Shepstone about it; but I must not conceal this, that I felt very surprised, and thought that Mr. Shepstone was not about to do well to the Zulu nation. (This kraal I got built while the Boers were troubling me and shooting down my subjects). . . .

Mr. Shepstone then came down to where the country was disputed by the Boers, and called the Zulu chiefs to a conference about to settle as to the disputed land. The chiefs came in large numbers, about 800, mostly men with rings [headrings, indicating mature men]; but there were some young men who followed their fathers, and sat at some distance from the assembly. When my chiefs had arrived where Mr. Shepstone was awaiting them, Mr. Shepstone said, "Men, I too have come here to see this tract of country arranged." Mr. Shepstone then asked us as to the boundary of Zululand since the Boers are troubling you so much, and so much disturbance has been created. The chiefs then said, "On the Natal side it used to extend as far as the Umkomazi; above, it used to extend as far as Pretoria, where the Zulus overthrew the chief Umzilikazi [Mzilikazi]." . . . My chiefs told Mr. Shepstone that all this country used to be theirs; but that Mpande had left Natal to the Boers, and that the English had then taken it away from the Boers.

Mr. Shepstone then said to my chiefs, "Specify the boundary of the country that is yours now, as you think fit." The Zulus then said, "The boundary of our country now by rights is that it is bounded on the Natal side by the Tugela [Thukela], and then by the Umzinyati (Buffalo River) along the Umzinyati as far as Ukahlamba (Drakensberg); then it bends off, and goes up as far as Kwamlambo next to the plain of Dedanganhlala (the plain is about six days' walk from Pretoria); then bends off from the last place down to the Maswazi country, taking in these hills, viz., the hill of Kwamlambo and Ntabande; and then it extends to Enkulunge, a hill the other side of the river Igwa (all this country is inhabited by the King's people, a people that do work for the King); it then curves down to the Pongolo river, excluding the Amaswazies; and then extends down along the Pongolo." Mr. Shepstone then said, "Men, you have extended your boundary too much." My chiefs said, "No, we have not; did you not ask us to tell you the boundary of our country? We have simply told you the boundary of our country before the Boers came and took it away from us by force." Mr. Shepstone then said, "Supposing another man stand up and mark out the boundary of your country where you do not like, what then?" My chiefs said, "No, Mr. Shepstone, we have come to you to ask you to arrange our country for us that we may stay at peace and be quiet. We wish to live in peace as we used to, and in our own country. We wish you to make the Boers leave our country that we may live in peace; the Boers always create disturbance." Mr. Shepstone then said, "Supposing I said your boundary was at Inhlazatye, what then?" The chiefs then replied and said, "You would not then be settling matters for us by cutting off our country like the Boers, who took it away from us by force. This tract of our country would then belong to the same men that trouble us and take our country from us." . . .

I say it will be good for Mr. Shepstone to tell the English nation, in order that the English nation may know what he is doing, when he is destroying my country, taking it away from, throwing me out of it, and giving it to the Boers. . . . The English then said that the Boers had been beaten by the Zulu chiefs in argument; and they said also, "We see now that you Boers are in the wrong, and that you have taken the land from the Zulus by force." They said also to my chiefs, "Go home now, chiefs, and tell your king that you have beaten the Boers, and that we are convinced that the land claimed by you is rightly yours, has been taken from you by force, and that we are now going home to tell the English nation of this, and that when we come again it will be for the sake of putting your country to rights for you." When my chiefs came to me they told me all the above words. I listened to them, and then sat down quietly awaiting the English that were coming to arrange my country for me. . . .

I now beg you to discuss my case and not keep me any longer from my wives, children, and all. . . .

I wish you to know that the ultimatum was never brought to me and that its contents I know not of. It must have been kept by those that were looking out for my overthrow. All what is mine in Zululand has been overturned and spoiled. My children and wives have been put in misery by the chiefs now ruling, specially Dunn [a white Zulu chief]. The English were merciful, but not the chiefs now ruling. I wish the English to look to this.

Cetewayo Ka Mpande.

P.S. My father Mpande belonged to the English, and when anything happened to him he used to report it to the English, and he made a move when he had heard from the English. I have been doing the same and why am I now here? I never for a moment thought that the English would invade my country.

Note

The explanations in parentheses were added by the previous publisher and are not part of the original document. The bracketed insertions are new to this edition.

Industrial Johannesburg

Violet Markham

Large-scale gold mining began in the late 1880s along an area that came to be known as the Witwatersrand ("Rand") in the Boer South African Republic (Transvaal), ruled by State President Paul Kruger. Within a few years, thousands of people began flocking to the region, leading to the creation of the city of Johannesburg. The gold boom unfolded in what was a poor agrarian economy with a poorly developed infrastructure to support industry. Almost immediately, tensions began emerging between the Boers and Anglo-identified industrial magnates such as Cecil Rhodes, as well as with newly arrived immigrants from around the world.

Industrializing South Africa also attracted a number of English social reformers, many from highly privileged families. Violet Markham (1872–1959), the wealthy daughter of an industrialist, became an important writer and reformer dedicated to education and welfare. An Antisuffragist and a fervent imperialist, Markham arrived in South Africa just before the outbreak of war in 1899. Like many imperialists at the time, Markham believed in racial hierarchy and in the need for the British Empire to govern the "weaker races." The reading is a good example of a description of Johannesburg during the 1890s, a crucial period in the gold-mining industry when the extraction of ore began taking place at deeper levels, which necessitated huge amounts of labor and large infusions of capital. Mine owners became concerned with issues such as consumption of alcohol by Africans and work discipline. Mine owners also began a process of consolidation and reorganization that resulted in the adoption of a modified version of the compound system pioneered in Kimberley, which Markham signals toward at the end of the text.

Johannesburg, the leading city of South Africa, has been described such countless times that most English people feel that they are as familiar with its main features as with those of London. It is an extraordinary place this Aladdin's City sprung up, so to speak, from nowhere in the night, and the incongruities of its surroundings are very striking. For three days the traveller from Cape Town traverses a desert containing few signs of human life and none of human industry. The "towns" passed on the way, Bloemfontein included, are only villages. Consequently, the numerous chimneys along the line of the Main Reef, which announce the neighbourhood of Johannesburg, are fairly startling in their sudden evidence of man's activity in this district. A chimney is a familiar object in England, execrated only for its ugliness; but a tall chimney in the heart of the African veldt [veld; countryside] seems very remarkable and thoroughly out of place. The different chimneys, of course, mark the different mines, and the galvanised-iron engine-houses, together with the great white heaps of cyanide tailings attached to each mine, add to the extraordinary appearance of the scene. Quite suddenly, so it seems, the desolation and silence of the veldt have given place to all the stir and activity of a great industrial centre. People, as I have said before, generally take life quietly in Africa; but at Johannesburg the press and turmoil of modern existence are distinctly felt. Every one is in a hurry, every one is on the rush, and the mania for speculation is universal. Johannesburg is the most unlovely as well as the largest city in South Africa. It is full of architectural contrasts. On the one hand there are huge meretricious [flashy] buildings, generally mining offices or banking establishments, as remarkable for their costliness as for their utter lack of artistic merit; on the other, the tin shanties of an earlier epoch still survive, as at Kimberley, in all stages of dilapidation. The streets are badly paved, drained, and lighted, and when the wind is blowing—and it generally blows hard, for Johannesburg is perched on a bleak spot 5,000 feet or more above sea-level—the dust storms, impregnated with cyanide of potassium from the tailings heaps, are most disagreeable and injurious. Still, it is all very wonderful when one remembers that the Rand was only declared a goldfield in 1886, and that this marvellous development has taken place in the short space of fourteen years. . . .

The Witwatersrand gold basin is about 130 miles long by thirty wide. This basin contains various reefs of greater or lesser value; but the bulk of the Rand output is obtained from the mines on what is known as the Main Reef series, a district twenty-six miles in length, which stretches from Boksburg on the east to Roodepoort on the west. The Main Reef series lie east and west of Johannesburg, and it is often declared that the town itself is built on the richest portion of the reef. It is this little district which has revolutionised South Africa.

The mineral wealth of the Witwatersrand is unique, and unsurpassed by that of any other known gold-fields in the world. It is unique for the reason that the precious metal is extracted from a conglomerate body consisting of a series of pebble beds, whereas in all other countries gold is extracted from quartz lodes. The irregularity of quartz reefs, and their liability to suddenly "pinch out," are two circumstances which in all ages have made gold-mining operations a highly speculative business. The conditions of gold mining on the Witwatersrand are in every respect the antithesis of those which have prevailed hitherto. Owing to the extraordinary nature of the deposits, the industry has passed for the first time in history from a speculative to a certain stage. The industry on the Rand is not so much gold mining as gold manufacturing. . . .

The Witwatersrand Goldfields were discovered in 1885, and were proclaimed as such in 1886. The discovery has already brought great wealth and prosperity not only to the Transvaal but to the whole of South Africa. It seems difficult to estimate the possibilities of the future when a sound and just government is established. An enormous development of the industry will inevitably follow better economic conditions. Gold-mining operations in the Witwatersrand are not more speculative than coal mining in Great Britain. . . .

Interest in Johannesburg is centred on two classes—the capitalists and the workmen. It is necessary to examine the status of both, especially the former, who are often held unjustly to be responsible for the [South African] war.

A great many erroneous ideas exist as to the powers wielded by the capitalists. It is generally supposed that the wealthy mine proprietors have derived their wealth from the goldfields. This belief is incorrect. With few exceptions, the wealthy men had made considerable fortunes on the diamond fields long before the discovery of the Witwatersrand. It is true that they have largely increased their fortunes in the Transvaal, but it is an absurd contention on the part of the pro-Boer party that the Rand capitalists owe their prosperity to the sweetness and light diffused by President Kruger's Government. On the contrary, the Transvaal owed its past existence to the energy and ability of many of these much-abused men, who developed the industry in face of opposition of a peculiarly ignorant character. . . .

The leading group of capitalists, Messrs. Beit, Rhodes, Robinson, Neumann, Farrar, Phillips, Eckstein, and a few others, undoubtedly work in an honest manner the large group of mines which they respectively control. It would not pay them to do otherwise, for the confidence and trust of European investors are their chief considerations in order that capital may always be available for new flotations. . . .

Very different, of course, is the position and career of the mushroom capitalists. These are individuals having neither reputations to gain nor to lose, who collect the sweepings cast aside by the respectable men, and in so doing have brought discredit on the industry. . . .

Turning now to the working classes of Johannesburg, one is immediately struck by their high standard of respectability. There is practically little or nothing of the mining camp about the place. Johannesburg, like all other large cities, contains a criminal section, but the police returns prove that the great majority of the population are a law-abiding community. There are certainly fewer drunken men to be seen about the streets than in many of the large industrial centres in Great Britain. The workmen on the Rand—and this is a fact seldom realized—are of an entirely different type from those to be found on any other goldfields. The reason of this is twofold. Firstly, banket mining entails regular and constant work; secondly, highly skilled workmen are required to manage the extremely complicated and delicate gold-mining machinery, and to deal with the ore in the many stages of reduction. In no district of the British Empire is there a mining equipment to compare with the plants on the Rand. The credit for the latter is due chiefly to American engineers. The exigencies of the industry have entailed these costly equipments, for the leading men soon realised that the only successful method of reducing the low-grade ores was by erecting the best machinery that money could buy. It is hardly necessary to add that highly-skilled artisans capable of handling such machinery are not recruited from the loafing disreputable classes. . . .

One of the most important and difficult questions on the Rand is that of native labour, which is closely connected with the liquor scandal. "Forced labour in South Africa" is an evil the enormities of which are constantly expounded by the Exeter Hall [antislavery] and Little England [anti-imperialist] people. This statement is wholly untrue as regards the mining industry. It is necessary to say at once that there is not a single Kaffir working on the Witwatersrand Goldfields or at Kimberley who has not chosen to work of his own free will. It is perfectly true, however, that in the country districts the pastoral Dutch farmer forces the Kaffir to work for him, the Kaffir receiving no consideration for the same save a liberal supply of sjambok [whips]. I have spoken elsewhere of that system prevailing among the Boers euphemistically called "apprenticeship," which is slavery under another name. The natives are slaves in every sense of the word in the Transvaal, and the apprentice system was devised in order to circumvent the [Sand River] Convention. My brother tells me that when travelling in remote parts of Africa he has seen Boer farmers tie up Kaffirs to a waggon wheel and flog them in a most terrible manner for the smallest offence. As regards the supply of labour at Johannesburg, the most imitable Kaffirs for mining purposes come from Portuguese East Africa, a few from Cape Colony, and a very consider-

Dormitory room in a mine compound, Gauteng, twentieth century. Photographer unknown. Courtesy of Campbell Collections of the University of KwaZulu-Natal, B47/049.

able number from Northern Rhodesia. My brother has met many parties of Kaffirs as far north as the Zambesi [Zambezi River] marching down to Kimberley and Johannesburg in order to find employment. Every traveller in South Africa can substantiate his statement, which does not bear out the allegation of forced labour.

The compound system prevailing at Kimberley, which I have described in the previous chapter, has been assailed by many purists as an attack on the liberty of the subject. Yet that system is in every respect superior to the one prevailing on the Rand. The use made by the Kaffir of his "freedom" in the latter case is a very terrible object-lesson. The curse of drink, which is the ruin of the natives at Johannesburg, is unknown at Kimberley. Under the compound system the managers are able to control the Kaffirs; at Johannesburg there is no control whatever. Twenty-five per cent of the natives on the Rand are daily incapacitated owing to the effect of liquor. A native when sober is easily managed, but when intoxicated he becomes literally like a wild beast. The following extract from a report of the Native Labour Commissioner, Mr. Grant, may perhaps convince even the Exeter Hall party that the compound system at Kimberley is preferable to the conditions prevailing on the Rand Goldfields:

> When consulted a year ago by the State Attorney I expressed the opinion that the one and only cure was total prohibition, and I continue to

adhere to this. It is almost superfluous to point out the grave and diaboli-
cal effect caused by what is practically free trade in liquor. The native
personally becomes degraded, and with the loss of his self-respect van-
ishes all care and regard for his home. His family in numberless cases
are left to the mercy of friends and outsiders, with the natural consequence that for many consecutive months not a penny is remitted for
their sustenance. Drink is undoubtedly the mainspring of three-fourths
of ordinary crime, and particularly that abhorrent crime—attempts on
white women. Faction fights almost invariably spring from the same
cause. Government mining inspectors assert that a large proportion
of deaths from accidents are occasioned by natives attempting to discharge their duties under the influence of liquor.

The foregoing statement is a most powerful argument in favour of the
compound system, horrors of this nature being unknown at Kimberley.
Many of the Kaffirs from Portuguese East Africa remain for years on the
Rand mines, expending the whole of their wages in drink. At Kimberley, on
the contrary, they are well housed and properly cared for; Government supervision of the compounds protecting them against the possibility of despotic treatment at the hands of the compound managers. The Kaffir returns
home at the end of his term of service healthy in body and mind, provided
with blankets, boots, concertinas, and other charms dear to the Bantu (African) heart, and also the wherewithal to buy two oxen, which will in turn
purchase him a wife. Unfortunately, however, every influence, not only in
the Transvaal but in the colonies, will be brought to bear against the application of the compound system on the Witwatersrand, the chief reason
being that it would destroy the trade of the small stores and canteens. . . .

A Model Compound Manager

Douglas Blackburn

In order to control illicit diamond buying, and also to impose tight labor discipline, mine owners at Kimberley housed workers in closed compounds. Black mine workers were confined in these compounds for the duration of their service, normally six months. The gold mines also eventually housed their workers in compounds, but these were "open," allowing for a flow of workers and goods, especially liquor, between the city and the mines. An elaborate system of corruption and patronage enabled the supply of liquor, nominally illegal, to black workers. White compound managers stood at the interface between the mines and the supply of workers and goods. As the following excerpt from a contemporary satirical novel illustrates, this provided ample opportunity for managers to enrich themselves and abuse their positions. In deadpan comic tones, the piece also succinctly informs us about the poor living conditions and harsh labor conditions of the gold mines.

Sidney Dane, Compound Manager of the New Yankee Gold Mining Company, Limited, was, of course, a Natalian. The mine compound is as much the preserve of the Natalian as the engineroom of a steamship is of Scotsmen; for the very sufficient reason that the youth of the miscalled "Garden Colony" are the only South Africans who learn native languages.

Dane had acquired his position by virtue of his intimate acquaintance with the kaffir, and, incidentally by paying his predecessor two hundred sovereigns in cash and ten pounds a month for five months, which was a fair premium to pay for a billet carrying a salary of £40 per mensem [month], and considerably less than the sum asked by the compound manager of an older and larger mine for which Dane had negotiated.

Mine magnates if asked why it is the custom to buy and sell these appointments, would probably express surprise, and even deny that such a traffic existed; nor would their ignorance be improbable. A mine is a large community, containing a much greater area and population than many a Colonial village. To expect directors who reside in Johannesburg, and probably spend less than fifty hours a year on their property, to know all that was going on there, would be unreasonable. If they did know of these transactions, they would have a ready and simple explanation. Life on a mine at £40 per month with quarters can be as nearly idyllic as anything in the sordid, ugly environment of the Rand. The compound manager is less subject to irritating supervision than any other employee. He is practically his own master; his comings in and goings out are not recorded in a time book, and so long as the required number of boys are turned out to go on shift, that almighty personage, the mine manager, has no occasion to talk business or otherwise assert his authority.

Then there is another great attraction, which appeals to the thrifty, careful young Natalian. He can save money. There have been compound managers who have saved a hundred pounds a month out of their salary of forty or fifty; but that has necessitated very strict, almost grinding economy and self-denial; consequently they are the exception rather than the rule. But he would be unworthy the traditions of his class who did not know how to limit his expenditure and restrain his desire for luxuries sufficiently to save nearly all his salary.

Sidney Dane was not of the stingy, cheeseparing type. He was free with his money, but not extravagant; content to possess a smart trap, pony, and riding horse, attend the local races, join a shooting party up country for a week or so during the season, and spend a modest fiver on a Saturday night's amusement in Johannesburg. What was left after paying his board and liquor bill, he put away and never grumbled if it was not more than thirty-five pounds.

That happened to be the amount he had estimated to pay in to his deposit account the day that Weldon brought his batch of boys [black adult male workers] and received a cheque for sixty pounds, but he found himself nearly ten pounds short. Being a man of action, Dane went into "camp," as most of the old hands still call Johannesburg, and hunted up the labour agent. He found him in the bar of the Grand National Hotel, "sobering up" on small brandies and large sodas. The young man looked annoyed, but invited the compound manager to join him in a drink.

"I was coming out to pay you, old chap, but have been awfully seedy," he began volubly.

Mr Dane took his drink to a table away from the crowd and beckoned Weldon to follow.

"Now, Mr Weldon," he began, "I don't know what you call this, but I tell you straight these games won't go down with me. You got your cheque three days ago, and promised faithfully to let me have my bit as soon as you had cashed it. I want thirty-two five-bobs, which is eight sovereigns, and I tell you that if this is the sort of business you do, you sell no more boys to the Yankee or any other mine, for I shall just pass the word round to the other compound managers, and your game will be finished. Let's understand one another. This is our first deal, but it looks like being the last. You are not the only labour agent in the country, so don't you forget it."

Weldon did something very unusual. He told the truth. He had got drunk, he said, as soon as he cashed the cheque, expressed contrition and paid over eight sovereigns.

"Now have a drink with me and listen to what I've got to say," Dane said, as he signalled to the barman.

"Our people will be taking a thousand boys during the next two months, and they are prepared to pay two pounds a head. I don't want to be greedy, but as it rests with me to accept or reject, I expect something for my trouble. These are my terms: Four shillings for every boy up to fifty, four-and-six for all over that number, cash down the day you get your cheque."

Weldon was disposed to haggle. Dane finished his drink and got up.

"Take it or leave it," he said with the air of a man who meant it. "I get those terms from the other agents, and they are quite satisfied. Mind, I pass no boy into my compound for a penny less."

Weldon capitulated.

"While I'm in camp I may as well pay exes," Dane soliloquised as he left the hotel. "I'll give Ikey a call."

He walked to Commissioner Street and turned up a passage leading to the side entrance of a shabby but obviously prosperous bar, entered and called for a whisky which was not served to him.

The barman nodded and indicated with his eyebrows a private door. Dane walked into a small room, furnished partly as an office, partly as the proprietor's snuggery. A well-dressed young man of Jewish appearance sat at the table, busy with a pile of invoices. He greeted the visitor cordially and took down a whisky bottle and box of cigars.

The opening remarks were casual, bearing principally on matters horsey. Then Mr Ikey Bernstein changed the subject abruptly.

"Everything goin' right?"

"Yes. We had one of our directors on the property on Monday. He was a bit curious to know how many boys were off work. I had about two hundred of 'em getting sober, but as luck would have it they were mostly quiet in their quarters. I had shut the doors in case of stray prowlers, so the old chap didn't see anything. I told him there were too many off for my liking, but that things were improving. I gave him a hint that what liquor got into the compound was supplied by Barzinsky."

Ikey grinned. "We mustn't shove Barzinsky off, you know. We ain't afraid of him. I suppose we sell ten bottles to his one. Let him have the credit of supplying the lot. How about the police?"

"Blind as owls in the sunshine. I gave two kaffirs into custody for drunk and disorderly yesterday. We mustn't be too lenient. I've got to study my character as a strict manager, you know."

Both men laughed. Mr Bernstein had taken something out of a cash-box and pushed it with his be-diamonded finger towards Dane.

"That'll help to pay exes in town tonight," he said.

Dane carelessly slipped the ten sovereigns into his waistcoat pocket.

"Thanks. Are you satisfied?"

Mr Bernstein put out his hand. Dane shook it and rose.

"You might give a hint to that new man you've got in the canteen not to be so cocky with the kaffirs. He has knocked several of my boys about, and they don't like it. The beggars are artful as monkeys. They know that the police are on the look-out, and they might turn spiteful and speak too loud. I just mention it as a hint. We can't be too careful. The local newspaper has been saying things lately about the Sunday drunks."

Mr Bernstein nodded knowingly.

"It's all right. They're only playing up for a bit of sugar. They'll be sweetened presently. We're going to give them a big advertisement of our bottle store in the township."

"That's right. I can't afford to have them on my track. One of my directors has got the illicit liquor business on the brain just now. I suppose you saw his speech at the last meeting of the Chamber of Mines?"

Mr Bernstein nodded and winked, and put out his hand again.

Mr Dane shook it and helped himself to a cigar.

"Take a dozen, man."

He obliged, and said good morning.

As he passed out of the passage he felt and recounted the coins in his pocket.

"A darned sight freer with his cigars than his quids," he thought, "but the quids are good; that's more than his cigars are. Never mind, I can give them away at the smoker tonight."

"The genial Sid Dane," as the local newspaper invariably described the compound manager of the New Yankee, was to take the chair that evening

at a smoking concert on an adjacent mine. The circumstance was unimportant, but significant as an evidence of the popularity of the cheery, frank,
open-handed C.M. In the ordinary course the compliment should have been
paid to John Fraser, who held on the Belmont the corresponding position
to Dane on the Yankee, but Fraser lacked the geniality of his rival and was
in every respect his antithesis. Dane's motto was "Make things as pleasant
for everybody as you can," and he acted up to it consistently. The result was
that things were made very pleasant for him.

The tradesmen who held contracts for the supply of food and such material as was required for the compound agreed in regretting that there were
not more managers like Dane. He never fussed or wrote letters threatening
to "inform my chief" if the bread or meat happened to be a few hundred
pounds short of weight or not up to sample. At the worst he would call in at
the office and remark, in his casual, jocular way, "Awful rotten stuff that last
parcel; I reckon you didn't lose much on that deal." Or to the bread man, "I
fancy there's something gone wrong with the multiplication table you use;
I'm about a thousand rations short on the month." And the butcher would
explain that he had picked up a carcase or two very cheaply as it was a bit
off, and playfully ask Dane to accept a fiver for calling attention to the poor
quality, while the baker would express astonishment and regret and beg to
be allowed to reimburse Dane to the extent of a few sovereigns for having
the trouble to call.

Fraser having none of the tact of Dane, and being too petty-minded to act
up the "live and let live" axiom, never failed to count and weigh everything
before signing a receipt, and had no scruples about keeping the delivery
man hanging about the compound while he checked and doubly checked
the consignment. When remonstrated with for wasting the valuable time
of other people's employees he would reply in his sneering way that he was
studying the interests of the tradesman by making sure that he was not
wronging himself by delivering more than he would be paid for.

In the little amenities of neighbourliness Dane shone conspicuously. If
one of the contractors wanted the use of a few boys for nothing, the loan or
gift of a bit of timber, coal or other trifle, Dane could always be relied upon
to oblige, while Fraser was as certain to rebuff the applicant by a curt excuse
to the effect that he could not give away the property of the company—a
company with a capital of half a million and paying dividends of thirty and
forty per cent., unable to spare the use of a few of its kaffirs or a paltry load
of wood from the piles on piles encumbering the ground!

The same mania for magnifying trifles was manifested by Fraser in the
handling of the details of the compound. When an unusually heavy rain-

storm had made a bit of a mess of the boys' sleeping quarters, Fraser worried the manager by alarmist pictures of flooded floors and leaking roofs into spending a couple of hundred pounds on repairs. Even then he was not satisfied, but coolly attributed a slight outbreak of pneumonia and typhoid that occurred about a week later to the dilapidated condition of the compound. The rather heavy mortality among the natives was commented upon by one of the papers, which sent a reporter to interview Fraser. Seeing a chance to get a little cheap notoriety, instead of ordering the man off the premises, he showed him round. The result was a scandalous article under the sensational heading, "How Mine Kaffirs are Killed. Housed worse than Pigs." Fraser pleaded that he was not responsible for what the reporter wrote; that he had only given him permission to look round for himself. The directors very generously accepted this feeble excuse, but warned him to be careful. His show of studying the interests of the company had had its desired effect in persuading some of the board that they had a conscientious servant in Fraser.

Sid Dane's treatment of the matter was in keeping with his light-hearted disposition and systematic refusal to go half way to meet trouble. When the kaffirs went to him and complained that the rain fell on their sleeping places and drenched them, he laughed good-humouredly, and pointed out that they had received a good washing which they much needed, and if the roof was broken in parts it was an advantage, as they would know when it rained without the trouble of getting up and going outside to look.

Dane was rarely worried by the complaints and imaginary grievances of his boys. They knew him too well to emulate the whining schoolboy. A new hand now and then would go to him with some nonsensical story of oppression, but he rarely went twice. A new cook after a week's experience of his duties had the temerity to suggest that the meat supplied by the contractor was many pounds short.

"What have you done with it?" the manager asked.

"Never had it, baas; every day boys come to me and say they have not had enough. Often I cannot give them all meat."

"I think your memory is a little bit out of order," Dane replied; "I must try to mend it."

He put the cook in the stocks, with a native to stand by with a sjambok [whip] to see that the victim did not endeavour to relieve the strain on his muscles by lying on his back.

The inventor of that ancient form of mild restraint has never received proper recognition of his ingenuity in producing an instrument of torture so innocently harmless in appearance that its application has always been regarded as a fit subject for humour. What could look less like a tortured creature than a man sitting on the ground with ankles merely passed through two large holes that do not pinch or compress the flesh half as much as a pair of handcuffs? Nobody but the victim notices that the ankles are raised six or eight inches from the ground, forcing the body into a position that strains the muscles of the back and brings on excruciating pains that last for hours, even days after release.

The stocks at the New Yankee had been designed by Mr Dane, who had introduced a great improvement. The holes for the ankles were placed six, twelve, eighteen, twenty-four and thirty-six inches apart. As the intensity of the torture is increased by widening the distance, the degree of punishment could be regulated to a nicety.

The cook was given the maximum stretch, and two hours in which to test its efficacy as a mnemonic stimulant.

At the end of that time he declared with many groans and moans he remembered that he must have used the meat without noticing it. An hour more of the torture and he would have remembered and admitted having eaten the missing four hundred pounds at one surreptitious meal.

The implied imputation against the *bona fides* of the meat contractor having been withdrawn by the frank confession of the real culprit, he was released, and went about his work for two days with body bent at an angle of sixty.

Nobody who knew the genial Dane would ever accuse him of cruelty. He was firm, because he "knew kaffirs," but, as he often said, he did not believe in brutality. That is why he rarely handed over recalcitrants to the police. Magistrates were so absurdly official. They expected every statement made against an accused kaffir to be borne out by a witness, which meant taking boys, and even white men, to town to waste the day hanging about the court over a case which probably ended in the infliction of a fine the kaffir could not pay, and had to work out in jail, and a remand for further evidence, or even an acquittal. The latter was fatal to discipline on the mine. The triumphant boy would return to boast of his victory and put on airs and consequences that invariably resulted in Dane having to take the impudent rascal into a quiet shed and convince him, by two dozen from a sjambok well laid on, that his acquittal was a mistake and jubilation premature.

The natives have a name for every compound manager on the Rand, always descriptive, generally amusingly accurate. By it the owner is known in every kraal in kaffirdom that yields its overplus of manhood to the mines, and thousands who have never seen him are familiar with his personality and characteristics, even as the British peasant in some remote village knows well political celebrities whom he has heard of only through the descriptive reporter. "Genial Sid Dane" was famous by a name difficult to write and impossible of pronunciation by Europeans. It meant the man who is a gentle fawn by daylight but a tiger-cat by night.

Building a Nation from Words

Isabel Hofmeyr

Afrikaner nationalism began in the late nineteenth century with the formation of some of South Africa's earliest political parties, such as the Cape Afrikaner Bond (Union), which was established in 1881. Nationalism entailed defining an Afrikaner identity as a nation and making claims on controlling the state as a way of ensuring its historic realization. The first union-wide party emerged in 1914 with the founding of the National Party, two years after the creation of the African National Congress. Early Afrikaner nationalism had an important basis in farming communities and in the Dutch Reformed Church. Newspapers and intellectuals, many of whom wrote historical tracts imagining a racially pure Afrikaner identity deep into South Africa's past, used the issue of the Afrikaans language to mobilize the volk *(people), as this selection discusses.*

By the nineteenth century the language Dutch-Afrikaans was extremely diverse by region, dialect and social class. This diversity of dialect had partly to do with the historical trajectory of the lowland Dutch dialects spoken by the seventeenth-century settlers. In confronting the language of the slaves—Malay and Portuguese creole—along with Khoesan speech, this Dutch linguistic cluster had partly creolised. In later years it picked up shards of German, French and Southern Nguni [Xhosa] languages and a goodly layer of English after 1806.

This linguistic interaction led to loosely related dialects which spread out with master and servant into the regional economies that migrant farmers set up in the Cape and subsequently the two republics. By the late 1800s the Cape could be divided into a dialect map whose boundaries approximated provincial divisions. In addition, dialect tended to modulate according to social class. The poorer the community, the more their language varied from that of the "civilised" Western Cape.

This social and regional variation of language increased with the rapid stratification brought about by the proletarianisation which occurred both before the mineral discoveries and, at an accelerating rate, thereafter. Linguistically this social differentiation expressed itself in an upper and middle class who spoke English. Included in their number were wealthy Dutch families who manipulated a variety of linguistic registers. These stretched from what passed for High Dutch, through more informal discourse to a language for servants, workers and farm labourers. These workers, along with "the poor," were rapidly accumulating in jumbled racial communities, in which the language "Afrikaans" was emerging quite clearly. The variety of terms by which Afrikaans was known all pointed to a strong association with poorness and "colouredness." Some of these terms included "hotnotstaal" (Hottentot language), "griekwataal" (Griqua language), "kombuistaal" (kitchen language), "plattaal" (vulgar language) and "brabbeltaal" (patois / lingo). In the 1870s another term was to be added to this list: "patriots" or, as it was pronounced in the Cape, "patterjots." . . .

Die Afrikaanse Patriot . . . began in 1876 and was the first publication to use "Afrikaans" systematically. The publication was the organ of Die Genootskap van Regte Afrikaners (GRA) (Fellowship of True Afrikaners) and we must look briefly at the background of this movement for the developments of the early twentieth century were to draw on its work. . . .

The organisation arose in the 1870s from a closely knit group of teachers and clerics from wine farming backgrounds in and around Paarl. This concentration, even "overproduction," of educated men was a common feature of Cape social life where commerce and government were British dominated. The Dutch intelligentsia tended to congregate in those professions—church, school, journalism—which cushioned them from the more irritating aspects of discrimination. Increasing British investment in the diamond fields seemed only to aggravate this discrimination. Enlarged state revenue flowed more towards wealthy urban English schools than to poorer rural Dutch schools. Also in the air was talk of a scheme to remove state stipends to church ministers. To certain Dutch-speakers, British imperialism appeared to be more of a hindrance than a help.

Other people in the Cape, however, were doing extremely well out of British imperialism. Dutch and English farmers, merchant interests and an emerging class of mining capitalists looked to the British imperial economy as the basis for their existence. But politically the constitutional changes bringing responsible government [granting more political autonomy to the Cape Colony] activated these various groups to new possibilities and alliances. The GRA or Pêrelspan (Paarl bunch), as they were known, were quick to respond to these political opportunities. The GRA group under S. J.

du Toit floated the Afrikaner Bond and its initial programme called for the establishment of small banks, boycotts of "foreign" traders and more funds for Dutch education. At the same time, the *Patriot* gave this populist vision some cultural and historical substance. Written in a Paarl dialect of "Afrikaans," the magazine attempted to define white Afrikaners in terms of a cultural, organic nation. . . .

It was in the space opened up by the *Patriot* that the Second Language movement was to begin. Again this movement was to be loose and uneven, and it was to be started by a small group of men in the north who found themselves in conditions broadly analogous but more extreme than their Paarl counterparts. . . .

The social geography of the north . . . fell into three broad groupings: the landed notables, those with tenuous land rights and the entirely landless. The processes underlying this stratification . . . involved a combination of rising land prices, inheritance law and natural disaster. Land prices had risen sharply after the intrusion of the mines into the Transvaal and the notables made good these speculative opportunities because of their hold on key government posts. Through this concentration of land, wealthy farmers swallowed up numerous [smaller landowners] . . . who then became bywoners [white tenant farmers], a term which covered a multitude of social relationships.

Whatever their precise form, these landlord/tenant ties involved humiliating relationships of subordination, whose friction was diffused through ideological mechanisms of *familie* (kinship), *huisgesin* (the household) and the church. Landlords were, after all, wealthy relations, church officials or in close association with religious authority, and they used these positions to ransom the acquiescence of their tenants.

Standing between the landed and the landless was a group of small farmers who stood to gain from these kinship/authority networks. By manipulating their ties to wealthier landed notables, these small farmers could glean the smaller pickings of government office. They could also, in turn, extract rent from their smaller number of tenants.

It was with changes and divisions like these that the two republics went to war in 1899. The crisis and chaos of the war fused the emerging differences and prised these divisions open even further. Some bywoners followed their landlords into war and supported them throughout. But others, and often the most numerous group, made use of the war to express their feelings. Thirteen per cent refused to heed commando call-ups. Others laid down arms and declared their neutrality while, on average, one in five actively joined the British.

After the war these divisions were to sharpen as the landowners moved quickly and decisively to reconstitute themselves often at the direct expense of the landless bywoners whom many landlords refused to take back. . . . [T]he social web of authority in Boer communities was beginning to wear thin. In general terms these changes expressed themselves as a hardening interface between bywoners and landlord. In 1906 one of an increasing number of indigency commissions noted: "The bywoners are no longer on the old terms of familiarity with the landowners but are becoming a separate and inferior class of society."[1] Kinship ties which had previously bound the two groups together were shrivelling. Within the *huisgesin* itself, authority began to crumble along lines of age and sex as it so often does in a "proto-industrial" situation. The logical strategy for some families was to send their young women to the cities from whence they could remit part of their wage to the household economy. Other families no doubt moved together, first to a small town and then to a city, where initially there might have been some opportunity to utilise their skills. But the city's employment profile had very little room for unskilled white male adults, and even less for old men. Teenagers, often by virtue of their greater physical strength, stood a better chance of employment, no matter how mean or temporary, than their parents.

In the towns and cities young people, and particularly young women, were in a position to question the authority of their fathers. This many people began to do by deserting the Dutch Reformed Churches in large numbers to join the growing number of apostolic sects. The disparaging referred to these church meetings as *lawaaigedoentes* (noisy affairs), but many must have discovered there an emotional satisfaction which they had failed to find in the joylessness of Calvinism. Others sought solace in a working-class culture of sport, liquor and popular entertainment which provided some compensation for the harshness of industrial life. Within this working-class environment, non-Afrikaner white men greatly outnumbered white women, and at least some Afrikaner women must have married non-Afrikaners.

All of these changes and realignments began to alarm a large section of the urban and rural community. Some of these people belonged to that legion of middle-class moral brokers who took it upon themselves to spread the imperial gospel of the family which appeared to be disintegrating under the impact of industrialisation. Within this ensemble were various Dutch-Afrikaners who had greater cause for alarm. Not only was the family under stress but the Afrikaner community itself appeared to be falling apart. One does not wish to overemphasise this disintegration. In places like Johannesburg, ordinary Afrikaners congregated in a reasonably defined community that filled the western suburbs. The church, one of the few Afrikaner institutions to survive the war intact, also remained a strong force which could shore up some of the cracks in the community. After the war, the church's position was enhanced when it played an important part in reconstructing poor Afrikaners—a class which neither the notables nor the British had any overriding desire to rehabilitate. Yet to many clerics the situation still appeared dire. For many years they had depended for their livelihood on the smooth functioning of kinship and religious patterns of authority in the community. By the early 1900s, these patterns seemed to be crumbling.

Another group who felt some anxiety about the changing texture of the Boer community was the small farmers. This group regarded the chasm that was growing between landlord and tenant with economic and social apprehension. In 1905 one of these small farmers spoke for many when he lashed out against the rich landowners. "These rich farmers," he wrote, "these selfish, self-righteous bloodsuckers! . . . Even our great generals who make such nice speeches, oppress the poor in private and enrich themselves from the impoverished." If these developments went unchecked, there would remain a social world of "the rich and the desperately poor: the bosses and the white kaffirs. God forbid!"[2] . . .

By 1905 journalists in various centres throughout the four colonies had started using "Afrikaans" in their papers, many . . . to expand their circulation. These various developments were first systematically drawn together by Gustav Preller in his by now famous series of articles: "Laat T Ons Toch Ernst Wezen" (Let's take this matter seriously). In these pieces he pointed to the gap which separated the spoken and written language of Dutch Afrikaners. The latter was a type of High Dutch, the former, according to Preller, was "Afrikaans" and he argued strongly for its adoption as a professional, written discourse. His ideas have generally been construed as an act of nationalist altruism, an acute feeling for *land*, *volk* and *taal*, and this was part of the story, particularly in the wake of the Anglo-Boer War. But Preller in his articles was also pleading for the professionalisation of Afrikaans and for its adoption in newspapers, books and schools. However, editors and publishers who could realise such developments prefer hard facts and figures to the warm sentiments of *volksgevoel*. These figures Preller provided. He alluded first to the poor circulation records of papers printed in Dutch, and claimed that no such paper had exceeded sales of about 1,000. He then referred to the *Patriot*'s high readership figures, and finally pointed to the tantalising possibilities in terms of markets and circulation: "We have a white adult population of at least 300,000 of whom a good 200,000 speak Afrikaans."[3] The figures might have been misfounded, but the essential point remained. Out there somewhere was an audience waiting to be captured by the enterprising, the imaginative and the adventurous. To give his argument more depth, Preller also pointed to those who had already glimpsed the business opportunities that went with Afrikaans.

> One of them is the practical businessman. If he wishes to reach the buying and commercial public, he tells the publishers of his adverts, "In Boer-language, otherwise people won't understand." And, good heavens, what linguistic abominations result. Quite enough to make one ill. But, my trusted reader, these are the commercial Boers, they are the voice of a dumb nation.

Preller, then, was trying to motivate Afrikaans as a professional industry in which many could find occupational mobility on the basis of their linguistic and cultural skills. But to professionalise Afrikaans was no small task. Before this goal could be attained, a number of preliminary battles had to be fought on various fronts. The first of these was to make Afrikaans respectable, to reinvent it as a standard language, *'n algemeen beskaafde taal* (a standard language). To accomplish this aim one had to shake off the very strong associations of poverty and particularly "colouredness" which clung to the language. The second task entailed giving the language some substance by creating books and written material in Afrikaans. These, in turn, required markets, publishers, printers and distributors. . . .

The columns of Preller's paper *De Volkstem* soon began to carry innumerable articles which began the long task of making Afrikaans respectable. Some of these spoke about "Taal en Self-Respek" [language and self-respect]. Others attempted to legitimate an Afrikaans language struggle by referring to similar developments in other parts of the world, most notably Flanders but also Quebec, Wales and Ireland. Subsequent articles began to emphasise the links between Dutch and Afrikaans, which made the latter a "white man's language," and gave it an entree via Dutch into that font of civilisation, the Graeco-Roman tradition.

Through these debates carried out in various journals, the people involved refined their objectives. The first was to try and standardise a middle-class variant of Afrikaans. The point was made in many ways, but nowhere more clearly than in the following sentences:

> Language unity is the natural outcome of national unity, the necessary precondition for a national culture. In a situation where there are a vari-

ety of dialects, language unity can only be achieved when one of these
dialects becomes hegemonic.[4]

To achieve such a "civilised" discourse, Preller and others realised that
Afrikaans needed massive injections of Dutch to save it from the English
and "Coloured" structures which permeated it. . . .

The whole issue of Afrikaans had to wait until Union before it could
make any significant advances. Firstly, in the negotiations preceding Union,
people interested in Dutch grouped together in the Academy for Language,
Literature and Art. In this powerful body with access to resources, the Afrikaans lobby could make its voice heard. But secondly, and more importantly, the massive ideological labours around Union with its emphasis on
white unity, citizenship, national symbols and generally its growing infrastructure of press, common taxation, education and postal system, created
an atmosphere propitious for the advancement of Afrikaans. . . . In 1911
Dutch-Afrikaans student bodies formally added their support to Afrikaans
and through it they must have glimpsed a partial solution to their clogged
careerist mobility. In 1914 the provincial councils promulgated a ruling allowing Afrikaans to be taught up to standard IV. This, in turn, required
materials production for schools; linguistic engineers to produce a standard
language; printers, publishers and distributors.

Afrikaans, too, found a fertile base amongst the many Afrikaner wom-
en's organisations which had arisen both during and after the Anglo-Boer
War. Middle-class women grouped together in these associations to try and
right the particular disabilities and discrimination which they experienced
as a sex. They took as their constituency the poor and specifically poor Afrikaner women. These eminent *volksmoeders* worked in an atmosphere where
poverty was increasingly being ethnicised. These welfare initiatives along
ethnic lines must, in turn, have influenced sections of the poor who derived
benefits from identifying and presenting themselves as "white Afrikaners."

Post-Union political development also aided the cause of the language
lobby. The unity of Union was short-lived. The ruling South African Party
(SAP) seemed increasingly to be at the beck and call of the mine magnates.
The wealthy Transvaal farmers in the SAP gained from lucrative maize
agreements with the mines—agreements which excluded the Free State
Farmers. In addition, wealthy landowners continued to swallow up small
farmers. On the Rand, Afrikaner workers competed with unskilled black labour, and when white workers struck to protect their relative privilege, they
came up against the full force of the state. When, in 1914, General J. B. M.

Hertzog broke away to form the National Party (NP), he drew all these disaffected groups behind him.

The language lobby flocked to join the new party. Hertzog had courted the language men throughout and in the NP they found something of a political home from whence they could continue with their work of forging a language and a literature.

The outbreak of the First World War also fuelled the language issue. When the SAP took South Africa into the war on the British side, certain sections of Afrikaner society rebelled. For many rural poor whites who supported the rebellion [against the government's decision to support Britain in the war], it took on the character of a messianic movement. But instead of the promised kingdom on earth, they found themselves and their leaders in prison or facing fines. In this atmosphere there was an increasingly sharpening definition of an Afrikaner—a development that happened on several organisational levels. One thinks, for example, of the opening of Die Vrouemonument [the Women's Monument] in 1913. There was also the Helpmekaar (Cooperation) movement which paid the rebels' fines, ensuring that many received concrete benefits for having behaved as "Afrikaners." The movement reputedly raised £180,000 in two months, and some of this money went "to endow certain Afrikaner cultural organisations."[5] The pattern of competitive donation used in this campaign was copied during the First World War to help set up Nasionale Pers, the publishing house for the NP. In addition, the canonisation of Jopie Fourie, the executed rebel, led to a spate of orally circulated poetry. Within the organisational shelter afforded by these institutions, it became immeasurably easier for the Afrikaner petty bourgeoisie to press their claims for a language and literature. Their successes soon assumed the shape of a rapidly rising graph as dictionaries and books appeared in great numbers. In 1918 Afrikaans became a subject in two universities. In the same year Afrikaans achieved legal recognition as a type of third language when legislation was passed to the effect that the word "Dutch" in Article 137 of the constitution included Afrikaans for all state and official purposes outside, but not inside the House. This legislation represented a small legal victory, but its effects on the ground were limited. The Civil Service continued to be English dominated despite 1912 legislation which stipulated Dutch-English bilingualism after five years in the service. The Nationalist coalition victory in 1924 improved the prospects of Afrikaans considerably. Dr Malan steered through legislation which conferred full official status on Afrikaans and on 8 May 1925 the motion was carried unanimously by both Houses in an atmosphere of goodwill and *toenadering* [cordiality]. . . .

Notes

1. *Report of the Transvaal Indigency Commission, 1906–1908* (Pretoria: TG 13-1908), 74.

2. *Die Volkstem*, November 1, 1905.

3. Gustav Preller, "Laat't Ons Toch Ernst Wezen," reprinted in Daniel Jacobus Conradie Geldenhuys, *Pannevis en Preller* (Johannesburg: Voortrekkerpers, 1967), 54–89.

4. Quoted in Eduard Christiaan Pienaar, *Taal en Poësie van Twede van die Twede Afrikaanse Beweging* (Cape Town: Nasionale Pers, 1926), 142.

5. T. R. H. Davenport, "The South African Rebellion, 1914," *English Historical Review* 78, no. 306 (1963): 93.

A Century of Wrong

Francis William Reitz

Francis William Reitz's (1844–1934) remarkable career included serving in the Cape Colony parliament, as president of the Orange Free State, and as secretary of state of the South African Republic (Transvaal) during the South African War (1899–1902). He later became president of the senate in the Union of South Africa, which was formed in 1910. Reitz was raised on a farm but pursued a legal degree in London; he then moved to Bloemfontein and for a time worked as a diamond prospector. He began his political career in 1873 and became deeply involved in Afrikaner nationalist politics, heading one of the movement's first parties, the Afrikaner Bond (Afrikaner Union).

A Century of Wrong, issued soon after the outbreak of war, is perhaps the most famous Afrikaner anti-imperialist polemic of the late nineteenth century. In the widely circulated tract, Reitz traces the conflict as the inevitable outcome of British imperialism while outlining a sacred history of the Afrikaners going all the way back to 1652. A Century of Wrong would become a central text in the rise of Afrikaner nationalism. Reitz helped draft the Treaty of Vereeniging, which brought an end to the South African War, though he preferred exile to swearing allegiance to the British. He returned to South Africa from the Netherlands and reentered politics while remaining true to his distaste of the British and supporting the cause of the Afrikaners.

In 1886 gold was discovered in great quantities and in different parts of the South African Republic, and with that discovery our people entered upon a new phase of their history. The South African Republic was to develop within a few years from a condition of great poverty into a rich and prosperous State, a country calculated in every respect to awaken and inflame the greed of the Capitalistic speculator. Within a few years the South African Republic was ranked among the first gold-producing countries of the world. The bare veldt [veld; countryside] of hitherto was overspread with large townships [cities] inhabited by a speculative and bustling class brought together from all corners of the earth. The Boers, who had hitherto followed pastoral and hunting pursuits, were now called upon to fulfill one of the most difficult tasks in the world, namely, the management of a complicated administration, and the government of a large digging population, which had sprung up suddenly under the most extraordinary circumstances. . . .

The development of British policy in South Africa had hitherto been influenced at different times, and in a greater or less degree, by the spirit of Jingoism, and by that zeal for Annexation which is so characteristic of the trading instincts of the race. It . . . might be justified by the argument that it was necessary in the interests of the Empire. But Capitalism was the new factor which was about to play such an important role in the history of South Africa. The natural differences in men find their highest expression in the varieties of influence which one man exercises over another; this influence can either be of a religious, moral, political, or purely material nature. Material influence generally takes the form of money, or the financial nexus, as an English writer has termed it. An unusual combination of this form of influence leads to Capitalism just as an unusual combination of political influence leads to tyranny, and an unusual combination of religious influence to hierarchical despotism. Capitalism is the modern peril which threatens to become as dangerous to mankind as the political tyranny of the old Eastern world and the religious despotism of the Middle Ages were in their respective eras.

In a part of the world so rich in minerals of all descriptions as the Transvaal, it is natural that Capitalism should play a considerable role. Unfortunately, in South Africa it has from the very first attempted to go far beyond its legitimate scope; it has endeavoured to gain political power, and to make all other forms of government and influence subservient to its own ends. The measure of its success can be clearly gauged by the fact that all South Africa is standing to-day on the brink of a great precipice, and may be hurled into the abyss before the ink on these pages is dry.

The spirit of Capitalism found its incarnation in Mr. Cecil Rhodes, who was able to amalgamate the pressing and conflicting interests of the Diamond Fields into the one great Corporation [De Beers] of which he is the head.

Although he probably had no exceptional aptitude for politics, he was irresistibly drawn towards them by the stress of his interests. By means of his financial influence, together with a double allowance of elasticity of conscience, he succeeded so far as to become Prime Minister of the Cape Colony, and was powerfully and solidly supported by the Africander [Afrikaner] party. The Africanders believed in him because they were really and deeply imbued with the necessity of the co-operation and fusion of the two

The Rhodes Colossus.
Punch, v. 103, December
10, 1892.

white races in South Africa, and he, as a loyal Englishman, but fully possessing the confidence of Colonial Africanderdom, seemed to them just the very
person to realise their ideal.

To a careful observer the alliance between Africanderdom and Capitalism was bound to lead to a rupture sooner or later. Deeply rooted and pure
national sentiment as well as burning conviction form the basis of Africander Policy, and it was obvious that in the long run it would be discovered that
this policy could never be made subservient to purely financial interests.

But there was another factor. There was that debased form of patriotism
called Jingoism. It is a form of party politics without solid convictions or
real beliefs, which puffs itself out with big words, and with the froth of
high-sounding ideas and principles. It is a policy, nevertheless, which appeals most strongly to the instincts of self-interest and to the illegal appropriation of other people's property. It revels in the lust of boasting, so deeply
ingrained in human nature. In a word, it is a policy which is in direct opposition to the true spirit of religion, to the altruistic ideals of humanity, and
to that sentiment of humility and moderation which is the natural basis of
all morality.

Here, indeed, were the elements of an enduring alliance—an alliance between Capitalism, with its great material influence, but barren of any one single exalted idea or principle on the one hand, and Jingoism, sterile, empty, soulless, but with a rich stock-in-trade of bombastic ideas and principles, prompted by the most selfish aspirations, on the other hand.

The one was eminently calculated to form the complement of the other, thus creating a natural alliance which is rapidly becoming a menace, all the world over, to the best and most enduring interests of humanity.

This Capitalistic Jingoism is the tree from which it is the lot of our unfortunate South Africa to gather such bitter fruit to-day.

Mr. Rhodes, with that treacherous duplicity which is an enduring characteristic of British policy in South Africa, co-operated publicly, and in the closest relationship, with the Colonial Africanders, while he was secretly fomenting a conspiracy with Jingoism against the Cape Africanders and the South African Republics. He already had the Africanders in the Cape Colony under his sway; his aim was now to gain the same influence in the South African Republic, with its rich gold mines—not so much, perhaps, for himself personally as for Capitalism, with which his interests were so closely identified. In case of success, he would obtain his personal aim, and Capitalism would be absolutely despotic in South Africa. With an eye to this end he, with other Capitalists, began in 1892 to foment a political agitation in Johannesburg against the Republic. In a place like Johannesburg, where drink is consumed in great quantities, and where the high altitude and the stress of business all tend to keep people's spirits in a constant state of excitability, it was easy enough, with the aid of money, to bring about a state of political ferment in a very short time, especially as just that measure of grievances existed to give a colour of truth to the imaginary ones. . . .

The secret conspiracy of the Capitalists and Jingoes to overthrow the South African Republic began now to gain ground with great rapidity, for just at this critical period Mr. Chamberlain became [British] Secretary of State for the Colonies. In the secret correspondence of the conspirators, reference is continually made to the Colonial Office in a manner which taken in connection with later revelations and with a successful suppression of the truth, has deepened the impression over the whole world that the Colonial Office was privy to, if not an accomplice in, the villainous attack on the South African Republic.

It is unnecessary to dwell at length on the Jameson Raid [1895–96]; the world has not yet forgotten how the Administrators of a British province, carrying out a conspiracy headed by the Prime Minister of the Cape Colony, attacked the South African Republic with an armed band in order to assist the Capitalist revolution of Johannesburg in overthrowing the Boer Government; how this raid and this revolution were upset by the vigilance of the Boers; how Jameson and his filibusters were handed over to England to stand their trial—although the Boers had the power and the right to shoot them down as robbers; how the whole gang of Johannesburg Capitalists pleaded guilty to treason and sedition; how, instead of confiscating all their property, and thus dealing a death blow to Capitalistic influence in South Africa, the Government dealt most leniently with them (an act of magnanimity which was rewarded by their aiding and abetting a still more dangerous agitation three years later).

Nor has the world forgotten how, at the urgent instance of the Africander party in the Cape Colony, an investigation into the causes of the conflict was held in Westminster; how that investigation degenerated into a low attack upon the Government of the sorely maligned and deeply injured South African Republic, and how at the last moment, when the truth was on the point of being revealed, and the conspiracy traced to its fountain head in the British Cabinet, the Commission decided all of a sudden not to make certain compromising documents public.

Here we see to what a depth the old great traditions of British Constitutionalism had sunk under the influence of the ever-increasing and all-absorbing lust of gold, and in the hands of a sharp-witted wholesale dealer, who, like Cleon of old, has constituted himself a statesman. Treachery and violence not having been able to attain their objects, "Constitutional means" were to be invoked (as Mr. Rhodes openly boasted before the aforesaid Commission), so as to make Capitalistic Jingoism master of the situation in South Africa. . . .

In this awful turning point in the history of South Africa, on the eve of the conflict which threatens to exterminate our people, it behoves us to speak the truth in what may be, perchance, our last message to the world. Even if we are exterminated the truth will triumph through us over our conquerors, and will sterilise and paralyse all their efforts until they too disappear in the night of oblivion.

Up to the present our people have remained silent; we have been spat upon by the enemy, slandered, harried, and treated with every possible mark of disdain and contempt. But our people, with a dignity which reminds the world of a greater and more painful example of suffering, have borne in silence the taunts and derision of their opponents; indeed, they elected out of a sense of duty to remedy the faults and abuses which had crept into their public administration during moments of relaxed vigilance.
. . .

During this century there have been three periods which have been characterised by different attitudes of the British Government towards us. The first began in 1806, and lasted until the middle of the century. During this period the chief feature of British policy was one of utter contempt, and the general trend of British feeling in regard to our unfortunate people can be summarised by the phrase, "The stupid and dirty Dutch." But the hypocritical ingenuity of British policy was perfectly competent to express this contempt in accents which harmonised with the loftiest sentiments then prevailing. The wave of sentimental philanthropy then passing over the civilised world was utilised by the British Government in order to represent the Boers to the world as oppressors of poor peace-loving natives, who were also men and brethren eminently capable of receiving religion and civilisation.

It may seem inexplicable that the Power which stood up boldly at the Treaty of Utrecht as the shameless champion of negro slavery was the very one which was celebrated in South Africa for its morbid love of the natives; the explanation, however, is that it was not so much love for the native that underlay the apparent negrophilistic policy as hatred and contempt of the Boer. As a result of this hatred of the Boer, disguised under the veneer of philanthropy in regard to the aborigines, the natives were employed as police against us; they were provided with arms and ammunition to be used against us; they were incited to fight us, and, wherever it was possible, they murdered and plundered us. In fact, our people were forced to bid farewell to the Cape Colony and all that was near and dear to them, and seek a shelter in the unknown wilderness of the North.

As an ultimate result of this hatred, our people had to pursue their pilgrimage of martyrdom throughout South Africa, until every portion of that unhappy country has been painted red with the blood, not so much of men capable of resistance as with that of our murdered and defenceless women and children.

The second period lasted until the year 1881. The fundamental principle then underlying British policy was no longer one of unqualified hatred. Results had already proved that hatred was powerless to subdue the Africander; it had, on the other hand, contributed largely to the consolidation of Africanderdom and to the fact that they spread over the whole of South Africa, thus forming the predominant nationality almost everywhere. In a moment of disinterestedness or absent-minded dejection England had concluded treaties with the Boers in 1852 [Sand River Convention] and 1854 [Bloemfontein Convention], by which they were guaranteed in the undisturbed possession of certain wild and apparently worthless tracts of territory.

The fundamental sentiment which governed the policy of the second period was a feeling of regret at having made this mistake, coupled with the firm determination to set aside its results. These wild and useless tracts, which had been guaranteed to the Boers, appeared to be very valuable after the Boers had rescued them from barbarism, and opened them up for civilisation. It was felt that they ought to gleam amongst the jewels of Her Majesty's Crown, notwithstanding the obstacle in the treaties that had been concluded with the Boers. This was the concealed intention. As far as the means were concerned—they were, from the very exigency of inborn hypocrisy, partly revealed and partly concealed; the one differing from the other, as light from darkness. The secret means consisted in arming the Kaffir tribes against us in the most incredible manner, and in inciting them to attack us in violation of solemn treaties and promises. If this policy succeeded the real objects and means could be suppressed, and England could then come forward and pose openly as the champion of peace and order, and as the guardian angel of civilisation in this part of the world. The Republics could then be annexed under cover of these plausible pretexts. This policy failed as far as the Orange Free State was concerned, because the brave burghers of the neighbouring Republic succeeded, after great difficulty, in over-coming Moshesh [Moshoeshoe, king of Basutoland], notwithstanding the fact that their arms and ammunition had been illegally stopped by the British Government. England was compelled in that case to confine itself to the protection of its "Basuto" tools. The British, however, succeeded in preventing the Boers from reaping the legitimate fruits of their victory, and in annexing the Diamond Fields—a flagrantly illegal act.

As far as the South African Republic is concerned, it was unfortunate that the burghers were not vigilant enough to foresee and prevent the crafty policy of the enemy. As the Transvaal Boers had subdued the most powerful Kaffir tribes, they never dreamt that the insignificant Kaffir wars in which they had been involved through English intrigue would have been seized as a pretext to annex their country to the British Crown. . . .

The Annexation [1877] was brought about. It was announced that the extension of Her Majesty's sway and protection over the South African Republic could alone secure unity of purpose and trade, as well as open out a prospect of peace and prosperity. In these words of [Sir Theophilus] Shepstone's proclamation we see in all its repulsive nakedness the hypocrisy which openly masqueraded in the guise of the disinterested and pitiful Samaritan, while its true and secret object was to inflict a fatal wound upon the burgher Republic.

The third period of our history is characterised by the amalgamation of the old and well-known policy of fraud and violence with the new forces of Capitalism, which had developed so powerfully owing to the mineral riches of the South African Republic. Our existence as a people and as a State is now threatened by an unparalleled combination of forces. Arrayed against us we find numerical strength, the public opinion of the United Kingdom thirsting and shouting for blood and revenge, the world-wide and cosmopolitan power of Capitalism, and all the forces which underlie the lust of robbery and the spirit of plunder. Our lot has of late become more and more perilous. . . .

And as the brain of the onlooker reels, and as his thoughts fade away into uneasy slumbers, there arises before him in a dream the distant prospect of Bantu children playing amongst the gardens and ruins of the sunny south around thousands of graves in which the descendants of the European heroes of Faith and Freedom lie sleeping.

For the marauding hordes of the Bantu are once more roving where European dwellings used to stand. And when the question is asked—why all this has happened? Why the heroic children of an heroic race, to which civilisation owes its most priceless blessings, should lie murdered there in that distant quarter of the globe? An invisible spirit of mockery answers, "Civilisation is a failure; the Caucasian is played out!" and the dreamer awakens with the echo of the word "Gold! gold! gold!" in his ears. . . .

The justice to which Piet Retief appeals when our fathers said farewell to the Cape Colony, and to which Joachim Prinsloo called aloud in the Volksraad of Natal when it was annexed by England; the justice to which the burghers of the Transvaal entrusted their case at Paarde Kraal in 1880, remains immutable, and is like a rock against which the yeasty billows of British diplomacy dissolve in foam. . . .

Africanders, I ask you but to do as Leonidas did with his 300 men when they advanced unflinchingly at Thermopylae against Xerxes and his myriads, and do not be disturbed by such men as [Alfred] Milner, [Cecil] Rhodes, and [Joseph] Chamberlain, or even by the British Empire itself, but cling fast to the God of our forefathers, and to the Righteousness which is sometimes slow in acting, but which never slumbers nor forgets. Our forefathers [in the Netherlands] did not pale before the terrors of the Spanish Inquisition, but entered upon the great struggle for Freedom and Right against even the mighty Philip, unmindful of the consequences.

Nor could the rack and the persecuting bands of Louis XIV tame or subdue the spirit of our fathers. Neither Alva nor Richelieu were able to compass the triumph of tyranny over the innate sentiment of Freedom and

Independence in our forefathers. Nor will a Chamberlain be more fortunate in effecting the triumph of Capitalism, with its lust for power, over us.

If it is ordained that we, insignificant as we are, should be the first among all peoples to begin the struggle against the new-world tyranny of Capitalism, then we are ready to do so, even if that tyranny is reinforced by the power of Jingoism. . . .

As in 1880, we now submit our cause with perfect confidence to the whole world. Whether the result be Victory or Death, Liberty will assuredly rise in South Africa like the sun from out the mists of the morning, just as Freedom dawned over the United States of America a little more than a century ago. Then from the Zambesi [Zambezi River] to Simon's Bay it will be

"AFRICA FOR THE AFRICANDER."

A Boer Commando

Deneys Reitz

Commando: A Boer Journal of the Boer War, *written by the son of Francis William Reitz, remains one of the most vivid texts of the experiences of Boer fighters. Deneys Reitz (1882–1944) entered the South African War of 1899–1902 at the age of seventeen and continued fighting until the cessation of the conflict. He participated in the Battle of Elands River of September 1901, recounted in the reading, in which the Boer commando headed by J. C. Smuts (later the prime minister of South Africa and a founder of the League of Nations and United Nations) defeated British forces. Like his father, Reitz went into exile following the war, living for a short time in Madagascar and writing the first draft of* Commando. *He returned to South Africa in 1906, joining the First World War effort in 1914 as a loyal member of the British Empire, of which the Union of South Africa remained a part. Reitz served as deputy prime minister of South Africa (1939–43) and then as high commissioner in London, where he died.*

When we reached Pretoria, affairs were moving to a climax. Peremptory notes had been exchanged between the Transvaal and the British Governments, and public excitement was rising as each cable and its reply was published. Already the Transvaal capital was an armed camp. Batteries of artillery paraded the streets, commandos from the country districts rode through the town almost daily, bound for the Natal border, and the crack of rifles echoed from the surrounding hills where hundreds of men were having target practice. Crowded trains left for the coast with refugees flying from the coming storm, and business was almost at a standstill.

Looking back, I think that war was inevitable. I have no doubt that the British Government had made up its mind to force the issue, and was the chief culprit, but the Transvaalers were also spoiling for a fight, and, from what I saw in Pretoria during the few weeks that preceded the ultimatum, I feel sure that the Boers would in any case have insisted on a rupture. . . .

I was seventeen years old and thus too young to be enrolled as a burgher. President Kruger himself solved this difficulty for me. One morning when

Transvaal artillery. Photographer unknown. Courtesy of Free State Archives Photographic Collection, VA178.

I was at the Government buildings, I met him and my father in the corridor and I told the President that the Field-Cornet's office had refused to enrol me for active service. The old man looked me up and down for a moment and growled, "Piet Joubert [commandant general of the South African Republic] says the English are three to one—*sal jij mij drie rooi-nekke lever*" (Will you stand me good for three of them?). I answered boldly, "President, if I get close enough I'm good for three with one shot." He gave a hoarse chuckle at my youthful conceit and turning to my father, asked how old I was. When he heard my age he said, "Well then, Mr. State Secretary, the boy must go—I started fighting earlier than that," and he took me straight to the Commandant-General's room close by, where Piet Joubert in person handed me a new Mauser carbine and a bandolier of ammunition, with which I returned home pleased and proud. . . .

Our military organization was a rough one. Each commando was divided into two or more field-cornetcies, and these again were sub-divided into corporalships. A field-cornetcy was supposed to contain 150 to 200 men, and a corporalship nominally consisted of 25, but there was no fixed rule about this, and a popular field-cornet or corporal might have twice as many men as an unpopular one, for a burgher could elect which officer he wished to serve under, and could even choose his own commando, although generally he would belong to one representing the town or district from which he came.

In the Pretoria Commando, we divided ourselves into corporalships by a kind of selective process, friends from the same Government department or from the same part of the town pooling their resources in the way of cooking utensils &c., and in this manner creating separate little groups that in course of time came to be recognized as military units. One of the number would be elected corporal, to act as the channel through which orders were transmitted from above, and much the same system held in all the other commandos. The commissariat arrangements were equally simple. Our Field-Cornet would know the approximate number of men under his command, and in order to maintain supplies all he needed to do was send a party to the food depot, stacked beside the railway line, where they would break out as many bags of meal, sugar, and coffee as they considered necessary, load them on a wagon, and dump them in the middle of the camp for each corporalship to satisfy his requirements. The meat supply consisted of an immense herd of cattle on the hoof, from which every commando drew as many animals as it wanted for slaughter purposes. This system, though somewhat wasteful, worked fairly well; the men were plainly but adequately fed on much the same diet as they were accustomed to at home, and there was little grumbling. Officers and men had to supply their own horses, rifles, clothing, and equipment, and nobody received any pay.

Ever since the Jameson Raid the Transvaal Government had been importing large quantities of Mauser rifles from Germany which were sold to the burghers at a nominal figure, and as great stores of ammunition had likewise been accumulated, the commandos were very efficiently equipped. The two republics had mobilized between 60,000 and 70,000 horsemen, at this moment distributed west and east, ready to invade the Cape Colony and Natal at the given word. This great force, armed with modern weapons, was a formidable fighting machine which, had it been better led, might have made far other history than it did.

How many troops the British had in South Africa I do not know, but they were pouring reinforcements into the country, and I think our leaders underestimated the magnitude of the task on which they were embarked.

So far as our information went in regard to Natal, the nearest British troops lay at the town of Dundee, some 50 miles away. This force we subsequently found to be about 7,000 strong, and still further south at Ladysmith they had over another 6,000 or 7,000 men, but with fresh troops being landed every day it was difficult to say how soon the scale would dip against us.

On the 10th of October a great parade was held in honour of President Kruger's birthday. We mustered what was then probably the largest body of mounted men ever seen in Africa. It was magnificent to see commando after commando file past the Commandant-General, each man brandishing hat or rifle according to his individual idea of a military salute. After the march-past we formed in mass, and galloped cheering up the slope, where Piet Joubert sat his horse beneath an embroidered banner. When we came to a halt he addressed us from the saddle. I was jammed among the horse-men so could not get close enough to hear what he was saying, but soon word was passed that an ultimatum (written and signed by my father) had been sent to the British, giving them twenty-four hours in which to with-draw their troops from South Africa, failing which there was to be war. . . .

As for the. English force on Nicholson's Nek, orders were sent to the Free State commandos, coming up from the west to attack them, and by seven o'clock we heard the popping of rifle shots from that direction, but for the next hour or two we could spare them no thought, for tall pillars of dust were rising from Ladysmith, and soon long columns of infantry de-bouched [emerged] into the plain before us. The Transvaal Staats Artillery had dragged a 6-inch Creusot gun ("Long Tom") up Pepworth Hill, a mile to the left, and they had installed several smaller guns there as well, and all these now began to fire on the approaching troops. . . .

The soldiers, paying little heed to the shells that dropped amongst them, advanced without a halt, although many now fell dead and wounded, while in the rear, battery after battery unlimbered. We saw the horse-teams rid-den back, and then, to cover the progress of their troops, heavy fire was opened and there came the sound, once heard never forgotten, of shells tearing towards us and exploding around us, and overhead, with deafening concussions.

By now, what with the thunder of the British guns and of our own, the crash of bursting shells and the din of thousands of rifles, there was a volume of sound unheard in South Africa before. I was awed rather than frightened, and, once I had got over my first impression, I felt excited by all I saw and keenly joined in the firing. We were so successful that by the time the foremost infantrymen came within 1,200 yards of us, many fallen dotted the veld, and their advance wavered before the hail of bullets. They did not run away, but we saw them taking cover behind ant-heaps and such other shelter as the ground afforded. From there they directed a heavy fire on us, but their progress was definitely stayed, and our line held for the rest of the day. . . .

More dead lay about and wounded men were sheltering with the rest in the lee of the parapet [during the Battle of Ladysmith, October 1899]. I liked the spot so little that I tried to persuade my brother to return with me to our own commando, but, although he was somewhat shaken by this ordeal, he refused to come, and I had to admit that he was right. As there was no object in my remaining I bade him good-bye, and taking advantage of a slackening in the British gun-fire I made my way down. Below I found Dr. Holz, lying in a heap, struck dead by a shell while helping the wounded. A fresh ambulance-wagon came up just then and I lent a hand at loading the casualties before I sought out my horse, fortunately unscratched, and made haste to get away. I found the Pretoria men still holding the ridge on which I had left them, and on the plain before them the situation had not materially altered. . . .

As we gained ground we began to come on their dead and wounded, and realized what heavy losses we were inflicting, for behind almost every rock lay a dead or wounded man, and we knew that we should have possession of the hill before long.

Towards noon, as we were increasingly hustling our opponents, we heard a bugle ring clear above the rifle-fire, and at the same time a white flag went up.

Hundreds of khaki-clad figures rose from among the rocks and walked towards us, their rifles at the trail. We stood up to wait for them. The haul was a good one for there were 1,100 prisoners, mostly Dublin Fusiliers. . . .

Shortly after the surrender I was talking to some of the captured officers when I heard one of them exclaim, "My God; look there!" and turning round we saw the entire British force that had come out against us on the plain that morning in full retreat to Ladysmith. Great clouds of dust billowed over the veld as the troops withdrew, and the manner of their going had every appearance of a rout. There were about 10,000 soldiers, but General Joubert had far more than that number of horsemen ready to his hand, and we fully looked to see him unleash them on the enemy, but to our surprise there was no pursuit. I heard Christian de Wet mutter, *"Los jou ruiters; los jou ruiters"* (loose your horsemen—loose your horsemen), but the Commandant-General allowed this wonderful opportunity to go by, a failure that cost us dear in the days to come.

Judging by the disorderly appearance of the retreat he could have driven the English clean through Ladysmith and out beyond, and he would have lost fewer men in the doing of it than we lost in the subsequent siege, but the English went hurrying back unmolested, save for an occasional shell from Pepworth Hill, where our guns had sprung into life again, and, with the whole Boer Army looking on, no attempt was made to exploit the victory that had been gained. . . .

Dead and wounded soldiers lay all around, and the cries and groans of agony, and the dreadful sights, haunted me for many a day, for though I had seen death by violence of late, there had been nothing to approach the horrors accumulated here. . . .

On the surface things looked prosperous. Five months ago we had come into this western country hunted like outlaws, and to-day we practically held the whole area from the Olifants to the Orange River four hundred miles away, save for small garrison towns here and there, whose occupants could not show themselves beyond the range of their forts without the risk of instant capture at the bands of the rebel patrols told off to watch them, while we roamed all the territory at will. We had enjoyed a number of successes which the British probably regarded as minor incidents, but which our men looked upon as important victories, and all this had greatly raised their spirits. Unfortunately, while matters stood thus well with us, the situation in the two Republics up north was far otherwise. Lord Kitchener's relentless policy of attrition was slowly breaking the hearts of the commandos. . . .

That evening (April 1902) he [General Smuts, later the prime minister of the Union of South Africa] showed me the dispatch. It was a communication from Lord Kitchener to say that a meeting between the English and Boer leaders was to be held at Vereeniging, on the banks of the Vaal River, with a view to discussing peace terms, and he was summoned to attend. A safe-conduct was enclosed, under which he was to proceed through the English lines to Port Nolloth, whence he would be taken by sea to Capetown, and from there by rail to the Transvaal. . . .

The men were the real tragedy. They had endured against great odds, facing years of peril and hardship without pay or reward, and they still had so much faith in the cause for which they were fighting that, when the news trickled through next day that General Smuts was to go to a peace conference, they were convinced that the British were suing for terms and were ready to restore our country.

It was pitiful to listen to their talk, and to see their faces light up when they spoke of having won through at last and I, for one, had not the heart to disillusion them, or even to hint at a result other than favourable, so steadfast was their trust.

General Smuts lost no time. Next morning a messenger was sent into O'Okiep, to advise the garrison that both sides were to refrain from active military operations while the Congress lasted, and the two British officers went on ahead to Steinkopf, to warn the relief force collecting there that we were shortly passing through their pickets.

The day after that the commando came in from the outlying posts to say good-bye to their leader. The men paraded before the Court House, each man sitting his horse, rifle at thigh, while General Smuts addressed them. He briefly told them of the object of his going, and asked them to be prepared for disappointment if need be, but there were only cheers and shouts of courage, as they pressed from all sides to wish him farewell.

I steered through the throng to shake hands with such as I could reach, waving to others beyond, and in this way I saw the last of many good friends and companions.

Concentration Camps

Emily Hobhouse

Soon after the outbreak of war and frustrated by Boer guerrilla tactics, Lord Her-
bert Kitchener, who commanded the British war effort, began a scorched-earth pol-
icy of destroying Boer farms and forcing people into so-called refugee camps. The
camps were also referred to as "concentration camps," one of the first uses of the
term. British forces created upward of forty-five camps for Boer internees, in addi-
tion to sixty camps for Africans. Women and children composed the majority of the
camps' population.

Camp conditions swiftly deteriorated. Internees suffered from inadequate food
and water supplies and from diseases, such as typhoid and dysentery. More than
28,000 perished from a white inmate population of 118,000, mostly women and chil-
dren. Mortality rates in the African camps may have been even higher, reaching as
high as 436 per 1,000 inmates. By the time the war ended, the conflict claimed more
than 22,000 imperial soldiers, 35,000 Boers, and 20,000 Africans, and it cost the Brit-
ish government more than 200 million pounds sterling.

A prominent British social welfare activist, Emily Hobhouse (1860–1926) traveled
to South Africa shortly after the outbreak of war. She worked tirelessly to protest the
conditions of the camps and criticizing the British conduct of the war. Hobhouse
was criticized by many upon her return to England, but she nonetheless managed
to have her claims of British maltreatment in the camps investigated by Parliament.
Hobhouse attempted to return to South Africa in 1901 but was deported by the Cape
government. The excerpts here are from her letters and memoir.

These are but a few lines to say I am really off to Bloemfontein on Tuesday
and hope to begin dispensing food and clothes before long. From that base
I can hope to work Edenburg, Kroonstad, Norvals Pont and other camps.
There are numbers of them. . . .

All day I have been loading my big truck. I have taken a great quantity of foodstuffs and all the clothing which had come from our English
sources. The food came to nearly £200. . . . It was such a pity not to have
been able to cram the great truck full, as I have been allowed it carriage-free

[no transportation charge], and I want to make myself a big base of supplies in Bloemfontein and work up to Johannesburg from there as soon as I can wheedle Lord Kitchener into giving me a further permit.

The state of Johannesburg Camp is a scandal. My host has just returned from Kimberley and up-country and describes the British Army—sick, weary, worn, spiritless, fit for nothing. The Boers have seldom had a better chance than they have at this moment. For instance, they were simply *let* through into the Colony by a man who had 15 miles of frontier to guard, but who had neither the wit nor the energy left to put patrols on that piece of line. I wish you could hear the accounts from eyewitnesses of some of the engagements lately fought.

After Nooitgedacht [a battle in December 1900 that resulted in a British defeat] the other day 7 000 Boers raised another Memorial—each man brought a stone, put his mark on it, and solemnly swore to fight for independence till death.

I think if you could see these people you would see their spirit is wholly unquenchable, while the spirit of our soldiers is gone out like a candle.

I have been meeting Mr. Fichardt, a charming young man, educated in England of course and lately Mayor of Bloemfontein. He was wounded and taken prisoner soon after Paardeberg, he was one of the 1 200 who rode out and escaped from Cronje's laager through 40 000 British troops. He is here on parole. His family are people of position in Bloemfontein and he has asked his mother to put me up when I get there on Friday. They housed both Milner and Kruger with their attendants at the memorable Conference. A year ago he [Fichardt] was superior in command to De Wet. He gave me thrilling accounts of the early battles.

The more I see and hear the more cruel I think it is to our men to let the war go on. They are so tired and ill. They know they will never catch [the Boer guerrilla leader] De Wet and frankly say so.

How grieved everyone here is about the Queen's illness; all wish she would express the dying wish that the war should end and that could be made an excuse for giving it up. . . .

A line which will probable be read by the [military] Censors, just to say I am here and am well and hard, very hard at work—no time to write now as fully as I should like. I can only send a line hoping the Boers, the Censors, Martial Law and all other impediments will let it catch the mail at Cape Town because I know you will be anxious to have some tidings.

I am preparing a really long account of things for next week if possible. Meantime, do get them to remit the Fund to Cape Town and hurry up with clothing, which is greatly needed.

I have a family of nearly 2000 here, leave alone other places.

Heat, mosquitoes and extreme fatigue prevent more—I am so busy I can only write scraps this week. But I have much to tell—so much, my pen won't go quickly enough.

I do hope you are both keeping well. I am, in spite of the heat, etc., and people are so very kind. . . .

It appears these camps are to be run with Civil money though by Military order—and each wants to shift the onus onto the other. But this I will say—I do think they all want to make matters as sanitary as possible; but nothing done in that way can undo the thing itself and the best must be bad. The chief officials strongly disapprove the policy but men like Captain Hume and that grade of official cannot see the cruelty to women and children and think any means justified that would end the war. Now they are angry because they find it did not end the war.

Their line generally is to speak of "refugee" camps and make out the people are glad of their protection. It is absolutely false. They are compelled to come and are wholly prisoners. In fact, I consider we are all more or less prisoners in Bloemfontein. We cannot move without passes. Everything is censored—spies abound—barbed wire and picquets surround the town—newspapers nearly all prohibited—we have no news and know nothing but vaguest rumours. Nevertheless, with all this rigour, General De Wet knows everything that goes on, in which case, I asked him [Hume], what was the use of wearing out the patience and ruining the business of the inhabitants by this deadening Martial Law? It is only making the people more determined and more bitter. If De Wet gets the news he wants anyhow, just as well relax the rigour. . . .

The women's camp is already one-third of the population of Bloemfontein itself, and there is also a large camp of Natives (Kaffirs)—about 500—to be looked after. A ring of soldiers' camps extends all round the town so all put together it's a large population to feed and water, with diminishing supplies, and unusual drought. The dry weather, though making scarcity of fodder, may be a blessing in disguise, for a great outbreak of typhoid is expected with the rains. Already there is plenty of it. . . .

Today I returned Bishop Webb's call. He is a dear old man. He knew my Father in Cornwall and of course Uncle Edmund's [the Anglican bishop of New Zealand] name was familiar to him. He was sent out here again last September to "conciliate." He calls once a week on Mrs. Fichardt for this purpose, to tell her it is wrong to sympathize with her people. He gave me a pamphlet which he had written many years ago on the settlement of South Africa. In his opinion all would settle down if it were not for Olive Schreiner, Mr. Merriman, the Bond and all Colonial agitators. In fact if you turned all the other side out of the country, I suppose.

He said one of his Sisters of Mercy had visited the camp some time ago and reported that all that was needed was a little cotton and a little soap. They were happy and well off otherwise.

Then I went straight to my camp and just in one little corner this is what I found. Nurse Kennedy underfed and overworked, just sinking onto her bed, hardly able to hold herself up after coping with some thirty typhoid and other patients with only the untrained help of two Boer girls—cooking as well as nursing to do herself. Next I was called to see a woman panting in the heat just sickening for her confinement. Fortunately I had a nightdress in my bundle to give her and two tiny baby-gowns. Next tent, a little six months' baby gasping its life out on its mother's knee. The doctor had given it powder in the morning but it had taken nothing since. Two or three others drooping and sick in that tent. Next, a child recovering from measles sent back from the hospital before it could walk, stretched on the ground white and wan, three or four others lying about. Next, a girl of 24 lay dying on a stretcher. Her father, a big gentle Boer, kneeling beside her while in the next tent his wife was watching a child of six also dying and one of about five also drooping. Already this couple had lost three children in the hospital and so would not let those go, though I begged hard to take them out of the hot tent. "We must watch these ourselves," they said. Captain Hume had mounted guard over me—he thinks I am too sympathetic—but I sent him flying to get some brandy and get some down the girl's throat. But for the most part you must stand and look on helpless to *do* anything, because there is nothing to do anything with. Then a man came up and said "Sister [nurse]," (they call me Sister) "come and see my child, sick for nearly three months." It was a dear little chap of four and nothing left of him except his great brown eyes and white teeth from which the lips were drawn back too thin to close. His body was emaciated.

"Captain Hume," I said, "you shall look." And I made him come in and shewed him the complete child-skeleton. Then at last he did say it was awful to see the children suffering so. The little fellow had craved for fresh milk, but of course, there had been none until the last few days and now our fifty cows only give four buckets, so you can imagine what feed there is for them. I sent Captain Hume for some of this and then made them lay the child outside on a pillow to get the breeze that comes up at sunset.

I can't describe what it is to see these children lying about in a state of collapse—it's just exactly like faded flowers thrown away. And one hates to stand and look on at such misery and be able to do almost nothing. . . .

From all accounts the mass of the Boer prisoners are determined never to live under British rule and now this camp system with all that led up to it

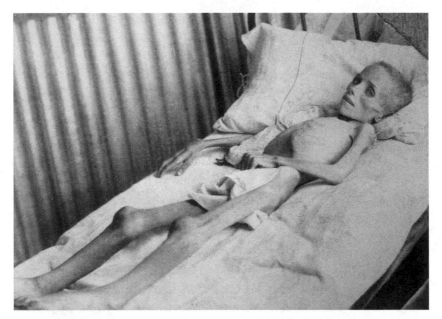

Lizzie van Zyl, photographed in a concentration camp, Bloemfontein. Photographer unknown. Courtesy of Free State Archives Photographic Collection, VA299.

has consolidated the feelings of the women into one strong desire to retain at all costs the independence of their country. . . . Not that, as far as I can discover, they hate the English at all. The English hate the Dutch and take every opportunity of shewing it and of saying so, but the Dutch women, though aghast at the barbarities committed by what they believed to be a civilized nation, bear no hatred and are quite prepared to be friendly with any English individually, though determined not to have their rule. This is quite clear everywhere. . . .

For the number of deaths which were increasing daily more forced attention—at first I had hardly realized their significance. I began to compare a parish I had known at home of 2,000 people where a funeral was an event and usually of an old person. Here some 20 to 25 were carried away *daily*. Captain Trollope remarked on it too, and when I asked him what a normal death-rate was, shewed himself disturbed. The full realization of the position dawned upon me—it was a death-rate such as has never been known except in the times of the great plagues. To produce such a tale of deaths practically everyone was below par—the majority sick, and the dying on all sides. The whole talk was of death—who died yesterday, who lay dying today, who would be dead tomorrow. . . .

It was all kept very quiet; after a while the corpses were carried away at dawn, and instead of passing through the town approached the cemetery another way. Many were buried in one grave. The little canvas tents covered their tragedy, and the little tin hospitals—but there was a man who kept a list of the deaths, and only those who kept in close touch with the people themselves and with the vital statistics of the camp knew what was passing. For some cannot read what is graven on the human countenance. . . .

I think that bad as the camp at Mafeking was and terrible as the death-rate continued to be—in so much that 500 died in the few weeks between the first and second visit of the Ladies' Commission and the Superintendent was dismissed—yet the appalling tragedy of it all came home to me in the sight I witnessed at and near Warrenton both going and returning.

Those truck-loads of women and children unsheltered and unfed, bereft of home, bearing the vivid recollection of their possessions in the flames; and that mass of the "sweepings" of a wide military "drive"—flocks and herds of frightened animals bellowing and baaing for food and drink, tangled up with waggons and vehicles of all sorts and a dense crowd of human beings—combined to give a picture of war in all its destructiveness, cruelty, stupidity and nakedness such as not even the misery of the camps (with their external appearance of order) could do. . . .

My camp work grows so fast and so rapidly that I feel it is almost impossible to cope with it. Here there are now 4 000 or double the number I left six weeks ago. At Springfontein I left a manageable little camp of 500, now it has swelled to 3 000 and as we passed yesterday morning there was a train-load in the station of 600 more. . . .

If only the camps had remained the size they were even six weeks ago, I saw some chance of getting them well in hand, organizing and dealing with the distress. But this sudden influx of hundreds and thousands has upset everything and reduced us all to a state bordering on despair. I feel para-lyzed in face of it. I feel money is of little avail, and there are moments when I feel it would be wisest to stop trying and hasten home to state plain facts and beg that a stop may be put to it all. . . .

The women there clung to me. One said: "There is an old lady and her husband here, aged aunt and uncle to Paul Kruger. She has no skirt. They were in the Great Trek (of 1836)—Van der Walts." I found the old couple near 90 years of age, and, slipping off my underskirt, put it on the old woman. In those days we wore sensible clothes and an underskirt was a long full gar-ment, making ample covering. The old lady was so pleased. They sketched in outline the vicissitudes of their life. And now in their last days had come this shattering blow—their home destroyed, and they carried they knew not whither. Where their fate lay was plain enough and within two weeks they found a grave in Bethulie Camp. He was, I am told, the first to be buried there. Brave and dignified old people, they faced their final uprooting as "the will of the Lord."

They belonged to a type fast disappearing if not already vanished from the plains and uplands of South Africa. You, dear Mrs. Steyn, must have known many such. I wonder if you too will be fearing, as you look over the country, that present-day life fails to produce such strong self-reliance and simple dignity.

The people massed there had no tents. Some crept under the railway trucks while some had begged bits of sailcloth from Tommies and sticking two or three sticks in the ground threw the canvas over, thus making a rude shelter in which, however, one could seldom stand upright.

To such a shelter I was called to see a sick baby. The mother sat on her little trunk with the child across her knee. She had nothing to give it and the child was sinking fast. I thought a few drops of brandy might save it, but tho' I had money there was none to be had. I thought of the Superintendent of the camp—a mile off—and sent a hasty message to ask him to let me have some for a sick child, but the reply was that his supplies were only for his camp. There was nothing to be done and we watched the child draw its last breath in reverent silence.

The mother neither moved nor wept. It was her only child. Dry-eyed but deathly white, she sat there motionless looking not at the child but far, far away into depths of grief beyond all tears. A friend stood behind her who called upon Heaven to witness this tragedy and others crouching on the ground around her wept freely.

Africans in the South African War

S. M. Molema

Few European observers discussed the African role in the South African War. Many Africans believed that British victory would result in political benefits, including a relaxation of strict labor laws. The war also nurtured African discontent of Boer rule, so that some areas of the South African Republic (Transvaal) teetered on outright rebellion. Africans contributed to the British war effort as irregular troops and in a variety of roles, such as scouting and transport; numbers totaled nearly 135,000, including Africans, Coloureds, and Indians. (A very small number of Africans aided the Boers.) Approximately twenty thousand died, many of them in camps. A member of a leading Barolong (Tswana) chiefly family, S. M. Molema (1891–1965) studied medicine in Glasgow and became the president of the African Races Association of Glasgow. In South Africa Molema became a friend of Solomon T. Plaatje, who famously wrote of the Boer siege of Mafeking. Molema's The Bantu Past and Present *was an early attempt by an African intellectual to consider the position of black people in South Africa in a sweeping narrative of the country's past and present. The excerpt describes the African contribution to the British defeat of the Boers and the sense of betrayal with how little came of their efforts.*

It is not generally known, beyond the shores of South Africa, that the South African War of 1899–1902 was not fought exclusively between the Boers and the British but that, on the other hand, very many Bantu people—the natives of South Africa—participated in it, fighting side by side with the British forces, in the same or separate regiments, winning battles and relieving besieged towns. . . .

The little town of Mafeking! the words conjure up before the mind's eye a conglomeration of bungalows, meagre mud and brick houses roofed with corrugated iron—not one of them substantial, perhaps—wide streets, very short, very few, and very dusty; unpavemented foot walks and pepper trees everywhere. That is the European quarter. Three-quarters of a mile to the west of it is a larger and more promiscuous and irregular aggregation of huts—all round and grass-thatched—a few more bungalows, walls, rocks,

and boulders, no regular streets, sand and dirt, and all kinds of trees. That is
the native staadt or town of 6000 souls. Let a river pass below the European
quarter on the south side to run through the native town. That constitutes
the famous little town of Mafeking, famous purely by accident, or, if you
like, by a dramatic achievement. The Barolong, as the Bantu who make up
the bulk of the population are called, upon learning that Mafeking was to
be an objective of their hereditary enemies, the Boers, approached the Civil
Commissioner stationed among them, and requested that they be supplied
with firearms so that they might defend their homes against the impending
invasion. The Civil Commissioner expressed himself in accordance with the
prevailing and unavailing sentiment then as now, that, as the war was one
of whites against whites, it would be wrong and impolitic to arm the blacks.
This reply of the magistrate was confirmed by the military headquarters at
Cape Town. In the meantime the Republican forces were fast approaching
the little town of Mafeking, which formed the junction of the British North
and South Rhodesia and Cape Colony approaching fast so as to surprise the
town, capture it by a coup de main, and isolate Rhodesia.

Within two days of the outbreak of hostilities 7000 Boer commandos
had crossed the western border of the Transvaal, and were assembled under
the supreme command of General Piet Cronje, above what they deemed
the ill-fated town, for Cronje and his subordinates, Snyman and De la Rey,
made no doubt but that Mafeking would fall an easy prey to them. Before
bombarding the town, however, the gallant and compassionate general,—
for Cronje is allowed to have been humane, and averse to causing needless
suffering—advised General Baden-Powell of Mafeking to surrender, and so
avoid unnecessary suffering. Getting no satisfaction, however, he turned
his Krupp guns arid Vickers-Maxim automatic guns on to Mafeking, and,
in a week, added to these a heavy Creusot monster of 94-lb. shell. By this
time General Baden-Powell, not seeing the logic of refusing the Barolong a
means of self-defence, had enrolled about five hundred of them, and armed
them with Snider rifles. These joined the British in the defence of the black
and the white quarters. At the same time they gladly welcomed the opportunity of doing what they could to conquer the Queen's enemies, as also
to settle old scores with the Boers. Regiments of Barolong volunteers were
formed and placed under their chiefs and headmen, who received orders
from the staff of Baden-Powell. Besides this, many Barolong volunteered for
the very serviceable but risky duties of carrying despatches. By this means
the besieged garrison was not only kept in constant communication with
forces under Plumer in the north, but the movements of the Boers around
Mafeking were also made known. On the 25th October the Boers tried to

force a way into the little puzzle of Mafeking by the native town on the south-west side, by what thus far was the heaviest practice of their field pieces. They, however, got a lively reception from the Barolong artillery, and were obliged to retire in confusion and, no doubt, irritation, especially as this step cost the Boers a good few men. The idea, further, that this Boer disaster should be caused by the blacks was galling to the Boers, who, at the beginning of the war, had done their best, first to draw the natives to their side, and, failing that, to keep them neutral. . . .

The *Cape Boy Contingent* was another body of coloured men who helped in the defence of Mafeking. These served with the Police Force, both being under the command of Sergeant Currie. . . . Throughout the seven months of the investment of Mafeking the coloured contingent displayed courage, soldierliness and valour in the field. With the Cape Police they captured from the Boers a five-pounder gun which now stands below the siege obelisk erected in front of the Mafeking Town Hall. It is said, in fact, that the gun was seized by the *coloured* Sergeant Bell, and two other coloured subalterns of the Cape Boy contingent. . . .

The part some members of the Bantu race played on behalf of Great Britain is thus by no means a small one. In fact, it was an important one and so it was recognised, not only by the British officials and rulers, but also, to their annoyance and discomfiture, by the Dutch.

The following excerpts from the speeches of the Boer leaders in their conference of 1902, to consider peace negotiations, speak for themselves. They are contained in General De Wet's book, *Three Years' War*, on the South African War.

Among other things Commandant General Botha said: "The Kaffir question was becoming from day to day more acute. At Vrijheid, for instance, there was a Kaffir commando which had already made several attacks upon the burghers. This attitude of the Kaffir population was producing a very dispiriting effect upon the burghers."

Mr. Birkenstock: "There is also continual danger from the Kaffirs, whose attitude towards us is becoming positively hostile. . . . One morning recently a Kaffir commando, shortly before daybreak, attacked a party of our men, who lost fifty-six killed out of a total of seventy." . . .

Yet another point; is, that the black troops were allowed by the . . . British to fight because their territories had been violated by the Boers, or they had suffered in some way or other, as inevitably they must, from the enemy, and the fairest thing was to allow the sufferers to retaliate. Thus it is that the Barolong, who suffered most, received the fullest liberty to strike back. . . .

Whether Great Britain could or could not have won the war without the help of the "black nations" seems idle to discuss.

What is a more practical question, and one that has more bearing upon our subject is—whether the Bantu people benefited, or did not benefit, by the Anglo-Boer War, i.e. by its peace terms. . . . [I]t might be expected that the rulers would earnestly seek to better the Bantu materially after the war. It is a fact, however, a regrettable fact, that the position of the Bantu after the South African War was worse than before it. It is a fact that their condition has grown worse and worse every year, their rights, never many, nor mighty, have been curtailed systematically since then to now; and the future is dark and dreary.

V

United and Divided

Eight years after the South African War (1899–1902), Britain's most vicious and costly imperial conflict, the Act of Union of 1910 amalgamated the various colonies and former republics into a unitary state composed of more than four million Africans, one million whites (who had a near-monopoly on political rights), half a million Coloureds (people of mixed-race descent), and 150,000 Indians. The union became a British dominion along with Canada, Newfoundland, New Zealand, and Australia, largely autonomous but still part of the empire.

The Union of South Africa also set the course for the history in the twentieth century of white supremacy in South Africa. Tense politics, particularly between Afrikaner political leaders and those representing British interests, marked the period between the Peace of Vereeniging that ended the war and the drafting of a new countrywide constitution. A small group of liberal politicians attempted to have the Cape's nonracial male franchise extended to the rest of the country. Had they succeeded, South Africa's modern history would have been radically different. The Act of Union provided for a sovereign, bicameral legislature. The constitution excluded virtually all black South Africans as well as all women from voting. White women received the franchise in 1930 (the last of the settler societies of the Commonwealth) at precisely the same time when black men in the Cape were being stripped of theirs.

The new state committed itself to addressing the so-called native question. This meant developing uniform policies affecting Africans living in territories conquered over the course of the nineteenth century (defined variously as "native reserves," "scheduled areas," and, under apartheid, "homelands" or "Bantustans") as well as blacks living in what was coming to be defined as "white" South Africa. South Africans borrowed the term *segregation* from the Southern United States, which imposed a strict color line and stunted black citizenship granted in the Reconstruction era after the Civil War. However, South Africa's era of Jim Crow was far more

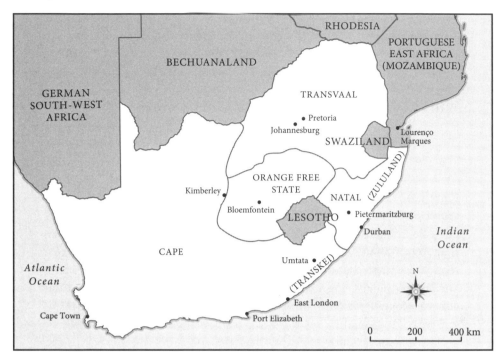

The Union of South Africa, ca. 1910. University of Wisconsin Cartography Lab

pervasive. Most black South Africans still lived in one of the impoverished and increasingly overcrowded native reserves, though they increasingly depended on labor on white farms and in cities. Black urbanization grew steadily through the twentieth century. In the native reserves, Africans continued to be governed as colonial subjects through a system of indirect rule, in which whites imposed political order through ostensibly traditional institutions such as chiefship, much as in other parts of Africa.

Segregation unfolded within the context of fractious white politics and the formation and reformation of various political parties, marked most especially by the rise of Afrikaner nationalist organizations. A very small minority of liberals remained committed to nonracialism. For the great majority, however, the issue was not whether to insist on white hegemony. The issue was its exact specifications. South Africa was to be a white man's country.

Legislation flowed from the new state immediately following union, and especially in the 1920s with the Pact Government (1924–33), formed by the National Party, headed by J. B. M. Hertzog and representing Afrikaners, and the Labour Party, representing the interests of white workers. Laws ranged from color bars in the major sectors of employment to urban housing and transport. Building on earlier legislation that racially segmented the work-force, the Native Labour Regulation Act of 1911 marked a commitment by capital and the state to use cheap, exploited migrant labor in the key mining industry. This and other legislation combined to suppress African wages and made it difficult for workers to organize. White wages moved in the opposite direction: in the early 1920s, white workers earned fifteen times black wages. The discrepancy remained stubbornly wide, hovering around a factor of ten to one well into the apartheid era.

A web of laws, including most notoriously the Natives' Land Act of 1913, created a political geography organized on the basis of racial and tribal terri-torial segregation. In the rural native reserves, areas of gut-wrenching pov-erty, Africans remained colonized subjects. Laws provided the Department of Native Affairs and African chiefs with unprecedented powers, and they organized rule on the basis of tribal or customary law. The Native Adminis-tration Act of 1927 was especially draconian, permitting the Department of Native Affairs to rule by decree.

South Africa's population grew dramatically in the twentieth century, from nearly six million in 1911 to double that thirty-five years later. Cities grew rapidly, with Johannesburg housing more than 1.5 million people by the 1950s. Farming continued to be a vital part of South Africa's economy, particularly sheep, wine and fruit in the Cape, and maize in the Orange Free State and in parts of the Transvaal. The mining sector remained South Af-rica's largest employer, but over the course of the century secondary indus-tries began developing across the country, in part related to the demands of diamonds and gold but much of it arising from the needs of urban dwellers. Labor movements emerged among blacks and whites, though race typi-cally trumped class. The Africanization of Christianity that began in the nineteenth century continued apace, with millions of black South Africans joining independent African-led "Ethiopian" and "Zionist" churches. Today, the largest church is the Zion Christian Church with well over four mil-lion members. Subcultures developed across the country. Despite racially discriminatory laws, a black middle class, also with roots in the nineteenth century, emerged in the country's urban centers, establishing social and cul-tural clubs, publishing newspapers and books, and forming political orga-nizations, most notably the African National Congress. Most striking was the lively world of black townships: the illegal bars (shebeens); the *marabi* music played on pianos, guitars, and concertinas; kwela music played on thin pennywhistles; and the emergence of a remarkable generation of black writers.

The selections that follow in this part seek to give readers a sense of the profound changes unfolding in the decades following the creation of South Africa: the continued impoverishment of the African countryside and the effervescent rough-and-tumble growth of cities; inequality and intolerance; the stirring of African and Afrikaner nationalism; and the looming problems of racial discrimination—developments that would profoundly shape South Africa's history into the era of apartheid and well beyond.

The 1913 Natives' Land Act

Solomon T. Plaatje

The Natives' Land Act of 1913 immediately followed on the heels of the Union of South Africa and created the basis of a territorially segregated South Africa. Under the legislation, Africans were prohibited from buying or renting land outside the native reserves or "scheduled areas." These areas accounted for less than 7.7 percent of the combined land in the country, and eventually expanded to about 13 percent. The act also prohibited African sharecropping. White farmers in the Orange Free State and in part of the Transvaal helped push the legislation through parliament. In doing so they were able to attack the economic livelihoods of thousands of African sharecroppers and rent tenants (both referred to as "squatters") who lived on lands owned by white farmers.

Draconian in its intents, the legislation was enforced haphazardly throughout the union. In a few areas, African sharecropping continued well into the 1950s. The act nonetheless became a galvanizing force for the newly formed African National Congress. Sol Plaatje, the first general secretary of the African National Congress, wrote Native Life in South Africa *during his trip in 1914 to England, where he hoped to convince politicians and other "friends of the natives" of the evils of segregation in South Africa. The act remained in force, however, and was regularly updated until the end of apartheid in the early 1990s; as such, it formed an important symbol of oppression for most of the twentieth century. Current land-restitution law in postapartheid South Africa aims toward reversing the effects of the act of 1913 and subsequent legislation and state action that expropriated land from black owners.*

Awaking on Friday morning, June 20, 1913, the South African native found himself, not actually a slave, but a pariah in the land of his birth.

The 4 500 000 black South Africans are domiciled as follows: one and three-quarter millions in locations and reserves, over half a million within municipalities or in urban areas, and nearly a million as squatters on farms owned by Europeans. The remainder are employed either on the public roads or railway lines, or as servants by European farmers, qualifying, that is, by hard work and saving to start farming on their own account.

A squatter in South Africa is a native who owns some livestock and, having no land of his own, hires a farm or grazing and ploughing rights from a landowner to raise grain for his own use and feed his stock. . . . As a rule many farm tenancies expire at the end of the half-year, so that in June 1913, not knowing that it was impracticable to make fresh contracts, some natives unwittingly went to search for new places of abode, which some farmers, ignorant of the law, quite as unwittingly accorded them. It was only when they went to register the new tenancies that the law officers of the Crown laid bare the cruel fact that to provide a landless native with accommodation was forbidden under a penalty of £100, or six months' imprisonment. Then only was the situation realized. . . .

[In addition, there] are the native locations which were reserved for the exclusive use of certain native clans. They are inalienable and cannot be bought or sold, yet the Act says that in these "Scheduled Native Areas" natives only may buy land. The areas being inalienable, not even members of the clans, for whose benefit the locations are held in trust, can buy land therein. The areas could only be sold if the whole clan rebelled; in that case the location would be confiscated. But as long as the clans of the location remain loyal to the Government, nobody can buy any land within these areas. Under the respective charters of these areas, not even a member of the clan can get a separate title as owner in an area—let alone a native outsider who had grown up among white people and done all his farming on white man's land.

If we exclude the arid tracts of Bechuanaland, these locations appear to have been granted on such a small scale that each of them got so overcrowded that much of the population had to go out and settle on the farms of white farmers through lack of space in the locations. Yet a majority of these legislators, although well aware of all these limitations, and without remedying any of them, legislate, shall we say, with "its tongue in its cheek" that only natives may buy land in native locations. . . .

Before reproducing this tyrannical enactment it would perhaps be well to recapitulate briefly the influences that led up to it. When the Union of the South African Colonies became an accomplished fact, a dread was expressed by ex-Republicans that the liberal native policy of the Cape would supersede the repressive policy of the old Republics, and they lost no time in taking the definite steps to force down the throats of the Union legislature, as it were, laws which the Dutch presidents of pre-war days, with the British suzerainty over their heads, did not dare enforce against the native people then under them. With the formation of the Union, the Imperial Government, for reasons which have never been satisfactorily explained,

The South African Native National Congress delegation to England, June 1914. Courtesy of the William Cullen Library, University of the Witwatersrand, Molema / Plaatje Collection, A1384.

unreservedly handed over the natives to the colonists, and these colonists, as a rule, are dominated by the Dutch Republican spirit. Thus the suzerainty of Great Britain, which under the reign of Her late Majesty Victoria, of blessed memory, was the natives' only bulwark, has now apparently been withdrawn or relaxed, and the Republicans, like a lot of bloodhounds long held in the leash, use the free hand given by the Imperial Government not only to guard against a possible supersession of Cape ideals of toleration, but to effectively extend throughout the Union the drastic native policy pursued by the province which is misnamed "Free" State and enforce it with the utmost rigour.

During the first year of the Union, it would seem that General [Louis] Botha [the first prime minister of South Africa] made an honest attempt to live up to his London promises, that are mentioned by [the former Cape Colony prime minister John X.] Merriman in his speech (reproduced elsewhere) on the second reading of the bill in Parliament. It would seem that General Botha endeavoured to allay British apprehensions and concern for the welfare of the native population. In pursuance of this policy General Botha won the approbation of all natives by appointing Hon. H. Burton, a Cape minister, to the portfolio of Native Affairs. That the appointment was a happy one, from the native point of view, became manifest when Mr Burton signalized the ushering in of Union, by releasing Chief Dinizulu-ka-Cetywayo [the Zulu king], who at that time was undergoing a sentence of imprisonment imposed by the Natal Supreme Court [in connection with the Bhambatha Rebellion], and by the restoration to Dinizulu of his pension of £500 a year. Also, in deference to the wishes of the Native Congress, Mr Burton abrogated two particularly obnoxious Natal measures, one legalizing the "Sibalo" system of forced labour, the other prohibiting public meetings by natives without the consent of the Government. These abrogations placed the natives of Natal in almost the same position as the Cape natives though without giving them the franchise. So, too, when a drastic Squatters' Bill was gazetted early in 1912, and the recently formed Native National Congress [later the African National Congress] sent a deputation to interview Mr Burton in Cape Town; after hearing the deputation, he graciously consented to withdraw the proposed measure, pending the allotment of new locations in which natives evicted by such a measure could find an asylum. In further deference to the representations of the Native Congress, in which they were supported by Senators the Hon. W.P. Schreiner, Colonel Stanford and Mr Krogh, the Union Government gazetted another bill in January 1911, to amend an anomaly which, at that time, was peculiar to the "Free" State: an anomaly under which a native can neither purchase nor lease land, and native landowners in the "Free" State could only sell their land to the white people.

The gazetted bill proposed to legalize only in one district of the Orange "Free" State the sale of landed property by a native to another native as well as to a white man, but it did not propose to enable natives to buy land from white men. The object of the bill was to remove a hardship, mentioned elsewhere in this sketch, by which a "Free" State native was by law debarred from inheriting landed property left to him under his uncle's will. But against such small attempts at reform, proposed or carried out by the Union Government in the interest of the natives, granted in small instalments of a teaspoonful at a time—reforms dictated solely by feelings of justice and equity—ex-Republicans were furious.

From platform, press, and pulpit it was suggested that General Botha's administration was too English and needed overhauling. The Dutch peasants along the countryside were inflamed by hearing that their gallant leader desired to anglicize the country. Nothing was more repellent to the ideas of the backveld Dutch, and so at small meetings in the country districts resolutions were passed stating that the Botha administration had outlived its usefulness. These resolutions reaching the press from day to day had the effect of stirring up the Dutch voters against the ministry, and particularly against the head. At this time General Botha's sound policy began to weaken. He transferred Hon. H. Burton, first Minister of Natives, to the portfolio of Railways and Harbours, and appointed General [J. B. M.] Hertzog, of all people in the world, to the portfolio of Native Affairs.

The good-humoured indulgence of some Dutch and English farmers towards their native squatters, and the affectionate loyalty of some of these native squatters in return, will cause a keen observer, arriving at a South African farm, to be lost in admiration for this mutual good feeling. He will wonder as to the meaning of the fabled bugbear anent [concerning] the alleged struggle between white and black, which in reality appears to exist only in the fertile brain of the politician. Thus let the new arrival go to one of the farms in the Bethlehem or Harrismith districts for example, and see how willingly the native toils in the fields; see him gathering in his crops and handing over the white farmer's share of the crop to the owner of the land; watch the farmer receiving his tribute from the native tenants, and see him deliver the first prize to the native tenant who raised the largest crop during that season; let him also see both the natives and the landowning white farmers following to perfection the give-and-take policy of "live and let live," and he will conclude that it would be gross sacrilege to attempt to disturb such harmonious relations between these people of different races and colours. But with a ruthless hand the Natives' Land Act has succeeded in remorselessly destroying those happy relations.

First of all, General Hertzog, the new Minister of Native Affairs, travelled up and down the country lecturing farmers on their folly in letting ground to the natives; the racial extremists of his party hailed him as the right man for the post, for, as his conduct showed them, he would soon "fix up" the natives. At one or two places he was actually welcomed as the future Prime Minister of the Union. On the other hand, General Botha, who at that time seemed to have become visibly timid, endeavoured to ingratiate himself with his discontented supporters by joining his lieutenant in travelling to and fro, denouncing the Dutch farmers for not expelling the natives from their farms and replacing them with poor whites. This became a regular ministerial campaign against the natives, so that it seemed clear that if any native could still find a place in the land, it was not due to the action of the Government. In his campaign the Premier said other unhappy things which were diametrically opposed to his London speeches of two years before; and while the Dutch colonists railed at him for trying to anglicize the country, English speakers and writers justly accused him of speaking with two voices; cartoonists, too, caricatured him as having two heads—one, they said, for London, and the second one for South Africa.

The uncertain tenure by which Englishmen in the public service held their posts became the subject of debates in the Union Parliament, and the employment of Government servants of colour was decidedly precarious. They were swept out of the railway and postal service with a strong racial broom, in order to make room for poor whites, mainly of Dutch descent. Concession after concession was wrung from the Government by fanatically Dutch postulants for office, for Government doles and other favours, who, like the daughters of the horse-leech in the Proverbs of Solomon, continually cried, "Give, give." By these events we had clearly turned the corner and were pacing backwards to pre-Union days, going back, back, and still further backward to the conditions which prevailed in the old Republics, and (if a check is not applied) we shall steadily drift back to the days of the Old Dutch East Indian [Dutch East India Company] administration.

The bill which proposed to ameliorate the "Free" State cruelty, to which reference has been made above, was dropped like a hot potato. Ministers made some wild and undignified speeches of which the following spicy extract, from a speech by the Rt Hon Abraham Fischer to his constituents at Bethlehem, is a typical sample:

"What is it you want?" he asked. "We have passed all the coolie [contemptuous South African term for British Indians] laws and we have passed all the Kaffir laws. The 'Free' State has been safeguarded and all her colour laws have been adopted by Parliament. What more can the Government do for you?" And so the Union ship in this reactionary sea sailed on and on and on, until she struck an iceberg—the sudden dismissal of General Hertzog.

To the bitter sorrow of his admirers, General Hertzog, who is the fearless exponent of Dutch ideals, was relieved of his portfolios of Justice and Native Affairs—it was whispered as a result of a suggestion from London; and then the Dutch extremists, in consequence of their favourite's dismissal, gave vent to their anger in the most disagreeable manner. One could infer from their platform speeches that from their point of view, scarcely anyone else had any rights in South Africa, and least of all the man with a black skin.

In the face of this, the Government's timidity was almost unendurable. They played up to the desires of the racial extremists, with the result that a deadlock overtook the administration. Violent laws like the Immigration Law (against British Indians and alien Asiatics) and the Natives' Land Act were indecently hurried through Parliament to allay the susceptibilities of "Free" State Republicans. No minister found time to undertake such useful legislation as the Coloured People's Occupation Bill, the Native Disputes Bill, the Marriage Bill, the University Bill, etc., etc. An apology was demanded from the High Commissioner in London for delivering himself of sentiments which were felt to be too British for the palates of his Dutch employers in South Africa, and the Prime Minister had almost to apologize for having at times so far forgotten himself as to act more like a Crown Minister than a simple Africander [Afrikaner]. "Free" State demands became so persistent that ministers seemed to have forgotten the assurances they gave His Majesty's Government in London regarding the safety of His Majesty's coloured subjects within the Union. They trampled underfoot their own election pledges, made during the first Union General Election, guaranteeing justice and fair treatment to the law-abiding natives.

The campaign, to compass the elimination of the blacks from the farms, was not at all popular with landowners, who made huge profits out of the renting of their farms to natives. Platform speakers and newspaper writers coined an opprobrious phrase which designated this letting of farms to natives as "Kaffir-farming," and attempted to prove that it was almost as immoral as "baby-farming." But landowners pocketed the annual rents, and showed no inclination to substitute the less industrious "poor whites" for the more industrious natives. Old Baas [Boss] M-, a typical Dutch landowner of the "Free" State, having collected his share of the crop of 1912, addressing a few words of encouragement to his native tenants, on the subject of expelling the blacks from the farms, said in the Taal [language, referring to Afrikaans]: "How dare any number of men, wearing tall hats and frock coats, living in Cape Town hotels at the expense of other men, order me to evict my natives? This is my ground; it cost my money, not Parliament's, and I will see them banged (barst) before I do it."

It then became evident that the authority of Parliament would have to be sought to compel the obstinate landowners to get rid of their natives. And the compliance of Parliament with this demand was the greatest ministerial surrender to the Republican malcontents, resulting in the introduction and passage of the Natives' Land Act of 1913, inasmuch as the Act decreed, in the name of His Majesty the King, that pending the adoption of a report to be made by a commission, somewhere in the dim and unknown future, it shall be unlawful for natives to buy or lease land, except in scheduled native areas. And under severe pains and penalties they were to be deprived of the bare human rights of living on the land, except as servants in the employ of the whites—rights which were never seriously challenged under the Republican regime, no matter how politicians raved against the natives.

Bhambatha Rebellion

Msime ka Beje

In 1906 Africans in Natal rebelled over the imposition of a new tax, the poll tax. The rebellion is known as the Zulu Rebellion or the Bhambatha Rebellion, after a chief who was one of its leaders. The crushing of the revolt involved spectacularly vicious assaults on the rebels using mechanized weaponry. This occurred in the context of the wider European scramble for Africa, in many areas an equally bloody affair, and a number of revolts in southern and East Africa in the first decade of the twentieth century. In the aftermath of the revolt of 1906, their fields and herds destroyed, thousands of young Zulu men were thrown on the labor markets of the Rand.

Msime ka Beje, some of whose brothers had joined the rebellion, and who had attended the trial of one of the rebel chiefs, spoke to the colonial official James Stuart about the rebellion in late 1906. In the portion of the interview excerpted here, Msime discusses the variety of colonial affronts in early twentieth-century Natal that led to the rebellion. These included the poll tax, which people said had the effect of separating sons from their fathers by treating them as separately taxable individuals, as opposed to the principle of taxing a homestead through its head. One important dynamic of the rebellion was the rejection by young men of obedience to elders whom they saw as overly compliant with, and benefiting from, the colonial order.

We were told a census was required of the number of people. We said, "What people want knowing, for we are all recorded in the books? We register our wives [under the marriage law], and none of us have hidden our huts" (from hut tax). The authorities said, *"It is nothing to be disturbed about. The king says he wants to know how many people he has."* We said, *"This is a nuisance." They saw this as insubordination. So we accepted it.* There is no matter we can speak about satisfactorily; all reply is (considered to be) of the nature of argument or contention. After this we were told, *"Let all the children who have been born be reported. Let all who have died be reported. If anyone does not do this, he will be punished."* And, true enough, he was punished.

We were afterwards told that people living on the reserves would be taxed at the rate of £3 a hut. We were astonished at this, feeling it was op-

Sigananda, a chief taken prisoner during the Zulu Rebellion (third from right). Photographer unknown. Courtesy of Campbell Collections of the University of KwaZulu-Natal, A50/018.

pressive. (I personally do not live on the reserves.) Some of these were imprisoned for not paying, and whilst such action was being taken, we were told about the poll tax.

The Poll Tax Act did not begin by being proclaimed among the chiefs, but among the young men of Durban and the towns. We heard that the young men of Durban had *created a disturbance* in Durban when collected to notify to them the provisions of the poll tax. We also heard that a disturbance occurred in Pietermaritzburg when a similar statement was made. We said, "What is the meaning of this?" The men of the tribe said, "What is the meaning of our children being addressed in this way in the towns?" By so doing *their children were being taken away from them.* The men said, *"So are we not going to pay tax?* For the boys won't agree to give us money to pay." . . .

People are *caused to be resentful by the whites*—a cause of rebellion— because *unexplained things* are brought about daily. What is desirable is to *listen to one another and to answer one another.* All *the things of which we complain have emerged* recently. Before, men like Misjana [John Shepstone], Gallwey, Windham decided our *lobola* [bridewealth] claims satisfactorily. The road-party work [forced labor] is a grievance. This is called month after month. *The young people are now deserting their fathers* because of the *isibalo* (forced labor), *because they are very much afraid of it.* The work is hard. They *earn* nothing, and are *given little* food.

Most of the people like the white people; they do not care for [the Zulu king] Dinuzulu. Things go wrong in our own mouths. The wrongs from which the people suffer are of the Europeans' own making. *"You treat them badly."*

Dog tax—this is an *inexplicable thing,* for they catch no bucks; and these bucks, we have specially provided, shall not be touched. *We come right into the homes of the people.* We make *kolwas* [African Christians], and when a *kolwa* is merely an *induna* [headman] of a missionary, we make a *chief* of him and give him a *district (isifunda)* in the middle of tribal lands of his chief. *Kolwas* have *destroyed* our kraals. *Kolwas* say they are sent by missionaries. The result is our children and our women have taken to dress, and in the midst of all we are at a loss as to what to say.

We are *surprised and concerned about* the whites buying land and charging heavy rentals from an *isifunda* (tribe) that pays the government far less, even though this *isifunda* is living alongside the farm in question.

We find police put in at the magistrate's office. These go out at will to arrest natives, although no one has gone to report to them that anything wrong has happened. . . . A country cannot be governed by children and lads—Europeans and natives. For the *induna* at the court house is a *boy,* and he *plays about with us.* A European boy too is unsuitable. Why appoint over us hot-tempered magistrates in whom we cannot have confidence?

No consideration is shown to men like myself who have no sons to work for them. I, for instance, might be given a place or post where I could make some money. Things are not as before, when I could go to the court and get a job—now police have usurped this position, and strut about wearing their "caps on their very cheeks." They wrongfully arrest time after time, as at a beer drink; they take beer, and then go and effect arrests—without warrants.

The Bulhoek Massacre

Anonymous

Radical separatist Christianity had begun in the nineteenth century, in some cases in the earliest years of European missionizing. In the late nineteenth century and especially in the twentieth century, however, Africans began exploring new ways of understanding their world, often by elaborating a vision that combined Christian eschatology with earlier ways of explaining misfortune. The worldwide influenza pandemic of 1918 created panic across South Africa's rural communities. Religious change also formed part of an Atlantic-wide religious revolution that connected black South Africans with adherents of new churches in the Caribbean and in the United States, particularly the African Methodist Episcopal Church, which was introduced from the United States in the early 1890s.

By the early 1920s, dozens of African independent churches existed throughout both rural and urban parts of the country. The Eastern Cape was an especially rich ground of religious and political innovation, with dozens of mission stations and a history of conversion going back to the early years of the nineteenth century. The newly created African National Congress had just held its annual meeting in Queenstown, just a few miles from Bulhoek, where a congregation known as the Israelites gathered on the location commonage. People across the broader region came to Bulhoek, attracted to the religious teachings that explained poverty and misfortune and promised everlasting peace. Reported in the newspaper excerpted here, the violence that unfolded that fall day in 1921 would be South Africa's first modern political massacre.

A fair day in May in the year 1921—to be precise, it was Empire Day, the 24th saw the end of the Israelite menace, as far as the now famous Ntabelanga Village is concerned; at any rate it is hardly likely that anybody will have the temerity to endeavour to re-establish the movement on this historic site for a good many years to come, if ever.

Many people will, doubtless, be under the impression that this so-called Israelite sect was confined merely to the Bullhoek locality. That, however, is quite a mistaken idea, for the Head Office of the Israelite organisation in South Africa is at Bloemfontein. It must be pointed out though, that the Prophet, Enoch Mgijima, or, as he styled himself, the "Watchman," was, in the words of the Head Office, "discommunicated" from the Church. The headquarter's scribe, of course, meant "excommunicated," and it was alleged that the reason for this "drastic" punishment was the fact that Enoch had been guilty of the crime of disobedience. . . . [T]his alleged prophet set about raising a congregation of his own, and there is no doubt that he succeeded in his object only too well, and managed to gull quite a large number of the natives of this country into believing his hare-brained prophecies.

The new religion captured the imagination of the womenfolk, with its procedure of baptism by total immersion at midnight, its kiss of peace, its Sabbath day, while the younger men did not look askance on it because of its assertion that the black people would be led by a prophet from among themselves, and that they were God's chosen. . . .

Ntabelanga Village, which is some twenty miles or so from Queenstown, is set amidst most picturesque surroundings, in a pleasant valley with towering mountains and boulder-strewn kopjes [hills] of rugged grandeur on every side, while standing out boldly, and in close proximity is Ntabelanga Mountain (the Mountain of the Rising Sun). . . . Standing on a slight eminence, just below a ridge which runs down from the slopes of Ntabelanga, were long rows of small, but neat, houses—very different from the ordinary round wattle and daub but constructed of unburned bricks, generally with thatched roofs, though iron formed the covering for one or two of the more pretentious. Some attempt was made at ventilation, and the occupants had displayed a certain amount of ingenuity in making a use of waste materials for building operations. For instance, a bicycle wheel was made to serve the purpose of quite a useful window, while old tins, after being flattened out, were employed in the construction of chimneys.

The property of Enoch, as, perhaps, was only to be expected, was the most imposing in the village, and, judging by appearances, the "Watchman" must have lived fairly comfortably. There are several buildings on his property, including storerooms, etc. The word "are" is used advisedly, for these buildings have not shared the fate of so many others, and are still standing. "Bishop" Enoch's dwelling, iron roofed, consists of several rooms, and one at least of these is papered, though the effect is somewhat incongruous, for the patterns on the same walls differ widely, sample papers having evidently been employed for the purpose. . . .

Those who have read the accounts of what occurred at Bullhoek on the fateful 24th May, will have observed reference to the Tabernacle. This was used for religious purposes, meetings, etc., and on the date in question it was located in the vicinity of the Prophet's dwelling. It was not a very magnificent affair; in fact, consisted of a number of tent poles covered over with canvas, which at the time of the affray presented a somewhat tattered and torn appearance. . . . The seating accommodation in the Tabernacle consisted of wooden benches, not unlike some church pews. Enoch had a Throne, so-called, not a very elaborate piece of work, to say the least of it, and obviously home-made, but, no doubt, it answered the purpose. To put it briefly, the Throne was nothing more or less than a fairly high chair, rough and ready in appearance, with arms and a foot rest. . . .

On May 23, 1917, Mr. Gladwin [a local official] wrote to Enoch, stating that the latter was well aware that, when he asked permission to erect a few huts of a temporary nature, to be used while they held their Passover, he promised to demolish these erections when the passover was finished. He had inspected Bullhoek that morning, and had found that the promise had not been carried out. Furthermore, he was erecting a large square building (the "Watchman's" residence) under an iron roof, on the commonage. On May 28, 1917, Mr. Gladwin sent Enoch the following: "Take notice that . . . you are hereby instructed to remove from the commonage all new buildings erected thereon by your orders on or before June 7, 1917." According to Mr. Nightingale, none of the 26 occupants of the huts mentioned were registered hut-tax payers, though some of them were quitrent payers, having lands away from the location. In his time there were no temporary structures there; he considered they were all permanent buildings.

One of the customs of the Israelites was to hold their Passover in the month of April in each year. In 1918 they made application to the Superintendent, through Attorney Brinkman, and were granted permission to hold the Passover. The camp remained for about six weeks, after which the people dispersed, tents and other temporary erections were taken down, and the place was left as it was before. In the following year their intention was to hold the Passover at Shiloh, but the Mission Board refused permission. Then a deputation of the Israelites from Enoch went to the Superintendent, and asked for permission to hold their Passover on the same spot as in 1918, on the Kamastone commonage. Owing, however, to the severe drought, and the consequent scarcity of water and pasturage, he told them he could not see his way clear to grant permission. The Israelites, who used to come to the Passover in wagons, brought in large numbers of stock, including their milk cows. Later they applied to him again, and enquired if there would be any objection to the Passover being held at Ntabelanga. He agreed to the request, and it was duly held there. As usual, after it was over, all the people departed for their homes, and all temporary structures were removed.

In February, 1920, Enoch went to see Mr. Nightingale at his office, and they had a general conversation. The Israelite "seer" broached the subject as to whether they would be able to have the Passover at Ntabelanga again in April. He was asked why they were making such early application, fully two months beforehand, and the reply was that people had to come from long distances away, and Enoch wanted to be able to give them notice as to where the Passover was to take place. The Superintendent took the opportunity of saying to the Prophet: "I'm glad you raised this question, because it has come to my notice that a certain number of people have moved into the Bullhoek Location from other districts, and are at present living in the tents of the residents at Ntabelanga and in its vicinity, and I have been credibly informed that these people have sold off all their property, and have come to take up their permanent residence in the Bullhoek Location."

Referring to Charles Mgijima, the Superintendent of Locations said he was Enoch's elder brother, and he just came in contact with him when the second batch of summonses were issued. Before he came to Ntabelanga, Charles was Court Interpreter at De Aar. He was not aware that this member of the Mgijima family was in receipt of any pension, as he understood he resigned from the service. When the people did not disperse, Mr. Nightingale was instructed, in October of last year, to make a register of all residents of the Bullhoek Location, and to commence with Ntabelanga first. A sergeant and two constables of the S.A.P. [South African Police] were detailed to accompany him, and they proceeded to Ntabelanga on October 20. When near the village they met some Israelites. These people were aware of the visit, as information had been sent them to that effect the previous evening. When they got near the village they saw a marquee [tent] had been erected some 200 yards from it, and they were told to wait there, as that was the place where the meeting would be held. Soon after their arrival Charles Mgijima, Edward Mpatane and other leaders came along, and altogether about 150 Israelites met them at the tent. Mr. Nightingale explained his instructions from the Native Affairs Department in regard to the register, and told them what information he would require. Several speakers rose one after the other, and said this thing had come on them as a surprise, and they would like time to consider it. The meeting was adjourned for half an hour, and on re-assembling, and before entering the tent, a hymn was sung.

After the singing had concluded, Edward Mpatane got up and said they had considered the matter during the Superintendent's absence, and they had come to the decision that they could be taken by him, as their names were written in God's book, and as God was greater than man, they were powerless to give him their names. Other speakers got up, and emphasised that that was the unanimous decision of those present. When Mr. Nightingale enquired whether that was definite, the reply was in the affirmative, so he informed the gathering there was nothing more for him to do but to report to the Government, which he duly did. The meeting was brought to a close with another hymn.

[This paragraph concerns a commission appointed by the Department of Native Affairs to look into the situation at Ntabelanga.] The proceedings commenced by the Commission explaining that it had been appointed to look after the interest of the native population of the Union. That they were the Prime Minister's counsellors in such matters; that [the prime minister] Gen. Smuts had sent them specially in connection with the position which had arisen at Ntabelanga; that they had come as the true friends of the natives, and they hoped that before leaving they would come to some friendly agreement which would be pleasing to the Prime Minister and to all parties. A discussion then ensued. The members of the Commission pointed out that the present state of affairs could not be allowed to continue, that the law was being broken, that the Government had to respect the rights of all natives. They asked the Israelites to be reasonable men, and to discuss such matters as the boundaries of their settlement at Bullhoek, the number of houses necessary for worship, and the limits of time of their residence here. It was impossible to get the Israelites to discuss the matter from a mundane point of view. They replied that:

God had appointed one of them to show how He should be worshipped; that man was the Prophet.

The Prophet spoke God's wishes, and they obeyed them.

It was God's desire that they should assemble at Ntabelanga; the speakers had no power to send people away, seeing the latter were influenced by Jehovah.

The Scriptures contained God's promise to gather His people together; those following the Prophet were His chosen.

They wished to obey the law of the land, but Jehovah was more powerful than the law, and they feared to offend Him by disregarding His wishes and obeying the laws of men.

They desired to injure no one, and only wished to serve God in the way in which He had shown.

Ntabelanga was the place for the assembling of God's chosen, but was not their permanent abiding place, and they awaited the command of Jehovah.

The punishment of Jehovah would soon fall on unbelievers, and the end of the world was near, and so they had gathered at this place of God's choosing to prepare for this day.

Colonel Truter had the following served on the Prophet under date Queenstown, May 21, 1921, and over his signature:—To Enoch Mgijima and all associated with him, styling themselves "Israelites," at Ntabelanga: You are hereby notified that, upon instructions of the Government, I have come to Queenstown, and will arrive at Ntabelanga on Monday, 23rd inst., with an adequate force to carry out certain orders, which are detailed hereunder, namely:—To arrest certain men against whom warrants have been issued, in order that they should be dealt with according to law.

To see that all unauthorised residents leave Ntabelanga, and go back to where they came from.

To destroy all houses erected without authority.

On completion of these operations, a force will be left on Ntabelanga to prevent any unauthorised resident squatting there.

Everyone's person and property will be respected. You are warned, however, that any resistance to lawful authority will be drastically dealt with.

The following message was received from the Prophet by Colonel Truter on Sunday, May 22:—

Sir,—Yours of the 21st inst. Duly to hand, I feel glad that to-day I am able to express myself to you how God has sent me to His people. On the 19th of April, 1907, the Lord God did appear to me by a vision. I was only a hunter of game and a sinner before God, but the God of heaven and earth appeared to me, and sent me to His people. And whosoever shall hear His word, saying: Do you hear the sound from the west? I said: I do hear, Lord. That is the war which shall be in the world, said He. A great sound was roaring from the west. The Lord informed me that the war will begin in 1914, and from thence there shall be no peace on earth. The Lord God also informed me from what side it shall appear when it comes in Africa. You are just on its track as you now stand. This war is not for the kings nor the rulers of this world, but it is the war of the Lord God of Israel. I, the servant of the Lord, inform you, therefore, that this war is not caused by me, nor by any earthly king.

I understand that you, Sir, intend to come out to Ntabelanga with an adequate force. May it therefore be known by you and all that the arms and forces shall be ruled by God. As for myself, I am a messenger before the blood. The whole world is going to sink in the blood. I am not the causer of it, but God is going to cause it. I am a man of blood, said my God, the Lord of Hosts is His name. The time of Jehovah has now arrived. All nations are invited to the marriage of the Lord God of heaven and earth, and also to the occupier of the God of heaven and earth (Rev. xix., 17–18; Ezek. xxxix., 17–20). . . .

Ninety per cent of the fighting force of the natives were dressed in white uniforms—a sort of smock affair—shorts and sandals, while many of them affected collars, both of the linen and celluloid varieties, the latter predominating, and in varying stages of cleanliness. . . . The Israelites, who, by the way, have their heads shaven for some reason or other, carried short double-edged swords of extreme keenness, and with very sharp points—altogether a very dangerous weapon. Car springs seem to have been found very useful in the manufacture of these highly dangerous implements of warfare, and files were also extensively utilised. Whether the Israelites purchased these files or acquired them in other ways in not quite clear, but what is certain is that on one sword, made from a file, was found the mark of a garage which has a penchant for stamping an identification sign on the tools used on the premises. The hilts were neatly constructed of wood, while the swords were carried in sheaths made from petrol or paraffin tins. These weapons varied in length, but they were evidently modeled on a brass hilted short sword of German origin, with leather scabbard, and dated 1917, which was captured from one who was apparently a leader in the enemy's ranks. Another favourite weapon was a broad-bladed assegai [spear], while knobkerries [wooden clubs] and villainous-looking knives also formed part of the armament. Sheep shears divided and well-sharpened made implements very villainous in appearance. Considering the facilities at the disposal of the Israelites, the weapons were remarkably well made, and it did not require a veteran in warfare to recognise that they would be particularly formidable wielded at close quarters by a determined enemy. . . .

As soon as he saw the Israelites were deploying for the attack, Colonel Woon ordered No. 2 Troop of A Squadron, consisting of about 25 rifles, to fire one volley, hoping to check their charge. They were then spreading out and advancing towards him, some breaking into a run and others still deploying. Knowing they had no experience of modern rifle fire, the Colonel thought one volley would stop them, and break them up, but this volley, apparently, had no effect as he did not see any Israelites drop. . . . The Israelites then advanced at a fast run, and the front line—two squadrons— were ordered to open five rounds rapid, which they did. There were two machine guns in the line, but they were not brought into action. As soon as fire opened from the two squadrons—it was very deadly fire—the charging fanatics began to drop in numbers, but it did not retard their charge in the slightest. Those who could still run continued charging, and even wounded men were getting up and staggering along into the charge. It was not until they were about twenty yards from the line that the rush was broken. The foremost Israelites who got to within twenty yards of the Police were all shot. When the officer commanding saw the attack was broken he whistled the "Cease Fire," and firing at once stopped all along his line. About fifty or sixty of the natives who had attacked, some of them wounded, were seen slowly walking back towards the village. They were within 200 yards of the force, but not a shot was fired at them. It was then noticed that the Israelites on the left flank were retiring along the ridge towards the village. No shots were fired at them either. The party in the red cloak had disappeared, while the man in the red sash on horseback was shot. Colonel Woon detailed three men to shoot this man, thinking he was the leader, and he saw him come down, horse and all. This order was given when the five rounds rapid was fired. . . .

Three natives came from the village with a flag of truce. They had their uniforms on, but had put on old coats to cover their white smocks. They were still wearing shirts and sandals. They asked permission to assist their wounded, which was given readily, and they were told they could send out as many parties as they liked, provided they came out with white flags. . . .

A curious thing was that among these deluded people were many of the better class, some of them educated. The woman with the wheelbarrow, for instance, had been a teacher. Among the killed and wounded were found some well-known store boys from Queenstown, even an attorney's clerk. By 2 P.M. on the following day he [Sergeant Major Bench] had collected 120 dead, and they were buried in one grave. Later, he collected another 34 dead, and buried them in a common grave. That made 163 buried in all. There were 129 wounded, and the prisoners numbered 95, excluding Enoch, who was removed to Queenstown and lodged in jail. Before the graves were closed up, the natives were given the right to hold a burial service, which they did. . . . It was estimated—though the number is by no means certain—there were about 500 armed Israelites in all, and it is believed a considerable number of them escaped.

Mine Workers' Songs

Anonymous

Africans migrated from all over southern Africa to work in the diamond and gold mines. Many tens of thousands quite literally walked hundreds of miles before the extension of railroads made travel easier. By the 1940s the gold mines employed nearly four hundred thousand black miners, many of them from South Africa's Transkei native reserve and from Mozambique. The diamond mines in Kimberley depended especially heavily on workers from the nearby mountain kingdom of Lesotho (formerly Basutoland). Early migrants used their wages to purchase guns to defend the kingdom from Boer predations and British imperial advances, leading to the Basotho Gun War of 1880–81.

By the early twentieth century, communities in Basutoland depended on mine wages, as did an increasing number of areas throughout southern Africa. The country had extremely high rates of migrancy—virtually all adult men engaged in mine labor, taking contracts of six or nine months or longer per year. A man might have owned a small number of sheep and cattle, and farm a small plot, but he likely spent most of his adult life moving between rural Basutoland and South Africa's industrial cities.

Rich subcultures emerged from migrant labor. Men departing for the mines were reminded of their responsibilities, and of the importance of not squandering their money at the mines on women and alcohol. Migrancy became an important part of masculinity: "Mines make the man," went one popular saying. In Lesotho, migrants developed a sung oral poetry known in the Sotho language as sefela sa litsamaea- naha *(inveterate traveler's songs), which they often performed in bars. These three songs, recorded by the anthropologist David Coplan and reproduced here, speak to the ways that migrant workers understood a world of hard and dangerous labor and of their experience of marginality and manhood.*

1.

It is now that we shall really travel the country;
Men of my home we're in for a forced march.
Distinguished sirs, we travel in a troop;
Poverty has dispersed us from our homes.
I call dogs to go hunting;
The hunters are caught by hunger in the farms.
The plan of traveling men:
Sharpen your sticks; we'll make spears.
Dig out the little mongoose; we need provisions.
Wind from the bushes is piercing us;
It is blowing in the high mountains.

2.

We came to the railway magistrate;
We came and asked him where our deserter's [train] was.
He said it was still in the stable, the favorite cow—
Its herders are still polishing it.
Instantly it came down from Bloemfontein, short-cutting hyena.
You know, I said, sons of my father,
You enter it through sides here;
It's the horse of our distant forefathers;
It was tamed by the Boers, in times of old.
You know, there when young men feared to ride,
I rode it, I, Child of Rakhali.
When that train moved, it performed miracles;
It began to do amazing feats:
Rail spikes popped, joints jumped up and down.
You know, at the sidings it passed in a hurry,
Well, it took notice of no one . . .
. . . When it leaves here, it will run fast—yes, the train.
It showed it was ridden by a wandering man.
When it left, it went wandering,
It went wandering as if it had stolen [something] away.
It coughed as if it might spit;
It murmured as if it would speak.
The train rattled like the dying Chief Makhaola.

You know when it entered Bloemfontein Sengae,
That's when it began to knock [at the door].
The managers in charge at Bloemfontein
Opened all the crossings,
The train showed it was ridden by a true wandering man.
Up spoke the Madam, wife of the whiteman,
"What's wrong with this train?"
"Haeka! It runs Number 17 [too fast]."
You know, a poor Boer was running,
His cap twisted sideways.
A lion was running, its colors [hide] turned inside out,
You know, when it came to the other side,
[To] Tikoe, the European place [mines],
I was saying these whitethorn trees would spear it.
Whitethorns, the train pierced the spear-sharp whitethorns.
A Bushman's ghost jumped from the culvert—With our own eyes we
     saw it;
The ghost of the Bushman was dreadful.
Girls herding there headed for the train to stop it;
It did not even wait.
They insulted it, saying, "You [ass]hole Boer's train."
Do you know where you are filing to?
A madman with iron legs,
Hyena, it rocked side to side.
You listen, my fathers,
My friends, I feel I want to praise a train.
You say a train does not know [appreciate] it?
You come to me, Rakhali's Child;
I may reveal for you things about the train . . .
     . . . It saw Francolins [birds] hopping quickly;
It saw sheep grazing;
It took fright at a hyena and lost the rails.
Its whitemen, you will see they put these iron [blinkers] on its cheeks;
It's so that it gets used to looking down the road.
Why should I speak this way?
My fathers, my parents,
My heart is in pain.

3.

 I am already running long distances:
 I [recite] as long as the cable pulling ore-buckets around the
      scotch—winch.
 I refuse [to empty] into the collecting drum,
 Even back down to the diggings still full.
 These mine compounds, I've long worked them . . .
      . . . What do I say to you, gamblers?
 I am a dog's stomach;
 I don't get cooked.
 I am skin with lice; I am not worn.
 I am a nest of mites; I am not entered.
 I'm like a charge that remained in the ore-face [unexploded]—
      Look, that stopped the drill boy from working.
 Drill boy, I slashed his head;
 Drill guide, I slashed his hand.
 It's then the drill guide started to scold:
 "You, charge-setter; you, timber boy,
 Shut off the water, so you stop the steam.
 These cables have burned us;
 Men's blood is mixed with the stones.

Women's Labour

Olive Schreiner

The politics of the newly formed Union of South Africa mainly concerned native policy aimed at minimizing the cost of African labor, while also denying most rights of citizenship to Africans. At the same time, the South African state denied voting rights to white women until 1930, and the South African economy excluded women from most opportunities in management, business, and professions such as law and medicine, with the feminized exceptions of nursing and teaching. Like her contemporaries in the West, the South African writer Olive Schreiner (1855–1920) argued that the changed economic conditions of an industrial economy had freed women from many of their traditional forms of work but that men prevented women from taking up intellectual work. Schreiner's text, published only two years before African women protested the extension of passes to women in Bloemfontein, is an important early articulation of feminist concerns in South Africa. These racially separate feminist movements would begin to overlap in the nationwide struggle against women's passes in the 1950s (see part VI). Gender discrimination remained entrenched and legal until the enactment of a progressive postapartheid constitution in 1996.

I had always been strangely interested from childhood in watching the condition of the native African women in their primitive society about me. When I was eighteen I had a conversation with a Kaffir woman still in her untouched primitive condition, a conversation which made a more profound impression on my mind than any but one other incident connected with the position of woman has ever done. She was a woman whom I cannot think of otherwise than as a person of genius. In language more eloquent and intense than I have ever heard from the lips of any other woman, she painted the condition of the women of her race; the labour of women, the anguish of woman as she grew older, and the limitations of her life closed in about her, her sufferings under the condition of polygamy and subjection; all this she painted with a passion and intensity I have not known equalled; and yet, and this was the interesting point, when I went on to question her, combined with a deep and almost fierce bitterness against life and the unseen powers which had shaped woman and her conditions as they were, there was not one word of bitterness against the individual man, nor any will or intention to revolt; rather, there was a stern and almost majestic attitude of acceptance of the inevitable; life and the conditions of her race being what they were. It was this conversation which first forced upon me a truth, which I have since come to regard as almost axiomatic, that, the women of no race or class will ever rise in revolt or attempt to bring about a revolutionary readjustment of their relation to their society, however intense their suffering and however clear their perception of it, while the welfare and persistence of their society requires their submission: that, wherever there is a general attempt on the part of the women of any society to readjust their position in it, a close analysis will always show that the changed or changing conditions of that society have made woman's acquiescence no longer necessary or desirable. . . .

In that clamour which has arisen in the modern world, where now this, and then that, is demanded for and by large bodies of modern women, he who listens carefully may detect as a keynote, beneath all the clamour, a demand which may be embodied in such a cry as this: Give us labour and the training which fits for labour! We demand this, not for ourselves alone, but for the race. . . .

Man had his work; we had ours. We knew that we upbore our world on our shoulders; and that through the labour of our hands it was sustained and strengthened—and we were contented. . . .

The changes which have taken place during the last centuries, and which we sum up under the compendious term "modern civilisation," have tended to rob woman, not merely in part but almost wholly, of the more valuable of her ancient domain of productive and social labour; and, where there has not been a determined and conscious resistance on her part, have nowhere spontaneously tended to open out to her new and compensatory fields.

It is this fact which constitutes our modern "Woman's Labour Problem."
. . .

Year by year, day by day, there is a silently working but determined tendency for the sphere of woman's domestic labours to contract itself; and the contraction is marked exactly in proportion as that complex condition which we term "modern civilisation" is advanced. . . .

Every mechanical invention which lessens the necessity for rough, untrained, muscular, human labour, diminishes also the social demand upon woman as the producer in large masses of such labourers. Already throughout the modern civilised world we have reached a point at which the social demand is not merely for human creatures in the bulk for use as beasts of burden, but, rather, and only, for such human creatures as shall be so trained and cultured as to be fitted for the performance of the more complex duties of modern life. . . .

Looking round, then, with the uttermost impartiality we can command, on the entire field of woman's ancient and traditional labours, we find that fully three-fourths of it have shrunk away for ever, and that the remaining fourth still tends to shrink.

It is this great fact, so often and so completely overlooked, which lies as the propelling force behind that vast and restless "Woman's Movement" which marks our day. It is this fact, whether clearly and intellectually grasped, or, as is more often the case, vaguely and painfully felt, which awakes in the hearts of the ablest modern European women their passionate, and at times it would seem almost incoherent, cry for new forms of labour and new fields for the exercise of their powers.

Thrown into strict logical form, our demand is this: We do not ask that the wheels of time should reverse themselves, or the stream of life flow backward. We do not ask that our ancient spinning-wheels be again resuscitated and placed in our hands; we do not demand that our old grindstones and hoes be returned to us, or that man should again betake himself entirely to his ancient province of war and the chase, leaving to us all domestic and civil labour. We do not even demand that society shall immediately so reconstruct itself that every woman may be again a child-bearer (deep and over-mastering as lies the hunger for motherhood in every virile woman's heart!); neither do we demand that the children whom we bear shall again be put exclusively into our hands to train. This, we know, cannot be. The past material conditions of life have gone for ever; no will of man can recall them; but this is our demand: We demand that, in that strange new world that is arising alike upon the man and the woman, where nothing is as it was, and all things are assuming new shapes and relations, that in this new world we also shall have our share of honoured and socially useful human toil, our full half of the labour of the Children of Woman. We demand nothing more than this, and we will take nothing less. This is our "WOMAN'S RIGHT!"

Workers of the World, Unite and Fight for a White South Africa

William Urquhart

White and then black mine workers went on strike in the years immediately follow-ing the creation of the Union of South Africa. Labor unrest continued across much of South Africa, particularly in the 1920s. Tens of thousands of black workers migrated to the gold mines, where they protested wage and labor conditions in a massive strike in 1920; state repression and industry practices, such as migrant-labor recruit-ing and the compound system, would prevent further African mine-worker strikes until 1946. The mines employed nearly twenty-five thousand white workers in the 1910s, when white miners began unionizing, but soon faced volatile world gold prices and rising costs. White workers, particularly Afrikaners, felt threatened by the em-ployment of blacks in semiskilled positions and with the possible weakening of the "colour bar" (under the Mines and Works Act of 1911) within the mining industry, which guaranteed whites the best jobs and vastly higher wages.

In late 1921, the Chamber of Mines began insisting that white wages be reduced, wage rates negotiated, and lower-skilled whites replaced with black workers. The strike and urban revolt that followed lasted for eight weeks. Prime Minister Jan Smuts deployed the military, including twenty thousand troops and aerial bombard-ment, to crush the revolt. More than two hundred people died, including a number of blacks who were hunted down by white workers. The crisis that followed led to the formation of the Pact government in the elections of 1924, recognition of white unions, and an entrenchment of South Africa's colour bar.

When in October, 1921, it became apparent that the gold premium was on the down grade, the crisis that threatened the low grade mines caused grave concern to the industry and the Government. The Government interested itself on behalf of the community in seeing in what directions savings could be effected. In one direction an opening presented itself by which, while avoiding for the time being any drastic cut in remuneration of workers, a saving in cost by means of increase in efficiency might be made. It was found that on several mines native shifts underground were not only not working their full eight hour shift, but were actually two or three hours short, owing to having to wait for the white "baas" [boss]. Experiments had been made on some mines as a result of consultation between the managers and the workers with a view to getting fuller value out of the native shifts. The difficulty in applying this arrangement generally was due to one of the mining regulations which made it incumbent on the white man, as the responsible certificated man in charge, himself to examine and make safe the working places of the native shift before it was allowed to enter and commence work. The work involved in clearing away all dangerous rock from the walls and roof sometimes resulted in a considerable portion of the shift being lost.

After a series of conferences in October and November, 1921 between the Prime Minister [Jan Christian Smuts] and the Chamber of Mines and the Mine Workers, all parties accepted the Prime Minister's proposal for an alteration in the regulation by which in future the examination and making safe of each working place was to be done by a skilled miner working with experienced natives in a previous early morning shift of the natives available for the work of ore production.

In the course of these conferences it was stated by the Prime Minister that the "colour bar" was not to be touched; he was no party to any attack on the colour bar. The Chamber at the same time stated that there were other matters in connection with the working efficiency underground upon which it would require to negotiate with the white miners, such as the employment of whites in the semi-skilled occupations referred to in the *status quo* agreement, contract rates and general organisation of underground work. The Prime Minister expressly stated that these should be subject to subsequent discussion, as he recognised with all others connected with the industry that a large measure of reorganisation of underground work would be necessary to make the low grade mines independent of the rapidly failing gold premium—but in no case was any attack on the colour bar contemplated. Subsequently a further sharp fall in the price of gold in December from 103s. [shillings] 2d. [pence] to 98s. produced a crisis by placing a number of mines in an actual position of non-payability. The working profit made by the gold mines fell from £980,000 in November, 1921, to £680,000 in December. Fifteen mines made a loss or negligible profit.

[In brief, the position was this: the unpayable mines had to be worked more economically or go under, with the immediate result that between 8,000 and 10,000 white men would be thrown out of employment.]

At the end of December, a week after it had fully explained to the Federation the class of men who would be involved by the abandonment of the

status quo agreement, the Chamber of Mines wrote the letter described by
the Federation as an "ultimatum" and by Mr. Tielman Roos, M.L.A. [Member of Legislative Assembly], as "a declaration of war on the workers." It
gave one month's notice of the Chamber's intention "without prejudice to
discussion" to abolish the *status quo* agreement and to reconsider the contract system underground. The Chamber denied that it intended this letter
as an ultimatum. It was the notice which they were bound to give under the
Transvaal law dealing with industrial disputes. . . .

The men's view on this point, as contained in a statement prepared by
a sub-committee of the Federation, was that the chief objection to the contract system lay in the very large earnings of some contractors, often due
not so much to the skill of the men as to the exceptionally good breaking
conditions of the ground. Hence the common saying, "Good ground makes
a good miner." A good man in a bad stope would have difficulty in working his contract at a small profit, whilst a man of much less ability in good
ground might be making large cheques. . . .

Time and again the writer was informed by men along the Reef that if
the Chamber would only annul its decision to cancel the status quo agreement every other difficulty would fly away and industrial peace would be
restored. Whether that result would have ensued or whether the men would
have interpreted the concession as a sign of weakness is open to debate. In
any event the *status quo* was the crux of the whole dispute. One, however,
seldom heard a reference to the *"status quo."* Everywhere the cry was: "The
Chamber of Mines is trying to abolish the colour bar," and amongst the
more ignorant: "The Chamber of Mines is going to work the mines with
kaffirs and give us the push." Along the Reef the strikers were convinced
that it was a fight for their survival on the goldfields, and men amongst
them with ideals spoke freely and feelingly about preserving the heritage
the Voortrekkers had handed down to them and "keeping South Africa a
white man's country." "A White South Africa." That was the slogan of the
leaders and the words were emblazoned in gold on many red banners that
were carried proudly at the head of processions of strikers.

Purity of race

[Any encroachment by coloured people, whether Natives or Indians, either industrially, socially or politically, is quickly resented by people in the
northern provinces of the Union—the Transvaal and Orange Free State.
Had it not been that the Voortrekker, one of the finest types of pioneer the
world has known, had always before him the ideal of preserving the purity
of his race, the backveld would today be peopled by half-castes.] His antipathy to mixing with the black has been inherited by his descendants, except
those whose souls have perished in the slums of Johannesburg.

Politically the colour bar is enforced. Though in the Cape the native enjoys the franchise, in the north he has no representatives in the Union Parliament or Provincial Council; neither body neglects to tax him.

Industrially, the "colour bar" is weakening. His own efficiency, which the native cannot hope to equal for many years, makes the position of the white skilled artisan quite secure. In the field of unskilled or semi-skilled labour the native has the pull, though not the monopoly, because Europeans are continually ousting him: from Government work, as a result of political manoeuvring; from municipal employment, in order that councillors may advertise themselves as upholders of a "White South Africa"; and from the mines, as a result of practice, agreement and regulations. Large numbers of Europeans are in periods of depression also employed on unskilled labour in relief works.

[Will the black man oust or overwhelm the white?]A fear that he will is implied in the hysterical cry of "A White South Africa." In point of fact, considered ethnologically, South Africa is black and has been black right back to legendary days. The Europeans in the country have always been greatly outnumbered, and the native gives no indication of dying out like the Red Indian or Maori. The white man here wants to hold what has been handed down to him by his forefathers. Well, socially the matter is in his own hands. Politically, he may ignore the native until his conscience reproves him, for the natives are incapable of uniting. Industrially, if he had to depend on statutory regulations and political expediency to hold his own, he may as well pack up his tools and quit the country, for these artificial barriers will have crumbled away before his children grow up. The restrictions on native employment on the mines may prove a fruitful source of trouble in the near future. The difficulty cannot be avoided. If the white employees do not create difficulties, the coloured will as they learn to combine industrially. Agitation for removal of the colour bar has begun in the Cape. The friction that has already been produced on the mines between the employers and the miners as a result of these colour restrictions makes one thankful that no parallel regulations apply in the country, where the rule holds good that no farming work shall be done by white labour if cheaper black labour is available.

The leaders of the mining industry have never made an attempt to remove the colour bar on the mines. To put it quite bluntly, they know that it is not practical politics. They are impressed no doubt as much as most other fair-minded Europeans by its economic absurdity and inherent inequity. At the end of December, just before he sailed for England, Sir Lionel Phillips [a South African mine owner] was interviewed by a representative of the *Star* who asked, "Are you in favour of the abolition of the colour bar, Sir Lionel?" "Yes," was the candid reply, "it is both immoral and irrational. While this artificial restriction should disappear in time, I am not in favour of any sweeping or sudden change." This expression of opinion was twisted in various ways to further the suspicion that the mines intended to embark on a policy of wholesale substitution of Europeans by natives. . . .

The idea that there was a conspiracy against the white miner and against the white worker throughout South Africa was sedulously fostered. At Springs, on Saturday, January 14th, Mr. R. Waterston, M.L.A., said that "if the removal of the colour bar went on, native police would replace white." At Boksburg the same day he averred that "If the Chamber of Mines had its way 90 per cent of the white employees would be eliminated by the removal of the status quo." The Rev. Mr. Mullineux, M.L.A., declared that the Chamber was above the law. "It might alter and change at will without regard to the interests of the people. It might lower at once the whole standard of white civilisation."

General [J. B. M.] Hertzog [the National Party leader], speaking to the Strike Committee at Witbank, on January 31st, said: "I understand that one of the main issues is the colour bar, and in regard to this I believe you have the sympathy of 90 per cent of the country people, and will retain it as long as there are no disturbances."

Interviewed on February 9th, General Hertzog said: "The Government has clearly revealed that in truth where it concerns the mines it has no desire to make of South Africa a country where the white man can find an existence, with the exception perhaps of the mine owners. It is scarcely an exaggeration to say that the strike hinges entirely on the question of the colour bar." . . .

The cry of "A White South Africa" pitched in the right key, was more calculated to win sympathy from the farmers than any other. Efforts were made with considerable success to enlist sympathy in the country.

The mine workers undertook a big propaganda movement in the rural districts. A pamphlet printed in Dutch and which was widely distributed, accused the Chamber of Mines of an "artful scheme" to remove the colour bar, and continued:

> Every Afrikander of whatever descent feels that the Chamber of Mines in this respect is going too far, and that the price is too high to pay. It threatens the soul of the nation.
>
> Every Afrikander also feels that in no circumstances can he support the mine owners in this. A lie has to be wrapped up in the mask of truth

and patriotism. If the mine workers decide to strike as a protest against the introduction of such a disgraceful institution, and the Government should support the capitalists, and consequently equal rights for Kaffirs, then any Afrikander with a grain of patriotism in him will keep away out of the struggle rather than go with the Government, because if he goes with the Government the strikers will suffer defeat, with all the resultant consequences that the Kaffir in the future will take up the place of the white man, and then we are doomed to national annihilation.

The first thing will be that the Kaffir, through his equal status with the white man in the industrial domain, will claim his franchise and political equality, and the question is whether, under the circumstances, it would be possible to refuse that.

There are perhaps people who think it will not go as far as that, but, then, who, a couple of years ago, would have thought that the mines would be applying to remove the colour bar?

As the Kaffirs will get higher wages when they start to do the work of white people, they will also take up a certain position in society, with the result that many white girls, embarrassed by the removal of the colour bar, will enter into marriage with coloured people—a danger against which the Afrikander is always fighting.

The agricultural industry will suffer because the demand for their products will decrease in proportion as the white people are replaced by coloured. The whole agricultural industry will suffer the consequences of this, and Kaffir labour on farms will almost become unobtainable.

So the cry of "A White South Africa" convinced the strikers that they were suffering for a noble cause and that they were engaged in a life and death struggle with the Chamber of Mines, while it created an immense amount of sympathy for them throughout the country.

"Man is a creature who lives not upon bread alone, but principally by catchwords." So it may happen that a headline may find the mark when a leading article falls short. Catchwords have sustained revolutions. [Robert Louis] Stevenson said scornfully and truly they were stages on the road to nowhere but second childhood and the grave. A White South African has filled many graves.

The Persecution of Indians

Mohandas K. Gandhi

Indians came to South Africa in the second half of the nineteenth century primarily as indentured laborers for the sugarcane farms of Natal Colony. Most traveled from the southern parts of the subcontinent, with a significant minority from northern areas such as Gujarat. Others arrived independently, many with the hope of establishing businesses that served the Indian communities. Total immigration numbered approximately 150,000 between 1860 and the early 1900s. From Natal, Indians moved elsewhere in South Africa, particularly to cities such as Port Elizabeth, Cape Town, and Johannesburg.

Indians experienced legal discrimination in the South African Republic and Orange Free State as early as the 1880s, with increasing persecution elsewhere in South Africa, especially Natal where they were most numerous. There, in the 1890s, Indians formed the Indian Committee to protect their interests, enlisting the support of the young attorney Mohandas K. Gandhi, who would help found the Natal Indian Congress to protest racial discrimination. In 1915 Gandhi returned to India and introduced his methods of nonviolent resistance, forged in South Africa, to the Indian independence struggle. .

On the seventh or eighth day after my arrival, I left Durban. A first class seat was booked for me. It was usual there to pay five shillings extra, if one needed a bedding. Abdulla Sheth insisted that I should book one bedding but, out of obstinacy and pride and with a view to saving five shillings, I declined. Abdulla Sheth warned me. "Look, now," said he, "this is a different country from India. Thank God, we have enough and to spare. Please do not stint yourself in anything that you may need."

I thanked him and asked him not to be anxious.

The train reached Maritzburg [Pietermaritzburg], the capital of Natal, at about 9 P.M. Beddings used to be provided at this station. A railway servant came and asked me if I wanted one. "No," said I, "I have one with me." He went away. But a passenger came next, and looked me up and down. He saw that I was a "coloured" man. This disturbed him. Out he went and came in again with one or two officials. They all kept quiet, when another official came to me and said, "Come along, you must go to the van compartment."

"But I have a first class ticket," said I.

"That doesn't matter," rejoined the other. "I tell you, you must go to the van compartment."

"I tell you, I was permitted to travel in this compartment at Durban, and I insist on going on in it."

"No, you won't," said the official. "You must leave this compartment, or else I shall have to call a police constable to push you out."

"Yes, you may. I refuse to get out voluntarily."

The constable came. He took me by the hand and pushed me out. My luggage was also taken out. I refused to go to the other compartment and the train steamed away. I went and sat in the waiting room, keeping my hand-bag with me, and leaving the other luggage where it was. The railway authorities had taken charge of it.

It was winter, and winter in the higher regions of South Africa is severely cold. Maritzburg being at a high altitude, the cold was extremely bitter. My over-coat was in my luggage, but I did not dare to ask for it lest I should be insulted again, so I sat and shivered. There was no light in the room. A passenger came in at about midnight and possibly wanted to talk to me. But I was in no mood to talk.

I began to think of my duty. Should I fight for my rights or go back to India, or should I go on to Pretoria without minding the insults, and return to India after finishing the case? It would be cowardice to run back to India without fulfilling my obligation. The hardship to which I was subjected is superficial—only a symptom of the deep disease of colour prejudice. I should try, if possible, to root out the disease and suffer hardships in the process. Redress for wrongs I should seek only to the extent that would be necessary for the removal of the colour prejudice.

So I decided to take the next available train to Pretoria.

The following morning I sent a long telegram to the General Manager of the Railway and also informed Abdulla Sheth, who immediately met the General Manager. The Manager justified the conduct of the railway authorities, but informed him that he had already instructed the Station Master to see that I reached my destination safely. Abdulla Sheth wired to the Indian merchants in Maritzburg and to friends in other places to meet me and look after me. The merchants came to see me at the station and tried to comfort me by narrating their own hardships and explaining that what had happened to me was nothing unusual. They also said that Indians travelling first or second class had to expect trouble from railway officials and white passengers. The day was thus spent in listening to these tales of woe. The evening train arrived. There was a reserved berth for me. I now purchased at Maritzburg the bedding ticket I had refused to book at Durban. . . .

The train reached Charlestown in the morning. There was no railway, in those days, between Charlestown and Johannesburg, but only a stage-coach, which halted at Standerton for the night *en route*. I possessed a ticket for the coach, which was not cancelled by the break of the journey at Maritz-burg for a day; besides, Abdulla Sheth had sent a wire to the coach agent at Charlestown.

But the agent only needed a pretext for putting me off, and so when he discovered me to be a stranger, he said, "Your ticket is cancelled." I gave him the proper reply. The reason at the back of his mind was not want of accom-modation, but quite another. Passengers had to be accommodated inside the coach, but as I was regarded as a "coolie" [a derogatory term for Indians] and looked a stranger, it would be proper, thought the "leader," as the white man in charge of the coach was called, not to seat me with the white pas-sengers. There were seats on either side of the coachbox. The leader sat on one of these as a rule. Today he sat inside and gave me his seat. I knew it was sheer injustice and an insult but I thought it better to pocket it. I could not have forced myself inside, and if I had raised a protest, the coach would have gone off without me. This would have meant the loss of another day, and Heaven only knows what would have happened the next day. So, much as I fretted within myself, I prudently sat next the coachman.

At about three o'clock the coach reached Pardekoph. Now the leader de-sired to sit where I was seated, as he wanted to smoke and possibly to have some fresh air. So he took a piece of dirty sack-cloth from the driver, spread it on the footboard and, addressing me said, "*Sami* [another derogatory term for Indians], you sit on this, I want to sit near the driver." The insult was more than I could bear. In fear and trembling I said to him, "It was you who seated me here, though I should have been accommodated inside. I put up with the insult. Now that you want to sit outside and smoke, you would have me sit at your feet. I will not do so, but I am prepared to sit inside."

As I was struggling through these sentences, the man came down upon me and began heavily to box my ears. He seized me by the arm and tried to drag me down. I clung to the brass rails of the coachbox and was deter-mined to keep my hold even at the risk of breaking my wristbones. The pas-sengers were witnessing the scene—the man swearing at me, dragging and belabouring me, and I remaining still. He was strong and I was weak. Some of the passengers were moved to pity and exclaimed: "Man, let him alone. Don't beat him. He is not to blame. He is right. If he can't stay there, let him come and sit with us." "No fear," cried the man, but he seemed somewhat crestfallen and stopped beating me. He let go my arm, swore at me a little more, and asking the Hottentot servant who was sitting on the other side of the coachbox to sit on the footboard, took the seat so vacated.

The passengers took their seats and, the whistle given, the coach rattled away. My heart was beating fast within my breast, and I was wondering whether I should ever reach my destination alive. The man cast an angry look at me now and then and, pointing his finger at me, growled: "Take care, let me once get to Standerton and I shall show you what I do." I sat speechless and prayed to God to help me. . . .

In the Orange Free State the Indians were deprived of all their rights by a special law enacted in 1888 or even earlier. If they chose to stay there, they could do so only to serve as waiters in hotels or to pursue some other such menial calling. The traders were driven away with a nominal compensation. They made representations and petitions, but in vain.

A very stringent enactment was passed in the Transvaal in 1885. It was slightly amended in 1886, and it was provided under the amended law that all Indians should pay a poll tax of £3 as fee for entry into the Transvaal. They might not own land except in locations set apart for them, and in practice even that was not to be ownership. They had no franchise. All this was under special law for Asiatics, to whom the laws for the coloured people were also applied. Under these latter, Indians might not walk on public footpaths, and might not move out of doors after 9 P.M. without a permit. The enforcement of this last regulation was elastic so far as the Indians were concerned. Those who passed as "Arabs" were, as a matter of favour, exempted from it. The exemption thus naturally depended on the sweet will of the police.

I had to experience the effect of both these regulations. I often went out at night for a walk with Mr. Coates, and we rarely got back home much before ten o'clock. What if the police arrested me? Mr. Coates was more concerned about this than I. He had to issue passes to his Negro servants. But how could he give one to me? Only a master might issue a permit to a servant. If I had wanted one, and even if Mr. Coates had been ready to give it, he could not have done so, for it would have been fraud. . . .

The consequences of the regulation regarding the use of footpaths were rather serious for me. I always went out for a walk through President Street [in Pretoria] to an open plain. President Kruger's house was in this street—a very modest, unostentatious building, without a garden, and not distinguishable from other houses in its neighbourhood. The houses of many of the millionaires in Pretoria were far more pretentious, and were

surrounded by gardens. Indeed President Kruger's simplicity was prover-
bial. Only the presence of a police patrol before the house indicated that it
belonged to some official. I nearly always went along the footpath past this
patrol without the slightest hitch or hindrance.

Now the man on duty used to be changed from time to time. Once one
of these men, without giving me the slightest warning, without even asking me to leave the footpath, pushed and kicked me into the street. I was
dismayed. Before I could question him as to his behaviour, Mr. Coates, who
happened to be passing the spot on horseback, hailed me and said:

"Gandhi, I have seen everything. I shall gladly be your witness in court
if you proceed against the man. I am very sorry you have been so rudely
assaulted."

"You need not be sorry," I said. "What does the poor man know? All
coloured people are the same to him. He no doubt treats Negroes just as
he has treated me. I have made it a rule not to go to court in respect of any
personal grievance. So I do not intend to proceed against him."

"That is just like you," said Mr. Coates, "but do think it over again. We
must teach such men a lesson." He then spoke to the policeman and repri-
manded him. I could not follow their talk, as it was in Dutch, the policeman
being a Boer. But he apologized to me, for which there was no need. I had
already forgiven him. . . .

The incident deepened my feeling for the Indian settlers. I discussed with
them the advisability of making a test case, if it were found necessary to do
so, after having seen the British Agent in the matter of these regulations.

I thus made an intimate study of the hard condition of the Indian settlers,
not only by reading and hearing about it, but by personal experience. I saw
that South Africa was no country for a self-respecting Indian, and my mind
became more and more occupied with the question as to how this state of
things might be improved. . . .

Practice as a lawyer was and remained for me a subordinate occupation.
It was necessary that I should concentrate on public work to justify my stay
in Natal. The despatch of the petition regarding the disfranchising bill was
not sufficient in itself. Sustained agitation was essential for making an impression on the [British] Secretary of State for the Colonies. For this purpose
it was thought necessary to bring into being a permanent organization. So
I consulted Sheth Abdulla and other friends, and we all decided to have a
public organization of a permanent character.

To find out a name to be given to the new organization perplexed me
sorely. It was not to identify itself with any particular party. The name
"Congress," I knew, was in bad odour with the Conservatives in England,

and yet the [Indian National] Congress was the very life of India. I wanted to popularize it in Natal. It savoured of cowardice to hesitate to adopt the name. Therefore, with full explanation of my reasons, I recommended that the organization should be called the Natal Indian Congress, and on the 22nd May [1894] the Natal Indian Congress came into being.

Dada Abdulla's spacious room was packed to the full on that day. The Congress received the enthusiastic approval of all present. Its constitution was simple, the subscription was heavy. Only he who paid five shillings monthly could be a member. The well-to-do classes were persuaded to subscribe as much as they could. Abdulla Sheth headed the list with £2 per month. Two other friends also put down the same. I thought I should not stint my subscription, and put down a pound per month. This was for me no small amount. But I thought that it would not be beyond my means, if at all I was to pay my way. And God helped me. We thus got a considerable number of members who subscribed £1 per month. The number of those who put down 10 s. [shillings] was even larger. . . . The Colonial-born Indian Educational Association was founded under the auspices of the Congress. The members consisted mostly of these educated youths. They had to pay a nominal subscription. The Association served to ventilate their needs and grievances, to stimulate thought amongst them, to bring them into touch with Indian merchants and also to afford them scope for service of the community. It was a sort of debating society. The members met regularly and spoke or read papers on different subjects. A small library was also opened in connection with the Association. . . .

In the same year, 1894, the Natal Government sought to impose an annual tax of £25 on the indentured Indians. The proposal astonished me. I put the matter before the Congress for discussion, and it was immediately resolved to organize the necessary opposition.

At the outset I must explain briefly the genesis of the tax.

About the year 1860 the Europeans in Natal, finding that there was considerable scope for sugarcane cultivation, felt themselves in need of labour. Without outside labor the cultivation of cane and the manufacture of sugar were impossible, as the Natal Zulus were not suited to this form of work. The Natal Government therefore corresponded with the Indian Government, and secured their permission to recruit Indian labour. These recruits were to sign an indenture to work in Natal for five years, and at the end of the term they were to be at liberty to settle there and to have full rights of ownership of land. Those were the inducements held out to them, for the white then had looked forward to improving their agriculture by the industry of the Indian labourers after the term of their indentures had expired.

But the Indians gave more than had been expected of them. They grew large quantities of vegetables. They introduced a number of Indian varieties and made it possible to grow the local varieties cheaper. They also introduced the mango. Nor did their enterprise stop at agriculture. They entered trade. They purchased land for buildings, and many raised themselves from the status of labourers to that of owners of land and houses. Merchants from India followed them and settled there for trade. . . .

The white traders were alarmed. When they first welcomed the Indian labourers, they had not reckoned with their business skill. They might be tolerated as independent agriculturists, but their competition in trade could not be brooked.

This sowed the seed of the antagonism to Indians. Many other factors contributed to its growth. Our different ways of living, our simplicity, our contentment with small gains, our indifference to the laws of hygiene and sanitation, our slowness in keeping our surroundings clean and tidy, and our stinginess in keeping our houses in good repair—all these, combined with the difference in religion, contributed to fan the flame of antagonism. Through legislation this antagonism found its expression in the disenfranchising bill and the bill to impose a tax on the indentured Indians. Independent of legislation a number of pinpricks had already been started.

The first suggestion was that the Indian labourers should be forcibly repatriated, so that the term of their indentures might expire in India. The [British] Government of India was not likely to accept the suggestion. Another proposal was therefore made to the effect that

1. the indentured labourer should return to India on the expiry of his indenture; or that
2. he should sign a fresh indenture every two years, an increment being given at each renewal; and that
3. in the case of his refusal to return to India or renew the indenture he should pay an annual tax of £25.

A deputation composed of Sir Henry Binns and Mr. Mason was sent to India to get the proposal approved by the Government there. The Viceroy at that time was Lord Elgin. He disapproved of the £25 tax, but agreed to a poll tax of £3. I thought then, as I do even now, that this was a serious blunder on the part of the Viceroy. In giving his approval he had in no way thought of the interests of India. It was no part of his duty thus to accommodate the Natal Europeans. In the course of three or four years an indentured labourer with his wife and each male child over 16 and female child over 13 came under the impost. To levy a yearly tax of £12 from a family of four—

husband, wife and two children—when the average income of the husband was never more than 14s. a month, was atrocious and unknown anywhere else in the world.

We organized a fierce campaign against this tax. If the Natal Indian Congress had remained silent on the subject, the Viceroy might have approved of even the £25 tax. The reduction from £25 to £3 was probably due solely to the Congress agitation. But I may be mistaken in thinking so. It may be possible that the Indian Government had disapproved of the £25 tax from the beginning and reduced it to £3, irrespective of the opposition from the Congress. In any case it was a breach of trust on the part of the Indian Government. As trustee of the welfare of India, the Viceroy ought never to have approved of this inhuman tax.

The Congress could not regard it as any great achievement to have succeeded in getting the tax reduced from £25 to £3. The regret was still there that it had not completely safeguarded the interests of the indentured Indians. It ever remained its determination to get the tax remitted, but it was twenty years before the determination was realized.[And when it was realized, it came as a result of the labours of not only the Natal Indians but of all the Indians in South Africa. . . .]

But truth triumphed in the end. The sufferings of the Indians were the expression of that truth. Yet it would not have triumphed except for the unflinching faith, great patience and incessant effort. Had the community given up the struggle, had the Congress abandoned the campaign and submitted to the tax as inevitable, the hated impost would have continued to be levied from the indentured Indians until this day, to the eternal shame of the Indians in South Africa and of the whole of India.

The Journey to Pretoria

Naboth Mokgatle

Descended from the paramount chief of the Bakwena, Naboth Mokgatle (1911–85) grew up in poverty in Phokeng, a small town in what would become the Bophuthatswana homeland and what is today North West Province. In 1930 Mokgatle moved to Pretoria, where he began a long career as a political activist, trade unionist, and writer, beginning with an antipass campaign that year. The pass system required African men to carry a document with them at all times, specifying their employment and residence while working in "white" South Africa. The system became one of the most powerful ways that the state enforced racial segregation. The first pass laws began in the mid-eighteenth century as a way of controlling the movement of slaves. They were extended to Africans particularly in the following century and were constantly updated until their repeal in 1986. With the entrenchment of segregation under apartheid in the 1950s, officials extended the "dom pas" or "dumb pass" system to black women and to Indians.

Mokgatle, who was increasingly hounded by the police for his political activities and banned between 1952 and 1954, went into exile and settled in London, where he lived until his death three decades later. The Autobiography of an Unknown South African forms part of a genre of autobiographical writings by black South Africans, including for instance Nelson Mandela's, that recount the experience of urbanization and their political awakening. In this selection Mokgatle recounts his early days in Pretoria during the height of segregation. The 1920s and early 1930s also marked a moment of black radicalization with the spread of Garveyism and the meteoric rise of the Industrial and Commercial Workers' Union.

The Urban Areas Act forbids Africans in the urban areas from making or brewing beer to their own natural tastes, to drink it or possess it in their homes without the permission of the municipality under which they live. When I arrived in Pretoria I knew nothing about this, I had no idea that it placed me and my life at the mercy of the European native commissioners. We walked to where my friend lived. When we got near the place I began to see a large concentration of Africans moving about. We were in the area of

"Pretoria Municipal Unmarried" compounds, for men without their wives in Pretoria. There were three large buildings, all of them compounds. The street was called Proes Street, in the area called Pretoria West. It was not outside Pretoria, but in the centre, towards the south, next to the old European grave-yard and next to a location for coloured people and Indians called the Cape Location or Reserve, or the Indian Bazaar.

On the northern side of Proes Street was the Municipal African Workmen's Hostel, where men were housed rent-free and women were not allowed. Next to it was a large block consisting of rooms let out to Africans employed in Pretoria paying monthly rents. Non-residents and women were not allowed, especially women. Male visitors could go in provided they obtained a permit at the office which was at the entrance. All the rooms were communal; tenants only hired a concrete bunk and they lived twelve in a room, six sleeping on each side. At the end of the room facing the door were large steel cabinets where they stored their belongings.

There was also a communal kitchen where they cooked their meals. At night the municipal police had to go round to see that no strangers were being given shelter in the rooms. On the west side of Proes Street right opposite was another large building, the reception depot. Strangers to Pretoria like myself were required to sleep there until they had found jobs and obtained places for themselves. I knew nothing about all that. My friend was an occupant of the hostel, where he paid rent. He occupied a room with two other tribesmen of ours, both my close relatives, whom I did not know were in Pretoria. They were Godfrey Mokgatle and his brother Mafito. The three of them took me in as their guest and obtained a permit for me to be with them for several hours. They gave me a tasty meal but before ten o'clock, the time when both the gates of the hostel and the reception depot were shut, they told me that they had to take me to the reception depot.

I was disheartened but I had no choice. At the reception depot, where they took me, the man in charge was from another tribe married to a girl of our tribe and friendly to everyone from our tribe because of his wife. His name was Mogotsi. He was not employed by Pretoria Municipality but by the Native Commissioner's Department. He was a policeman. They introduced me to Mogotsi and left. After taking me in he asked me if I knew his wife's people, which I did. He then took me to a room, showed me an empty concrete bunk in a room full of completely strange men from nearly all the tribes in the country. He then warned me to be careful with my belongings because others might help themselves to them. The building was double-storeyed and full of men seeking work. Mogotsi instructed me to be early at the reception office next morning with my blankets and other things neatly

Thokoza Hostel, East Rand, November 1980, © BAHA, photograph by Drum Photographer, dm2001082014. Used by permission of Bailey's African History Archive (BAHA).

folded for safe keeping, and for a rubber stamp showing that I had spent the night at the reception depot as required by law. Without such a stamp on my travelling pass or on my native commissioner's permit to seek work, the police could arrest me and get me charged for not having spent the night at the reception depot.

That was an eye-opener for me. At last I began to realise that I was in the white man's place, as Dan Branke had remarked earlier in my adult life.

Municipal hostels and reception depots for unmarried African workmen, the direct results of the Native Urban Areas Act of 1923, are instruments designed purely to put into operation the doctrine of Apartheid. Before its introduction, African workmen—who are largely migrants from tribes—who went into towns and cities to seek work, leaving their families behind, were housed by their employers close to their places of work. They lived in the centre of cities and towns, but the authorities, who are always the first to incite the European population into thinking that Africans living next to them are a menace and ought to be removed far away from the areas defined as European areas, began to make a law by which they could compel the municipalities to build such hostels and reception depots. They then arrested Africans if they failed to sleep there, or for trespassing into European residential areas.

Nineteen-thirty was a year of depression. Many Africans were out of work and could not find any; some of them were thrown out of their jobs to make room for European workers. Hard manual jobs like working on the railways, road making, digging trenches and sweeping streets, which were considered suitable for Africans only were taken away from them and given to the Europeans. In cities like Pretoria where I lived, the authorities were even inciting European families to boycott factories, bakeries, butcher shops, laundries and others which kept on employing African labour instead of European labour. Notices appeared in the windows of many places stating that the work done there was only by white labour.

Being placed in such a situation, I was faced along with many others with the dilemma of being arrested for being in a European city without work. An African seeking work was allowed fourteen days within which to find it, and after that the local native commissioner was entitled to refuse him another chance to try his luck. Once your pass was stamped with a refusal stamp you knew that your next home would be the police cell. The next morning you would be before the same native commissioner who refused you a chance, and you would be sent to prison if you could not pay the fine.

. . .

I was about to celebrate my twentieth birthday, but when I left Rustenburg the native commissioner's official, without asking my age, stamped my travelling pass "Not Liable for Tax." When Mr. Malherbe in Pretoria issued me with a permit to seek work, he also stamped my pass with his large stamp "Not Liable for Tax." In fact I ought to have been liable when I was eighteen, but because of that stamp I did not pay poll tax until I was twenty-three. Armed with a permit to seek work I went to Nchotlho Diale's place for lunch and to start my future in Pretoria. I didn't know that one of my school friends from another tribe who had been sent to Phokeng by his parents to learn English was also in Pretoria working. Diale told me of him, gave me his address and told me how to get there. After lunch I set out to find my friend Titus Diphoko. I found him working for a butcher in Esselen Street, Sunnyside. He was out collecting orders but I was told to wait, that he would arrive at any time.

I did not wait long before Titus Diphoko arrived to find me, leaning against his master's shop. Surprise was coupled with happiness. After laughs and warm handshakes he invited me into the yard to introduce me to his fellow workers who were all from tribes far away from Rustenburg. Their master, Mr. Herbert George How, was having an afternoon sleep and was due to get up at four o' clock to see that everything was in order for the next day. Mr. How was a fairly old man who, I was told, came to South Africa during the Anglo-Boer war, decided to stay, married a Dutch woman, but never bothered to learn the language. He understood everything said in it but always replied in English. Titus and Phoshoko Thsetla were the only two who spoke English among the African workers, who numbered more than fifteen. Both Titus and Phoshoko agreed to introduce me to their master to see if he could give me a job. When he got up and found me amongst his men he asked what I was doing there. Titus explained that I was looking for a job. "Can he speak English?" Mr. How asked. I replied, "Yes, sir, I can." That was enough. . . .

I worked ten months for Mr. How, but his insistence that I should wait for the wholesalers and cook dripping while others went freely where they liked, and do the Sunday work in the tennis court, forced me to give him notice to leave his employ at the end of July nineteen-thirty-one. It seems to me, looking back, that August was a month of movements for me. I left Mr. How's employ at the beginning of the month after struggling for my release for four days. I refused to change my mind when he urged me to, saying that in future he would see that we took turns in cooking the dripping. I was, in addition, tired of getting up early in the mornings and hoped to find a job where I could get up later than four o'clock. Reluctantly, after first refusing to sign off my pass, he did so and threw it at me, saying, "Don't come here again."

During November nineteen-thirty, when I had been in Pretoria two months, I undertook a journey one Sunday to find my mother's cousin who lived in one of Pretoria's African locations, Bantule. When I left home Mother had told me to search for her so that when I experienced difficulties I could call on her for help. From Sunnyside to Bantule was a long walk, and as we were not allowed to use delivery bicycles on Sundays I had to start early to get there, find her and stay with her before returning to my place of work.

I did not reach Bantule that day as I intended to. On the way, walking westward through the old and famous African location Marabastad and the Indian Bazaar (on open ground at the end of Boom Street) at about two o'clock in the afternoon, I saw a large gathering of people with police nearby, some standing next to their motor-cycles. I went to see what was taking place. For the first time I attended a political meeting, but I had no idea that was what it was. I found four groups holding a joint open-air meeting. They were the African National Congress, the ICU (the Industrial and Commercial Workers' Union of Africa), the Radicals and the Garveyites. The speakers were taking turns delivering their addresses. The ICU were represented by Ismael Moroe, the Radicals by George Daniels, the Garvey-

A. W. G. Champion
(left), head of the ICU
in Natal, and the ICU
founder Clements
Kadalie (right), n.d.,
© BAHA, photograph
by Drum Photographer,
dm2001052105. Used by
permission of Bailey's
African History Archive
(BAHA).

ites by a man whose name was also Garvey, a follower and admirer of Mar-
cus Garvey, and the Congress by Simon Peter Matseke, who later became
President of Congress in the Transvaal.

Their theme was the burning of passes by Africans on the sixteenth of
December nineteen-thirty, Dingaan's day. Such agitation against the passes
was in full swing in all major cities of the country. The emphasis was that
on that day all Africans must burn their passes and never carry them again.
The police were taking notes, and the speakers were speaking in very high
tones charged with high emotions. I was surprised by the bravery displayed
in the presence of the police. The speech which impressed me most was
made by the Radical, George Daniel.

[J. B. M.] Hertzog's government was in power at the time and his minister of justice was Oswald Pirow, the man who prosecuted in the famous
treason trial [see part VI] of nineteen-fifty-six. During his speech Daniels
said, and repeated it three times, "Pirow, Pirow, Pirow, I am not going to

call him Minister of Justice, but Minister of Injustice." He went on to attack Hertzog, his government, Pirow and the whole system of pass laws, urging every African present to respond to the call to burn the passes on the day. While he went on I expected the police to rush to arrest him for saying such things against the government and those who were running it. Nothing of the kind happened. Daniels' speech and attacks inspired me greatly and I did not leave the meeting until darkness had fallen and everyone dispersed. Bantule was not far away, I could see it on the hill to the north-west of where I attended the meeting, but I returned without having reached it.

The day on which the passes were to be burnt remained in my memory, and I made sure that I remembered it, so that I too should be there to throw my pass into the flames. I did not attend further meetings after that but on the sixteenth of December I left my place of work, telling the others that I was going to visit my aunt. I listened to my fellow-workers discussing the burning of passes, but all warned that if you burn your pass the police will arrest you and those who urged you to burn it will do nothing for you. But I remained convinced that if I did burn my pass I would have freed myself from the pass system. I never told my friends that I was going to burn my pass on that day. Dingaan's Day was a public holiday in South Africa at that time and I went carrying my monthly contract pass with me but forgetting that its duplicate was with Mr. How. I got there in good time before the ceremony and a large number of Africans turned up, but I think that the majority were the unemployed and those who were refused a chance to seek work who were eager to get rid of their passes because they were exposing them to the police. The meeting started with singing the African national anthem, Nkosi-Sekele-Africa, and thereafter the burning started in the presence of the police. As I threw my pass into the flames with the others, Hertzog and Pirow's effigies were also held in the flames. Compared with the number of Africans employed and living in Pretoria those of us who performed the burning were like a tiny drop in the ocean.

After the burning, columns of passless Africans were rounded up by the police in the streets, arrested, brought before the native commissioner's court, charged for being without lawful documents, and some spent days and weeks in prison. All pleaded the loss of their passes, including myself. With me it was easy because of the duplicate which Mr. How held, and I got another one. Some who went to prison came back with prison documents and the lucky ones got permits to search for work once more. Some had a very hard time and had to go back to their tribal homes to go through the old procedure of making their way back to Pretoria and other cities and towns. I never told my friends or Mr. How that I was a pass-burner.

It may be said that it was a useless effort, but I have always held the view that, though the burning did not in any way mean the ending of the pass system, if only the Africans had made a gesture by burning some of their papers they would have demonstrated their hatred for the badge of slavery, the pass, which restricted their movements since its inception. The pass denies the African privacy, choice, dignity, movement and everything which makes a man. . . .

Township Life, Marabastad, Pretoria

Es'kia Mphahlele

Es'kia Mphahlele (1919–2008) ended up in exile because of his political activities, as did many of the country's black writers. Banned from teaching in 1951, Mphahlele left South Africa in 1957 before returning two decades later, when he took up a position at the University of the Witwatersrand in Johannesburg. Mphahlele published his first fiction in 1947. In the 1950s he helped edit the hugely important magazine Drum. *Mphahlele's writings influenced later generations of black intellectuals. In this selection, Mphahlele describes life in Marabastad ("Maraba City," named after Pedi Chief Maraba), one of the rough-and-tumble slums near the center of Pretoria: amalaita gangs (often male migrant domestic workers), African independent churches, American jazz and movies, and especially the exuberant marabi (a type of music) world that emerged in and around the shebeens (illegal bars).*

Like many townships in the first half of the twentieth century, such as Sophiatown and District Six, ethnic and racial diversity characterized Marabastad, including a sizeable Indian population. Particularly in the 1940s, the state began relocating Africans and Coloureds to racially defined townships outside the city center. This racial gerrymandering would accelerate throughout South Africa during the apartheid era.

We were getting used to Second Avenue life, my brother, sister and I. Avenues and streets were new to us. Now why would people go and build houses all in a straight line? Why would people go to a bucket in a small building to relieve themselves? Why would people want to be cut off from one another by putting up fences? It wasn't so at Maupaneng. Houses didn't stand in any order and we visited one another and could sit round the communal fire and tell one another stories until the cocks crowed. Not in Second Avenue. And yet, although people didn't seem to be interested in one another, they spoke with a subtle unity of voice. They still behaved as a community. . . .

Here the young men who migrate to the cities to work still fight as they did on moonlight nights in the country. And so every Sunday afternoon they march with big broad slabs of human flesh they called feet to some place outside the city. They moved in rival teams. In Pretoria these "Malaita" were provided with a piece of ground and they marched under police guard. In this way, the "Natives let off steam," as the Pretoria City Council said.

Our house faced Barber Street. It was a family recreation to sit on the veranda on Sunday afternoons. The malaita beat on the tar with their large feet past our house; the police dispersed in front of our house before going each to his beat; visiting domestic workers from the suburbs passed our house before they swept into the location, and passed in front of our house again on their way out. It was a common Sunday afternoon spectacle for a policeman to pass in front of our house propelling a man by the scruff of the neck to the police-station. Women particularly fascinated us in their various styles of dress. Some hobbled past in awkward high heels, evidently feeling the pinch; others were really smart [well-dressed] and enviable.

Our fence needed constant pulling up because it was always falling. Grandmother said how she wanted to plant flowers. We tried valiantly, but none of us had the guts to fetch water for the plants. We gave it up. The best we ever got to doing was set up a grape-vine creeper which made pleasant shade for the family to do washing. The rusty iron gate was a particular nuisance. The ants kept eating up the standards underneath, and we kept digging in the poles until we, the gate and everything else about it resigned ourselves to an acute angle and we piled stones around the standards to maintain the *status quo*. We swept the yard, however, a ten-foot border on all sides of the corrugated walls. The women made a lovely path from the gate to the front door, branching off to the back of the house. This was skirted on either side by small mud walls, and the floor was paved with mud smoothened with a slippery stone and then smeared with dung. Small pebbles had been worked in repeated triangular patterns. A small wall separated this path from our ash dump, where we constantly scratched for coke to use again in our braziers. The ash we then poured into the garbage can. Towards the front end of our yard, facing Barber Street and Second Avenue, we often planted maize. From this patch we harvested exactly seven cobs most years. We, the smaller members of the family, netted half a cob each. Our backyard was fenced with a four-foot mud wall. The floor of the yard was paved with mud because that was where we cooked—we and the tenants in the two back rooms. These rooms, together with our passage that ran from the back to the front doors, opened on to a small veranda. This we used as a kitchen in the winter. Our kitchen table stood at a corner, for as long as I can remember, where we had found it when we came from Pietersburg. The floor of this porch, not more than six feet deep, was laid in broken

Zulu traditional healers with their medicines, Durban, 1945. Photographer unknown. Courtesy of Campbell Collections of the University of KwaZulu-Natal, D7/159.

uneven slabs of slate. No matter how hard we scrubbed the slabs, there were always spots of candle wax which stuck out like carbuncles.

At another corner Mathebula kept his blankets and the sack on which he slept on a soap box. He slept in the porch. He was a witch doctor and had dropped in one day to ask for shelter. It turned out that he had come from Shanganaland in the north and was homeless. Grandmother had kept him. The ash around the fire-place was a perennial problem. The corrugated-iron walls were always sooty, except towards the edge of the porch, where Chipile, the Indian soft-goods hawker, often penciled his invoice. At one end of the backyard Mathebula could be seen any morning sitting on a mat, his bones scattered in front of him while he mumbled magic words in Shangana. All of us, visitors alike, tried, as much as room allowed, to move clear of Mathebula's sphere of influence.

I did most of the domestic work because my sister and brother were still too small. My uncles were considered too big. I woke up at 4.30 in the morning to make fire in a brazier fashioned out of an old lavatory bucket. I washed, made breakfast coffee for the family and tea for grandmother as she did not take coffee. "That's how I stopped taking coffee," said grandmother, telling us the story of how when she was a girl, someone hit her with a stone and drew blood from the temple. She had picked up the stone and a witch doctor had treated it with some medicines, but this hadn't helped because since then she was unable to eat beef or drink coffee. They made her so sick.

After morning coffee, which we often had with mealie-meal porridge from the previous night's left-overs, we went to school. Back from school I had to clean the house as Aunt Dora and grandmother did the white people's washing all day. Fire had to be made, meat had to be bought from an Indian butchery in the Asiatic Reserve. We were so many in the family that I had to cook porridge twice in the same big pot. We hardly ever bought more than a pound of mutton in weight. Weekdays supper was very simple: just porridge and meat. When there was no money we fried tomatoes. We never ate vegetables except on Sundays. We never had butter except when we had a visitor from Johannesburg. Same with custard. And then I don't remember ever seeing a pound of butter. We bought a tickey's—three pence worth—when we did. On such days we, the children, made a queue to have grandmother smear a sparing layer of butter on one slice only of bread.

At breakfast bread was cut up. The grown-ups were given theirs first in saucers. Then I rationed the remainder in slices and bits of slices. Our youngest uncle, not much older than I, picked his first, which was the greatest quantity. Then I followed, and my brother and then my sister. We ate supper out of the same plate, we children, and meat was dished out in varying sizes and the ritual was repeated. We never sat at table. Only a visitor was treated to such modern innovations.

On Monday mornings, at about four o'clock, I started off for the suburbs to fetch washing for Aunt Dora. Thursday and Friday afternoons I had to take back the washing. If I was lucky enough I borrowed a bicycle from a tenant of ours we called simply "Oompie"—uncle—when he was not using it on his rounds in the location collecting numbers from gamblers for the Chinaman's fah fee [number game]. If I couldn't get the bicycle for the morning or afternoon I carried the bundles on my head and walked—about seven miles' single journey. Like all the other tenants, Oompie sometimes quarrelled with grandmother over tidiness. I was sure, then, that I wasn't going to get the bicycle. When I walked I couldn't use the pair of tennis shoes I'd been bought for Sunday wear. Winter mornings were most trying when the air penetrated the big cracks round the edges of my feet.

When I came back I went to school, I could never do my homework until about ten o'clock at night when I had washed up and everybody else had gone to bed. We all slept in the same room which had boxes of clothing and a kitchen dresser. My aunt and her husband slept in the room which had a table and chairs.

Because we were so many in the family, there was only one bedstead—a three-quarter institution occupied by grandmother and Aunt Dora's children. The wooden floor of the room we slept in had two large holes. There was always a sharp young draught coming up from underneath the floor. Coupled with this our heads were a playground for mice which also did havoc on food and clothing.

Sometimes I stole cooked meat and put it in my pocket. I forgot all about it until I was reminded by a large hole in the pocket where our night visitors had celebrated their jubilee. Early winter mornings a large cold drop of water fell on your cheek or into your ear from the iron roof and you woke up with a start. The only window there was misty because it had been shut all night. You heard the sharp whistle of the regular steam train passing, from Pietersburg. You heard the coal-black Nyasa police corporal yell his drill commands on the police station premises in First Avenue. You also heard his whistle. Soon, you knew, they'd be marching with heavy booted strides up Barber Street, past our house. Then they'd stop and disperse to yet another yell, and go each to his own beat on the row of Indian and Chinese shops facing the location. They hardly ever entered the location on their regular beats. If all this happened while you were in bed you knew you were late in getting out of the blankets and the rest of the morning was going to be a headlong rush to the accompaniment of grandmother's mumblings and moanings. You soon learned that it was never wise to leave a window open in Marabastad, even on thick mothy summer nights. We were always scared of burglars and what grandmother called "wicked night-prowlers who've no respect for creatures made in the image of God." These were witches. . . .

For all that it mattered, the depression of the early thirties did not seem on the surface to add an ounce of pressure more to the poverty of the Black man.

We still had one tarred street for the police to patrol and for the white superintendent of the location to drive his sleek shining car along. There were still a few electric lights dotted about street corners and none in the houses; the smell from the sewerage centre in the plantation below us still came in a suffocating wave. Of course fewer of us went to the Dougall Hall bioscope [movie theater] because the market and the gold links were scantier and the white people didn't want to pay as much as they used to. They brought the price down from nine pence to six pence for carrying vegetables five miles to Sunnyside suburb. Children still squatted in the street to relieve themselves, chicken still came to peck at the stools with relish.

There was much less to eat at home, and boys and girls of our age group raided Indian hawkers' backyards for discarded fruits, bread and vegetables in garbage bins. But then we had always done that after school. We planned our strategy of entering through the back gate. Some of the hawkers were vicious with the sjambok [whip], especially Cassim Hassim. Some of the women connived at our acts; others poured rice crust and water on us from the balconies, just to have a laugh. Often we looked up to the balconies and laughed with them while we shook down rice grains from out of our shirts. We returned to rummage again. Little Links and Danie, the noisiest boy down Second Avenue whom we could seldom trust to "pull off a job" with a sense of duty becoming a Fox, raided one yard. Ratau and China went to Moosa's wholesale establishment for "tin-my-Moosa." This meant they would ask Moosa to off-load vats of bananas from a truck and get a tin of black-skinned overripe bananas for it. Ratau was the quietest and steadiest of us and said little; China came of parents who always dressed smartly and were reputed to be well off. For Ratau this was a "decent" assignment, and for China—a kind of sport. Moloi and Issac, the round-faced boy who came from Bantule, another location two miles away, and I, struck elsewhere. Issac attended school with us and preferred to play with the Foxes. And so we fanned out over the Asiatic Bazaar.

At the end of the raid we met at the river, just below the police station, with a good haul of oranges, sponspecks [cantaloupes], carrots, tomatoes, bananas and other items: all rotten in parts. We went to the tap at the corner of the police tennis court and washed off as much rot as we could. After the meal we got dry sticks and ran them the whole length of the corrugated-iron wall of Fung Prak, the Chinaman's yard. He made malt and sold it to the local shops for illicit home beer-brewing in the locations. Our little game annoyed his vicious bulldog inside and it followed the rat-tat-tat, barking ineffectually all the time. There were days when we divided the booty and took it home.

Twice a week we took sacks and made a long journey to the municipal ash dump in the last suburb west of town. There we scratched and scrounged for coke for use in our home braziers. We came back all white with ash. And when we washed our cracked scaly feet, we felt like dancing a jig from the stinging pain when the feet dried.

It was during those years that I began to regard the Indian as someone who was also privileged to have more money than us or the Coloured people. He traded among us, and yet he kept aloof from our sufferings, unmoved by them. He appeared to me, in those years, as somebody who could never suffer; who didn't die; who couldn't cry or care. We laughed and joked with him in his shop; he played with the breasts of some of our girls just to annoy them; we called each other pet names; but it seemed that we could never project ourselves into each other's lives and share certain things. But then we didn't care to. The Chinaman, on the other hand, was a surly, disgruntled creature who just dragged his feet about and moved with a sinister stoop. How could we not believe our parents when they told us never to venture beyond the counter of a Chinaman's shop because he ate human flesh? Fung Prak's tiny wife would stand on her veranda until customers came in. She stood there, her arms folded, laughing at the heavy-booted African policemen marching past, their buttocks stretching the slit at the back of the coat. She hardly had any buttocks. There she was, her lower teeth receding as her upper row was advancing; and as she turned to walk into the shop the hem of her dress clung to the woollen stockings, on one leg and then on the other.

I couldn't consciously probe into the attitudes of the Asiatics; I simply felt a barrier beyond a certain point of contact.

There were other and deeper changes at work in Marabastad, in Bantule to the west of us, in Lady Selborne, six miles farther, in Cape Location next to the Asiatic Bazaar, and in the peri-urban locations east of town. Boys of our age were getting rough and knife-happy. Scores of them left school and joined the won't-works and some of those who had lost their jobs. They stood about on shop verandas, made rude jokes and guffawed with broken voices, chewed bubble-gum impudently and smoked insolently. Boeta Lem (Brother Blade) from down our street easily collected a nice bunch of hangers-on about him. They hero-worshipped him as an ex-convict. They brought him food and money from their homes. They spoke a lot about the wonderful performance of their counterparts "on the Rand." Somewhere in the Golden City, we felt, big evil things were going on. And our parents blamed it all on this mystical bond.

"If I see you again listening to what that Boeta Lem says, I'll chop your neck into pieces, pieces, pieces with an axe!" grandmother warned us. "He's a heathen, his mouth smells like the sewerage down in those trees. His father can't do a thing with him any more, and heathen too, if you want to know. All he does is sit there in his house, kill lice between his nails just because his son would rather go about sweeping God's streets with his tattered trousers and go about rooting in garbage cans instead of working. He doesn't even know which way the church door's facing by Titus who lies in his grave. Both of them will soon be eating rats and dogs." Titus was my grandpa, her late husband.

Marabastad seemed to be turning inside out, showing all her dirty underwear. "The world is coming to an end," grandmother said with a sigh, "as sure as Titus sleeps in his grave. What we see today is a sign of God's anger. When I was young there wasn't so much hate; boys and girls didn't insult their elders like this; and we helped one another during famine. The world is nearing an end." She frightened me that way.

"Nonsense, Hibila," Old Rametse from the lower end of the street said, "this is the beginning of a new world. I worked for a white farmer, Van Wyk his name was. 'Petros,' he used to say, 'listen here, Outa, if ever your children go to the city, know it's the end of them. My son Koos is long gone, and now Grieta is going, and I know they're lost. But thank God in the heavens they come of an upright and God-fearing house. If they throw away their Bible teaching, God forgive them. I've written to Dominee [pastor] Brink at the Groote Kerk [church] to look after them.'" Old Rametse chuckled.

> Ah, Hibila, that Van Wyk was a kind man but still a big Baas. I've been here now—let me see—ten plus five years—how many?—fifteen, and only last year I saw young Koos in town with a girl hanging on his arm. They were both drunk but not so bad. He's a fellow with a big shadow now, and you think he'd know me? Ha-ha, I stopped him and I said, Greetings, Kleinbaas [little boss], remember Petros from the farm? I saw in those eyes that he remembered me, but he said, "Get out of my way, Kaffir!" and he passed on. Now I ask you, Hibila, if the white man goes on like this and he has everything, farms money, good clothes, clean face, what were you and I—we who live on borrowed things? Give me that mug of coffee, my boy.

It was a special privilege he enjoyed, to be given coffee in our home. When I wasn't feeling so good, as often happened when he was around, he reminded me.

"Borrowed things, borrowed things," Aunt Dora said after he had left. "He thinks we were born yesterday. Everybody knows he has a lot of money hidden somewhere. And yet such a miser too. Look at the khaki clothes he wears—a man with so much money."

No one really knew how rich old Rametse was, if that was true. But people spoke of it as a fact. A few days later he came to our house waving his arms madly. "You've never seen such a thing. That *skelm* [rascal] has done it again. It's me this time. Son of a rat, son of a pig, son of a heathen, son of a baboon, son of a crocodile without a name, son of a runaway mother!"

"Who's that?" grandmother asked.

"That piece of filth called Boeta Lem. Stole all my money from under my mattress. My woman saw him, saw him run out of the house, saw him with her eyes. I've worked for years for my money, long before his mother carried that lump of sin in the womb. His hands are getting mouldy in his pockets because instead of doing honest work he wants to ruin other people. Little Shepherd, he has taken my life away with the money!"

"Go to the police station," Aunt Dora suggested.

"Where do you think I'm going?"

Aunt Dora laughed secretly. He made his way out towards the police station, talking aloud and gesticulating. "Modisana!" [Little Shepherd (Jesus)] he kept saying.

The police did not or could not prosecute, although the Blade was taken to the station. "God's no fool. He'll stumble and fall one day. You'll see." That was grandmother's ruling. Ma-Lebona, Ma-Janeware, and even the cross-eyed woman next door, said grandmother couldn't have been more right. "God will deal with him." Old Rametse's story of how much had been stolen changed much. He said it was five pounds, then twenty, then ten. And still people didn't know how rich or poor he was.

It seems God did catch up with the Blade. One Saturday night he raped a teen-aged girl in a dark field near the Dougall Hall. He had forced the girl, at the point of a knife, from the door of the cinema to the field. The girl ran home to report, and the police got on Boeta Lem's tracks. He was picked up at the Columbia. He still had the girl's knickers [panties] in his pocket.

The next week, on a Sunday, Second Avenue residents swarmed at the gate of the Blade's home, where he lived with his father and stepmother. The people were angry. He had been bailed out, and they didn't like it. Aunt Dora went, not grandmother, who said she was sorry her leg was sore, otherwise she'd go and tell "the heathen Blade a thing or two, roll him in the dust a few times and lower his price on the market."

"Let him come out!"

"Let us see him!"

"We don't want animals here!"

"What, he gets a lawyer to speak for a criminal!"

"And it's his father, he knows his son's a criminal!"

"He's giving his son more pluck to do bigger crimes!"

"That lad will kill another man yet God's my witness!"

"What is it you want to do with the lad?" Old Rametse asked a knot of people at one end.

"Are *you* going to ask that, you whose money he stole?"

"I know, but I also want to know why I should be here."

"We want to take him back to the police station. They must keep the dog chained until it goes to court."

Old Rametse nodded understandingly.

"Speak to his father," said the Blade's stepmother, panting and waving her apron this way and that as if to disown the Blade.

At last the father came out of his hovel, his son's hand in the grip of his, sinewy and trembling.

"Speak to them, speak to them," the stepmother babbled, her fat hands fidgeting with the hem of the apron. "I've long been talking about this boy of yours. I'm weary of it, Jehovah knows in the heavens. Speak to them."

"God's people!" the man began. The noise gradually subsided.

I always remember how dignified the Blade's father looked on that day, even in the state of agitation.

"God's people!" he repeated, "what do you want of me?"

"We want your son, he must go back to the police cells," a woman said.

"That's right," another echoed. "You've no right to keep a criminal in your house!"

"And even hire a lawyer for him."

"If he'd raped a white girl he'd have been kept locked up until he should hang."

"You must deliver him."

For a few minutes Boeta Lem's father seemed lost for words. Then, "God's people, hear me. You men and women here have children. You're lucky some of them are not like this lad here. You're lucky some of them haven't raped and stolen. It hurts me when a boy of my own blood makes life miserable for other people. For every stab he gives a victim I get a hundred in my heart, not so easy to heal. You say if I'm willing to pay a lawyer to try to set him free, it means I like the dirty crime he has committed, and others before that."

He paused, and I could see he was weeping. His son stood there beside him, with a dirty sleeved vest for a shirt, and a wide flannel bag for trousers, out of which his long bare toes peeped. He looked both frightened and defiant.

"Whoever thinks that is a cruel person. Why do I hire a lawyer then? I don't know. I can't tell you."

"What about my money?" Old Rametse said, his Adam's apple pushing out sharply, and the sinews and veins in his neck telling a story of pain.

"That is a matter for the police, Son of Rametse," the Blade's father said. "I've brought him outside with me so that he should know what people think of his wickedness."

A wave of mumbling swept through the crowd, and they dispersed, threatening doom, predicting chaos, invoking God's instruments of punishment. "We leave you to chain your own dog then," one said, throwing up his arms.

Boeta Lem subsequently appeared in court. He was sentenced to ten years' hard labour.

"You see," grandmother said. "They hanged a man for doing what a white woman asked him to do in her own bed, and this is what they do to us! You go away from here, Es'ki, or you'll be telling your mates fat lies after hearing this!" I took myself off.

Columbia Hall cuddled in the centre of a row of Indian houses in the Asiatic Bazaar, just wedged between Marabastad and the Cape Coloured Reserve. It was an old building, with sooty walls that were painted and re-painted time after time to give the deception of attractiveness. On either side of the low platform that was meant to be a stage, was a door leading to a lounge room that covered the breadth of the hall in length and was par-titioned into cubicles, each fitted with a couch. The lights of the Columbia were never bright.

We often did odd jobs in the hall for the manager for pocket money, and breathlessly we examined every part of the interior. Breathlessly, be-cause few parents liked the sound of the name "Columbia." We were told in doubtful terms that it was an evil place where immoral practices went on behind the cloak of a dance or concert. Boys who were not tethered to their homes told us gleefully what dancers and concert performers did in the cubicles backstage. The men paid money for the convenience of using the couches with their girls. At the sight of the couches, my head turned round, aflame with all sorts of pictures, and I promised myself the opportunity of finding out what it was grandmother and Aunt Dora didn't want us to see. That is, if I should get the chance of attending a function.

The opportunity came. Talking pictures had just arrived in Pretoria. A new Indian-owned bioscope hall, the Star Picture Palace, opened for the first time in the Asiatic Bazaar with a showing of *The Singing Fool*, featuring Al Jolson. Excited crowds flocked at the cinema to see the new wonder in the history of the film.

We were permitted to go—my little uncle and I, escorted by an older uncle and Aunt Dora. Every night there was something on at the Columbia. What better night could there be for going there? But then I doted on the movies, and it would break my heart to hear the other boys recall among themselves what they had seen at the Picture Palace. I had a little money I had made at the market, and I could afford the admission fee of a shilling at the Columbia. So, once I had been given my ticket, I lost myself in the crowd and dashed to the Columbia just round the block. There would be an introductory programme of shots and a silent film before Al Jolson.

Penny whistler, n.d., © BAHA, photograph by Drum Photographer, dm2004060803. Used by permission of Bailey's African History Archive (BAHA).

I was let into the Columbia. I came face to face with the U-NO-MES dance band, whose music had before only floated to our ears as we passed the hall; violently, noisily, but vigorously. Thinking back on it now I remember the sad note of depravity, self-abandon, sweet, sensuous dissipation "Marabi" jazz sounded. The small jazz combos like U-NO-MES and the Merrymakers beat out a new two-to-the-bar jazz, the second note in which was accentuated by a bang on the drum. The name "Marabi" came from Marabastad. From there it went to the Reef. Handbills in pink or green or white could be seen on electric poles and rusted corrugated-iron walls which read:

THINGS ARE UPSIDE-DOWN!
AND WHY? 'CAUSE THERE'S GALORE SENSATIONAL,
FANTASTICAL, SCINTILLATING, REVERBERATING
JAZZ EXTRAVAGANZA
BRING YOUR GAL, SPIN YOUR GAL FOR THE
PALPITATING MARABI RHYTHM OF U-NO-MES
AT A
DAYBREAK DANCE AT COLUMBIA EVERY NIGHT

I stood against the wall in that misty hall of dim lights. Couples clung to each other very tightly, swayed sideways and backwards and forwards at the hips. Their faces were wet with perspiration. Occasionally a man or girl wiped it off with the back of the hand. They swayed to the monotonous tune, seeming to hear or see nothing, lost in the savagery of the band's music. They might even be blissfully unaware of the fact that just round the block, Al Jolson was bringing the magic of the age—the sound film. I continued to stand there, drinking in all the dust that rose from the concrete floor, the dim lights, the smell of perspiration and tobacco smoke. That was the Columbia, the name that spelled horror and damnation to those who concerned themselves with human conduct.

Everyday Life in Soweto:
The Photography of Santu Mofokeng

Patricia Hayes

Patricia Hayes is a professor of history at the University of the Western Cape. Her research concerns the relationship between photography and history in southern Africa, both in the colonial archive and in the late stages of the antiapartheid struggle. Her publications include The Colonising Camera *(1998) and* Bush of Ghosts *(2010).*

Santu Mofokeng was born in Newclare, outside Johannesburg, in 1956. His mother wrote *Soweto* on the birth certificate as a claim to some future in the city. This and his father's status as "resident alien" in Johannesburg point to some of the uncertainties of ordinary existence in South Africa during apartheid. Many people were excluded from urban rights and even citizenship of their own country, at risk of being deported to one of the new Bantustans. Mofokeng grew up in Orlando East in Soweto, and also spent time in Sophiatown. By his own unsentimental account, living conditions were tough. After his father died, the whole family lived in one room and eventually moved to a house in the White City Jabavu section of Soweto. His widowed mother did various things to support her children, and Mofokeng recalls her improvisations, like the clothes she made, which marked them out from other children. To him, the streets, everything around the early childhood home, remain important somehow, imaginatively.

In recent years Mofokeng has said explicitly that, in his photographs, he tries to "depict anxiety."[1] In a medium that is supposedly about realism, he is instead "chasing shadows." The expression of a range of affective states marks his photography over a long period of time. The term *affect* is more appropriate in his case than *emotion*, because it is more indeterminate. His pictures might convey a sense of nebulous uncertainty, like the *Concert at Sewefontein*, where some viewers have seen nonexistent bullet holes in the

Concert at Sewefontein, Bloemhof, ca. 1988. Photograph by Santu Mofokeng (b. 1956). Silverprint. © Santu Mofokeng. Image courtesy of Lunetta Bartz, MAKER, Johannesburg.

Church of God, Motouleng, Free State, 1996. Photograph by Santu Mofokeng (b. 1956). Silverprint. © Santu Mofokeng. Image courtesy of Lunetta Bartz, MAKER, Johannesburg.

Golf in Zone 6, Diepkloof, 1987. Photograph by Santu Mofokeng (b. 1956). Silverprint.
© Santu Mofokeng. Image courtesy of Lunetta Bartz, MAKER, Johannesburg.

wall (in the 1980s), and others have seen spirits in the blur of one figure next to sharper ones (in the 2000s).

We can say this now about Santu Mofokeng, for there is an accumulated impact from the three decades of his photographic essays that have taken us from late apartheid well into postapartheid time. But what about his early work, especially his depictions of everyday life in Soweto? Here too things are often ambiguous, though it may not be immediately apparent. It is more like a saltiness of the visual language about the place, people's relations to each other, and to the things around them. Irony is often present, or a twist to social expectations, like the unexpected golfers in Soweto looking for balls, or the man in a suit listening to a radio cassette recorder outside a church hall, or the view of a performance from the viewpoint of the performer (Ray Phiri of Stimela). There is also the odd presence of a police photographer looking back at Mofokeng like a gunfighter in *Police with Sjamboks, Plein Street, Johannesburg, ca. 1986.*

Sometimes he did not get the shot he most obviously should have, but the result had something more. Perhaps he missed a funeral service and then caught the disappearing cortège. Or he did a portrait of Jakobus Maine, brother of Kas, the sharecropper, only to have the man's horse fill the frame.

Church in Mamelodi, Pretoria, ca. 1987. Photograph by Santu Mofokeng (b. 1956). Silverprint. © Santu Mofokeng. Image courtesy of Lunetta Bartz, MAKER, Johannesburg.

Ray Phiri, Leader of Stimela Music Band at Shareworld, near Soweto, ca. 1986. Photograph by Santu Mofokeng (b. 1956). Silverprint. © Santu Mofokeng. Image courtesy of Lunetta Bartz, MAKER, Johannesburg.

Police with Sjamboks, Plein Street, Johannesburg, ca. 1986. Photograph by Santu Mofokeng (b. 1956). Silverprint. © Santu Mofokeng. Image courtesy of Lunetta Bartz, MAKER, Johannesburg.

Chief More's Funeral, GaMogopa, 1989. Photograph by Santu Mofokeng (b. 1956). Silverprint. © Santu Mofokeng. Image courtesy of Lunetta Bartz, MAKER, Johannesburg.

Maine Talking to His Horse, Vaalrand, 1988. Photograph by Santu Mofokeng (b. 1956). Silverprint. © Santu Mofokeng. Image courtesy of Lunetta Bartz, MAKER, Johannesburg.

Mofokeng worked with all this in the darkroom. The darkroom is where he spent many years, as if incubating, before becoming a recognized photographer himself. Today, after thirty years of chasing shadows, as it were, he is at times able to articulate his way of looking very clearly. In particular, Mofokeng sets himself up in contrast to the world-renowned David Goldblatt. Mofokeng has said that Goldblatt photographs the *is-ness* of things. "There's no question what he's looking at. . . . And I'm not like that," Mofokeng says. For Mofokeng, it is not *what it is*, but *what it might be*, or *what we never knew it might be*, or even *what it is not*. "I am interested in the ambiguity of things," he says. "This comes not from a position of power but of helplessness."

Mofokeng matriculated at Morris Isaacson High School, in an environment that finally ignited in the Soweto protests and repression of 1976. Mofokeng was not an activist and hated violence, and yet through most outside lenses, his township world was completely suffused with politics. This did not mean that ordinary things were not important. In fact they seem to take on a heightened resonance with Mofokeng. To understand this, it is important to go through the multiple trajectories that produced the career of this photographer.

In his autobiographical text, "Trajectory of a Street Photographer," Mofokeng describes the sense of envy and attraction aroused by anyone having a camera among his school friends.[2] University was out of the question, and for some time he tried to make a living as a street photographer, also photographing weddings and other family occasions, because these were the kinds of pictures people wanted. It is from this time that he maintains that people in Soweto sought to show what they had, not what they lacked—the latter being the focus of much photojournalism. Mofokeng became a darkroom assistant, and in 1986 he was invited to join the photographic collective Afrapix. This brought together progressive photographers who pooled images for distribution to various organizations (including overseas), and who also ran photographic training workshops. Mofokeng's first exhibitions and photographic essays date from this time. He worked for the *New Nation* newspaper and then took up an appointment at the Oral History Documentation Centre at the University of the Witwatersrand, where he photographed the subjects of social-history research like the sharecropper Kas Maine. In the 1990s he began to work on commission and did a number of residencies in the United States and Europe, with his work increasingly showing in international galleries.

Parts of Mofokeng's work exemplify a tension that exists in South African photography. A certain photographic discourse had begun to forcefully emerge by the mid-1980s. This represented a narrowing down of larger social-documentary ideas and practices and fed off a photojournalistic demand. This coincided with large-scale political mobilization and organization across urban areas and especially the formation of the United Democratic Front in 1983. This discourse was produced locally but reinforced internationally, with big media forces at play. There was a market for a certain kind of photography and a certain coding of images. The latter included what Mofokeng frequently describes as the white-cop-black-youth code, where the more white cops beating a black youth in the picture, the better it sold. Commercial newspaper forces wanted this image, but so did solidarity movements and other organizations outside South Africa in a more generalized antiapartheid set of activities and campaigns. Other desired images were of political funerals, sites of mourning and mobilization with young activists showing clenched fists and strong emotions.

Behind this code is a much deeper visual genealogy of white or Euro-American viewers looking at black subjects whose struggle is worthy, who are deserving, maybe even powerless, and who require intervention and possibly redemption. In fact such images redeem the viewer who might be moved to sympathize or contribute to the salvation of these subjects from their harsh fate at the hands of white police or the state, implicitly read as racist. The police in these images appear forceful, armed, and strong, and somehow out of step with the rest of the world that accepted decolonization in Africa long ago.

Mofokeng entered this discourse when he joined Afrapix and newspaper photojournalism in the mid-1980s. Afrapix sought to expose the often secret or hidden dealings of the apartheid state toward its mostly black citizens. One could argue that the boundaries were firm and the codes of meaning very clear. But from Mofokeng's standpoint, why photograph the increasingly generic, which often put you in the firing line where black life (including your own) was cheap? In addition, there were practical obstacles for someone like Mofokeng, such as the lack of ready access to a car, which left him behind the better-resourced photographers. To some extent he was simply out of the running. But in fact he had little desire to be an action photographer in "the A-Team," as he put it. The photographs that were in demand had come to constitute a strong and memorable genre that was named "struggle photography," or latterly and not totally accurately, "documentary photography" (which was in fact underpinned by multifold ideas). In the manner of all successful genres, it needed new twists but remained largely stable within its boundaries.

We could say this was a photography complex of the political. This might help to explain the successful, persistent, and at times overwhelming nature of what Njabulo Ndebele calls the spectacular in South Africa of the 1980s.[3] Because photographs were fed into networks that traveled quickly and reached people around the world, this helped to shape transnational political sensibilities. There is a predictable array of meanings that attach to certain kinds of content. These become easily recognizable, and productive in terms of building support. In South Africa in the 1980s, these would include scenes of conflict, often photographed in proximity, with heightened emotional impact. A public was being constituted and in a sense educated.

Being part of this discourse however, as many Afrapix photographers were, does not mean they were unambiguous or uncritical of it. These networks and what the photographs implied, in fact became less and less satisfactory to many photographers. A number of them speak about how they chafed within these parameters, or sought to do their own private or personal projects alongside this growing system of signs. Thus the discourse around documentary photography was in fact highly differentiated.

The problem is that such a recognizable range of signs has its limits. There are drawbacks to exposure in a literal sense, to making things visible. This is where the work of Mofokeng stands out. In his photographic terrain, vision is seared through with night, shadow, smoke, mist, blurring, occlusion, and abeyance. There is something about this tension between ex-

Limbless Doll, Jakkalsfontein, 1989. Photograph by Santu Mofokeng (b. 1956). Silverprint. © Santu Mofokeng. Image courtesy Lunetta Bartz, MAKER, Johannesburg.

pected images and the contingencies of the world that helps us understand some of the force of Mofokeng's depiction of everyday life within the wider frame of South African photography at the time. But it is not only through the occlusions in Mofokeng's photographs: there is a second feature, and that is objects themselves—things—that often seem larger than life. I have argued elsewhere that with Mofokeng there is "a tangibility to the atmosphere of a space. There is also, strangely, the aliveness of objects, things, even detritus. Ironically, the proximities of black urban life in South Africa seem to liberate these tendencies."[4]

Mofokeng loosely conceptualizes the pictures of everyday life in Soweto as a fictional or metaphorical biography. The work is neither literal nor expository but touches on things that could have happened in Mofokeng's own life, or were familiar to him. With the heightened framing around the objects of everyday life, though, the familiar is often rendered unreal. Things

(above) Old Man,
Dukathole, ca. 1988.
Photograph by Santu
Mofokeng (b. 1956). Sil-
verprint. © Santu Mofo-
keng. Image courtesy of
Lunetta Bartz, MAKER,
Johannesburg.

*(left) Near Maponya's Dis-
count Store,* Dube, 1985.
Photograph by Santu
Mofokeng (b. 1956). Sil-
verprint. © Santu Mofo-
keng. Image courtesy of
Lunetta Bartz, MAKER,
Johannesburg.

Winter in Tembisa, ca. 1989. Photograph by Santu Mofokeng (b. 1956). Silverprint.
© Santu Mofokeng. Image courtesy of Lunetta Bartz, MAKER, Johannesburg.

are not what they are supposed to be; they are altered, formally dislodged. A doll takes on its own grotesque life of parody; or a stooping elderly figure is as important as a rivulet of dirty water. Perhaps this is what the excesses of inequality did to people's lives, and these uncomfortable photographs some-how bring out this level of existence.

Consumerism itself is rendered strange. The photograph of Maponya's discount store, for instance, gives more attention to a boy urinating in the dark amid smoke than to the business itself. Due to attacks on stores from 1976 and the later boycotts and consumer campaigns, the store has slits in-stead of windows. The goods are shrunken out of view.

Mofokeng has a long interest in advertising billboards, which offer life-changing goods and services in an unpropitious, unlikely environment. This started with *Winter in Thembisa, ca. 1989*, where the mist heightens a few details, and one man walks slightly hunched over, presumably from cold but seemingly wrapped up in his own thoughts. Mofokeng enjoys a little joke around the way some European viewers have read the Omo washing-powder billboard in the picture, in relation to the man in the frame: *huomo* (pronounced *omo*) means "man" in Italian. The billboard product is blown completely out of scale to the emptiness around it, and appears very sharp. This is capitalism in focus.

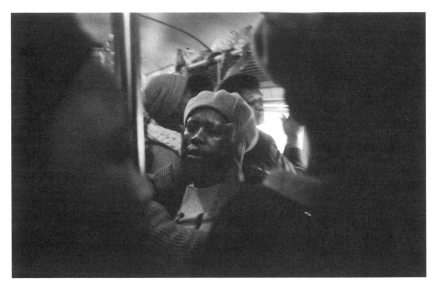

Laying of Hands, Johannesburg-Soweto Line, 1986. Photograph by Santu Mofokeng
(b. 1956). Silverprint. © Santu Mofokeng. Image courtesy of Lunetta Bartz, MAKER,
Johannesburg.

Supplication, Johannesburg-Soweto Line, 1986. Photograph by Santu Mofokeng
(b. 1956). Silverprint. © Santu Mofokeng. Image courtesy of Lunetta Bartz, MAKER,
Johannesburg.

The Book, Johannesburg-Soweto Line, 1986. Photograph by Santu Mofokeng
(b. 1956). Silverprint. © Santu Mofokeng. Image courtesy of Lunetta Bartz, MAKER,
Johannesburg.

Mofokeng is not usually a one-shot man; he does not believe in the "decisive moment." Or so he says. Instead, he likes to assemble a number of images and make a narrative that can be read in various ways. The first proper
photographic essay he did as a member of Afrapix was called *Train Church*.
For Mofokeng, it touched on two issues that were absolutely central to the
life of most South Africans: commuting and spirituality.

In 1986 Mofokeng used to take a train from Soweto as part of a complicated
commute to distant Randburg. He would then catch a ride from Maureen
Isaacson, who was editing the text that photographer Jurgen Schadeberg
was compiling from the Jim Bailey *Drum* archives at his countryside villa
northwest of Johannesburg. Mofokeng worked in the darkroom. While getting there, his attempts to sleep on the train were disrupted by what he calls
"gyrations," for the train is not just a train; it is a church. People seize the
opportunity of motion, transition, travel, and being in-between to gather
for worship. There is the laying on of hands, transmitting some force between one body and another; there is a preacher with the "book"; there
are hands beating the panels of the compartment like a drum, tapping the
insides, evoking other forces.

Mofokeng also took photographs of young men in *Riding Staff on
Johannesburg-Soweto Line*, sometimes called "stealing trains." They are flying

The Drumming, Johannesburg-Soweto Line, 1986. Photograph by Santu Mofokeng (b. 1956). Silverprint. © Santu Mofokeng. Image courtesy of Lunetta Bartz, MAKER, Johannesburg.

Riding Staff on Johannesburg-Soweto Line, 1986. Photograph by Santu Mofokeng (b. 1956). Silverprint. © Santu Mofokeng. Image courtesy of Lunetta Bartz, MAKER, Johannesburg.

through the air holding on to the outside of the train, like spirits clinging to a thing of metal and speed.

This tenacity, this holding on to the outside because you cannot be inside, evokes other associations in a metaphorical biography. There is the "resident alien" status of Mofokeng's father. There is also the sense of dispossession when his mother and her six children were confined to one room in a "three-room mansion" in Orlando East, which for Mofokeng represented "a shrinking closet which became alien to [him] as [he] grew."[5]

With regard to photographing the troubled townships in the 1980s, the question was asked of Mofokeng: "What's the difference between an insider and an outsider?" In terms of photojournalism, he answers, there is no difference whether you are from Soweto or another country. But there are several dimensions to such a question. In a text suggestively titled "Distorting Mirror / Townships Imagined" (2011), Mofokeng argues that to counter the state's propaganda image of blacks as dangerous and unstable, radical photographers tended to portray them with dignity, but suffering from a lack or absence. In his view, this distorts "the reality of life in the townships." To Mofokeng, these images are incomplete. Social documentary work that remains within "monotony, gloom and despair" is unable to acknowledge that people in the townships might have rich and full lives; "You can't just say it's about poverty."[6]

Mofokeng often plays with a notion of a third way. He recently quipped that the root of third is *tri*, which is associated with triviality. "I don't know why I said that," he then comments. Especially in this Freudian slip, something less obvious and hierarchical is suggested, that is on the edge of consciousness.

The question about South African photography in the 1980s is not best posed by the superficial notion that there are insiders and outsiders. This is an old issue rooted in anxiety over the politics of representation. A more interesting question is that of *interiority*, which is about the inside, but of quite another order. There is the interiority of insiders that makes them outsiders. Outsiders, that is, in the dominant culture of secular, rational modernism, whether advocated by the exclusionary apartheid state or the inclusionary nationalist movement that was seeking to oust apartheid in the 1980s.

Mofokeng's photographs of African spirituality do not come from any desire to celebrate the traditions of his people. By contrast, he stresses the importance of simply "finding a way to talk about this thing, this way of being." He claims he is not an expert, and while not a believer, strictly speaking, this does not mean that he does not believe in spirituality. In South Africa there are many contemporary artists who have tried to represent

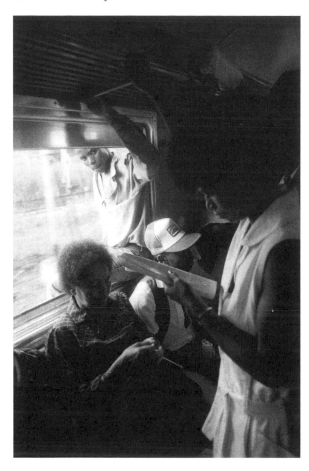

Staff Rider,
Johannesburg-Soweto
Line, 1986. Photograph
by Santu Mofokeng
(b. 1956). Silverprint.
© Santu Mofokeng.
Image courtesy of
Lunetta Bartz, MAKER,
Johannesburg.

spirits and to acknowledge the communicative medium of dreams. These works call into question an order of colonial knowledge that writes out or skews what is deemed to be nonrational in the past, and which deeply affects the present. It is no wonder, then, that Mofokeng often refers to a sense of schizophrenia, or a series of disjunctures, that he associates with his own moving between worlds.

Notes

1. Quotations by the photographer Santu Mofokeng come from a variety of recorded interviews, workshops, exhibition walkabouts, and informal conversations with the author, together with postgraduate students in visual history at the University of the Western Cape and other audiences between 2005 and 2011. When the photographer is quoted from a separate published source, this is indicated.

2. Santu Mofokeng, "Trajectory of a Street Photographer," in Pascal Martin Saint Leon, N'Goné, and Jean Loup Pivin, eds., *Anthology of African and Indian Ocean Photography* (Paris: Revue Noire, 1998), 264–71. Biographical details can be found in Santu Mofokeng, *Santu Mofokeng* (Johannesburg: David Krut Publishers, 2001); and Santu Mofokeng, *Chasing Shadows: Thirty Years of Photographic Essays* (Munich: Prestel, 2011). See also Santu Mofokeng, *Santu Mofokeng*, Taxi Series 004 (Johannesburg: David Krut Publishers, 2001); Patricia Hayes, "Night, Shadow, Smoke, Mist, Blurring, Occlusion and Abeyance: Santu Mofokeng," *Art South Africa*, 8, no. 2 (2009): 66–71.

3. Njabulo Ndebele, *Rediscovery of the Ordinary: Essays on South African Literature and Culture* (Pietermaritzburg: University of KwaZulu Natal Press, 2006).

4. Patricia Hayes, "Santu Mofokeng, Photographs: 'The Violence Is in the Knowing,'" special issue on history and photography, *History and Theory* 48, no. 4 (Fall 2009): 50.

5. Mofokeng, *Santu Mofokeng*, 26.

6. Santu Mofokeng, *Distorting Mirror / Townships Imagined* (Johannesburg: Worker's Library, 1995).

VI

Apartheid and the Struggle for Freedom

In 1948 a dejected Jan Smuts ceded power to the leader of the National Party, D. F. Malan. Many observers of South African politics had not expected the rapid ascendance of Afrikaner nationalists, who came to power on the strength of the votes of Afrikaner workers threatened by African competition and Afrikaner farmers alarmed by African urbanization and calling for a tightening of the pass laws that controlled black people's movement in "white" South Africa. The National Party soon consolidated its control of the state, which it ruled for nearly fifty years. Shortly after the election, the National Party government began passing laws that transformed South Africa into an authoritarian society based on racially discriminatory legislation known as *apartheid* (apartness) and turned the country into a worldwide pariah. A mere 19 percent of the population ruled South Africa ruthlessly and with a determination that created enormous suffering and lasting injury.

South Africa before apartheid already deprived black South Africans of political rights and kept them in segregated rural and urban poverty. Apartheid was a much more brutal and more tightly enforced system of white supremacy, but its basic elements were all foreshadowed under segregation. Huge numbers of Africans had streamed into Johannesburg and other cities during the years of the Second World War seeking opportunities provided by the wartime boom, escaping rural poverty, and taking advantage of a relaxation of the pass laws during the war. Many apartheid policies would be aimed at controlling ongoing black urbanization in the country. In addition, an important part of apartheid dogma rested on the idea that humanity was naturally composed of racial and ethnic groupings that should form the basis of any social and political order. Beginning in 1951 the government introduced laws that created a system of local and regional government in the native reserves, which would become self-governing "homelands," mocked as Bantustans. These policies came to be known as *separate development* or *grand apartheid*. Transkei ostensibly became independent in 1976, though it had very little support among black South Africans and no international

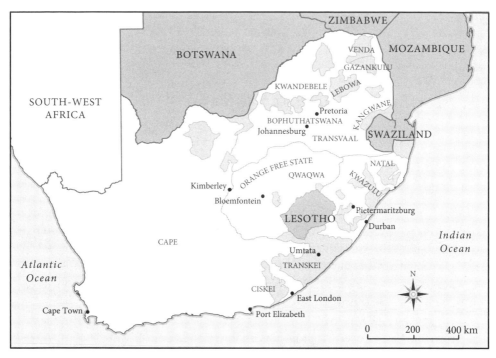

The Bantustans. University of Wisconsin Cartography Lab

recognition. Three other South African homelands (as well as two in South Africa's colony, South West Africa, which became independent Namibia in 1990) eventually attained a similar pseudo-independence in a South African attempt to persuade the world that it too was engaged in decolonization even as it deprived millions of Africans of any political rights outside the homelands.

Prosecuting grand apartheid involved an enormous commitment by the state and resulted in massive social dislocation through forced removals and resettlement that included at least three million people, nearly one-fifth of South Africa's population in 1960. In the homelands, resistance to grand-apartheid policies, especially the Bantu Authorities Act, led to the outbreak of open rebellion in the northern reserve of Sekhukhuneland, and particularly in Pondoland in the Transkei. There the military intervened, followed by the declaration of a state of emergency that remained in effect throughout much of the apartheid era. Authorities arrested more than 3,500 people and sent more than twenty men to the gallows. They also tortured roughly 150 people, the first use of torture in modern South Africa's history.

Other laws enforced spatial segregation in South Africa's towns and cities, particularly the Group Areas Act of 1950; these policies are sometimes

Black worker passes sign indicating petty apartheid regulations. Photographer unknown. © Reuters / Corbis, R89004009. Used by permission of Corbis Images.

referred to as *petty apartheid*. The enactment of Group Areas led to the destruction of various communities throughout the country and the formation of segregated townships, most famously the leveling of Sophiatown and the creation of South Western Townships, or Soweto, outside Johannesburg. South Africa's cities had grown steadily in the post–Second World War years. By 1951 more than two million Africans lived in overcrowded urban slums. The new battery of laws led to increased police harassment. Yearly convictions for failure to produce a proper pass, which Africans had to carry at all times, increased from just over two hundred thousand in 1951 to nearly seven hundred thousand in the late 1960s. Race laws permeated society, extending to schools and amenities such as beaches, post offices, and hospitals. The Prohibition of Mixed Marriages Act of 1949 and the Immorality Act of 1950 prohibited marriage and sexual relations between whites and people defined as "nonwhite." The apartheid government also stripped Coloureds of the vote within the Western Cape. In less than two decades South Africa became a police state.

Until the late 1940s, the African National Congress (ANC) remained a relatively small organization composed primarily of elite men. The end of

Sharpeville massacre, March 1960, © BAHA, photograph by Ian Berry, dm2004011404. Used by permission of Bailey's African History Archive (BAHA).

the decade and the early years of the 1950s saw increased radicalization of black politics, especially the growing prominence of young activists, like Nelson Mandela, in the ANC Youth League, which in 1949 adopted a more radical position in the Programme of Action. In 1952 the ANC and other organizations staged the peaceful Defiance Campaign to defy apartheid laws. Support for the ANC increased meteorically. The apartheid government responded by arresting protesters and passing authoritarian laws restricting political dissent. After the ANC and other groups met and adopted the Freedom Charter in 1955, the government arrested 156 activists, including Mandela, and charged them with treason. The case kept black political figures hamstrung for several years, but by 1961 all those against whom charges had not already been dismissed were found not guilty, much to the state's frustration.

Resistance politics in the 1950s involved complex alignments among various organizations ranging from the ANC, the Communist Party, the South African Indian Congress, and the Coloured People's Congress to a number of smaller groups scattered across the country. Women became eligible to be full members of the ANC in 1943 and took a more prominent role in politics, culminating in 1956 when twenty thousand women marched on Pretoria to protest the extension of pass laws to women. Disagreements within the resistance movements abounded, ranging from tactics, the role of whites in alliance with the ANC, to the very definition of the "struggle." Was it a fight for civil rights, for national liberation, or against class oppression? How did South Africa stand in relation to the wave of decolonization then sweeping the world? These questions extended far beyond intellectual debates to matters of organization and strategy. In 1959 a group of so-called Africanists broke away from the ANC to form the Pan Africanist Congress (PAC), headed by Robert Sobukwe.

The government response to increasing radicalization of politics involved arrests, charges of treason and other high crimes, bannings and house arrests, the declaration of groups such as the ANC as "unlawful organizations," and ultimately the use of torture as a political weapon. In 1960, following the massacre in Sharpeville of sixty-nine people in an antipass protest organized by the PAC, the government declared a nationwide state of emergency and banned the ANC and PAC. (The Communist Party had been declared illegal in 1950.) Under the leadership of Prime Minister Hendrik Verwoerd, who was the architect of apartheid, South Africa became a republic and withdrew from the British Commonwealth. Mandela and others formed an armed wing of the ANC, Umkhonto we Sizwe (Spear of the Nation, or MK), which set off small bombs at government facilities in late 1961. The following year police arrested Mandela, and in 1963 they captured most of the top leadership near Johannesburg. As many others fled the country, MK fell apart. The government convicted Mandela and the others and sentenced them to life in prison on Robben Island near Cape Town.

The selections that follow in this part cover this tumultuous and still contested period in South Africa's modern history. Contemporary politics and culture remain profoundly shaped by the years of apartheid's creation and early efforts to resist it. More than five decades later, South Africans argue about whether the current ANC government has turned its back on the principles enshrined in the Freedom Charter of 1955. Politicians mythologize and lay claim to this period, particularly moments such as the Defiance Campaign, the Sharpeville Massacre, and the armed struggle. Reincorporating the former homelands, particularly the chiefs and "traditional authorities" who formed the cornerstone of grand apartheid, poses difficult challenges to creating a democracy. How South Africans see themselves today remains shaped by their historical consciousness of this traumatic past.

Requiem for Sophiatown

Can Themba

Can Themba (1924–68) was born in Marabastad township (depicted in Es'kia Mphahlele's Down Second Avenue*) (see Part V), and his life is most famously associated with Sophiatown and* Drum *magazine, founded in 1951. Just over four miles from the Johannesburg city center, Sophiatown grew tremendously during the 1930s and 1940s, with more than thirty thousand residents by the end of the Second World War. Exempted from the Urban Areas Act of 1923 and a place where Africans could own property, Sophiatown became a mixed community with Indian shop owners, a smattering of poor white residents, and a vibrant African culture.*

In the years around the ending of the Second World War, an artistic revolution unfolded in South Africa's townships, which were growing rapidly. The creation in Johannesburg of the Polly Street Art Centre in 1952 helped nurture black visual artists. Perhaps the most visible development centered on print culture: newspapers, magazines, and fiction. An already rich musical culture expanded with the emergence of jazz and other bands playing in venues across the country, particularly in the Johannesburg area, where artists such as Hugh Masekela and Miriam Makeba made their early careers. South African jazz had its formative moment in Sophiatown, where musicians kept abreast of American musical styles, which they blended into local musical traditions.

Sophiatown was at the very center of South Africa's postwar black cultural renaissance. Many of the country's black artists and intellectuals lived in Sophiatown, including Dr. A. B. Xuma, president of the African National Congress (ANC), and the young Nelson Mandela. The apartheid government targeted the community for removal under the Group Areas Act, beginning in 1955. Sophiatown's destruction was completed in 1960, and it became a white suburb named Triomf (Triumph). The postapartheid government restored the community's original name in 2006.

Realism can be star-scattering, even if you lived your whole unthinking life in reality. Especially in Sophiatown, these days, where it can come with the sudden crash of a flying brick on the back of your head.

Like the other day when Bob Gosani and I sneaked off towards our secret shebeen [illegal bar] in Morris Street. We were dodging an old friend of ours whom we call the Leech, for he is one of those characters who like their drink—any amount—so long as someone else pays for it.

Well, this secret shebeen in Morris Street was a nice place. You take a passage through Meyer Street over haphazard heaps of bricks where houses have been broken down, you find another similar passage that leads you from Ray Street into Edith Street, where you find another passage, neater, having always been there, between the Coloured School and Jerusalem-like slum houses, you go down a little, and suddenly there it is.

Quite a fine place, too. A little brick wall, a minute garden of mostly Christmas flowers, a half-veranda (the other half has become a little kitchen) and the floor of the veranda polished a bright green.

Inside, the sitting room may be cluttered with furniture, it is so small, but you sink comfortably into a sofa as one of the little tables that can stand under the other's belly is placed before you, and you make your order. Half a jack of brandy!

How often have Bob and I not whooped happily: "Yessus! The Leech will never find us here." So, though there were directer routes to this place, we always took the passages. They say these people can smell when you are going to make a drink.

But that day, as we emerged into Morris Street, it was as if that brick had just struck us simultaneously on our heads. That sweet, little place was just not there. Where it should have been was a grotesque, grinning structure of torn red brick that made it look like the face of a mauled boxer trying to be sporting after his gruel. A nausea of despair rose up in me, but it was Bob who said the only appropriate thing: "Shucks."

Here is the odd thing about Sophiatown. I have long been inured to the ravages wreaked upon Sophiatown. I see its wrecks daily and, through many of its passages that have made such handy short cuts for me, I have stepped gingerly many times over the tricky rubble. Inside of me, I have long stopped arguing the injustice, the vindictiveness, the strong-arm authority of which prostrate Sophiatown is a loud symbol.

Long ago I decided to concede, to surrender to the argument that Sophiatown was a slum, after all. I am itchingly nagged by the thought that slum clearance should have nothing to do with the theft of freehold rights. But the sheer physical fact of Sophiatown's removal has intimidated me.

Moreover, so much has gone—veritable institutions. Fatty of the Thirty-nine Steps. Now, that was a great shebeen! It was in Good Street. You walked up a flight of steps, the structure looked dingy as if it would crash

Miriam Makeba, performing with the Manhattan Brothers, 1955, © BAHA, photograph by Gopal Naransamy, dm2004101123. Used by permission of Bailey's African History Archive (BAHA).

down with you any moment. You opened a door and walked into a dazzle of bright electric light, contemporary furniture and massive Fatty. She was a legend. Gay, friendly, coquettish, always ready to sell you a drink. And that mama had everything: whisky, brandy, gin, beer, wine—the lot. Sometimes she could even supply cigars. But now that house is flattened. I'm told that in Meadowlands she has lost the zest for the game. She has even tried to look for work in town. Ghastly.

Dwarf, who used to find a joke in everything. He used to walk into Bloke's place, catch us red-handed playing the music of Mozart. He used to cock his ear, listen a little and in his gravel voice comment: "No wonder he's got a name like that." There is nothing that Dwarf loved more than sticking out his tongue to a cop and running for it. I once caught him late at night in his Meadowlands house washing dishes. He still manfully tries to laugh at himself.

And Mabeni's, where the great Dolly Rathebe once sang the blues to me. I didn't ask her. She just sidled over to me on the couch and broke into song. It was delicious. But now Dolly is in Port Elizabeth, and Mabeni, God knows where.

These are only highlights from the swarming, cacophonous, strutting, brawling, vibrating life of the Sophiatown that was. But it was not all just shebeeny, smutty, illegal stuff. Some places it was as dreams are made on.

I am thinking of those St. Cyprian's School boys who a decade ago sweatingly dug out the earth behind the house of the Community of the Resurrection, in order to have a swimming pool. It still stands, and the few kids left still paddle in it. Some of those early schoolboys of St. Cyprian's later went up to Father Ross or Father Raynes or Father Huddleston who wangled a bursary for them to go to St. Peter's, then on to Fort Hare and later even Wits [University of the Witwatersrand], to come back doctors.

Their parents, patiently waiting and working in town, skimped a penny here, a tickey there, so that they might make the necessary alteration to their house, or pay off the mortgage. And slowly Sophiatown was becoming house-proud.

Of course, there were pressures too heavy for them. After the war, many people came to Johannesburg to seek for work and some hole to night in. As they increased they became a housing problem. As nobody seemed to care, they made Sophiatown a slum.

But the children of those early Sophiatonians—some of them—are still around. It is amazing how many of them are products of the Anglican Mission at St. Cyprian's. I meet them often in respectable homes and we talk the world to tatters. Mostly we talk of our lot in life. After all, too often we have been told that we are the future leaders of our people. We are the young stalwarts who are supposed to solve the problems of our harassed world.

"Not political unity, we need," one would say; "our society is too diverse and unwieldy for that. Just a dynamic core of purified fighters with clear objectives and a straightforward plan of action. That is all."

Another: "No! We must align ourselves with the new forces at play in Africa today. There already is the dynamicity. The idea of a one Africa has never been put as powerfully as at Accra [capital of Ghana] recently. You see, Africans, wherever they are, have not a territorial, a local loyalty: they don't feel that they belong to a South Africa or a Federation or a Tanganyika or a Kenya or a West Africa; but with Africans in the whole of Africa. In fact, many of us are wondering if Arabs and Egyptians are also Africans. They probably are."

Still another: "But if the boys in the North are getting busy, shouldn't we start something here ourselves?"

"Waal, you see, our ANC here has been caught with its pants down. The Africanists are claiming that Accra has proclaimed their stand. And the ANC representative there could only discuss the tactical difficulties of the ANC in South Africa with her special conditions."

"Ya. But this African Personality idea, how does it mean to us? What does it mean, anyway?"

"I'll tell you. In the world today are poised against each other two massive ideologies: of the East and of the West. Both of them play international politics as if we're bound to choose between them. Between them only. We have discovered just that we can choose as we like, if we grow strong in our own character. But there's more to this. The West has had a damned long time to win us. Win us over to Western thinking, Western Christian way of living. Their ideas of democracy and their Christian ideals were wonderful, but they did not mean them.

"Let me explain. We are quite a religious people. We accept the idealism of Christianity. We accept its high principles. But in a stubborn, practical sense we believe in reality. Christian Brotherhood must be real. Democracy must actually be the rule of the people: not of a white hobo over a black MA [master's degree].

"To us, if a witch doctor says he'll bring rain, we not only want to see the rain fall, but also the crops sprout from the earth. That's what a rainmaker's for, nay? If the bone-thrower says he'll show up the bastard who's been slinging lightning at me, I expect him to swing that bolt of lightning right back. So if the priest says God's on my side, I'd like to see a few more chances and a little less whiteman's curses.

"But in any case, Christianity is now an anaemic religion. It cannot rouse the ancient in me—especially the Shaka instinct I still have. Now, you and I are educated guys. We don't go for the witchcraft stuff. And we don't want to go for the jukebox stuff. But much as we deny, we still want the thrill of the wild blood of our forefathers. The whites call it savagery. Ineradicable barbarism. But in different degrees we want the colour and vigour and vibrant appeal of it all. So the tsotsi [gangster] seeks in the cowboy the way to strut across the streets with swaying hips and a dangerous weapon in each hand. So the Zionist thumps his drum and gyrates his holy fervor up the streets. So you and I and these guys here discuss politics, teasingly dancing around the idea of violence.

"All it means is that in wanting to express her demand for democratic

Member of the "Americans" gang, September 1954, © BAHA, photograph by Bob Gosani, dm2000042608. Used by permission of Bailey's African History Archive (BAHA).

self-determination, Africa is also releasing her ancient most desire to live life over the brim. That's how come we sometimes seem to talk in two voices."

"Wait a minute," another shrieks, "wait a minute. We're not all like that. Some of us would like to get things right and start anew. Some piece of social engineering could get things working right, if our moral purposes were right, not just vengeful."

"Sure, but our masters have taught this damned thing violence so well by precept—often practice—that they get you to believe that it's the only way to talk turkey to them."

We do not only talk about this particular subject. Our subjects are legion. Nkrumah [the first president of Ghana] must be a hell of a guy, or is he just bluffing? What about our African intellectuals who leave the country just when we need them most? But is it honestly true that we don't want to have affairs with white girls? What kind of white supremacy is this that cannot stand fair competition? What will happen if a real topmost Nat gets caught by the Immorality Act? In fact, all those cheeky questions that never get aired in public.

But it always ends up with someone saying, "Aw shut up, folks, you got no plan to liberate us."

Somewhere here, and among a thousand more individualistic things, is the magic of Sophiatown. It is different and itself. You don't just find your

Last days of Sophiatown, November 1959, © BAHA, photograph by Drum Photographer, dm2005020219. Used by permission of Bailey's African History Archive (BAHA).

place here, you make it and you find yourself. There's a tang about it. You might now and then have to give way to others making their ways of life by methods not in the book. But you can't be bored. You have the right to listen to the latest jazz records at Ah Sing's over the road. You can walk a Coloured girl of an evening down to the Odin Cinema and no questions asked. You can try out Rhugubar's curry with your bare fingers without embarrassment. All this with no sense of heresy. Indeed, I've shown quite a few white people, "the little Paris of the Transvaal"—but only a few were Afrikaners.

What people have thought to be the brazenness of Sophiatown has really been its clean-faced frankness. And, of course, its swart jowl against the rosy cheek of Westdene [a neighboring white suburb].

Ay, me. That was the Sophiatown that was.

I shall have to leave these respectable homes of my friends and stumble over the loose bricks back to my den. I hear tell that Blackie is still about in his shack behind the posh house in devastated Millar Street.

Blackie's landlord is still facing it out, what the hell for? Since the Rathebe case most of the standholders have decided to capitulate. They are selling out like rats letting the passengers sink. Solly got caught in this—the newest racket. His landlord told him nothing. Waited for him to pay the next month's rent, although he knew that he was planning to sell out. The Resettlement Board has been very sympathetic with such cases; it has told tenants not to pay landlords rent any more, for they may suddenly be given yesterday's notice and the GG [government vehicles] will come to break down the house over their heads.

Solly was not at home when the landlord trekked. When he got there he found his furniture was left outside and a policeman was guarding the house. Poor Solly had to rush about looking for some place to put his stuff for the night. Half a dozen friends helped.

And I still wander among the ruins, trying to find one or two of the shebeens that Dr. Verwoerd [the prime minister] has overlooked. But I do not like the dead eyes with which some of these ghost houses stare back at me. One of these days, I, too, will get me out of here. Finish and clear!

Mr. Drum Goes to Jail

Henry Nxumalo

Drum, *a popular South African magazine aimed at a black urban readership, had
its heyday in the 1950s. It highlighted the work of black fiction writers and investigative journalists, such as Can Themba and Henry Nxumalo (1917–57). While much
of the magazine's content was devoted to glamorous photographs of African musicians like Miriam Makeba and sensationalist journalism about gangsters,* Drum
*also offered a forum for black writers to investigate the social ills and injustice
of apartheid South Africa. Henry Nxumalo wrote a number of these investigative
pieces under the name "Mr. Drum."*

*For this selection, Nxumalo deliberately got himself arrested so that he could
investigate conditions in a prominent urban jail, Johannesburg Central. Getting arrested was the easy part. By the time the piece was published, a quarter of a million
South Africans were sent to jail every year, mostly for pass offenses. Effectively, the
pass laws made criminals of all Africans. Nxumalo's piece uncovers the appalling
conditions and rampant violence of South African jails, which confronted petty violators like the author as well as long-term inmates.*

I served five days' imprisonment at the Johannesburg Central Prison from
January 20 to January 24. My crime was being found without a night pass
five minutes before midnight, and I was charged under the curfew regulations. I was sentenced to a fine of 10s. [shillings] or five days' imprisonment.

Two constables arrested me at the corner of Rissik and Plein Streets. I
was taken to Marshall Square Police Station, charged, searched, given two
blankets and locked up in the cells together with 37 others. The night was
long. The prison doors kept clanging as more prisoners trickled in during
the night. The cell itself was dark. I couldn't tell the day from the night.
Only the familiar shout of the young constable carrying a noisy bunch of
prison keys told us it was morning.

We had roll-call, breakfast, got back our personal effects and were packed
like sardines—over 40 of us—in a truck and delivered to the cells below
the magistrate's court. When we got off the truck into the cells below the

courts, one elderly-looking prisoner was a little slow to climb off. The prisoners were jostling to get off at once and blocking the way, and when the old man reached the ground he nearly missed the direction the other prisoners were taking. He looked about and S. saw him. He hit him with his open hand on the temples and told him to wake up. Before we appeared in court I asked one of the black constables to allow me to phone my employers and my family. He said: "Go on, voetsek!" [get lost]. Meanwhile white prisoners in the opposite cells were phoning their families and their employers without trouble from a wall telephone near the warder.

After our cases had been heard by the magistrate, we were sent back to the cells. Convicted prisoners who couldn't raise enough money to pay their fines employed various methods to get money. They either borrowed from those who had much less or bartered their clothes, promising to release their benefactors as soon as they were out. Discharged prisoners took messages to relatives of convicted prisoners.

This lasted about two hours; we were checked and taken to Johannesburg Central Prison by truck. We arrived at the prison immediately after one o'clock. From the truck we were given orders to "shayisa" (close up), fall in twos and "sharp shoot" (run) to the prison reception office. From then on "Come on, Kaffir" was the operative phrase from both black and white prison officials, and in all languages.

Many of us who were going to prison for the first time didn't know exactly where the reception office was. Although the prison officials were with us, no one was directing us. But if a prisoner hesitated, slackened his half-running pace and looked round, he got a hard boot kick on the buttocks, a slap on his face or a whipping from the warders. Fortunately there were some second offenders with us who knew where to go. We followed them through the prison's many zig-zagging corridors until we reached the reception office.

The reception office had a terrifyingly brutal atmosphere. It was full of foul language. A number of khaki-uniformed white officials stood behind a long cement bar-like curved counter. They wore the initials "PSGD" on their shoulders. When they were not joking about prisoners, they were swearing at them and taking down their particulars. Two were taking fingerprints and hitting the prisoners in the face when they made mistakes.

Five long-term prisoners attended to us. One came up to me and said he knew me. I didn't know him. He asked for cigarettes, but I didn't have any. Another told us to take off our watches and money and hold them in our hands. These were to be kept separate from our other possessions. Another asked me for 2s. 6d. [pence]; but I had 5d. only and he wasn't interested. He noticed I had a copy of *Time* magazine in my hand and asked for it. I gave it to him. He hid it under the counter so the warders couldn't see it. Later he asked me what paper it was, how old it was and whether it was interesting. After we had undressed, one long-term prisoner demanded my fountain pen.

"That's a fine pen you've got, eh?" he asked. "How about giving it to me?" I said: "I'm afraid I can't; it's not my pen, it's my boss's pen." "Hi, don't tell me lies, you bastard," he said, "what the hell are you doing with your boss's pen in prison? Did you steal it?" he asked. I said I hadn't stolen it. I was using it and had it in my possession when I was arrested. "Give it here. I want it for my work here; if you refuse you'll see blood streaming down your dirty mouth soon!" I was nervous, but didn't reply. "Look, you little fool, I'll see that you are well treated in prison if you give me that pen." The other prisoners looked at me anxiously. I didn't know whether they approved of my giving my pen or not; but their anxious look seemed to suggest that their fate in prison lay in that pen. I gave it away. . . .

After this we were marched down to the main court of the prison in double time. Here we found different white and black warders and long-term prisoners, who took charge of us. Again we undressed and had our second shower in 30 minutes. I was unable to make out my own clothes after the shower and the skipping. The African warder kicked me in the stomach with the toe of his boot. I tried to hold the boot to protect myself, and fell on my face. He asked if I had had an operation to my stomach. I said no. He looked at me scornfully. I got up, picked up the clothes in front of me and ran to join the others squatting on the floor.

After another roll-call we were marched to the top of the court to collect our food. The dishes were lined in rows and each prisoner picked up the dish nearest to him. The zinc dishes containing the food were rusty. The top of my dish was broken in three places. The food itself was boiled whole mealies with fat. We were marched to No.7 cell, given blankets and a sleeping mat and locked in.

We ate. The time was about 4.30 P.M. Clean water and toilet buckets were installed. But that water wasn't enough for 60 people. The long-term prisoners warned us not to use the water as if we were at our own homes. An old man went to fetch water with his dish at one stage and the long-term prisoner in charge of the cell swore at him. The old man insisted that he was thirsty and continued scooping the water. The long-term prisoner took the water away from him and threw it all over the old man's face.

There was a stinking smell when prisoners used the toilet bucket at night without toilet paper. At 8 P.M. the bell rang and we were ordered to be quiet and sleep. Some prisoners who had smuggled dagga [marijuana] and matches into the cell started conversing in whispers and smoking. The blankets were full of bugs; I turned round and round during the night without being able to sleep, and kept my prison clothes on for protection against bugs.

We were up at about six o'clock the following morning. I tried to get some water to wash my dish and drink. The dish was full of the previous night's fat, and I didn't know how I was going to do it. But the long-term prisoner shouted at me and ordered me to leave the water alone. I obeyed. He swore at me in Afrikaans, and ordered me to wipe the urine which was overflowing from the toilet bucket with a small sack cloth. I did so. He said I must wipe it dry; but the cloth was so small that the floor remained wet.

He told me to find two other prisoners to help me carry the toilet bucket out, empty it and clean it. It was full of the night's excrement. There were no volunteers, so I slipped to a corner and waited. He saw me and rushed at me. "What did I tell you, damn it; what did I say?" He slapped me on my left cheek with his right open hand as he spoke. He said he could have me put in solitary confinement if he wished. He could tell the chief warder that I had messed the floor and I would get an additional punishment. I kept quiet. I had done nothing of the sort. Finally he ordered two other prisoners to help me.

We emptied the bucket and washed it as the other prisoners were being lined up in readiness for breakfast. One of my colleagues tried to wash his hands after we had emptied the bucket. The white warder saw him and slashed him with the strap part of his baton. The dish containing my porridge—and many others—still had the previous night's fat. It had been washed in cold water. The breakfast itself was yellow porridge with half-cooked pieces of turnips, potatoes, carrots and other vegetables I could not recognise. No spoons are provided; so I had my breakfast with my stinking soiled hands. I didn't feel like eating, but feared that I would be inviting further trouble. . . .

One night I didn't have a mat to sleep on. Long-term prisoners in charge of the cells sometimes took a bundle of mats to make themselves comfortable beds, to the discomfort of other prisoners. In practice, a prisoner never knows where he will sleep the next day. It is all determined by your speed in "tausa" [body search], food and blanket queues. Invariably a prisoner is always using another prisoner's dirty blankets every night.

In the four days I was in prison—I got a remission of one day—I was kicked or thrashed every day. I saw many other prisoners being thrashed daily. I was never told what was expected of me, but had to guess. Sometimes I guessed wrong and got into trouble.

Long-term and short-term prisoners mixed freely at the prison. For example the famous A-D-, of Alexandra Township, who is doing a "10-year sentence for various crimes," was one of the most important persons in prison during my time. He was responsible for the in and out movements of other prisoners and was respected by prisoners and warders. Though I was a short-term prisoner, I, too, took orders from A-.

It was a common practice for short-term prisoners to give their small piece of meat to long-term prisoners on meat days for small favours such as tobacco, dagga, shoes (which are supposed to be supplied to Coloured prisoners only), wooden spoons—or to ensure that they were always supplied with sleeping mats.

Many other prisoners shared the same fate. There are no directions or rules read or posted in prison. At least I didn't see any. Thrashing time for warders was roll-call and breakfast time as well as supper time. For long-term prisoners it was inside the cells at all times. Long-term prisoners thrashed more prisoners more severely and much oftener than the prison officials themselves, and often in the presence of either white or black warders. All prisoners were called Kaffirs at all times.

Repeal the Pass Laws!

ANC Women's League and the Federation
of South African Women

One of the main goals of apartheid was to control the movement of Africans into urban areas, which the state had long considered to be fundamentally white space. Apartheid's social engineers took this to a new level by trying to allow only the number of Africans needed by white employers and no more. This plan, called "influx control," entailed a much more draconian system of pass-law enforcement. As part of the plan, the National Party government adopted the ironically named Abolition of Passes Act, which consolidated a variety of pass controls into one document. It also declared that African women, for the first time, would be required to carry passes. Women organized much of the opposition to the pass laws in the 1950s, arguing that not only were the pass laws in general unjust but that the requirement for women to carry them was an affront to female dignity and a threat to their role as mothers.

After the government declared its intention to enforce the requirement for women to carry passes beginning in 1956, the African National Congress (ANC) Women's League and the Federation of South African Women led a march of twenty thousand women to deliver the following petition, with one hundred thousand signatures, to the prime minister's office in Pretoria. They sang a song directed at the prime minister, J. G. Strijdom, telling him, "you have tampered with the women, you have struck a rock," a phrase that has been a byword of women's movements in South Africa ever since. The protest fell on deaf ears, however, and by the end of the decade, the authorities had succeeded in imposing the new burden. Protest against the pass laws peaked with demonstrations organized by the Pan Africanist Congress in 1960. The government met these demonstrations with armed force, resulting in the Sharpeville Massacre and the banning of all the liberation movements.

We, the women of South Africa, have come here today. We represent and we speak on behalf of hundreds of thousands of women who could not be with us. But all over the country, at this moment, women are watching and thinking of us. Their hearts are with us.

Women's march at Union buildings, Pretoria, © BAHA, photograph by Drum Photographer, dm2005020718. Used by permission of Bailey's African History Archive (BAHA).

We are women from every part of South Africa. We are women of every race, we come from the cities and the towns, from the reserves and the villages. We come as women united in our purpose to save the African women from the degradation of passes.

For hundreds of years the African people have suffered under the most bitter law of all—the pass law which has brought untold suffering to every African family.

Raids, arrests, loss of pay, long hours at the pass office, weeks in the cells awaiting trial, forced farm labour—this is what the pass laws have brought to African men. Punishment and misery—not for a crime, but for the lack of a pass.

We African women know too well the effect of this law upon our homes, our children. We, who are not African women, know how our sisters suffer.

Your Government proclaims aloud at home and abroad that the pass laws have been abolished, but we women know this is not true, for our husbands, our brothers? Our sons are still being arrested, thousands every day, under these very pass laws. It is only the name that has changed. The "reference book" and the pass are one.

In March 1952, your Minister of Native Affairs denied in Parliament that a law would be introduced which would force African women to carry passes. But in 1956 your Government is attempting to force passes upon the African women, and we are here today to protest against this insult to all women. For to us an insult to African women is an insult to all women.

- We want to tell you what the pass would mean to an African woman, and we want you to know that whether you call it a reference book, an identity book, or by any other disguising name, to us it is a PASS. And it means just this:—That homes will be broken up when women are arrested under pass laws
- That children will be left uncared for, helpless, and mothers will be torn from their babies for failure to produce a pass
- That women and young girls will be exposed to humiliation and degradation at the hands of pass-searching policemen
- That women will lose their right to move freely from one place to another.

In the name of women of South Africa, we say to you, each one of us, African, European, Indian, Coloured, that we are opposed to the pass system.

We voters and voteless, call upon your Government not to issue passes to African women.

We shall not rest until ALL pass laws and all forms of permits restricting our freedom have been abolished.

We shall not rest until we have won for our children their fundamental rights of freedom, justice, and security.

Programme of Action

ANC Youth League

A new generation infused the African National Congress (ANC) with youthful energy in the 1940s. Future leaders of the organization, such as Walter Sisulu, Oliver Tambo, and Nelson Mandela, came to the fore as a result of the changing social and political conditions of the 1940s. These included the rise of dynamic black urban communities like Sophiatown and a spirit of protest from boycotts of buses over fare increases to a huge black mine-workers' strike in 1946, which was crushed by the mines and government. The ANC Youth League, formed in 1944, began to challenge the tradition of the ANC as an elite body that politely petitioned white authorities and was left with nothing to show for it. After the apartheid government came to power in 1948, the ANC Youth League proposed a program of action that would harness the energy of black urban protest over social and economic conditions and put it toward a black nationalist agenda that was in sync with movements sweeping across colonial Africa after the Second World War.

The Programme of Action committed the ANC to nonviolent direct protests, including strikes, boycotts, and civil disobedience, aimed at achieving political rights. This approach was inspired by the methods Mohandas Gandhi (see part V) had pioneered on behalf of Indians in South Africa and later infused into India's independence struggle, which achieved its goal in 1947. The Programme of Action led to the Defiance Campaign of 1952, in which activists from the ANC, the South African Indian Congress, and other antiapartheid organizations engaged in civil disobedience against apartheid laws. Membership in the ANC, heretofore small, shot up to one hundred thousand during the campaign. This approach brought world renown and mass membership to the ANC but did not succeed in stopping the onslaught of ever-more repressive apartheid legislation and brutal enforcement. Mass protest would become a hallmark of the ANC until it and its offshoot, the Pan Africanist Congress, were banned in 1960.

The fundamental principles of the Programme of Action of the African National Congress are inspired by the desire to achieve national freedom. By national freedom we mean freedom from White domination and the attain-

Nelson Mandela in traditional dress portrait (wearing a Xhosa beadwork collar), 1950, Eli Weinberg Collection, UWC-Robben Island Mayibuye Archives, EW007-3-1. Courtesy of the Robben Island Museum.

ment of political independence. This implies the rejection of the conception of segregation, apartheid, trusteeship, or white leadership which are all, in one way or another, motivated by the idea of white domination or domination of the white over the Blacks.

Like all other people the African people claim the right of self-determination. With this object in view, in the light of these principles we claim and will continue to fight for the political rights . . . such as:

1. The right of direct representation in all the governing bodies of the country—national, provincial and local—and we resolve to work for the abolition of all differential institutions or bodies specially created for Africans, viz. representative councils, present form of parliamentary representation

2. To achieve these objectives the following Programme of Action is suggested:
   a. the creation of a national fund to finance the struggle for national liberation.
   b. the appointment of a committee to organise an appeal for funds and to devise ways and means therefor.
   c. the regular use of propaganda material through:
      i. the usual press, newsletter or other means of disseminating our ideas in order to raise the standard of political consciousness;
      ii. establishment of a national press.

3. Appointment of a council of action whose function should be to carry into effect, vigorously and with the utmost determination, the Programme of Action. It should be competent for the council of action to implement our resolve to work for:
   a. the abolition of all differential political institutions, the boycotting of which we accept, and to undertake a campaign to educate our people on this issue and, in addition, to employ the following weapons: immediate and active boycott, strike, civil disobedience, non-co-operation and such other means as may bring about the accomplishment and realisation of our aspirations.
   b. preparations and making of plans for a national stoppage of work for one day as a mark of protest against the reactionary policy of the government.

4. Economic:
   a. The establishment of commercial, industrial, transport and other enterprises in both urban and rural areas.
   b. Consolidation of the industrial organisation of the workers for the improvement of their standard of living.
   c. Pursuant to paragraph (a) herein, instructions be issued to Provincial Congresses to study the economic and social conditions in the reserves and other African settlements and to devise ways and means for their development, establishment of industries and such other enterprises as may give employment to a number of people.

5. Education:
   a. Raising the standard of Africans in the commercial, industrial and other enterprises and workers in their workers' organisations by means of providing a common educational forum wherein intellectuals, peasants and workers participate for the common good.
   b. Establishment of national centres of education for the purpose of

training and educating African youth and provision of large scale scholarships tenable in various overseas countries.

6. Cultural:
   a. To unite the cultural with the educational and national struggle.
   b. The establishment of a national academy of arts and sciences.

7. Congress realises that ultimately the people will be brought together by inspired leadership, under the banner of African nationalism, with courage and determination.

Khoesan rock art showing settlers with guns and horses. Rock Art Centre, University of the Witwatersrand, IZI RSA BEH1 1. Reproduced with permission, Iziko Museums of Cape Town Social History Collections Department, South Africa. http://www.sarada.co.za.

Klaarwater, later known as Griquatown. Painting by William John Burchell. Courtesy of the Collection of the Parliament of the Republic of South Africa, 125 Burchell Klaarwater.

Long Street, Cape Town, in 1845. Painting by Wilhelm Heinrich F. L. Langschmidt.
Courtesy of Izikio Social History and Art Collections, CD 115.

Orator at the Great Trek reenactment, 1988. Photography by Gideon Mendel.
© Gideon Mendel / Corbis, AAKA002070. Used with permission of Corbis Images.

"Don't Vote in Apartheid Elections!" UDF poster, 1984.

Informal settlement near township houses, Soweto, 2007. Photograph by Thomas McClendon.

Migrant worker hostel, Johannesburg, 2007. This hostel is near the city center. Hostels situated in or near townships were implicated as centers of violence by IFP-aligned migrant workers from KwaZulu-Natal against township dwellers. Photograph by Thomas McClendon.

Storefront of a traditional healer, Mai Mai market, Johannesburg, 2011.
Photograph by Thomas McClendon.

Women's Charter

Federation of South African Women

Throughout the twentieth century, women actively protested unfair burdens imposed by the state, and they also sought improved economic conditions. In 1913 African women in Bloemfontein demonstrated against an early attempt there to impose passes on them. In the 1920s African women in Natal protested against municipal monopolies on brewing and supplying traditional-style beer to African men. Starting in the 1930s, as black and white women entered the textile industry in large numbers, many organized in trade unions (some affiliated with the Communist Party) to seek better wages and conditions. In the 1950s urban women who had been active in labor struggles and in the Defiance Campaign came together in a large nonracial grouping, the Federation of South African Women, to fight for women's rights.

At the launch of the Federation of South African Women in April 1954, delegates adopted the Women's Charter. The document is a call for full legal rights for women of all races, arguing that ongoing legal disabilities for women were antiquated holdovers from the past that restrained progress for society as a whole in the modern industrial present. The charter also complains that men within the liberation movements had been guilty of opposing progress for women in attaining equal rights. In addition, the document demands vastly improved social services and education. Women continued organizing throughout the decade, culminating in the march on Pretoria in 1956.

Preamble: We, the women of South Africa, wives and mothers, working women and housewives, African, Indians, European and Coloured, hereby declare our aim of striving for the removal of all laws, regulations, conventions and customs that discriminate against us as women, and that deprive us in any way of our inherent right to the advantages, responsibilities and opportunities that society offers to any one section of the population.

*A **Single Society***: We women do not form a society separate from the men. There is only one society, and it is made up of both women and men.

As women we share the problems and anxieties of our men, and join hands with them to remove social evils and obstacles to progress.

Test of Civilisation: The level of civilisation which any society has reached can be measured by the degree of freedom that its members enjoy. The status of women is a test of civilisation. Measured by that standard, South Africa must be considered low in the scale of civilised nations.

Women's Lot: We women share with our menfolk the cares and anxieties imposed by poverty and its evils. As wives and mothers, it falls upon us to make small wages stretch a long way. It is we who feel the cries of our children when they are hungry and sick. It is our lot to keep and care for the homes that are too small, broken and dirty to be kept clean. We know the burden of looking after children and land when our husbands are away in the mines, on the farms, and in the towns earning our daily bread.

We know what it is to keep family life going in pondokkies [houses made of tin, reeds, and salvaged materials] and shanties, or in overcrowded one-room apartments. We know the bitterness of children taken to lawless ways, of daughters becoming unmarried mothers whilst still at school, of boys and girls growing up without education, training or jobs at a living wage.

Poor and Rich: These are evils that need not exist. They exist because the society in which we live is divided into poor and rich, into non-European and European. They exist because there are privileges for the few, discrimination and harsh treatment for the many. We women have stood and will stand shoulder to shoulder with our menfolk in a common struggle against poverty, race and class discrimination, and the evils of the colour bar.

National Liberation: As members of the National Liberatory movements and Trade Unions, in and through our various organisations, we march forward with our men in the struggle for liberation and the defence of the working people. We pledge ourselves to keep high the banner of equality, fraternity and liberty. As women there rests upon us also the burden of removing from our society all the social differences developed in past times between men and women, which have the effect of keeping our sex in a position of inferiority and subordination.

Equality for Women: We resolve to struggle for the removal of laws and customs that deny African women the right to own, inherit or alienate property. We resolve to work for a change in the laws of marriage such as are found amongst our African, Malay and Indian people, which have the effect of placing wives in the position of legal subjection to husbands, and giving husbands the power to dispose of wives' property and earnings, and dictate to them in all matters affecting them and their children.

We recognise that the women are treated as minors by these marriage and property laws because of ancient and revered traditions and customs which had their origin in the antiquity of the people and no doubt served purposes of great value in bygone times.

There was a time in the African society when every woman reaching marriageable stage was assured of a husband, home, land and security.

Then husbands and wives with their children belonged to families and clans that supplied most of their own material needs and were largely self-sufficient. Men and women were partners in a compact and closely integrated family unit.

Women who Labour: Those conditions have gone. The tribal and kinship society to which they belonged has been destroyed as a result of the loss of tribal land, migration of men away from the tribal home, the growth of towns and industries, and the rise of a great body of wage-earners on the farms and in the urban areas, who depend wholly or mainly on wages for a livelihood.

Thousands of African women, like Indians, Coloured and European women, are employed today in factories, homes, offices, shops, on farms, in professions as nurses, teachers and the like. As unmarried women, widows or divorcees they have to fend for themselves, often without the assistance of a male relative. Many of them are responsible not only for their own livelihood but also that of their children.

Large numbers of women today are in fact the sole breadwinners and heads of their families.

Forever Minors: Nevertheless, the laws and practices derived from an earlier and different state of society are still applied to them. They are responsible for their own person and their children. Yet the law seeks to enforce upon them the status of a minor.

Not only are African, Coloured and Indian women denied political rights, but they are also in many parts of the Union denied the same status as men in such matters as the right to enter into contracts, to own and dispose of property, and to exercise guardianship over their children.

Obstacle to Progress: The law has lagged behind the development of society; it no longer corresponds to the actual social and economic position of women. The law has become an obstacle to progress of the women, and therefore a brake on the whole of society.

This intolerable condition would not be allowed to continue were it not for the refusal of a large section of our menfolk to concede to us women the rights and privileges which they demand for themselves.

We shall teach the men that they cannot hope to liberate themselves from the evils of discrimination and prejudice as long as they fail to extend to women complete and unqualified equality in law and in practice.

Need for Education: We also recognise that large numbers of our women-folk continue to be bound by traditional practices and conventions, and fail to realise that these have become obsolete and a brake on progress. It is our duty and privilege to enlist all women in our struggle for emancipation and to bring to them all realisation of the intimate relationship that exists between their status of inferiority as women and the inferior status to which their people are subjected by discriminatory laws and colour prejudices.

It is our intention to carry out a nation-wide programme of education that will bring home to the men and women of all national groups the realisation that freedom cannot be won for any one section or for the people as a whole as long as we women are kept in bondage.

An Appeal: We women appeal to all progressive organisations, to members of the great National Liberatory movements, to the trade unions and working class organisations, to the churches, educational and welfare organisations, to all progressive men and women who have the interests of the people at heart, to join with us in this great and noble endeavour.

Our Aims

We declare the following aims:

This organisation is formed for the purpose of uniting women in common action for the removal of all political, legal, economic and social disabilities. We shall strive for women to obtain:

1. The right to vote and to be elected to all State bodies, without restriction or discrimination.
2. The right to full opportunities for employment with equal pay and possibilities of promotion in all spheres of work.
3. Equal rights with men in relation to property, marriage and children, and for the removal of all laws and customs that deny women such equal rights.
4. For the development of every child through free compulsory education for all; for the protection of mother and child through maternity homes, welfare clinics, creches and nursery schools, in countryside and towns; through proper homes for all, and through the provision of water, light, transport, sanitation, and other amenities of modern civilisation.

5. For the removal of all laws that restrict free movement, that prevent or hinder the right of free association and activity in democratic organisations, and the right to participate in the work of these organisations.

6. To build and strengthen women's sections in the National Liberatory movements, the organisation of women in trade unions, and through the peoples' varied organisation.

7. To cooperate with all other organisations that have similar aims in South Africa as well as throughout the world.

8. To strive for permanent peace throughout the world.

My Spirit Is Not Banned

Frances Baard and Barbie Schreiner

*Women were central as organizers and activists in the antiapartheid struggles of
the 1950s. Many of the women who were leaders in these efforts came to national
politics from the direct material struggles around conditions and wages in the factories as part of the trade-union movement. One such leader was Frances Baard
(1909–97). Baard shows the linkages among the union movement, the effort to organize as women in the Federation of South African Women and the African National Congress (ANC) Women's League, and other political movements. Along with
other leaders from the Federation of South African Women and the ANC Women's
League, Baard was one of the leaders of the women's antipass march in Pretoria in
1956. She also came under the sharp eye of the authorities. As one of the drafters of
the Freedom Charter, she became a defendant in the Treason Trial of 1956 and in the
1960s served a five-year sentence for ANC activities.*

*Here Baard describes union organizing and the obstacles raised by the Group
Areas Act, and she describes the role of women in the ANC. She also recalls the
apartheid state's imposition of Bantu Education, which imposed state control over
education (formerly provided mainly by missionaries) and severely diminished the
curriculum's academic content. Apartheid theorists argued that Africans should
only receive enough education to be good servants and low-level workers. Though
opponents initially lost the struggle against Bantu Education, it was to become a
focus of opposition in the 1970s and 1980s as schoolchildren, frustrated by these limitations, took to the streets.*

There was a certain lady from Cape Town who was a trade unionist. She
was Ray Alexander. In 1948 she came to Port Elizabeth and she came to talk
to us at the factory about trade unions and about how to organize the workers. She came to the factory at lunch time one day and she called all those
of us who were outside having lunch. She held a meeting with us. She told
us that she's the organizing secretary, general secretary of the food and canning union and she wants to open a branch here. We were very interested
to listen to her, and she told us everything how the unions work. She was a

very brave lady. She was always organizing the workers. She began to come to the factory every day to talk to us. Then she picked some people from the workers to help her organize the other workers, and she picked me. I started organizing since that time. . . .

It was Ray who helped us to start the trade union in the canning factories in Port Elizabeth. She taught us how to run the union, and we learnt administration and taking minutes, how to chair a meeting, and about shop stewards and so on, so that the union should be properly run. She was a wonderful person, Ray Alexander. We used to call her our mother. When the government banned her in 1953, the workers came out on strike to say no, they can't do this to our mother, they cannot make her leave the trade unions like this. . . .

We found it was not so difficult to get the workers interested in the trade union because they knew that they were getting very little money, and when the union was telling them that "If you are united you can fight for more wages," they knew they must come together to make things better. We used to have meetings at lunch time at the factory to talk to the workers. Not all the workers had lunch at the same time, and so we had to have little meetings all at different times.

After a time we decided that we must now have our own somebody to look after the workers, we must have a committee and a secretary for ourselves, a person who can organize the workers. So we had a meeting in a big hall and many of the workers were called to that meeting. When the workers got there, we decided that someone must be elected for the office. I was the first person to be elected for organizing secretary in Port Elizabeth, for the African Food and Canning Workers Union. Then I had to leave the factory and go to work at the trade union office. There were three of us women working at the office. We had a big office in Korsten—that was a coloured area there—and the coloured desk was this side, and the African desk this side, in the same office.

You see, there were really two unions there, the one for coloured people and the one for Africans, because there was this law from the government that would not allow us to be one union. So there was my union, the African Food and Canning Workers Union, and then there was the Food and Canning Workers Union. But we worked together all the time like we were one union. We always had our meetings and discussions together, and all our strikes we did together too. . . .

At the meetings or at the factories, the workers would tell us their complaints, and we see what are the worst problems. Sometimes we have a complaint which we must take to the management with the committee.

Police checking passes in 1960, © BAHA, photograph by Drum Photographer, dm2004011308. Used by permission of Bailey's African History Archive (BAHA).

We had a committee in each factory. When I get to the one factory they tell me this and this is wrong, and then I talk to the other committee as well, and then the two committees decide that we have to see the management. That was how the two sides worked together all the time.

It was whenever the season was strong and there was lots of fruit coming into the factory that we bring a lot of complaints because then we knew that the management would just help, help, and give us what we want because he can't afford that we should stop work at that time.

But sometimes the management would not give us what we want. They say no, they are not going to do anything about our problems. Then the workers have a meeting, and we take a vote with all the members of the union. They put up their hands at the meeting, yes they want this strike, or no they don't want it. Maybe they take a decision that we are going to strike if what we want from the employers is not met. We go back to the management, even if it is for high wages, or anything, and if he doesn't want to take up our grievances, then the only alternative we have is to strike. We used to try again, try to talk to them, because we didn't like strikes because the workers used to be dismissed and some used to be arrested when we went on strike, so we always try to talk to the management first. If we have a strike, all the workers would stand outside the factory. Nobody would go in. And those who wanted to go in, they were afraid of the others, and we did not allow them to work, because when you are fighting for high wages, when the money goes up, everyone is going to get it, so everyone must support the strike.

The workers would tell other people in the townships, "There's a strike at such-and-such a place, and not a single person must go there and look for work." So then the other people would not go there for scab labour. . . .

All this time things were going very nicely for us in that little house in New Brighton [Port Elizabeth] until in 1952, my husband suddenly passed away. . . . I went to see him at the hospital, and I found when I got there that he had already passed away. He just collapsed. I think it was high blood pressure and a heart attack. It was such a shock. I couldn't understand so young a person to die like that of high blood pressure. And so quick too. And suddenly I was alone in the house to look after the children. . . .

We had our offices there in Korsten. It was a coloured area, but we had our offices together, African and coloured. Then came this legislation which was passed in parliament, the Group Areas Act.

This Group Areas Act was a terrible thing. It was so us Africans were told not to be in a coloured area any more. The police came to raid our office where we were, to tell us the coloureds must be alone there, and the Africans must move. We didn't want to separate ourselves. We had worked together for a long time. But they came to our office and they told me I must take my union somewhere in the location.

It was impossible to move to the location because it is very far for the workers to go from the factory for meetings and complaints during lunch times and so forth. Korsten was most central for those workers at Jones and at Langeberg and they used to come to the offices. So we decided to stay in Korsten. We refused to separate. And because we stayed together the special branch [secret police] used to watch us. They used to run after us. Every time we want to hold a meeting, they would be there, at the place, watching us. We don't even know who told them we are having a meeting; we just see them there. If we wish to hide ourselves and go and have our meeting somewhere they don't know, they will hunt the whole night until they find us, or they don't find us. That was how we held our meetings. Sometimes when they found us they would charge us with public nuisance or something. Then you must go to the charge office, and then to the magistrate's court where maybe you will be fined, or maybe discharged. But most of the time they used to disperse the meeting, or maybe take our names and tell the people to go home. . . .

Another time I went to organize some workers at East London. We used to do a lot of organizing at East London, talking to the workers and so on to help them there because they were not as well organized as our branch. When I got to East London, I thought well, the best thing to do, since there is this permit thing, I must go to the commissioner's office and get a permit. So I was given a permit so I could stay for the week-end, or for a few days maybe, without I must worry about the police. Early the next morning I was still sleeping at the hotel. I hear—shoo! loud!—"The police! the police! the police!" They were checking the hotel. I thought, well there's no worry this time; I've got a permit now. They were going from room to room checking the permits of the other people and leaving them. All that time they wanted me! When they came to me at last I took out my permit, and I thought no, it's all right, I've got a permit. They look at my permit. Then they look at me. Then the one says, "Kom aan [come on]. We want you."

"*Ag* what for now? I've got a permit *mos*."

Well, I was taken to the charge office and I was charged there, I don't know what for because they didn't catch me at the factory or anything, they just caught me at the hotel where I was sleeping. I didn't even address any meetings yet. The magistrate gave me one hour to leave East London. . . .

For a long time the women were not proper members of the ANC. They only changed that in 1943 when the women were allowed to join properly. That was when the Women's League started. So it was a very big thing for us to organize the women like that.

We used to go out in the evening mainly when everyone is home from work, and we walk from house to house in the location and talk to the women. We knock on the door, and when they open we tell them we are from the Women's League and can we talk to them. We talk about the problems they have—maybe it's high rent or no money for food. The women were always worried about their sons and their husbands being arrested for passes all the time. And they are worried maybe they will lose their houses. Also there were things that the people as a whole did not like, things that were very strong in their lives like housing and jobs and passes (some people could not get jobs because their passes were not right) and we used to talk to the women about these things too. The women had lots of problems. It is always the women who are trying to feed the family and look after them, and there is too little money and so on. We tell them how we want to do something about these troubles, and how they must join us so we can be strong and go to the authorities about all these things. After a while we had a group of women behind us who all wanted to help. Then we started to have big meetings. We would tell the women that there was going to be a meeting at the hall and they should come. Sometimes we used to have pamphlets to tell them about the meeting, or else we used to make an announcement about the women's meeting at the general meeting on Sunday.

There were a lot of women who did join us and they brought a lot of complaints about all the things that they wanted made better, and we had a lot of work to do. We used to take up complaints about everything we didn't like in the location, and we used to go and see the superintendent often about our problems to tell him to fix this thing or that thing. Sometimes we were successful with our complaints, and there were a lot of things we had improved. One of the first things we dealt with was the single men's quarters. We went to see the superintendent about it and he told us it was an old building and it was too small. He said that there were many people coming to town to look for work and many of them came there looking for somewhere to sleep. He said there were too many people and not enough space, but there was nothing he could do about it. We asked him if they couldn't build a bigger place, but he said that was not for him to answer; he had to take that to his superiors. But after a time they did build another hostel and those people were given a place to stay there.

But us women, even when we did things like this, we never used to work by ourselves, because we were part of the ANC as a whole. We used to have our own meetings, just the women, and talk about what we wanted to do and how to do it. Then we would go to the general meeting and tell them, "Such and such a thing is so and so, and we want to do this and this."

And we would tell them exactly what we wanted to do to put this thing right. We would discuss it all together at the general meeting and decide on it, and we would get a mandate from them. We couldn't do things by ourselves; we had to work together so that everyone knew what we were going to do, and everyone agreed.

We women had a lot of problems at that time which the men didn't have to worry about. I remember there was one thing which we all used to worry about. If a woman's husband died they used to chase her out of the house, or tell her to get another husband, because only married women can have houses. I had a case with one woman who came to me one day. Her husband had just died and they chased her out of the house she lived in. She came to me and told me how they chased her out. I went and spoke to them and said, "But how can you let a woman go out of her house and yet she's got children? Where must she go?"

Then they tell me, "No, she must go back to the kraal; there will be a husband waiting for her there." . . .

In 1953 the government passed the Bantu Education Act which the people didn't want. We didn't want this bad education for our children. This Bantu

Education Act was to make sure that our children only learnt things that would make them good for what the government wanted: to work in the factories and so on they must not learn properly at school like the white children. Our children were to go to school only three hours a day, two shifts of children every day, one in the morning and one in the afternoon, so that more children could get a little bit of learning without government having to spend more money. Hawu! [expression of surprise] it was a terrible thing that act. Verwoerd—he was the minister that time—he wanted the Africans to stay in the reserves except when they had to come and work for the white people. He didn't want our children to get a proper education; he wanted to keep them down with this education system. Before that time the education was a little bit better, mostly the schools were run by the missionaries, but now all the schools were going to be run by the government.

In December 1954 at the ANC conference we rejected this new education plan and we started to organize for a boycott of government schools. I used to go about with other people exclaiming to the parents what Bantu Education is about, what does it mean, and how are the children going to be affected, because some of them didn't understand. And we told them, "If you agree with us that this education is bad for our children then we are going to boycott this education by taking our children out of schools to show the government we are not satisfied."

Many parents were anxious too. They didn't want their children to get that Bantu Education. They took their children out of the schools so much that in the government schools there was no child who attended school. But we couldn't leave the children like that, out of school and learning nothing. So every morning we used to have buses standing to collect all the children to take them to the veld. We used to take them there and get some teachers to teach them. We called them cultural clubs because we weren't allowed to call them schools, and we weren't allowed to have teachers either; we had to call them club leaders. It was illegal to have a school that wasn't registered with the government, so we had to pretend that the cultural clubs weren't schools. We weren't allowed to have books or blackboards or anything like that either. Some other people organized things for the children to be taught, (I know Helen Joseph [an important member of the antiapartheid movement and a defendant in the Treason Trial] was very involved in that) and we used songs and stories to teach the children. They would sing a song about history, Dingaan or Shaka or whatever, or there would be a story they can hear about geography or what. The teachers would draw in the sand instead of writing on a blackboard. And they went on like that. . . .

Protest against the introduction of Bantu Education, 1955, © BAHA, photograph by
Drum Photographer, dm2002032703. Used by permission of Bailey's African History
Archive (BAHA).

All this time there was still this thing of passes for women going on, and
the women still protesting. Quite soon after the Congress of the People [po-
litical summit of the Congress Alliance in 1955] there was a big conference
of the women overseas called the Congress of Mothers. We had a conference in Port Elizabeth in solidarity with that conference, and they had one
in Johannesburg too. That was in August 1955. At that conference we also
endorsed the Freedom Charter. Lilian [Ngoyi] went to that conference overseas and when she came back she came to Port Elizabeth and we organized
a big meeting for her to speak against the passes. You know there were
maybe 6,000 people at that meeting! It was outside and Lilian stood on the
back of a truck to talk to the people; we had no stage or anything.

Then in October many women in the Transvaal went to the Union Buildings to protest to Strijdom, the prime minister, that we didn't want these
passes. That was a very strong protest, 2000 women of all races at the Union
Buildings. In Port Elizabeth we had a meeting of the women to support the
Transvaal women in this thing.

This protest to the Union Buildings was so good that the next year the
Federation decided that we should do it again but this time we would send

thousands of women from all over South Africa, black and white, to tell Strijdom the same thing. So each of us in her own place had to organize the women for this protest. We only had a few months to prepare for this but we wanted to send many, many women so that Strijdom would know that we really meant what we were saying. The first thing that we did in Port Elizabeth after the decision had been made was to call a meeting of all the women. We told them what had been decided and that we are going to the Union Buildings to protest, and that we will have to work very hard to do this.

We went from branch to branch organizing the women. Florence Matomela and I used to organize together for most of the campaigns, and we worked together on this one too. She would take one section of the location, and I would take another, and we would each work in that portion. . . .

But before we went to Pretoria we got all the women who couldn't go to sign petitions to say that they also didn't want these passes. Every woman who was on that train took those petitions with her to give to Strijdom.

It is two days by train from Port Elizabeth to Pretoria. Two days on the train sitting in the railway carriage, singing all the way. First we went to Johannesburg and we slept the night in Soweto, and then the next day, it was August 9th, we went to Pretoria. Some took buses, some trains, some taxis, anything to get to Pretoria. Some people were volunteers who were to look after everyone and make sure that everything went smoothly. They had to see that the women got to the Union Buildings, either by bus or on foot. They told the women walking not to walk like it is a procession because otherwise the police would have stopped them before they got there. We had to walk like we were all going somewhere by ourselves, not like we were a group. Then we all walked into the yard of the Union Buildings and we waited there for all the women coming from other places: Lady Selborne, and all through the Transvaal, and through the Cape and so on. We all had those protest forms with us and there were some extra ones for those who hadn't brought them. We waited until all the women were gathered there. It was about 20 000 of us altogether!

Then we went up into the place there in front of the buildings, what they call the amphitheatre. It took a long time, maybe nearly two hours or more for all the women to walk up the steps to that place. Some of us had been chosen, Lillian, Helen, Rahima Moosa, myself and some others, eight of us, we took all those petitions that had been signed, piles and piles of them, and we marched up to Strijdom's office to give them to him. The secretary told us that Strijdom was not there and that we were not allowed in anyway because we were black and white together. They said he was not there, just like that. But we knew that he was just too scared to see us! We walked past the secretary and into his office and we put those pamphlets on his desk, and on the floor, and the room was full of them. You know, they say Strijdom never even looked at those petitions; the special branch just took them away!

Then we walked outside again and joined the other women who were waiting in the amphitheatre. All the women were quiet. 20 000 women standing there, some with their babies on their backs, and so quiet, no noise at all, just waiting. What a sight, so quiet, and so much colour, many women in green, gold and black [ANC colors], and the Indian women in their bright saris! Then Lilian started to speak. She told everyone that the prime minister was not there and that he was too scared to see us but that we left the petitions there for him to see. Then we stood in silence for half an hour. Everyone stood with their hands raised in the salute, silent, and even the babies hardly cried. For half an hour we stood there in the sun. And not a sound. Just the clock striking. Then Lilian started to sing and we all sang with her. I'll never forget the song we sang then. It was a song especially written for that occasion. It was written by a woman from the Free State. It went: "Wena Strijdom, wa'thinthabaJazi, Wathint'embokotho, uzokuJa!" That means: "You Strijdom, you have touched the women, you have struck against rock, you will die." Of course he did die, not long after that.

Freedom Charter

Congress of the People

In 1955 a coalition of antiapartheid organizations aligned with the African National Congress (ANC) met in Kliptown (now part of Soweto) as the Congress of the People and adopted the Freedom Charter. It quickly became a key point of reference for the struggle against apartheid, and it remains an important touchstone for South African political discourse. Organizations representing all racial groups, as well as labor unions, sent three thousand delegates to the meeting, which was held in the open air for two days in June. While the meeting was in progress, police photographed the participants and took notes of the speeches. They eventually moved in to seize documents and broke up the meeting. The state charged 156 of the organizers with treason. All were eventually acquitted, but the trial and banning orders made political activity nearly impossible.

The Freedom Charter offers a utopian vision of an open and democratic society in which all would have access to political and legal rights, housing, education, and economic opportunity. In other words, it is a call for a South Africa that was opposite to that being created under apartheid. In keeping with the politics of other national liberation movements and newly decolonized nations at the time, the charter is a plea for the wealth of the land and its minerals to be restored to the people. In recent years, populists like the ANC Youth League leader Julius Malema (see part VIII) have pointed to this language to call for nationalization of the mines and redistribution of farms, contrary to the procapitalist policies of the ANC in power. A recent breakaway party from the ANC trumpeted its claim on the ideals of the Freedom Charter by naming itself the Congress of the People.

We, the People of South Africa, declare for all our country and the world to know:

That South Africa belongs to all who live in it, black and white, and that no government can justly claim authority unless it is based on the will of all the people;

That our people have been robbed of their birthright to land, liberty and peace by a form of government founded on injustice and inequality;

That our country will never be prosperous or free until all our people live in brotherhood, enjoying equal rights and opportunities;

That only a democratic state, based on the will of all the people, can secure to all their birthright without distinction of colour, race, sex or belief;

And therefore, we, the people of South Africa, black and white together, equals, countrymen and brothers adopt this Freedom Charter;

And we pledge ourselves to strive together, sparing neither strength nor courage, until the democratic changes here set out have been won.

The People Shall Govern!

Every man and woman shall have the right to vote for and to stand as a candidate for all bodies which make laws;

All people shall be entitled to take part in the administration of the country;

The rights of the people shall be the same, regardless of race, colour or sex;

All bodies of minority rule, advisory boards, councils and authorities shall be replaced by democratic organs of self-government.

All National Groups Shall have Equal Rights!

There shall be equal status in the bodies of state, in the courts and in the schools for all national groups and races;

All people shall have equal right to use their own languages, and to develop their own folk culture and customs;

All national groups shall be protected by law against insults to their race and national pride;

The preaching and practice of national, race or colour discrimination and contempt shall be a punishable crime;

All apartheid laws and practices shall be set aside.

The People Shall Share in the Country's Wealth!

The national wealth of our country, the heritage of South Africans, shall be restored to the people;

The mineral wealth beneath the soil, the Banks and monopoly industry shall be transferred to the ownership of the people as a whole;

All other industry and trade shall be controlled to assist the well-being of the people;

All people shall have equal rights to trade where they choose, to manufacture and to enter all trades, crafts and professions.

The Land Shall be Shared Among Those Who Work It!

Restrictions of land ownership on a racial basis shall be ended, and all the land re-divided amongst those who work it to banish famine and land hunger;

The state shall help the peasants with implements, seed, tractors and dams to save the soil and assist the tillers;

Freedom of movement shall be guaranteed to all who work on the land;

All shall have the right to occupy land wherever they choose;

People shall not be robbed of their cattle, and forced labour and farm prisons shall be abolished.

All Shall be Equal Before the Law!

No-one shall be imprisoned, deported or restricted without a fair trial;

No-one shall be condemned by the order of any Government official;

The courts shall be representative of all the people;

Imprisonment shall be only for serious crimes against the people, and shall aim at re-education, not vengeance;

The police force and army shall be open to all on an equal basis and shall be the helpers and protectors of the people;

All laws which discriminate on grounds of race, colour or belief shall be repealed.

All Shall Enjoy Equal Human Rights!

The law shall guarantee to all their right to speak, to organise, to meet together, to publish, to preach, to worship and to educate their children;

The privacy of the house from police raids shall be protected by law;

All shall be free to travel without restriction from countryside to town, from province to province, and from South Africa abroad;

Pass Laws, permits and all other laws restricting these freedoms shall be abolished.

There Shall be Work and Security!

All who work shall be free to form trade unions, to elect their officers and to make wage agreements with their employers;

The state shall recognise the right and duty of all to work, and to draw full unemployment benefits;

Men and women of all races shall receive equal pay for equal work;

There shall be a forty hour working week, a national minimum wage, paid annual leave, and sick leave for all workers, and maternity leave on full pay for all working mothers;

Miners, domestic workers, farm workers and civil servants shall have the same rights as all others who work;

Child labour, compound labour, the tot system [paying farm workers with alcohol] and contract labour shall be abolished.

The Doors of Learning and Culture Shall be Opened!

The government shall discover, develop and encourage national talent for the enhancement of our cultural life;

All the cultural treasures of mankind shall be open to all, by free exchange of books, ideas and contact with other lands;

The aim of education shall be to teach the youth to love their people and their culture, to honour human brotherhood, liberty and peace;

Education shall be free, compulsory, universal and equal for all children;

Higher education and technical training shall be opened to all by means of state allowances and scholarships awarded on the basis of merit;

Adult illiteracy shall be ended by a mass state education plan;

Teachers shall have all the rights of other citizens;

The colour bar in cultural life, in sport and in education shall be abolished.

There Shall be Houses, Security and Comfort!

All people shall have the right to live where they choose, be decently housed, and to bring up their families in comfort and security;

Unused housing space to be made available to the people;

Rent and prices shall be lowered, food plentiful and no-one shall go hungry;

A preventive health scheme shall be run by the state;

Free medical care and hospitalisation shall be provided for all, with special care for mothers and young children;

Slums shall be demolished, and new suburbs built where all have transport, roads, lighting, playing fields, creches and social centres;

The aged, the orphans, the disabled and the sick shall be cared for by the state;

Rest, leisure and recreation shall be the right of all:

Fenced locations and ghettoes shall be abolished, and laws which break up families shall be repealed.

There Shall be Peace and Friendship!

South Africa shall be a fully independent state which respects the rights and sovereignty of all nations;

South Africa shall strive to maintain world peace and the settlement of all international disputes by negotiation—not war;

Peace and friendship amongst all our people shall be secured by upholding the equal rights, opportunities and status of all;

The people of the protectorates Basutoland, Bechuanaland and Swaziland shall be free to decide for themselves their own future;

The right of all peoples of Africa to independence and self-government shall be recognised, and shall be the basis of close co-operation.

Let all people who love their people and their country now say, as we say here:

THESE FREEDOMS WE WILL FIGHT FOR, SIDE BY SIDE, THROUGHOUT OUR LIVES, UNTIL WE HAVE WON OUR LIBERTY.

The Manifesto of Paramount Chief
K. D. Matanzima, 1963

K. D. Matanzima

The government first introduced grand apartheid, or separate development, in the Transkei, the country's largest "native reserve" and important source of migrant labor. The new policies began in the 1950s with the Bantu authorities system, a pyramidical and overlapping structure of local and territorial governance organized on the basis of tribes headed by hereditary chiefs and locally appointed headmen who controlled individual locations. Separate development operated under the assumptions that Africans belonged to discrete tribes who inhabited given territories and that these areas should be politically autonomous. In this sense, Africans would achieve their independence much as the rest of Africa in what was the era of decolonization. The South African government passed the Bantu Self Government Act in 1959, which led to elections in 1963 and the creation of a Transkei parliament. The homeland became nominally independent in 1976, with its capital at Umtata (now Mthatha), though it had no international recognition.

Chief Kaiser Daliwonga Matanzima (1915–2003) headed the Transkei government until 1987. He was also recognized by the South African government as the tribal head of the Emigrant Thembu. Matanzima, a nephew of Nelson Mandela, attended Fort Hare University to study law. He entered Transkei politics in 1948 and became a stalwart supporter of apartheid. Mandela and others in the African National Congress and allied movements condemned Matanzima. In 1962 he survived an assassination attempt by the armed wing of the Pan Africanist Congress. Matanzima issued his manifesto the following year. He ruled the Transkei dictatorially and with the support of the South African government, banning and arresting opponents. Widespread evidence of corruption forced him into retirement and internal exile.

As the future Chief Minister of the Transkei I wish the people to know that:

1. I stand for the policy of separate development which is the cornerstone of the Transkei Constitution Act which has granted self-government to the Transkei.

2. Chieftainship should be preserved and, in order to do so, chiefs should participate in the body that makes the laws—the Transkei Legislative Assembly.

3. The Transkei should have its own industries but no European private enterprise should be allowed. Initially the Transkei government acting with the Republican government [of South Africa] on the commonwealth relationship should start industries which can later be taken over by Bantu companies or individuals.

4. All the land in the Transkei should belong to the Bantu including municipal land in the 26 villages of the Transkei. This will be done by the gradual elimination of the white. In other words, the land that formerly belonged to the British King (Crown land) and later to the South African Native Trust, will be transferred to the Transkeian government and land held on freehold title by whites should be purchased by the Republican government for occupation by Bantu in terms of the 1936 legislation [an amendment of the Natives' Lands Act of 1913]. Municipalities will be zoned on a gradual process until they are wholly occupied by Bantu. Additional land formerly occupied by Bantu will, after consultation with the Republican government, be added to the Transkeian territories. I refer to such land as in the districts of Queenstown, Lady Frere, Indwe, Maclear, Elliot, Ugie, Mount Currie, Harding and Port Shepstone.

5. The Department of Education in the Transkei should be solely responsible for the nature and standard of education to be given to the Bantu child. The Republican government should stop interfering. The people of the Transkei should decide on the medium of instruction and syllabi.

6. The Transkei civil service should be entirely black and the salaries paid to the staff should compare favourably with those paid to the white civil servants in the Republic of South Africa. The principle of equal pay for equal work would be demanded if the Transkei were a multi-racial society, but since the Transkei is to be a black state we can only promise high salaries for our staff and compare these with those of the whites in the Republic. This is my objective.

7. Agriculture should be put on a high standard. It means that every able-bodied man owning land should use modern methods of farming. The whole country should be completely rehabilitated. Irrigation schemes, such as that under construction at Qamata, should be undertaken. Soil erosion should be stopped. Dams should be constructed. Stock should be of good quality.

8. Roads and bridges should be so well constructed that quick communication will be facilitated.

9. The Transkei will require financial stability. Good relations with the Republican government will have to be maintained in order to facilitate the flow of money from that country to the Transkei by way of grants and employment of the people of the Transkei in the border industries and elsewhere.

10. The expeditious transfer of the departments presently left in the care of the Republican government will be considered. The Department of Public Health and Labour should be the first to be transferred as soon as conditions become favourable.

11. I propose to make representations to the Republican government for the establishment of a Bantu battalion of the Transkei government in the Republican defence force: The object is to train our young men for military service in the event of war involving Africa and to prepare for the establishment of a Department of Defence in the Transkei.

12. I will strive to induce the Republican government to employ Bantu men and women in all the departments that have not been transferred to the Transkei government so as to train them for independence.

13. In granting licences for trading, Bantu traders will receive first consideration and the radius rule between Bantu and European trading stations will be abolished.

As a graduate of the University of South Africa in Arts, having majored in Roman Law and Politics with English II, Latin I, Psychology I, Native Law, South African criminal Law and Roman Dutch Law as subsidiary subjects and having passed the Attorneys Admission Examination, obtaining the first position amongst Cape candidates, I feel positive that I will be able to discharge my duties as head of the Transkei government with all the competence that is expected from a distinguished statesman. My achievement in piloting discussions between the Transkeian Territorial Authority Executive Committee and the Minister of Bantu Education, resulting in the appointment of an all black Commission of Inquiry into complaints levelled against Bantu Education is sufficient evidence of my statesmanship and is a pointer to the achievement of much greater things for my people in future.

As an administrator with 23 years' service, I am competent to deal with any situation on a national or international level. My colleagues, the chiefs of the Transkei, will admit that their status socially [and] economically improved as soon as the Bantu Authorities Act was introduced. In 1954 the United Transkeian Territories General Council resolved unanimously that the Transkei did not want Bantu Authorities. But as soon as I joined the Bunga [Council] in 1955 a motion from Emigrant Tembuland challenged the 1954 decision and asked for the abolition of that puppet body, the Bunga, and the substitution therefor of Bantu Authorities—hence Proclamation No. 180 of 1958.

If anybody wants to see what I have done for my people during the last 23 years of service to them, let him visit Emigrant Tembuland for personal observation. The present Act was piloted by me. During the struggle for self-government, Paramount Chief Botha Sigcau [of Eastern Pondonland, Transkei] and I experienced the most trying and difficult time resulting from revolts engineered by communists. Were it not for our bravery and statesmanship, the position of the chiefs and other colleagues who assisted us would have been in jeopardy. We should be allowed to continue our work until men of similar calibre appear who are prepared to carry on similar work. There is no room for Communists and Liberals in the Transkei.

Actions speak louder than words.

The Peasants' Revolt

Govan Mbeki

The implementation of the Bantu Authorities Act of 1951 provoked widespread re-sistance, most famously in the Transkei, which erupted in open revolt in 1960. The South African government deployed the armed forces and in November declared a state of emergency, which remained in effect for nearly three decades. The police and army detained more than 3,500 people. More than 280 people died.

Govan Mbeki (1910–2001), the father of South Africa's second president, Thabo Mbeki, grew up in the Transkei and, like many African leaders, attended Fort Hare University. He became involved in resistance politics from the 1940s. Govan Mbeki was a member of the African National Congress and the South African Communist Party, and he was imprisoned with Mandela on Robben Island; he was released in 1987, after twenty-four years. Throughout his life Mbeki played a central role in call-ing attention to the economic and social conditions of Africans in South Africa, in-cluding in the homelands, about which he wrote an influential booklet that reported on the Transkei revolt. In the excerpt here, Mbeki describes the policies of apartheid and the divisive politics of tribalism in South Africa.

The Transkei is Dr Verwoerd's answer to world-wide criticism of apart-heid. Upon this area, smaller than Togo, the smallest independent African state, but bigger than Basutoland on which it borders, the South African government's claims for its racial policy stand or fall. To those who say that apartheid is discriminatory and oppressive, the South African government replies that it provides the only chance the African people have ever had to "develop along their own lines," in their own areas; that the establishment of a Bantustan in the Transkei is to give that country an independence more meaningful and secure than the independence attained elsewhere in Africa during the last decade.

The establishment in South Africa of Bantustans is based on the apart-heid supposition that certain areas of the country belong to the Whites, and others, generally known as the reserves, to the Africans, with neither people able to enjoy rights in the areas belonging to the other. . . .

Pondo men on the way to listen to the official report on recent Pondoland disturbances, October 16, 1960, © BAHA, photograph by Drum Photographer, dm2001091903.
Used by permission of Bailey's African History Archive (BAHA).

The so-called White state is a contiguous land area, containing practically all the natural resources and advanced development secured by the
labour and skill of all South Africans—the majority of whom, of course,
are Africans. This territory includes all the large cities, the seaports, the
harbours; the airfields, the areas served well by railways, main roads, power
lines, and major irrigation schemes. It contains the enormously rich gold
mines, the diamond mines, the coal mines. It includes all the main industries, maintained largely by African labour, in this industrially advanced
country. It includes the best and most fertile farmlands.

The Bantu "homelands" consist of 260 small and separate areas scattered
throughout the country. They are South Africa's backwaters, primitive rural slums, soil-eroded and under-developed, lacking power resources and
without developed communication systems. They have no cities, no industries, and few sources of employment. They are congested and permanently
distressed areas where the inhabitants live on a narrow ledge of starvation,
where a drought, as experienced recently in the northern areas, leads inevitably to famine. They are areas drained of their menfolk, for their chief export is labour, and while the men work on white-owned farms and in mines
and industry, their women-folk and old people pursue a primitive agriculture incapable of providing even subsistence. The "homelands" are mere

reserves of labour, with a population not even self-sustaining, supplying no more than a supplement to the low wages paid on the mines and farms. . . .

The Nationalist government cannot deny the discrimination that it practises against Africans. Like the old Salvation Army song that promises "pie in the sky when you die," apartheid promises the African persecuted by pass laws and police that he will get rights one day back home in the Transkei.

Meanwhile he must expect fewer rights, no rights at all, in the so-called white areas. The 1964 Bantu Laws Amendment Bill is rooted in this premise, stripping from Africans their last remaining right to reside in the urban areas at all. It is long-declared government policy that African family groups should be prohibited from establishing themselves in the urban areas. The African worker permitted there must be a migrant, a temporary sojourner, who can at any time be sent back to his home reserve. The new measure sets up "depots" in which Africans will be detained both while seeking work and while awaiting repatriation if they have been ordered out of an urban area. The African migrant labour force was always large; now every African capable of work is to be turned into a migrant labourer. So-called citizenship rights in the Bantustans are to be paid for by the complete loss of citizenship and occupation rights in the rest of the country.

What are the rights of this Transkeian citizen, the man who is no alien and yet is treated as an alien, without the privileges granted to the immigrant settling from abroad in the Republic? The Transkeian citizen may live in White territory, if he works for the White man and if he pays taxes, but he may have no say whatsoever in the government that rules him. In the Transkei he can vote for a Legislative Assembly in which 64 appointed chiefs over-rule the wishes of the 45 elected members. The chiefs can generally be relied upon to toe the government line because they are officials of the Republic's government, responsible to that government and not to the Transkeian citizen.

Back home in the Transkei, the African may dream of some future economic and political well-being, but the dream shows little signs of ever turning into reality. The Transkei is as firmly subject to the demands of white supremacy as ever it was. The people of the Transkei had no say in the drafting of their constitution. The elections held in 1963 took place under a state of emergency: which imposed a ban on all meetings of more than ten persons, laid down severe penalties for statements disrespectful to chiefs, and permitted the indefinite detention, without warrant or trial, of political opponents. . . .

The Nationalist Government has succeeded in gaining the support of a few Africans at least, the Transkei Chiefs who fear for their jobs. For the time being, with arbitrary arrests, banishments, and countless restrictions on individual liberty, the government will hold in check those who reject separate development and demand full rights for all within South Africa.

But even the Chiefs are split. Matanzima and his supporters hold power by a slender majority. If all the elected members were to break away from the Chiefs, they could form a solid block and hold the balance of power in the Legislative Assembly. Even with consolidated Matanzima control, the government will be forced to make concessions to popular demands, on such issues as the removal of mother-tongue instruction in Bantu Education.

But the Transkei scheme, rooted in tribalism and the sway of the Chiefs, is corrupting itself from within. A victory for Matanzima, paradoxically enough, could result in tribalism as an institution collapsing more swiftly in the Transkei than anywhere else. The government has no option but to work through the Chiefs who, like the Nationalists, have a mortal fear of change and the will of the common peasants. Conservatism is the lifeblood of the chieftainship system, and change threatens the positions of power that the Chiefs and the government enjoy. Chiefs and government therefore, have common aims: to resist movements advocating multi-racialism and modern social development. Because the Chiefs hold an overall majority in the new Assembly, the alliance between Chiefs and government seemed safe enough. But the Nationalists underestimated the deep hatred of apartheid among the peasants. The great majority of the voters went to the polls not to signify a meek obedience to their Chiefs, but their opposition to apartheid policies. This opposition has been clearly expressed. When the Chiefs elevated Matanzima to power, despite his minority rating in the election, they opted not to express the viewpoint of their people, but to keep favour with the government that pays them. This denied the long-established tribal tradition that a Chief is merely the embodiment of his people, and it must result in the commoners turning with increasing distaste from their Chiefs. If their traditional leaders fail them, the peasants will inevitably seek other ones. Yet this is precisely what the government hoped that the Transkei plan would prevent.

Three Tembu aristocrats, two still living in the Transkei, the third serving a life sentence after the [1964] Rivonia case, are the main antagonists for and against Verwoerd, symbolizing three different ways of life and struggle in the Transkei. All three are drawn from the Tembu Royal House, share a common grandfather, and were groomed for chieftainship by the same tutor. They are Kaizer Matanzima, promoted against tribal custom from a minor chieftaincy to head of the Emigrant Tembus when Nationalist Party administrators cut Tembuland into two paramountcies, in a blatant divide and rule policy; Paramount Chief Sabata Dalindyebo, head of the Tembu tribe; and Nelson Mandela, uncle of Sabata, underground leader of the African National Congress and hero of the African youth.

Matanzima, arrogant and ambitious, explains his acceptance of the Bantustan programme on the grounds that the Transkei could in this way become South Africa's first independent Black state. Yet in practice Matanzima is playing the role of the classic collaborator, as the strong man groomed by the White government to keep down the peasantry, to destroy the political fighters of the Transkei who, outlawed and persecuted in the Matanzima kingdom, are becoming throughout the country an inspiration to resistance. It has been suggested that apart from his collaborationist role, there is another course open to Matanzima: that he could try to last a little longer in a Transkei hostile to his despotism by demanding that the Nationalist talk of independence must be made a reality; that he must find a way to keep his footing in a Transkei that will not long be satisfied to levy local taxes, but will need to find large capital sums for development; that he will head a Transkei that will not be satisfied with the right to rubber-stamp Nationalist policies, and pass petty decrees, but will demand the power to repeal those laws which so disable the Transkei and indeed all Africans. The Matanzima way, it has been suggested, will be to call the bluff of the Nationalists, to bite the apartheid hand that feeds and protects him. Ambition will undoubtedly drive him to demand a larger share of the takings. But Matanzima knows the Nationalist government full well—for he is not untutored in stratagems of "Bantu" administration; he must know that real independence, granted by a Nationalist government, is impossible, and that if he defies the machine which has made him, he will be destroyed by it.

If there are two courses open to Matanzima—and men who know him well discount the course of bluff and eventual defiance—both place him in a nasty dilemma. Terror against the people will in time range across the whole of the Transkei, and counter-terror will threaten the authority, and the lives, of all the Chiefs who range themselves with White authority against their people. But demanding that the Nationalist government give the Transkei real independence will be just as disastrous for the Matanzimas. For the Bantustan promises to be fulfilled, so that Transkeians have factories and dams and power stations, and their old worn, over-worked labour reserve is turned into an economically viable state, millions of pounds must be voted and spent; but the White taxpayer will never tolerate this. The Transkei is an under-developed region and the recipe for advancement is simple enough; but White supremacy in South Africa will not supply the ingredients. The Transkei has the labour, but no power, no transport, no communications, no capital. The millions recommended by the Tomlinson Commission [a government report from 1955 on the economic crisis in the African reserves] for a scheme of development are a nightmare memory to the Nationalists.

The truth is that apartheid is losing its stake fast in the Transkei. Open terror, imposed for too long, will fire violent resistance. If, in a desperate, though unlikely, bid to save itself and apartheid from the acid test of the Transkei, the Nationalists try to push ahead with industrialization and urbanization, they will create in the Transkei, faster than ever, new forces that will rise to destroy them—those forces now represented by the Mandela leadership; African workers, removed from the land and based in factories, who will turn from Chiefs and tribal loyalties to trade unions and political parties. The more earnestly the Nationalists try to make their fantastic scheme work, the more forces they will release to resist and eventually bring them down. The harder the Nationalists set their faces against development, and lean on forces of conservatism and stagnation, the more farcical becomes the talk of development, of self-government, of Transkei independence.

The Transkei, show-place of the Bantustan scheme, could well be the first battlefield on which apartheid will be defeated.

The Discarded People

Cosmas Desmond

Apartheid policies resulted in the forced removal of three and a half million black people from cities and farms. The "discarded people," as Cosmas Desmond's ground-breaking book from 1971 named them, were moved to unfamiliar new neighborhoods, far from employers and social networks, or to desolate rural slums with no means of livelihood and few amenities. The government removed people from their homes under the Group Areas Act, which declared some formerly black urban neighbor-hoods, such as Sophiatown (in Johannesburg) and District Six (in Cape Town), to be reserved for whites. It also removed huge numbers under the policy of influx control, which sought to permit no more blacks in urban areas than the minimum number needed for white employers, declaring the rest surplus. In addition, some farms that had long been under black ownership were declared "black spots" and expropriated in a futile effort to completely separate white and black territories in South Africa. Finally, mechanization of white farms resulted in eviction of large numbers of labor tenants (farm tenants who secured their places by providing labor to the owner).

In The Discarded People, *Desmond attempted to document the extent of these unjust removals. This selection describes a squalid resettlement camp in Ciskei (a former Bantustan that is now part of the Eastern Cape), long one of the poorest and most overcrowded parts of the country. Desmond puts a human face on the suffering associated with a variety of apartheid policies aimed at social engineering to main-tain white supremacy. These included the policy that attempted to keep Africans east of an arbitrary line, the "Kat-Fish line," reserving the Western Cape and the economic opportunities of Cape Town for whites and Coloureds.*

Much as they desire apartheid, the Whites of the Eastern Cape have a price-less economic asset in their impoverished Black neighbours, in terms of the vast labour pools of the adjoining Transkei, the most politically advanced and the only geographically consolidated of the Government's Bantustans, and the Ciskei, which exists as a scattered collection of seventeen separate pieces of land threading through the "white" areas of the Eastern Cape.

The Ciskei is backward, impoverished, little short of a rural slum with

Destruction of huts in Weenen, Natal, during forced removals, June 1958, © BAHA, photograph by Peter Magubane, dm2001051008. Used by permission of Bailey's African History Archive (BAHA).

an average population density of more than 80 per square mile (according to the Tomlinson Commission), which is considerably in excess of its carrying capacity. In figures, there are about half a million Africans crowded into the Ciskei's 1,035,903 morgen [approximately 3,440 square miles, or slightly larger than the state of Delaware].

The territory is further handicapped by the Government's policy of removing Africans from the Western Cape. Many of these have been resettled in the Eastern Cape, at places which will be described later. The first Government plan was to remove all Africans who were living to the west of the "Eiselen Line" (Kimberley / Colesburg / Humansdorp). This includes quite a sizable portion of the Cape Province, but later the line was drawn much further to the east and so the African inhabitants of Middelburg, Burgersdorp, Cradock, and many other towns were doomed. This is known as the "Kat-Fish Line"; it runs from Aliwal North, through Sterkstroom to the Fish River. The Government has in recent years become increasingly coy about furnishing statistics relating to the number of people being moved in terms of its policy so it is impossible to estimate how many new arrivals have been resettled in the Eastern Cape, particularly in the Ciskei. The usual pattern that emerges is that the newcomers are unable to find work, so soon return to the Western Cape towns or go to the Rand as contract labourers, leaving the women, the aged, and the children behind them for long periods to exist as best they can. . . .

Limehill has become symbolic of the plight of Natal's rural Africans. In the same way, Mnxesha has become a symbol for the Ciskei. As I travelled from Cape Town eastwards, the name kept recurring. Obviously conditions in this resettlement camp were more than usually atrocious. . . .

There were the familiar, tiny one or two-roomed houses, many with a number of ragged, hungry-looking children or a bent old woman sitting outside. It was not quite true that I could no longer be shocked or disturbed. I was, in particular, by the sight of one tiny baby, a virtual skeleton, unable to move or even to cry and covered with flies. I have been through the children's wards in African hospitals throughout the country and, over the past ten years have seen thousands of starving, dying children. But I doubt whether I have ever seen anything worse than this. It was as bad as any of the horror pictures from Biafra [the Nigerian Civil War of 1967–70]. . . .

Mnxesha is about ten miles from King William's Town, on the road to Alice. From the main road you can see that there is some kind of settlement, but the worst parts are not visible. The first people were "settled" there in December 1967 with the aim of eventually accommodating 1,800 families, (about 10,000 people). But by July 1968 there were only about seventy families. The main influx took place between December 1968 and February 1969. . . .

The first arrivals were put into wooden huts, with zinc roofs. The huts measured roughly 10 feet by 16 feet and are 10 feet high, with no ceilings or floors. There are 99 of these which are still in use. In one of these, chosen at random, there were three adults and four children; this, I was assured, was less than in some of the others. These people are mainly pensioners and indigents who do not pay rent. Obviously such huts are extremely hot in summer and cold in winter and the earth floors become very damp, even wet, in the rainy season. . . .

The signs of malnutrition are obvious throughout the settlement and there have been many deaths. In May 1969 there were over 90 graves, of which over 70 were children's. The bulk of the population only arrived in December–February 1969.

There are now taps in the streets. These first appeared in February 1969. Until then water was brought in once a day Monday to Friday, twice on

Saturday and not on Sunday. The people were told to boil the water before drinking it. Pit latrines are provided but they appear to be very shallow and are prone to overflowing.

We have already seen from the Minister's figures that almost half of the men are migrant workers. The only employment in the area is on the building of houses in the settlement, for which men are paid R16.50 a month. Women are paid R6 a month for such work as planting grass in the settlement; this "wage" is officially considered as Government aid. In the beginning there was some employment in the settlement for one person from almost every house. But now there are many with no wage earner.

People complained that the rations were issued irregularly and that it appeared they were being cut down. Some said that the rations lasted them only two weeks: "After that we have to pawn our clothes in order to buy food at the European store." There are no shops in the settlement. The nearest one, which is White-owned, is about two miles away; there is another one and a Post Office about four miles away. The Border Council of Churches is subsidising the sale of milk and soup powders.

There is no fuel available in the area; I passed some children carrying wood four miles from the settlement. At first wood was being sold for 35 cents a bag and then for 25 cents. It is now being sold for 15 cents, the balance being paid by a relief organisation. But even with this subsidy, wood was piling up with the distributor because the people could not afford it. . . .

The sufferings of the people at Mnxesha are exemplified in the case of Mrs. E. M.: She arrived at Mnxesha from Burgersdorp in December 1968, with her six children. By May 1969 two of the children had died; two others, aged 13 and 6 years, had "gross pellagra," according to a doctor; another younger child was in hospital with malnutrition. She is a widow and was supporting herself in Burgersdorp by doing domestic work; now she has no employment. She is only 37 years old and so does not receive a pension. As Mnxesha is a rural area she cannot get a child maintenance allowance. Since she went to Mnxesha she had had no source of income apart from the few cents which she manages to earn by collecting wood from miles away and selling it in the settlement. She has taken her children to the nurse several times but because she did not have the 20 cents they were not attended to. She was receiving Government rations, which were obviously inadequate.

The Pan Africanist Congress

R. M. Sobukwe

Robert Mangaliso Sobukwe (1924–78) was the founding leader of the Pan African-
ist Congress (PAC), which broke away from the African National Congress (ANC)
in 1959. Many members of the ANC Youth League, including Nelson Mandela, had
been attracted to the ideals of Africanism in the 1940s. Africanism, like the Negri-
tude of Aimé Césaire and Leopold Senghor, posited the virtues of African traditions,
fostering what would later be known as black pride or Black Consciousness. In
South Africa, Africanists argued that it was dangerous to work with white liberal
and radical allies, as they might exercise undue domination and lead the liberation
movement away from African ideals. As apartheid unfolded after 1948, however,
most in the ANC came to believe that it was practical to work with allies in all racial
groups and that alliances were the best counter to the hyperracialism of apartheid.
Those who remained unconvinced, and remained wary of the influence of whites,
decamped to the PAC. The PAC organized the antipass campaign of March 1960
that was met with the Sharpeville Massacre and the banning of all the liberation
movements. Sobukwe was imprisoned on Robben Island until 1969 and was tightly
restricted after his release.

The following selection comes from Sobukwe's inaugural address at the launch
of the PAC. The speech argues for unity of all Africans and calls for a United States
of Africa as the only way to contend with large powers like the United States and
the Soviet Union. However, Sobukwe also argues against the "myth" of distinct
racial groups as opposed to historically formed "national groups" like Europeans
and Indians in South Africa and says that anyone who is primarily loyal to Af-
rica is an African. In many respects, this is the position that the ANC eventually
adopted during the antiapartheid struggle as it opened itself to white membership
and called for a nonracial South Africa.

Sons and Daughters of the Soil, fighters in the cause of African freedom,
we are living today in an era that is pregnant with untold possibilities for
both good and evil. In the course of the past two years we have seen man
breaking asunder, with dramatic suddenness, the chains that have bound

his mind, solving problems which for ages it has been regarded as sacrilege even to attempt to solve. However, in spite of all these rapid advances in the material and physical world, man appears to be either unwilling or unable to solve the problem of social relations between man and man. Because of this failure on the part of man, we see the world split today into two large hostile blocs, the so-called Capitalist and Socialist blocs represented by the U.S.A. and the Soviet Union respectively.

These two blocks are engaged in terrible competition, use tough language and tactics, employ brinkmanship stunts which have the whole world heading for a nervous breakdown. They each are armed with terrible weapons of destruction and continue to spend millions of pounds in the production of more and more of these weapons. In spite of all the diplomatic talk of co-existence, these blocks each behave as though they did not believe that co-existence was possible.

The question then arises, where does Afrika fit into this picture and where, particularly, do we African nationalists, we Africanists in South Afrika, fit in? There is no doubt that with the liquidation of Western imperialism and colonialism in Asia, the Capitalist market has shrunk considerably. As a result, Afrika has become the happy-hunting ground of adventuristic capital. There is again a scramble for Afrika and both the Soviet Union and the United States of America are trying to win the loyalty of the African States. Afrika is being wooed with more ardour than she has ever been.

There is a lot of flirting going on, of course, some Africans [are] flirting with the Soviet camp, and others with the American camp. In some cases the courtship has reached a stage where the parties are going out together; and they probably hold hands in the dark but nowhere has it yet reached a stage where the parties can kiss in public without blushing. This wooing occurs at a time when the whole continent of Afrika is in labour, suffering the pangs of a new birth and everybody is looking anxiously and expectantly towards Afrika to see, as our people so aptly put it ukuthi iyozala nkomoni (what creature will come forth). We are being wooed internationally at a time when in South Africa the naked forces of savage Herrenvolkism [master-race ideology] are running riot; when a determined effort is being made to annihilate the African people through systematic starvation; at a time when brutal attempts are being made to retard, dwarf and stunt the mental development of a whole people through organised "miseducation"; at a time when thousands of our people roam the streets in search of work and are being told by the foreign ruler to go back to a "home" which he has assigned them, whether that means the breakup of their families or not; at a time when the distinctive badge of slavery and humiliation, the "dom pass"

Robert M. Sobukwe, © BAHA, photograph by Drum Photographer, dm1999121303. Used by permission of Bailey's African History Archive (BAHA).

[pass book] is being extended from the African male dog to the African female bitch.

It is at this time, when fascist tyranny has reached its zenith in South Afrika, that Afrika's loyalty is being competed for. And the question is, what is our answer? Our answer, Mr. Speaker and children of the Soil, has been given by the African leaders of the continent. Dr. Kwame Nkrumah has repeatedly stated that in international affairs, Afrika wishes to pursue a policy of positive neutrality, allying herself to neither of the existing blocs but, in the words of Dr. Nnamdi Azikiwe of Nigeria, remaining "independent in all things but neutral in none that affect the destiny of Afrika." Mr. Tom Mboya of Kenya has expressed himself more forthrightly, declaring that it is not the intention of African states to change one master (western imperialism) for another (Soviet hegemony). . . .

Our relation to the States in Afrika may be stated precisely and briefly by quoting from George Padmore's book, "Pan Africanism or Communism." Discussing the future of Afrika, Padmore observes that "there is a growing feeling among politically conscious Africans throughout the continent that their destiny is one, that what happens in one part of Afrika to Africans must affect Africans living in other parts." We honour Ghana as the first independent state in modern Afrika which, under the courageous nationalist leadership of Dr. Nkrumah and the Convention People's Party, has actively interested itself in the liberation of the whole continent from White domination, and has held out the vision of a democratic United States of Afrika. We regard it as the sacred duty of every African state to strive ceaselessly and energetically for the creation of a United States of Afrika, stretching from Cape to Cairo, Morocco to Madagascar. The days of small, independent countries are gone. . . .

Beside the sense of a common historical fate that we share with the other countries of Afrika, it is imperative, for purely practical reasons that the whole of Afrika be united into a single unit, centrally controlled. Only in that way can we solve the immense problems that face the continent's people.

It is for the reasons stated above that we admire, bless and identify ourselves with the entire nationalist movements in Afrika. They are the core, the basic units, the individual cells of that large organism envisaged, namely, the United States of Afrika; a union of free, sovereign independent democratic states of Afrika. For the lasting peace of Afrika and the solution of the economic, social and political problems of the continent, there needs be a democratic principle. This means that White supremacy, under whatever guise it manifests itself, must be destroyed. And that is what the nationalists on the continent are setting out to do. They all are agreed that the African majority must rule. In the African context, it is the overwhelming African majority that will mould and shape the content of democracy. Allow me to quote Dr. [W. E. B.] DuBois, the father of Pan Africanism: "Most men in the world," writes Dubois, "are coloured. A belief in humanity means a belief in coloured men. The future of the world will, in all reasonable possibility, be what coloured men make it." As for the world, so for Afrika. The future of Africa will be what Africans make it.

And now for the thorny questions of race. . . . The Africanists take the view that there is only one race to which we all belong, and that is the human race. In our vocabulary therefore, the word "race" as applied to man, has no plural form. We do, however, admit the existence of observable physical differences between various groups of people, but these differences are the result of a number of factors, chief among which has been geographical isolation.

In Afrika the myth of race has been propounded and propagated by the imperialists and colonialists from Europe, in order to facilitate and justify their inhuman exploitation of the indigenous people of the land. It is from this myth of race with its attendant claims of cultural superiority that the doctrine of white supremacy stems. Thus it is that an ex-engine driver can think of himself as fully qualified to be the head of the government of an African state, but refuse to believe that a highly educated black doctor, more familiar with Western culture than the White premier is, cannot even run a municipal council. . . .

In South Africa we recognise the existence of national groups, which are the result of geographical origin within a certain area as well as a shared historical experience of these groups. The Europeans are a foreign minority group, which has exclusive control of political, economic, social and military power. It is the dominant group. It is the exploiting group, responsible for the pernicious doctrine of White Supremacy, which has resulted in the humiliation, and degradation of the indigenous African people. It is this group which has dispossessed the African people of their land and with arrogant conceit has set itself up as the "guardians," the "trustees" of the Africans. It is this group which conceives of the African people as a child nation, composed of Boys and Girls, ranging in age from 120 years to one day. It is this group which, after 300 years, can still state with brazen effrontery that the Native, the Bantu, the Kaffir is still backward and savage etc. But they still want to remain "guardians," "trustees," and what have you, of the African.

In short, it is this group which has mismanaged affairs in South Africa just as their kith and kin are mismanaging affairs in Europe. It is from this group that the most rabid race baiters and agitators come. It is members of this group who, whenever they meet in their Parliament, say things, which agitate the hearts of millions of peace-loving Africans. This is the group, which turns out thousands of experts on that new South African Science the Native mind. . . .

The freedom of the African means the freedom of all in South Africa, the European included, because only the African can guarantee the establishment of a genuine democracy in which all men will be citizens of a common state and will live and be governed as individuals and not as distinctive sectional groups. . . .

Against multi-racialism we have this objection, that the history of South Africa has fostered group prejudices and antagonisms, and if we have to maintain the same group exclusiveness, parading under the term of multi-racialism, we shall be transporting to the new Afrika these very antagonisms and conflicts.

Further, multi-racialism is in fact a pandering to European bigotry and arrogance. It is a method of safeguarding white interests, implying as it does, proportional representation irrespective of population figures. In that sense it is a complete negation of democracy. To us the term "multi-racialism" implies that there are such basic insuperable differences between the various national groups here that the best course is to keep them permanently distinctive in a kind of democratic apartheid. That to us is racialism multiplied, which probably is what the term truly connotes. We aim, politically, at government of the Africans by the Africans, for the Africans, with everybody who owes his only loyalty to Afrika and who is prepared to accept the democratic rule of an African majority being regarded as an African.

We guarantee no minority rights, because we think in terms of individuals, not groups. Economically we aim at the rapid extension of industrial development in order to alleviate pressure on the land, which is what progress means in terms of modern society. We stand committed to a policy guaranteeing the most equitable distribution of wealth. Socially we aim at the full development of the human personality and a ruthless uprooting and outlawing of all forms or manifestations of the racial myth.

Statement from the Dock

Nelson Mandela

After the state banned the African National Congress (ANC) and the Pan Africanist Congress in the aftermath of the Sharpeville Massacre of 1960, each organization came to the conclusion that resistance within the bounds of South African law had become impossible and that they needed to deploy armed struggle as part of their strategy to end apartheid. They made this decision as most of Africa was sweeping to independence and as anticolonial armed struggles were in progress from Algeria to Vietnam. Similar struggles were launched in other parts of white-ruled southern Africa in the early 1960s. Nelson Mandela (1918–) and others in the ANC formed an armed wing, Umkhonto we Sizwe (Spear of the Nation; known as MK), to carry out acts of sabotage against government facilities. They planned their attacks to minimize loss of life but gain maximum publicity, for instance by bombing power pylons. Mandela traveled to Ethiopia and Algeria for military training and solicited support from newly decolonized African nations. On December 16, 1961, MK carried out its first attacks. This was the date of the Afrikaner nationalist holiday known as Dignane's Day or the Day of the Vow, commemorating the Boer's defeat of the Zulu army during the Great Trek. (The date is now celebrated as the Day of Reconciliation.) In July 1963 South African police raided a farm in Rivonia (near Johannesburg) where top leaders of the ANC were planning MK's attacks. The state charged the defendants with acts of sabotage and planning for violent revolution. They were convicted and sentenced to life imprisonment on Robben Island near Cape Town.

At the conclusion of the trial, Mandela made the following statement to justify the ANC's turn to armed struggle and recounted a history of African resistance to white rule, noting that the organization had exhausted all legal means available and arguing that their aim was to bring about negotiations with the white government. He repeated his stirring conclusion, in which he affirms his willingness to die in the cause of freedom, in the speech he gave upon his release from prison in 1990.

In my youth in the Transkei I listened to the elders of my tribe telling stories of the old days. Amongst the tales they related to me were those of wars fought by our ancestors in defence of the fatherland. The names of Dingane and Bambata, Hintsa and Makana, Squngthi and Dalasile, Moshoeshoe and Sekhukhuni, were praised as the glory of the entire African nation. I hoped then that life might offer me the opportunity to serve my people and make my own humble contribution to their freedom struggle. This is what has motivated me in all that I have done in relation to the charges made against me in this case. . . .

I was one of the persons who helped to form Umkhonto. I, and the others who started the organization, did so for two reasons. Firstly, we believed that as a result of Government policy, violence by the African people had become inevitable, and that unless responsible leadership was given to canalize and control the feelings of our people, there would be outbreaks of terrorism which would produce an intensity of bitterness and hostility between the various races of this country which is not produced even by war. Secondly, we felt that without violence there would be no way open to the African people to succeed in their struggle against the principle of white supremacy. All lawful modes of expressing opposition to this principle had been closed by legislation, and we were placed in a position in which we had either to accept a permanent state of inferiority, or to defy the Government. We chose to defy the law. We first broke the law in a way which avoided any recourse to violence; when this form was legislated against, and then the Government resorted to a show of force to crush opposition to its policies, only then did we decide to answer violence with violence.

But the violence which we chose to adopt was not terrorism. We who formed Umkhonto were all members of the African National Congress, and had behind us the ANC tradition of non-violence and negotiation as a means of solving political disputes. We believe that South Africa belongs to all the people who live in it, and not to one group, be it black or white. We did not want an interracial war, and tried to avoid it to the last minute. If the Court is in doubt about this, it will be seen that the whole history of our organization bears out what I have said, and what I will subsequently say, when I describe the tactics which Umkhonto decided to adopt. I want, therefore, to say something about the African National Congress.

The African National Congress was formed in 1912 to defend the rights of the African people which had been seriously curtailed by the South Africa Act [creating the Union of South Africa], and which were then being threatened by the Native Land Act [of 1913]. For thirty-seven years—that is until 1949—it adhered strictly to a constitutional struggle. It put forward demands and resolutions; it sent delegations to the Government in the belief that African grievances could be settled through peaceful discussion and that Africans could advance gradually to full political rights. But White Governments remained unmoved, and the rights of Africans became less instead of becoming greater. . . .

Even after 1949, the ANC remained determined to avoid violence. At this time, however, there was a change from the strictly constitutional means of protest which had been employed in the past. The change was embodied in a decision which was taken to protest against apartheid legislation by peaceful, but unlawful, demonstrations against certain laws. Pursuant to this policy the ANC launched the Defiance Campaign, in which I was placed in charge of volunteers. This campaign was based on the principles of passive resistance. More than 8,500 people defied apartheid laws and went to jail. Yet there was not a single instance of violence in the course of this campaign on the part of any defier. I and nineteen colleagues were convicted for the role which we played in organizing the campaign, but our sentences were suspended mainly because the Judge found that discipline and non-violence had been stressed throughout. This was the time when the volunteer section of the ANC was established, and when the word "Amadelakufa" [death defiance] was first used: this was the time when the volunteers were asked to take a pledge to uphold certain principles. Evidence dealing with volunteers and their pledges has been introduced into this case, but completely out of context. The volunteers were not, and are not, the soldiers of a black army pledged to fight a civil war against the whites. They were, and are, dedicated workers who are prepared to lead campaigns initiated by the ANC to distribute leaflets, to organize strikes, or do whatever the particular campaign required. They are called volunteers because they volunteer to face the penalties of imprisonment and whipping which are now prescribed by the legislature for such acts.

During the Defiance Campaign, the Public Safety Act and the Criminal Law Amendment Act were passed. These Statutes provided harsher penalties for offences committed by way of protests against laws. Despite this, the protests continued and the ANC adhered to its policy of non-violence. In 1956, 156 leading members of the Congress Alliance, including myself, were arrested on a charge of high treason and charges under the Suppression of Communism Act. The non-violent policy of the ANC was put in issue by the State, but when the Court gave judgement some five years later, it found that the ANC did not have a policy of violence. We were acquitted on all counts, which included a count that the ANC sought to set up a communist state in place of the existing regime. The Government has always sought to

Walter Sisulu burns his pass book, 1960, Eli Weinberg Collection, UWC-Robben Island Mayibuye Archives, EW014-2-1. Courtesy of the Robben Island Museum Mayibuye Archives.

label all its opponents as communists. This allegation has been repeated in the present case, but as I will show, the ANC is not, and never has been, a communist organization.

In 1960 there was the shooting at Sharpeville, which resulted in the proclamation of a state of emergency and the declaration of the ANC as an unlawful organization. My colleagues and I, after careful consideration, decided that we would not obey this decree. The African people were not part of the Government and did not make the laws by which they were governed. We believed in the words of the Universal Declaration of Human Rights [by the United Nations General Assembly in 1948], that "the will of the people shall be the basis of authority of the Government," and for us to accept the banning was equivalent to accepting the silencing of the Africans for all time.

The ANC refused to dissolve, but instead went underground. We believed it was our duty to preserve this organization which had been built up with almost fifty years of unremitting toil. I have no doubt that no self-respecting White political organization would disband itself if declared illegal by a government in which it had no say.

In 1960 the Government held a referendum which led to the establishment of the Republic. Africans, who constituted approximately 70 per cent of the population of South Africa, were not entitled to vote, and were not even consulted about the proposed constitutional change. All of us were apprehensive of our future under the proposed White Republic, and a resolution was taken to hold an All-In African Conference [held in Pietermaritzburg in 1961] to call for a National Convention, and to organize mass demonstrations on the eve of the unwanted Republic, if the Government failed to call the Convention. The conference was attended by Africans of various political persuasions. I was the Secretary of the conference and undertook to be responsible for organizing the national stay-at-home which was subsequently called to coincide with the declaration of the Republic. As all strikes by Africans are illegal, the person organizing such a strike must avoid arrest. I was chosen to be this person, and consequently I had to leave my home and family and my [law] practice and go into hiding to avoid arrest.

The stay-at-home, in accordance with ANC policy, was to be a peaceful demonstration. Careful instructions were given to organizers and members to avoid any recourse to violence. The Government's answer was to introduce new and harsher laws, to mobilize its armed forces, and to send Saracens, armed vehicles, and soldiers into the townships in a massive show of force designed to intimidate the people. This was an indication that the Government had decided to rule by force alone, and this decision was a milestone on the road to Umkhonto. . . .

It must not be forgotten that by this time violence had, in fact, become a feature of the South African political scene. There had been violence in 1957 when the women of Zeerust were ordered to carry passes; there was violence in 1958 with the enforcement of cattle culling in Sekhukhuniland; there was violence in 1959 when the people of Cato Manor protested against pass raids; there was violence in 1960 when the Government attempted to impose Bantu Authorities in Pondoland. Thirty-nine Africans died in these disturbances. In 1961 there had been riots in Warmbaths, and all this time the Transkei had been a seething mass of unrest. Each disturbance pointed clearly to the inevitable growth among Africans of the belief that violence was the only way out—it showed that a Government which uses force to

Mandela (center) in Algeria for military training, IDAF Collection, UWC-Robben Island Mayibuye Archives, AT040–13. Courtesy of the Robben Island Museum Mayibuye Archives.

maintain its rule teaches the oppressed to use force to oppose it. Already small groups had arisen in the urban areas and were spontaneously making plans for violent forms of political struggle. There now arose a danger that these groups would adopt terrorism against Africans, as well as Whites, if not properly directed. Particularly disturbing was the type of violence engendered in places such as Zeerust, Sekhukhuniland, and Pondoland amongst Africans. It was increasingly taking the form, not of struggle against the Government—though this is what prompted it—but of civil strife amongst themselves, conducted in such a way that it could not hope to achieve anything other than a loss of life and bitterness.

At the beginning of June 1961, after a long and anxious assessment of the South African situation, I, and some colleagues, came to the conclusion that as violence in this country was inevitable, it would be unrealistic and wrong for African leaders to continue preaching peace and non-violence at a time when the Government met our peaceful demands with force. . . .

Umkhonto was formed in November 1961. When we took this decision, and subsequently formulated our plans, the ANC heritage of non-violence and racial harmony was very much with us. We felt that the country was drifting towards a civil war in which Blacks and Whites would fight each other. We viewed the situation with alarm. Civil war could mean the destruction of what the ANC stood for; with civil war, racial peace would be more difficult than ever to achieve. We already have examples in South African history of the results of war. It has taken more than fifty years for the scars of the South African War to disappear. How much longer would it take to eradicate the scars of inter-racial civil war, which could not be fought without a great loss of life on both sides?

The avoidance of civil war had dominated our thinking for many years, but when we decided to adopt violence as part of our policy, we realized that we might one day have to face the prospect of such a war. This had to be taken into account in formulating our plans. We required a plan which was flexible and which permitted us to act in accordance with the needs of the times; above all, the plan had to be one which recognized civil war as the last resort, and left the decision on this question to the future. We did not want to be committed to civil war, but we wanted to be ready if it became inevitable. . . .

Four forms of violence were possible. There is sabotage, there is guerrilla warfare, there is terrorism, and there is open revolution. We chose to adopt the first method and to exhaust it before taking any other decision.

Umkhonto had its first operation on 16 December 1961, when Government buildings in Johannesburg, Port Elizabeth and Durban were attacked. The selection of targets is proof of the policy to which I have referred. Had we intended to attack life we would have selected targets where people congregated and not empty buildings and power stations. The sabotage which was committed before 16 December 1961 was the work of isolated groups and had no connection whatever with Umkhonto. In fact, some of these and a number of later acts were claimed by other organizations.

The Manifesto of Umkhonto was issued on the day that operations commenced. The response to our actions and Manifesto among the white population was characteristically violent. The Government threatened to take strong action, and called upon its supporters to stand firm and to ignore the demands of the Africans. The Whites failed to respond by suggesting change; they responded to our call by suggesting the laager. In contrast, the response of the Africans was one of encouragement. Suddenly there was hope again. Things were happening. People in the townships became eager for political news. A great deal of enthusiasm was generated by the initial successes, and people began to speculate on how soon freedom would be obtained. But we in Umkhonto weighed up the white response with anxiety. The lines were being drawn. The whites and blacks were moving into separate camps, and the prospects of avoiding a civil war were made less. The white newspapers carried reports that sabotage would be punished by death. If this was so, how could we continue to keep Africans away from terrorism?

Already scores of Africans had died as a result of racial friction. In 1920 when the famous leader, Masabala, was held in Port Elizabeth jail, twenty-four of a group of Africans who had gathered to demand his release were killed by the police and white civilians. In 1921, more than one hundred Africans died in the Bulhoek affair [see part V]. In 1924 over two hundred Africans were killed when the Administrator of South-West Africa led a force against a group which had rebelled against the imposition of dog tax. On 1 May 1950, eighteen Africans died as a result of police shootings during the strike. On 21 March 1960, sixty-nine unarmed Africans died at Sharpeville.

How many more Sharpevilles would there be in the history of our country? And how many more Sharpevilles could the country stand without violence and terror becoming the order of the day? And what would happen to our people when that stage was reached? In the long run we felt certain we must succeed, but at what cost to ourselves and the rest of the country? And if this happened, how could black and white ever live together again in peace and harmony? These were the problems that faced us, and these were our decisions. . . .

I have always regarded myself, in the first place, as an African patriot. After all, I was born in Umtata, forty-six years ago. My guardian was my cousin, who was the acting paramount chief of Tembuland, and I am related both to the present paramount chief of Tembuland, Sabata Dalindyebo, and to Kaizer Matanzima, the Chief Minister of the Transkei.

Today I am attracted by the idea of a classless society, an attraction which springs in part from Marxist reading and, in part, from my admiration of the structure and organization of early African societies in this country. The land, then the main means of production, belonged to the tribe. There were no rich or poor and there was no exploitation.

It is true, as I have already stated, that I have been influenced by Marxist thought. But this is also true of many of the leaders of the new independent States. Such widely different persons as Gandhi, Nehru, Nkrumah, and Nasser all acknowledge this fact. We all accept the need for some form of socialism to enable our people to catch up with the advanced countries of this world and to overcome their legacy of extreme poverty. But this does not mean we are Marxists.

Indeed, for my own part, I believe that it is open to debate whether the

Communist Party has any specific role to play at this particular stage of our political struggle. The basic task at the present moment is the removal of race discrimination and the attainment of democratic rights on the basis of the Freedom Charter. In so far as that Party furthers this task, I welcome its assistance. I realize that it is one of the means by which people of all races can be drawn into our struggle.

From my reading of Marxist literature and from conversations with Marxists, I have gained the impression that communists regard the parliamentary system of the West as undemocratic and reactionary. But, on the contrary, I am an admirer of such a system.

The Magna Carta, the Petition of Rights, and the Bill of Rights are documents which are held in veneration by democrats throughout the world.

I have great respect for British political institutions, and for the country's system of justice. I regard the British Parliament as the most democratic institution in the world, and the independence and impartiality of its judiciary never fail to arouse my admiration.

The American Congress, that country's doctrine of separation of powers, as well as the independence of its judiciary, arouses in me similar sentiments.

I have been influenced in my thinking by both West and East. All this has led me to feel that in my search for a political formula, I should be absolutely impartial and objective. I should tie myself to no particular system of society other than of socialism. I must leave myself free to borrow the best from the West and from the East. . . .

Our fight is against real, and not imaginary, hardships or, to use the language of the State Prosecutor, "so-called hardships." Basically, we fight against two features which are the hallmarks of African life in South Africa and which are entrenched by legislation which we seek to have repealed. These features are poverty and lack of human dignity, and we do not need communists or so-called "agitators" to teach us about these things.

South Africa is the richest country in Africa, and could be one of the richest countries in the world. But it is a land of extremes and remarkable contrasts. The whites enjoy what may well be the highest standard of living in the world, whilst Africans live in poverty and misery. Forty per cent of the Africans live in hopelessly overcrowded and, in some cases, drought-stricken Reserves, where soil erosion and the overworking of the soil makes it impossible for them to live properly off the land. Thirty per cent are labourers, labour tenants, and squatters on white farms and work and live under conditions similar to those of the serfs of the Middle Ages. The other 30 per cent live in towns where they have developed economic and social habits which bring them closer in many respects to white standards. Yet most Africans, even in this group, are impoverished by low incomes and high cost of living. . . .

Poverty goes hand in hand with malnutrition and disease. The incidence of malnutrition and deficiency diseases is very high amongst Africans. Tuberculosis, pellagra, kwashiorkor, gastro-enteritis, and scurvy bring death and destruction of health. The incidence of infant mortality is one of the highest in the world. According to the Medical Officer of Health for Pretoria, tuberculosis kills forty people a day (almost all Africans), and in 1961 there were 58,491 new cases reported. These diseases not only destroy the vital organs of the body, but they result in retarded mental conditions and lack of initiative, and reduce powers of concentration. The secondary results of such conditions affect the whole community and the standard of work performed by African labourers.

The complaint of Africans, however, is not only that they are poor and the whites are rich, but that the laws which are made by the whites are designed to preserve this situation. There are two ways to break out of poverty. The first is by formal education, and the second is by the worker acquiring a greater skill at his work and thus higher wages. As far as Africans are concerned, both these avenues of advancement are deliberately curtailed by legislation. . . .

Africans want to be paid a living wage. Africans want to perform work which they are capable of doing, and not work which the Government declares them to be capable of. Africans want to be allowed to live where they obtain work, and not be endorsed out of an area because they were not born there. Africans want to be allowed to own land in places where they work, and not to be obliged to live in rented houses which they can never call their own. Africans want to be part of the general population, and not confined to living in their own ghettoes. African men want to have their wives and children to live with them where they work, and not be forced into an unnatural existence in men's hostels. African women want to be with their menfolk and not be left permanently widowed in the Reserves. Africans want to be allowed out after eleven o'clock at night and not to be confined to their rooms like little children. Africans want to be allowed to travel in their own country and to seek work where they want to and not where the Labour Bureau tells them to. Africans want a just share in the whole of South Africa; they want security and a stake in society. Above all, we want equal political rights, because without them our disabilities will be permanent. I know this sounds revolutionary to the whites in this country, because the majority of voters will be Africans. This makes the white man fear democracy.

But this fear cannot be allowed to stand in the way of the only solution which will guarantee racial harmony and freedom for all. It is not true that the enfranchisement of all will result in racial domination. Political division, based on colour, is entirely artificial and, when it disappears, so will the domination of one colour group by another. The ANC has spent half a century fighting against racialism. When it triumphs it will not change that policy.

This then is what the ANC is fighting. Their struggle is a truly national one. It is a struggle of the African people, inspired by their own suffering and their own experience. It is a struggle for the right to live. During my lifetime I have dedicated myself to this struggle of the African people. I have fought against white domination, and I have fought against black domination. I have cherished the ideal of a democratic and free society in which all persons live together in harmony and with equal opportunities. It is an ideal which I hope to live for and to achieve. But if needs be, it is an ideal for which I am prepared to die.

VII

From Soweto to Liberation

Across the world, colonialism and statutory racial discrimination eroded in the decades following the Second World War. In 1954 the U.S. Supreme Court overturned the "separate but equal" doctrine that formed the basis of Jim Crow segregation. Much of Africa rapidly decolonized, catalyzed by Ghana's independence in 1957. By the early 1960s, formal European imperialism had largely collapsed.

Southern Africa went in the opposite direction. Portuguese colonialism became more entrenched during the 1950s. Southern Rhodesia (Zimbabwe) generally followed South Africa's path of white domination. In 1960 white voters passed a referendum declaring South Africa a republic; the following year South Africa left the British Commonwealth. Throughout the 1960s and into the following decade, the government vigorously pursued its apartheid policies. The Transkei became nominally independent in 1976, followed by the Ciskei two years later. The state enforced policies such as Group Areas, in one notorious example forcibly removing upward of sixty thousand people from District Six just outside Cape Town's city center. The ruling National Party completed its creation of a security state, forming agencies such as the Bureau for State Security and passing laws permitting detention without trial. In the 1970s, with the collapse of colonialism and white supremacy in Angola, Mozambique, and Southern Rhodesia (Zimbabwe), apartheid's rulers began zealously intervening in regional affairs, including maintaining apartheid's illegal control over South West Africa (Namibia).

Despite an enormous commitment of state resources, none of the state's apartheid policies succeeded. Separate development failed miserably. The "homelands" system had little support among black South Africans and no support internationally. Economically, the homelands were a disaster, with gut-wrenching levels of poverty and little promise of sustainable development. Black urbanization continued, despite the state's zealous prosecution of pass laws. South Africa's economy rested on black labor, whose wages were kept artificially low owing to racial laws and the prohibition of unionization. White South Africans enjoyed one of the world's highest standards of living, but the skewed distribution of wealth and apartheid policies stunted the growth of an African middle class and warped economic growth. Some ruling National Party leaders who were committed to white supremacy nonetheless soon began to realize that apartheid no longer worked. The reforms they proposed would fracture Afrikaner politics.

With its movements outlawed and its leaders in jail or in exile, black resistance entered a quiescent period. The external African National Congress (ANC) had little ability to conduct its armed struggle; the Pan Africanist Congress had much less. Within South Africa, a new generation of political activists began emerging in the late 1960s, some with ties to the struggles of the late 1950s, others middle and high schoolers. In early 1973, wildcat strikes spread throughout Durban; this was the most important working-class movement since the mine workers' strike of 1946. Militancy and organization spread across the country, including to the crucial mining industry. The government soon legalized black unionization. In 1982 miners formed the National Union of Mine Workers, which joined the Congress of South African Trade Unions at its formation three years later.

A second wave of resistance crystalized around South Africa's black students. This culminated in a massive movement in 1976 and the massacre of June 16 in Soweto (the Soweto Uprising), followed by state persecution across the country. Enrollment had increased steadily, with nearly four million African children in school by the early 1970s, most in the country's major urban centers. University students formed the South African Students Organisation in 1969, partly in response to the white-dominated National Union of South African Students. Students, faced with atrocious conditions and increasingly connected to events unfolding across the world, particularly the liberation struggles in neighboring countries, increased their militancy. The South African Students Organisation would become critical to the development and spread of the Black Consciousness movement led by Steven Biko. The nature and content of Black Consciousness continue to be debated, but in general it espoused the inward transformation of people's souls as a necessary condition to fighting oppression. Black Consciousness drew on a variety of beliefs such as negritude, African self-reliance, and American black power. Banned and hounded by the authorities, Biko died in 1977 from beatings he received while in police custody.

The apartheid state initiated reform policies beginning with changes in township governance and culminating with a new constitution that created a tricameral parliament in 1984 that gave Coloureds and Indians the vote. The tricameral parliament, which still denied the vote to the vast majority of South Africans, led to widespread resistance and the formations of literally scores of organizations, most famously the umbrella United Democratic Front, followed by an intensification of political repression that included the deployment of the army throughout the country's black townships. Tens of thousands of people died in violence that spread across South Africa; many more ended up in prison. Torture became commonplace. The state also used vigilante and other "third force" groups to prosecute violence, particularly the Inkatha movement, which was associated with Chief Gatsha Buthelezi. Intolerance increased within the townships, with "comrades" aligned with the United Democratic Front in organizing kangaroo courts and murdering suspected informers, often in gruesome public rituals known as "necklacing." The economy entered a prolonged decline partly as a result of international sanctions. Most observers believed there were slim chances of a peaceful resolution to South Africa's political crisis. In 1989, however, the new state president, F. W. de Klerk, unbanned the ANC and other organizations and followed soon after with the release of political prisoners and the beginning of negotiations.

South African history between the Soweto Uprising of 1976 and the release of Nelson Mandela in 1990 remains fiercely contested and would come under public scrutiny with the Truth and Reconciliation Commission hearings beginning in 1996. Questions abound. What was the relationship between the exiled ANC and political movements such as the United Democratic Front? Were government leaders committed to real change or simply to reengineering white supremacy, joining Indians and Coloureds to "white" South Africa while continuing to confine African citizenship to the pseudo-decolonized Bantustans? To what extent did the ANC engage in gross human rights violations? The selections that follow in this part introduce the reader to this tumultuous period that saw apartheid's unraveling and the withering of white supremacy, a period of extraordinary violence and disorder, but also of hope and excitement. The next and final part returns to these years and to the uncertain years of South Africa's young democracy.

White Racism and Black Consciousness

Steven Biko

When the Rivonia Trial court sentenced Nelson Mandela and his fellow defendants to life terms in 1964, the apartheid state had succeeded in imprisoning or driving into exile all the major leaders of the liberation movements. Although foreign commentators and international organizations regularly condemned apartheid, the South African economy was thriving and the government seemingly went unopposed as it implemented grand apartheid through forced removals and the Bantustan policy. In the late 1960s, however, a new generation came to the fore with a new approach to liberation: instilling pride and dignity through the cultivation of "Black Consciousness." This came to be known as the Black Consciousness movement; one of its most articulate leaders was Steve Biko (1946–77). Black Consciousness drew on the ideas of Africanism, arguing that whites could not be reliable allies as they were inevitably beneficiaries of apartheid. But the movement argued that all who were oppressed by apartheid, including Coloureds and Indians, were black, thereby forging alliances across groups that apartheid strove to keep divided. In 1969 black students broke away from the multiracial National Union of South African Students to form the South African Students Organisation (SASO). Black Consciousness infused energy into students, community-development activists, and labor organizers and helped to fuel the student movement that led to the Soweto Uprising in 1976. The following year, the state banned all Black Consciousness organizations and detained their leaders. Police severely beat Biko in jail, resulting in his death. Twenty thousand people attended his funeral in his hometown, King William's Town, in the Eastern Cape.

In this selection, written for a student conference in 1971, Biko explains why blacks should not rely on white liberals in the struggle against apartheid and argues that the emergence and cultivation of Black Consciousness is the only hope for the true liberation of blacks. He also argues that Black Consciousness and the defeat of the inferiority complex instilled by apartheid institutions is a necessary precondition for progress in South Africa. Biko's piece suggests that Black Consciousness is both inspired by and parallels decolonization in the rest of Africa, which was beginning to put Africans on a more equal footing with the West in international

Steven Bantu Biko,
© BAHA, photograph
by Drum Photographer,
dm2000041408. Used by
permission of Bailey's
African History Archive
(BAHA).

relations. In South Africa the growth of Black Consciousness organization and
rhetoric was further spurred by the independence of Mozambique and Angola from
Portuguese colonial rule in 1975 and the ongoing liberation struggles in Namibia and
Rhodesia (Zimbabwe).

The white man's quest for power has led him to destroy with utter ruthlessness whatever has stood in his way. In an effort to divide the black world
in terms of aspirations, the powers that be have evolved a philosophy that
stratifies the black world and gives preferential treatment to certain groups.
Further, they have built up several tribal cocoons, thereby hoping to increase inter-tribal ill-feeling and to divert the energies of the black people
towards attaining false prescribed "freedoms." Moreover, it was hoped,
the black people could be effectively contained in these various cocoons
of repression, euphemistically referred to as "homelands." At some stage,

however, the powers that be had to start defining the sphere of activity of these apartheid institutions. Most blacks suspected initially the barrenness of the promise and have now realised that they have been taken for a big ride. Just as the Native Representative Council [a preapartheid advisory body] became a political flop that embarrassed its creators, I predict that a time will come when these stooge bodies will prove very costly not only in terms of money but also in terms of the credibility of the story the Nationalists are trying to sell. In the mean-time the blacks are beginning to realise the need to rally around the cause of their suffering—their black skin—and to ignore the false promises that come from the white world.

Then again the progressively sterner legislation that has lately filled the South African statute books has had a great effect in convincing the people of the evil inherent in the system of apartheid. No amount of propaganda on Radio Bantu [a government radio station directed at black audiences] or promises of freedom being granted to some desert homeland will ever convince the blacks that the government means well, so long as they experience manifestations of the lack of respect for the dignity of man and for his property as shown during the mass removals of Africans from the urban areas. The unnecessary harassment of Africans by police, both in towns and inside townships, and the ruthless application of that scourge of the people, the pass laws, are constant reminders that the white man is on top and that the blacks are only tolerated—with the greatest restraints. Needless to say, anyone finding himself at the receiving end of such deliberate (though uncalled for) cruelty must ultimately ask himself the question: what do I have to lose? This is what the blacks are beginning to ask themselves.

To add to this, the [white] opposition ranks have been thrown into chaos and confusion. All opposition parties have to satisfy the basic demands of politics. They want power and at the same time they want to be *fair*. It never occurs to them that the surest way of being unfair is to withhold power from the native population. Hence one ultimately comes to the conclusion that there is no real difference between the United Party [the official opposition party in Parliament] and the Nationalist Party. If there is, a strong possibility exists that the United Party is on the right of the Nationalists. One needs only to look at their famous slogan, "White supremacy over the whole of South Africa," to realise the extent to which the quest for power can cloud even such supposedly immortal characteristics as the "English sense of fair play." Africans long ago dismissed the United Party as a great political fraud. The Coloured people have since followed suit. If the United Party is gaining any votes at all it is precisely because it is becoming more explicit in its racist policy. I would venture to say that the most overdue political step in South African White politics is a merger between the United and Nationalist Parties.

The flirtation between the Progressive Party [a white liberal party] and blacks was brought to a rude stop by legislation. Some blacks argue that at that moment the Progressives lost their only chance of attaining some semblance of respectability by not choosing to disband rather than lose their black constituents. Yet I cannot help feeling that the Progressives emerged more purified from the ordeal. The Progressives have never been a black man's real hope. They have always been a white party at heart, fighting for a more lasting way of preserving white values in this southern tip of Africa. It will not be long before the blacks relate their poverty to their blackness in concrete terms. Because of the tradition forced onto the country, the poor people shall always be black people. It is not surprising, therefore, that the blacks should wish to rid themselves of a system that locks up the wealth of the country in the hands of a few. . . .

We now come to the group that has longest enjoyed confidence from the black world—the liberal establishment, including radical and leftist groups. The biggest mistake the black world ever made was to assume that whoever opposed apartheid was an ally. For a long time the black world has been looking only at the governing party and not so much at the whole power structure as the object of their rage. In a sense the very political vocabulary that the blacks have used has been inherited from the liberals. Therefore it is not surprising that alliances were formed so easily with the liberals.

Who are the liberals in South Africa? It is that curious bunch of nonconformists who explain their participation in negative terms; that bunch of do-gooders that goes under all sorts of names—liberals, leftists, etc. These are the people who argue that they are not responsible for white racism and the country's "inhumanity to the black man"; these are the people who claim that they too feel the oppression just as acutely as the blacks and therefore should be jointly involved in the black man's struggle for a place under the sun; in short, these are the people who say that they have black souls wrapped up in white skins.

The liberals set about their business with the utmost efficiency. They made it a political dogma that all groups opposing the *status quo* must *necessarily* be non-racial in structure. They maintained that if you stood for a principle of non-racialism you could not in any way adopt what they described as racialist policies. They even defined to the black people what the latter should fight for.

With this sort of influence behind them, most black leaders tended to rely too much on the advice of liberals. For a long time, in fact, it became the occupation of the leadership to "calm the masses down," while they engaged in fruitless negotiation with the *status quo*. Their whole political action, in fact, was a programmed course in the art of gentle persuasion through protests and limited boycotts and they hoped the rest could be safely left to the troubled conscience of the fair-minded English folk.

Of course this situation could not last. A new breed of black leaders was beginning to take a dim view of the involvement of liberals in a struggle that they regarded as essentially theirs, when the political movements of the blacks were either banned or harassed into non-existence. This left the stage open once more for the liberals to continue with their work of "fighting for the rights of the blacks."

It never occurred to the liberals that the integration they insisted upon as an effective way of opposing apartheid was impossible to achieve in South Africa. It had to be artificial because it was being foisted on two parties whose entire upbringing had been to support the lie that one race was superior and others inferior. One has to overhaul the whole system in South Africa before hoping to get black and white walking hand in hand to oppose a common enemy. As it is, both black and white walk into a hastily organised integrated circle carrying with them the seeds of destruction of that circle—their inferiority and superiority complexes.

The myth of integration as propounded under the banner of the liberal ideology must be cracked and killed because it makes people believe that something is being done when in reality the artificially integrated circles are a soporific to the blacks while salving the consciences of the guilt-sticken [*sic*] white. It works from the false premise that, because it is difficult to bring people from different races together in this country, achievement of this is in itself a step towards the total liberation of the blacks. Nothing could be more misleading.

How many white people fighting for their version of a change in South Africa are really motivated by genuine concern and not by guilt? Obviously it is a cruel assumption to believe that all whites are not sincere, yet methods adopted by some groups often do suggest a lack of real commitment. The essence of politics is to direct oneself to the group which wields power. Most white dissident groups are aware of the power wielded by the white power structure. They are quick to quote statistics on how big the defence budget is. They know exactly how effectively the police and the army can control protesting black hordes—peaceful or otherwise. They know to what degree the black world is infiltrated by the security police. Hence they are completely convinced of the impotence of the black people. Why then do they persist in talking to the blacks? Since they are aware that the problem in this country is white racism, why do they not address themselves to the white world? Why do they insist on talking to blacks?

In an effort to answer these questions one has to come to the painful conclusion that the liberal is in fact appeasing his own conscience, or at best is eager to demonstrate his identification with the black people only so far as it does not sever all his ties with his relatives on the other side of the colour line. Being white, he possesses the natural passport to the exclusive pool of white privileges from which he does not hesitate to extract whatever suits him. Yet, since he identifies with the blacks, he moves around his white circles—white-only beaches, restaurants, and cinemas—with a lighter load, feeling that he is not like the rest. Yet at the back of his mind is a constant reminder that he is quite comfortable as things stand and therefore should not bother about change. Although he does not vote for the Nationalists (now that they are in the majority anyway), he feels secure under the protection offered by the Nationalists and subconsciously shuns the idea of change.

The limitations that have accompanied the involvement of liberals in the black man's struggle have been mostly responsible for the arrest of progress. Because of their inferiority complex, blacks have tended to listen seriously to what the liberals had to say. With their characteristic arrogance of assuming a "monopoly on intelligence and moral judgement," these self-appointed trustees of black interests have gone on to set the pattern and pace for the realisation of the black man's aspirations.

I am not sneering at the liberals and their involvement. Neither am I suggesting that they are the most to blame for the black man's plight. Rather I am illustrating the fundamental fact that total identification with an oppressed group in a system that forces one group to enjoy privilege and to live on the sweat of another, is impossible. White society collectively owes the blacks so huge a debt that no one member should automatically expect to escape from the blanket condemnation that needs must come from the black world. It is not as if whites are allowed to enjoy privilege only when they declare their solidarity with the ruling party. They are born into privilege and are nourished by and nurtured in the system of ruthless exploitation of black energy. For the 20-year-old white liberal to expect to be accepted with open arms is surely to overestimate the powers of forgiveness of the black people. No matter how genuine a liberal's motivations may be, he has to accept that, though he did not choose to be born into privilege, the blacks cannot but be suspicious of his motives.

The liberal must fight on his own and for himself. If they are true liberals they must realise that they themselves are oppressed, and that they must fight for their own freedom and not that of the nebulous "they" with whom they can hardly claim identification. . . .

In South Africa political power has always rested with white society. Not only have the whites been guilty of being on the offensive but, by some skilful manoeuvres, they have managed to control the responses of the blacks to the provocation. Not only have they kicked the black but they have also told him how to react to the kick. For a long time the black has been listening with patience to the advice he has been receiving on how best to respond to the kick. With painful slowness he is now beginning to show signs that it is his right and duty to respond to the kick *in the way he sees fit.*

[In the 1950s] there was emerging in South Africa a group of angry young black men who were beginning to "grasp the notion of (their) peculiar uniqueness" and who were eager to define who they were and what [Biko is referring to the Pan Africanist Congress]. These were the elements who were disgruntled with the direction imposed on the African National Congress by the "old guard" within its leadership. These young men were questioning a number of things, among which was the "go slow" attitude adopted by the leadership, and the ease with which the leadership accepted coalitions with organisations other than those run by blacks. The "People's Charter" [Freedom Charter] adopted in Kliptown in 1955 was evidence of this. In a sense one can say that these were the first real signs that the blacks in South Africa were beginning to realise the need to go it alone and to evolve a philosophy based on, and directed by, blacks. In other words, Black Consciousness was slowly manifesting itself.

It may be said that, on the broader political front, blacks in South Africa have not shown any overt signs of new thinking since the banning of their political parties; nor were the signs of disgruntlement with the white world given a real chance to crystallise into a positive approach. Black students, on the other hand, began to rethink their position in black-white coalitions. The emergence of SASO (South African Students Organisation) and its tough policy of non-involvement with the white world set people's minds thinking along new lines. This was a challenge to the age-old tradition in South Africa that opposition to apartheid was enough to qualify whites for acceptance by the black world. Despite protest and charges of racialism from liberal-minded white students, the black students stood firm in their rejection of the principle of unholy alliances between blacks and whites. A spokesman of the new right-of-middle group, NAFSAS [National Federation of South African Students], was treated to a dose of the new thinking when a black student told him that "we shall lead ourselves, be it to the sea, to the mountain or to the desert; we shall have nothing to do with white students."

The importance of the SASO stand is not really to be found in SASO per se—for SASO has the natural limitations of being a student organisation with an ever-changing membership. Rather it is to be found in the fact that this new approach opened a huge crack in the traditional approach and made the blacks sit up and think again. It heralded a new era in which blacks are beginning to take care of their own business and to see with greater clarity the immensity of their responsibility.

The call for Black Consciousness is the most positive call to come from any group in the black world for a long time. It is more than just a reactionary rejection of whites by blacks. The quintessence of it is the realisation by the blacks that, in order to feature well in this game of power politics, they have to use the concept of group power and to build a strong foundation for this. Being an historically, politically, socially and economically disinherited and dispossessed group, they have the strongest foundation from which to operate. The philosophy of Black Consciousness, therefore, expresses group pride and the determination by the blacks to rise and attain the envisaged self. At the heart of this kind of thinking is the realisation by the blacks that the most potent weapon in the hands of the oppressor is the mind of the oppressed. Once the latter has been so effectively manipulated and controlled by the oppressor as to make the oppressed believe that he is a liability to the white man, then there will be nothing the oppressed can do that will really scare the powerful masters. Hence thinking along lines of Black Consciousness makes the black man see himself as a being, entire in himself, and not as an extension of a broom or additional leverage to some machine. At the end of it all, he cannot tolerate attempts by anybody to dwarf the significance of his manhood. Once this happens, we shall know that the real man in the black person is beginning to shine through.

I have spoken of Black Consciousness as if it is something that can be readily detected. Granted this may be an over-statement at this stage, yet it is true that, gradually, the various black groups are becoming more and more conscious of the self. They are beginning to rid their minds of imprisoning notions which are the legacy of the control of their attitude by whites. Slowly, they have cast aside the "morality argument" which prevented them from going it alone and are now learning that a lot of good can be derived from specific exclusion of whites from black institutions. . . .

The growth of awareness among South African blacks has often been ascribed to influence from the American "Negro" movement. Yet it seems to me that this is a sequel to the attainment of independence by so many African states within so short a time. In fact I remember that at the time I was at high school, Dr Hastings Kamuzu Banda [the independence leader of Malawi] was still a militant and used to be a hero of a friend of mine. His often quoted statement was, "This is a black man's country; any white man who does not like it must pack up and go." Clearly at this stage the myth of the invincibility of the white man had been exposed. When fellow Africans were talking like that how could we still be harbouring ideas of continued servitude? We knew he had no right to be there; we wanted to remove him from our table, strip the table of all trappings put on it by him, decorate it in true African style, settle down and then ask him to join us on our own terms if he liked. This is what Banda was saying. The fact that American terminology has often been used to express our thoughts is merely because all new ideas seem to get extensive publicity in the United States.

National consciousness and its spread in South Africa has to work against a number of factors. First there are the traditional complexes, then the emptiness of the native's past and lastly the question of black-white dependency. The traditional inferior-superior black-white complexes are deliberate creations of the colonialist. Through the work of missionaries and the style of education adopted, the blacks were made to feel that the white man was some kind of god whose word could not be doubted. As [Frantz] Fanon puts it [in *The Wretched of the Earth*]: "Colonialism is not satisfied merely with holding a people in its grip and emptying the Native's brain of all form and content; by a kind of perveted [*sic*] logic, it turns to the past of the oppressed people and distorts, disfigures, and destroys it." At the end of it all, the blacks have nothing to lean on, nothing to cheer them up at the present moment and very much to be afraid of in the future.

The attitude of some rural African folk who are against education is often misunderstood, not least by the African intellectual. Yet the reasons put forward by these people carry with them the realisation of their inherent dignity and worth. They see education as the quickest way of destroying the substance of the African culture. They complain bitterly of the disruption in the life pattern, non-observation of customs, and constant derision from the non-conformists whenever any of them go through school. Lack of respect for the elders is, in the African tradition, an unforgivable and cardinal sin. Yet how can one prevent the loss of respect of child for father when the child is actively taught by his know-all white tutors to disregard his family's teachings? How can an African avoid losing respect for his tradition when in school his whole cultural back-ground is summed up in one word: barbarism?

To add to the white-oriented education received, the whole history of the black people is presented as a long lamentation of repeated defeats. Strangely enough, everybody has come to accept that the history of South Africa starts in 1652. No doubt this is to support the often-told lie that blacks arrived in this country at about the same time as the whites. Thus, a lot of attention has to be paid to our history if we as blacks want to aid each other in our coming into consciousness. We have to rewrite our history and describe in it the heroes that formed the core of resistance to the white invaders. More has to be revealed and stress has to be laid on the successful nation-building attempts by people like Shaka, Moshoeshoe and Hintsa.

Our culture must be defined in concrete terms. We must relate the past to the present and demonstrate an historical evolution of the modern African. We must reject the attempts by the powers that be to project an arrested image of our culture. This is not the sum total of our culture. They have deliberately arrested our culture at the tribal stage to perpetuate the myth that African people were near-cannibals, had no real ambitions in life, and were preoccupied with sex and drink. In fact the widespread vice often found in the African townships is a result of the interference of the White man in the natural evolution of the true native culture. "Wherever colonisation is a fact, the indigenous culture begins to rot and among the ruins something begins to be born which is condemned to exist on the margin allowed it by the European culture" [Fanon, *The Wretched of the Earth*]. It is through the evolution of our genuine culture that our identity can be fully rediscovered.

We must seek to restore to the black people a sense of the great stress we used to lay on the value of human relationships; to highlight the fact that in the pre-Van Riebeeck days we had a high regard for people, their property and for life in general; to reduce the hold of technology over man and to reduce the materialistic element that is slowly creeping into the African character. . . .

In this age and day, one cannot but welcome the evolution of a positive outlook in the black world. The wounds that have been inflicted on the black world and the accumulated insults of oppression over the years were bound to provoke reaction from the black people. Now we can listen to the Barnett Potters [a South African newspaper editor] concluding with apparent glee and with a sense of sadistic triumph that the fault with the black man is to be found in his genes, and we can watch the rest of the white society echoing "amen," and still not be moved to the reacting type of anger. We have in us the will to live through these trying times; over the years we have attained moral superiority over the white man; we shall watch as time destroys his paper castles and know that all these little pranks were but frantic attempts of frightened little people to convince each other that they can control the minds and bodies of indigenous people of Africa indefinitely.

Reporting from Soweto, 17 June 1976

Nat Serache and Derrick Thema

In the 1970s the economic and social contradictions built into the system of apartheid begin to erupt in confrontational politics spearheaded by students and workers. Migrant workers and other wage earners were caught between long-stagnant wages and a rising cost of living. In 1973 workers in Durban staged a series of wildcat strikes. They refused to name leaders so as to prevent employers from co-opting their spokesmen. Employers pressed for legalization of black unions in order to have more predictable industrial relations. Bantu Education combined with a growing population meant that increasing numbers of students received deliberately inferior education, and the rise of Black Consciousness gave them rhetorical tools to analyze and challenge their position and to criticize their elders' resignation. In 1974 the government began to enforce a requirement that schools employ Afrikaans equally with English as a medium of instruction. Students bridled at this, seeing Afrikaans as the "language of the oppressor" and realizing that English was the key to economic opportunity. On June 16, 1976, students in Soweto marched against the language policy. The police tried to stop the march with armed force, setting off a major uprising that spread to black townships around South Africa and lasted for many months. The Soweto Uprising was a major turning point in South African history. The government responded by enacting reforms, such as legalizing black unions and encouraging the growth of a black middle class, while keeping a tight lid on black politics through repression.

Based in Johannesburg, the Rand Daily Mail *provided some of the most detailed coverage of the uprising. Long known for reporting on the impact of apartheid policies on black South Africans and for exposing government corruption, the newspaper employed a number of prominent black reporters, many of whom lived in Soweto. Their work exposed them to near-constant police harassment and arrest. Following the uprising, police arrested and tortured Nat Serache (1944–) under the Suppression of Communism Act. He later fled to Botswana and joined the African National Congress. In 1985 Serache narrowly survived an assassination attempt when the members of the Special Forces blew up his house in a cross-border raid. The* Rand Daily Mail *closed in 1985. A few of its reporters formed the newspaper the* Mail *and*

Guardian, *which has continued South Africa's tradition of progressive investigative journalism. Serache later served as the South African envoy to Botswana.*

"Police Fired—Then I Saw Four Children Fall," by Nat Serache

Police threw teargas canisters and fired shots into a crowd of about 10 000 people demonstrated outside the Orlando West Junior Secondary School yesterday against the use of Afrikaans as a medium of instruction.

At least one pupil was killed during the shooting and a White official was clubbed to death by students who called for revenge after their colleague was shot dead by the police.

About 30 000 pupils ranging in age from seven to 19 and from most of the secondary and high schools in Soweto, together with a few primary schools marched from different points in Soweto to Orlando West Junior Secondary School.

Senior pupils on several occasions warned the boys and girls not to be violence [*sic*].

About 10 000 had assembled outside the school were singing "Moreno Boloka Sechaba" when police arrived in vans and with dogs.

I did not hear the police give any order to disperse before they threw teargas canisters into the crowd of singing school children.

The children scattered in all directions while some were dazed and blinded by the teargas.

The pupils then regrouped and when the police charged again they threw stones at the police.

The police then fired a few shots, some in the air and others into the crowd. I saw four schoolchildren fall to the ground.

The mob then charged the shooting policemen and when a police dog was let loose it was stabbed with knives. As it lay writhing on the ground it was beaten with stones and bricks.

A white man was dragged from a West Rand Road vehicle beaten with stones, clubbed with sticks and left dead. He was later picked up by students and thrown into a rubbish bin. Some remarked "That is where he belongs."

Pupils then ran into the school yard to ask teachers at the Orlando West Junior Secondary School who had cars to take the injured students to hospital. The teachers refused.

Dr. Aaron Matlhare, a Soweto doctor, and Mr. Pankle Khabela, a sportsman, volunteered to take the injured in their cars to the hospital.

The students then formed road blocks and stoned cars. Drivers had to

Protest during the Soweto Uprising, Naledi Township, southwestern Soweto, © BAHA, photograph by Mike Mzileni, dm2002040407. Used by permission of Bailey's African History Archive (BAHA).

show the clenched fist and shout "Power!" or "Amandla" before they were allowed to pass.

The first road block was reinforced by thousands more students marching along Potchestroom Road, via Dube, from schools in Naledi and many other outlying parts of Soweto.

Some policemen were forced to run out of their vans and at least two such vans were set alight.

The police then came back, threw some more teargas canisters at the students and ran away.

Meanwhile, about 25 police vehicles formed a road block above the bridge between Orlando East and Orlando West.

I saw a white policeman chase two students in White City carrying anti-Afrikaans posters. One of the posters read: "If we must do Afrikaans, Vorster must do Zulu."

The policeman fired three shots, but the students managed to escape.

The same policeman was later seen arresting a woman in Orlando after the woman had shouted "power" when a military helicopter landed outside Orlando Police Station.

All the bakery vans that went to deliver in Soweto yesterday were stopped and their cargos of bread removed by youths and adults who later joined the road block.

The students ordered the Black drivers out of the vans without injuring them.

They would then help themselves to everything in the vans—from biscuits to bread.

Those drivers who refused were dragged out of their vans and some youths were seen joyriding in some of the vans.

"I Saw Death at the Hands of Child Power," by Derrick Thema

I saw a man dragged from his van and stoned to death in Soweto. I saw another battered to near-death. But he was saved because he was Chinese, not White as the mob first thought.

I saw an African attacked. He was a policeman.

I saw four White women in a small car escape a barrage of bricks and big stones.

I saw children lying shot in the street.

I saw mob anger. And it was ugly. I saw Black Power in its most violent mood. And, ironically, it was child power. Many were younger than seven—throwing stones. About half were between seven and 14, the rest still in their teens.

Shortly after 8 am yesterday Orlando West and Westcliff Extension were alive with thousands of schoolchildren.

I gathered they were on the way to Orlando Stadium for a mass demonstration.

They carried "Afrikaans is terrorism" and "We don't want Afrikaans yet."

They shouted "power, power." They were confronted by police near the Orlando West High School. The police, Whites and Africans armed with sticks, blocked the road. There were not many police at this point.

The crowd stopped and turned back as the police advanced. They started running away. There was shouting. The rioters stopped and faced the police.

They threw stones, bottles and whatever missiles they could lay their hands on.

Suddenly shooting broke out. There was chaos. Children and youths ran in every direction. Many fell, many hid up side streets.

I saw two boys who were shot in the legs. They were helped into taxis. As police retreated over the Orlando Bridge, the rioters regrouped. But they turned their anger on Whites and African policemen.

Hector Pieterson, the first victim in the Soweto Uprising. Photograph by Sam Nzima. Used by permission of The Bailey Seippel Gallery.

Taxi drivers could only pass after shouting the Black Power slogan and raising clenched fists. Buses were stopped. . . .

The police were forced to retreat across the river going into Orlando East from Phefeni. They were reinforced by many more, some in camouflage uniforms.

A car driven by a White woman with three White passengers was stoned as it drove down Kumalo Street from Phefeni Station. The occupants crouched. Windows were smashed. Students scattered as the car swept through the rioters.

A White van driver whom I believe worked for the West Rand Board, was hit continually as he drove down from Phefeni and forced to stop at the Phefeni clinic. He was dragged out and stone to death near his van. The rioters then set the van on fire.

An African policeman was stoned and pulled from his van. He was hand-cuffed with his own cuffs and beaten. As he ran towards the police, he was stoned again. . . .

Students and the Soweto Uprising

Khotso Seatlholo

Students were among the most important new voices of political protest during the 1970s. They elaborated critiques of the apartheid system, which they tied to racism and imperialism across the world. Khotso Seatlholo (1958–2004) attended Naledi High School in Soweto where he became deputy president of the Soweto Students Representative Council. Seatlholo took an increasingly visible position after the council president, Tsietse Mashinini (1957–1990), fled the country. Seatlholo organized strikes and boycotts throughout the Soweto Uprising. He was shot by the police, and he would later join Mashinini in Botswana in 1977. Profoundly influenced by Black Consciousness, Seatlholo returned to South Africa on clandestine missions to recruit members for the armed wing of the Soweto Students Representative Council, the South African Youth Revolutionary Council. Seatlholo served fifteen years in prison after being captured in 1981 and convicted under the Terrorism Act. He was released in 1990 along with many other political prisoners. Seatlholo is buried alongside his friend and comrade Mashinini.

There are a few points which, on behalf of the Black youth and students of South Africa, I wish to make clear—what we think about them, and what our stand is.

It is a pity that I speak at a time when there is no happiness in the Black community; at the crucial moment when the whole country is plunged into a period of unrest and bloodshed. This is the time when the whole of Black Azania [South Africa] has gone into mourning for their dead sons and daughters who have been killed by White police gangsters. Yet, at this serious moment when Rome has gone up in flames, the Hon. Chief Kaiser Matanzima and other stooges of the South African Government, have decided to go feasting with meat and wine while their Black brothers are being shot and killed at their grave yard.

I wish to start with the most recent event, which is:

Transkei Independence: 26th Oct, 1976

The Black youth of Azania totally reject the whole idea of the independence of the Transkei; and that of any Homeland. We see this as the final product of the policy of Separate Development, and the culmination of a political fraud. We see Chief Matanzima as being seduced by the White racist Government to fall for the political joke of the year. We regard him as a betrayer of Black peoples' political aspirations by selling out our birthright to the White minority Government.

We reject the policy of Separate Development in toto. We are opposed to the fragmentation of our Mother-land into some ethnic political entities that are neither politically nor economically viable. We see this policy as the basis for the creation of tribal colonies that would still remain in all aspects dependent on the main colonial power, the so-called White South Africa. Our fear is that this might be the creation of rivalries that might end up in the creation of another "Biafra" tribal conflict in South Africa.

Besides, we are simply opposed to the division of the Black nation into some ethnic sovereign states. We see this as the breaking of Black solidarity and power. We see it as the "divide and rule" method designed to subjugate Black people politically and otherwise. Blacks in the Homelands shall, forever, remain subservient to the White Government; and they will be used as tools for cheap labour in order to maintain the White man's economic power and political domination.

We take the acceptance of the policy of Separate Development by the so-called Homeland leaders as shameful give-in and a betrayal of the Black struggle for the achievement of political freedom and economic independence. We see the step that [Kaiser] Matanzima [the leader of the Transkei] has taken as a grave act of political blunder that we, the youth of today and even those of the coming generation shall never forgive him.

We thus do not recognize the Transkei Independence as meaning anything to us and the Black people as a whole. To us, Azania belongs to us in whole. It is our land. It is our birthright. All the wealth of Azania belongs to all its citizens irrespective of ethnic group, race or colour of the skin. We have an inalienable right to live and die on this land. We shall not accept any policy that is designed to rob us of our birthright.

Therefore, we see the Hon. Chief Matanzima, the so-called Prime Minister of the Transkei, and the rest of the Homeland leaders as political cowards, stooges and puppets who could not hold their own in the fight and defence of their birthright.

They are sell-outs who were just too ready to capitulate to the oppressor and collaborate with the exploitative, oppressive and suppressive system.

They shall go down into annals of Black history as Judas Iscariots who sold the Black nation down a political drain.

The blood of our brothers and sisters who died in the struggle for the liberation of Blacks shall be on their heads until eternity. We shall carry on with the fight for our freedom and ultimate peace in this country.

Present Unrests

Many people, including the Vorster Government, [Minister of Justice] Jimmy Kruger's police and some fascist Government's secret agents, have attributed the present unrests in Soweto and all over the country, to the ANC [African National Congress], PAC [Pan Africanist Congress] or some subversive Communist organisations. Some Government officials have even had the guts to point a finger at the Black Consciousness movements who have to date operated overboard in broad daylight. If this be true that the above organizations are the cause of the upheavals, then we take off our hats for the South African Security force. They seem to be efficiently inefficient in their detective work. They deserve a Noble Price [*sic*] for being too fast to accuse, and faster to find a scapegoat.

We tried to locate symptoms of the above revolutionary organizations, we failed. We worked hard to unearth the communist agitators who caused so much loss of life and bloodshed in our peaceful Black community, we found none. Then our main task was to find the real cause of the unrest and riots all over the country. We found it. It was glaring right into our face—it was the *WHITE FASCIST MINORITY GOVERNMENT OF JOHN VORSTER* and his gang of pro-Nazi Ministers.

It is a pity that Mr. Kruger and his security police could not see this monstrous beam in his regime's eye and racial policies. When we were born, we found our fathers struggling under the yoke of oppression. We found ourselves ushered into a socio-economic and political situation which neither of our fathers' nor of our making. Black people have never been consulted in the making of laws that are today oppressing us; and have made South Africa the stink-cat (meerkat) of the world. We cannot afford to be ostracised from the world community because of no fault of our own. We strongly reject the subservient heritage that our fathers have handed down to us. Our fathers stood up to speak and fight for their rights, they were given Robben Island as eternal place of residence. Their peaceful pleas were answered with ruthless violent acts of suppression, and they lived on as a politically crippled nation.

We came. We saw. We judged and ACTED or REACTED to the whole system of oppression [sic] discriminatory racist laws. We refuse to bend down [so] that the White man can ride on our back. We have the full right to stand up erect and reject the whole system of apartheid. We cannot accept it as our fathers did. We are neither carbon nor duplicate copies of our fathers. Where they failed, we shall succeed. The mistakes they made shall never be repeated. They carried the struggle up to where they could. We are very grateful to them. But now, the struggle is ours. The ball of liberation is in our hands. The Black student shall, fearlessly, stand up and take arms against a political system which is stinking with immoral policies that we have found distasteful and unacceptable to us. We shall rise up and destroy a political ideology that is designed to keep us in a perpetual state of oppression and subserviency. We shall oppose the economic system that is keeping us in non-ending state of poverty. We shall not stand a social system of discrimination that has become an insult to our human dignity. We shall reject the whole system of Bantu Education whose aim is to reduce us, mentally and physically, into "hewers of wood and drawers of water" for the White racist Masters. Our whole "being" rebels against the whole South African system of existence, the system of apartheid that is killing us psychologically and physically. The type of education we receive is like poison that is destroying our minds.

It is reducing us into intellectual cripples that cannot take seat within the World community of academics. It is killing inherent sense of creation in us and thus, it is frustrating us.

Twenty years ago, when Bantu Education was introduced, our fathers said: "half a loaf is better than no loaf." But we say, "half a Gram of poison, is just as killing as the whole gram." Thus we strongly refuse to swallow this type of Education that is designed to make us slaves in the country of our birth.

The Afrikaans question that made us to stand together, as students in one Solidarity to voice our grievances, was just but [sic] "Achilles heel" in the whole system of Bantu Education. The enforcement of Afrikaans as a medium of instruction was the last straw on the camel's back.

We wish to remind the government that it was the extra charge of a tickey (3d [pence]) that broke the British Empire (Boston Tea Party). In the same manner through the rejection of Afrikaans we are prepared to break the spine of the whole immoral White Apartheid Empire. Morality and the

World is [*sic*] on our side. Black Students are determined to die for the Fatherland, the land of AZANIA. The White fascist regime shall be blamed for all the blood shed and misery that shall take place in this country.

The main causes of the present unrests are:

(1) The White racist government's discriminatory racial policies. They have caused unbearable suffering to many Blacks socially economically and politically.

(2) The White man's arrogance in their [*sic*] refusal to listen to Black man's grievances; and their unpreparedness to consult with Blacks in the making of laws that govern the country.

(3) Lack of contact and communication between Black and White at local and National levels because of the Apartheid policy.

(4) The White man's avarice and readiness to amass all the economic wealth in the country and keep Black races in a perpetual state of destitute and poverty. We cannot live on charity and patronisation by Whites.

(5) The undermining of the Students' Power and their determination to free themselves from the oppressive system of education and Government.

If Mr. Vorster, Jimmy Kruger, [W. C.] Ackermann [the Bantu Education Department official] and all their gangsters had paid attention to our cry and warnings by our parents and Black leaders, there would never have been any riots in the country. Instead, they became stubborn. They used ruthless methods of oppression. They arrested, detained, imprisoned or banned nearly all our political and even Cultural leaders. They drove us like dumb cattle to jails. They thought they had solved the problem. What a mistake! Anyway, those whom the gods wish to destroy, they first make them mad. The White government is on the brink of insanity. Our task is how to save them, and thus save the whole of South Africa—the land of AZANIA.

Riots Strikers and Shootings

(1) When Adolf Hitler's Nazi Government liquidated the Jews in the "Final Solution," the whole world rose up in arms to crush the Nazis because lives of a White race were in jeopardy.

(2) When Idi Amin threatened to take the life of Mr. [Denis] Hills in Uganda, the whole World raised a furious cry because a White skin was in danger.

(3) When a White Doctor was killed during the Soweto riots on June 16th

1976 the White press, local and overseas, played the murder for weeks on end because White blood had been shed.

(4) The destruction of West Rand Board's and government property: Beerhalls, Bottle Stores and the bombing of the Jabulani Police Station, received more publicity and emphasis because the White man's property had been destroyed.

The World abhored Hitler's atrocities, the cruelty of Idi Amin and the heartlessness of students in the killing of just one White doctor and the wanton destruction of symbols of White oppression.

But, when Jimmy Kruger's White terrorists shot down the innocent, defenceless school children in a peaceful demonstration when they killed our colleagues in the streets, on the football grounds in the school yards, classrooms and even in the grave yards, the whole World goes silent because the 10 year old child was throwing stones at the well-armed white police; and the police had no alternative but to shoot in self-defence(?). The police who were attacked by the Black mob with some stones and brick missiles, have such strong hippo skins that these stones had to bounce back like rubber balls without leaving any wounds.

Still it was the Black child that was shot down. It was the Black skin that was destroyed. It was the Black life that was taken in defence and protection of the burning car, the beer hall or bottle store that went up in flames. It is nothing!

It was all done in self-defence—In defence of a system that does not value human life especially if that life is Black.

It was in the defence of the White racist system and policies that have turned the land of AZANIA into a blood bath. These incidents show a clash of sense of values between the Black and White races of South Africa.

For the last four months of unrests in Soweto and other areas, apart from the destruction of the White man's property in the Black man's ghetto, Blacks have neither killed nor harmed any Whites. We took our demonstration right into the heart of Johannesburg City, we shed no White blood. We proved our degree of discipline, dignity and value of human life whether it be Black or White.

If there were any casualties, they were very minor. But, the White South African Police have shot and killed hundreds of my Black brothers and sisters; they shot, wounded and maimed thousands of Black school children and adults; their prison cells are teeming with hundred thousands of Black students and leaders detained or imprisoned for having dared to oppose the Monster-Policy of Apartheid.

Black students have never taken any human life; but White police have triumphed in assault and murder of harmless kids. This is a proof to us Blacks that Whites value material property more than human life. They are materialists—a godless race that find pleasure in the violation of human or Christian values. They are sadists who derive satisfaction in the shedding of human blood. They are worse than Communists.

We organise a peaceful march protest against the use of Afrikaans in our schools, they levelled guns at us and shot us down. We called upon a non-violent peaceful stay-at-home strike, they mobilised Black hostel inmates to club us to death and smash our houses and furniture. They set Black to kill Black. We neither begrudge nor feel any bitterness against our poor Black brothers in the hostels. We know it that they have been mentally raped, seduced and corrupted by the Police agitators of Jimmy Kruger. We forgive them.

We held the within-campus protest against the visit of [U.S. Secretary of State] Dr Henry Kissinger to South Africa, then [they] shot and killed our brothers in the school yards. They slaughtered six students plus a Black housewife who was hanging washing in her yard for the reception of Dr Kissinger. And, the so-called American peace-maker never uttered a word of protest at this atrocity and bloodshed.

We carried our dead, whom they killed in the streets or prison cells, to bury, they opened fire at us at the grave-yard—killing further more seven including one of our most respectable Funeral undertakers, Mr. Sydney Kgaye. They desacreded [*sic*] the dead without even a sense of shame or remorse. We cannot even bury our dead brothers without fear of arrest or death. Shall we leave them to rot in the streets like dogs, cats or rats?

Our fathers know what the White man has done for them. They know the good things that Whites did for them. The White man gave them jobs, *banzela* money [small bonuses], second hand clothes—and he did them many other favours. Our fathers may forgive Whites. But, there is only one thing that I, as a Black student and Youth of this country, know. That is: the White police shot and drove a bullet through the head and brain of my 10 year old brother. That the White police shot and killed hundreds of my colleagues; that they shot, wounded and maimed my father, mother, brother and sister at the graveyard; that they terrorise the streets of my ghetto and I can find no peace to rest my head.

This is what I know of the White man; and I cannot forgive him. I smelled the smoke of a gun. I felt the sting of a bullet. I tasted blood. I suffered wounds. I became a fugitive in the country of my birth. I cannot forget. I can't forgive the White man.

The struggle for my freedom shall go on until each and every one of us drops dead. This is a vow, the vow that the Black youth have taken over the dead bodies, and written with the blood of our wounded brothers.

Thus, from Nov. 1st–5th 1976 we are calling on all Blacks of Azania: coloured, Indians, and Africans to go on a 5 day National Stay-at-home Strike. This call must be obeyed by all parents, students and workers. We also call upon all police to join us, to park their hippos [armored vehicles] and remain peacefully in their barracks. Businessmen should not interfere with Workers and thus cause confrontation between us and them.

In this national strike, we call upon Mr. John Vorster, Jimmy Kruger and their White fascist, racist, oppressive regime to:

(a) Resign en bloc
   —They have mismanaged the rule of Azania. They have plunged the country into violence, blood bath, loss of human life.
   —They killed thousands of Black children and thus causing racial hostility in our peaceful country.
(b) Release all political detainees—Students and Black leaders rotting in your jails all over the country.
(c) Open détente with our Black parents in order to plan a future South Africa where there shall be justice, happiness and peace for all.
(d) Stop killing our brothers in the ghetto. We are prepared to stop unrest as soon as you take a move toward consultation, settlements and peace.

To all black people of Azania we say:
   Take heart, have courage.
   Victory is ours!

SOLIDARITY AND POWER!

AMANDLA!

The United Democratic Front

Allan Boesak

Grand apartheid aimed to define South Africa as a white country, allowing Africans to have political aspirations only in rural homelands. With the rethinking forced by the Soweto Uprising and other events of the 1970s, the apartheid state sought to co-opt some groups. In 1983 President P. W. Botha proposed a new constitution with a tricameral parliament, which would include a house for Coloureds, one for Asians (Indians), and a white chamber that could outvote the other two, along with enhanced executive power for the president. Africans remained without political rights, except to vote for township councils that were made responsible for collecting rents and delivering services. Opponents of apartheid denounced these reforms as further entrenchment of apartheid, and hundreds of NGOs, churches, unions, and other groups came together as the United Democratic Front (UDF), a loose nonracial federation, to oppose the new constitution. For the remainder of the 1980s, the UDF, with its distinctive red, yellow, and black colors and its slogan "UDF Unites, Apartheid Divides," was the public face of the antiapartheid struggle in South Africa and in many ways functioned as an above-ground wing of the banned African National Congress. The UDF was banned in 1988.

Reverend Allan Boesak (1945–), an activist proponent of black liberation theology, was one of the patrons of the UDF and gave the following speech at its launch in Mitchell's Plain (a Coloured township in the Cape Town area) in 1983. Boesak denounces the reform proposals as a sham designed to disguise apartheid but not to change any of its fundamental features. He also seizes the moment to justify the idea of a coalition of groups that includes whites, returning to the nonracialism of the Freedom Charter. Boesak builds on the Black Consciousness idea that the struggle must be between those oppressed by apartheid and those who support it, but he argues that whites are among those oppressed and that some blacks are among those supporting and benefiting from apartheid. This idea was a key element of the struggle for the remainder of the decade.

We have arrived at a historic moment. We have brought together under the aegis of the United Democratic Front the broadest and most significant coalition of groups and organizations struggling against apartheid, racism, and injustice since the early 1950s. We have been able to create a unity among freedom-loving people this country has not seen for many years. I am particularly happy to note that this meeting is not merely a gathering of individuals. No, we represent organizations deeply rooted in the struggle for justice, deeply rooted in the hearts of our people. Indeed, I believe we are standing at the birth of what could become the greatest and most significant people's movement in more than a quarter of a century.

We are here to say that the government's constitutional proposals are inadequate and that they do not express the will of the vast majority of South Africa's people. But more than that, we are here to say that what we are working for is one, undivided South Africa that shall belong to all of its people, an open democracy from which no single South African shall be excluded, a society in which the human dignity of all its people shall be respected. We are here to say that there are rights that are neither conferred by nor derived from the state. You have to go back beyond the dim mist of eternity to understand their origin; they are God-given. And so we are here not to beg for those rights, we are here to claim them.

In a sense, the formation of the United Democratic Front both highlights and symbolizes the crisis apartheid and its supporters have created for themselves. After a history of some 331 years of slavery, racial discrimination, dehumanization, and economic exploitation, what they expected were acceptance of the status quo, docility, and subservience. Instead they are finding a people refusing to accept racial injustice and ready to face the challenge of the moment.

After more than three decades of apartheid, they expected humble submission to the harsh rule of totalitarianism and racial supremacy. Instead they find a people ready at every level of society to fight this evil system.

After more than twenty years of apartheid education they expected to see totally brainwashed, perfect little hotnotjies [little Hottentots] and kaffertjies [little kaffirs] who knew their place in the world. Instead they find a politically conscious generation of young people determined to struggle for a better future.

After the draconian measures of the 1960s and the ever harsher oppression of the so-called security laws, they expected a people immobilized by the tranquilizing drugs of apathy and fear. Instead they find a rising tide of political and human consciousness that swept away complacency and shook South Africa to its very foundations.

After the tragic happenings of the 1970s—the banning of our organizations and so many of those who struggle for justice; the torture and death of so many in detention; the merciless killing of our children on the streets of the nation—they expected surrender. Instead, here we are at this historic occasion telling South Africa and the world: we are struggling for our human dignity and for the future of our children—we shall never give up!

In all of this, those in power in this country have made the fundamental mistake of all totalitarian regimes who do not depend on the loyalty of the people but on the power of the gun: they have not reckoned with the determination of a people to be free. Because they depend on propaganda, deceit, and coercion, they have forgotten that no lie can live forever and that the fear of the gun is always overcome by the longing for freedom. They have forgotten that it is true you can kill the body, but you cannot kill the spirit and the determination of a people.

The most immediate reason for our coming together here today is the continuation of the government's apartheid policies as seen in the constitutional proposals. In recent weeks some people have asked me with greater urgency than before (and I am sure this question has been put to you also), "Why do you not see the positive side of apartheid?" Now when you are white and your children's education is guaranteed and paid for by the state; when your job is secure and blacks are prevented from being too much competition; when your home has never been taken away and your citizenship of the country of your birth is not in danger; when your children don't have to die of hunger and malnutrition; and when your over privileged position is guaranteed by security laws and the best equipped army on the continent, then I can understand why some people believe that apartheid has its positive side.

But for those of us who are black and who suffer under this system there is no positive side. How can we see something positive in a system which is built on oppression, injustice, and exploitation? What is positive about a system which destroys, systematically and by design, the human dignity of people, which makes as irrelevant and unimportant a thing as skin color the basis of society and the key to the understanding of human relationships, political participation, and economic justice? How can apartheid be positive when in the name of Christianity it spawns policies which cause little children to die of hunger and malnutrition, which break up black family life, and which spell out a continuous, hopeless death for millions of black people?

How can apartheid be positive when it keeps part of South Africa's children manacled in the chains of unfreedom and the other part in the chains of fear? The time has come for white people to realize that their destiny is inextricably bound with our destiny and that they shall never be free until we are free. I am so happy that so many of our white brothers and sisters are saying this by their presence here today.

It is true: people who think that their security and peace lie in the perpetuation of intimidation, dehumanization, and violence, are *not* free. They will never be free as long as they have to kill our children in order to safeguard their over privileged positions. They will never be free as long as they have to lie awake at night worrying whether a black government will one day do the same to them as they are doing to us, when white power will have come to its inevitable end.

But we must also ask the question: what is positive about the government's constitutional proposals? In order that there should be no misunderstanding, let me as clearly and briefly as possible repeat the reasons why we reject these proposals.

- Racism, so embedded in South African society, is once again written into the constitution. All over the world, people are beginning to recognize that racism is politically untenable, sociologically unsound, and morally unacceptable. But in this country, the doctrine of racial supremacy, although condemned by most churches in South Africa as heresy and idolatry, is once again enshrined in the constitution as the basis upon which to build the further development of our society and the nurturing of human relationships.
- All the basic laws, those laws which are the very pillars of apartheid, indeed, those laws without which the system cannot survive—mixed marriages, group areas, racial classification, separate and unequal education, to name but a few—remain untouched and unchanged.
- The homelands policy, which is surely the most immoral and objectionable aspect of the apartheid policies of the government, forms the basis for the wilful exclusion of 80 percent of our nation from the new political deal. Indeed, in the words of the proposals made by the president's council, the homelands policy is to be regarded as "irreversible." So our African brothers and sisters will be driven even further into the wilderness of homeland politics; millions will have to find their political rights in the sham independence of those bush republics; millions more will continue to lose their South African citizenship; and millions more will be forcibly removed from their homes into resettlement camps.
- Clearly the oppression will continue, the brutal breakup of black family life will not end. The apartheid line is not at all abolished; it is simply shifted so as to include those so-called coloreds and Indians who are willing to cooperate with the government.

- Not only is the present system of apartheid given more elasticity, making fundamental change even harder than before, but in the new proposals the dream of democracy to which we strive is still further eroded.
- So while the proposals may mean something for those middle class blacks who think that the improvement of their own economic position is the highest good, it will not bring any significant changes to the life of those who have no rights at all, who must languish in the poverty and utter destitution of the homelands, and who are forbidden by law to live together as families in what is called "white South Africa."

It cannot be repeated often enough that all South Africans who love this country and who care for its future, black and white, Jew and Gentile, Christian and Muslim, have no option but to reject these proposals. . . .

To be sure, the new proposals will make apartheid less blatant in some ways. It will be modernized and streamlined, and in its new multicolored cloak it will be less conspicuous and less offensive to some. Nonetheless, it will still be there. And we must remember, apartheid is a thoroughly evil system. As such it cannot be modified, modernized, or streamlined; it has to be irrevocably eradicated. And we must continue to struggle until that glorious day shall dawn when apartheid shall exist no more.

And so, to those who ask *why* we are not satisfied and *when* we shall be satisfied we must say in clear, patient terms: we shall not be satisfied as long as injustice reigns supreme on the throne of our land. We shall not be satisfied as long as those who rule us are not inspired by justice but dictated to by fear, greed, and racialism. We shall not be satisfied until South Africa is once again one, undivided country, a land where there shall be meaningful participation in a democratic process of government for all our people.

We shall not be satisfied until the wealth and riches of this country are shared by all. We shall not be satisfied until justice rolls down like waters and righteousness like a mighty stream.

We must turn to one other important question, namely the question of whites and blacks working together. This has been mentioned as a reason why the United Democratic Front has been so severely attacked by some and why they have refused to give their cooperation.

They are saying to us that white people cannot play a meaningful role in the struggle for justice in this country because they are always, by definition, the oppressor. Because the oppression of our people wears a white face, because the laws are made by a white government, because we are suffering so much under a system created and maintained by white people, they say there can be no cooperation between white and black until all of this is changed.

I would like to say to those who think this way that I understand the way they feel. We have seen with our own eyes the brutalization of our people at the hands of whites. We have seen police brutality. We have experienced the viciousness and the violence of apartheid. We have been trampled on for so long; we have been dehumanized for so long. But it is not true that apartheid has the support of all white people. There are those who have struggled with us, who have gone to jail, who have been tortured and banned. There are those who have died in the struggle for justice. And we must not allow our anger for apartheid to become the basis for a blind hatred for *all* white people. Let us not build our struggle upon hatred, bitterness, and a desire for revenge. Let us even now seek to lay the foundation for reconciliation between white and black in this country by working together, praying together, struggling together for justice.

No, the nature and the quality of our struggle for liberation cannot be determined by the color of one's skin, but rather by the quality of one's commitment to justice, peace, and human liberation. And in the final analysis, judgment will be given, not in terms of whiteness or blackness, whatever the ideological content of those words may be today, but in terms of the persistent faithfulness we are called to in this struggle.

Besides, the very fact that we are talking about the constitutional proposals already reveals the paradox in this argument. The government has been pushing ahead with these proposals precisely because they have been supported and accepted by some people from the black community who think that the short-term economic gains and the semblance of political power are more important than the total liberation of all South Africa's people. So our struggle is not only against the white government and their plans, but also against those in the black community who through their collaboration seek to give credibility to these plans. . . .

South Africa belongs to all its people. That is a basic truth we must cling to tenaciously for now and for the future. This country is our country, and its future is not safe in the hands of people who—white or black—despise democracy and trample on the rights of the people. Its future is not safe in the hands of people—white or black—who depend upon economic exploitation and human degradation to build their empires. Its future is not safe in the hands of people—white or black—who need the flimsy and deceitful cloak of ethnic superiority to cover the nakedness of their racialism. Its future is not safe in the hands of people—white or black—who seek to secure their unjustly required privileged positions by violent repression of the weak, the exploited, and the needy. Its future is not safe in the hands of people—white or black—who put their faith simply in the madness of growing militarism. So for the sake of our country and our children, whether *you* be white or black, resist those people, whether *they* be white or black.

So let us not be fearful of those who sit in the seats of power, their lips dripping with the words of interposition and nullification. Let us not be intimidated by those who so arrogantly, so frighteningly, echo their master's voice.

We are doing what we are doing not because we are white or black, we are doing what we are doing *because it is right*. And we shall continue to do so until justice and peace embrace and South Africa becomes the nation it is meant to be. . . .

As we struggle on let us continue to sing that wonderful hymn of freedom: Nkosi Sikilel' iAfrika. I know: today we are singing that hymn with tears in our eyes. We are singing it while we are bowed down by the weight of oppression and battered by the winds of injustice. We are singing it while our old people languish in the resettlement camps and our children are dying of hunger in the homelands. We are singing it now while we suffer under the brutality of apartheid and while the blood of our children is calling to God from the streets of our nation.

But we must work for the day when we shall sing it when we are free. We shall sing it when our children shall no longer be judged by the color of their skin but by the humanness of their character.

We shall sing it on that day when we even here in this country, in Johannesburg and Cape Town, in Port Elizabeth and Durban, the sanctity of marriage and family life shall be respected, and no law shall require of man to put asunder what God has joined together.

We shall sing it on that day when in this rich land no child shall die of hunger and no infant shall die untimely, and our elderly shall close their eyes in peace, and the wrinkled stomachs of our children shall be filled with food just as their lives shall be filled with meaning.

We shall sing it when here in South Africa white and black will have learned to love one another and work together in building a truly good and beautiful land.

With this faith, we shall yet be able to give justice and peace their rightful place on the throne of our land; with this faith, we shall yet be able to see beyond the darkness of our present into the bright and glittering daylight of our future; with this faith we shall be able to speed up the day when all of South Africa's children will embrace each other and sing with new meaning:

NKOSI SIKILEL' IAFRIKA

GOD BLESS AFRICA—GUIDE HER RULERS—BLESS HER CHILDREN— GIVE HER PEACE!

Sanctions and the Armed Struggle

Oliver Tambo

After the Soweto Uprising in 1976, the African National Congress (ANC) was able to revive the armed struggle with an infusion of new recruits to Umkhonto we Sizwe (Spear of the Nation, or MK), and it also began to receive support from newly independent "frontline states" in southern Africa, including Mozambique and Angola. The ANC also pursued a worldwide diplomatic strategy, rallying public opinion in the West against apartheid and urging countries and international organizations to put pressure on South Africa through economic and cultural sanctions. The ANC and its allies, including the United Democratic Front and the trade union federation Congress of South African Trade Unions, intensified the campaign for sanctions after the township uprising that began in 1984 and a state of emergency was imposed in 1985.

Oliver Tambo (1917–93), Nelson Mandela's former law partner, had led the ANC in exile since the 1960s. On the tenth anniversary of the Soweto Uprising, Tambo spoke at the UNESCO headquarters, in Paris, to rally support for the antiapartheid movement and to justify the ANC's armed struggle, and to pressure Western powers to impose sanctions. A few months after this speech, the U.S. Congress voted to override President Reagan's veto of a comprehensive sanctions bill. Sanctions and other economic pressures, along with the unrelenting pressure and cost of quelling the township uprising, helped force the South African government to enter negotiations with the ANC.

We thank the United Nations, the Organisation of African Unity and the Non-Aligned Movement for summoning this conference at this critical time in the struggle to free Namibia and South Africa. We extend to everyone present here the greetings of the ANC and the beleaguered people of South Africa. To you all we bring assurance that racism and colonialism in southern Africa cannot survive much longer. At the same time, we carry with us the simple message that the times demand of all of us, drawn from all quarters of the globe, that we sue for victory now rather than later, today and not tomorrow, tomorrow rather than the day after. The long awaited victory is within our grasp. . . .

The result of our common efforts is that today there are no people any-where in the world who do not know what apartheid means, who are not aware of the evil nature of this man-hating system. There are today very few people who will not oppose the apartheid monster by word or deed, who are unwilling to do that little more which will bring the monster to its knees. In reality, even the argument in favour of sanctions has been won bar those who, for reasons of racist principle or avaricious self-interest, continue to argue that the Pretoria regime must be treated as an errant child—lovingly kept within the bosom of the family of nations, occasion-ally, gently chided and offered sweets as an inducement to mend its way-ward behaviour.

It would therefore seem clear to us that from these successes, which are truly significant, we can in fact enhance the isolation of apartheid South Africa in a meaningful way. Taking advantage of mass, popular sentiment in favour of sanctions, governments that are committed to anti-racism and truly interested to minimise the bloodshed and usher in an era of peace, freedom and justice in southern Africa, can and must take further steps to-wards the imposition of comprehensive sanctions.

Equally, this feeling in favour of meaningful action against the apartheid regime provides the basis for public organisations such as political parties, trade unions, churches, anti-apartheid movements and others to mobilise for the imposition of sanctions by the people themselves.

Surely, it has by now become patently clear to all thinking people that unless the world takes decisive action now, a bloodbath in South and south-ern Africa is inevitable.

We meet on the day of the tenth anniversary of the Soweto uprising, which is today South Africa Youth Day. To honour our youth who were killed ten years ago and to advance the cause for which they perished, the African National Congress and all other democratic forces in our country called for a national general strike, which is a resounding success, as well as commemorative mass rallies and meetings.

As all of us present here know, the apartheid regime has, in response, taken unprecedented measures to place itself in a position where it can, this very day, massacre our people in their tens of thousands. Huge numbers of armed soldiers and policemen have been deployed in both black and white areas of our country. The enemy hopes that through sheer use of terror, it will force our people to go to work, and having done so, not to engage in mass demonstrations in the centres of towns and cities.

Nobody knows what the situation will be when this day ends. It is, how-ever, perfectly clear that by this massive deployment of brute force to sup-

Students opposing the state of emergency, IDAF Collection, UWC-Robben Island Mayibuye Archives, LA598–2-4. Courtesy of the Robben Island Museum Mayibuye Archives.

press peaceful actions, the apartheid regime is blatantly telling our people, as it told them ten years ago, that we can never achieve our objective of a united, democratic and nonracial South Africa except through armed struggle. Pretoria is saying this in very clear terms, that only armed resistance on our part will win the day.

When the racist rulers communicated this message ten years ago, our youth understood it fully. Today that message is being conveyed to the whole nation clearly and unequivocally. It will similarly be understood fully. Those who sow these seeds will surely reap the whirlwind.

Death has become so much a part of our daily lives that it can no longer serve as deterrence discouraging struggle. Indeed, death has become so much part of our daily lives that the urgent necessity to end the murderous system of apartheid presses on us with the greatest insistence. Therefore, having learnt the lessons that the enemy seeks to teach us today, our people will join the armed offensive in even greater numbers, displaying the same bravery and same contempt for death that they have shown in the last two years and before.

We speak here not in triumph that the Botha regime has dragged our country into the situation which we witness today. The prospect of growing numbers of our people killed and injured does not fill us with joy. We view it as a sombre prospect and wish it could have been avoided.

However, we have also learnt to look reality in the face. That reality demands that in order to win our liberty we must be prepared to make the necessary sacrifices. It also demands that we should steel ourselves for war with all the consequences that implies. We are certainly not prepared to live as slaves and will therefore continue to intensify our offensive for the victory of the cause of democracy, national liberation and peace in our country.

The certainty of greatly increased violence is not confined to South Africa. It is a prospect which faces the peoples of southern Africa. Already many people have died in our region and enormous destruction has been caused by the aggression of the apartheid regime. As this regime grows more desperate, so will it seek to wreak more havoc throughout the region.

The major Western Powers and in particular the United States, Great Britain, the Federal Republic of Germany and France cannot avoid taking the blame for this inevitable and terrible outcome. It is they who have, above all, shielded the apartheid regime from decisive international action. They have aided and abetted this regime in the past and continue to do so today. Current reports confirm that these governments remain determined to persist in this ignoble and dishonourable role as allies of a truly murderous regime.

The African National Congress and the masses of the people it leads are committed to the victory of the cause of democracy in our country. There should be no doubt whatsoever that with your support, we shall emerge victorious. Already, reports coming out of South Africa today confirm that despite all the extraordinary measures of state terrorism that the Botha regime has adopted, our people have observed the call for a general strike in their millions. In action our people are saying we shall never be terrorised into submission. Practically they are rejecting the legitimacy of the Pretoria regime and affirming their recognition of the African National Congress and the rest of the democratic movement of our country as their leaders, the authentic political force that represents all the people of South Africa.

These masses, and their organisation, the ANC, would have dearly loved to liberate our country from a racist tyranny by peaceful means, including negotiations. Indeed, over many years, we tried again and again to achieve this result, to no avail. The Commonwealth Group of Eminent Persons has now added its confirmation that the Botha regime is not prepared to resolve the problem of South Africa by negotiations. It is instead as committed as ever to maintain the system of white minority domination.

This surely must lay to rest the illusion that negotiations are an option available to us and confirms the hollowness and bankruptcy of arguments that decisive action should be avoided in the interests of promoting the chances of a negotiated settlement. The call made on us to renounce violence, as it is put, is nothing but a ruse to render us impotent precisely for the purpose of ensuring the perpetuation of the apartheid system. We shall certainly not fall into that trap.

To achieve change we must and will continue to intensify our political and military offensive. We owe it to ourselves as a people and to the thousands who died before, during and after June 16th, 1976. We owe it to the peoples of southern Africa, Africa and the rest of the world. We count on your all-round support, as the representatives within South Africa of the objectives contained in the Charter of the United Nations and the Universal Declaration of Human Rights. The obligation to choose to be on the side of the oppressed people of our country and their national liberation movement can no longer be avoided.

On behalf of the ANC and the struggling people, we greet all participants at this timely World Conference on Sanctions against Racist South Africa. We extend our heartfelt thanks to all who have acted to help end the apartheid system. Over many years you have stood side by side with us because you would not countenance the commission of a crime against humanity. We call on you on this important day in our history, the tenth anniversary of the Soweto uprising, when it is possible that yet more massacres are taking place, that you act decisively now for the total isolation of the apartheid regime.

Sanctions Now!

Our Common Victory is Assured!

The Church and the Struggle

Desmond Tutu

South Africa's mainstream Christian churches, including the Anglicans, Method-
ists, and Catholics, grew from the missionary encounter in the nineteenth century
discussed in part III. These churches were important allies and bases of institutional
support for the antiapartheid movement, especially in the 1970s and 1980s. Churches
and church leaders put themselves on the line to offer theological justification and
moral and material support for the struggle. One of the most remarkable and cele-
brated church figures supporting the liberation movements was Desmond Tutu
(1931–), who was the secretary-general of the South African Council of Churches
from 1978 to 1985 and later the Anglican archbishop of Cape Town. He was awarded
the Nobel Peace Prize in 1984 in support of his and the churches' role in the struggle.

Tutu used the world stage offered to him by the Nobel Peace Prize ceremony to give
a short course in the injustice and horrors of apartheid, so that his audience would
understand that South Africa lacked peace because it lacked justice. The churches
took a firm stand in support of Christian nonviolence (and civil disobedience) but
offered their sympathetic understanding to the leaders of the liberation movements
who had concluded from the time of the Sharpeville massacre in 1960 that there was
no reasonable alternative to the use of armed struggle. Tutu's Christian theology and
rhetoric provided him with common ground with many in the West, especially in
the United States, where Christian activism had also been an important element of
the struggle for black rights.

In pursuance of apartheid's ideological racist dream, over 3,000,000 of God's
children have been uprooted from their homes, which have been demolished, whilst they have then been dumped in the bantustan homeland resettlement camps. I say dumped advisedly: only things or rubbish is dumped,
not human beings. Apartheid has, however, ensured that God's children,
just because they are black, should be treated as if they were things, and not
as of infinite value as being created in the image of God. These dumping
grounds are far from where work and food can be procured easily. Children
starve, suffer from the often irreversible consequences of malnutrition—

Tutu addresses the End Conscription Campaign rally, Cape Town, 1987, IDAF Collection, UWC-Robben Island Mayibuye Archives, LA578-2-3. Courtesy of the Robben Island Museum Mayibuye Archives.

this happens to them not accidentally, but by deliberate Government policy. They starve in a land that could be the bread basket of Africa, a land that normally is a net exporter of food.

The father leaves his family in the bantustan homeland, there eking out a miserable existence, whilst he, if he is lucky, goes to the so-called white man's town as a migrant, to live an unnatural life in a single sex hostel for 11 months of the year, being prey there to prostitution, drunkenness, and worse. This migratory labor policy is declared Government policy, and has been condemned, even by the white Dutch Reformed Church, not noted for being quick to criticize the Government, as a cancer in our society. This cancer, eating away at the vitals of black family life, is deliberate Government policy. It is part of the cost of apartheid, exorbitant in terms of human suffering.

Apartheid has spawned discriminatory education, such as Bantu Education, education for serfdom, ensuring that the Government spends only about one tenth on one black child per annum for education what it spends on a white child. It is education that is decidedly separate and unequal. It is to be wantonly wasteful of human resources, because so many of God's children are prevented, by deliberate Government policy, from attaining to their fullest potential. South Africa is paying a heavy price already for this iniquitous policy because there is a desperate shortage of skilled manpower, a direct result of the short-sighted schemes of the racist regime. It is a moral universe that we inhabit, and good and right equity matter in the universe of the God we worship. And so, in this matter, the South African Government and its supporters are being properly hoisted with their own petard.

Apartheid is upheld by a phalanx of iniquitous laws, such as the Population Registration Act, which decrees that all South Africans must be classified ethnically, and duly registered according to these race categories. Many times, in the same family one child has been classified white whilst another, with a slightly darker hue, has been classified colored, with all the horrible consequences for the latter of being shut out from membership of a greatly privileged caste. There have, as a result, been several child suicides. This is too high a price to pay for racial purity, for it is doubtful whether any end, however desirable, can justify such a means. There are laws, such as the Prohibition of Mixed Marriages Act, which regard marriages between a white and a person of another race as illegal. Race becomes an impediment to a valid marriage. Two persons who have fallen in love are prevented by race from consummating their love in the marriage bond. Something beautiful is made to be sordid and ugly. The Immorality Act decrees that fornication and adultery are illegal if they happen between a white and one of another race. The police are reduced to the level of peeping Toms to catch couples red-handed. Many whites have committed suicide rather than face the disastrous consequences that follow in the train of even just being charged under this law. The cost is too great and intolerable.

Such an evil system, totally indefensible by normally acceptable methods, relies on a whole phalanx of draconian laws such as the security legislation which is almost peculiar to South Africa. There are the laws which permit the indefinite detention of persons whom the Minister of Law and Order has decided are a threat to the security of the State. They are detained at his pleasure, in solitary confinement, without access to their family, their own doctor, or a lawyer. That is severe punishment when the evidence apparently available to the Minister has not been tested in an open court— perhaps it could stand up to such rigorous scrutiny, perhaps not; we are never to know. It is a far too convenient device for a repressive regime, and the minister would have to be extra special not to succumb to the temptation to circumvent the awkward process of testing his evidence in an open court, and thus he lets his power under the law to be open to the abuse where he is both judge and prosecutor. Many, too many, have died mysteriously in detention. All this is too costly in terms of human lives. The minister is able, too, to place people under banning orders without being subjected to the annoyance of the checks and balances of due process. A banned person for 3 or 5 years becomes a non-person, who cannot be quoted during the period of her banning order. She cannot attend a gathering, which means more than one other person. Two persons together talking to a banned person are a gathering! She cannot attend the wedding or funeral of even her own child without special permission. She must be at home from 6:00 PM of one day to 6:00 AM of the next and on all public holidays, and from 6:00 PM on Fridays until 6:00 AM on Mondays for 3 years. She cannot go on holiday outside the magisterial area to which she has been confined. She cannot go to the cinema, nor to a picnic. That is severe punishment, inflicted without the evidence allegedly justifying it being made available to the banned person, nor having it scrutinized in a court of law. It is a serious erosion and violation of basic human rights, of which blacks have precious few in the land of their birth. They do not enjoy the rights of freedom of movement and association. They do not enjoy freedom of security of tenure, the right to participate in the making of decisions that affect their lives. In short, this land, richly endowed in so many ways, is sadly lacking in justice. . . .

It is against this system that our people have sought to protest peacefully since 1912 at least, with the founding of the African National Congress. They have used the conventional methods of peaceful protest—petitions, demonstrations, deputations, and even a passive resistance campaign. A tribute to our people's commitment to peaceful change is the fact that the only South Africans to win the Nobel Peace Prize are both black. Our people are peace-loving to a fault. The response of the authorities has been an escalating intransigence and violence, the violence of police dogs, tear gas, detention without trial, exile, and even death. Our people protested peacefully against the Pass Laws in 1960, and 69 of them were killed on March 21, 1960, at Sharpeville, many shot in the back running away. Our children protested against inferior education, singing songs and displaying placards and marching peacefully. Many in 1976, on June 16th and subsequent times, were killed or imprisoned. Over 500 people died in that uprising. Many children went into exile. The whereabouts of many are unknown to their parents. At present, to protest that self-same discriminatory education, and the exclusion of blacks from the new constitutional dispensation, the sham local black government, rising unemployment, increased rents and General Sales Tax, our people have boycotted and demonstrated. They have staged a successful two-day stay away. Over 150 people have been killed. It is far too high a price to pay. There has been little revulsion or outrage at this wanton destruction of human life in the West. In parenthesis, can somebody please explain to me something that has puzzled me. When a priest goes missing and is subsequently found dead, the media in the West carry his story in very extensive coverage. I am glad that the death of one person can cause so much concern. But in the self-same week when this priest is found dead, the South African Police kill 24 blacks who had been participating in the protest, and 6,000 blacks are sacked for being similarly involved, and you are lucky to get that much coverage. Are we being told something I do not want to believe, that we blacks are expendable and that blood is thicker than water, that when it comes to the crunch, you cannot trust whites, that they will club together against us? I don't want to believe that is the message being conveyed to us. . . .

There is no peace in Southern Africa. There is no peace because there is no justice. There can be no real peace and security until there be first justice enjoyed by all the inhabitants of that beautiful land. The Bible knows nothing about peace without justice, for that would be crying "peace, peace, where there is no peace." God's Shalom, peace, involves inevitably righteousness, justice, wholeness, fullness of life, participation in decision-making, goodness, laughter, joy, compassion, sharing and reconciliation. . . .

Unless we work assiduously so that all of God's children, our brothers and sisters, members of our one human family, all will enjoy basic human rights, the right to a fulfilled life, the right of movement, of work, the freedom to be fully human, with a humanity measured by nothing less than the humanity of Jesus Christ Himself, then we are on the road inexorably to self-destruction, we are not far from global suicide; and yet it could be so different.

When will we learn that human beings are of infinite value because they have been created in the image of God, and that it is a blasphemy to treat them as if they were less than this and to do so ultimately recoils on those who do this? In dehumanizing others, they are themselves dehumanized. Perhaps oppression dehumanizes the oppressor as much as, if not more than, the oppressed. They need each other to become truly free, to become human. We can be human only in fellowship, in community, in koinonia, in peace.

Crossing the Rubicon

P. W. Botha

On July 20, 1985, President P. W. Botha (1916–2006) declared a state of emergency in response to the township uprising that had begun the preceding year. Under emergency regulations, the army occupied the black townships and the government restricted or detained tens of thousands of people, many of them children, and heavily censored the dissemination of news. With one brief gap in 1986, the emergency remained in force until 1990. With repression firmly in place, the leaders of the National Party turned to reform aimed at quieting external critics. Less than a month after declaring the emergency, Botha addressed a party congress and declared that the government was "crossing the Rubicon" by committing itself to reform. Although Botha raised expectations prior to the speech, its content showed that the government was still unwilling to contemplate reforms that would bring a real end to apartheid and introduce democracy, as internal and external critics demanded. The liberation movements and their allies dismissed Botha's Rubicon speech as a sham.

The speech shows apartheid's leaders moving toward a new strategy in a bid to hold on to power. Instead of discussing a white minority and a black majority, Botha tries to emphasize a multiplicity of ethnic groups (all minorities, in his view), implicitly referencing whites, Zulus, Sothos, and Indians, among others. The idea is that the interests of each minority group, including whites, must be protected and that people have rights only as parts of groups, not as individuals. He also states the government's willingness to work with compliant black leaders, such as the heads of the Bantustans (which he calls "National States") and those who denounce violence, justifying the continued imprisonment of Nelson Mandela as a leader who embraces violence.

We are not prepared to accept the antiquated, simplistic and racist approach that South Africa consists of a White minority and a Black majority.

We cannot ignore the fact that this country is a multicultural society—a country of minorities—White minorities as well as Black minorities.

While the National Party accepts and respects the multicultural and poly-ethnic nature of South Africa's population, it rejects any system of horizontal differentiation which amounts to one nation or group in our country dominating another or others. . . .

It is my considered opinion that any future constitutional dispensation providing for participation by all South African citizens, should be negotiated.

But let me point out at once that since South Africa freed itself from colonialism, democracy has already been broadened and millions of people who never had a say in Governmental affairs under the British Colonial system, have it today.

I am pressed by some who mean it well and those who wish to destroy orderly government in this country, to make a Statement of Intent. I am not prepared to make it, not now and not tomorrow.

I say it would be wrong to be prescriptive as to structures within which participation will have to take place in the future.

It would also be wrong to place a time limit on negotiations. I am not going to walk into this trap—I am responsible for South Africa's future.

However, I believe that the majority of South Africans as well as independent states, which form our immediate neighbours, have much in common apart from our economic interests.

We believe in the same Almighty God and the redeeming grace of His Son, Jesus Christ.

And I know what I am talking about, because only a few months ago I stood before an audience of 3 million Black people [a meeting of the avowedly apolitical Zion Christian Church], proving the truth of what I am saying now. I don't know whether one of our critics ever saw 3 million people together in a meeting. I did.

We believe and wish to uphold religious freedom in South Africa. This is a country of religious freedom.

We believe in democratic institutions of government and we believe in the broadening of democracy.

We believe our great wealth of divergent population groups must speak to each other through their elected leaders, not self-appointed leaders.

We believe that our peace and prosperity is indivisible.

We believe in the protection of minorities. Is there anybody in this hall who would get up and say he is not for the protection of minorities? Let me see how such a fool looks.

We know that it is the hard fact of South African life, that it will not be possible to accommodate the political aspirations of our various population groups and communities in a known defined political system, because our problems are unique. . . .

Now let me state explicitly that I believe in participation of all the South African communities on matters of common concern. I believe there should exist structures to reach this goal of co-responsibility and participation.

I firmly believe that the granting and acceptance of independence by various Black peoples within the context of their own statehood, represent a material part of the solution. I believe in democratic neighbours, not neighbours that call out elections and then stop them in their mysterious ways.

I would, however, like to restate my Government's position in this regard, namely that independence cannot be forced upon any community. Should any of the Black National States [Bantustans] therefore prefer not to accept independence, such states or communities will remain a part of the South African nation, are South African citizens and should be accommodated within political institutions within the boundaries of the Republic of South Africa. This does not exclude that regional considerations should be taken into account and that provision be made for participation in institutions on a regional and / or group basis. We must be practical in this regard.

But I know for a fact that most leaders in their own right in South Africa and reasonable South Africans will not accept the principle of one-man-one-vote in a unitary system. That would lead to domination of one over the other and it would lead to chaos. Consequently, I reject it as a solution.

Secondly, a so-called fourth chamber of Parliament is not a practical solution and I do not think responsible people will argue in favour of it.

We must rather seek our solutions in the devolution of power and in participation on common issues.

But I admit that the acceptance by my Government of the permanence of Black communities in urban areas outside the National States, means that a solution will have to be found for their legitimate rights.

The future of these communities and their constitutional arrangements will have to be negotiated with leaders from the National States, as well as from their own ranks. . . .

I am not prepared to lead White South Africans and other minority groups on a road to abdication and suicide.

Destroy White South Africa and our influence, and this country will drift into faction strife, chaos and poverty. . . .

We have had to contend with escalating violence within South Africa, and pressure from abroad in the form of measures designed to coerce the Government into giving in to various demands.

Our enemies—both within and without—seek to divide our peoples.

They seek to create unbridgeable differences between us to prevent us from negotiating peaceful solutions to our problems. Peaceful negotiation is their enemy. Peaceful negotiation is their enemy, because it will lead to joint responsibility for the progress and prosperity of South Africa. Those whose methods are violent, do not want to participate. They wish to seize and monopolize all power. Let there be no doubt about what they would do with such power.

One has only to look at their methods and means. Violent and brutal means can only lead to totalitarian and tyrannical ends.

Their actions speak louder than their words. Their words offer ready panaceas such as one-man-one-vote, freedom and justice for all. Their actions leave no doubt that the freedoms that we already have—together with the ongoing extension of democracy in South Africa—are the true targets of their violence. . . .

From certain international as well as local quarters, appeals are being made to me to release Mr Nelson Mandela from jail.

I stated in Parliament, when put this question, that if Mr Mandela gives a commitment that he will not make himself guilty of planning, instigating or committing acts of violence for the furtherance of political objectives, I will, in principle, be prepared to consider his release.

But let me remind the public of the reasons why Mr Mandela is in jail. I think it is absolutely necessary that we deal with that first of all. When he was brought before court in the sixties, the then Attorney-General, Dr Yutar, set out the State's case inter alia as follows:

> As the indictment alleges, the accused deliberately and maliciously plotted and engineered the commission of acts of violence and destruction throughout the country . . .
>
> The planned purpose thereof was to bring about in the Republic of South Africa chaos, disorder and turmoil . . .
>
> They (Mr Mandela and his friends) planned violent insurrection and rebellion.

The saboteurs had planned the manufacture of at least seven types of bombs: 48 000 anti-personnel mines, 210 000 hand grenades, petrol bombs, pipe bombs, syringe bombs and bottle bombs. . . .

The violence of our enemies is a warning to us. We, who are committed to peaceful negotiation, also have a warning to them. Our warning is that our readiness to negotiate should not be mistaken for weakness.

I have applied much self-discipline during the past weeks and months. I have been lenient and patient. Don't push us too far in your own interests,

I tell them. Reform through a process of negotiation is not weakness. Talking, consulting, bargaining with all our peoples' leaders is not weakness. Mutual acceptance of and joint responsibility for the welfare and stability of our country is not weakness. It is our strength.

Our strength is the courage to face and accommodate the problems bequeathed to us by history. The reality of our diversity is a hard reality. We face it, because it is there. How do we accommodate it? How do we build a better future out of cultures, values, languages which are demonstrably real in our heterogeneous society?

We are resolved, we are committed, to do so in two fundamental ways.

Firstly—by letting the people speak. By letting the people speak through their leaders.

By negotiation between all these leaders. I go out of my way, and my colleagues know that I am working all hours every day of my life. Negotiation in which we will all endeavour to improve our common well-being. Negotiation in which there will be give and take. We will not prescribe and we will not demand—to do so would be to take only. We will give so that others can also give—towards a better future for each and everyone.

Secondly—the overriding common denominator is our mutual interest in each other's freedoms and well-being. Our peace and prosperity is indivisible. Therefore, the only way forward is through co-operation and co-responsibility.

If we ignore the existence of minorities; if we ignore the individual's right to associate with others in the practice of his beliefs and the propagation of his values; if we deny this in favour of a simplistic "winner-takes-all" political system—then we will diminish and not increase the freedoms of our peoples. Then we would deny the right of each and everyone to share in the decisions which shape his destiny.

Between the many and varied leaders in this country, in the National States and the independent states neighbouring on our borders, in our urban areas I recognise this, but I also know that their love for South Africa is intense as my own. I am therefore in no doubt that working together, we shall succeed in finding the way which will satisfy the reasonable social and political aspirations of the majority of us. . . .

We have never given in to outside demands and we are not going to do so now. South Africa's problems will be solved by South Africans and not by foreigners.

We are not going to be deterred from doing what we think best, nor will we be forced into doing what we don't want to do. The tragedy is that hostile pressure and agitation from abroad have acted as an encouragement to the militant revolutionaries in South Africa to continue with their violence and intimidation. They have derived comfort and succour from this pressure.

My Government and I are determined to press ahead with our reform programme, and to those who prefer revolution to reform, I say they will not succeed. If necessary we will use stronger measures but they will not succeed.

We prefer to resolve our problems by peaceful means: then we can build, then we can develop, then we can train people, then we can uplift people, then we can make this country of ours a better place to live in. By violence and by burning down schools and houses and murdering innocent people, you don't build a country, you destroy it.

Despite the disturbances, despite the intimidation, there is more than enough goodwill among Blacks, Whites, Coloureds and Asians to ensure that we shall jointly find solutions acceptable to us.

But I say it is going to take time. Revolutionaries have no respect for time, because they have no self-respect. Look what they have done to Africa, a continent that is dying at present. I can tell you, because I know what is happening in many of these countries. I have the facts and I am not going to hand South Africa over to these revolutionaries to do the same to this lovely country.

I am encouraged by the growing number of Black leaders who are coming forward to denounce violence. Any reduction of violence will be matched by action on the part of the Government to lift the State of Emergency and restore normality in the areas concerned.

Moreover, as violence diminishes, as criminal and terrorist activities cease, and as the process of dialogue and communication acquires greater momentum, there would be little need to keep those affected in detention or prison.

The implementation of the principles I have stated today can have far-reaching effects on us all. I believe that we are today crossing the Rubicon. There can be no turning back. We now have a manifesto for the future of our country, and we must embark on a programme of positive action in the months and years that lie ahead. The challenges we face call for all concerned to negotiate in a spirit of give and take. With mutual goodwill we shall reach our destination peacefully.

Never Give In

Andries Treurnicht

After the Soweto Uprising, the ruling National Party moved toward limited reforms to the structure of apartheid with the aim of mollifying international critics and co-opting portions of the black population. Though opponents of apartheid considered most of the reforms a sham or a further entrenchment of apartheid, true believers in apartheid among the Afrikaner population felt increasingly threatened. In 1982 Andries Treurnicht (1921–93), a member of Parliament, led a breakaway from the National Party to form the Conservative Party, with a platform of retaining and strengthening apartheid. The new party attracted the support of many rural and working-class Afrikaners and government workers. In the election of 1987, it surpassed the white liberal Progressive Federal Party to become the official opposition.

In this speech from 1985, Treurnicht, known as "Dr. No," decries the inclusion of Coloureds and Indians under the constitution of 1983 and argues that the government is on a slippery slope toward the inclusion of Africans. In his view, this would result in an unthinkable loss of autonomy for the "white community."

What is the future of the white race in South Africa? What is your future and my future as a particular community, a white community in this country? Zimbabwe, the former Rhodesia of Mr. Ian Smith, is a footnote of history! In Mozambique, the Portuguese had to flee when the government turned Marxist. There is no corporate political self-determination for any white group or community in any African country. The whites of South West Africa [Namibia] were subject to experiments with power sharing and mixed marriages, and their freedom as a people was betrayed.

In South Africa the self-determination of the white man was cleverly taken away from him in the same co-responsibility, joint decision-making, grand words and phrases, reconciliation, peace and cooperation, you name it, and to escape from the threat of revolution. That was done by persuading people to accept the new constitution, to accept a multi-racial parliament and to accept a mixed cabinet for whites, coloureds and Indians. During the last few years, Mr. Chris Heunis [the minister of constitutional reform] propagated his consensus politics, his power sharing and the conviction that every man should be able to take part in the government of the country in which he lives.

Whites, coloureds and Indians were declared one nation by Mr. P.W. Botha. But for the one nation in the one country there could be only one government. And now the line of joint decision making and power sharing has been drawn right through to include blacks outside their homelands. Just listen to a few quotes from the speech made by the State President, opening parliament.

Here's a booklet published by the Department of Cooperation and Development, you better call it: cooperative co-existence, cooperative suicide. The State President said: "Give all the countries' people a say in decision making that affects their interests." This applies to all the population communities of South Africa, including the blacks. He says: "The government accepts the permanency in the Republic of South Africa of the large numbers of members of black population communities who found themselves outside the national states." Yes, about ten million black people inside the Republic of South Africa outside the national states. Of that 10 million only 13 per cent accepted citizenship of their homelands, of the national states. That means about 8 million 700 thousand are still in the Republic of South Africa not willing to accept citizenship of their own countries.

The State President says of those staying in the Republic of South Africa, large numbers, they are considered permanent residents. They are a permanent part of the population of this country according to the government. Next he says, not all those people can express themselves politically beyond the local level via the government structures of the national states. That means those people living inside the Republic of South Africa, instead of linking them with their own ethnic groups and their own governments, their own national states. The State President says they cannot express themselves politically at a higher level than local level in their own national states! So where is that to happen? That is to happen in yours and my country! He says such communities must be given political participation and a say at higher levels and he concludes by saying the government decided that they should have a say in the decision making about their own affairs up to the highest level.

The Conservative Party's argument with the government—the coalition government, the mixed government—is this: The highest level in a country is the parliament and the cabinet. So either you have a black parliament in South Africa—if they are to have a joint *say* at the highest level and either they have a black parliament and a black cabinet, alongside the present coalition cabinet and the present parliament. Or you give them representation in the present cabinet and the present parliament. Mr. Heunis and Mr. P.W. Botha exclude a black parliament and a black cabinet. The only option left is representation in our parliament and in our cabinet.

The Conservative Party says: Black peoples should not be divided into homeland blacks and urban blacks and I agree with Chief Buthelezi [the leader of the KwaZulu Bantustan] who warned the government not to make such a division between the so called urban blacks and the homeland blacks. Treat the Zulu nation for example, as a whole, as [an] entity and give the blacks of black residential areas their own local government. But we say: Don't cut their cultural and political ties with their ethnic groups and their own governments. It will be absolutely disastrous, it will be political suicide for whites, coloureds and Indians to include millions and millions of blacks in the same political dispensation, in the same political structures with whites, coloureds and Indians. But evidently the State President is willing to accept this as a possibility! It will be absolutely disastrous if blacks are included in the same political system and the same parliament and the same government.

We of the Conservative Party say: There is no acceptable alternative to separate development. We say this constitution must be changed to restore white self-determination, a white parliament, and a white cabinet and to let coloureds have the full political self-government, to have their own parliament and their own cabinet, governing themselves in their own territories which they have this very moment. And the same principle applies to the Indians and to the various black nations.

Never give in!

We have not come to give our support to Mr. P.W. Botha but to say to him: "Gentleman we're going to fight you!" And if you think that until the next general election, we're going to give in, we wish to remind you of the message given by the famous Winston Churchill to a group of young persons in England. And he said: "My message to you is: Never give in!"

Never give in! Never! Never!

The Future of South Africa

Mangosuthu Gatsha Buthelezi

While critics dismissed black homeland leaders as puppets, Chief Mangosuthu Gatsha Buthelezi (1928–) used his position as leader of the KwaZulu homeland to build a wider following. He tried to position himself as a moderate black leader who could steer a middle course between apartheid and revolution. In 1975 Buthelezi and other KwaZulu leaders formed the Zulu nationalist group Inkatha (renamed Inkatha Freedom Party in 1990) as the ruling party of the homeland, advocating cultural liberation in line with Black Consciousness. The African National Congress (ANC) initially supported the formation of Inkatha. However, Inkatha repressed rebellious youths when the Soweto Uprising spread to KwaZulu (intertwined with Natal), and the organizations decisively split in 1979. A violent struggle broke out between United Democratic Front– and ANC-aligned youths and Inkatha-aligned elders in KwaZulu and Natal beginning in 1985. Buthelezi and Inkatha staked a position as moderates, refusing apartheid's phony independence for KwaZulu but allying with capitalist interests against the socialist-oriented liberation movements and opposing the ANC's armed struggle. With these positions, Buthelezi and Inkatha became the darlings of white moderates and conservatives in South Africa and in the West. The U.S. press lionized Buthelezi. Throughout this period, Inkatha received clandestine support from the South African government.

In the second year of the state of emergency, Buthelezi addressed the conservative Heritage Foundation in Washington, D.C. With considerably greater rhetorical skill than that deployed by P. W. Botha, Buthelezi undermines the ANC's image as a group seeking democracy and civil rights and argues that it is engaged in violent revolution aimed at securing a one-party socialist state. Ironically, what Buthelezi argued "white South Africa" wanted in 1986, that is, "a normalization of South Africa as a modern, multi-party, industrial democracy," is what ANC rule since 1994 has achieved.

The idiom of the American media and the content of American debate on South Africa indicates to me that people in the United States just have not grasped the extent to which the politics of negotiation is under siege in

South Africa. Some would retort: What politics of negotiation? And they would point to white political recalcitrance and the refusal of the State President [P. W. Botha] to actually get going with meaningful reform. Such people have to understand that the politics of negotiation is started a long time before people actually sit around a negotiating table. The actual negotiations around that table will be a culminating event of the politics of negotiation. It is the process that leads to negotiation that is now so threatened in South Africa. . . .

What prospects are there then for negotiations to get off the ground in South Africa? This is not my question, ladies and gentlemen. It is a skeptical American question. There is pessimism about the politics of negotiation now in South Africa because these Americans I am referring to are drawing parallels about what happened in Mozambique and Zimbabwe and about what is happening in South Africa. People like Mr. Randall Robinson [the head of TransAfrica, an antiapartheid organization in Washington, D.C.] already in fact believe that, if the ANC is not the central negotiating party on the side of blacks, there is no prospect of successful negotiations being concluded. This was also the view of the Commonwealth Eminent Persons Group. They too saw the ANC Mission in Exile as a prime negotiating partner in South Africa, and they persist in seeing the ANC as a prime negotiating partner, or perhaps the only black negotiating power, and they retain some kind of idealistic belief or perhaps hope that, if Pretoria started to move toward the negotiating table, the ANC Mission in Exile would soften its approach and participate in black democracy which must surround negotiations. They fail to see that the ANC has now smelt blood and is driving in for what they think will be the final kill, and they are totally convinced that they will be a government returned from exile to establish a one-Party socialist State in South Africa. They see negotiation as something that will rob them of that final reward of their revolutionary endeavors.

Americans must necessarily make their own judgments about what kind of an organization the ANC is and what its real intentions are. I do not want to use this platform today to mount a personal attack on the ANC. I am simply being analytical and telling Americans what happens in our African circumstances. I am laying before you the facts of the matter, and the facts of the matter are that the ANC's stand is that the only thing to negotiate about is the handing over of power to the people, that is, to themselves. They are not interested in negotiating for an open general election from which they will be able to compete as equals. They are not interested in negotiating the kind of constitution which must necessarily be finalized before such an election could be held. Those are the facts of the matter. They see themselves as a government in a future one-Party state and they envisage themselves evolving a constitution once they are in that position. The politics of negotiation in South Africa really is under siege.

Ladies and gentlemen, this is not an attack on the ANC Mission in Exile. You cannot attack an organization by telling the world what its cherished hopes are and what it is actually doing. You cannot attack an organization by telling the world: this is what they themselves are saying. The problem comes when the world does not know what the ANC Mission in Exile is saying; and in the West, the problem comes when the West only knows what the ANC is saying to the West. I am not a Westerner. I am a son of Africa, a son of South Africa and I know what the ANC Mission in Exile is saying to black South Africans. That is where they are fighting their revolution and that is where they say what they really mean.

They spend millions saying what they really mean to black Africa. They have a massive propaganda machine and all one has to do is to examine closely the texts of their actual broadcasts to South Africa made daily on Radio Freedom from Addis Ababa [the capital of Ethiopia]. Those broadcasts are formulated by the political and publicity brains of the ANC Mission in Exile. They are really the authentic voice of the Mission in Exile. Those broadcasts do not reflect media opinion about what they are saying. The broadcasts are authentically what they say. In these broadcasts they promote the slogan again and again: "Every patriot a combatant and each combatant a patriot." They exhort black South Africa to spread violence from black areas into white areas. They exhort our youth to take up arms. They call on workers to destroy their factories, and again and again they call on black South Africa to destroy black leaders who refuse to toe the ANC Mission in Exile line to pursue violent confrontation. They tell black South Africa that they reject any concept of a National Convention. They tell black South Africa that there is nothing to negotiate about and an analysis of what they say will show very clearly that they will continue to do their damndest to make sure that successful negotiations do not take place before they have won their military victory. Of course once that victory is won, there will be no need to negotiate. There never is in a one-Party state.

Wherever I go in the United States I find a kind of noble and romantic view of the black struggle in South Africa. Apartheid is so hideous and repulsive that any protest against it which is not yet a protest in which people are actually throwing bombs, planting hand grenades, and laying land-mines is praised. For Americans oppression must lead to protest, and all protest against apartheid for them is praiseworthy. For Americans, failed protests are seen as lost skirmishes in a battle which will be won by protest. They see even protest bordering on violence as that which stays the inevitability of violence. Protest rhetoric sounds beautiful to many American ears, and a protest leader dramatically proclaiming the hideousness of apartheid and the indomitable spirit of blacks who have not been crushed by it is praised as a hero of the struggle.

But again, ladies and gentlemen, do not hear me as criticizing protest politics in South Africa. It is an essence which lies deep in the very guts of the black struggle for liberation. In our circumstances, however, protest politics is no more than a phase in the development of the true black struggle in South Africa that must be left behind sooner or later. Protest politics can be beautiful, but even a beautiful, chubby cheeked little boy must grow up. Protest is exciting because it shows the indomitability of the human spirit. Protest has immense value because it mobilizes people, and as protest gathers momentum, people are encouraged to do something about their terrible circumstances because they see they are not alone. They find strength and succor in protest. Protest builds up morale. I myself am the political product of the great surge of protest which took place in the 1950s under Chief Albert Luthuli's leadership [Luthuli was the former president of the ANC]. I do not condemn protest, but we cannot go on protesting forever.

The problem I see with the American perception of protest politics in South Africa is that they see it with the same eyes that they saw protest in the black civil rights movement in the United States. They simply fail to understand that protest politics in the United States led to incorporation. Protest politics in South Africa cannot lead to incorporation. Protest politics in South Africa must go somewhere, and there is a deep cleavage between black South Africans on the question of where protest ought to go. There is a kind of natural progression for protest in circumstances such as ours. . . .

The radicalization of protest deepens and begins to polarize society itself, and an onward march to use violence in protest continues. Protest eventually becomes the means of mobilizing violent action. Protest becomes that which you must organize in order to get people to kill and burn and when this happens, revolutionaries claim protest as their child. They see protest as the kindergarten of the armed struggle and indeed it is by then just that. After June 1976 when protest met with violent reaction and when the first schoolboy Hector Petersen was shot dead as he walked in front of school mates in a simple school protest march, violent protest spread. When the spreading of violent protest was crushed by massive State power, there was a vast spin-off of young black refugees fleeing South Africa to escape the brutality of the State. ANC Mission in Exile recruiters for the armed struggle had a field day. Radicalized protest suits revolutionaries very well. Protest is so much more in South Africa than it ever was in the American civil rights struggle.

Radicalized protest in South Africa has begun to seek a political home. I made the point earlier that protest must go somewhere if it does not lead to incorporation. Violent protest must seek a home in violent politics, and this is happening. The ANC Mission in Exile has claimed as its own the violent protest movement in South Africa. The violent protest movement in South Africa now proclaims the ANC as the true liberators of the country, and thus the whole of South Africa is shaping up for a revolutionary future and moving towards violent solutions. The politics of negotiation really is under siege.

American idealism about protest politics in South Africa is understandable. Protest is justifiable. It is essential. It performs a vital task, and its radicalization is inevitable. If radicalized protest were a force working with all other democratic opposition to apartheid strengthening non-violent tactics and strategies, the struggle for liberation in South Africa would by now have been a great deal further advanced than in fact it is. Radicalized protest challenges the State without engaging the State. It endorses itself out of institutionalized politics. It is non-cooperative with some of the country's parliamentary forces working for the same change that Americans see protest politics working for. Radicalized protest politics in South Africa does not set itself the task of strengthening the hand of the Progressive Federal Party [a white liberal party]. It does not set itself the task of strengthening opposition to apartheid in institutionalized South Africa. Radicalized protest is not only extra-parliamentary, it is extra-institutional. As it occupies this position, it endorses itself out of the politics of negotiation.

Non-cooperation has become more than a tactical issue. Non-cooperation is now a principle of radical protest politics. It has thus far only confronted. Radicalized protestors despise those who do not protest. They claim the right to make everyone protest. Radicalized protest now freely uses intimidation, and this again is incompatible with the politics of negotiation. Let me say rather bluntly that black South Africa has the choice between the politics of negotiation and the politics of violence. If the choice is for the politics of negotiation, then it must ultimately be negotiations with the ruling National Party government. The politics of negotiation from the black side involves driving the South African government to the negotiating table. This will not be done by only mounting confrontation and conflict. It must also be done by undermining the basis of the government's own power.

The politics of negotiation must make ever deeper incursions into the seat of power. This is possible, and it is happening. The power of the gov-

Gatsha Buthelezi address-
ing a crowd of support-
ers, IDAF Collection,
UWC-Robben Island
Mayibuye Archives,
LA592-5-3. Courtesy of the
Robben Island Museum
Mayibuye Archives.

ernment is no longer monolithic. The total solidarity of Afrikaner support, which forms the guts of government power, is beginning to fragment. Government power has always rested in South Africa on the total control of the country's institutional life. This is no longer happening. Big business is not under government control. They are challenging the government. The trade union movement is not under government control. It is challenging the government. The government is being challenged even by its own first and second tier levels of government in white society.

There is now vast scope for democratic opposition to apartheid, which mobilizes institutionalized forces to drive the government to the negotiating table. White South Africa has finally seen that apartheid is totally unworkable and that it is destabilizing the whole of South Africa. White South Africa wants a normalization of South Africa as a modern, multi-party, industrial democracy. It sees that apartheid has threatened the very basis of the free enterprise system. Whites can now be mobilized into participating in bringing about radical change, and because this is now in fact the case, revolutionaries have to make a very concerted attempt to spread violence to inhibit the politics of negotiation.

I come again to my statement that protest politics has to go somewhere if it does not lead to incorporation. I have given in the briefest outline how protest politics has become radicalized and developed into violent confrontation. That is not the only development in protest politics. Protest politics as we know it today crystallized in the early seventies. The same black foment that produced June 16, 1976, produced Inkatha. Inkatha was also fashioned by protest politics, and there is an alternative to both incorporation and to violence. This is the Inkatha option. It is the option of once again establishing a mass democratic organization that now cannot be smashed by the State in the way the State smashed the ANC.

The yearning for organization which I said protest politics produces, the yearning for collective action which I said it produces and the tendency in protest politics to become objective oriented as I so briefly outlined all culminated in the formation of Inkatha. And that, ladies and gentlemen, is why Inkatha is in fact the largest political organization ever to have been formed in the history of South Africa. Inkatha plays in the league above protest politics. It has entered constituency politics as the only base from which mass black power can be mobilized in favor of the politics of negotiation. Inkatha actually engages the State. That engagement is a far more effective confrontation with the State than violent street-corner protest. We engage the State in KwaZulu and thump the State there. . . .

We employ our power to say: Mr. State President, unshackle black democracy first and then we will join you. We say to the State President: Release Dr. Nelson Mandela, Mr. Zeph Mothopeng [a Pan Africanist Congress leader], and other political prisoners and then we will join you. We say to the State President: Declare the death sentence on the Tricameral Parliament and then we will join you. We engage the State in this confrontation between mass black power and mass State power.

History in South Africa has thrown up the radicalized protest movement, and it has thrown up Inkatha. Both are the products of the same history of the same people, both are legitimate. One can only be finally effective in non-violent change and the other can only be finally effective in violent change. The West must now decide which they want. While the West cannot fight our battles for us, how the West now behaves may well determine how we fight our own battles.

Violent Times

Emma Mashinini

The township uprising that began in 1984, initially as a protest over rents, marked a new and intensely violent phase of the struggle against apartheid. The state cracked down with increasing force, both through police and the army deployed in the townships and through covert operations against activists, including bombings, kidnappings, torture, and assassinations. Government agents bombed the headquarters of the Congress of South African Trade Unions (COSATU), the largest union federation and an affiliate of the United Democratic Front, and the South African Council of Churches, and they assassinated union activists, political leaders, and university professors. While unions, churches, and NGOs in the townships organized to replace the functions of illegitimate township councils that were under attack, township youths calling themselves "comrades" struck out at people they believed to be collaborators with apartheid or anyone they saw as preying on the community. Comrades, sometimes joined by criminal opportunists, meted out rough street justice, sometimes to the point of execution by "necklacing," burning the victim with a gasoline-soaked tire.

In 1989 Emma Mashinini (1929–) wrote about her experiences as a union member and leader. After the resurgence of labor activism in the early 1970s and the government's decision to legalize black unions in 1979 as part of the post-Soweto reforms, union activists were among the most important figures in the struggle against apartheid in the 1980s. Mashinini was one of the founders of COSATU, in 1985. It played an important role in calling for sanctions and disinvestment, and, along with the wider United Democratic Front, was one of the key organizations working above ground to help bring about a new dispensation in South Africa.

One of the most important victories for the trade union movement, and one which for me closed a chapter that had opened when I first tried to meet with management as a trade union leader, was in 1986, when I came up against my old friend Ray Ackerman, of Pick n Pay [the country's largest supermarket chain]. We in South Africa were appealing to trade unionists in

Australia to stop the expansion of Pick n Pay in their country. We regarded the move to develop in Australia as grossly unfair. I myself had had many disputes with Pick n Pay, over a number of years, concerning their exploitation of black workers. I now felt strongly that it was on the strength of the profits of this exploitation that they were opening new markets in Australia. It angered me that these multinational companies, instead of using their wealth to bring an end to apartheid, were instead benefiting from it, and at the same time cushioning themselves against the eventuality of black liberation and the fairer distribution of the wealth of the country. They are building up fortunes outside of South Africa so that come what may they can continue their luxuries and comforts elsewhere.

I was elated when the Australian trade unions showed solidarity with our cause, and was thrilled to read in the London *Financial Times*, on 20 February 1986, that "industrial action by an Australian union [the Plumbers' and Gasfitters' Union] has compelled Pick n Pay to abandon plans to build a hypermarket in Melbourne."

Once again the Australian trade unions had risen to the challenge, and had demonstrated their solidarity that an injury to one is an injury to all. It reminded me again that in April 1982, after the DPSC [Detainees' Parents Support Group] had battled that those of us who were imprisoned without charge or trial, and in solitary confinement, should be allowed to have transistor radios, Tom had brought one to me and I had been able to hear of Neil Aggett's "suicide" [Aggett was a white trade unionist who died while in police detention], and that trade unions in Australia were refusing to unload South African goods in protest.

That March I was invited, as a trade unionist and also as a member of Women Against Apartheid, to a meeting with the Commonwealth Eminent Persons Group (EPG). This group consisted of distinguished leaders of the Commonwealth, and had been allowed into South Africa as a fact-finding team. They were granted access to all the political forces in South Africa, and were even allowed to visit Nelson Mandela.

I was very pleased to be at that meeting, because I wanted to challenge Malcolm Fraser, ex-Prime Minister of Australia and Co-Chairman of the Group, regarding South African multinationals opening in his country. I reminded him that while trade unionists had prevented Pick n Pay from opening in Melbourne, Pick n Pay still had a branch in Brisbane, which had opened the previous year, and that when the Brisbane branch opened the prices were so competitive that there was a stampede and one person died as a result. I pointed out that the reason they could price themselves so low was simply that the exploitation of their black workers in South Africa enhanced their profits. Mr Fraser listened attentively to my comments, which were supported by the general meeting.

The findings of the EPG were published in 1986. They have not been acted upon by the South African government.

You can never relax in this country, this South Africa. With each step forward comes a step backwards. They gave the black unions the right to register, and then they swooped on the leaders and arrested those in the forefront of the black trade union movement. And now, with the stronger position of black unions and improving industrial relations, they are bringing in a new plan, which they are calling Racial Mix.

Before I left CCAWUSA [Commerical, Catering and Allied Workers Union of South Africa] I one day received information pushed under my door, at my office and at home, about this Racial Mix. Workers are very good characters. They will gather information, and even when they don't want you to know who actually delivered it they will get it to you. So here was a circular letter with the heading "Racial Mix." It said that from now on, henceforth, every black worker should be replaced with a worker of another race. You must mix the races on the shop floor, because during work stoppages the blacks are the ones that support stoppages most. Therefore, never replace a black with a black. They didn't necessarily say, "Replace them with a Coloured, Indian or white," and this was deliberate, because when you speak with people who do not have all the information you find that "Racial Mix" is seen as a symptom of development in South Africa. . . .

As we make strides towards further change, this government is also making preparations to counter our every move. Take, for example, the bombing of COSATU House, in May of 1987. To destroy that building—the building I was involved in finding, that was our centre as workers—well, whoever did that deed made sure that that building was utterly destroyed, and that trade unions were fragmented all over again in their efforts to find a place in which to gather. And then, towards the end of August 1988, I attended a board meeting in Namibia on behalf of the Department of Justice and Reconciliation. We had spent three days in the north, which is the war zone, and on our return to Windhoek we learnt that a massive bomb explosion had devastated Khotso House [the headquarters of the South African Council of Churches]. The explosion took place on 31 August at 1.03 AM, and damage to the building was estimated at 1 million rand. Fortunately no one was hurt, although all the workers who were asleep on the sixth floor were severely shocked. Before leaving for Namibia I had asked a colleague to park my car in the underground garage of Khotso, for "safety." Now, on the TV news, I saw my car mashed under the rubble of the building.

As soon as the board received the news of this attack it was decided that we would go and pray in one of the parishes in Windhoek. On our way back to the conference centre after the service we witnessed a building blown up in front of our eyes, and as a result of that bomb blast two people were killed, and others injured. We are thankful to God that no one was hurt in Khotso House.

A few months after Khotso House was bombed, the Catholic church in Pretoria was burnt down. In South Africa, when the darkest forces of evil arraign themselves in this way against the work of God, the culprits are never found or arrested. There is no place for neutrality in this crisis we find ourselves in. We are all too aware that these blasts take place in an atmosphere of hatred, which is generated against all organisations and church bodies opposed to apartheid. We are forced to join the growing squatter community in their pain of having nowhere to stay, and we know full well that in this country, where black people are treated as less than human, the question of human rights and dignity can never arise.

The police have now made an announcement that the bomb was put into Khotso House by the people who work there, and that it inadvertently went off before being used on its intended target. They claim to be looking for several ANC [African National Congress] members. The Church has protested strongly at the suggestion that they might be involved in bombings.

Sadly, as black determination to be free increases, so does the virulent right wing grow in number. Their fear and greed increases their hatred. The numerous right-wing organisations in South Africa may differ on certain issues of policy, strategy and tactics, but one idea is common to them all: they identify blacks as the enemy. The grotesque slaughter in Pretoria in 1988 epitomises the right wing. Mr Strydom, a member of the [neofascist] Afrikaner Weerstand Beweging (AWB), simply woke up one morning and with his sawn-off shotgun went on a hunting expedition. He killed seven innocent black people and wounded many others. He is a man in his twenties. He has been declared sane and will stand trial. He smiles and waves to his family and friends in the courtroom and looks distinctly proud of his achievement on behalf of the Boere Volk (Boer Nation). One lives in a constant state of fear of these people. They cannot be underestimated, and as their numbers grow they remain a very real and dangerous threat to black people, and even to those white people who stand up to be counted with us in the struggle and are labelled by their right-wing white brethren as Communists and Kaffir-boeties (black brothers).

This is the kind of violence which surrounds the apartheid regime. This is the kind of society we live in—a society where children disappear, where mothers go from prison to prison to try and find their children, where some of those picked up by the troops or the police are as young as eleven years old. And in this kind of society it is not difficult to fan hatred, mistrust and revenge. The authorities have skilfully manipulated black people, creating ethnic divisions by encouraging malicious rumours, and turning black against black rather than against their real enemy, which is apartheid. The horror of South Africa is that the life of a black person is very cheap. Under this brutal regime, the saddest tum of all is that some of our own people have become brutalised and a prey to violent feelings.

This has hit me personally very recently, when as a result of a long and unsubstantiated article in the *Sowetan* five undertakers were killed in different parts of Soweto on Friday, 4 March 1988. One of them was my dear son-in-law, Aubrey, the husband to my daughter Molly, father of her children.

Aubrey's death took place in Mshenguville, in Molofo, one of the most squalid and overcrowded of the squatter camps which have mushroomed in the ghetto of Soweto in the last two years. Hundreds and hundreds of homeless people have constructed tin shacks in which to live, in conditions in which it is hard to keep up human dignity. The government provides houses for the "upwardly mobile" black middle class who can afford to pay their prices, but the homeless and the unemployed are left to rot. In such an area of despair, paranoia and hatred can easily be inflamed.

Aubrey was thirty-seven when he was killed. He had returned to South Africa in 1987 after studying in West Germany for the previous six years. He had obtained his BSC degree in agriculture at Fort Hare in South Africa and was then granted an Anglican Church scholarship to complete his Master's degree in Agriculture at the Technical University of Berlin. Molly and Aubrey had a very loving and close relationship, and it was made even closer by those many years living in a foreign country, far from their home.

They returned to their country, with their two children, Mphoentle (Beautiful Gift), aged thirteen, and Rirandzu (Love), aged eight, all speaking fluent German and with great excitement, with high hopes for their future. My grandchildren are very clever, and they can speak German so well that they have found a way to express their disapproval of me in that language, which I cannot understand. The other day, while sharing a meal, they said to their mother in German, "You always told us not to talk with food in our mouths, so why is Gogo (Gran) doing that now?"

Aubrey had applied for a lectureship at a university, and while waiting for an interview he was helping his family in their undertaking business. In February 1988 the *Sowetan* published articles claiming that a terror gang driving an ambulance was abducting children in the townships, and then that as well as an ambulance there was a hearse, and that the abductors of innocent children were undertakers.

On that terrible Friday, 4 March 1988, Molly was driving home from work, having collected the children from school. She was driving past Mshenguville when she saw large crowds and billowing smoke. In the confusion of the crowd she suddenly spotted Aubrey, who approached her car and asked her to return home immediately and phone the police to come quickly because there was violence in that area. He said the man who was being assaulted was the driver, Alson Twala, an elderly man who had worked for Aubrey's parents for many years, and that the black smoke ahead of them was the burning hearse. Molly asked Aubrey where he was going, and he explained that he was going to plead with the assailants. He reassured Molly that he would be returning home in a short while.

Molly and the children returned home, which was less than five minutes' drive, and phoned Jabulani police station, who said that Mshenguville was not their area geographically. She phoned another police station, in Moroka, but they also failed to respond. Molly finally drove to the police station and pleaded with the police to come. Finally they agreed. By now the crowds had grown bigger, but still Aubrey had not returned home. As Molly pursued her way through the crowds to look for him, neighbours were stopping her from going closer to the burning hearse. The neighbours already knew that Aubrey was dead, and they did not wish Molly to see his burnt-out body.

Molly returned home and called me to say that she was anxious about her husband, who had still not returned. Nomsa and myself immediately drove to Molly's house. The neighbours were gathered outside, and they asked me not to leave Molly and the children there, but to take them back to my house. As we were driving off, one neighbour approached the car and whispered to me that my son-in-law was dead. With the shock, I gave it a deaf ear, and said nothing to Molly, but drove home.

At home I immediately phoned Roger, Molly's father, and told him that he must go in search of Aubrey. I still could not accept that he was dead. I then phoned the Mageza family and Aubrey's mother came to my house. Aubrey's family and Roger went in search, but returned within a short while to say that the whole area was barricaded off by the police, but they had insisted on going through and had seen the charred remains of Alson Twala and Aubrey. They were so badly burnt there was no body to bury.

Two weeks after Aubrey's death an unknown man came to visit Molly, and through him we learnt what happened that day. The man said he was a final year student at university. He said he was part of the huge crowd witnessing the horror of the assault and the burning of the hearse when a well-dressed young man very politely patted him on the shoulder and said, "Excuse me, would you let me pass through." He stood aside for this young man, who was Aubrey, and then witnessed my son-in-law raise his arms above his head and say, "Peace, peace, gentlemen, please don't kill this old man." To his horror he witnessed the first stab under Aubrey's armpit. He says that he cannot forget that day. He is now unable to concentrate to study, because the vision which will not leave his head is of giving way to this polite, well-dressed young man so that he could go to his death that day.

At the time of Aubrey's murder I was working closely with Sheena Duncan [the leader of the Black Sash, a white women's antiapartheid group] and a committee on the "Save the Sharpeville Six Campaign," to fight against the death penalty. And I must confess that for a brief time I was in a moral conflict. I did not know whether I wanted the death penalty for those who had murdered those innocent people, Aubrey and Alson. Only with time can such a wound heal. But my conclusion was that I wanted those people who committed that atrocity to be brought to justice, but never to be barbarically hanged.

This was my conclusion, and it is one I will hold to. But my concern for the increasing violence among my own people grows daily. It was expressed so well by a journalist writing for the *Sowetan* on 8 March 1988, four days after Aubrey's death:

> Dammit. We have to stop passing the buck. Something is happening in our community and instead of trying to come to grips with it, we continue to find the usual scapegoat, apartheid. We are eating into ourselves; all respect for human life is gone.
>
> Only the other day it was Maki Skhosana ruthlessly roasted in front of TV cameras. Who can forget that obscene image?
>
> We continue to scream, demanding justice from white South Africa; we continue to protest against detention without trial; we continue demanding democracy. But we also continue to deny ourselves these things.
>
> We refuse to give the other man a hearing.
>
> We continue to be prosecutors, judges and executioners.
>
> And all this turns our struggle for justice into a mockery.

The Funeral of ANC Guerrilla
Thanduxolo Mbethe

Anonymous

The township uprising of 1984 was sparked by a combination of material depriva-tion, the new tricameral parliament, and new policies concerning the administra-tion of townships. The uprising led to states of emergency in 1985 and 1986–91 and marked a new and more sustained phase of struggle against the apartheid state and its agents, especially black collaborators such as the township councils that were now expected to raise and collect rents to finance dismal services. With the state of emergency, security forces occupied the black townships and policing concentrated on stifling political opposition through attacks on protesters as well as assassina-tions of activists. The armed struggle also intensified as guerrillas like Thanduxolo Mbethe, many of whom had left the country during the Soweto revolt of 1976 to join the African National Congress (ANC) or Pan Africanist Congress in exile, infiltrated back into the country.

From the time of the Soweto Uprising of 1976 until the first democratic elections in 1994, the funerals of those killed in political protest or in armed struggle were turned into occasions for mass political theater, with prominent display and per-formance of the symbols, songs, and slogans of the banned ANC, its armed wing Umkhonto we Sizwe (MK), and other banned organizations such as the Communist Party as well as the newly legal union organizations. In many cases, even though the authorities allowed the funerals to proceed, they attacked the mourners as they left the site, leading to more deaths and more political funerals. Because there was no le-gal outlet for political expression during the state of emergency, funerals such as the one documented here became one of the main ways for crowds to gather and openly show their support for the banned organizations and imprisoned leaders. Mbethe's funeral was in the town of Uitenhage in the Eastern Cape, an area of particularly intense struggle. The bracketed notes are by Mark Swilling, the researcher who tape recorded the event.

[The church is packed to absolute capacity. People stand singing with their hands in salute. COSATU (Congress of South African Trade Unions) banners are up. There are political T-shirts all over, and a banner that says "go well comrade Thanduxolo Mbethe—your blood will water the tree of liberation that will grow."]

Song [in Xhosa]:

Nobody can stop us!
CROWD: We are the future!
Nobody can stop us!
CROWD: We are the future!

Song [in Xhosa]:

Look, there is Tambo (repeated 3 times)
There he comes from Zimbabwe
This burden is heavy
Look, there is Tambo (repeated 3 times)
There he comes from Zimbabwe (repeated 2 times)

M.C.: Viva Mandela viva!
CROWD: Viva!
M.C.: Amandla! [Power]
CROWD: Awethu! [is ours]
M.C.: iAfrika!
CROWD: Mayibuye! [Let it come back]

[The shouting of these slogans is done as the coffin is coming into the church. It is held high with clenched fists and is put down in front.]

THE PRIEST: Glory be to God. This body which is here today is the shadow of God. I am the first and the last. Our children are being shot every day, but we will shoot their children too.

SPEAKER: We feel grieved to have lost this courageous and brave proletarian, but comrades let it be known to everyone that we shall take from where this comrade left [off] to a free nonracial South Africa. We shall strive to heighten the insurgent activities, and this is the only means to achieve peace and stability in our country. We shall [imitate?] this comrade if need be for total abolition of all forms of exploitation [unintelligible] and for crushing the spirit of individualism and aggrandisement and power by individual groups and classes, to eradicate all forms of materialism for a free egalitarian society. Comrades, let the death of comrade

Thanduxolo serve as a motivation factor and let us rededicate ourselves to the struggle for a free South Africa. Amandla!

CROWD: Awethu!

Song [in Xhosa]:

Mandela, Mandela (repeated 3 times)
Mandela bring freedom in this land of Africa (repeated 3 times)

Poet:

Our mothers are weeping
Our fathers are weeping
They are crying against imperialists
They are crying against their suffering as workers
Our mothers are crying for their sons, who are being shot as students
    by the SA [South African] minority regime
Our mothers are crying, demanding their sons and daughters in prison
Our mothers are crying for those who died, killed by this fascist regime
Comrades, remember the cry of Namibian mothers, when they cried for
    their sons and daughters who have been doomed by the SA regime
They were crying, shouting: Come guerrilla, come SWAPO [South West
    People's Organization]
Comrades, remember in [1982] in the Lesotho raid when the Comrades
    were burying their compatriots, they were singing
Over the river we shall go and catch their sons

SPEAKER: Comrades, compatriots, I am proud today. Thanduxolo Mbethe is a freedom lover, he is a freedom fighter. My countrymen, I call this murder and I remember the Sharpeville Massacre. I wonder why in the land of our birth must we suffer like this. They refuse an education, they want to poison our minds. We are prepared to die; our blood will water the tree of liberation. Comrades, I am saying forward ever.

[CROWD: Forward ever!]

Comrades this is the time to sacrifice, it is the time to go forward, it is the time for Umkhonto we Sizwe [MK] which was formed in 1961. Comrades we know that this year is the year of the MK. We know that Oliver Tambo is the leader of the people. He was voted for by the people for the people.

CROWD: Viva!

SPEAKER: Mayibuye!

CROWD: iAfrica!

UDF supporters at the funeral of Guguletu 7, IDAF Collection, UWC-Robben Island Mayibuye Archives, LA582-2-3. Courtesy of the Robben Island Museum Mayibuye Archives.

SPEAKER 3: Comrades; Thanduxolo Mbethe left the country to go and join the ANC. Today Thanduxolo is here; Thanduxolo has fallen, comrades. But there is only one thing, comrades; his blood is going to water the tree of liberation. The ANC was formed in 1912, in 1950 [1955] the Freedom Charter was drawn.

The Charter said the doors of learning and culture shall be open. Years went by with Mandela and [Walter] Sisulu peacefully negotiating with the government, but the SA government refused to listen. In Tanzania the Congress decided that it should have an educational policy because the people must learn, and must know that education is not a privilege but a right. The South African government must understand one thing, that when we say the doors of learning and culture shall be open we mean that the government shall serve the needs of the people.

The establishment of Solomon Mahlangu Freedom College in Tanzania in 1978 means today our comrades at Solomon Mahlangu are learned. All the schools in South Africa must be named after our leaders. We don't want Bantu Education, we demand a people's education. Today our schools are closed. The government is demanding that our parents must report to the inspectors why the schools are closed. We can't report to these criminals. From the people's education we are moving to people's power, and we are going to rename one school as Thanduxolo High School. We are also demanding that soldiers must be removed from our schools, because they are turning our schools into police stations.

Comrades, we must never be divided. Our demands are there and they have not been met. The State of Emergency must not divide because our demands have not been met. A decade has gone since this generation of students have witnessed and participated in the struggle for a non-racial education in South Africa. This has gone by accompanied by numerous clashes between the students of the oppressed population in this country and the group of criminals and gangs who have employed ruthlessness against the revolting students. The confrontation has turned out to be an endless one, despite all the repressive measures used against the students. Our people have been tear gassed, baton charged, brutally killed; but all that has failed in subjugating the youth. Instead it has infused in us a greater militancy.

That is why we are here today saying we are proud of Amabutho [militarized UDF (United Democratic Front) youth]. We are very proud of Amabutho as a people's army, and we are engaged in a battle in our streets. The most interesting part of it all is that the government has failed to break us. I heard that there are roadblocks all over but today I see thousands of people here. It means they have failed and they are going to fail.

During all this period of confrontation, our parents who are fortunately workers in this country, have been left out in the struggle because they disapprove of our militancy. Gone is the time of moderation and meekness. Time has come for our parents not to stand by and watch coldly as their children are dying. Our parents must also realise that the slogan "education before liberation" is nothing else than the first big step into the hands of the oppressive regime.

The government is also progressing and becoming even more sophisticated. We must therefore not play into the hands of the system. The unity of the working class shall never be crushed. This must be clear to the imperialists and the capitalists. Comrades, there is one thing that you must never forget—I am talking to students and parents. Non-involvement in the political struggle on the part of the oppressed students is something that the oppressors hold dear to their hearts. There is no way we can accommodate people who are standing on [the] fence in our struggle. It is better to die fighting than to live the miserable life of a slave.

Unban COSAS [Congress of South African Students] Unban!

CROWD: Unban!

SPEAKER 4: Viva ANC Viva!

CROWD: Viva!

SPEAKER: Viva the spirit of Umkhonto we Sizwc Viva!

CROWD: Viva!

SPEAKER: Viva the spirit of Oliver Tambo Viva!

CROWD: Viva!

SPEAKER: Viva the spirit of Nelson Mandela Viva!

CROWD: Viva!

SPEAKER: Amandla!

CROWD: Awethu!

SPEAKER: Ngawethu!

CROWD: Amandla!

SPEAKER: Viva to you comrade Thanduxolo!

CROWD: Viva!

SPEAKER 4: I thank you all in the name of the [mothers], the domestic workers union of Port Elizabeth (PEDWU). This union is fighting for the right of domestic workers to be recognised as workers in South Africa. The domestic worker leaves early in the morning to work for the white man and they come back in the evening to look after their children and husbands and the wages they get is peanuts. We are pledging all domestic workers to stand up and fight for a decent wage and better working conditions. We also don't get our maternity leave pay. When the white man first came to South Africa the domestic workers looked after them and their children, and yet the conditions of the domestic workers are still worse and they refuse to recognise us as workers.

So stand up domestic workers and fight. Time is running out, workers. We demand our pension pay, maternity leave and better wages. We arc tired of being slaves. There is a mother here in PE [Port Elizabeth] who worked for a certain family for eighteen years. When she asked for a raise she was [treated] as a dog. For eighteen years this woman has been paid twenty-six rand. So I am asking all domestic workers to join the UDF and fight for their rights and better working conditions!

Viva the spirit of no surrender viva!

CROWD: Viva!

SPEAKER 5: Viva ANC viva!

CROWD: Viva!

SPEAKER 5: We are the future!

CROWD: Nobody can suffer!

SPEAKER 5: We are the future!

MIKE [ODOLO?], VICE PRESIDENT OF PEYCO [PE YOUTH CONGRESS]: Comrades, I am requesting that people should listen. Last week Saturday we lost comrade Moses Mabhida. I want you to know that Moses Mabhida is remembered all over the world. Even in Robben Island the comrades have gathered today to commemorate his death. Moses Mabhida is a tried and tested revolutionary for the South African struggle. AMANDLA! [*Crowd:* Awethu!] Parents, before we start today. Because Moses Mabhida represents the most conscious sector of the working class today, and the South African Communist Party today is a true alliance of the people because it represents the true aspirations of the working class. Comrades, in respect for Moses Mabhida, I am requesting all of us to stand up and observe a moment of silence. Despite his departure the struggle continues. AMANDLA!

CROWD: Awethu!

SPEAKER: You can sit down. Long live the South African Communist Party, long live!

CROWD: Long live!

SPEAKER: Long live the alliance of the ANC and SACP, long live!

SPEAKER: Comrades, today is a historic day in the struggle for liberation in South Africa. The people's organisation, the ANC and its military wing of Umkhonto we Sizwe, is here today. Comrade Thanduxolo has fallen. He has left his AK-47 which we must pick up and continue with the struggle. When the people attend these meetings they must listen to the direction which is given. The leaders, [Mkhuseli] Jack and [Henry] Fazzie who are not here today, we don't believe that the banning of Jack and Fazzie is going to stop the struggle. Political organisations are united. Surely they don't believe that we are going to stop the consumer boycott. When the consumer boycott was started women wearing white dresses led the boycott. We know that we are going to win.

We know that we are going to push for their unbanning. We are not divided, it is the whites who are. They must unban Jack and Fazzie because they aren't the ones who are to blame for the boycotts. We are the ones, the people who are here in this hall today. The ANC believes that blood must be shed. We don't hurt anyone but they hurt us. We are only defending ourselves. When they say you must not go to town it is for your own good, because they are going to "hit the bird with the tree." If you are in town you are going to be caught in the crossfire.

If you don't listen to the streets and area committee, where are you going to get the message from? People are urged to listen to their street committees. The March stayaway is on the 16th, 17th and 18th. People must observe the call for the stayaway. We are a force to be reckoned with. The forthcoming stayaway on Monday, people must listen to their street committees for direction and instructions. There are going to be no more meetings, but only street committee meetings. This is an effort to stop the government from infiltrating our organisations.

Song [in Xhosa]:

Shoot guerrilla shoot (repeated 3 times)
Shoot, shoot (repeated many times)

SPEAKER: Viva NEUSA [National Education Union of SA] Viva!
CROWD: Viva!
SPEAKER: Down with Botha regime down!
CROWD: Down!
SPEAKER: Amandla!
CROWD: Awethu! . . .

Song [in Xhosa]:

We will fight for our land South Africa
We will leave our parents
We will go to Angola to train
We will fight for our land (repeated several times)

THE M.C.: This man who is lying here is a man of truth. One day [foreigners] came here, and asked to be accepted in our house. The government is saying it is the ANC who made the Freedom Charter but I am saying it is the people who made the Freedom Charter. Our children leave our country to go and train to come back and take the country. Thanduxolo went for training, then he came back and served the people until he died. The world is on fire. They say that they are going to keep Mkhuseli Jack and Henry Fazzie for five years; they say that for five years they must not talk. If they shoot all our children, then the women must take the AK-47 and shoot back. Women must join PEWO [PE Women's Organisation]. I know that there are people [informers] who are going to take what I have been saying to the Le Grange building [security police headquarters]. Amandla!
CROWD: Awethu!

[One person, believed to be an informer, was singled out by singing and shouting with everyone pointing their fingers and whistling.]

Song [in Xhosa]:

Shoot, workers, shoot
Come, workers, come, come through Umkhonto we Sizwe
Shoot, shoot with a bazooka (repeated several times)

SPEAKER: Today we are marching towards a nonracial and a free democratic South Africa. I greet you in the name of the struggle for total liberation, not only in South Africa but the world over. Comrades, I am addressing myself to the workers. The people shall be free to form trade unions, to elect officers. The state shall recognise the right and existence of unions. There shall be a forty-hour working week, the miners, the domestics, and the civil servants shall have a right to a pay raise as any other person. These are the demands of the people. The time has come for action.

Struggle Songs

Various

Group efforts in Africa, from work parties to political protest, are often accompanied by group singing. As recounted in the documentary Amandla! A Revolution in Four-Part Harmony *(2002; directed by Lee Hirsch), songs infused the struggle against apartheid. In the 1950s, Africans sang with irony a happy lilt about moving from the destroyed Sophiatown to Meadowlands in Soweto. They also mournfully asked, "Senzenina?" (what have we done to deserve this oppression?). Songs were also an important part of the training of militants in Umkhonto we Sizwe (MK) and other groups carrying out armed struggle. With the revival of mass protest in the 1970s and its explosion in the 1980s, songs of resistance were in the air. People generated and reflected a common spirit as they sang at union rallies, meetings of civic associations, marches, and political funerals. Songs, often in a call-and-response format, ranged from the mournful to the defiant and joyful.*

The following are the lyrics of a few such songs collected by Alton Pollard. Some political organizations have continued to use struggle-era songs as rallying points in the postapartheid era. In one instance, the African National Congress Youth League president Julius Malema (who was expelled from the party in 2012) revived the song "Ayesaba Amagwala" (The cowards are afraid), which includes lyrics calling on listeners to "shoot the Boer." A court ruled this hate speech in the context of postapartheid South Africa. President Jacob Zuma continues to rally his supporters with the song "Umshini Wami" (Bring me my machine gun), which recalls his rise to prominence as an MK stalwart. Less controversial is the nineteenth-century hymn and common feature of antiapartheid protest "Nkosi Sikelel' iAfrika" (Lord, bless Africa; see part III), which is now part of the national anthem.

1. *"Senzeni Na?" (What have we done?)*

Senzeni na senzeni na
Senzeni na senzeni na
Senzeni na senzeni na
Senzeni na kulomhlaba?

Amabhulu azizinja
Amabhulu azizinja
Amabhulu azizinja
Amabhulu azizinja
Kuyisono 'kubamnyama
Kuyisono 'kubamnyama
Kuyisono 'kubamnyama
Kuyisono kulelizwe
[What have we done, what have we done?
What have we done, what have we done?
What have we done, what have we done?
What have we done in this country (world)?
Boers are dogs
Boers are dogs
Boers are dogs
Boers are dogs
It's a sin to be black
It's a sin to be black
It's a sin to be black
It's a sin in this country (world)]

2. *"Hamba Kahle" (Safe journey)*

Hamba kahle mkonto
Wemkhonto
Mkhonto wesizwe
Thina bantu bomkhonto siz'misele
Ukuwabulala
Wona lamabhulu
[Safe journey spear
Yes spear
Spear of the nation
We, the members of Umkhonto are determined
To kill
These Boers]

3. *"Chant by the Militants"*

> Company
> Tshela wena, tshelu uTambo
> Siyal'thatha, kulonyaka
> Tambo ye, yicomanda
> NoMandela, basemajele
> NoSisulu, basemajele
> Sibakhulule
> Lenj'u Botha
> Usengozini
> No Kruger
> Usengozini
> No LeGrange
> Usengozini
> Shoot to kill! Guerilla!
> [Company
> Tell, tell, Tambo
> We'll take our country this year
> Tambo is our commander
> And Mandela, in jail
> And Sisulu, in jail
> We will release them
> That dog Botha
> Is in danger
> And Kruger
> Is in danger
> And LeGrange
> Is in danger
> Shoot to kill! Guerilla!]

"Reforms" and Revolution in South Africa

Joe Slovo

In the early 1980s, President P. W. Botha's National Party government attempted to persuade the world that it was engaged in a process of reform. The liberation struggle in the 1980s included mass protest as well as armed struggle. But it was also a struggle to persuade the world that the reforms were empty and that the African National Congress (ANC) was necessarily involved, with its allies, in a revolutionary struggle for fundamental transformation of South Africa. The ANC needed to persuade a sympathetic audience in the West that it was justified in the use of violence and in rejection of the so-called reforms.

In 1984 Joe Slovo (1926–95) addressed these issues in a lecture series devoted to the memory of his wife, Ruth First, whom apartheid agents had murdered with a parcel bomb two years earlier. Slovo, a Lithuanian immigrant to South Africa, was a lawyer and the commander of Umkhonto we Sizwe (MK) and a high-level member of both the South African Communist Party and the ANC. He became the minister of housing after the transition to democracy in 1994. Here he provides a careful theoretical analysis to explain that Botha's reforms, while not inconsequential, did nothing to change the fundamental bases of apartheid. In addition, he argues that blacks in South Africa were engaged in a struggle for national liberation, like other decolonization struggles in Africa and Asia, not a mere struggle for civil rights or against apartheid. In a line that may haunt the ANC as today's ruling party, he warns, "national liberation implies more than formal participation in the electoral processes and more than the replacement of black faces for white ones in the Mercedes Benz!"

In troubled times, theory and basic concepts are also at high-risk [for] potential casualties, and need to be jealously guarded. I have selected a few of the concepts which have a fundamental bearing on our perspectives of struggle, and I have been influenced in my selection by the fact that of late some questioning voices are being raised about aspects of our strategy; voices which have to be taken seriously since they come from friends and brothers. The theses I propose touching on and arguing for tonight are the following:

- Firstly, that the Botha regime is not a reformist regime bent on a retreat from apartheid. On the contrary, it has gone further than any previous regime in South Africa's history in an advance towards the implementation of the essentials of apartheid.
- Secondly, that while, historically, political control of the country has shifted from an externally based to an internally based ruling class, the colonial status of the Blacks has, in substance, been maintained (albeit in different forms) from 1910 until now.
- Thirdly, that the immediate struggle in South Africa is not just against apartheid or merely to achieve civil rights, but is a struggle for national liberation in the full meaning of that term.
- Fourthly, that the element of revolutionary violence (as an integral part of the political struggle) is an imperative imposed on us by South African reality and that, like every other similar struggle, it of necessity implies both an external and internal factor, and
- Fifthly, that the dramatic advance and massive impact of the ANC-led liberation movement in the post-Soweto period is a tribute to the strategic and tactical approaches, and that the situation created by this impact is forcing Pretoria and its Western friends to probe for other ways to cope with the ANC. . . .

The very foundation of apartheid—the Bantustan creations and the fragmentation of South Africa (with one of the fragments, covering 87% of its area and 99% of its riches, going to the Whites)—has been pursued by the Botha regime with more vigour than by any of their predecessors.

It is under Botha that the door of access by Africans to central state power has been slammed with a deadening finality.

It is through the duct of Botha and [the defense minister General Magnus] Malan (in pursuit of apartheid's total strategy) that every surrounding country has felt the blows of military intervention and the chaos of bandit armies created and sustained by them. And it is during their time that Black political opposition has felt a heightened level of brutality.

It is only if words lose all conventional meaning that we can describe the Botha regime as one which is straining at the leash to move away from apartheid. It is in fact straining at the leash to be left in peace to take apartheid (in its real meaning) to its ultimate conclusion.

How then do we explain what is generally referred to as the reforms? Are they merely cosmetic? More time would be needed to reflect exhaustively on the complex mosaic of the reforms and the social needs and tendencies which they express. But, in brief, they must not be seen either as flowing from the same set of causes or as having the same significance.

Some reforms are indeed cosmetic and represent gestures to placate embarrassed allies or (as for example in the sporting arena) to cope with international isolation.

Other reforms are designed to co-opt Black collaboration, particularly from the middle strata, and (as in the case of the new constitutional dispensation) to break the unity of the Black opposition.

Yet other reforms are the achievements of people in bitter class and national struggles, as for example in the trade union field.

Some reflect the new type of labour needs of sectors of the ruling class, which are poised to break into the technological age.

Nevertheless, the fact remains that the reforms do touch on the daily lives of sections of our people. . . .

It is, however, one thing to be sensitive to the impact of the reforms on the unfolding of the day-to-day struggle, and quite another thing to encourage the illusion that we have a regime in South Africa which has the potential to break with those ingredients of apartheid which constitute its real essence. Indeed, it is precisely because apartheid has been rooted so firmly in the recent period that steps can be contemplated which would have met with more universal revulsion and opposition from the White community, especially its Afrikaner section. Before fragmentation had reached such an advanced level with the creation of the Bantustans, the defence of White cohesion had to be carried out in communities which, although segregated, were sharing common urban and rural territory. The pressures for a common South African society were not yet counterbalanced with its institutionalised creation of a dozen separate so-called countries. In these circumstances, among the early lines of defence of the purity and cohesion of the White laager were institutions which prevented inter-race mobility, such as the Immorality Act, the Mixed Marriages Act and so on. These mechanisms no longer play the same important role as they previously did in perpetuating White exclusiveness.

One further point needs to be emphasised. What Botha thinks, says, or believes in is of some interest and importance. But at the end of the day, what counts decisively are what he does, and, more especially, the economic aspirations he represents at the political level. . . .

In general, capitalist exploitation and race domination are not symbiotically linked. They can exist without one another. But in every phase of South African capitalism, from its emergence to its stabilisation and to its growth and development, race and class have been inextricably and inseparably joined together. Primitive accumulation in South Africa involved internal national conquests and dispossession. The creation and consolidation of cheap labour reserves were "virtually" completely colour-based. And today not only does the race factor continue to play a dominating role at the level of the relations of production, but also the very survival of the ruling class—its continued monopolistic hold on the land, mines and other means of production—depends upon maintaining and even reinforcing the mechanisms which guarantee White race political control and domination. That is why even the Oppenheimers [owners of De Beers], with all their enlightened talk against the excesses of apartheid, do not show a readiness to eliminate the Bantustans and to risk the immediate grant of full political and economic rights to the indigenous people.

The great divide between liberal and radical analysis in South Africa has always been a liberal belief that race discrimination is an obstacle to capitalist development, and that, in time, racist practices will be inevitably eroded by capitalist economic forces. The last two decades have demonstrated more clearly than before that this thesis is a false one. It is during this period that we have witnessed the most dramatic advance in the South African economy, and it is also during this period that we have witnessed the most intense application of the worst features of apartheid and race discrimination. . . .

Those who are sceptical about the internal colonial thesis should perhaps have another look at the way it is actually handled in the Programme of the South African Communist Party, a programme which, in the best tradition of Marxist methodology, uses basic concept, not as a dogma, but as a tool to enable it to cope with concrete reality.

The programme spells out the duality of South Africa's socio-economic formation, which has unique features. It actually uses the following words, and I quote:

> South Africa is not a colony but an independent state. Yet masses of our people enjoy neither independence nor freedom . . . On one level, that of "White South Africa," there are all the features of an advanced capitalist state in its final stage of imperialism. But on another level, that of "non-white South Africa," there are all the features of a colony. The indigenous population is subjected to extreme national oppression, poverty and exploitation, lack of all democratic rights, and political domination by a group which does everything it can to emphasise and perpetuate its alien European character.

The latter face of South Africa (i.e. the social, political and economic status of Africans) is deliberately not described simply as colonialism, for the reason that it does not conform to the classic colonial model. It is described as colonialism of a special type or as internal colonialism. The term might not suit everyone's verbal tastes. But the reality is almost self-evident. It would be an interesting exercise for any of us to sit across the table with a South African Black and convince him that his status as a colonial subject has substantially altered since the shift of political power from London to Pretoria. Every single disability—whether it be access to real political power, ownership of land, the right to free movement and to live and work where a Black man pleases, etc. etc.—attaches to him, not as a member of a class, but because he is part of the indigenous, conquered and colonised people. And the ruling class, which is internally based and drawn from the White group, relies, in the first place (like all imperialist ruling classes) on its kith and kin, to whatever class they belong, to keep the native in his place. "The validity of the colonial thesis as an analytical concept has perhaps been reinforced by the process, which is taking place under our very eyes, of institutionalising the colonial status of the Black people through the creation of territorial entities—the Bantustans—which are developing some of the more classical attributes of colonies and neo-colonies."

"Colonialism of a special type" or "internal colonialism" is, I think, the closest we can come in our search for an accurate description of the South African reality. But it is not merely a desire for analytical delicacy, which requires us to grasp this unique reality. A grasp of the institutionalised national oppression which characterises South Africa is the starting point for elaborating the perspectives of our revolutionary practice, and leads to the conclusion that the main content of the immediate struggle is to achieve complete national liberation for the racially dominated and racially exploited Black communities.

The organisation which stands at the head of the alliance and which leads this struggle is the ANC, and its description as a national liberation movement is not a careless slip of the tongue; it actually describes correctly the main goal of the immediate revolutionary process, which is national liberation.

The populist slogan of the struggle against apartheid has its place; it helps the world to identify the most extreme manifestation of race domination, and provides a platform which can, on occasions, be shared by a revolutionary and a liberal. This is of some positive value, but only if we understand that, for example, Mrs [Helen] Suzman [a white, liberal member of Parliament] and I may both be against apartheid but we are certainly not both for liberation.

Apartheid is, broadly speaking, the post-1948 mechanism for maintaining racial domination. It has specific features which merit careful analysis. But it is necessary to emphasise that it is not apartheid which fathered race discrimination and domination, but the other way about. The struggle against apartheid and against race domination is not the same. We are not engaged in a struggle just to end apartheid; that is to go back to the pre-1948 days when the inferior and colonial status of the Blacks was underwritten by a policy called segregation rather than apartheid. We must therefore be on the alert lest the slogan which concentrated only on apartheid becomes an excuse to denude the struggle of its revolutionary content by restricting it merely to the excesses of the Nationalist regime and therefore keeping it purely within the arena of reformist politics.

What I have said about apartheid applies with equal force to the question of the struggle for civil rights. This is a term, which, in the recent period, once again gained currency in the struggle by Black Americans to assert their rights in terms of the US constitution. There are no civil rights which South African Blacks can hope to assert in terms of the South African constitution. It is a constitution which is specifically designed to exclude all Africans (whatever class they belong to) from all political and civil rights. It is a constitution which creates a power framework, which closes the door to even the remotest possibility an advance by blacks to democratic rights through anything resembling a constitutional process which is implied by the phrase, "struggle for civil rights."

In any case, especially in the South African context, national liberation implies more than formal participation in the electoral processes and more than the replacement of black faces for white ones in the Mercedes Benz!

We cannot talk seriously of ending race domination and leave undisturbed the ownership and control by the existing ruling class of virtually all the means of production—a control which is the real source of its power to exploit and to maintain its domination.

You don't have to be a Communist or a Marxist—you just need to be an honest Black patriot with a justified sense of national grievance—to accept that liberation in our country has little or no meaning without a return of the land and its wealth to the people. And this reality reinforces the conclusion that we cannot restrict the struggle objectives to the bourgeois democratic concept of civil or democratic rights. . . .

The extraordinary impact which the ANC has made both inside and outside the country since 1976 has been precisely as a result of its strategy of combining mass political struggle with revolutionary violence which has, for the first time since the indigenous wars of resistance, inculcated into our people a belief and a conviction that the seemingly all powerful White state can indeed be dealt with. This factor has, perhaps more than any other, created the psychological and inspirational atmosphere in which the people themselves have made such dramatic advances in the field of mass organisation, trade union struggle, UDF [United Democratic Front], etc., etc.

There is a new and refreshingly revolutionary arrogance abroad amongst the Blacks, particularly amongst the youth, precisely because they have seen their compatriots abandoning their meekness and showing a readiness to challenge the enemy with weapons it has monopolised for 350 years. It is abundantly clear to us, and even more clear to our enemy, that an abandonment or a weakening of our policy of armed activity will have a most negative effect on the process of mass political opposition, resistance and organisation. . . .

The regime's attempts, through external pressures, to spike the guns of the ANC-led liberation movement has demonstrably failed, precisely for the reason that the arena of our struggle is amongst our people, deep inside our country.

It would, of course, be unrealistic to assert that the external factor of this struggle is irrelevant. There has not been a single people's armed struggle in Africa, or elsewhere for that matter, which has not depended in some degree on rear bases in fraternal and friendly countries (FNLA [National Liberation Front] of Algeria-Morocco and Tunisia; PAIGC [African Party for the Independence of Guinea and Cape Verde] of Guinea-Bissau-Guinea Conakry; MPLA [People's Movement for the Liberation of Angola] of Angola-Congo Brazzaville; ZANU [Zimbabwe African National Union] of Zimbabwe-Mozambique). One wonders whether we should be sitting here without Tanzania's grant of exclusive and massive external rear base facilities for FRELIMO [Front for the Liberation of Mozambique].

In this connection I wish to emphasise two points. Firstly, in each of the countries mentioned the struggle was fought out and won inside their own national territory, and this assertion remains valid despite the fact that they were helped by outside friends to meet any enemy who (by the way) also depended upon its external allies. So when we assert the imperatives of the external factor for our struggle, this must not be construed as detracting from the obvious objective that it must grow from inside and engage the enemy inside. . . .

We have concentrated on internal growth deep inside the country around a core of trained revolutionary politico-military cadres in both rural and urban areas. We have deliberately avoided the pattern of using adjacent territory to hit close to the border and to run back.

The second point of emphasis is the special role in our conditions of ur-

AND WE WISHED TO BE GRACIOUS TO THOSE WHO WERE BEING OPPRESSED IN THE LAND, TO MAKE THEM LEADERS AND MAKE THEM HEIRS.

(AL — QUR'ĀN)

THE NATION THAT LOVES MARTYRDOM CANNOT BE ENSLAVED Imam

MARTYRDOM IS VICTORY

Muslim funeral for victims of Trojan Horse shooting, Athlone, Cape Town, October 1985, IDAF Collection, UWC-Robben Island Mayibuye Archives, LA584-5-3. Courtesy of the Robben Island Museum Mayibuye Archives.

ban guerrilla warfare and sabotage. This needs to be noted particularly in relation to the existence in our country of a relatively advanced capitalist economy and a working class which is the most important force in our revolutionary process. But above all, our starting point has always been on the political struggle, political organisation and underground leadership. It has always been our objective to work for the creation in all parts of our land of political revolutionary bases out of which people's war will grow and be sustained. And we see organised-armed blows against the enemy as playing an indispensable role in stimulating the emergence of such political, revolutionary bases. . . .

I have kept away from an analysis of the current exciting happenings in widespread areas of South Africa. But let me add one word. Victory may not be around the corner, but events have demonstrated that the ANC-led liberation front has taken [ineradicable] root among the people, and that there can be no long-term solution without the ANC. This explains the many pronged hints of dialogue with the ANC; hints which are coming from various sources such as USA official visitors to Southern Africa, the South African English press, the government supporting *Die Burger* [a newspaper], Pik Botha [the minister of foreign affairs] and others.

In the first place this is recognition of the place we have won as leaders of the liberation struggle. But it also spells danger. They are no doubt prepared to talk, but they want to talk to an ANC which is different to the one we know—an ANC which will abandon its internal and international allies, an ANC which will jettison its advanced revolutionary nationalism and agree to work within the suffocating framework of Botha's dispensations. Whilst it is infantile to mechanically reject all dialogue with an enemy, we must frankly state that we do not trust Botha's current dialogue offensive. It is designed to advance and not to compromise his policies.

Comrade Chairman, there is of course no way to compensate for the loss of a person such as Ruth, to whose memory we have dedicated this talk. But when we look at the situation of revolutionary ferment which is developing in our country, it is clear that she has an important place among those whose dedication in life and martyrdom in death will bring the day of People's Victory that much nearer.

Politics and Violence

Rian Malan

In many of South Africa's black townships, violence in the 1980s degenerated into civil war and thuggery. The African National Congress (ANC) espoused the idea of making the townships "ungovernable." Groups that were aligned with the ANC and the United Democratic Front (UDF) began advocating the practice of "necklacing," in which people suspected of being police informers or "collaborators" were beaten and set on fire using rags, gasoline, and discarded tires. The government itself fomented violence in the townships by arming anti-ANC and UDF groups, especially Inkatha. Gangs borrowing the slogans of the various resistance movements extorted money from innocent people and engaged in terrific violence. Uncontrolled violence and the criminalization of politics extended, most famously, to Winnie Mandela and the Stompie Moeketsi murder. The Truth and Reconciliation Commission would allege that Winnie Mandela was implicated in at least eighteen instances of gross human rights violations, including eight murders. She denied the charges.

This selection comes from Rian Malan's (1954–) best-selling memoir My Traitor's Heart, *first published in 1989. Malan, a journalist from a prominent Afrikaans family, fled South Africa to avoid compulsory military conscription. He returned in the 1980s and began writing about race relations and the extraordinary violence sweeping across the country. In the excerpt, Malan explores the ubiquity of violence in which nearly everyone, it seemed, had blood on their hands.*

This other civil war in Soweto was a largely subterranean affair, covered desultorily by the press. From time to time the papers noted the violent death of some BC [Black Consciousness] activist at the hands of faceless "groups of youths" or "members of a rival organization," but the killing was seldom if ever attributed to supporters of the UDF—not at the outset, at any rate. "There was a very, very heavy bias," said George [an activist who had been involved in Black Consciousness during the 1970s]. He ascribed this to a "rightist" conspiracy in the media, but a simpler explanation suggested itself to me. The UDF was a supposedly nonviolent, democratic movement, and a fount of hope and righteousness in the eyes of many reporters. It was inconceivable that such an organization should be implicated in a campaign of extermination, so the cutting questions went unasked, which was probably just as well. As far as many UDF leaders were concerned, there was no war at all; the black community was simply cleansing itself of collaborators and right-wing vigilantes.

"They didn't see anything," George said bitterly. "Murphy Morobe, Terror Lekgota, Albertina Sisulu—they never *ever* acknowledged that there was this internecine warfare. They never *ever* tried to stop it." George's movement condemned the violence, but the UDF was slow to follow suit.

And then George's house was burned down, and young Fana Mhlongo abducted from the ruins. George was thirty-six years old on the day it happened, and he'd been a revolutionary for sixteen years. There was nothing else. He had given his entire adult life, every working day, every waking hour, to the cause of BC, the cause of black pride, black power, and total noncollaboration. Azapo [Azania People's Organization, a Black Consciousness group founded in 1978] did not court favorable coverage in the white-controlled media and disdained the use of the white courts, even for purely strategic ends. There came a time, however, when such pure doctrinarism was no longer affordable.

And so, in the wake of Fana's abduction, George Wauchope took a step that must surely have broken his heart: He appeared, cap in hand, before a white Supreme Court judge, and asked the white judicial system to protect him and his family from further Warara attacks.

The word *Warara* was not mentioned in the pleading, of course. In the pleading, George claimed to be under attack by members of the Soweto Students Council, an affiliate of the UDF. Four individuals were identified by name. They didn't show up to defend themselves, so the judge granted a temporary injunction restraining the Charterists [people and organizations affiliated with the ANC and in support of the Freedom Charter] from further violent acts. It made a handy hook for newspaper stories, but otherwise the court order wasn't worth the paper it was printed on—not in Soweto, in 1986. "It just went on and on," the BC leader said.

There were more attempts on George's own life. One of his aunts was kidnapped, another threatened with death. His mother, Ethel, never recovered from the trauma of the firebombing and died within the month of a heart attack. One of his uncles was the target of an attempted assassination. Another uncle was shot dead. One of his nephews was shot in the face, another stabbed in the hand. By the time it was over, George's family was devastated. Most surviving Wauchopes had fled to a township on the far side of the Witwatersrand, and young Byron had been sent to school in a quiet country town. Another relative, seventeen-year-old Ephraim Zilba, was in jail on a murder rap, arising from a killing he maintained was an act of self-defense.

As for George himself, he'd recently stepped down as Azapo's general secretary, and his political career appeared to have come to a tragic end. There were killings on both sides in Soweto's other civil war, and now one was being blamed on him; he was about to stand trial for murder, in a country where convicted murderers were usually hanged.

I asked what had happened, but George just shook his head. "I don't want to talk about it," he said. There was no pain or anger in his voice. Indeed, he seemed curiously dispassionate, as if something inside him was already dead.

There was so much horror in my country, and it came in so many forms. There was the white horror, the horror of black protesters shot down in the streets—412 of them that year. But there was another kind of horror too, the horror blacks inflicted on one another. It was there from the very beginning, from the day it all started, back in September 1984, in the township of Sebokeng. The very first casualty of the great uprising was a black community councilor, a supposed sellout, hacked and burned to death by a black mob. After that, it grew and grew, until it equalled and ultimately eclipsed the white horror. As the grip of the white state weakened, blacks turned on one another in a bloody power struggle that has since claimed close to three black lives for every martyr cut down by apartheid's riot police.

The white state blamed the carnage on a cold-blooded Marxist plot to exterminate the center, and the Mandela Charterists, in a manner of speaking, agreed. Government spokesmen referred to the dead as "moderates" or "law-abiding citizens," Charterists called them "stooges" or "sellouts," but the difference was largely semantic; both sides would have had you believe that there was some sort of overarching logic to the madness, and both sides were talking complete shit.

When that terrible year was done, statisticians in the service of the liberal Institute of Race Relations counted only 79 "perceived collaborators" among 1,302 unrest fatalities. Of the remaining deaths, 265 were attributed to "internecine conflict" among blacks, a further 98 to "unexplained conflict." And beyond that, beyond internecine and inexplicable violence, beyond "accidents" (10 deaths) and "indeterminate" (31), lay the black hole of "burned bodies found"—231 of them in all, the anonymous burned alive by the faceless, under circumstances no one dared examine too closely.

Who on earth were those people? Who ordered their deaths? The ANC initially encouraged the burnings of collaborators, but changed its mind in

February 1986, and issued a statement condemning the practice. The sole result was a massive rise in the number of necklacings. Azapo termed the necklace "a crime against humanity," so it was surely not to blame. Bishop Tutu's UDF was supposedly nonviolent. So was Inkatha, Chief Buthelezi's Zulu political movement. So who was doing the killing? Who was telling the truth? Who were the good guys? Who ordered Fana's abduction and execution? Were the UDF comrades who allegedly carried it out disciplined by their nonviolent organization? Indeed, where were the comrades who did it? Where were the police? Who was really in charge—the reasoned and rational black leaders who sat behind the desks, or the teenagers on the streets? There were no clear answers to any of these questions, in the South African winter of 1986.

The only place where the country really made sense was in the pages of the world's enlightened white newspapers, where the struggle was usually portrayed as a rather fastidious affair. In this other, largely imaginary South Africa, "anti-apartheid activists" waged a "nonviolent" and "intensely principled" struggle against white evil in the name of democracy or civil rights. The reality on the streets was so much darker, so much darker. The comrades' ends were just, to be sure, but their means were sometimes as ruthless as the Boers'. They lopped people's ears off for breaking boycotts, forced pacifist Zionists to eat their metal badges. People were dragged behind cars or forced to drink detergent for violating don't-buy-white campaigns. Thousands of moderate, middle-aged blacks were herded to funerals and rallies by young comrades shaking boxes of matches—a not-so-subtle warning of what awaited those who approached the struggle with insufficient enthusiasm. These grim facts of black life tended to undercut the horror of children tortured or shot dead in the streets, so the Western media downplayed them whenever possible, sometimes barely mentioned them at all.

Consider this clipping from the *New York Times*, dated April 15, 1986. At the top of the page is a fourteen-inch story about Desmond Tutu's election as Archbishop of Cape Town, and thus head of South Africa's Anglican Church. It is an elegant piece of writing, intended to evoke a cathedral mood, a reverent silence in which one might hear stirring the most noble aspects of the human spirit, unquenchable in its thirst for freedom and justice. "The doors were suddenly opened. Light poured from the chapel into the darkness . . . and Bishop Tutu stepped into the cool air" to deliver his moving victory speech. He called upon South African churches to transform "religious belief into political code," and rededicated himself to the pursuit of "fundamental change."

Beneath the Tutu story is a minute headline reading, "Eleven Die in

Night of Violence," and a squib of copy summarizing the government's overnight "unrest report." The police shot and killed five black people, and six anonymous burned bodies were found. And *beneath* that, unheralded by any headline, are two cryptic little sentences about the discovery, in a place called Sekhukuniland, of something horrible beyond comprehension; the remains of thirty-two African women, hurled alive into pits of flame. This was the worst mass murder in South African history, and it took place in a context that the *Times* clearly could not bring itself to explain. The seventy-six black youths arrested in connection with the massacre were all members or supporters of the UDF—the supposedly nonviolent liberation movement led by the Nobel Peace Laureate at the head of the page. The thirty-two victims were suspected of using sorcery to retard the freedom struggle, and were incinerated in the name of fundamental change.

Looking at this shred of newsprint, my brain yaws at South Africa's amazing reality. I don't intend to deride Bishop Tutu or suggest he was in any way complicit in those killings. I can even find it in my heart to forgive those witch-burning comrades, because I cannot judge an action that lies so far beyond my own understanding. I don't hate any of the black men who appear in this clipping, and yet the sight of it makes me choke with rage. I think I should rest my case right here, for fear that I lose control, leap off the page, and tear out the throat of the nearest enlightened white man.

It is ancient and primordial, this rage of mine; it is the spirit of Slagters-nek—spirit of the futile 1815 rebellion that marked the start of the war of words and the moral recrimination between Boers and other white men. What are we fighting over? Over the doctrine of the brotherhood of man, which holds that all men are born the same and, given the same environment and opportunities, would turn out to be exactly alike. This is a fundamental tenet of the Great Church of Western Thought, and I believe it; I believe it is true. I'm just not sure what it means in a country such as mine. In South Africa, we must evolve a definition of human brotherhood broad enough to embrace an African of Bishop Tutu's stature as well as tribal youths who burn witches in his name; broad enough to grant the justice of black political aspirations and yet ease the fears of whites so apprehensive of Africa that they vow to die rather than accept fundamental change. That's no easy task. It's so much easier for critics to preserve their moral rectitude by looking the other way.

Consider these color photographs, introduced as evidence in a South African trial virtually ignored by the outside world. They show the scarred and mutilated torsos of two teenage torture victims, brothers named Peter and Phillip. (Peter was only sixteen, so the brothers' last name was withheld by the court in accordance with South African law.) Peter and Phillip claim they were roused from their beds in the dead of night by masked gunmen and taken to a prefabricated shack in someone's Soweto backyard, where they were accused of treachery to the struggle and ordered to confess. When they balked, Peter was hanged by the neck from the rafters until the rafters broke. Then the torturers put a plastic bag over his head and half drowned him in a bucket of water. After that, some women tied Phillip's hands behind his back and forced him to sit in a chair. A man produced a penknife and started carving freedom slogans onto the boy's body: a big "M" for Mandela on his chest, "Viva ANC" on his thigh. And finally, someone fetched a car battery and the wounds were etched into Phillip's flesh with sulphuric acid.

It was just another atrocity in a season of atrocities in most respects save one: It allegedly took place at the home of Mrs. Winnie Mandela, first lady of the Charterist movement and Nobel Peace Prize nominee; subject of ten thousand hagiographic newspaper and magazine profiles, several sycophantic books, at least three prospective Hollywood movies and an on-again, off-again miniseries to be produced by Harry Belafonte. "A woman of extraordinary faith and love of God and of country," gushed Senator Edward Kennedy, deeply moved by Mrs. Mandela's "gentleness and firmness, in a touching but meaningful way."

As I write, the newspapers are full of tales of another dark deed in Mrs. Mandela's backyard—this time, murder; the murder of Stompie Mokhetsie Seipie, a fourteen-year-old soldier in the anti-apartheid struggle who somehow fell out with his own side. He was allegedly abducted by Mrs. Mandela's bodyguards, tied up, whipped under her supervision, dropped repeatedly on his head until half-conscious, and finally dumped in the veld with a slit throat. The Western media is aghast with shock and dismay at this news, but theirs are crocodile tears. Stompie's murder was the third attributed to members of Mrs. Mandela's entourage, and remarkable only in that the Western media chose to cover it. Two earlier killings and numerous allegations of thuggery and intimidation were resolutely ignored by Mrs. Mandela's media sympathizers—for fear, one assumes, of undermining a myth of their own creation.

Schoolchildren in Mrs. Mandela's neighborhood grew so tired of being bullied by her thugs that they eventually burned her house down in broad daylight while her neighbors looked on indifferently, none bothering to throw so much as a cup of water onto the flames. Every journalist in Johannesburg knew the gory details, but no newspaper that I know of printed them—not at the time, at any rate. Why? I'll tell you why. Because white reporters and editors didn't want to be branded racists, and black reporters were "paralyzed by fear," to use George Wauchope's phrase. If you lived in Soweto, there were some things you dared not say for fear of being labelled a sellout. Sellouts did not live long. One of the township's most prominent black journalists chuckled bleakly when I asked why the full story of the arson attack on Winnie Mandela's home hadn't yet been written. "You write it," he said. "You're white, you might get away with it."

Am I upsetting you, my friend? Good. Do you want to argue? Do you want to tell me about the evil of apartheid? Do you want to talk about democracy and the allied civil and human rights that fall under the umbra of its name? Okay. Let's open my bulging files of tales of ordinary murder. You choose your weapons and I'll choose mine, and we'll annihilate the certainties in one another's brains.

We're in the capital, Pretoria. In the distance stands the Voortrekker Monument, a towering blunt chunk of gray concrete, symbolizing the remorseless resolve of the Boer founding fathers. And here comes a Boer now, strolling down the sidewalk, calmly shooting every black person he passes. The trail of bodies behind him is three blocks long—twenty-nine blacks are down, and six of them are dead. The woman beside us is black and she says something very strange. She says the terrorist is "beautiful." A Boer holy warrior, with a beatific smile on his face.

We're in Orlando West, Soweto, outside the home of the lovely Masabata Loate, a beauty queen in a more light-hearted era. She's what the Western press would call an anti-apartheid activist. She's just spent five years on Robben Island for agitating for the downfall of the apartheid state. She expected to be welcomed home as a heroine, but her politics are out of fashion these days. Here she comes now, running for her life, with a pack of rival "anti-apartheid activists" on her heels. She falls, is stabbed, rises and runs on again, screaming for help. She pounds on the doors of neighbors, but they're too scared to let her in. She goes down for the last time on her grandmother's doorstep, where she's hacked to pieces with pangas.

We're in Beaufort West in the Karroo, listening to bangs, thuds and screams from inside a black man's humble shack. The door opens and a UDF leader named Kratshi comes staggering outside, blood pouring from wounds in his head. A white cop follows, motioning his brother officers to stand aside. He says something like, "I'm going to shoot this pig." And he does. Dead.

We're in yet another township, at the funeral of a young black boy who became a burned body found. The bereaved father asked the comrades to stay away, but they don't like being told what to do. So they throw the father into his son's grave and hit him with shovels when he tries to climb out again. The old man eventually gives up and sits down on his dead son's coffin, cradling his bloody head in his hands. The comrades bury him alive.

Are you sick and confused, my friend? I'll make you sick yet. I'll hold you down and pound these images into your brain, like Simon [a serial killer] pounded white skulls with his hammer, and I'll keep on pounding until they poison you the way they poisoned me.

We're in a forest in the homeland Venda, watching an African father hack off his living daughter's arms. She says, "Please father, let me go, I won't tell anyone," but her father just keeps hacking. A political power struggle is under way in Venda, and he needs her body parts for battle medicine.

We're in a stronghold of the South African Police, discussing the security situation with a Boer colonel. We're speaking the tongue of my tribe, a guttural bastard Dutch in which the r's roll like thunder and the g's grate like a shovel in cold gravel. It is a brutal language, so violent on the tongue that Americans would quail when I tried to teach them the odd word or two. Colonel Viljoen is eyeing us warily. He is thinking, this Malan looks a little weird for a Boer, and he's been out of the country too long to be entirely wholesome, but maybe he's okay. I know the look in his eyes. It is a look of recognition. It says, *maybe I can trust him; maybe he's one of us.* When I fall silent, the colonel says nothing, just takes a card from his wallet and slides it wordlessly across the desk. I pick it up. It is professionally printed and lovingly laminated. It bears a saying of Albert Schweitzer's: "Any white man who comes to work in Africa must understand that these people are subhuman," or words to that effect.

We're on a farm in Bonnievale, witnessing subhuman behavior. An elderly white woman has been raped, and her son has captured a black suspect. The white man puts a shotgun in the black man's face, hands him a pig-castrating tool, and orders him to use it. The black man refuses, so the white shoots him in the leg. At that, the black man unbuckles his blood-drenched trousers and uses the castrating knife on himself. The white man uses a stick to flick the testicles away.

We're in Pietermaritzburg, staring at something the police have seized: a trunk full of human body parts and testes, cut out of corpses by a gang of African holy warriors for use in potions to give their side victory in the struggle for fundamental change.

We're at a roadblock near Soweto, where white soldiers have stopped a car driven by a light-skinned black man. They ask him, "Why are you so white?" Then they beat him to death with their helmets. "They didn't say why," says a witness. "I think they were just doing it for fun."

I could go on, but I'll spare you. Let's stop at this photograph, which appeared on the front page of a black newspaper called *City Press*. The picture was taken on the streets of some sub-tropical township. There are palm trees in the background. In the foreground, in a pool of molten rubber tar, lie the burning bodies of two nameless young black men. The fire has singed all their hair off. Their skulls and limbs are as smooth and shiny as baked ceramic. They look like department store mannequins toppled over on their sides, all twisted and contorted in death. Behind them stands a young black schoolgirl, laughing and clapping her hands. I spent hours staring at this picture, trying to read the girl's avid expression, studying the positioning of her school shoes in relation to her shadow. I can't be sure, but I think she was rising into the air as the shutter clicked. I think she was dancing.

The headline says, "This Is the Face of Today's South Africa."

So I dunno, my friend. I dunno what to say anymore. When I came home to face my demons, I heard a song called "Reggae Vibes Is Cool," as sung by Bernoldus Niemand, "Bernard Nobody," the world's first exponent of Boer New Wave rock and roll. His song was a Boer reggae song, the music of black suffering sung in the vernacular of white supremacy, and its chorus had a line that broke my heart. It ran, "How do I live in this strange place?" That seemed a very valid question to me. I had never learned how to live in my own country. I ran away because it was too strange to bear, and when I came home, it was stranger than ever. Everyone had blood on their hands.

Chief Gatsha Buthelezi's Inkatha movement was trying to crush the Mandela Charterists, and the Charterists were reciprocating. Traditionalists were killing modernists, radicals killing moderates. Those who said Mandela were killing those who said Biko, and vice versa. Conservative vigilantes known as Fathers were killing their comrade sons, and everyone was exterminating those they regarded as traitors. All the blacks were killing each other, and atop the boiling roil sat the Afrikaner tyrants, playing the various forces against one another and killing anyone who survived to challenge them. South African politics had turned into a hall of mirrors in which every reflection was a mockery of itself, and in the center of it all stood a sphinx saying yes: the answer to everything is yes. Yes, the black cause is just. Yes, the Boers are barbaric. Yes, the blacks are barbaric too. Yes, things are bad now. Yes, they can only get worse. The time had come to make choices, but there was nothing on the market but rival barbarities and absurd ideologies.

"A new era of freedom has begun," declared State President Botha, standing atop a pile of corpses.

"The Soviet Union is a torchbearer for all our hopes and aspirations,"

Winnie Mandela told TASS [Telegraph Agency of the Soviet Union] at the height of what was supposedly a struggle for freedom. "In Soviet Russia," she said, "genuine power of the people has been transformed from dreams into reality."

The time had come to make choices, but there were no rational choices at all.

But that was politics. Beyond politics, there was mythology, and rival myths to live and die by: for some whites, the myth of white supremacy, and for others, the myth of brave and noble Africans in heroic struggle against unspeakable evil. If you were white, you had to embrace one of those two myths, and let it guide your way. If you believed in neither, the paradox fractured your skull and buried its poisonous claws in your brain.

Preparing Ourselves for Freedom

Albie Sachs

During the most intense phase of the fight against apartheid, in the 1970s and 1980s, many in the liberation movements argued that "culture is a weapon of struggle." This meant not only that they strived to isolate South Africa through cultural and sports boycotts, as part of the broad effort to pressure the government to enter negotiations, but that creators of art, music, and theater should produce work supporting the movement's message. Theater especially became a lively forum for propagating an antiapartheid message within South Africa and in the wider world. In 1991 Albie Sachs (1935–), a lawyer who was detained in the 1960s for African National Congress (ANC) activities and who was attacked by South African operatives and seriously injured with a car bomb in 1988, took direct aim at the idea of culture as a weapon of struggle. Sachs was involved in drafting a new constitution for South Africa and in 1994 became a member of the Constitutional Court; he has since retired from the court.

In this selection, Sachs argues that instead of culture being seen as a tool for specific ends, it must instead be appreciated in its rich variety as the essence of democratic humanity. South Africa would be strengthened by a wide variety of cultural expression, supported by a strong bill of rights. While these notions are familiar, as ideals, to Americans and to postapartheid South Africans, they were challenging in a South Africa just emerging from a revolutionary period of literally life and death struggle. Critically, Sachs opposes the apartheid idea of separate cultural silos and instead argues that South African cultural communities overlap and enrich each other.

We all know where South Africa is, but we do not yet know what it is. Ours is the privileged generation that will make that discovery, if the apertures in our eyes are wide enough. The problem is whether we have sufficient cultural imagination to grasp the rich texture of the free and united South Africa that we have done so much to bring about; can we say that we have begun to grasp the full dimensions of the new country that is struggling to give birth to itself, or are we still trapped in the multiple ghettos of the apartheid imagination? Are we ready for freedom, or do we prefer to be angry victims?

The first proposition I make—and I do so fully aware of the fact that we are totally against censorship and for free speech—is that we should ban ourselves from saying that culture is a weapon of struggle. I suggest a period of, say, five years.

Allow me, as someone who has for many years been arguing precisely that art should be seen as an instrument of struggle, to explain why suddenly this affirmation seems not only banal and devoid of real content, but actually wrong and potentially harmful. It is not a question of separating art and politics, which no one can do, but of avoiding a shallow and forced relationship between the two.

In the first place, repeated incantation of the phrase results in an impoverishment of our art. Instead of getting real criticism, we get solidarity criticism. Our artists are not pushed to improve the quality of their work; it is enough that it be politically correct. The more fists and spears and guns, the better. The range of themes is narrowed down so much that all that is funny or curious or genuinely tragic in the world is extruded. Ambiguity and contradiction are completely shut out, and the only conflict permitted is that between the old and the new, as if there were only bad in the past and only good in the future. . . . We line up our good people on the one side and the bad ones on the other, occasionally permitting someone to pass from one column to the other, but never acknowledging that there is bad in the good, and, even more difficult, that there can be elements of good in the bad; you can tell who the good ones are, because in addition to being handsome of appearance, they can all recite sections of the Freedom Charter or passages of Strategy and Tactics at the drop of a beret.

In the case of a real instrument of struggle, there is no room for ambiguity: a gun is a gun is a gun, and if it were full of contradictions, it would fire in all sorts of directions and be useless for its purpose. But the power of art lies precisely in its capacity to expose contradictions and reveal hidden tensions—hence the danger of viewing it as if it were just another kind of missile-firing apparatus.

And what about love? We have published so many anthologies and journals and occasional poems and stories, and the number that deal with love do not make the fingers of a hand. Can it be that once we join the ANC we do not make love anymore, that when the comrades go to bed they discuss the role of the white working class? Surely even those comrades whose tasks deny them the opportunity and direct possibilities of love, remember past love and dream of love to come. What are we fighting for, if not the right to express our humanity in all its forms, including our sense of fun and our capacity for love and tenderness and our appreciation of the beauty of the world? . . .

Listen in contrast to the music of Hugh Masekela, of Abdullah Ibrahim, of Jonas Gwanga, of Miriam Makeba and you are in a universe of wit and grace and vitality and intimacy; there is invention and modulation of mood, ecstasy and sadness. This is a cop-free world in which the emergent personality of our people manifests itself. Pick up a book of poems, or look at a woodcut or painting, and the solemnity is overwhelming. No one told Hugh or Abdullah to write their music in this or that way, to be progressive or committed, to introduce humor or gaiety, or a strong beat to denote optimism. Their music conveys genuine confidence because it springs from inside the personality and experience of each of them, from popular traditions and the sounds of contemporary life; we respond to it because it tells us something lovely and vivacious about ourselves, not because the lyrics are about how to win a strike or blow up a petrol dump. It bypasses, overwhelms, ignores apartheid, establishes its own space. So it could be with our writers and painters, if only they could shake off the gravity of their anguish and break free from the solemn formulas of commitment that people (like myself) have tried for so many years to impose upon them. . . .

Culture is not something separate from the general struggle, an artifact that is brought in from time to time to mobilize the people or prove to the world that, after all, we are civilized. Culture is us, it is who we are, how we see ourselves and the vision we have of the world. In the course of participating in the culture of liberation, we constantly remake ourselves. Organizations do not merely evince discipline and interaction between their members; our movement has developed a style of its own, a way of doing things and of expressing itself, a specific ANC personality. And what a rich mix it is. . . .

African tradition, church tradition, Gandhian tradition, revolutionary socialist tradition, liberal tradition, all the languages and ways and styles of the many communities in our country; we have black consciousness, and elements of red consciousness (some would say pink consciousness these days), even green consciousness (long before the Greens existed, we had green in our flag, representing the land). Now, with the dispersal of our members throughout the world, we also bring in aspects of the cultures of all humanity. Our comrades speak Swahili and Arabic and Spanish and Portuguese and Russian and Swedish and French and German and Chinese, even Japanese, not because of Bantu [apartheid] Education, but through ANC Education. Our culture, ANC culture, is not a picturesque collection of separate ethnic and political cultures lined up side by side, or mixed in certain proportions; it has a real character and dynamic of its own. When we sing our anthem, a religious invocation, with our clenched fists upraised, it is not a question of fifty-fifty, but an expression of an evolving and integrative interaction, an affirmation that we sing when we struggle and we struggle when we sing. When we dance the toyi-toyi [protest-march dance] we tell the world and ourselves that we are South Africans on the road to freedom. This must be one of the greatest cultural achievements of the ANC, that it has made South Africans of the most diverse origins feel comfortable in its ranks. . . .

The fact is that the cultural question is central to our identity as a movement: if culture were merely an instrument to be hauled onto the stage on ceremonial or fund-raising occasions, or to liven up a meeting, we would ourselves be empty of personality in the interval. Happily, this is not the case—culture is us, and we are people, not things waiting to be put into motion from time to time. . . .

We want to give leadership to the people, not to exercise control over them. This has significant implications for our cultural work, not just in the future but now. We think we are the best (and we are!), that is why we are in the ANC. We work hard to persuade the people of our country that we are the best (and we are succeeding!). But this does not require us to force our views down the throats of others. On the contrary, we exercise true leadership by being non-hegemonic, by selflessly trying to create the widest unity of the oppressed and to encourage all forces for change, by showing the people that we are fighting not to impose a view upon them, but to give them the right to choose the kind of society they want and the kind of government they want. We are not afraid of the ballot box, of open debate, of opposition. One day we will even have our Ian Smith equivalents protesting and grumbling about every change and looking back with nostalgia to the good old days of apartheid, but we will take them on at the hustings. In conditions of freedom we have no doubt who will win, and if we should forfeit the trust of the people, then we deserve to lose.

Release from Prison

Nelson Mandela

In 1989, President P. W. Botha suffered a stroke. F. W. de Klerk (1936–) succeeded him in office that September; he would be the last leader of the apartheid era. De Klerk's rise to power came during a time of domestic and international crisis. South Africa teetered on the edge of civil war and revolution. The economy was in a protracted collapse. Foreign governments, under pressure from political movements demanding international sanctions and calling for companies to divest from South Africa, increasingly criticized the country's police and military violence. In southern Angola, South African Defense Forces were forced from the strategic town of Cuito Cuanavale, where Cuban forces had come to the defense of the Angolan government, which also had the aid of the South West African Peoples Organization, fighting for Namibian independence, and the armed wing of the African National Congress (ANC). International negotiations would soon begin, leading to the withdrawal of South African forces and the independence of Namibia in March 1990. During this time the National Party government had also begun secret talks with the ANC and Nelson Mandela.

The fall of the Berlin Wall in 1989 and the collapse of the Soviet Union two years later fundamentally transformed the international political situation. South Africa, suffering from international sanctions, could no longer claim that it was engaged in a struggle against a Soviet-directed communist conspiracy. At the same time, the ANC and Umkhonto we Sizwe (MK) lost the support of Eastern Bloc nations. The apartheid state and the liberation movements were in a stalemate with no end in sight. At the opening of the next parliamentary session, on February 2, 1990, de Klerk stunned the world by announcing that he was unbanning the ANC, the Communist Party, the Pan Africanist Congress, and other political organizations and seeking negotiations for a new political dispensation. Nine days later, Nelson Mandela walked out of Victor Verster Prison, near Cape Town, as a free man.

That evening, Mandela spoke to a large crowd gathered in front of Cape Town City Hall. He used his address to acknowledge the broad movement that had secured his release and brought the National Party to the negotiating table. He also assured his allies that he had not cut a deal to secure his own freedom. He affirmed the ANC's *alliance with the Communist Party and its ongoing commitment to armed struggle. He ended by quoting the famous lines from his "Statement from the Dock" (see part VI), proclaiming his willingness to die in the cause of freedom.*

Friends, comrades and fellow South Africans.

I greet you all in the name of peace, democracy and freedom for all.

I stand here before you not as a prophet but as a humble servant of you, the people. Your tireless and heroic sacrifices have made it possible for me to be here today. I therefore place the remaining years of my life in your hands.

On this day of my release, I extend my sincere and warmest gratitude to the millions of my compatriots and those in every corner of the globe who have campaigned tirelessly for my release.

I send special greetings to the people of Cape Town, this city which has been my home for three decades. Your mass marches and other forms of struggle have served as a constant source of strength to all political prisoners.

I salute the African National Congress. It has fulfilled our every expectation in its role as leader of the great march to freedom.

I salute our President, Comrade Oliver Tambo, for leading the ANC even under the most difficult circumstances.

I salute the rank and file members of the ANC. You have sacrificed life and limb in the pursuit of the noble cause of our struggle.

I salute combatants of Umkhonto we Sizwe, like Solomon Mahlangu and Ashley Kriel who have paid the ultimate price for the freedom of all South Africans.

I salute the South African Communist Party for its sterling contribution to the struggle for democracy. You have survived 40 years of unrelenting persecution. The memory of great communists like Moses Kotane, Yusuf Dadoo, Bram Fischer and Moses Mabhida will be cherished for generations to come.

I salute General Secretary Joe Slovo [of the Communist Party], one of our finest patriots. We are heartened by the fact that the alliance between ourselves and the [Communist] Party remains as strong as it always was.

I salute the United Democratic Front, the National Education Crisis Committee, the South African Youth Congress, the Transvaal and Natal Indian Congresses and COSATU [Congress of South African Trade Unions] and the many other formations of the Mass Democratic Movement.

I also salute the Black Sash and the National Union of South African Students. We note with pride that you have acted as the conscience of white South Africa. Even during the darkest days in the history of our struggle you held the flag of liberty high. The large-scale mass mobilisation of the past few years is one of the key factors which led to the opening of the final chapter of our struggle.

I extend my greetings to the working class of our country. Your organised strength is the pride of our movement. You remain the most dependable force in the struggle to end exploitation and oppression.

I pay tribute to the many religious communities who carried the campaign for justice forward when the organisations for our people were silenced.

I greet the traditional leaders of our country—many of you continue to walk in the footsteps of great heroes like Hintsa and Sekhukune.

I pay tribute to the endless heroism of youth, you, the young lions. You, the young lions, have energised our entire struggle.

I pay tribute to the mothers and wives and sisters of our nation. You are the rock-hard foundation of our struggle. Apartheid has inflicted more pain on you than on anyone else.

On this occasion, we thank the world community for their great contribution to the anti-apartheid struggle. Without your support our struggle would not have reached this advanced stage. The sacrifice of the frontline states will be remembered by South Africans forever.

My salutations would be incomplete without expressing my deep appreciation for the strength given to me during my long and lonely years in prison by my beloved wife and family. I am convinced that your pain and suffering was far greater than my own.

Before I go any further I wish to make the point that I intend making only a few preliminary comments at this stage. I will make a more complete statement only after I have had the opportunity to consult with my comrades.

Today the majority of South Africans, black and white, recognise that apartheid has no future. It has to be ended by our own decisive mass action in order to build peace and security. The mass campaign of defiance and other actions of our organisation and people can only culminate in the establishment of democracy. The destruction caused by apartheid on our subcontinent is incalculable. The fabric of family life of millions of my people has been shattered. Millions are homeless and unemployed. Our economy lies in ruins and our people are embroiled in political strife. Our resort to the armed struggle in 1960 with the formation of the military wing of the ANC, Umkhonto we Sizwe, was a purely defensive action against the violence of apartheid. The factors which necessitated the armed struggle still exist today. We have no option but to continue. We express the hope that a climate conducive to a negotiated settlement will be created soon so that there may no longer be the need for the armed struggle.

I am a loyal and disciplined member of the African National Congress. I am therefore in full agreement with all of its objectives, strategies and tactics.

The need to unite the people of our country is as important a task now as it always has been. No individual leader is able to take on this enormous task on his own. It is our task as leaders to place our views before our organisation and to allow the democratic structures to decide. On the question of democratic practice, I feel duty bound to make the point that a leader of the movement is a person who has been democratically elected at a national conference. This is a principle which must be upheld without any exceptions.

Today, I wish to report to you that my talks with the government have been aimed at normalising the political situation in the country. We have not as yet begun discussing the basic demands of the struggle. I wish to stress that I myself have at no time entered into negotiations about the future of our country except to insist on a meeting between the ANC and the government.

Mr De Klerk has gone further than any other Nationalist president in taking real steps to normalise the situation. However, there are further steps as outlined in the [ANC's] Harare Declaration that have to be met before negotiations on the basic demands of our people can begin. I reiterate our call for, inter alia, the immediate ending of the State of Emergency and the freeing of all, and not only some, political prisoners. Only such a normalised situation, which allows for free political activity, can allow us to consult our people in order to obtain a mandate.

The people need to be consulted on who will negotiate and on the content of such negotiations. Negotiations cannot take place above the heads or behind the backs of our people. It is our belief that the future of our country can only be determined by a body which is democratically elected on a non-racial basis. Negotiations on the dismantling of apartheid will have to address the overwhelming demand of our people for a democratic, non-racial and unitary South Africa. There must be an end to white monopoly on political power and a fundamental restructuring of our political and economic systems to ensure that the inequalities of apartheid are addressed and our society thoroughly democratised.

It must be added that Mr De Klerk himself is a man of integrity who is acutely aware of the dangers of a public figure not honouring his undertak-

Mandela is released from prison, February 11, 1990. Originally titled *Nelson Mandela and Wife Winnie Saluting.* Photographer unknown. © Reuters / CORBIS, R90053040. Used by permission of Corbis Images.

ings. But as an organisation we base our policy and strategy on the harsh reality we are faced with. And this reality is that we are still suffering under the policy of the Nationalist government.

Our struggle has reached a decisive moment. We call on our people to seize this moment so that the process towards democracy is rapid and un-interrupted. We have waited too long for our freedom. We can no longer wait. Now is the time to intensify the struggle on all fronts. To relax our efforts now would be a mistake which generations to come will not be able to forgive. The sight of freedom looming on the horizon should encourage us to redouble our efforts.

It is only through disciplined mass action that our victory can be assured. We call on our white compatriots to join us in the shaping of a new South Africa. The freedom movement is a political home for you too. We call on the international community to continue the campaign to isolate the apart-heid regime. To lift sanctions now would be to run the risk of aborting the process towards the complete eradication of apartheid.

Our march to freedom is irreversible. We must not allow fear to stand in our way. Universal suffrage on a common voters' role in a united democratic and non-racial South Africa is the only way to peace and racial harmony.

In conclusion I wish to quote my own words during my trial in 1964. They are true today as they were then:

I have fought against white domination and I have fought against black domination. I have cherished the ideal of a democratic and free society in which all persons live together in harmony and with equal opportunities. It is an ideal which I hope to live for and to achieve. But if needs be, it is an ideal for which I am prepared to die.

White Referendum

F. W. de Klerk

Even though none of the reforms advanced by the National Party in the 1970s and 1980s changed the fundamental fact of white supremacy, the breakaway Conservative Party challenged the ruling party from the right. The government's opening of negotiations with the African National Congress, whose members it had long denounced as terrorists, shook the foundations of white South Africa. Between the first and second round of formal negotiations, known as the Convention for a Democratic South Africa, the National Party government sought to shore up its political foundations. It did this both to ensure its own political survival against a potential challenge from the right and to give it credibility in the talks by showing that it had popular backing among the white population. In early 1992 President F. W. de Klerk asked white voters to endorse his choice to negotiate. A very tense atmosphere preceded the vote, with many dire predictions about what would happen if voters rejected the proposition. In the end, whites voted to endorse negotiations, 69 percent to 31 percent. Befitting the last election under apartheid, no blacks were permitted to vote. After the breakdown of negotiations later that year, the African National Congress organized a massive two-day stay away, to show its broad-based support among blacks, that many referred to as the "black referendum."

Although negotiations were in progress, South Africa in 1992 was engulfed in violence, much of it fomented by elements within the government that sought to sow chaos in the townships and portray the National Party government as the only hope to restore order. In his euphoric speech announcing the results of the referendum, de Klerk paints himself as the leader of a vast majority of South Africans who opposed radicalism and who were united in their love of the land. It is clear in retrospect, however, that the government was playing a double game that would soon send the country close to the brink.

Ladies and gentlemen, today will be written up as one of the most fundamental turning points in the history of South Africa. Today we have closed the book on apartheid. That chapter is finally closed.

There were those who objected, in one way or another, to the fact that this was an all-White Referendum. I think it reflects an element of justice that we who began this long chapter in our history, should have been called upon to close the book on apartheid.

What started out with idealism in the quest for justice, for that was the starting point of the policy of separate development, failed to attain justice for all South Africans and, therefore, had to be abandoned and be replaced by the only viable policy able to work in this country. And that is power-sharing, co-operation, the building of one nation in one undivided South Africa.

It does not happen often that in one generation a nation gets the opportunity to rise above itself. The White electorate has risen above itself in this Referendum. The White electorate has reached out, through this landslide win for the YES-vote, to all our compatriots, to all other South Africans and the message of this Referendum is: Today, in a certain sense, is the real birthday of the real new South African nation. . . .

We are on the eve of really penetrating negotiations. Ladies and gentlemen, in standing on this threshold we face a future full of challenges. Nothing is going to be easy but we have chosen our direction. We have laid the foundation on which to build real reconciliation, long-term stability and peace and progress for all. Therefore, I say: "Let us look forward. Let us take hands. Let us use this magnificent result as a great impetus for that which we have to do and what we are about to do." . . .

We shall build a new South Africa that has room and a place for all its people, that will offer security to those who have much to lose and offer those who have not yet been able to share fully in democratic rights and other areas of opportunities, equal opportunities, full participation and true citizenship together with all others.

Our future, ladies and gentlemen, lies in bringing together those who really want peace and in forging this nation together into an overwhelming majority against radicalism, from whatever source. There is a risk, now, of radicalism both from the left and from the right because radicals do not want us to succeed in building one nation. They do not really want peace.

It is up to us the 90% or 95% of the South African nation from every walk of life, to take hands and stand firm against radicalism; to reach out and build a new future for all our people.

Record of Understanding

F. W. de Klerk and Nelson Mandela

The CODESA (Convention for a Democratic South Africa) II talks collapsed in June 1992 following the horrific massacre on Boipatong township, where at least forty-six people were murdered. Reports immediately implicated the Inkatha Freedom Party and the South African government. The United Nations and foreign governments called for an investigation into the massacre. The African National Congress (ANC) withdrew from the negotiations and began a new wave of resistance it called "rolling mass action." In September 1992, and amid increasing radicalization, ANC leaders led a march on the capital of the Ciskei homeland in a move they believed would topple the homeland government and accelerate the political overthrow of apartheid. Ciskei soldiers opened fire on the demonstrators, killing twenty-six.

Key negotiators worked frantically to restore negotiations between the ANC and the National Party. A summit between Nelson Mandela and President F. W. de Klerk in late September ended with their signing the "Record of Understanding" excerpted here. The agreement restarted talks and outlined the process that would result in the final unraveling of apartheid and lead the way forward to South Africa's first democratic elections in 1994.

The Government and the ANC agreed that there is a need for a democratic constituent assembly / constitution-making body and that for such a body to be democratic it must:

- be democratically elected;
- draft and adopt the new constitution, implying that it should sit as a single chamber;
- be bound only by agreed constitutional principles;
- have a fixed time frame;
- have adequate deadlock breaking mechanisms;
- function democratically[,] i.e. arrive at its decisions democratically with certain agreed to majorities; and be elected within an agreed predetermined time period.

Within the framework of these principles, detail would have to be worked out in the negotiation process.

The Government and the ANC agreed that during the interim / transitional period there shall be constitutional continuity and no constitutional hiatus. In consideration of this principle, it was further agreed that:

- the constitution-making body / constituent assembly shall also act as the interim / transitional Parliament;
- there shall be an interim / transitional government of national unity;
- the constitution-making body / constituent assembly cum interim / transitional Parliament and the interim / transitional government of national unity shall function within a constitutional framework / transitional constitution which shall provide for national and regional government during the period of transition and shall incorporate guaranteed justiciable fundamental rights and freedoms. The interim / transitional Parliament may function as a one or two-chambered body.

The two parties are agreed that all prisoners whose imprisonment is related to political conflict of the past and whose release can make a contribution to reconciliation should be released. The government and the ANC agreed that the release of prisoners, namely, those who according to the ANC fall within the guidelines defining political offences, but according to the government do not, and who have committed offences with a political motive on or before 8 October 1990 shall be carried out in stages (as reflected in a separate document; "Implementation Programme: Release of Prisoners") and be completed before 15 November 1992. To this end the parties have commenced a process of identification. It is the Government's position that all who have committed similar offences but who have not been charged and sentenced should be dealt with on the same basis. On this question no understanding could be reached as yet and it was agreed that the matter will receive further attention.

As the process of identification proceeds, release shall be effected in the above-mentioned staged manner. Should it be found that the current executive powers of the State do not enable it to give effect to specific releases arising from the above identification the necessary legislation shall be enacted.

The Goldstone Commission [appointed by the government in 1991 to investigate ongoing political violence] has given further attention to [migrant-worker] hostels and brought out an urgent report on certain matters and developments in this regard. The Commission indicated that the problem is one of criminality and that it will have to investigate which localities are affected. In the meantime some problematic hostels have been identified and the Government has undertaken as a matter of urgency to address and deal with the problem in relation to those hostels that have been associated with violence.

Further measures will be taken, including fencing and policing to prevent criminality by hostel dwellers and to protect hostel dwellers against external aggression. A separate document ("Implementation Programme: Hostels") records the identification of such hostels and the security measures to be taken in these instances.

Progress will be reported to the Goldstone Commission and the National Peace Secretariat. United Nations observers may witness the progress in co-operation with the Goldstone Commission and the National Peace Secretariat.

In the present volatile atmosphere of violence, the public display and carrying of dangerous weapons provokes further tension and should be prohibited. The Government has informed the ANC that it will issue a proclamation within weeks to prohibit countrywide the carrying and display of dangerous weapons at all public occasions subject to exemptions based on guidelines being prepared by the Goldstone Commission. The granting of exemptions shall be entrusted to one or more retired judges. On this basis, the terms of the proclamation and mechanism for exemption shall be prepared with the assistance of the Goldstone Commission.

The Government acknowledges the right of all parties and organisations to participate in peaceful mass action in accordance with the provisions of the National Peace Accord and the Goldstone Commission's recommendations. The ANC for its part reaffirms its commitment to the provisions of the Code of Conduct for Political Parties arrived at under the National Peace Accord and the agreement reached on 16 July 1992 under the auspices of the Goldstone Commission as important instruments to ensure democratic political activity in a climate of free political participation. The two parties also commit themselves to the strengthening of the Peace Accord process, to do everything in their power to calm down tension and to finding ways and means of promoting reconciliation in South Africa.

Inaugural Address

Nelson Mandela

In April 1994 people waited hours and hours in lines that snaked for two or three miles to vote for the first time in their lives. In the space of four remarkable years, Nelson Mandela had been released from nearly three decades in prison and South Africa's politicians negotiated the end of apartheid. Voting took place over three days and was closely monitored by international organizations. Most systematic voter intimidation took place in the Kwazulu-Natal area, the bastion of the Inkatha Freedom Party and the scene of internecine struggles for several preceding years. The final results saw a victory for the African National Congress (ANC) and its strategic alliances with the labor federation Congress of South African Trade Unions and the South African Communist Party. The ANC, however, fell narrowly short of the two-thirds majority that would have permitted it control over constitution making in the new government. In addition, voters in the Western Cape, where whites and Coloureds were a majority, strongly supported the National Party over the ANC.

The interim constitution mandated the formation of a Government of National Unity composed of the major parties represented in the election results: the ANC, the National Party, and the Inkatha Freedom Party. Two weeks after the election, Mandela became South Africa's first black president. On a still day in Pretoria, surrounded by dignitaries and with fighter jets roaring across a blue sky, Mandela offered a conciliatory speech and outlined the promise of democracy on Africa's southern tip.

Today, all of us do, by our presence here, and by our celebrations in other parts of our country and the world, confer glory and hope to newborn liberty.

Out of the experience of an extraordinary human disaster that lasted too long, must be born a society of which all humanity will be proud.

Our daily deeds as ordinary South Africans must produce an actual South African reality that will reinforce humanity's belief in justice, strengthen its confidence in the nobility of the human soul and sustain all our hopes for a glorious life for all.

All this we owe both to ourselves and to the peoples of the world who are so well represented here today.

To my compatriots, I have no hesitation in saying that each one of us is as intimately attached to the soil of this beautiful country as are the famous jacaranda trees of Pretoria and the mimosa trees of the bushveld.

Each time one of us touches the soil of this land, we feel a sense of personal renewal. The national mood changes as the seasons change.

We are moved by a sense of joy and exhilaration when the grass turns green and the flowers bloom.

That spiritual and physical oneness we all share with this common homeland explains the depth of the pain we all carried in our hearts as we saw our country tear itself apart in a terrible conflict, and as we saw it spurned, outlawed and isolated by the peoples of the world, precisely because it has become the universal base of the pernicious ideology and practice of racism and racial oppression.

We, the people of South Africa, feel fulfilled that humanity has taken us back into its bosom, that we, who were outlaws not so long ago, have today been given the rare privilege to be host to the nations of the world on our own soil.

We thank all our distinguished international guests for having come to take possession with the people of our country of what is, after all, a common victory for justice, for peace, for human dignity.

We trust that you will continue to stand by us as we tackle the challenges of building peace, prosperity, non-sexism, non-racialism and democracy.

We deeply appreciate the role that the masses of our people and their political mass democratic, religious, women, youth, business, traditional and other leaders have played to bring about this conclusion. Not least among them is my Second Deputy President, the Honourable F.W. de Klerk.

We would also like to pay tribute to our security forces, in all their ranks, for the distinguished role they have played in securing our first democratic elections and the transition to democracy, from blood-thirsty forces which still refuse to see the light.

The time for the healing of the wounds has come.

The moment to bridge the chasms that divide us has come.

The time to build is upon us.

We have, at last, achieved our political emancipation. We pledge ourselves to liberate all our people from the continuing bondage of poverty, deprivation, suffering, gender and other discrimination.

We succeeded to take our last steps to freedom in conditions of relative peace. We commit ourselves to the construction of a complete, just and lasting peace.

We have triumphed in the effort to implant hope in the breasts of the millions of our people. We enter into a covenant that we shall build the society in which all South Africans, both black and white, will be able to walk tall, without any fear in their hearts, assured of their inalienable right to human dignity—a rainbow nation at peace with itself and the world.

As a token of its commitment to the renewal of our country, the new Interim Government of National Unity will, as a matter of urgency, address the issue of amnesty for various categories of our people who are currently serving terms of imprisonment.

We dedicate this day to all the heroes and heroines in this country and the rest of the world who sacrificed in many ways and surrendered their lives so that we could be free.

Their dreams have become reality. Freedom is their reward.

We are both humbled and elevated by the honour and privilege that you, the people of South Africa, have bestowed on us, as the first President of a united, democratic, non-racial and non-sexist South Africa, to lead our country out of the valley of darkness.

We understand it still that there is no easy road to freedom.

We know it well that none of us acting alone can achieve success.

We must therefore act together as a united people, for national reconciliation, for nation building, for the birth of a new world.

Let there be justice for all.

Let there be peace for all.

Let there be work, bread, water and salt for all.

Let each know that for each the body, the mind and the soul have been freed to fulfill themselves.

Never, never and never again shall it be that this beautiful land will again experience the oppression of one by another and suffer the indignity of being the skunk of the world.

Let freedom reign.

The sun shall never set on so glorious a human achievement!

God bless Africa!

VIII

Transitions and Reconciliations

Sixteen thousand people died in the four years between Nelson Mandela's release from prison and South Africa's first democratic elections in April 1994. This was some of the worst violence in the country's modern history. Political violence continued for another two years, bringing the total figure to over thirty-six thousand dead in less than a decade. In the elections, the African National Congress (ANC) received 63 percent of the vote; the National Party received 20 percent. Most whites and many Coloureds and Indians voted with the National Party. Two weeks after the election, Mandela became South Africa's first black president.

Conflict and suffering have been major themes in this anthology. After 1994, South Africans confronted the question of what to do about their traumatic history, particularly the nearly fifty years of racial engineering and political oppression. Well into the 1980s, ANC leaders believed in a punitive model similar to the Nuremberg Trials and the de-Nazification policies that had followed the end of the Second World War. In 1995, however, the ANC-led government passed legislation to create the Truth and Reconciliation Commission; the idea of the commission emerged out of the negotiations leading up to the elections of 1994. People who had committed gross human rights violations could apply for amnesty from criminal or civil prosecution; sworn testimony formed a central part of the process.

South Africans inherited a deeply violent and profoundly unequal society. Political violence subsided. Other forms of violence increased meteorically, particularly against women and foreigners. A wave of xenophobic violence in 2008 claimed more than sixty lives. South Africa has one of the very highest per capita incidences of rape in the world, including the rape of infants and children. Economic inequality increased after 1994. At least 40 percent of the population lives in poverty, many in outright destitution. Poverty is especially pronounced in the former homelands, where chiefs have reasserted their power and control many economic resources. The reincorporation of the homelands has in some ways reinscribed ethnicities and traditional patriarchies in conflict with the constitution's protection of gender rights. The economic challenges have frayed the ANC government's alliance with the Communist Party and especially with the trade union federation, the Congress of South African Trade Unions.

Doctors first diagnosed AIDS in South Africa in 1983. The disease spread rapidly in the 1990s and beyond. Currently, approximately six million people are infected by HIV, the largest number of any country in the world and more than one-tenth of South Africa's population. Infection rates exceed one-third among parts of the population. The government's slow and misguided response to the crisis generated extraordinary controversy, though recent government policy has improved, HIV-infection rates have leveled somewhat, and better treatment options are available.

The dismantling of apartheid has reshaped parts of South Africa's urban landscape. The small black elite that emerged rapidly after 1994 moved from poor townships to formerly exclusive white neighborhoods. City centers have been transformed into spaces dominated by the black working class. In less visible ways, the end of apartheid has produced tensions as people worry about their pasts and futures. Questions of identity have been especially pronounced among what had been defined as the Coloured population; many now refuse the appellation and have sought new identities based on claims to a Khoesan heritage. Many whites left the country; most who remain wonder what their futures hold. Across the country people seek explanations for their misfortunes: poverty, joblessness, HIV, and so on. South Africans are fiercely nationalistic—proud of the "rainbow nation" they have created, and they celebrate world events that have taken place in South Africa, such as the Rugby World Cup of 1995 and the FIFA [soccer] World Cup of 2010—even as they fret over the perennial question: what is South Africa, and what does it mean to be a South African?

The readings that close this volume illustrate the remarkable changes that South Africa has experienced over the past two decades. They connect to many of the themes covered in other parts: the politics of race and ethnicity; gender and women's struggles; poverty and inequality; and, less visible but not less important, matters of culture, identity, memory, and historical consciousness. South Africa's fragile democracy faces daunting challenges. Many of the world's most pressing issues lay at the southernmost tip of Africa. South Africa remains a work in progress, a bumptious, creative, extraordinary place, if also a troubling land of violence and suffering.

I Am an African

Thabo Mbeki

Two years after the first democratic elections, South Africa adopted a new constitution that enshrined democracy and individual rights. This was perhaps the high-water mark of the optimism and widespread good feeling that characterized the transition to democracy. Deputy President Thabo Mbeki (1942–), who would become president following Nelson Mandela's term, marked the adoption in 1996 of the constitution with the following speech. In lyrical tones, Mbeki, a scion of the African National Congress who usually presented himself as a technocrat, evoked the beauty of South Africa's land and celebrated the histories of its diverse peoples. Mbeki painted the constitution as a humanist African response to the historical injuries of conquest, exploitation, and apartheid. With the repeated phrase "I am an African," he captured some of the emotional appeal of Africanism and Black Consciousness. Through his insistence on South African diversity, however, he harnessed this appeal to a broader nationalism in tune with the African National Congress's embrace of nonracialism, while also reaffirming South Africa's position as an African nation.

I am an African.

I owe my being to the hills and the valleys, the mountains and the glades, the rivers, the deserts, the trees, the flowers, the seas and the ever-changing seasons that define the face of our native land.

My body has frozen in our frosts and in our latter day snows. It has thawed in the warmth of our sunshine and melted in the heat of the midday sun.

The crack and the rumble of the summer thunders, lashed by startling lightning, have been a cause both of trembling and of hope.

The fragrances of nature have been as pleasant to us as the sight of the wild blooms of the citizens of the veld.

The dramatic shapes of the Drakensberg, the soil-coloured waters of the Lekoa, iGqili noThukela [rivers], and the sands of the Kgalagadi [Kalahari], have all been panels of the set on the natural stage on which we act out the foolish deeds of the theatre of our day.

At times, and in fear, I have wondered whether I should concede equal citizenship of our country to the leopard and the lion, the elephant and the springbok, the hyena, the black mamba and the pestilential mosquito.

A human presence among all these, a feature on the face of our native land thus defined, I know that none dare challenge me when I say: I am an African!

I owe my being to the Khoi and the San whose desolate souls haunt the great expanses of the beautiful Cape—they who fell victim to the most merciless genocide our native land has ever seen, they who were the first to lose their lives in the struggle to defend our freedom and independence and they who, as a people, perished as a result.

Today, as a country, we keep an audible silence about these ancestors of the generations that live, fearful to admit the horror of a former deed, seeking to obliterate from our memories a cruel occurrence which, in its remembering, should teach us not and never to be inhuman again.

I am formed of the migrants who left Europe to find a new home on our native land. Whatever their own actions, they remain still part of me.

In my veins courses the blood of the Malay slaves who came from the East. Their proud dignity informs my bearing, their culture a part of my essence. The stripes they bore on their bodies from the lash of the slave-master are a reminder embossed on my consciousness of what should not be done.

I am the grandchild of the warrior men and women that Hintsa and Sekhukhune led, the patriots that Cetshwayo and Mphephu took to battle, the soldiers Moshoeshoe and Ngungunyane taught never to dishonour the cause of freedom.

My mind and my knowledge of myself is formed by the victories that are the jewels in our African crown, the victories we earned from Isandhlwana to Khartoum, as Ethiopians and as the Ashanti of Ghana, as the Berbers of the desert.

I am the grandchild who lays fresh flowers on the Boer graves at St Helena and the Bahamas, who sees in the mind's eye and suffers the suffering of a simple peasant folk: death, concentration camps, destroyed homesteads, a dream in ruins.

I am the child of Nongqause. I am he who made it possible to trade in the world markets in diamonds, in gold, in the same food for which my stomach yearns.

I come of those who were transported from India and China, whose being resided in the fact, solely, that they were able to provide physical labour, who taught me that we could both be at home and be foreign, who taught me that human existence itself demanded that freedom was a necessary condition for that human existence.

Being part of all these people, and in the knowledge that none dare contest that assertion, I shall claim that I am an African!

I have seen our country torn asunder as these, all of whom are my people, engaged one another in a titanic battle, the one to redress a wrong that had been caused by one to another, and the other to defend the indefensible.

I have seen what happens when one person has superiority of force over another, when the stronger appropriate to themselves the prerogative even to annul the injunction that God created all men and women in His image.

I know what it signifies when race and colour are used to determine who is human and who subhuman.

I have seen the destruction of all sense of self-esteem, the consequent striving to be what one is not, simply to acquire some of the benefits which those who had imposed themselves as masters had ensured that they enjoy.

I have experience of the situation in which race and colour is used to enrich some and impoverish the rest.

I have seen the corruption of minds and souls as a result of the pursuit of an ignoble effort to perpetrate a veritable crime against humanity.

I have seen concrete expression of the denial of the dignity of a human being emanating from the conscious, systemic and systematic oppressive and repressive activities of other human beings.

There the victims parade with no mask to hide the brutish reality—the beggars, the prostitutes, the street children, those who seek solace in substance abuse, those who have to steal to assuage hunger, those who have to lose their sanity because to be sane is to invite pain.

Perhaps the worst among these who are my people are those who have learnt to kill for a wage. To these the extent of death is directly proportional to their personal welfare.

And so, like pawns in the service of demented souls, they kill in furtherance of the political violence in KwaZulu-Natal. They murder the innocent in the taxi wars. They kill slowly or quickly in order to make profits from the illegal trade in narcotics. They are available for hire when husband wants to murder wife and wife, husband.

Among us prowl the products of our immoral and amoral past—killers who have no sense of the worth of human life; rapists who have absolute disdain for the women of our country; animals who would seek to benefit from the vulnerability of the children, the disabled and the old; the rapacious who brook no obstacle in their quest for self-enrichment.

All this I know and know to be true because I am an African!

Because of that, I am also able to state this fundamental truth: that I am born of a people who are heroes and heroines.

I am born of a people who would not tolerate oppression.

I am of a nation that would not allow that the fear of death, torture, imprisonment, exile or persecution should result in the perpetuation of injustice.

The great masses who are our mother and father will not permit that the behaviour of the few results in the description of our country and people as barbaric. Patient because history is on their side, these masses do not despair because today the weather is bad. Nor do they turn triumphalist when, tomorrow, the sun shines. Whatever the circumstances they have lived through—and because of that experience—they are determined to define for themselves who they are and who they should be.

We are assembled here today to mark their victory in acquiring and exercising their right to formulate their own definition of what it means to be African.

The Constitution whose adoption we celebrate constitutes an unequivocal statement that we refuse to accept that our Africanness shall be defined by our race, colour, gender or historical origins.

It is a firm assertion made by ourselves that South Africa belongs to all who live in it, black and white.

It gives concrete expression to the sentiment we share as Africans, and will defend to the death, that the people shall govern.

It recognises the fact that the dignity of the individual is both an objective which society must pursue, and is a goal which cannot be separated from the material well-being of that individual.

It seeks to create the situation in which all our people shall be free from fear, including the fear of the oppression of one national group by another, the fear of the disempowerment of one social echelon by another, the fear of the use of state power to deny anybody their fundamental human rights and the fear of tyranny.

It aims to open the doors so that those who were disadvantaged can assume their place in society as equals with their fellow human beings without regard to colour, race, gender, age or geographic dispersal.

It provides the opportunity to enable each one and all to state their views, promote them, strive for their implementation in the process of governance without fear that a contrary view will be met with repression.

It creates a law-governed society which shall be inimical to arbitrary rule.

It enables the resolution of conflicts by peaceful means rather than resort to force.

It rejoices in the diversity of our people and creates the space for all of us voluntarily to define ourselves as one people.

As an African, this is an achievement of which I am proud, proud without reservation and proud without any feeling of conceit.

Our sense of elevation at this moment also derives from the fact that this magnificent product is the unique creation of African hands and African minds. But it also constitutes a tribute to our loss of vanity that we could, despite the temptation to treat ourselves as an exceptional fragment of humanity, draw on the accumulated experience and wisdom of all humankind, to define for ourselves what we want to be.

Together with the best in the world, we too are prone to pettiness, petulance, selfishness and short-sightedness. But it seems to have happened that we looked at ourselves and said that the time had come that we make a super-human effort to be other than human, to respond to the call to create for ourselves a glorious future, to remind ourselves of the Latin saying: Gloria est consequenda—Glory must be sought after!

Today it feels good to be an African.

It feels good that I can stand here as a South African and as a foot soldier of a titanic African army, the African National Congress, to say to all the parties represented here, to the millions who made an input into the processes we are concluding, to our outstanding compatriots who have presided over the birth of our founding document, to the negotiators who pitted their wits one against the other, to the unseen stars who shone unseen as the management and administration of the Constitutional Assembly, the advisers, experts and publicists, to the mass communication media, to our friends across the globe: Congratulations and well done!

I am an African.

I am born of the peoples of the continent of Africa.

The pain of the violent conflict that the peoples of Liberia, Somalia, the Sudan, Burundi and Algeria suffer, is a pain I also bear.

The dismal shame of poverty, suffering and human degradation of my continent is a blight that we share.

The blight on our happiness that derives from this and from our drift to the periphery of the ordering of human affairs leaves us in a persistent shadow of despair.

This is a savage road to which nobody should be condemned.

This thing that we have done today, in this small corner of a great continent that has contributed so decisively to the evolution of humanity says that Africa reaffirms that she is continuing her rise from the ashes.

Whatever the setbacks of the moment, nothing can stop us now! Whatever the difficulties, Africa shall be at peace!

However improbable it may sound to the sceptics, Africa will prosper!

Whoever we may be, whatever our immediate interest, however much baggage we carry from our past, however much we have been caught by the fashion of cynicism and loss of faith in the capacity of the people, let us say today: Nothing can stop us now!

Mass Struggle, Negotiations, and the 1994 Elections

Alex Callinicos

In South Africa and beyond, observers called South Africa's first democratic elections in 1994 a "miracle." They celebrated the absence of violence while people voted and the peaceful transfer of power when Nelson Mandela took the oath of office as president. Commentators gave credit to two men: Mandela and President F. W. de Klerk. More thoughtful discussions broadened this to attribute the achievement of a new democratic order to the negotiators of the African National Congress and the former ruling party, the National Party, who had brought about the compromises that enabled the elections to go forward. (The Government of National Unity mandated by the interim constitution included the National Party and the Inkatha Freedom Party.) Alex Callinicos (1950–), a British leftist born in Zimbabwe, argues here that this narrative about the elections fails to give due credit to the township dwellers and union members who struggled through strikes, demonstrations, boycotts, and other forms of mass action to bring about change. He also argues that these people are right to expect real transformation in their material lives, not just the abstract democratic rights represented by elections.

Amid the cynicism and torpor that descended over the globe after it turned out that 1989 had not, after all, ushered in a new world order, South Africa's first democratic elections in April 1994 shone out like a beacon. In an era when politicians were generally held in profound contempt, the new State President, Nelson Mandela, towered like a colossus. Here at least there was a story that seemed to have a happy ending, as the new "rainbow nation" stepped proudly into the future.

The sweeping victory secured by the African National Congress (ANC) in the elections after all marked the climax of a struggle that had been going on since before the movement's foundation in 1912. It was a struggle for which Mandela had spent 27 years in prison, a struggle that had been revived by the great Soweto school students' rising of 16 June 1976, a struggle that, above all, had been taken to even greater heights by the township insurrections and workers' strikes of 1984–1986. Around the world millions had identified with the cause of the black majority in South Africa, had supported it by taking part in demonstrations and consumer boycotts, and now felt the ANC's triumph as theirs as well. Apartheid, the barbarous system of racial domination that had made South Africa (in the words of one of its own diplomats) "a polecat among nations," was finally gone.

It will soon be two years since that historic victory. How well has the ANC-led Government of National Unity (GNU) fulfilled the hopes raised by its entry to office? Commentators typically approach this question by launching a sort of pre-emptive strike. They talk about the problem of "expectations." By this they mean that the black people who voted for the ANC in April 1994 did so in the belief that the political transformation represented by black majority rule would rapidly usher in a social and economic transformation as well. Having won the vote, they expected from an ANC-dominated government jobs, houses, and schools as well. But—say the commentators—these expectations are "unrealistic." The GNU, like governments everywhere, has to worry about enhancing competitiveness and reducing public spending. The masses' hopes for a rapid improvement in their material conditions will have to be deferred, perhaps indefinitely.

If this argument is correct, it predicts a bleak future for South Africa. In 1990, 42 percent of the population lived in poverty. In 1991 South Africa had a Gini co-efficient, which measures the extent of income inequality, of .68, the highest in a group of 36 developing countries. That same year the poorest 40 percent of households earned 4 percent of national income, while the richest 10 percent received more than half. In 1995 unemployment among Africans was calculated to be 37 percent—almost certainly an underestimate.

The appalling economic plight of the black majority was summed up recently by the Socialist Workers Organisation of South Africa:

- Only one out of five African households have running water BUT every white household has running water.
- One quarter of all African households get less than R300 a month. Two thirds get less than the breadline—R900 a month. BUT two thirds of white households get more than R2000 a month.
- Two thirds of African children and half of Coloured children live in overcrowded houses BUT only 1 out of 100 white children live in overcrowded conditions.
- Less than half of African kids live in a proper brick house. The rest live in shacks or huts BUT most white children live in a brick house.[1] . . .

The elections of 26–29 April 1994 were the outcome of a strategic compromise between the two main political actors in South Africa—on the one hand, the African National Congress as the dominant force among the black majority and the embodiment of their aspiration for national liberation; on the other hand, the National Party (NP), the historic party of Afrikaner nationalism, in power since 1948, responsible for turning apartheid into a system, but now pursuing "reform" in close alliance with big business.

That compromise was embodied in the Interim Constitution finally agreed on at the Multi-Party Negotiating Forum in November 1993. This provided the basis on which the country's first one person, one vote elections were held the following April. Under the settlement, South Africa was to become a non-racial liberal democracy, subject to certain limitations. The most important of these was that during the five-year transition period in which the new National Assembly would draft a final constitution, a coalition government representing all the parties that won at least 5 percent of the vote would hold office. It is by virtue of this provision that the GNU comprises not merely the ANC, but also the NP, and the Zulu tribalist Inkatha Freedom Party (IFP).

The rationale for this compromise settlement reflected both sides' assessment of the balance of forces, and in particular their shared belief that neither could decisively defeat the other. The risings of 1984–1986—and the persisting strength shown by the black organised working class during the State of Emergency which brought the insurgency to an end—convinced key figures in the regime that they would have to negotiate with the ANC. After becoming State President in August 1989, the new NP leader, F W de Klerk, made the decisive move in February 1990 of unbanning the ANC, the South African Communist Party (SACP) and the Pan-Africanist Congress (PAC), and freeing Mandela, as a prelude to full scale talks.

In the meantime, many township and union activists had concluded after the defeat of the mid-1980s rebellion that the regime could be removed, not by mass insurrection, but by a negotiated settlement. This had always been the long-term objective of the exiled ANC leadership in the Zambian capital of Lusaka. Now the conditions were emerging in which this goal could realistically be pursued. But it is clear that the decisive initiative in making contact with the regime was undertaken independently by Mandela himself in Pollsmoor prison.

After an initial meeting with justice minister Kobie Coetsee during a spell in hospital in November 1985, Mandela was separated from his fellow ANC prisoners on his return to jail. He later recalled: "Immediately in my mind I said: 'Well, this would be a good opportunity to start negotiations with the government and to maintain this element of secrecy.' If you are a member of an organisation and your comrades say: 'Don't do this,' whatever your views are, that you have to accept, and that is what I feared. I wanted to confront them [the ANC] with a fait accompli.'"[2]

While still nominally a prisoner of the South African state, and ignoring the initial objections of the ANC leadership, Mandela held a total of 47 meetings with a secret committee set up by Coetsee on the instructions of State President P W Botha. Despite the ground that had thus already been covered by February 1990, the path to a negotiated settlement proved tortuous and very bloody.

The fundamental reason for this lay in the strategy pursued by de Klerk and the NP. It soon became clear that they were not negotiating in good faith. Their aim was, while conceding the formal principles of liberal democracy, to preserve the substance of white economic and political power. Initially, the regime harboured vain hopes of splitting Mandela off from what they believed to be the Communist-dominated ANC in exile.

Then the regime sought to create an electoral alliance between the NP and conservative black organisations, above all Inkatha. All-out warfare between ANC and IFP supporters, which had first developed in the townships and squatter settlements of Natal after the 1984–1986 risings, spread to the Pretoria-Witwatersrand-Vereeniging (PWV) region, the industrial and political heart of South Africa centred in Johannesburg, in July–August 1990. Overwhelming evidence rapidly accumulated of the role of a "third force," backed by the security forces and allied to Inkatha, in stoking up the violence. The effect was to disorganise the ANC's popular base and force it onto the defensive.

To counter this attack, the ANC leadership found itself compelled to turn to the masses. After a particularly revolting IFP massacre in the Vaal township of Boipatong in June 1992, the movement returned to the streets. The ANC and its allies in the Congress of South African Trade Unions (COSATU) had already launched the Mass Action Campaign after the collapse of the first attempt at formal all party talks, the Convention for a Democratic South Africa (CODESA), in May. Cyril Ramaphosa, secretary general of the ANC and the movement's chief negotiator, explained: "We needed to put the entire struggle on a completely different plane, and that plane had to be resorting back to the major power that we had, which was our people."[3] On 3–4 August some 4 million workers took part in a massive political general strike. After this demonstration of mass determination, the NP could harbour no illusions about the extent and the depth of the ANC's popular support.

For Mandela and Ramaphosa, however, the Mass Action Campaign was only a brief detour from the negotiating table, a means of showing the regime how strong the ANC's hand was, and a way of allowing their increasingly angry and impatient supporters to let off a bit of steam. The "Leipzig Option"—the strategy supported by some ANC and SACP leaders of using mass demonstrations to bring down de Klerk—was discredited after one of its main proponents, Ronnie Kasrils, was widely believed to have rashly led marchers into a massacre by soldiers of the Ciskei Bantustan at Bisho in September 1992.

The same month saw a public resumption of contacts between the ANC and the NP (private discussions between Ramaphosa and his government counterpart Roelf Meyer continued throughout the Mass Action Campaign). But in order to secure a summit with Mandela that would form the basis for carrying on with the negotiations, de Klerk had to make a symbolically crucial concession concerning the release of political prisoners. For Ramaphosa, that "without a doubt was the turning point of the whole negotiating process."[4] The ANC subsequently made its own major concession when Joe Slovo, chairperson of the SACP, persuaded it to accept the principle of "sunset clauses," i.e. temporary departures from strict democratic principles such as a transitional coalition government that would help to overcome white fears of majority rule.

The final settlement was, however, considerably more favourable to the ANC than de Klerk and his advisers had hoped. This outcome, however, did not derive chiefly from the negotiating skills of Mandela, Ramaphosa and Slovo. Once again it was a consequence of the intervention of the masses. In April 1993 a white fascist assassinated Chris Hani, general secretary of the SACP and one of the most popular ANC leaders. There followed a spontaneous explosion of popular anger. Two stayaways (political general strikes) and numerous demonstrations showed not only that the black masses overwhelmingly backed the ANC but that they might escape from anyone's control. The abyss was opening up before the regime. Mandela, not State President de Klerk, appeared on television to call for calm. Patti Waldmeir of the *Financial Times* argued that the assassination and the reaction had the effect of "permanently tilting the balance in the ANC's favour and allowing them to extract the concession that elections would be held on April 27 [1994]."[5]

There was, however, one final stage in the transition to democracy where the masses played a decisive role. The political realignment in 1992–1993 drew the ANC and the NP together, and left the IFP relatively isolated (although there is plenty of evidence of security-force complicity in the violence that continued to rage in the townships and squatter camps of Natal and the East Rand almost up to election day itself). Inkatha's leader, Chief Mangosuthu Buthelezi, Chief Minister of the KwaZulu Homeland, therefore threw his lot in with various other political forces threatened by the end of apartheid. These included principally the white far right. The angry black reaction to Hani's assassination terrified many whites, and rallied together right-wing opponents of de Klerk's policy in the Afrikaner Volksfront (AVF), under the leadership of General Constand Viljoen, ex-Chief of the South African Defence Force (SADF).

The Freedom Alliance, a strange coalition of Afrikaner and African ultra-conservatives, now took shape. Aside from the AVF and the IFP, the principal backers of the Freedom Alliance were the rulers of two "independent" Bantustans, the Ciskei and Bophuthatswana. Combined with Buthelezi's control of KwaZulu and of parts of Natal, this gave the opponents of the settlement an extensive territorial grip, and therefore the capacity substantially to disrupt the elections, which the Freedom Alliance threatened to boycott. Viljoen claimed to be training up a formidable military force, and could certainly count on plenty of sympathy in the ranks of the SADF.

The ANC responded to the far-right threat, and the escalation of violence as the elections drew near, by offering Viljoen, Buthelezi and their cronies significant constitutional concessions. The Johannesburg *Weekly Mail and Guardian* argued that these actually worked to de Klerk's benefit. "For the first time the NP will be able to claim some 'victories' at the negotiating table,"[6] the newspaper commented. It is hard to say how far this surrender to right-wing blackmail would have gone had not the masses intervened.

At the beginning of March 1994, student demonstrations and workers' strikes paralysed Bophuthatswana. As his police started to mutiny and join the rising, the Homeland's president, Lucas Mangope, appealed to his Freedom Alliance partner, Viljoen, for help. The general responded by sending thousands of AVF "farmers" to Bophuthatswana. What had been intended as a disciplined military operation disintegrated into chaos as the thugs of the fascist Afrikaner Weerstandsbeweging (AWB) joined the expedition, apparently against the wishes of Viljoen and Mangope. But they soon discovered they had chosen the wrong century. The glory days of the Boer republics were over, and their would-be heirs were confronting blacks ready and able to fight and win.

Bophuthatswana soldiers refused to supply the AVF with the weapons Mangope had promised them, and threatened to attack the right wingers. The AWB were persuaded to pull out of the Homeland, and were followed

Afrikaner Weerstandsbeweging (AWB) dead in Bophuthatswana, South Africa, Mafek-eng, 1994. Photograph by Greg Marinovich / South Photographs. © Greg Marinovich.

slightly later by the AVF force. As they drove in convoys through its capital, Mmabatho, the fascists fired indiscriminately at people in the streets. At a roadblock three AWB men got involved in a shoot out with rebel soldiers and policemen. That night the world saw on television their last moments, as the fascists begged ineffectually for their lives. In a few minutes a giant shadow that hovered threateningly over South Africa's transition to democracy since the late 1980s—the white far right—was dispersed.

The effects of the Bophuthatswana rising were enormous. Mangope was toppled, and Bophuthatswana was reincorporated into South Africa. Within a few days the Ciskei's military dictator, Oupa Gqozo, and his Bantustan had suffered the same fate. Viljoen, already uncomfortable with the more unsavoury or demented of his right-wing allies—the Nazis of the AWB and the pro-apartheid no hopers of the Conservative Party—used the pretext of the debacle to break with the AVF and launch the Freedom Front to represent the cause of traditional Afrikaner nationalism in the elections. Buthelezi now found himself isolated. Outmanoeuvred by the ANC, who were able to draw into their camp the Zulu King Goodwill Zwelithini—long impatient with his uncle and prime minister's tutelage—Buthelezi grudgingly agreed to end his boycott only a week before the elections.

The historic achievement of the April 1994 elections was thus a consequence less of the skill and determination of the ANC leadership (though no one could deny that they had plenty of both), than of mass struggle. It was the risings of the mid-1980s, and what they represented—not merely the incredible courage and elan of the township youth, but the strength and endurance of organised black labour—that had forced de Klerk to the negotiating table in the first place. But even after the great breakthrough of February 1990, further mass action, sometimes orchestrated from the top, more often a result of initiatives from below, was necessary first to strengthen the ANC's bargaining hand and then to knock out the far right. Mandela's words to the people as voting began on 26 April were truer than he perhaps knew: "This is your day."

Talk of the "problem of expectations" needs to be considered in this light. The oppressed and exploited—workers, students, unemployed, township and squatter camp dwellers—had won the great victory over apartheid. Whenever they were asked, they made it clear that they had been fighting for more than new laws and a new constitution. They had fought to change their lives dramatically for the better. Often they were prepared to put it in more theoretical terms by saying that they were fighting for socialism as well as national liberation. This was one reason why the red banners of the Communist Party had such a powerful attraction for the more militant workers and youth.

These aspirations deserve better than to be patronised by journalists and ex-Marxist academics who dismiss them as fantasies spun by those who fail to understand the "realities" of the global market and of the kind of voodoo economics promoted by the International Monetary Fund and the World Bank. It was the black masses who put Mandela in his official residence at Tuynhuys, all his ministers in their offices and limousines, the members of parliament and of provincial assemblies in their seats. Their "expectations" of a total liberation should serve as the benchmark by which the "New South Africa" is judged.

Yet even before the ANC took office in May 1994 it was already clear that it would introduce only limited changes in the social and economic structure of South Africa. The ANC and its close partner in the struggle, the SACP, had long been committed to what came to be known as the two-stage strategy. Derived ultimately from Stalinist orthodoxy, this sharply separated the struggle against apartheid from that against capitalism. Its political conclusion was: first win national liberation by means of a broad democratic alliance of all classes of the oppressed population plus anti-apartheid whites;

only once that has been achieved should the question of socialism come onto the agenda. . . .

Notes

1. *Socialist Worker* (Johannesburg), 11 October 1995.
2. Interview in *Death of Apartheid* (BBC-TV, 1995), Part 1.
3. Interview in *Death of Apartheid* (BBC-TV, 1995), Part 2.
4. Interview in *Death of Apartheid* (BBC-TV, 1995), Part 2.
5. *Financial Times*, 4 December 1993.
6. *Weekly Mail and Guardian*, 25 February 1994.

The Rape of Women

Antjie Krog

In the negotiations to bring about the democratic transition, the African National Congress (ANC), National Party, and other parties agreed that there should be a process for perpetrators of human rights abuses under apartheid, including agents of the state and those fighting against it, to apply for amnesty. The proponents of this idea argued that it would prevent a cycle of vengeance, free the courts from being overwhelmed with claims from the past, and, crucially, that it would secure the cooperation of apartheid's security forces in allowing the new democratic order to be born. Legislation in 1995 created the Truth and Reconciliation Commission, and the commission conducted hearings for the testimony of victims and the amnesty applications of perpetrators over the next several years. To be successful, applicants had to fully disclose their crimes and establish that they acted with a political motive. In the end, the Truth and Reconciliation Commission granted amnesty for only 849 people out of more than 7,000 applications, denying the others mainly on the grounds of lack of full disclosure. The hearings brought into the open the horrific abuses committed in secret by the security forces and also exposed the internecine violence of the township uprising in the 1980s.

Antjie Krog (1952–), a poet and journalist, reported on the Truth and Reconciliation Commission hearings for the South African Broadcasting Corporation and wrote about the commission in Country of My Skull, *from which the following selection is drawn. In this excerpt, Krog focuses on the role of women on all sides of the antiapartheid struggle and at the hearings themselves, and she highlights the rape of women by agents of the state and by male freedom fighters.*

There has been concern that so few women activists have come to testify before the Truth Commission. They have their reasons. "The day I became involved in the struggle . . . I made a choice and I fully understood the consequences of it. To run to the commission now just doesn't seem right." In an effort to draw in the experiences of women activists and get a fuller picture of the past, the commission creates special forums. At a hearing on prisons, Greta Appelgren, who drove the getaway car for Robert McBride when he planted the Magoo's Bar bomb, testifies. She is now known as Za-krah Nakardien:

"What bothered me were the rats. They were the size of cats and they were in the passage all the time. While I was eating, three of them would watch me. I took my clothes to block their access, but they ripped all that and came in, crawling up, until one night they reached my neck . . . I screamed the place down and they found me in a corner eating my T-shirt. This is how berserk I was.

"Isolation for seven months taught me something. No human being can live alone. I felt I was going deeper and deeper into the ground. It felt as if all the cells were like coffins full of dead people.

"I had to accept that I was damaged. That part of my soul was eaten away by maggots and I will never be whole again." . . .

"A group of six guys and myself in Sebokeng decided to form an organization to keep the senior comrades busy all the time. We rape women who need to be disciplined. Those who behave like snobs. They think they know better than most of us. And when we struggle, they simply don't want to join us."

A seemingly simple question like "What is rape?" can derail a whole discussion. South African law defines rape as occurring only between a man and a woman and involving the penetration of the penis into the vagina. Acts of forced oral or anal sex and penetration by foreign objects are not considered rape. [The law was reformed in 2007.] But the Truth Commission has to establish whether one can rape with a political motive and whether the raping of nonpolitical women to keep the comrades busy is indeed a political act. The Geneva Convention regards rape as a crime of war and prosecutions for rape in Bosnia have begun only because of its link to ethnic cleansing.

The Truth Commission might recommend that rapists should not be granted amnesty. But why would a rapist testify if he knows he won't get amnesty? Then again, few women have testified about rape, and fewer, if any, have named the rapists. So why would a rapist apply for amnesty at all? There seems to be a bizarre collusion between the rapist and the raped. Although rumors abound about rape, all these mutterings are trapped behind closed doors. Apparently high-profile women, among them Cabinet ministers, parliamentarians, and businesswomen, were raped and sexually abused under the previous dispensation—and not only by the regime, but by their own comrades in the townships and liberation camps. But no one will utter an audible word about it.

The silence is locked into loss and cultural differences, says clinical psychologist Nomfundo Walaza. "Women who have been raped know that if they talk about it now in public, they will lose something again—privacy, maybe respect. If you knew that a particular minister had been raped, what would go through your mind when you saw her on television? Another deterrent is that some of the rapists hold high political positions today—so if you spoke out you would not only undermine the new government you fought for, but destroy your own possibilities of a future. There is also a culture of not discussing these things with your own family."

"When they raped me, I was already torn and injured by electric shocks," testifies Thandi Shezi. "I hurt deep inside. I could tell nobody. My mother is sitting here—she is hearing it for the first time. I'm suffering from a womb that feels as if it's jumping. I'm frigid. I'm cold. When I get involved with a man, I get scared. I didn't tell a single soul about it. I don't want them to pity me. I don't want them to call me names."

Men don't use the word "rape" when they testify. They talk about being sodomized, or about iron rods being inserted into them. In so doing, they make rape a women's issue. By denying their own sexual subjugation to male brutality, they form a brotherhood with rapists that conspires against their own wives, mothers, and daughters, say some of those who testify.

There is a lot of ambiguity surrounding sexual torture, says Sheila Meintjes [a South African academic]. It is not difficult to understand why. "There is a hypothesis that the sexual torture of men is to induce sexual passivity and to abolish political power and potency, while the torture of women is the activation of sexuality. There is a lot of anger about women—because women do not have the authority, but often they have a lot of power."

The picture of Rita Mazibuko in her brown dress, beige cardigan, and neatly knotted *kopdoek* [headscarf] is in stark contrast with her story of rape, torture, and rejection. And neither she nor the Truth Commission is prepared for the storm that follows her testimony.

Mazibuko underwent military training in Angola and Mozambique, and was then placed in Swaziland to work out routes for cadres moving in and out of the country. When nine of these cadres were shot, suspicion fell on her. The fact that she had R35,000 (about $5,800) in her bank account was proof enough for the ANC that she worked for the apartheid regime. In reality, Mazibuko says, she earned the money by sewing and selling tracksuits. Accused of being a spy, she was taken to Tanzania and Zambia, and kept in a hole for six months—sleeping on pieces of cardboard.

"On the day I was taken out of that hole, they said I should go and wash. The clothes I was wearing at the time was the same dress for about six months—when I tried to take off the clothes, they were in tatters. When

I washed my hair, it fell out; my skin was greasy because I didn't wash for three months."

Two comrades, Jacob and Mtungwa, ordered her to pick one of them. She needed a man to take up her case, they said. Some comrades said she was guilty; others disagreed. They kept on torturing her.

"I refused to have sex with them. Then they tortured me between two chairs. I fell on the ground. They were kicking me across my face, they treated me like a donkey. . . . They pushed a pipe with a condom in and out of my vagina. While they did it, they asked how it felt. When I did not respond, it was put deeper and deeper—to satisfy me, they said . . . After being assaulted, I was bleeding from my mouth and nose, but still I was hanged, left dangling from a tree—they wanted to kill me that day. I was made to wear overalls so that if I messed myself up, they wouldn't catch sight of my mess. When they brought me down, they said: 'This dog is dead.'"

Afterward, Mazibuko wrote to comrade Mathews Phosa, because she had once shared a house with him and cooked for him. He spoke to a senator about her case, but the assaults continued: "At Sun City prison, someone called Desmond raped me nine times. Nine times. He is quite a young man—he was twenty-nine at the time. And I saw myself as his mother. Comrade Mashego was staying at Swaziland—when I met him, he raped me until I approached the authorities. And then Tebaga, who was also very young, he raped me and cut my genitals—he cut me through from number one to number two. And then he put me in a certain room, he tied my legs apart. He tied my neck and then poured Dettal [an antiseptic] over my genitals."

ANC members sold her house and furniture in Swaziland for R20,000 (about $3,300). "It's now Comrade Mike who sleeps in my bed and uses my dressing table," she says. When she finally returned from exile, she bumped into Jacob Zuma. He lent her money to report her case to Shell House [ANC headquarters, in Johannesburg]. But one of her former rapists took her from Shell House to Boksburg, where he again raped her for the whole night in a house with a "For Sale" sign in front of it. "He warned me that I would not get away. That he would kill me if I talk."

Mazibuko tells the commission that she doesn't have a cent to her name. She borrowed the clothes she has on. To crown it all, two weeks after she gave a written statement to the Truth Commission, she received a phone call from Mpumalanga premier Mathews Phosa, warning her not to testify—because then he would be obliged to defend ANC members against her claims.

"I fell in love with the late Chris Hani [the general-secretary of the South African Communist Party] and gave birth to his son Simphiwe. Hani showed this boy to his family but not to his wife. I gave the son to my sister-in-law to avoid a divorce from my husband." On Mazibuko's confidential written statement, the name of Simphiwe is underlined—a plea for extra reparation? I wonder.

It is strange testimony. Is this woman with the good-natured face, who speaks of rape as if it is water, who emphasizes the youth of her rapists, nothing more than a prostitute? And is her sexual history perhaps the reason why Phosa says afterward that he has never heard of Rita Mazibuko or "Mumsy Khuswayo"—her code name in the ANC?

When she leaves the witness table, she pulls her cardigan closed and folds her arms protectively over her body. As if she already knows that a mighty provincial premier is going to discredit her evidence repeatedly in public and threaten to take her to court. As if she knows no one will stand up for her. The Truth Commission does not utter a single word in Mazibuko's defense. Not one of the commissioners, not one of the feminists agitating for women's rights, stands up and says: "We respect the right of Rita Mazibuko to tell the truth as she sees it, just as we respect the right of Mathews Phosa to tell the truth as he sees it. But we expect him to do the same."

The Cradock Four

Testimony from the Truth and Reconciliation Commission

As resistance grew in the early 1980s, peaking with the township uprising that began in 1984, the South African state authorized its security forces to engage in secret campaigns of violence and intimidation aimed at activists and their organizations. In many cases, politicians at the highest levels of the state gave orders that anti-apartheid activists be permanently removed from society, that is, killed. One of the most notorious cases was that of the Cradock Four. In 1985 a hit squad with the Orwellian name Civil Cooperation Bureau abducted and killed Matthew Goniwe, Fort Calata, Sparrow Mkhonto, and Sicelo Mhlauli. Tens of thousands attended the funeral of the four, openly displaying banners and colors of the banned African National Congress (ANC) and Communist Party. The government answered this defiance by declaring a state of emergency.

The government successfully covered up its involvement in the murders until a second inquest in 1994. Seven former members of the security forces applied to the Truth and Reconciliation Commission for amnesty in connection with the murders; the commission granted amnesty to one, who had minor involvement, but denied the others for failure to truthfully and fully disclose their actions. The Truth and Reconciliation Commission proceedings concerning the case are covered in the documentary film Long Night's Journey into Day *(2000; directed by Deborah Hoffmann and Frances Reid). The following is an excerpt from the Truth and Reconciliation Commission testimony of Nomonde Calata, the widow of Fort Calata. Her testimony is notable for highlighting the minor resistance actions they had been involved in as young people and how these led to increasing harassment and imprisonments, culminating in deeper involvement in resistance and the assassination of Fort and his comrades. Her testimony also shows how the agents of the apartheid state preyed on the vulnerabilities of women left behind when their men were detained.*

MRS CALATA: I am Nomonde Calata, a wife to the late Fort Calata. My birthplace is in Cradock, I met Fort in 1974. . . .

495

MR SMITH: Thank you, now your husband Fort Calata has had quite a strong background in his family in so far as politics is concerned, is that right? Would you like to tell the Commission about it?

MRS CALATA: The grandfather to Fort was a general secretary to the ANC organisation during the [1950s] treason trial. Fort was born during that period. This name Fort was given by the grandmother, because she used to pay visits during the trial and she informed the grandfather that there is a child and he was named Fort, because at the time that he, the grandfather was at the Fort Prison [in Johannesburg]. . . .

In 1976 he was involved because it was the time of the struggle. Everybody was conscious now. During the time when he was at school, he typed a letter to the municipality in Cradock, trying to inform them about the way in which they were overworked, the streets were dirty and also how they used to carry on with the bucket system [for human waste]. He was detained for this involvement and for this explanation and then he was cross-questioned about why he wrote these letters, which he wrote anonymously, but they could trace that he was the source of these letters. . . .

MR SMITH: In 1983 you related a story that he came back from [teaching] school one day and he was very happy about a particular teacher that he met.

MRS CALATA: Yes he came back in 1983, he told us that there was a new teacher at school and he loves this teacher very much. . . . He introduced him as Matthew Goniwe. He and Fort then became friends thereafter.

[MRS CALATA]: Yes they started to be friends ever since. At that moment there were some houses that were being built there in Cradock, so we decided to get one of the houses and then we took it as accommodation. There was a sliding scale and rentals were charged according to earnings and it ranged from R24.99 to R89. Because my husband was a teacher he paid the R89. The community of Cradock felt that this was too much for them, because it is a small place and the people were not earning much, even if they were employed. So they decided to put this and present it to all the teachers there in Cradock, and tried to request them if they could assist in trying to negotiate for a reduction of the rentals. Then a meeting was organised to discuss this issue. That is where the committee was elected which was going to handle all this and Matthew was the chairperson of this Committee and Fort was a treasurer. There were also other members.

MR SMITH: You're referring to the formation of Cradora?

MRS CALATA: Yes. This organisation then started to become more important and then it was named as Cradock Residents Association, abbreviated as Cradora. There was also the youth organisation which was also in existence, and this organisation was trying to bring about discipline and morals to the youth which was beginning to disintegrate, and Fort was the president of that youth association. . . . As this carried on, preparing to challenge this in court, time went on, UDF [United Democratic Front] started. Our organisations decided that we should get into UDF because it was strong at that time, and it was the organisation with a vision, and we affiliated with the UDF. Whilst still affiliating with them, things went on and I was arrested in November 1983. I was fetched from work. I was wearing a T-shirt on which was printed, "Free Mandela." I was then arrested and charged just because of that T-shirt. . . .

MR SMITH: Did anything happen during the process of negotiations between the community and the authorities regarding Matthew's transfer [away from Cradock]?

MRS CALATA: During that time of negotiations with [the Department of] Education and Training to reinstate Matthew, instead of him receiving a letter telling him that his transfer will be cancelled, he only received a telegram saying he has been dismissed. . . . [When] the schools reopened, school boycotts started, pupils were not going to school, they wanted Matthew to be reinstated. Parents were at the same time negotiating with the Department of Education and Training. But you know nothing actually ever came up from the Department of Education, whether to reinstate Matthew or not. On the 31st of March, in 1984, it was 10 o'clock in the evening, we were sleeping, we heard lots and lots of cars outside, I said to my husband, "No let us not wake up, let's wait and see what happens." We heard knocks at windows at the front of the house, all over. Because I was always close to him I tried to be very strong. We stood up and lit up the house. I said to them. "If you are not going to knock at the door only, I'm not going to open." They knocked at the door, Mr Venter stepped in, he had a paper in his hands but he never showed it to me, what was written on it, he said to me, "Where is Mr Calata, we're here to detain him in terms of the Internal Security Act." . . . The following morning I woke up to go to work and tried to ask the police where they took him because I wanted to give him some [medicine] tablets. They said they would come and tell me and I went to work but there was absolute silence. I went for my own case on the 11th of April in 1984, the case was discussed and I was charged for three months imprisonment or a fine of R800. I paid R250 a month because I couldn't leave my children alone at home without their father. The following day I went to work after this case of mine. When I arrived at work, I was working at the Provincial Hospital at Cradock, they said the matron would like to see me. Well I went to the Superintendent with the matron, there was a form on the table which they said I must sign. I asked them to read me the form but they refused. They informed me that they want to make me leave the job. I asked them if we could wait until the case is finished, but they never gave me the chance and just dismissed me with immediate effect. They said that I shouldn't be seen anywhere around the premises in the hospital and I went home. . . .

The police came to tell me he was in Diepkloof Prison in Johannesburg. We applied for a permit to go and see him. I went to see him in May for the first time. The second time when I asked for a permit to visit him, it was after supper time, the police said to us they don't take permits after their meals. I went home, and just at the entrance police took me, and put me into their cars. I tried to shout to my dad that I am being taken by the police, because I could see him in the distance. At the police station, the head of the police asked to see my identity document. I gave them my document with the hope that I may see my husband. At that time I was carrying a so-called Coloured ID. They asked me, if I am going to vote now for the tricameral parliament. Before I could answer that question, they said that they knew that I could not even vote, because they knew that I'm a member of the ANC. I never gave them an answer, I just kept quiet. They were now threatening me, saying, "Your children long to see their father, hey, they will never see him." And I asked them what child doesn't want to see his or her father? They told me that I will never ever be employed in Cradock. What will we eat because my husband was in prison and my children had to go to school? I just kept quiet. Eventually at about six, when it was dark in the town, and I didn't have a permit to see my husband, I went to see Fort and I said to him that I have bad news for him. . . .

On the 27th of May in the early hours, I was woken up by the knocks and the lights of flashlights right in the house, and I went to open the door. I saw Mr Venter and Mr Gouws as well as many other policemen, horses, SADF [South African Defence Force], just full of military. They entered my house and said they want to search. They searched my bedroom for UDF documents and took everything. In their search Mr Venter asked me where my husband was. I told them that he was in Gauteng. He asked this in Afrikaans and he said, "The day we find him he's going to be in very big trouble." I was worried and scared but brave at the same time. I kept quiet looking at him. He stood up and said, "What is this bad after all?" After that they left my house, Matthew arrived and he said that they had visited all the executive members, taking all the documents from them. In April before Fort went to Johannesburg for his physio [physical therapy] treatment, he arrived from the UDF meeting at night, I was already in bed and he woke me up. He said, "Nomonde, I have to tell you this." I replied, "Speak." And he said "We were detained with Matthew for a few hours in Port Elizabeth. We left Sparrow in the car, we left Sparrow because we didn't want the car to be seen. Matthew and I were taken to SANLAM [South African National Life Assurance Company] building in Port Elizabeth. A security branch section was sitting there waiting for us. There was one of them who said, 'Lieutenant [*sic*], can we do it?' They asked questions after saying this. Matthew at the same time was being asked such questions[.]" He was clever enough to tell Fort that one guy . . . yes he was able to explain and said, "I think they plan something very big about us." . . .

MRS CALATA: Yes. On the 27th of June [1985] [Fort] informed me that he and Matthew would be going for a briefing in Port Elizabeth. . . . Yes he mentioned when they'll be coming back because they usually came back at eight but today he came in at 10 o'clock, but he said also, "We think that we'll be coming very late, maybe at 11 in the evening, I'll be here," I'm certain about that. . . . So I kept on, I was awake suffering from insomnia. When I looked out, there was a casper [armored vehicle] and vans. The casper was on the other street but not a single car moved around as they usually did. This was also an indication that something was wrong. . . . We slept uneasily on Friday as we did not know what happened to our husbands. Usually the [Port Elizabeth] Herald was delivered at home because I was distributing it. During the time that it was delivered I looked at the headlines and one of the children said that he could see that his father's car was shown in the paper as being burned. At that moment I was trembling because I was afraid of what might have happened to my husband, because I wondered, if his car was burned like this, what might have happened to him? . . . (sobbing)

MR SMITH: Mr Chairman, may I request the Commission to adjourn maybe for a minute, I don't think the witness is in a condition to continue at the present moment.

CHAIRPERSON: Can we adjourn for 10 minutes please?

OBSERVERS SINGING: What have we done? What have we really done? What have we done? . . .

MRS CALATA: Well of course, I arrived with other women at that place [Mrs. Goniwe's house]. Mrs Mkhonto was there with us, Mrs Goniwe was also there, people were very full in the house, and I heard the news that the bodies of Sparrow Mkhonto, and Mhlawuli have been discovered. I was wondering what happened to Matthew and Fort. . . . When I got home, the reverend from my church visited me. He had come to explain that the bodies of Fort and Matthew were found. . . . The community and the family members went out to identify the bodies. Mr Koluwe, the man we as families asked to go and identify the bodies, has passed away. He said that he had seen the bodies but he discovered that the hair was pulled out, his tongue was very long. His fingers were cut off. He had many wounds in his body. When he looked at his trousers he realised that the dogs had bitten him very severely. He couldn't believe it that the dogs already had their share. . . .

MR SMITH: Allow me please. There is an incident that happened after the funeral, when the police actually came to your house, I want you to tell the Commission what happened.

MRS CALATA: They were buried on the 20th of July, that time there was a declaration of a state of emergency. On the 8th of August I went to deliver my baby Tulani, I was used to giving birth in the normal way but Tulani was a caesarian. Well I gave birth to the child and went home the following day. A few days after the birth of this son, the security police arrived at home, the leader was Mr Labuschagne, and they said to me, "Don't you want us to be the father of this child?" I kept quiet, I didn't give them an answer. They waited a few minutes and then left. After a few minutes they came back. They said, "We want to evict you from this house. You do not have money to pay for the rent and we know you do not have money, you took out all your money in your bank. Even in Fort's account there is not a cent left, so we are here to take you out of the house." . . .

MR SMITH: During 1989 there was an inquest into the circumstances surrounding your husband's death. Can you recall what the findings of that inquest were?

MRS CALATA: Yes we had this inquest in 1989 at New Brighton. The finding was that, yes the court agreed they were killed but there's not enough evidence as to who killed them. Now the inquest will never be taken further. That was the end of it. We stayed at home with no knowledge until 1994, if I am right. There was a signal in the New Nation newspaper. Then the inquest was reopened.

MR SMITH: Is that the note where instructions were given for your husband to be removed from society, your husband and the other three?

MRS CALATA: Yes the signal, as I have mentioned, was written by Mr du Plessis, through Mr van Rensburg's instructions, he was also instructed by Brigadier van der Westhuizen. This signal, the three names were there, Fort Calata, Bulela Goniwe and Matthew Goniwe removed from society as a matter of urgency. . . .

MR SMITH: The inquest has made a very general finding about your husband and those who were responsible for his death. Would you want to know the identity of the person or persons who were responsible for your husband's death, and if so, why would you like to know who exactly killed your husband?

MRS CALATA: I'd be very glad to know this person. If I can know the individuals who are responsible for this I will be able to understand why they did it. Most of the time I can remember that this child, the third born, Tommy does not have a picture of his father and the last born has no idea at all and they always ask how he was and what he will be doing at this time. Tomani, the last born is a child who always wants attention, always wants to be hugged, and even if he's playing with the other children and talking about the others who always say that their fathers are coming at a certain time, you'll find that when he comes back he doesn't know what to say about his father. As a mother I always have to [try] to play the roles of both parents but I'll be really glad if I can know what happened so that my children can get an explanation from me, so that I can say it is so and so and so and so. This will probably make me understand. I do not know the reason for their cruelty, but I just want to know and my family will also be happy to know who really cut short the life of my husband. Not to say that when they are old I'm just teaching them to retaliate or to be revengeful, it's just to know who's done this and who changed our lives so drastically.

Amnesty or Impunity?

Mahmood Mamdani

The Truth and Reconciliation Commission (TRC) was most effective in bringing to light the activities of the South African security state, including the torture and assassination of political activists, as well as abuses by activists committed against community members. In this selection, Mahmood Mamdani (an African political scientist based in the United States) argues that the price of this focus on individual acts was a failure to understand apartheid as a systematic denial of rights to communities on the basis of race. As a result, the commission missed the larger truths of apartheid, especially the absence of a regime of law and rights in the rural areas where a large percentage of South Africa's people continues to reside. Mamdani does not address the practical issues that led to the formation of the TRC. For instance, Justice Albie Sachs has argued that the African National Congress needed to provide a path to amnesty for members of the security forces in order to ensure that those forces would not interfere with the elections in 1994. And one might wonder how one commission could address the entire history of apartheid. Mamdani alerts us to the narrowness of the TRC's approach, however, and calls our attention to the ongoing nondemocratic forms of rule through chiefs in the former homelands.

The TRC claimed to be different from its predecessors, whether in Latin America or Eastern Europe. It would practice neither impunity nor vengeance. It was therefore determined to avoid two pitfalls: on the one hand, reconciliation becoming an unprincipled embrace of political evil and, on the other hand, a pursuit of justice so relentless as to turn into revenge. To do so, the Commission was determined to address both "victims" and "perpetrators," not just one or the other.

This double determination was first written into the interim constitution that paved the way for the legislation that set up the TRC. First, there would be no blanket amnesty. Amnesty would be conditional. It would not be a group amnesty. Every perpetrator would have to be identified individually, and would have to own up to his or her guilt—the truth—before receiving amnesty from legal prosecution. Second, any victim who is so acknowledged would give up the right to prosecute perpetrators in courts of law.

Justice for the victim would thus not be criminal but restorative: acknowl-edgment would be followed by reparations. In sum, individual amnesty for the perpetrator, truth for the society, and acknowledgment and reparations for the victim—this was the pact built into the legislation that set up the TRC.

Since the Act did not clearly define "victim," however, the definition of "perpetrator" was unclear as well. The task of defining "victim" and "per-petrator" was left to the Commission and was the single most important decision that determined the scope and depth of the Commission's work. Without a comprehensive acknowledgment of victims of apartheid, there would be only a limited identification of perpetrators and only a partial understanding of the legal regime that made possible the "crime against humanity." . . .

The TRC individualized the victims of apartheid. Though it acknowl-edged apartheid as a "crime against humanity" which targeted entire com-munities for ethnic and racial policing and cleansing, the Commission majority was reluctant to go beyond the formal acknowledgment. The Com-mission's analysis reduced apartheid from a relationship between the state and entire communities to one between the state and individuals. Where entire communities were victims of gross violations of rights, the Commis-sion acknowledged only individual victims. If the "crime against humanity" involved a targeting of entire communities for racial and ethnic cleansing and policing, individualizing the victim obliterated this particular—many would argue central—characteristic of apartheid. Limiting the definition of harm and remedy to individuals center-staged political activists as victims of apartheid, as indeed happened with the victim hearings. The consequence was to narrow the TRC perspective to a political reconciliation between state agents and political activists, individual members of a fractured politi-cal elite, rather than the "national unity and reconciliation" mandated by the legislation that set it up. To pursue its actual mandate, the TRC needed to broaden its perspective: to work for a social reconciliation between per-petrators and victims required that the relationship between the state and the entire South African people be addressed.

Second, by focusing on individuals and obscuring the victimization of communities, the TRC was unable to highlight the bifurcated nature of apartheid as a form of power that governed natives differently from non-natives. If the apartheid state spoke the language of rights to the white population, it disaggregated the native population into tribal groups—each to be administered under a separate set of laws—in the name of enforcing custom. Rights and custom were two different and contradictory languages: the former claimed to circumscribe power, the latter to enable it. Whereas the former claimed to be a rule of law, the latter claimed the legitimacy of custom and tradition. The TRC's failure lay in focusing exclusively on the "civil" regime and in totally ignoring the "customary" regime. No wonder, then, that it failed even to recommend reforms that would put in place a single unitary regime—rule of law understood as formal equality before the law—for all South Africans in a postapartheid South Africa.

Finally, the TRC extended impunity to most perpetrators of apartheid. In the absence of a full acknowledgment of victims of apartheid, there could not be a complete identification of its perpetrators. To the extent that the TRC did not acknowledge the full truth, the amnesty intended to be individual turned into a group amnesty. For any perpetrator who was not so identified was a perpetrator who enjoyed impunity. . . .

From the outset, there was a strong tendency in the TRC not only to *dehistoricize* and *decontextualize* the story of apartheid but also to individualize the wrongs done by apartheid. Wynand Malan's minority report blamed this tendency on the religious messianism of the leadership in the Commission. This religious mode of thought received powerful international support from secular quarters. If the religious discourse was located in the churches that provided the leadership of the TRC, a parallel secular discourse was characteristic of the human rights community that provided the bulk of the technical assistance for the TRC, both as preparatory support before its constitution and as research and organizational support during its operation.

If the leadership of the TRC was eager to make the story of apartheid—especially the lessons of reconciliation—universally available, its ambitions were easy to reconcile with equally universalist aspirations of those in the human rights community who looked forward to framing the problem of apartheid as one of a violation of individual rights, albeit on a wide scale. Both shared the tendency to dehistoricize and decontextualize social processes, and to individualize their outcomes. For this reason, the confluence of two modes of thought—one religious, the other secular—around the project of the TRC should be of more than just historical interest. It is also of theoretical interest.

The Commission's Report did not just downplay apartheid, the "crime against humanity." It also showed little understanding of the legal machinery through which this crime against humanity was perpetrated in the guise of a rule of law. The Commission's limitations were reflected not only in its prognosis of the past, the story of apartheid, but also in its prescriptions of the—particularly legal—reform that is needed to dismantle the institutional legacy of apartheid in the legal domain.

Repeal the Black Authorities Act

Rural People's Movement

A central challenge of South Africa's new postapartheid government centered on the reincorporation of the former homelands (Bantustans) created during the apartheid era. In 2010 the government repealed the Bantu (later Black) Authorities Act of 1951 that established the administrative structure of local, regional, and territorial authorities of tribes and that resulted in the forced removal of millions of people from urban areas and white farms to the homelands. During the negotiations for a new constitution, however, traditional authorities represented in the Congress of Traditional Leaders of South Africa lobbied for their recognition within a new South Africa. The passage of legislation such as the Traditional Leadership and Governance Framework Act of 2003 ensured their continued power in the former homelands. Remarkably, chiefs are more powerful today than at the height of apartheid, which raises questions about the success of democratization and which leads to the emergence of groups such as the Rural Peoples Movement that have highlighted the legacy of apartheid, rising corruption, and the terrific inequalities faced by citizens living in the former homelands.

I am Nomonde Mbelekane. I am the President of the Rural People's Movement (RPM). I stay at the Ndlambe village, not far from the Great Fish River, under the Ngqushwa Municipality in the Eastern Cape. As I come to speak I am a bit relieved. I say so because between March and June this year, I had received death threats from those who did not like the work we do as RPM. At the time, we were busy raising the awareness to communities in Ngqushwa about the traditional council elections. I am now relieved because finally the Independent Complaints Directorate was able to investigate and address the failures of the police in properly investigating the death threats against me. I now feel I can come to parliament safely without any such problems.

In the last 2 weeks, we as the RPM went village by village to seek the opinions of our members, supporters and the broad community about the repeal of the Black Authorities Act (BAA). We went to the villages of Nobumba, Ndlambe, Pikoli, Ndwayana, Prudhoe and Mgababa. People were shocked that this law was still existing. They thought that we lived in a new South Africa. When we told them that this Act introduced tribal authorities they remembered all the pains they suffered under tribal authorities. They then asked us whether the repeal of this law will also mean the removal of the chiefs who are now coming back to rule them. We said that yes the BAA will go but the chiefs will remain. They were unhappy about this. They gave us one clear and loud voice: . . . The BAA has undermined the dignity of black people in South Africa. It caused so much sufferings. This law damaged the authority of chiefs. It changed them from being representatives of the people to collaborators with apartheid. They served the apartheid boss and not the people.

As the RPM, we see the Black Authorities Act as the mother of tribal authorities in rural areas. We also see it as something that gave powers to chiefs and put us under boundaries that made things difficult for us. This law led to the following:

a) The putting together of people under one chief even if that was not the case before;
b) Payments of levies and dues to chiefs by those under their rule;
c) The establishment of apartheid homelands;
d) Division and disunity amongst people even those who were related to each other[.]

We do not see the BAA as different from the new laws that do the same. These new laws are tripling the negative effects of controlling human lives in many different ways. Tribal leaders have been given more powers than they had under the BAA.

In particular, we are very angry about the Traditional Leadership and Governance Framework Act. This new Act gives tribal authority a new life. This is not what we fought for. We thought that we were free when Cyril Ramaphosa [as secretary-general of the African National Congress] came to Peddie in 1991 to dissolve all headman. We are now very surprised that our struggle has come to nothing, thanks to the Framework Act. We did not even get a chance to hear about this Framework Act. Why was it passed? Our views were not asked for. We see it with many problems and disadvantages for us. We see it as giving chiefs the same advantages as the BAA.

Chiefs believe that the land is theirs to own and control. Anyone who wants a site or a field has to go to the chief for an allocation.

We are now faced by traditional councils who also handle cases in Peddie. The Magistrate's Court in Peddie no longer takes cases from rural areas.

The Magistrate tells people to go back to get their cases discussed by their local chief. The Magistrate wants a letter from the chief first before they can take a case from people of rural Peddie. But this is not done for those who stay in the Peddie town or people from Peddie who stay in Grahamstown and King William's Town. Some of the chiefs in Peddie have said that women are unpure, dirty and involved in witchcraft. In Prudhoe village, an 8-months pregnant woman was called to the Dabi tribal court. She had tried to claim damages from the man who made her pregnant. The tribal court asked her to say who the man was. The court decided that she was just accusing the man and dirtying his name. The court said that the man's father is rich and important, he cannot just have his family name pulled through mud. She was then sentenced to corporal punishment.

This makes many women feel as it they do not have rights. In Pikoli village, no one can apply for a child support grant without the letter from the chief. We see this as wrong. These things make chiefs not to be wanted by the people. We do not understand why government has given them these powers. . . .

These traditional councils in Ngqushwa will face the same problems as the old tribal authorities. People do not want them. People will not work with them. We fear that if the chiefs insist with these traditional councils then there will be more problems. We therefore ask parliament to help keep peace in the Ngqushwa villages. Please come and do what Cyril Ramaphosa did: remove these unpopular tribal authorities.

a) We ask parliament and government to tell whether the Framework Act and Traditional Courts Bill are not children of the BAA. What does the constitution say about these new laws?

b) We ask government to ensure that the rights of rural people do not suffer.

c) As women, we do not really like chiefs that much. We voted for a democracy of the people by the people. We did not vote for individuals. We did not vote for apartheid.

d) We ask Minister Noluthando Mayende-Sibiya [of Women, Youth, Children, and People with Disabilities] to be clear about her role. We suffer as rural women. We suffer under the chiefs. We ask for her to hear our voices.

e) We see chiefs as filling their own stomachs.

f) We prefer municipalities. We see abuse only from chiefs. We do not want the government of the chiefs in rural areas.

g) What will now be the role of municipalities and ward councilors? Is government giving with the one hand and taking with the other? Is government removing the BAA whilst also keeping its tribal authorities in place?

h) We ask for a chance for our views to be heard. If not, it is going to be difficult for us to vote [for the African National Congress] again in the future.

The Myth of Timeless Africa
in the Game Parks

Shirley Brooks

Each year hundreds of thousands of middle- and upper-middle-class South Africans and foreign tourists enjoy the opportunity to visit the country's spacious and beautiful game parks and reserves. Most famous of these is the Kruger National Park, which covers a vast tract on the country's east side, bordering Mozambique. Here tourists can enjoy world-class amenities while looking for the "big five" (elephants, rhinos, buffalo, lions, and leopards) and other wildlife managed by renowned conservationists. This seemingly untouched natural world belies a more complicated past. In the 1970s the apartheid regime erected an electric fence on that border to prevent infiltration of guerrilla fighters; it was later an obstacle for undocumented immigrants. Though the fence has since fallen into disrepair, the government is now discussing reestablishing a ninety-mile section to combat poaching.

As Shirley Brooks argues in this selection, the tourism industry and Hollywood imagery lead visitors to see these spaces as somehow outside of historical time, rather than being part of a country with a long, complex, and conflicted past. Rural Africans who live near the parks, by contrast, bring their own understandings of these spaces as important sites of precolonial events and, more recently, as zones from which they have been forcibly excluded. Brooks's discussion can be generalized, but it draws particularly on the Hluhluwe-Umfolozi Game Reserve in KwaZulu-Natal, established in 1895, making it Africa's oldest game reserve.

Like other "natural spaces," the Hluhluwe-Umfolozi game reserve is often presented as being outside of time. Indeed, one could argue that the reserve is nestled in layers of timelessness, rather like the Russian doll that is opened to reveal yet another figurine inside each wooden shell.

First, Africa as a continent is commonly presented, in a reprisal of a familiar colonial trope, as a place without a history (other than perhaps that conferred upon it by the imperial encounter). Words that recur frequently in the ecotourism and safari marketing literature on East Africa—and increasingly in South Africa—are "primeval" or "primordial." Wild animals are essential to this presentation of Africa. . . .

This make-believe world of Disney Africa has featured in numerous films, the most recent of which is a Hollywood production recently released on circuit of Kuki Gallman's book *I Dreamed of Africa* (1992). The film stars the American actress Kim Basinger. While the book is set in Kenya, the movie was actually shot in the Hluhluwe-Umfolozi reserve. For purposes of the film, the park was recreated as the heterotopic space of the African game reserve. It was made to stand in for a generic East African savannah landscape, while providing a more accessible and possibly less costly venue for filming. . . .

In the case of the Hluhluwe-Umfolozi park, the marketing of the game reserve must be located within the overall marketing strategy of the KwaZulu-Natal region. Significantly, the recently launched KwaZulu-Natal tourism marketing initiative is called "Timeless Afrika"—the "k" presumably being used in preference to a "c" in Africa, in order to further exoticise the destination. The theme of timelessness, or being outside of time, has now been adopted as the official marketing strategy for KwaZulu-Natal.

A second element in the creation of a space outside of time, supplementary to "timeless Africa," is "timeless Zululand." This is a well-worn notion that long predates the launching of any marketing initiatives for the KwaZulu-Natal region as a whole. It is present, for example, in popular writing on the history of the Anglo-Zulu war. The message that Zululand was a space "outside of time" prior to the British invasion of 1879 may be conveyed quite subtly, as for example in the captions accompanying old photographs. . . .

In addition to wild animals, "timeless Zululand" is predicated on the persistence of an unchanging Zulu culture. At the tourist attraction of Shakaland, for example, one can expect, according to the tourist brochure, to "experience the essence of Africa, pulsating tribal rhythms, assegaai [spear] wielding warriors and the mysterious rituals of the Sangoma [diviner] interpreting messages from the Spirits."[1] Another brochure, produced by the Uthungulu and Zululand Regional Councils, combines a romanticised imperial history, a static and somehow magical Zulu culture, together with the spaces of conservation and nature:

> This land has witnessed one of the greatest challenges to the supremacy of the once mighty British Empire during the tragic but heroic days of the Anglo-Zulu War. It is also steeped in the fascinating culture of the people who call it home. Rich in symbolism and tradition, here the

heartbeat of Africa throbs with an almost mystic vitality. Zululand is also home to an astonishing variety of wild game. The many game reserves, parks and farms in the region are dedicated to the conservation and heritage of wildlife preservation.

Thirdly, the Umfolozi-Hluhluwe game reserve itself is often experienced as a space outside of time. The reserve is approached by most tourists as a place of pristine nature or wilderness in which one is effectively removed from history and society. This is particularly striking in the Wilderness Area of Umfolozi, a large section of the park (25,000 hectares) in which no development is allowed and to which the only access is on foot. The Wilderness Area was set aside in the 1950s on the initiative of former game ranger and well-known conservationist, Ian Player.

Player is a sophisticated writer whose constructions of Zululand and the game reserves are far more complex than the one-dimensional tourist marketing images discussed above. The Zululand reserves are intricately linked to Player's own personal history and he has written frankly about the politics of land dispossession involved in their maintenance. Nonetheless, Player has contributed both through his books and through the creation of the Wilderness Leadership School, to the linking of the Umfolozi reserve, in particular, with representations of a primeval Zululand wilderness.

Player's writing is infused with nostalgia. In an interview broadcast on South African public radio, Player's latest book, *Zululand Wilderness, Shadow and Soul* (1997), was described by the interviewer, John Richards, as follows: "It's an account of a remarkable inner journey, a pilgrimage, a friendship, against the background of the animals, the birds, the insects, the ancient wilderness of Africa."[2] The friendship to which Richards was referring is Player's relationship with a Zulu man, Magqubu Ntombela, who worked all his life as a game guard in the Zululand game reserves. . . .

[As Player remarked]:

> Well, I think it was an archetypal home for *mankind*. I mean, early man had been there, and the bushmen had been there. There are still remnants of bushman paintings. And one—when you walk on that landscape, you know that you are walking inside a very ancient part of yourself. But you need midwives—you need midwives to enable you to understand it. And that's where old Magqubu was so wonderful.

Player's [characterization] reveals his understanding of a sacred space of nature, outside the normal rules of time and social history. This space must be interpreted to outsiders by people who are "close to nature"—a construction of "the native" that Jane Jacobs has usefully discussed with respect to ecotourist presentations of the Aboriginal presence in Australia. What is being invoked here is, in Jacobs' words, a "general and variably expressed modern desire to (re)turn to Nature by way of indigenous cultures, to see indigenous peoples as the First Conservationists."[3]

Thus the transformation during his lifetime of the Zulu game guard, Magqubu Ntombela, into an ecological guru, the man whose sacred task it was to interpret the timeless wilderness of the Umfolozi game reserve for spiritually impoverished westerners, is part of a much wider—indeed global—process. The sacred space of the wilderness can be understood fully only by the native; but others, if they have the patience, may access it through his agency.

The notion that the Umfolozi-Hluhluwe game reserve falls outside of time, is not the only possible reconstruction of its past. Another and equally fascinating representation, one which emphasises a glorious history rather than the primeval or timeless character of the reserve, is woven around the nineteenth-century history of the area and in particular around the early nineteenth-century Zulu king Shaka.

Shaka remains a figure of fascination for western tourists and is still significant in the contemporary politics of the region. . . . The mythic status of Shaka and associated celebration of Zulu masculinity are central to the construction of a romanticised history of the Zululand game reserves. This history emphasises the stereotypically masculine activities of fighting and hunting. In particular, it claims the space of the reserves (especially the Umfolozi game reserve) in two ways. Umfolozi, according to popular histories of the reserve, was the site of past Zulu victories in battle, and it was also the royal hunting ground of King Shaka. These constructions resonate powerfully with a number of constituencies: not only tourists, but also local Zulu men, some of whom have served as game guards in the reserves, and white game rangers. . . .

For the tourist constituency, the comfortably remote history of an African monarchy, long since rendered unthreatening by the (now forgotten) violence of colonialism and capitalist transition, has irresistible romantic appeal. Game or nature reserves are the perfect places in which to digest this romantic past: the glories of Zulu history are much more easily imagined and assimilated by tourists in landscapes from which actual Zulu people have been removed, than they would be in the poverty-stricken tribal areas surrounding the reserves. Connections to the old Zulu monarch add mystique. . . .

In contrast to this rather superficial exposure, local Zulu men, operating within an oral history-telling tradition, also see the stories of past battles and hunts as important reminders of a glorious and now unattainable past. It is important to stress, therefore, that the stories . . . do not constitute an entirely "invented tradition," manufactured for the benefit of tourists (although this history is no doubt an embroidered one made up of stories that have now attained the status of legends in the region). The point is that local Zulu men have played a formative role in shaping the tourist narrative of the game reserves, and this history is important because it celebrates, for them, the pre-conquest past and their lost independence.

For white men too, this history has a deep resonance. Many of the men who, like Ian Player, spent their formative years as game rangers in the Umfolozi game reserve in particular, became deeply fascinated by the Zulu history taught to them by game guards like Magqubu Ntombela, Player's mentor. Magqubu's connections with the Zulu royal house uniquely qualified him to act as Player's guide to the sacred space of reserve. Player explains:

> Maklwana Ntombela was Magqubu's father. He was son of Nkovana, son of Bidankomo, son of Ngogo, who was an *induna* [advisor] of King Senzangakhona, an early Zulu king. Then he served Shaka and could imitate the way Shaka spoke. He passed this on to Magqubu. Magqubu would spend hours telling me his lineage and that of Zulu kings, his *indunas* and their praise names. Shaka was a hero of Magqubu's, and we were to walk for over thirty years together in Shaka's footsteps across the Zululand hills.[4]

The construction of white and black masculinities in the reserves is an important theme that deserves more attention than can be given here. The young white rangers who sat, metaphorically, at the feet of the older Zulu game guards and listened to stories about battles, or about hunting, responded positively to the tales of young Zulu warriors proving their masculinity. Their books are full of admiration for the physical strength and prowess of Zulu men. Versions like Player's have grown out of the interaction, over many years, between black men and white men *in place*, and it would be difficult to decide for whom, the white men or the black, the past is recreated with greater nostalgia. . . .

In these presentations of the Hluhluwe-Umfolozi reserve, other, less palatable histories are suppressed. These include, for example, large-scale slaughter of animals by the authorities during the anti-nagana [trypanomiasis] campaigns of the 1930s and 1940s; the removal of communities from the Corridor area between the two reserves, also in the 1940s; and a bitter history of conflict over land, particularly in the western section of the Um-folozi game reserve. The nostalgic journey tourists are asked to take when visiting the Hluhluwe-Umfolozi park is to the world of a century and a half ago. This is easy in a space where history has apparently been frozen, where nothing seems to have changed.

But preservationist discourses of nature are continually disrupted by those who remain outside them. In the twentieth-century history of the re-serves these constituencies have included local African people, white farm-ers and developers. In the post-apartheid climate, where land reform has gained new priority, some game reserves in the province are subject to land claims. These spaces are under threat and the nostalgic presentation of a pristine space of nature and / or romantic history is being challenged.

Yet the power of international ecotourism and conservation discourse—linked, of course, to a commoditised nature—remains immense. The "King-dom of the Zulu" is being marketed under the rubric of "Timeless Afrika." The Hluhluwe-Umfolozi game reserve, with its luxury camp Hilltop, is a conservation and tourism showpiece for the province and it seems unlikely that this major game reserve will be used for any form of land restitution or redistribution. Given this context, ways must be found to offer tourists and others more complex and inclusive interpretations of the history and landscape of the game reserves.

Notes

1. "Zululand Map," non-dated tourist brochure published by Azalea Promotions and avail-able in 1999 from Timeless Afrika, first floor, Tourist Junction, Old Station Building, Dur-ban.
2. Interview with Ian Player, "Total Exposure," South African FM Radio, broadcast January 1998.
3. J. Jacobs, *Edge of Empire: Postcolonialism and the City* (London: Routledge, 1996), 136.
4. I. Player, *Zululand Wilderness: Shadow and Soul* (Cape Town: David Philip, 1997), 128.

AIDS and Poverty

Thabo Mbeki

One of the most immense problems facing postapartheid South Africa is HIV/ AIDS. In recent years, epidemiologists have identified South Africa as the country with the highest number of infections—nearly six million—and one of the highest infection rates in the world. In the last years of apartheid and in the early years under democracy, when infection rates were small but growing, the South African government did little to prevent the spread of the disease. By the time Thabo Mbeki became president in 1999, it was clear that the country faced a serious public-health crisis that was likely to result in large numbers of deaths. Soon after coming to power, however, Mbeki threw the government's response even further off course as he latched on to the writings of Western scientists who dissented from the well-accepted theory that HIV infection is the cause of AIDS. He observed that Westerners tended to blame the AIDS crisis on African hypersexuality and understate the role that poverty played in public health. As a result of his denialism, the government was passive in its public-health efforts and hostile to mainstream science on AIDS in the face of an exponential rise in the number of infections and deaths, leaving many thousands of AIDS orphans across the country.

In July 2000 the annual International AIDS Conference for scientists and activists took place in Durban, South Africa. Mbeki addressed the conference to explain his views, arguing that the underlying cause of AIDS and other diseases in Africa was not HIV but poverty. While the impact of poverty on public health is clear, Mbeki's speech, excerpted here, downplayed and even denied the government's inadequate response to the AIDS crisis in terms of prevention and treatment.

Let me tell you a story that the World Health Organisation told the world in 1995. I will tell this story in the words used by the World Health Organisation [WHO].

. . .

The world's biggest killer and the greatest cause of ill-health and suffering across the globe is listed almost at the end of the International Classification of Diseases. It is given the code z59.5—extreme poverty.

Poverty is the main reason why babies are not vaccinated, why clean water and sanitation are not provided, why curative drugs and other treatments are unavailable and why mothers die in childbirth. It is the underlying cause of reduced life expectancy, handicap, disability and starvation. Poverty is a major contributor to mental illness, stress, suicide, family disintegration and substance abuse. Every year in the developing world 12.2 million children under 5 years die, most of them from causes which could be prevented for just a few US cents per child. They die largely because of world indifference, but most of all they die because they are poor . . .

Beneath the heartening facts about decreased mortality and increasing life expectancy, and many other undoubted health advances, lie unacceptable disparities in wealth. The gaps between rich and poor, between one population group and another, between ages and between sexes, are widening. For most people in the world today every step of life, from infancy to old age, is taken under the twin shadows of poverty and inequity, and under the double burden of suffering and disease.

For many, the prospect of longer life may seem more like a punishment than a gift. Yet by the end of the century we could be living in a world without poliomyelitis, a world without new cases of leprosy, a world without deaths from neonatal tetanus and measles. But today the money that some developing countries have to spend per person on health care over an entire year is just US $4—less than the amount of small change carried in the pockets and purses of many people in the developed countries.

A person in one of the least developed countries in the world has a life expectancy of 43 years according to 1993 calculations. A person in one of the most developed countries has a life expectancy of 78—a difference of more than a third of a century. This means a rich, healthy man can live twice as long as a poor, sick man.

That inequity alone should stir the conscience of the world—but in some of the poorest countries the life expectancy picture is getting worse. In five countries life expectancy at birth is expected to decrease by the year 2000, whereas everywhere else it is increasing. In the richest countries life expectancy in the year 2000 will reach 79 years. In some of the poorest it will go backwards to 42 years. Thus the gap continues to widen between rich and poor, and by the year 2000 at least 45 countries are expected to have a life expectancy at birth of under 60 years.

In the space of a day passengers flying from Japan to Uganda leave the country with the world's highest life expectancy—almost 79 years—

and land in one with the world's lowest—barely 42 years. A day away by plane, but half a lifetime's difference on the ground. A flight between France and Cote d'Ivoire takes only a few hours, but it spans almost 26 years of life expectancy. A short air trip between Florida in the USA and Haiti represents a life expectancy gap of over 19 years . . .

HIV and AIDS are having a devastating effect on young people. In many countries in the developing world, up to two-thirds of all new infections are among people aged 15–24. Overall it is estimated that half the global HIV infections have been in people under 25 years—with 60% of infections of females occurring by the age of 20. Thus the hopes and lives of a generation, the breadwinners, providers and parents of the future, are in jeopardy. Many of the most talented and industrious citizens, who could build a better world and shape the destinies of the countries they live in, face tragically early death as a result of HIV infection. [World Health Organization, "Executive Summary," The World Health Report 1995, available at http://www.who.int/whr/1995/media_centre /executive_summary1/en/index.html]

This is part of the story that the World Health Organisation told in its World Health Report in 1995. Five years later, the essential elements of this story have not changed. In some cases, the situation will have become worse.

. . . Because of your heavy programme and the limited time you will spend with us, what you will see of this city, and therefore of our country, is the more developed world of which the WHO spoke when it told the story of world health in 1995.

You will not see the South African and African world of the poverty of which the WHO spoke, in which AIDS thrives—a partner with poverty, suffering, social disadvantage and inequity.

As an African, speaking at a Conference such as this, convened to discuss a grave human problem such as the acquired human deficiency [sic] syndrome, I believe that we should speak to one another honestly and frankly, with sufficient tolerance to respect everybody's point of view, with sufficient tolerance to allow all voices to be heard.

Had we, as a people, turned our backs on these basic civilised precepts, we would never have achieved the much-acclaimed South African miracle of which all humanity is justly proud.

Some in our common world consider the questions I and the rest of our government have raised around the HIV-AIDS issue, the subject of the Conference you are attending, as akin to grave criminal and genocidal misconduct.

What I hear being said repeatedly, stridently, angrily, is—do not ask any questions!

The particular twists of South African history and the will of the great majority of our people, freely expressed, have placed me in the situation in which I carry the title of President of the Republic of South Africa.

As I sat in this position, I listened attentively to the story that was told by the World Health Organisation.

What I heard as that story was told, was that extreme poverty is the world's biggest killer and the greatest cause of ill health and suffering across the globe.

As I listened longer, I heard stories being told about malaria, tuberculosis, hepatitis B, HIV-AIDS and other diseases.

I heard also about micro-nutrient malnutrition, iodine and vitamin A deficiency. I heard of syphilis, gonorrhoea, genital herpes and other sexually transmitted diseases as well as teenage pregnancies.

I also heard of cholera, respiratory infections, anaemia, bilharzia, river blindness, guinea worms and other illnesses with complicated Latin names.

As I listened even longer to this tale of human woe, I heard the name recur with frightening frequency—Africa, Africa, Africa!

And so, in the end, I came to the conclusion that as Africans we are confronted by a health crisis of enormous proportions.

One of the consequences of this crisis is the deeply disturbing phenomenon of the collapse of immune systems among millions of our people, such that their bodies have no natural defence against attack by many viruses and bacteria.

Clearly, if we, as African countries, had the level of development to enable us to gather accurate statistics about our own countries, our morbidity and mortality figures would tell a story that would truly be too frightening to contemplate.

As I listened and heard the whole story told about our own country, it seemed to me that we could not blame everything on a single virus.

It seemed to me also that every living African, whether in good or ill health, is prey to many enemies of health that would interact one upon the other in many ways, within one human body.

And thus I came to conclude that we have a desperate and pressing need to wage a war on all fronts to guarantee and realise the human right of all our people to good health.

And so, being insufficiently educated, and therefore ill prepared to answer this question, I started to ask the question, expecting an answer from others—what is to be done, particularly about HIV-AIDS!

One of the questions I have asked is—are safe sex, condoms and anti-retroviral drugs a sufficient response to the health catastrophe we face!

I am pleased to inform you that some eminent scientists decided to respond to our humble request to use their expertise to provide us with answers to certain questions.

Some of these have specialised on the issue of HIV-AIDS for many years and differed bitterly among themselves about various matters. Yet, they graciously agreed to join together to help us find answers to some outstanding questions.

I thank them most sincerely for their positive response, inspired by a common resolve more effectively to confront the AIDS epidemic.

They have agreed to report back by the end of this year having worked together, among other things, on the reliability of and the information communicated by our current HIV tests and the improvement of our disease surveillance system.

We look forward to the results of this important work, which will help us to ensure that we achieve better results in terms of saving the lives of our people and improving the lives of millions.

In the meantime, we will continue to intensify our own campaign against AIDS, including:

- a sustained public awareness campaign encouraging safe sex and the use of condoms;
- a better focused programme targeted at the reduction and elimination of poverty and the improvement of the nutritional standards of our people;
- a concerted fight against the so-called opportunistic diseases, including TB and all sexually transmitted diseases;
- a humane response to people living with HIV and AIDS as well as the orphans in our society;
- contributing to the international effort to develop an AIDS vaccine; and,
- further research on anti-retroviral drugs.

You will find all of this in our country's AIDS action plan which I hope has been or will be distributed among you.

You will see from that plan, together with the work that has been going on, that there is no substance to the allegation that there is any hesitation on the part of our government to confront the challenge of HIV-AIDS.

However, we remain convinced of the need for us better to understand the essence of what would constitute a comprehensive response in a context such as ours which is characterised by the high levels of poverty and disease to which I have referred.

As I visit the areas of this city and country that most of you will not see because of your heavy programme and your time limitations, areas that are representative of the conditions of life of the overwhelming majority of the people of our common world, the story told by the World Health Organisation always forces itself back into my consciousness.

The world's biggest killer and the greatest cause of ill health and suffering across the globe, including South Africa, is extreme poverty.

Is there more that all of us should do together, assuming that in a world driven by a value system based on financial profit and individual material reward, the notion of human solidarity remains a valid precept governing human behaviour!

Global Day of Action

Treatment Action Campaign

As a result of President Thabo Mbeki's denial of the link between HIV and AIDS, the government's efforts toward prevention and treatment were grossly inadequate to the scale of the crisis. At the low point of the government's embrace of this position, the health minister Manto Tshabalala-Msimang suggested remedies such as beetroot and garlic as alternatives to antiretroviral (ARV) drugs, and the government was extremely slow to make ARVs available.

In 1998 activists formed the Treatment Action Campaign to pressure the government to do more to combat the epidemic and treat its victims. The organization was one of the most vocal in challenging Mbeki's inaction. Little changed, however, until Mbeki was forced out over other matters in 2008. Jacob Zuma, who became president in 2009, infamously claimed in his rape trial in 2006 that he had protected himself from HIV infection by showering after having sex with an HIV-positive woman. Nevertheless, his administration has radically changed course on HIV/AIDS and is making much greater efforts for prevention and treatment. The epidemic remains one of the country's most challenging problems. The following is a leaflet issued by the Treatment Action Campaign in 2006 to advocate for the Global Day of Action on HIV/AIDS.

+ STOP 1000 NEW HIV INFECTIONS DAILY
+ STOP 800 HIV DEATHS DAILY IN SOUTH AFRICA!
+ BUILD A GLOBAL UNITED FRONT FOR HIV PREVENTION AND TREATMENT

The Treatment Action Campaign (TAC) demands that President Mbeki and Deputy President Mlambo-Ngcuka:

1. CONVENE A NATIONAL MEETING AND PLAN FOR THE HIV/AIDS CRISIS NOW

    South Africa needs a new plan to deal with HIV/AIDS. Infection, illness, death, denialism and lack of leadership must be overcome. We need a meeting with everyone—community organisations, business, trade unions, faith-based organisations and health professionals, as long as they do not believe in AIDS denialism. It should put an end to the arguments that we have in South Africa over HIV/AIDS—we should be united!

2. END DEATHS IN PRISONS—PROVIDE TREATMENT, NUTRITION AND PREVENTION!

People in prison (inmates) who are sick must be treated as soon as possible. The longer we wait, the more will die. We also need a long term plan for all prisons. TAC and the AIDS Law Project are willing to help. We will keep pressurising the government in the courts and streets, because people are dying now.

3. DISMISS HEALTH MINISTER MANTO TSHABALALA-MSIMANG

In her actions on HIV/AIDS Manto has ignored the constitution. President Mbeki has a duty to fire her and the director-general Thami Mseleku. Because of her denial and incompetence, we have—

- The highest number of women who die giving birth in our recent history
- The highest number of infants and children who die mainly because of HIV
- Higher numbers of TB infections and deaths than under apartheid
- Confused, delayed and undermined the ARV roll out

4. RESPECT THE RULE OF LAW AND THE CONSTITUTION

Government must respect the rule of law. They must obey the courts and provide prisoners with ARVs. The Constitution says everyone has a right to life and health.

5. HEALTH FOR ALL—END HEALTH APARTHEID, BUILD A PEOPLE'S HEALTH SERVICE

We need to work together to ensure that everyone can be healthy. Communities and business need to work under government leadership. We must end health inequalities. We say again that we will work as hard as we can, with government, to do this.

HIV/AIDS is not under control! Every day, 1000 people in South Africa get HIV. HIV prevention in South Africa is failing. If people who are HIV positive do not get ARV medicines they get AIDS and die. Most people in South Africa know people who have died of AIDS. **More than 800 people in South Africa die of AIDS every day**.

We have known about ARVs for more than ten years. In many countries across the world, governments have given ARVs to their people and deaths from HIV have quickly fallen. This has not yet happened in South Africa because of the slow and confused roll-out.

Manto Tshabalala-Msimang became Health Minister in 1999. Since 1999, deaths have increased dramatically. The biggest increases are in women, children and young adults. . . .

WE NEED A HEALTH MINISTER—NOT CONFUSION.

Manto Tshabalala-Msimang is confusing the people. She makes people think that vegetables can be used to treat HIV instead of ARVs. She has said ARVs are poisons, but we know that thousands of people in the world are alive now because they are taking these medicines. Scientists and people with HIV all over the world agree that ARVs work!

GOVERNMENT BREAKS THE LAW—PEOPLE ARE DYING.

"Everyone who is detained, including every sentenced prisoner, has the right to conditions of detention that are consistent with human dignity, including at least, exercise and the provision at state expense of adequate accommodation, nutrition, reading materials and medical treatment." *South African Constitution*

The government does not look after sick people in prison. The Judicial Inspector of Prisons is a judge who is meant to look after inmates. His report shows that **five times more inmates die now than died in 1995**. Most of the prisoners do not die in fights or in accidents. They die of diseases caused by HIV. Nearly 1 in 10 of these deaths were in Westville Prison in Durban where 2 prisoners die of AIDS every week.

Thousands of people in prison have HIV. Many need ARVs now. Last year TAC and 15 inmates in Westville Prison protested to government. In April this year they took the government to court because there were still no ARVs. . . .

GOVERNMENT MUST ACT TO END 1000 NEW HIV INFECTIONS DAILY. END 800 HIV DEATHS DAILY IN SOUTH AFRICA!

On Thursday 24th August, TAC has called for a Global Day of Action. We have tried talking with the government. We have tried the courts. We cannot wait. We are beginning a global campaign of protest action. Some people may be arrested. Everyone must protest in peaceful demonstrations always.

Zuma's Rape Trial

Steven Robins

In late 2005, only a few months after being forced to resign as deputy president over corruption charges, Jacob Zuma was charged with rape. The complainant was a family friend who had spent the night at Zuma's house. The trial resulted in Zuma's acquittal. The case exposed sharp social and political fissures over the country's epidemics of rape and AIDS, as well as patriarchy, ethnicity and race, and Zuma's political future. (He became president in 2009, just after having corruption charges thrown out due to procedural deficiencies.) The complainant was HIV-positive, and Zuma, who argued that their sex was consensual, said that he had taken a shower afterward to protect himself from infection. He and his supporters also offered the classically sexist rape defense that the complainant seduced him through her manner of dress and added an ethnic twist that as a Zulu man he was honor bound to satisfy a woman who wanted sex. At the same time, some of the criticisms of Zuma were thinly veiled appeals to the idea that Africans, especially polygamous Africans like the traditionalist Zuma, are hypersexual. Meanwhile, supporters of Zuma contended that the rape and corruption charges were part of a conspiracy by then-president Thabo Mbeki and his backers to discredit a populist challenger who had the political backing of the African National Congress's left wing.

In the following selection, the South African anthropologist and cultural critic Steven Robins connects the many crosscurrents of politics and culture that converged at Zuma's trial. The trial helped to substantiate the former justice Albie Sachs's quip that all of South Africa's cultures have one thing in common: patriarchy. (It is also true that South Africa has strong feminists from all cultural backgrounds.) In a country convulsed by rape and AIDS, attacks on the character of the complainant forced her to flee the country for her safety. In the wake of this scandal, South Africa adopted a new and more progressive rape law that is more in keeping with its rights-oriented constitution.

The rise of AIDS, gay and gender activism has contributed towards transforming "private" sexual matters into contested public concerns. This "clash of values" around sexuality was very evident in Jacob Zuma's rape trial in May 2006. During the trial, which was held in the Johannesburg High Court, the former Deputy President and his defence counsel argued that the rape accuser had seduced Zuma by wearing "revealing clothes." The clothing referred to here was the kanga, a traditional African cloth that is worn in villages throughout the sub-continent. As the *Mail & Guardian* reporter Nicole Johnston pointed out, the African kanga "has been the hallmark of female modesty and respectability [and is] handed out at political rallies emblazoned with slogans and the faces of political leaders."[1] (During the trial, however, the mundane cotton kanga was sexualised and transformed into an object of seduction, much like the infamous cigar during the Monica Lewinsky and Bill Clinton scandal.) Responding to what they perceived to be a systematic attempt to discredit the rape accuser and portray her as an unscrupulous seducer, a small group of gender and anti-rape activists from the People Opposing Women Abuse (POWA) faced a huge crowd of jeering Zuma supporters when they demonstrated outside the Johannesburg High Court dressed in cotton kangas. As the journalist Johnston concluded, they were demonstrating to "re-appropriate their right to wear the kanga—anywhere, any time."

Zuma was ultimately acquitted by Justice Willem van der Merwe, and the complainant was portrayed by Zuma's legal counsel, and his supporters, as a psychologically disturbed, manipulative seductress, pathological liar and serial rape accuser. In his ruling, the Judge lashed out at the media, activists and Zuma supporters for prejudging the case and being more interested in sexual and gender politics than the actual evidence presented in the rape case. The Judge chastised pressure groups, NGOs, governmental organisations and the media for having "breached the sub judice rule."[2] In the preface to his 174-page judgment delivered in the Johannesburg High Court on 4 May 2006, the Judge argued that "it is not acceptable that a court be bombarded with political, personal or group agendas and comments." As one contributor to a daily newspaper correctly put [it]: "This trial is more about sexual politics and gender relations than it is about rape." In his final concluding statement, the white Judge also lambasted Zuma for having unprotected sex with an HIV-positive woman and being unable to control his sexual desires. Paraphrasing Kipling, Judge van der Merwe concluded, "If you can control your sexual urges, then you are a man, my son." This statement revealed how lingering colonial legacies of racial paternalism continued to discursively link sex, gender and race in post-apartheid South Africa.

This moralising tone from the white Judge, as well as similar utterances from other quarters, including the media, NGOs and religious leaders, provoked angry responses from Zuma's supporters. In a public statement on 25

May 2006, Senzeni Zokwana, the president of the National Union of Mine-
workers (NUM) attacked the hypocrisy of those who drew on "Christian
morality" to judge and condemn Zuma for his sexual behaviour. According to Zokwana, not all NUM's members were Christians, and not all of
them adhered to the "Ten Commandments," in particular the prohibition
on adultery. This statement, made in a deeply Christian country, unsurpris-
ingly unleashed heated discussions on the Friends of Jacob Zuma (FJZ) website about the relationship between sexuality, morality, Christianity and the
secular state. Many pro-Zuma website contributors belonging to the trade
union movement, the SACP [South African Communist Party] and ANC [Af-
rican National Congress] and Communist Party Youth Leagues supported
Zokwana's statement, and portrayed Zuma as a "man of the people," a heroic fighter for the liberation of the black working class, the downtrodden
and destitute. "Lekua," a vehemently pro-Zuma contributor to the website,
defended Zuma's moral integrity, and Zokwana's statement, in a posting on
25 May 2006:

> . . . On the selective morality, namely that it is alright for a woman to
> lay a false rape charge but it is uncalled for JZ [Jacob Zuma] to have
> breached his marriage vows, NUM [Zokwana] said: "NUM does not sub-
> scribe to the Ten Commandments, especially the one that says 'Thou
> shall not commit adultery.'" This hardline stance by Cosatu [Congress
> of South African Trade Unions] and its largest affiliate, NUM, clearly
> shows that *the whole nation is getting impatient with the hypocrites* who
> behave as if they are hollier [sic] than JZ and all of us. *Their dictatorial
> tendencies has [sic] inspired the whole nation into action to reclaim the* ANC
> *from the elites and restore it to the masses* who are still poor and destitute
> [sic]. (Emphasis added)[3]

Here we see how questions of sexual morality were reconfigured into a
populist rhetoric on African nationalism and the need "to reclaim the ANC
from the elites and restore it to the masses." This was yet another illustration about how "sex talk" and popular discourses of religion and morality
have increasingly come to shape political life in South Africa. These responses were set against the backdrop of bruising political battles between
supporters of President Thabo Mbeki and former Deputy President Zuma.
Zuma's supporters comprised a mix of trade unionists, communists, ANC
Youth League figures and Zulu neo-traditionalists. This powerful support
base, which succeeded in their campaign to elect Zuma to the position of
ANC President in December 2007, demanded that their leader should become the next President of the country, notwithstanding President Mbeki's

Zapiro, *"So You Plead Guilty . . ."* © 2006–2012 Zapiro (all rights reserved). Used with permission from www.zapiro.com.

dismissal, in 2005, of Zuma from his position as Deputy President. The dismissal followed the decision by the prosecuting authority to prosecute Zuma on corruption and, some months later, rape charges. These trials, as well as President Mbeki's calls for the next president to be a woman, were seen to be part of an elaborate anti-Zuma conspiracy orchestrated by the Office of the President. These conspirators were also portrayed on the Friends of Jacob Zuma Website as a part of President Mbeki's "Xhosa nostra," which was seen as determined to prevent a Zulu from becoming president. Postings on the website also claimed that President Mbeki wanted his female Xhosa-speaking Deputy President, Phumzile Mlambo-Ngcuka, to succeed him in order to prevent Zuma becoming the next president:

> So the president has spoken the next president of RSA should be a "woman." And every one knows that "woman" word read Ngcuka's wife [sic] . . . According to the intelligent Mbeki all men are unproductive and all women are [productive]. When are we going to have a gay or lesbian president? At present I do not see any woman that is ready to rule this country . . .[4]

Zuma supporters were especially upset with President Mbeki's introduction of quotas for women in political office and ANC structures. Mbeki's ANC government was also perceived to be undermining the powers of traditional leaders through local government reform. Demonstrations outside the court included the presence of *iinyanga* (traditional healers) using herbal medicines to ensure that Zuma was successfully acquitted in his trial. Meanwhile chiefs (*amakosi*) dressed in traditional skins occupied the front seats of the courtroom during proceedings.

The Friends of Jacob Zuma (FJZ) website was bombarded with postings alleging plots perpetrated by Mbeki's inner circle, the media, big business, neo-liberals, and even "Christians." These claims circulated on the FJZ website well after Zuma's acquittal on the rape charges. The Zuma rape trial became a key discursive site in an ongoing leadership struggle between Zuma's supporters, including the SACP and COSATU, on the one side, and President Mbeki and his followers on the other. These divisions became increasingly evident in the run-up to the December 2007 ANC Conference in Polokwane in Limpopo Province where Zuma and his supporters soundly defeated the Mbeki camp. These developments revealed that the ANC was split down the middle by ideological divisions as well as the rumours that Mbeki's inner circle were responsible for orchestrating Zuma's legal problems. This divide within the ruling party was widened by popular perceptions that President Mbeki was behind the introduction of new sexual and gender rights.

For media commentators and gender activists, the trial was a lens onto a deeply embedded authoritarian culture of patriarchy, misogyny, and sexual violence. However, few commentators reflected on the historical transformations that produced these cultural forms and social practices (see below). Instead, commentary was focused on the visceral immediacy of events inside and outside the court. For example, journalists covering the daily demonstrations outside the Johannesburg High Court reported on Zuma supporters who burnt photographs and effigies of the rape accuser and chanted "burn the bitch." Zuma's supporters, many of whom wore "100% Zulu Boy" T-shirts, were also accused of intimidating anti-rape activists protesting outside the court. The latter had launched a "One in Nine Campaign" to draw attention to the fact that so few women are prepared to report their rapes to the police. Rape activists highlighted the fact that there were 55,000 reported cases of rape in 2004/05 whereas the South African Law Reform Commission had provided estimates of 1.69 million rapes per year. Gender activists also questioned the judge's decision to permit the defence to lead testimony on the complainant's "sexual history," a decision that activists believed was designed to demonstrate that she had a history of false rape accusations going back to her childhood. As Nomboniso Gasa, a gender and political analyst, put it:

We are told that the "sexual history" of this person is being probed to show her lack of credibility as an accuser. In reality, what we have witnessed has been the rehearsing of a series of painful episodes in her life. You [Jacob Zuma] replicated your favourite song "give me my machine gun" and discharged fire without any holds barred. You have not only fed into the most backward sections of South African law, but you have deployed your training as an armed fighter in that arena against an unarmed individual. Are the weapons you have deployed compatible with that vision and appropriate to the target?[5]

The Judge thoroughly dismissed the complainant's evidence, and completely endorsed Zuma's claim that he had consensual sex at his home in November 2005. There was no room for any consideration of sexual ambiguity, which is often the result of such unequal power relations, in this judgment. Activists argued in the press that the judgment, and the treatment meted out to the rape accuser by Zuma's supporters, would simply reinforce this "one in nine" syndrome amongst rape victims.

After the judgment against the "kanga-clad seductress," gender activists appeared to have even stronger grounds for believing the judicial system would continue to be perceived by rape victims to be unsympathetic to their predicament. Some activists also claimed that the relentless cross-examination of the complainant by Zuma's defence lawyer constituted "secondary rape" of the victim by the criminal justice system. Zuma's acquittal, they argued, would also be interpreted by many of his followers as vindication of their patriarchal beliefs and claims that women are predisposed to fabricate rape in order to access money and power.

It was not only the gender activists who were enraged by Zuma's sexual behaviour. Zuma had also angered AIDS activists with his court testimony that he had sex without a condom with an HIV-positive woman because he had calculated that the risk of infection was low. Zuma also told the court that by showering after he had sex with the rape accuser he intended to reduce the risk of infection. According to AIDS activists, these statements contributed towards widespread confusion and misinformation about HIV/AIDS, including the proliferation of AIDS myths, dissident theories, and popular beliefs that sex with virgins could cure AIDS and that the disease was caused by witchcraft.

Gender and AIDS activists and media commentators argued that Zuma's trial highlighted the deeply entrenched character of patriarchy in South African society. They also claimed that the trial reflected the dismal failure of the national political leadership to confront sexual violence and HIV/AIDS. After all, Zuma had been the president of both the Moral Regeneration Campaign and the South African National AIDS Commission (SANAC), government bodies that activists regarded as entirely ineffectual. These failures of government were perceived to be especially disturbing in a country with a "rape pandemic" and an estimated 5.5 million people living with AIDS. So, notwithstanding a progressive constitution that promised sexual rights and gender equality, as well as better health care for all, there seemed to be deeply embedded social and cultural barriers in the way of realising these rights.

Notes

1. *Mail & Guardian*, 5 May 2006, p. 2.
2. For the full judgment see *Mail & Guardian* website: http:www.mg.co.za/specialreport.aspx?area=zuma_report.
3. http://www.friendsofjz.co.za/viewmessage.asp. [Bracketed *sics* in the original.]
4. Ndosi, 06/05/2006, http://www.friendsofjz.co.za/viewmessage.asp.
5. *Mail & Guardian*, 17 March 2006.

Lessons Learned

Bafana Khumalo and Dean Peacock

South Africa is notorious for its high levels of violent crime. The country has extremely high rates of rape, mostly committed against women and children. In one survey, more than a quarter of all men said that they had committed rape at least once, and 10 percent of the men also reported being the victims of rape by other men.[1] Violent and unwanted sexual contact of course compounds the HIV/AIDS epidemic. This situation stands in stark contrast to the postapartheid constitution's commitment to gender equality and the constitution's general emphasis on human dignity.

The following piece places South Africa's rape crisis in the context of the trial and acquittal of Jacob Zuma, who went on to become president of South Africa in 2009. This selection argues that South Africans need to address the rape problem through a variety of strategies, from increasing the capacity of police to investigate rape cases, to providing appropriate HIV-preventative medication to victims, to countering sexist mythologies that allow many men to assume that certain forms of women's dress or behavior constitute "consent" to sexual relations. It also calls for reform of the rape law, which was done in the aftermath of the Zuma trial, though rape continues to occur at appalling rates.

On March 5th, a day before the Jacob Zuma rape trial resumed[,] a fellow gender activist and friend of ours was raped in her home. On Monday the judge in the Zuma trial issued his verdict—and found that the prosecution had not proven beyond reasonable doubt that the former Deputy President [was guilty]. In reaching that verdict, he publicly rebuked the police for their shoddy investigation. For our friend there is no resolution to her case. The trauma inflicted upon her persists. For her and countless other rape survivors, the sleepless nights, the intermittent panic attacks whenever she is alone, the terror and hyper-vigilance on the streets and in the taxi on the way home and the devastating depression continue to gnaw at her sense of self and at the convictions that inspired her activism.

When the rapist broke in through her door and held a knife to her throat she did all she could to convince him to wear a condom. She finds some solace in the fact that she was able to persuade him to try and put a condom on—until, drunk and violent, he broke it. He then raped her. She is in her mid-twenties. It is the fourth time she has been sexually assaulted.

Fortunately, as a gender activist, she knew about the importance of post exposure prophylaxis [PEP] and was lucky enough to live near one of the few health service sites in Gauteng that stocks it. Almost exactly two months later and after taking her course of PEP she still is not certain of her HIV status. She'll have to wait until the window period closes before she knows for sure.

The two male police who arrived on the scene informed her that no women police were available despite existing policy that there should be and made little effort to secure forensic evidence. When she was taken to the sexual assault unit in Braamfontein there were no counsellors available to debrief her. Instead, a well meaning doctor told her how much worse it could have been and described in detail the ordeal of a gang rape survivor who had been brought to the centre earlier in the evening.

In the weeks following her rape she made repeated calls to the police and got no response at all—no call back, no additional questioning, nothing. And that despite the fact that the rapist had stolen and used her phone and in the process left a clear trail for the police, had they taken action. It turns out her investigating officer has over 60 cases at the moment, more than half of them children. Most of her colleagues are carrying even larger case-loads. They earn very little and are themselves often struggling with the after-effects of repeated exposure to stories of trauma and dehumanizing brutality. With that many cases, they are able to attend court cases but do almost no investigation.

Almost two months to the day since she was raped, our colleague has still heard nothing about her case. In all likelihood, her case will remain un-solved and the criminal justice system will send a silent message to the man who raped her and to many others like him that they can rape and brutalize women with impunity.

Whatever we may think of the outcome of the Zuma trial, the trial itself and the public debates it has generated have offered us important lessons about rape in South Africa. As a country, we have to act on these lessons. Failure to do so makes a mockery of our constitution—especially Section 12, subsection 2 of the bill of rights which states that "Everyone has the right to bodily and psychological integrity, which includes the right to security in and control over their body."

What have we learned? We have learned—or, more accurately, been reminded—that sexual violence is endemic and that very little is done to stop it. Like our colleague, the complainant in the Zuma case reports having been raped throughout her childhood. In neither case were the perpetrators held to account. In the case of the Zuma trial, this history of sexual abuse at the hands of much older men was cynically used to suggest that the complainant "cries rape" after supposedly engaging in consensual [sex].

It seems we still do not understand our own statutory rape laws. The Zuma rape case and the acquittal in the rape case against Orlando Pirates soccer star Bernard Vilikazi for having sex with a 15 year-old tell us we have lots of work to do to ensure that the Criminal Justice System complies with the countries [*sic*] statutory rape laws.

We have learned that our court rooms often serve to further brutalize women. A colleague reports that after watching news coverage of the trial her 15 year-old daughter told her that she would choose not to report rape rather than be subjected to the humiliating questions the Zuma complainant was forced to answer.

We have learned that men's violence against women is still explained away by crude victim blaming. Story after story in the media has shown us that women are still blamed for being raped if they do not forcibly resist, if they show their knees, if they talk about sex, if they have been previously raped, if they visit the house of a man after certain hours and if they don't have a boyfriend. Similar arguments, of course, are not made to blame victims of carjackings for having their windows open or victims of break-ins for not closing their curtains. What explains this double standard? Put simply, sexism.

Zuma's claims that sex between he and the complainant was consensual should sound alarm bells about men's understanding of what constitutes sexual consent and their sense of entitlement to women's bodies. In workshops across the country, we have heard many men argue that sexual consent is established when a woman gives her cell phone number, accepts a drink, dances closely, or comes back to their house. These definitions of consent then provide men with a convenient justification for not respecting women's right to say no to sex.

To address this, we need to educate young and adult men about the difference between consensual sex and date rape and make sure that men understand that women have the right to say no to sex—no matter what the relationship and no matter what signs they may think indicated an interest in sex. Most importantly, though, we need to create a society that encourages men to respect women.

Zuma's testimony should also serve to remind us that men who have multiple concurrent sexual partners and practice unsafe sex place themselves and all of their partners at risk and drive the rapid spread of HIV infection. To slow the spread of HIV and AIDS we will have to challenge the ways in which some men equate manhood with sexual conquest and risk taking. Uganda's much heralded HIV prevention strategy owed its success in large part to a "zero grazing" campaign aimed at men.

Two years ago on International Women's Day Kofi Annan [the United Nations secretary-general] said, "We must encourage men to replace risk-taking with taking responsibility." The Zuma trial has reinforced the urgency of that call.

This week the Sexual Offences Bill is likely to go before Parliament. As a result of the Zuma trial and as a result of what we have learned from our friend's ordeal, it is clear that this bill needs to be passed urgently. Despite prior commitments from senior government officials that it would be tabled, it has languished since 1998. It must be passed immediately. The Zuma trial has shown us that it must include provisions that protect rape survivors from further traumatisation in courts—whether on the stands or in the nearby streets.

To be meaningful, the new act must also include clear provisions for additional resources. The Criminal Justice System will need additional specialized sexual assault police with decent pay to be able to do their job properly and to avoid the kind of rebuke they received today. Rape survivors in every community across the country need easy access to fully staffed specialized sexual assault centres with easy access to PEP. The public needs swift and committed investigations to hold perpetrators accountable and to deter additional assaults. Without a commitment from the treasury to pay for these services, the law will be severely compromised.

In that same speech, two years ago Kofi Annan said, "Across all levels of society, we need to see a deep social revolution that transforms relationships between women and men." To achieve this, we must act on the lessons we have learned over the course of the last few months—no matter what verdict is issued today.

As men, we believe many other men also care deeply about women in their lives affected by rape or the threat of rape. We believe many men know that violence against women is wrong and would like to see it stop. We call especially on men, including men in parliament and government, to find the courage to act on their convictions and to take action to end the violence some men commit in our names.

Note

1. R. Jewkes, N. Abrahams, S. Mathews, M. Seedat, A. Van Niekerk, S. Suffla, and K. Ratele, *Preventing Rape and Violence in South Africa: Call for Leadership in a New Agenda for Action*, MRC Policy Brief, November 2009, 1–2.

Murder of Noxola Nogwaza

Ekurhuleni Pride Organizing Committee

The equality clause of South Africa's famously progressive constitution of 1996 guarantees freedom from discrimination on the basis of not only race, ethnicity, religion, and gender but also sexual orientation. As a result, the Constitutional Court ruled that same-sex marriage must be allowed, and this took effect in 2006. Despite these legal protections and a vibrant gay culture in South Africa's larger cities, prejudice and discrimination against LGBTI people is common. This all too often takes violent forms, including rape and murder, especially against black lesbians. In addition to other violent attacks on gay individuals, some men attack lesbians through "corrective" rape to "cure" them of their sexual orientation.

The following selection is a response by a black gay rights organization, the Ekurhuleni Pride Organizing Committee, to the rape and murder of one of its members. Though the violence suggests deep social pathologies in postapartheid South Africa, the efforts of groups like this one continue to draw on South Africa's tradition of collective action. Two thousand people attended Noxola Nogwaza's funeral to speak out against such acts of violence.

Today is the 17th anniversary of South Africa's independence but for Black lesbians there is little to celebrate as today we learn of the rape and murder of yet another young sister. The Constitution debated and formed to protect all South Africans has failed the majority of South Africans. It has shamefully failed the most vulnerable people in the country and in particular young Black lesbians. The body of Noxola Nogwaza was found on Sunday morning. This is just 4 weeks after the body of 20 year old Nokuthula Radebe was discovered and which has not even been reported in the media. The pain of these brutal attacks grows and my heart goes out to their family and friends. May both Nogwaza and Nokuthula Rest in Peace.

Ekurhuleni Pride Organizing Committee (EPOC), the key LGBTI organization in the township of Kwa-Thema, Gauteng, South Africa, and the Coalition of African Lesbians (CAL) condemn the brutal rape and murder, in cold blood, of a member of EPOC. . . .

The body of Noxolo Nogwaza, a 24 year old lesbian, was found lying in an alley in Kwa-Thema at about 9 AM on Sunday, April 24, 2011. Noxola's head was completely deformed, her eyes out of the sockets, her brain spilt, teeth scattered all around and face crashed beyond recognition. Witnesses say that an empty beer bottle and a used condom were stuck up her genitals. Parts of the rest of her body had been stabbed with glass. A large pavement brick that is believed to have been used to crash her head was found by her side.

Noxola was raped and murdered in a similar manner as that in which another member of EPOC was murdered almost three years ago (April 28, 2008). Eudy Simelane's body was also found in an open field in Kwa-Thema. It was clear that she had been raped and murdered afterwards, crimes that the perpetrators confessed to. Just last year, a gay man in the same township was attacked by eight men, who attempted to rape him. Luckily, he escaped the vultures. The men, as they attempted to rape him, were heard saying, "We are determined to kill all gay people in this area and we will do it."

It is very clear that these rapists are on a mission. We will however not rest until justice prevails. Eudy's case was not recognized as a hate crime against a lesbian and the same is not done in the cases of many other people who have been raped and/or murdered on the basis of their sexual orientation and gender identity/expression in South Africa. EPOC is determined to get to the bottom of the Noxola case and push for justice. . . .

EPOC and CAL call on the Tsakane Police Station, where the case has been reported, to carry out a quick and thorough investigation into the murder of Noxolo and deal with the perpetrators accordingly.

Noxola will be laid to rest at a cemetery in Kwa-Thema on Saturday, April 30, 2011. EPOC and CAL call on all your support in this time of grief and horror. Details of the burial will be sent out shortly. Please come and stand with us.

Ghosts of Sara Baartman

Clifton Crais and Pamela Scully

The end of apartheid has seen a resurgent politics of indigeneity across South Africa. In the former homelands, traditional leaders have made claims to ethnic pasts and have insisted that resources pass through their hands. In the Western Cape, individuals and groups have reawakened Khoesan history, in some cases changing their names in an attempt to imagine a more authentic identity in a postapartheid era. The return of Sara Baartman's remains from France in 2002 formed part of these complex and contested cultural politics. Baartman, a Gonaqua woman born on the violent South African frontier in the late 1700s, was exhibited as the "Hottentot Venus" throughout England and in Paris in the 1810s. Her life in England became the subject of widespread controversy concerning the way she was displayed to the public and whether or not she was a slave. Baartman died in Paris in late 1815; her body was dissected by the renowned scientist Georges Cuvier. Writings about Baartman shaped European ideas about race and sexuality. Efforts to repatriate Baartman's remains grew after the end of apartheid, culminating in a state funeral presided over by the then-president Thabo Mbeki. The following excerpt describes the politics surrounding Baartman's return, and the ways South Africans have debated their traumatic pasts and present.

How South Africans understood Sara's life and the history of the Hottentot Venus shaped discussions about democracy and identity, citizenship and ethnicity, about memory and how people might face, or efface, histories of violence and oppression. What was the "new" South Africa? Who was this woman trapped in a Paris museum? How would Sara Baartman be returned home? To whom did she belong?

It seemed as if one could touch worlds that lay broken and scattered across the horizon. For people of Khoesan descent, the promise of return and renewal had long been part of their sense of themselves and their history, no more so than in the years immediately after apartheid's collapse when earlier state and racialized ascriptions melted away. "Coloured" disappeared as a legal category. But who one was in history's detritus and in South Africa's political quagmires was less than clear.

For some there was the palpable feeling the prophecies people had kept alive for well over a century might finally come true. And there was a sense, a terrible fragile vague sense, that somehow one might connect the present to a now distant time before the violence and dispossession of colonial conquest . . . when Sara's parents had been a free people in the Camdeboo. What stories had they spoken, what stories did Sara hear—the winds, the moon carrying the soul away, the stars the spirits of departed women and children? Which star was Sara?

People saw in Sara and her return to South Africa the revelations from the book of Ezekiel where the Spirit becomes a wind blowing across the land that breathes the Lord God into our hearts. Ezekiel sees the bones of a genocide, a land of horrible violent death that annihilates memory and creates a holocaust so vast and lonely that the living are unable to care for the departed. But he also sees the promise of reconciliation and rebirth. In a valley "full of bones" the Lord God instructs Ezekiel to "prophesy unto the wind, prophesy, son of man, and say to the wind." These bones were "the whole house of Israel," and the wind "came into them and they lived." And the Lord God would bring the people of Israel "into their own land" and "make them one nation" again. The scattered bones of people once cursed reconnect, one bone bumping into another until each found its proper place. Muscles and skin reappear. Ligaments reunite what had been sundered apart. God's breath makes the dead come alive again.

Sara likely had heard of the words of Ezekiel during her years living in Cape Town. Those of her family that had survived the deafening silences of colonial violence believed in them. Now, almost exactly two centuries after she journeyed to the port city, people imagined in Sara Baartman the book of Ezekiel, in the violence perpetrated against her and in the redemptive possibilities of coming home. Baartman's return augured the arrival of a new era, for many Khoesan quite literally when the scattered bones of the oppressed might come together again and the chasms of history finally traversed.

People claiming Khoekhoe descent, and especially the Griqua, took the lead in claiming Sara as their own and in demanding her return, and they often did so through the words of Ezekiel. The Griqua emerged in the eighteenth and nineteenth centuries among people who fled colonial power and across the borders of the Cape Colony. Khoekhoe, slaves and others, initially had been known as "Bastards" or "Basters," an indictment of their mixed descent. Around 1813 they adopted the name "Griqua" and many recognized the strong leadership of men like Adam Kok and the Le Fleur family. Over the decades Boer and British chased them from one spot to another, from the Orange Free State to Griqualand East, later to Plettenberg Bay along the Indian Ocean and as far as Vanrhynnsdorp in the Western Cape. Each time the Griqua believed they had finally found a land of their own, the authorities pushed them away again.

For two centuries the Griqua have spoken of the stories and prophecies of Ezekiel and of their leader as "die kneg," as a servant of God. In 1889, A.S. Le Fleur received a calling from God to gather together the bones of the Griqua founder Kok as the first task of gathering the Griqua as a nation, "so that they can be my people and I their God . . . and that the word of Ezechiel be fulfilled."[1] Women have long fashioned blankets recalling their history of dispossession and scattering, bits and pieces of cloth which they wear around themselves during the winter, fragments of the past stitched together reminding them of their history and that, one day, their land shall be returned and restored.

Following his 1903 release from Robben Island on charges of sowing unrest, Le Fleur had a vision that God called him to a desolate place some three hundred kilometers to the north where the Griqua should gather, where the bones of the past would one day come alive again. A final trek led to the scrub of Namaqualand near Vanrhynnsdorp, where in the short spring the plants bloom to create an extraordinary quilt of brilliant yellow, oranges, azure blues, and magentas before disappearing back into the greens and browns of the veld. Here Le Fleur began to acquire part of the farm Kranshoek where they established their sacred site of Ratelgat, named after an animal that leads one to water. At the farm he prophesied a new world, that this barren dry land would become a Garden of Eden for the Griqua headed by his organization the Griqua National Conference (GNC). Since 1905, the Griqua have struggled to come together to reaffirm their history and conviction that the world will be made anew, that one day they will make blankets of whole cloth. In 1941, the Great Reformer died. The faithful buried Le Fleur at Ratelgat. Even this piece of land, as richly symbolic as it is barren, they lost to a white farmer who God later punished with a violent death.

Before the 1990s, no Griqua leader knew of Sara Baartman. A man named Mansell Upham brought her story, and the location of her remains in a Paris museum, to the attention of the Griqua leaders. An attorney by training, a former diplomat, and an extraordinarily skilled genealogist, Upham claims descent from Eva or Krotoa, the seventeenth-century Khoekhoe women who worked as a servant for Jan van Riebeeck and who, in 1664, married the

Roadside painting, Hankey, 2005. Photograph by Clifton Crais.

Dutch surgeon Pieter van Meerhof. In Sara Baartman, Upham conceived a Krotoa for the nineteenth century, the plight of indigenous peoples, and a story of dehumanization and the tragedies befalling black women in colonial societies. . . .

In Cape Town, Upham "alerted" the Griqua National Conference to the "Sarah Baartman issue as a possible indigenous people's issue."[2] The timing of the campaign to bring Sara Baartman home was perfect. The politics of Khoesan identity and history, and with it Sara Baartman's past and present, had become an international issue. It also dovetailed with local and national politics. In South Africa's first democratic elections in 1994, the African National Congress failed to win the Western Cape. Instead the province remained under the control of the National Party, the very party responsible for apartheid, for persecuting "Coloureds" even as it provided them with preferential treatment within the labor market. The "Coloured" vote swung the balance against the ANC [African National Congress].

Politics within the "Coloured" community remained fraught and fragile. Many thousands had fought against apartheid; hundreds had lost their lives. But many also shared much of the culture of white Afrikaners, including a language and a common, if also divided, history in the Cape. The movement of Africans into the Western Cape from the 1970s, an area previously under the "coloured labor preference policy," created anxieties and conflicts over jobs and housing. At least many in the older generation wondered if the wave of black nationalism and government declarations of an "African Renaissance" included them. Claims to ancient blood and land, and shameful histories like that of Sara Baartman, offered one way of negotiating an uncertain present.

Politicians clearly knew that securing the province for the ANC was impossible without the "Coloured" vote, and in the ensuing years they became acutely sensitive to the demands of Khoesan leaders. Khoesan claims began to receive the attention of government. In late 1995, GNC leader and Paramount Chief A.A.S. LeFleur II brought to the attention of President Nelson Mandela the issue of Sara Baartman and the importance of repatriating her remains. The GNC also formally appealed to the French Embassy in Pretoria, invoking the United Nation's Declaration of Human Rights and the Draft Declaration on the Rights of Indigenous People. Mandela subsequently raised the issue with French President Francois Mitterrand. . . .

In late February 2002, the [French] National Assembly unanimously passed a bill for her return. The final law came into effect as "Loi no 2002–323 du 6 mars 2002 relative a la restitution par la France de la depouille mortelle de Saartjie Baartman a l'Afrique du Sud." The legislation instructed the Museum to repatriate Sara Baartman's remains within two months. Sara was coming home.

In early 2002, the Department of Arts and Cultures (DAC) created a Reference Group to oversee the return, burial, and memorialization of Sara Baartman, or what many now referred to as "Mama Saartjie," the maternal figure of the new South Africa. [Phillip] Tobias [a paleoanthropologist and one of South Africa's leading scientists] became the most illustrious member of the group. The other twelve representatives appointed by the minister included members of the government, academics, the Deputy Chairperson of the Human Rights Commission, a representative of the Commission on Gender Equality, representatives of the Khoesan community, and the poet and University of Western Cape academic Diana Ferrus, who had written the widely distributed poem about Sara Baartman "I have come to take you home."[3]

DAC officials knew they were dealing with a potentially explosive issue, but also one that might serve multiple purposes in the "new" South Africa. An early project proposal noted that the "story of Ms Saartjie Baartman has become synonymous with the pain and suffering of a black woman of a colonised people,"[4] a prime example of the creation of the "Other." Returning her remains "has national as well as international significance." Officials concluded that Baartman's return might become an important moment for "nation-building and reconciliation." South Africa would, in effect, speak for Sara Baartman, defend her human rights, and in doing so claim her as a citizen of the fledgling democracy. DAC proposed an eighteenth month time frame and a budget of 8,700,000 South African Rands (Rds.); a later budget estimate extended the figure to a total of Rds. 10,350,000. . . .

The South African government decided that Sara Baartman would be laid to rest on 9 August 2002, to coincide with International Indigenous Peoples' Day and South Africa's Women's Day. The latter commemorated the famous 1956 march on Pretoria when nearly 20,000 women protested the pass laws and the introduction of apartheid and where the famous saying "You have struck the women, you have struck a rock" was born. In choosing Women's Day, the government recognized the contribution of individual women as leaders of the group that campaigned for Baartman's return, and sought to acknowledge the broader suffering of women under colonialism and apartheid.

The government's decision was not without dissent. Chief Jean Burgess of the "Chonaqua" (Gonaqua) House, and Chief Margaret Coetzee of the Inqua, believed that burying Baartman on National Women's day was "a great insult to us." Baartman "deserves," they continued,

> a day that belongs to her alone and not a day that will be clouded across the country with Women Day celebrations. She deserves a day that we will remember as the day that our Great Foremother has been buried.

Burgess and Coetzee invoked the Vermillion Accord on Human Remains that privileged local communities in the dispensation of remains. They insisted that Sara Baartman was first and foremost a "Khoesan . . . Icon, as she symbolized to us the abuse that our great foremothers were exposed to. . . . During her birth the blood that was shed was given to the earth and it is to the same earth that her remains needs to be laid to rest. . . . Ms Baartman deserves the peace that was never given to her spirit."

Their protests were met with indifference. By now the government had spent quite considerable funds in its negotiations with the French government and in organizing the Reference Group, and a small fortune planning for the funeral. Officials had every intention of staging the burial as an international event. Sara Baartman would be repatriated not to a family but to a nation that, during her own lifetime, didn't exist. "Media interest" had been "intense," coverage "huge," according to one internal document. "It would be difficult," the document continued, to over-rate both the national and international importance to South Africa of this event. It was a victory over colonialism, racism and sexism. It very visibly and publically restored the dignity of a South African woman exploited and humiliated in her lifetime. It brought together and united South Africans of all backgrounds in seeing justice done.

Internationally the return of Sara Baartman changed French political culture and "substantially contributed to the discussions and debates around the issue of human rights in French society," while also encouraging other countries "to pursue similar requests to have the remains of their nationals . . . repatriated."[5]

The government planned a small ceremony in Cape Town where Baartman would first arrive back in South Africa from Paris. This celebration, the enrobement or "Aantrek" ceremony, titled "Flowers for Sarah Bartmann [*sic*]," began on a Sunday afternoon on 4 August 2002. [Bridget] Mabandla, the Deputy Minister of Arts, Culture, Science and Technology; church members; Griqua National Conference leaders; and members and other representatives of the Khoesan Community, as well as the Reference Group, attended the ceremony. Women figured prominently in the somber welcoming of Baartman's return, [Yvette] Abrahams [a Khoesan activist] performing a putatively "traditional" San dance. A few days later [Baartman's] remains were flown east to Port Elizabeth.

On 9 August 2002, between seven and fifteen thousand people converged on the small village of Hankey to see and to participate in laying to rest the remains of Sara Baartman.[6] Foreign visitors, many of whom were women, flew to Hankey from the United States, Europe, and Asia. The South African Broadcasting Corporation provided full, uninterrupted coverage of the daylong funeral. The national and international importance of Baartman easily overwhelmed the concerns of the local Khoesan community who had wanted to bury her at a time that coincided with the moon. Baartman had become a national symbol and a symbol for women everywhere, though the ceremonies largely entailed men speaking on behalf of women and their rights as South African citizens.

As [Henry] Bredekamp [head of Iziko Museums] said at the funeral, "We are laying to rest a national icon, not just a Khoikhoi symbol, and Sarah's return should be elevated to a national celebration." For Deputy Minister Mabandla, the funeral signified an "end of oppression to women," the funeral part of the rebirth of Africa "out of the shackles of colonialism." For Tobias, Baartman was "an icon . . . a symbol . . . a victim" of an era that should be cast into the dustbin of history. For the poet Ferrus, Baartman was "a human rights icon." For Raymond Mhlaba, the veteran political activist and then Premier of the Eastern Cape, Sara Baartman's life "depicts the attitude of colonialism."

Mhlaba saw in the funeral nothing less than the arrival of a new historical consciousness. For too long South African history had been produced by white historians who spoke of the savagery of Africans and who had airbrushed, as it were, the many evils they had perpetrated. Baartman's funeral was an exercise in producing history from the other side, from the vantage of the poor and the oppressed.

Thabo Mbeki arrived in full presidential splendor, the helicopter arriving on the outskirts of the town, the motorcade winding its way up to the grave site. Following a "traditional" praise poem the president delivered a long speech that ranged from critiques of the Enlightenment, the history of American slavery, the legacies of colonialism and apartheid, the necessity of gender equality, to the poet Langston Hughes. For Mbeki, it was crucial that Sara Baartman was being laid to rest on National Women's Day. Her history reminded the world—and especially South Africans—of the long history of women's oppression. Mbeki spoke of the persistence of gender violence and of the necessity of gender equality to realizing a truly democratic South Africa. "We cannot undo the damage that was done to her," Mbeki said early in the speech.

> But at least we can summon the courage to speak the naked but healing truth that must comfort her wherever she may be. I speak of courage because there are many in our country who would urge constantly that we should not speak of the past. They pour scorn on those who speak about who we are and where we come from and why we are where we are today. They make bold to say the past is no longer, and all that remains is a future that will be. But, today, the gods would be angry with us if we did not, on the banks of the Gamtoos River, at the grave of Sarah Baartman, call out for restoration of the dignity of Sarah Baartman, of the Khoi-San, of the millions of Africans who have known centuries of wretchedness.

For the president, as it was for many others, Sara Baartman's story was the story of South Africa. It was, he said, the "story of the loss of our ancient freedoms . . . of the dispossession of our lands," and the reduction of once proud people into mere objects, a "people without a past." Reciting the history of Sara Baartman at her grave site formed part of a more widespread awakening of history in South Africa, a reclaiming of pasts too long denied. The "restoration" of the dignity of Sara Baartman was part and parcel of the restoration of the dignity of black South Africans, and especially of the Khoesan. "We need only start here, on the banks of the Gamtoos River, and advance to the rest of our country." The past is with us, Mbeki instructed the world, and because of this we have the burden of eradicating the legacies of colonialism and apartheid, of ensuring that Sara Baartman "did not suffer and die in vain."

Much of President Mbeki's speech took up the history of European co-lonialism, racism, and science. For the president, Europeans were the ones who were truly monstrous, the barbarism of people who considered them-selves "men *par excellence.*" Cuvier received the harshest words, the man most responsible for Sara Baartman being "sucked into the evil" of not simply Western science but the Enlightenment itself. From an indictment of Cuvier, Mbeki quickly expanded his condemnation to Montesquieu, Diderot, and Voltaire. These men were the barbarians, not the "defenseless" Sara Baartman who had been "ferried" to Europe.

Mbeki's attack on the West, especially Western science, was not simply an instance of presidential blather. Since coming to power in June 1999, the Mbeki government had regularly issued scathing denunciations of Western science as part of its denying the medical basis of the HIV/AIDS crisis in South Africa, where infection rates are among the highest anywhere in the world today. Sara Baartman already had been used to condemn science, in academic studies particularly as part of the rise of cultural studies, in artis-tic works, in the popular press, in public discussions across the world, and most immediately in the work of the Reference Group. Now the president of South Africa deployed Baartman and her history as part of a harangue against science and the West.

The president ended his speech announcing that Sara Baartman's rest-ing place would become a designated National Heritage site. Mbeki also promised that a fitting monument would be erected in Cape Town, where she had left Africa's shores on her fateful voyage to Europe. It was now time to finally bury Sara. She was laid to rest recognizing her Christian faith but still buried as a pure Khoekhoe woman. The coffin containing her skel-eton and remains was lowered into the ground with the due solemnity of a Christian burial. The top of the grave reproduced traditional Khoekhoe burial practices from the eighteenth century. A pile of stones marked her final resting place.

In the ensuing weeks and months people composed small messages or wrote their names on some of the stones, reminders of their visiting the grave, their allegiance to the dead. Within months, however, the grave site and memorial had fallen into disrepair. Graffiti marred the site, the cement boundaries had been chipped away, perhaps by those wanting relics. Some saw the state of the site as an "insult" to the Khoesan, as "totally degrading for Sarah and the Khoi-San people." Most seriously, the grave itself was vandalized. While it is impossible to determine the motives of the culprits, it may have been that the powerful symbolic site offered ritual specialists powerful *muti* (medicine) to cause harm, to ensure benefits, or to ward off witchcraft.

In September 2003, a four-year-old child, Makhumandile "Trompies" Bantom, was abducted by two men outside a day care center. The child's father had died, and Trompies was heir to the Rds. 150,000 inheritance, a vast sum in South Africa's impoverished Eastern Cape. His body was later found near Sara Baartman's grave; the child's throat had been slit, perhaps on the order of his mother, who had contested the will.[7]

Originally red African soil surrounded Baartman's grave. A simple cement rectangle marked the grave, on top of which were placed stones and the boegoe bush to purify her spirits, to reunite Baartman with the earth. The vandals changed all this. Officials decided to cement the area immediately around the grave. Tall green metal bars now surround the site on the hilltop overlooking the Gamtoos River Valley, the river Khoekhoe had named as "wily as a lion" as it wound its way down to the Indian Ocean. Returned to South Africa, Sara Baartman remains behind bars, imprisoned still.

Notes

1. Material on the Griqua movement can be found at http://www.toekncoin.com.lefleur.htm.
2. We thank Mr. Upham for responding to our written questions.
3. Diana Ferrus has a Web site at http://dianaferrus.blogspot.com.
4. Department of Arts and Culture, "Project Proposal: Return and Internment of the Remains of Ms Saartjie Baartman," n.d.
5. Department of Arts and Culture, "Final Report," n.d.
6. The following is based on the SABC broadcast of the Baartman funeral.
7. "Trompie's Murder," *Port Elizabeth Herald*, 13 Nov. 2003.

David's Story

Zoe Wicomb

The removal of all racially discriminatory laws and the emergence of democratic electoral politics raised important issues of identity, especially in the Western Cape and among the population that under apartheid had been categorized as "Coloured." In the 1980s thousands of Coloureds had joined in the popular revolt against apartheid. In the first postapartheid elections, however, the "Coloured" vote shifted to the National Party, which had been responsible for their racial oppression. The very category "coloured" became a topic of public cultural debate, with many intellectuals renouncing a history of cultural mixing for a claim to their indigenous roots in the Khoesan past. Born in the Western Cape, Zoe Wicomb (1948–) has been one of the most important voices in exploring historical memory and racial identity. David's Story (published in 2001) centers on former African National Congress (ANC) guerrillas in the years of political transition, David, who sets out in search of the past, and Dulcie, a woman whose luminous voice in the novel raises questions about gender and liberation in a country that remains deeply patriarchal, if not misogynist. In the excerpt here, Wicomb imagines the exuberant expectations—and looming anxieties—just as freedom arrived in South Africa.

David is not sure of what he remembers. They were difficult times, times best forgotten. He rubs his face with both hands. People could not, under those pressures, always afford to be cautious, he explains; it was crucial to act quickly. He does not say why he was at Quatro [an ANC prison camp in Angola], but yes, as in any movement beset by treachery there was bound to be paranoia, bound to be some mistakes, and yes, if his treatment had been a mistake it was soon rectified, nothing really serious, perhaps the odd excesses practised by the overwrought. God knows, it was difficult enough. It was war, for God's sake. Every movement produces its crackpots, its power-mongers who cross over into a corrupted version of the freedom they set out to defend. That does not discredit the Movement itself. If things go off course, that course is also determined by the very system we attack. And it's enemy tactics, he repeats, that produce corruption.

I raise an eyebrow.

Oh yes, he explains, by making us insecure about our own members so that we remain suspicious, incriminate the innocent, and do terrible things to our own people. Keeping your hands clean is a luxury that no revolutionary can afford; there's corruption in every institution. It's only you arty types who think of such problems as something special, something freakish that can bring about a climax in a story. Stick to the real world and you'll find the buzz of bluebottles deafening.

Leaning against the bronze horseman, I say nothing; David nevertheless turns on me, his movements stiff with distaste and resentment.

There is no justification for the likes of you to sneer. People who tend their gardens and polish their sensibilities in the morality of art have no idea about the business of survival out there in the bush with no resources. There things do get distorted and ideals do drift out of sight. You who are too fastidious to use the word *comrade*, what would you know about such things? Oh, you can talk about ambiguity or freedom, but you can't face putting the two together, not even from the sunny comfort of your garden chair. That's why you'll never understand about Dulcie; hers is another world altogether.

And when freedom comes, I ask, what are we meant to do with these different worlds? Which one will survive? Or rather, which one will you choose for me?

My dear girl, he says condescendingly, another bourgeois myth of niceness you've swallowed. There've always been other worlds; there always will be many, all struggling for survival. Then his tone changes. Look, he pleads, I've trusted you with a delicate job. The struggle is sacred; it's been my life. It must not be misrepresented. You know, as all sensible people do, that the fight against oppression is a just one, that it has been managed as justly as is possible in politics.

Together our eyes follow the movement of an ant, stumbling with its burden of an enormous breadcrumb.

Perhaps, I say, as the ant disappears down a crack, it's too difficult. Perhaps we should abandon the whole thing.

Oh no, David says anxiously, no need for that. It's just a matter of being careful, of not distorting things.

I try to think of my walled winter garden where the basil is still green and bushy and the bougainvillea never lets up on its purple rustle. But another image invades, one of worlds as a stack of so many dirty dinner plates that will not come unstuck as each bottom clings to another's grease. . . .

Capetown, 1991

There will be an ANC rally on Thursday in the centre of Cape Town.

As if everybody does not know it, there is this peculiar message on my answer-phone. There are no other messages.

As if the 1960s BBC-received pronunciation still used by SABC [South African Broadcasting Corporation] newsreaders is not humorous enough, there is something parodic about this newsreader's voice.

There will he an ANC rally on Thursday in the centre if Cape Town. Buses from the townships will arrive by ten A.M. and toyi-toying [a military-style dance] to the Parade is scheduled to settle down by midday when the crowds will be addressed by Bishop Tutu and Joe Slovo. You are most welcome to attend.

The sixteenth of June—Soweto Day—Youth Day—Bloomsday—Day of the Revolution of the Word—birthday of freedom. I do not usually attend rallies. Except, of course, the historic moment of Mandela's release. But I am impressed with this invitation. Has the Movement managed to infiltrate all the media in the official voice of the newscaster?

It is an invitation I cannot refuse. . . .

In the bus a young man ties large gold, green, and black rosettes to their jerseys and pretty ribbons around their hats, and although Ouma [grandmother] wishes to nurse her bad temper and her scepticism, the laughter and babble of the children, the guitar and the jolly singing, and Mrs. January pressing her to eat just a teeny-weeny frikkadel [meatballs] before they even get on to the highway, soon lift her spirits, so that in no time she is singing along, the children helping her with the funny black words, so old-fashioned, her little ones, they know everything about the struggle. How nice and jolly it is in the bus. Together the big women lift their arms and sway to the song, happy-y-y like the New Year Coon Carnival [Coloured New Year's festival in Cape Town] she saw on the TV last year—although that lot with their minstrel faces, she remembers in time, withdrawing the private comparison, are just a disgrace. Which for a while makes her compose herself as she concentrates on her dignity. But the mood is too infectious, and by the time they arrive in Castle Street where the buses park, Ouma Sarie tumbles toyi-toying out of the bus like everyone else.

It is a perfect winter's day with a jewel of a sun in a bright blue sky. If she had earlier doubted the wisdom of coming along, she now knows that God himself is smiling up there, for would he not have churned up the streets with proper Cape wind and rain if he had not approved? But this day is a sign that the young people have been right after all, that what the government these long years have told them was the straight and narrow path was all the time the ways of the devil. How could such a fine-looking gentleman like Nelson Mandela—she just knows that he must have good coloured blood in him—not be the voice of truth and justice. And so she toyi-toyis gaily up Buitenkant Street, where a contingent from one of the black townships joins in so that they all get mixed up together, actually holding onto the bony waist of a sisi [sister]—and oh, how good it is, with everyone out in the warm winter sunshine today. . . .

The children, trained in chanting, shout after her, Mandela's floor, Mandela's toilet. Another child takes over, Kill the Boer, kill the farmer, kill the bubbi in his pyjama, but he is soundly beaten over the head by a man in an old-fashioned red fez. All of which confuses Ouma, who has to be helped down the marble steps. Memories of 16 June 1976 and of Sharpeville before that buzz like persistent flies around her head, a memory of shooing everyone in-doors in case the three black men employed by the Logan Hotel were to go on the rampage. She swats Sharpeville aside decisively, intent on a new vision of peace and justice and harmony, just as Sally explained.

She may not catch all of the speech making, but knows that they are very, very good. Bishop Tutu, say what you like, is a fine, fine speaker, cutting a grand figure in his purple frock, a colour straight from heaven as she has always said, his voice like the engine of a train through a hilly landscape, just gathering steam and beauty as he speaks of those very good things, of rebuilding the country, of food and health and housing for all, of the forthcoming elections and, oh, even her Joop would not have minded his swaying and clapping like an Apostolic, for there comes a season, a time and a place, when even Apostolic behaviour must be overlooked. And what a sensible white man that Mr. Slovo is in his communist socks; she can only hope that he changes them from time to time, even though it's winter, cause since he's been back in the country the TV has been speaking nonstop about these red socks. Anyone can see his name in his oupa's [grandfather's] own language means the word—she read that somewhere—for the words that come tumbling out of his mouth are like the clear mountain stream of the Word which was with God and the Word that was God, a new beginning of light that shines in the darkness and the darkness has not overcome it. Before her very eyes the Word becomes flesh, full of grace and truth, so that the whole city, crammed into the Grand Parade and spilling over into the streets, beholds the glory of justice and freedom finally come, and she blushes for the white people's lies, Boer and English lies fed over the years and foolishly swallowed by her, and then her eyes fill with tears of shame for the poor Mrs. Slovo [Ruth First], a pretty woman, too, blown to bits, they say for standing up against those lies, even if they weren't married—

why else would she be called by some other name?—but what does she, old Sarie, care any more about such things in the face of abomination; she will honour the woman with the fine married name she deserves. That the man is a saint and not a communist at all is as clear as this wondrous day that God has given them to celebrate freedom.

As the food is shared around and the children dart about like dassies [rock rabbits], Ouma zealously holds her left fist up, stamps her feet, oblivious of the beer being smuggled under her very nose. There is a wonderful smell of herbal smoke in the air, much nicer than cigarettes; there is singing and dancing, and when the bishop sets free clutch after clutch of coloured balloons, lifted by the breeze and kept hovering just out of reach, Ouma, overcome by the beauty of it all, feels, first in her heart, the transformation, turning her inside out, turning her into a princess—yes, nothing short of a princess, waving her fist like a magic wand in this fairyland.

Nkosi sikilele iAfrika/Malu apanyiswe lumu lwayo.

Their voices swoop like summer swallows, weaving up through the balloons to circle the very top of Table Mountain.

The sun is a ball of fire and the sky is streaked with the holiest reds and gold by the time they are finally settled in the bus. Yes, what a business getting themselves together, all these people tired, lost, and jostled, as they must be even in fairyland, where she explains to the whining children, patience also must be practised. But now, as the engine starts up, they fall asleep with heavy bladders, the beauty of the day stamped on their chocolate-smudged faces.

Witchcraft in Soweto

Adam Ashforth

Although the triumph of the freedom struggle in 1994 was greeted with a national wave of euphoria, the introduction of democracy did not solve all of South Africa's problems. Moreover, the end of apartheid removed a large abstract force that people could point to, often with a great deal of justification, as the source of many of their problems. As the largest former liberation movement, the African National Congress, became the ruling party, a former source of unity became a focus of mundane politics. At the same time, the new system benefited some black South Africans—especially those who already had education and the right political connections—much more than others. For many, democracy meant continued un- or underemployment at the same time that many of their neighbors began to prosper. Many people explained their personal misfortunes through the traditional cosmology of witchcraft, and sought help from healers and diviners to protect them against their neighbors' use of evil forces against them. These African understandings of misfortune, which had persisted alongside adherence to Christianity, were on the lips of many people in South Africa's townships in the years after the end of apartheid.

Adam Ashforth, an Australian-born anthropologist, conducted participant-observation research in Soweto beginning in 1990 after Mandela's release. Ashforth worked closely with a friend, the man he refers to in this work as Madumo, who suffered from a variety of ills that he attributed to witchcraft and sought to remedy through the assistance of traditional healers.

As he began to glimpse the possibility of a passage through the torment he now knew to be wrought by witches, began to dare to hope, Madumo became convinced that he was not alone in falling victim to witchcraft in the new South Africa. All around he saw its evil presence. Every family seemed to be afflicted in some way, even those who appeared prosperous. Especially the prosperous! Stories circulated in whispers: this one is rich because he's made a deal with Mamlambo, the evil snake; he had to give Mamlambo his firstborn son so that Mamlambo would give him money. . . . Drawn by Madumo's growing obsessions, I too became steadily more aware of the fear of witchcraft lurking beneath the surface of everyday life. I would discreetly ask friends about their problems and learn that witchcraft was a worry to all. Madumo insisted that the "volume of witchcraft" was increasing enormously. I asked around. Most people agreed.

On our way back from the cash machine after visiting Mr. Zondi, we decided to make a closer study of this deluge of witchcraft. Madumo suggested that I tape an interview with him about his views on witchcraft in Soweto. We stopped at Lekoka Street to fetch my machine.

Over the years Madumo and I, along with Mpho, Thabo, and other friends, have recorded dozens of conversations about the situation in Soweto. When I was first here, in 1990, we used to gather with groups of comrades and talk about the Struggle, interview activists about their heroic deeds, and analyze endlessly the possibilities for the future. South Africa in those days was a center of world attention, and Sowetans felt themselves to be at the center of South Africa. As an outsider, I was assumed to be telling their story to the world and "exposing the Government." At the time I thought I was gathering material for a study of political transition. We called it Research. Then the war with Inkatha began. You can hear it in the background of some of our tapes. In 1992, I bought a video camera and we began to document the everyday currents of life lived in the wake of History. We taped interminable talk about politics and violence and freedom and crime. We were always taping something: a chat after breakfast; a rally; a riot. The tape was rolling when the police began shooting at the crowds mourning Chris Hani in the streets outside Protea Police Station in '93. On that tape, the picture stays steady and zooms towards the gunmen as the volleys ring out, before tumbling skywards and then back to the ground amongst the feet pounding in flight from tear gas and bullets towards the shelter of a neighboring yard. (In the stampede away from the bullets one of the "comrades" had the presence of mind to try stealing Mpho's camera, but Mpho fought him off while they were scrambling over a fence.) After a while the video camera, and its "cameraman," were mostly pressed into service by the local kids in Lekoka Street to "televise" their impromptu talent shows, beauty pageants, and soccer matches. In '94, when the elections came, Madumo and I, along with our other friends, talked on tape about freedom and democracy and the prospect of a better life for all. We interviewed neighbors on their way to vote. We taped ourselves celebrating at parties and rallies. I took photographs, too. Thousands of them. They reside still in albums all over Soweto. I used to fantasize about "doing something" with all this stuff, but never got around to it. Though fragments have appeared here and there over the years, the mass of it is still waiting in boxes in my study.

So, when Madumo suggested we tape our conversations about witch-craft, it seemed an ordinary enough thing to do—just a way of telling our-selves we were being serious, doing research like in the old days. Madumo felt it was something he could offer me in return for helping him with the money for his healer. We fetched the tape recorder and stopped at Moloi's bottle store for refreshments before returning to Madumo's room.

I set up the recorder. "When would you say it started increasing?" I asked Madumo when the machine was ready. "I mean, I don't remember people being so much bothered by witchcraft before." I shifted my weight and Ma-dumo's bed sagged. There was nowhere for me to put my glass. I couldn't get comfortable. My shoulder was cramping from sitting too long in the broken seat of the Dombolo while battling through throngs of commuters on the Old Potch Road from Southgate back to Soweto. I felt cramped, too, by the idea of being ON AIR and would much rather have stretched my legs out to where the microphone sat at the end of the bed and enjoyed my glass in peace.

Madumo, having organized the glasses and poured out two generous tumblers of whiskey, squatted in readiness on a beer crate beside the bed, focusing intently upon the microphone like a boxer in training setting up a rhythm on his speed ball. "This witchcraft?" he said. "I would reckon from '95 . . . January, January '95 . . . around that time . . . after the elections. . . . That was when we Africans, South Africans, Black South Africans . . . we just thought . . . generally like, we thought that now we are free. Free at last. Free from the hands of the White Man. Everybody then just told himself that 'Oh, we don't have any grudges with Whites—they're our brothers and all—now we're going to face each other, black and white together, since now we are all free. We're going to face each other.'" He paused for a mo-ment, studying his feet. "But instead, we found ourselves facing each other, black to black. . . ."

I found myself sitting upright, closely attentive.

"And one other thing that has caused this high volume of witchcraft," he continued, "is the lack of jobs. When other families are going well, their lives are compared. Then others become jealous of them and cause this harm. So it's lack of jobs."

"Let me get this straight," I said. "Freedom and democracy have caused the increased witchcraft because they've led to more jealousy. People are coming face-to-face with each other because they are no longer oppressed by the White Man. They are blaming each other now for their lack of success?"

"Ya," Madumo replied. "It's direct confrontation. Like, everyone is asking themselves: Who owns this? Who is having that? I don't know how to put it, really. Everything has changed. You know, in the past everyone was demanding their freedom. There was this slogan of 'We Want Freedom.' And everything was blamed on the National Party and the apartheid regime. Then the black leadership took over. So anybody with bad fates now, misfortunes like, is pointing the finger to someone else in a direct confrontation. There's no more of that old story of saying, 'I'm suffering because of apartheid, because of the White Man.' Now it's, 'I'm like this because of my neighbor.' It's all turned around."

While Madumo was speaking, his landlady's boyfriend, BraJohnny, appeared in the yard outside, stacking beer crates. A heavy-set man in his fifties with a light complexion and a clean-shaven skull, BraJohnny was dragging on a cigarette as he carried empty crates from the kitchen. Madumo greeted him and called him into the room. He showed him the bottle of Jameson Irish Whiskey I'd found in Moloi's. BraJohnny's eyes lit up. I switched off the tape and waited.

"It's special whiskey from overseas," said Madumo.

BraJohnny asked for a "tot" and Madumo said "sure." He filled a beer glass with whiskey. BraJohnny gulped a good mouthful and smacked his lips before exhaling a fiery gasp. "Phew!" he said. "That's hot stuff." Madumo laughed and drove the talk towards football, securing for himself thereby an invitation to the house to watch the big match between Kaiser Chiefs and Orlando Pirates on Sunday and the prospect of drinks in return. BraJohnny probably doesn't recognize Madumo as one of the crowd of faces on that day back in '86 when the young comrades disciplined him at a People's Court hearing. He'd been accused of mistreating his wife and taking up with a girlfriend—MaDudu. He was whipped almost insensate. While Madumo and BraJohnny speculated upon the outcome of Sunday's game and kicked about their memories of big matches past, I lost track of their talk and drifted into speculations of my own.

As Madumo says, habits of blaming apartheid were deeply ingrained here. And "Apartheid," named not just a government's policy or ideology but also the source and shape of a generalized misfortune: Why are we suffering? Because of Apartheid. The equation was too obvious to require elaboration. Even when un-stated, as it mostly was, such an axiom could encompass in a solidarity of suffering the likes of BraJohnny and his estranged wife as well as the comrades like Madumo who had whipped him mercilessly in the righteousness of their "people's power." And it sometimes seemed as if misfortune became more bearable for having such a name. Suffering the afflictions of Apartheid was all the more noble for serving the cause of destiny: Freedom. At the same time, the motive force behind the suffering—the "racist regime"—seemed, paradoxically, all the more powerful for the invocation of that awful word naming its cause. There was so much suffering about. Who could doubt that *something* must be behind it? In the gigantic scale of its manifest evil effects, that powerful something towered over other agents of misfortune such as witches.

Then the politicians pronounced the death of apartheid and the liberation Movement became the government. Freedom came and with it a chaos of possibility to fragment the meanings of misfortune. The solidarity of suffering was shattered as the question Why are we suffering? lost its distinctive hue. Blaming Apartheid and the White Man made less sense in an era of unparalleled social and economic advancement for black South Africans—*some* black South Africans. Cleaving to the old formulas would have made it imperative to ask: if the White Man is making our family suffer, why is he allowing another just down the street to prosper? And whereas in the old days the prosperous could be branded as "sellouts"—for no one prospered without the consent of the authorities—in the new South Africa everyone was supposed to be "progressing"; and the purpose of political power was to make that happen. The image of power no longer represented the White Man. Institutions of government slowly took the form of ordinary black men and women struggling, and mostly failing, to do good things against overwhelming odds (with the exception of Mandela, who always carried some kind of saintly aura). The sense of the enormous evil potential of government gradually withered away. If there was no longer a monumental force of evil named Apartheid in the new South Africa, there was no massive countervailing force of the good, either. In such a field, the lesser agents of misfortune, the witches, could flourish.

Somebody, probably MaDudu, called from the kitchen door across the yard. BraJohnny answered the call and left, concealing his glass of whiskey in a hand crooked behind his sleeve.

Madumo returned his attention to the tape recorder. I flicked on the switch.

"What was I saying?" he asked.

"What were you saying? I don't know, something about witchcraft," I replied.

"About this witchcraft . . ." he said pausing for a moment, "oh yes, I remember. It's also about jobs. It's the lack of jobs that's contributed to the high volume of witchcraft. Because if someone is having a job, then his neighbors become jealous and will witch him so as to make him lose that job. That's why we're having so much high unemployment, because of this witchcraft."

"It's a vicious circle, then this witchcraft business," I said, trying to gather my thoughts and return to the issue. "Witchcraft is causing people to lose their jobs, then the unemployment causes jealousy in those without jobs, so they then witch their neighbors who are more successful, causing them to lose their jobs, and that makes more unemployment, and then more jealousy. . . ."

Madumo paused for a moment. "Ya, it's like that."

"Yikes!" I said. We both laughed. "So nobody who loses his job thinks that it's just because of himself—he's lazy, say—or else because of the economy, or whatever? It always must be witchcraft?"

"No, not always. They're not always saying that. But it's difficult. If you lose your job, but then the other one doesn't, it's obvious you're going to suspect this thing. Obvious."

"So what is to be done?"

"Hey, we must ask Mr. Zondi [a traditional healer]. He can tell us that for sure. But the way I'm seeing it, I think these traditional healers must play a part. They're the ones who should be solving this thing. I mean, if we've got so many traditional healers, why do we have to suffer by becoming victims of evil forces?" Madumo remembered that at the inauguration of President Mandela in 1994 there had been hundreds of traditional healers massed at the Union Buildings at Pretoria to bless the new regime: "Who paid those thousands of healers at the Union Buildings? Why can't these healers protect our communities voluntarily? They can't just let our community be destroyed by this evil monster that is not seen, since they are in a position of curing it. They should form a club, like when they went to the Union Buildings for Mandela's inauguration and danced and burnt all the herbs for all South Africans—for Blacks, Whites, Indians, and all. They should go from location to location and pour herbs on the boundaries to keep out the witches. They should make rallies in the locations to sniff witches out. They should drive them out! They should protect the community by pouring their herbs in the street. We've got trucks and all. They should load in drums and drums of those herbs and pour them in the street. Sniff these people out. Definitely. I'm sure if they are going to protect us, witches won't be strong. If they just burn their substances, witches won't be strong." As a child of the era of mass action, Madumo thought it obvious that the healers should combine their efforts to struggle for the common good. "They should make rallies," he insisted again.

"But Madumo," I said, "I didn't think it worked like that. I mean, remember what Mr. Zondi said about his great-grand-father being the main man of his ancestors, the one from whom all his powers come? Wouldn't it be useless for Zondi to make a rally with other *inyangas* [healers] unless his great-grandfather approved? And who's going to organize all those dead ancestors? Hey, you'll have to wait until Mandela dies, then he can get together with Oliver Tambo and Slovo and organize the ancestors properly."

"And Hani! Don't forget Comrade Chris!" said Madumo, laughing.

"Yeah, of course Hani. They can build a nation of ancestors." I was joking, but the point was serious. In the past, ancestors of great chiefs and kings became ancestors of the whole nation, guiding and protecting their collective destiny. Not any longer. The casualties of colonialism in this part of the world had been felt not only amongst the living. Nowadays you are lucky if you know the name of your own father, let alone the ancestors of old.

"And another thing," said Madumo, returning to his theme with quiet intensity, "these *inyangas* are too jealous. That's why they don't organize. They're just in business for themselves; they don't care about anyone else. Why can't these people help with foreign investment? They've got the power to help with high escalating crime, help the police. Help the miners to produce more gold and prevent mines collapsing. And help fishermen down in wild seas. Help wineries in the Cape. Help with the different types of sickness that are found in the whole African continent. Sniff all the witches and destroy them from the society, since those witches are really cruel and destructive. And most important of all, they should stop supplying herbs to political organizations to strengthen them in fighting."

"But Madumo," I said, mischievously seeking to undermine his confidence in the enterprise of divination, "if these *inyangas* are so powerful, why couldn't they find that little girl in the East Rand?"

The seven-year-old child disappeared on the day before she was due to appear in court to testify against the man accused of raping her. Four months later, as a result of the usual police incompetence, the child had still not been found and the case became a cause célèbre in the Johannesburg press. The girl's mother, with financial assistance of the congress of civic associations, hired a *sangoma*, a diviner, to help find her. Diviners are supposed to be skilled at finding things. Indeed, one of the tests they are given before graduating through their *ukuthwasa* [spirit possession] involves finding a hidden object. No luck. A reward of ten thousand rands was posted by the police, but still the girl was missing. Shortly afterwards, the investigating officer convened a rally of diviners in a stadium near the child's home to determine her whereabouts. They were to become eligible for the reward. Few black South Africans would deny that the officer was acting responsibly. The diviners came in scores, with thousands of onlookers. They threw their bones, burnt their herbs, and communed with their ancestors. Then they sent the police off to the places pinpointed by the spirits. For the next week members of the South African Police Service searched houses, rivers, and swamps in diverse parts of the country in quest of the little girl.

The press reported the diviners' work with a mixture of irony and detachment. Black journalists are particularly skilled at striking a note in their writing that allows the believers to believe and the scoffers to scoff while preserving their own dignity as hard-nosed reporters amongst their white colleagues. My friends in Soweto especially enjoyed the coverage of the story of a diviner from the east of Johannesburg who made himself a laughing stock before a crowd of five thousand when he insisted that the girl was in a river nearby despite the failure of police divers to locate her. His spirits had told him she was there. The crowd insisted that he enter the water himself and retrieve the girl, but he was afraid of the snake. Bodies of water such as that river are widely believed to be the sanctuaries of magical snakes, and the diviner was terrified that if he entered the water without appeasing the snake he would be in peril of his life. The crowd had no sympathy, less patience. The very least he should do before entering the water, he insisted, was slaughter a goat to appease the snake. But there was no goat, nor time to delay. For even if under the water, the girl could still be alive. Most people here are convinced that the snake can keep people under water, alive, for years at a time. Indeed, many diviners insist upon having survived such an experience as a way of demonstrating their astonishing powers. The crowd at the river in Nyoni Park had no time for his fears. The diviner tossed a fifty-cent coin into the water in lieu of a sacrificial goat and began his search. A few seconds later he leapt from the water. The snake was after him, he shrieked. The police divers, burly Afrikaners, re-entered the water. They fished out a rusty exhaust pipe: the diviner's snake. The crowd was merciless; the diviner was miffed. "We do not need white people to interfere with this," he is reported to have said. "This is a black thing and needs the support of our people. All *inyangas* must come and coax the mamba so that we can take the child."

Reports of the divination fiasco occasioned much mirth amongst my friends in Soweto at the time, especially the story of the hapless diviner with his exhaust pipe. I wasn't surprised. People here tend to combine a deep faith in the general possibility of the divinatory enterprise with a hearty skepticism about particular diviners. Most people have received, or know someone who has received, false divination from these people. A granny I know, when her firstborn was an infant, discovered one of the baby's diapers to be missing—a potentially serious situation as witches could use the soiled nappy to perform their evil work on the child. She went to a diviner, who threw her bones and saw that the diaper had been taken by a woman neighbor to bewitch the child. After a terror-stricken week, during which she harbored all manner of plans for revenge should the infant die while she was trying to figure out how to pay for the treatment to protect the baby, the granny went to visit her sister and discovered the missing diaper safe and sound.

A couple of weeks after the spectacle of public divination in search of the child, the man accused of raping the child—whose trial had been aborted for want of a witness—was rearrested. Under the impression that he could apply to the Truth and Reconciliation Commission for amnesty, he confessed to murdering the girl and led the investigators to a grave miles from anywhere pinpointed by the diviners. The first official joint effort of police and diviners thus ended in a flop. But the failure of divination was not generally seen as proof of the futility of the whole enterprise of divination. All it proved was that the particular diviners who turned out to chase the reward money were phonies.

"No," said Madumo in reply to my question about diviners and the missing girl, "some of these people are just taking chances. You can't just trust them at all except if they prove their powers to you. That's why I trust Mr. Zondi. One hundred percent."

Nationalize the Mines

Julius Malema

*The mining sector that sparked South Africa's industrial revolution in the nine-
teenth century remains key to its economy and an important symbol of the country's economic might in the twenty-first century. As we saw in part VI, the Freedom
Charter of 1955 called for "the mineral wealth beneath the soil" to be "transferred to
the ownership of the people as a whole." This language has provided an opportunity for populists like Julius Malema (1981–), the African National Congress (ANC)
Youth League leader, to argue in recent years that the mines should be nationalized. As a ruling party since 1994, however, the ANC has embraced probusiness
policies in tune with a globalized economy. It has also continued the trend, begun
in the late apartheid years, of privatizing sectors of the economy, such as steel production, formerly controlled by the government. ANC economic policies, like those
in much of the post–Cold War world, have resulted in economic expansion but a
net loss of jobs and widening inequality. South Africa's unemployment rate hovers
near 25 percent, with the young suffering the worst unemployment. Malema and
others have therefore called for nationalization as a return to first principles, while
others, including leaders of the Communist Party, have argued that nationalization is not a viable policy.*

*Malema is a firebrand who has been at the center of several controversies, includ-
ing reviving the liberation-era song "Ayesaba Amagwala" (The cowards are scared)
that calls on listeners to "shoot the Boer" (for which he was convicted of hate speech)
and demanding the overthrow of neighboring Botswana's democratically elected
government. For these and other transgressions, the ANC in 2011 suspended him
from the party and from his post as leader of the Youth League. Malema was later
expelled, but he has remained in the public eye particularly in the aftermath of the
police massacre of striking miners at Marikana in 2012. The issues he has raised
(however cynically) about wealth and inequality are unlikely to go away.*

This forum is important because credible and evidence-based information
and data [are] brought and in most instances confirming what the ANC
Youth League has always said, particularly that 1) the people of South Af-

rica have not substantially benefitted from the country's mineral resources and 2) that South Africa remains the most lucrative mining territory in the entire world.

Most of you here might be aware of the research report released in April this year [2010], by the American banking Group, Citigroup, which said that South Africa is the richest in the world when it comes to mineral reserves.

We are indeed the richest country in the world when it comes to mineral resources because we are home to 70% of the world's platinum group metals, more than 70% of chrome, manganese, iron ore and many other critical precious and industrial metals.

Our massive minerals wealth and resources however co-exist with high levels of poverty, unemployment and starvation of particularly the black majority and Africans in particular.

While the economy grew over the last 16 years, not so many jobs were created to redeem the majority of our people from absolute poverty.

The ANC government's efforts to make sure that people have better and sustainable livelihoods have not succeeded because we have not changed the structure of South Africa's economy.

We have dedicated much time and efforts trying to deal with issues of service delivery within a very limited focus, but have not moved decisively to transform the economy.

The model of empowerment we adopted, in particular BEE [Black Economic Empowerment] has not succeeded in empowering the majority of our people. Instead, few and politically connected individuals are the ones who have reaped the fruits of Black Economic Empowerment.

When we went to Polokwane [conference of the ANC held in 2008, at which Jacob Zuma replaced Thabo Mbeki as leader], the question of few people benefiting from BEE deals was one of the issues we raised and one of the issues that led to the removal of the leadership that wanted to control and own the ANC forever.

If reports that such trends is repeating itself under the new administration are true, then we will again have a bigger problem, because our people are getting more impatient with slower and lack of economic emancipation and freedom.

The ANC has a strategic objective and vision on how it can best resolve these challenges of high levels of poverty, unemployment and starvation.

That vision and strategic objective is the FREEDOM CHARTER.

The Freedom Charter says that under the democratic government, the minerals [sic] wealth beneath the soil, monopoly industries and banks shall be transferred to the ownership of the people as a whole.

This Freedom Charter was re-affirmed in all ANC Conferences, including the 2007 52nd National Conference of the ANC in Polokwane, which said ANC's view on economic transformation takes as its starting point, the Freedom Charter's clarion call that the people shall share in the country's wealth.

We have been listening to leaders of the ANC who have been saying nationalisation is not the policy of the ANC. It is the policy of the ANC and we want to reactivate it so it becomes policy of the government.

A debate on whether to nationalise or not does not arise in the ANC, because all of us, who have joined the ANC, joined in order to realise the aims and objectives of the Freedom Charter, which amongst other things say Mines should be nationalised.

If you say it is not the policy of the ANC. . . . You are denouncing the Freedom Charter. . . . Everyone else junior and senior must respect the policies of the ANC.

Those in the ANC, who oppose Nationalisation of Mines, are in actual fact opposing what Nelson Mandela, Walter Sisulu, Govan Mbeki and many others were imprisoned for. Those who oppose Mines nationalisation in the ANC are opposing what O.R. Tambo, Robert Resha, Patrick Maoloa were exiled for. They are opposing what Chris Hani was killed for. Chris Hani was killed because he was not ready to sacrifice the Freedom Charter, and we will never betray him.

The ANC Youth League 1st National General Council, which happened between the 24th and 27th of August here in Johannesburg, took a very clear resolution on Nationalisation of Mines and how it is going to benefit all the people.

We re-affirmed our standing that Mines' Nationalisation should happen in order to achieve the following:

a. Increase the budget of the State for social development purposes, e.g. Health, Education, Rural development, fight against crime and job creation.
b. Lay a very firm basis for the country's minerals to be locally beneficiated and industrialised.
c. Change the South African economy from over-dependence and reliance of exporting of natural resources and importing of finished goods and services.
d. Create new economic centres of development outside of Johannesburg, Durban and Cape Town.
e. Could improve the working conditions and salaries of Mine workers.

The government revenue that is generated from taxes will not be able to build better lives for all South Africans. Government cannot solely rely on taxes to deliver better services to majority of our people. South African [*sic*] will not be able to deal with the housing backlog, free education access, better healthcare, safety and security, employment of particularly youth if we are not in control of the key and strategic sectors of the South African economy. The wealth of South Africa should benefit all who live in it.

It is an open secret that ordinary workers in Mines are the least beneficiaries of mining in South Africa either as recipients of salaries and stakeholders in mining. Mineworkers in South Africa are underpaid and work under difficult conditions and unsafe Mines. Their workplaces and socioeconomic existence expose these workers to fatal diseases and accidents. Nationalised Mines should be beacons of safer working environments and better working conditions, as they will not be in narrow pursuit of profits at the expense of community and human development.

With State ownership and control of Mineral Resources, South Africa will be able to attract industrial investors, who will contribute to the growth of the economy, transfer skills, education and expertise to locals and give them sustainable jobs. It can never be correct that an absolute majority of the Minerals we produce is exported to other countries, with very little efforts to build internal capacity to beneficiate these minerals.

Nationalisation of Mines will lead to greater local beneficiation, industrialisation, growth of the economy and jobs for majority of our people. The industrial strategy adopted by government will never succeed unless we have State control and ownership of the natural resources.

We need metals, iron ore, gold, platinum, coal, chrome, manganese and many other minerals to industrialise. South Africa's skills [and] development efforts should be dynamically (not exclusively) linked to the industrialisation of minerals wealth.

Although related to the above component, it is important to highlight the fact that the South African economy as it currently stands bears strong features of all colonial economies. Primarily, all colonial economies were positioned as sources and reserves of primary goods and services for the colonisers' economies.

Post political independence, many if not all postcolonial economies continued to function and operate in the same manner colonisers designed them—exporters of primary commodities and importers of finished goods and services. This pattern has a direct impact on the sustainability of postcolonial economies as they are heavily reliant on the demand of their goods and services by former colonisers and bigger market economies.

Xenophobic Violence

Nathan Geffen

With the dismantling of apartheid, large numbers of Africans from other countries began to settle in South Africa. In many cases, skilled people came to take up positions in South Africa that were now open to blacks. But larger numbers of people came as economic and political refugees from countries such as neighboring Zimbabwe, which suffered an economic meltdown in the mid-2000s, and the Democratic Republic of Congo, where civil war has raged since 1997. Poor South Africans in townships and informal settlements began to resent the presence of these foreigners, whom they saw as threatening their own fragile economic security. Although the postapartheid years saw economic growth in South Africa, this benefited wealthier members of society, including the new black economic elites, while leaving most people little better off in material terms than they had been before. In many cases, lower-level jobs disappeared as a liberalized economy put new pressure on South African industry. Resentments against foreigners boiled over in May 2008. South African mobs attacked settlements with concentrations of foreigners, and the foreigners were forced to flee to temporary camps set up by the government; at least sixty people died. The South African sci-fi film District 9 *(2009; directed by Neill Blomkamp) is a satire about this situation, while its title is a play on the black community in Cape Town, District 6, which was dismantled under apartheid.*

Nathan Geffen, a Treatment Action Campaign (TAC) activist, wrote at the time of the attacks, deploring not only the violence of South Africans against foreigners but also the inadequate and cynical response of the authorities. He argues that political maneuvering between the ruling African National Congress (ANC) and the Democratic Alliance, which controls Cape Town's government, left foreigners unprotected from further attacks. While the Democratic Alliance positions itself as a party devoted to protecting human and constitutional rights, Geffen maintains that in this instance its leader, Helen Zille, fanned the flames of xenophobia to seek her own political advantage. According to Geffen, the situation of a highly unequal society with a large number of foreigners is ripe for xenophobic violence, and he urges responsible political leaders to actively work against that outcome.

On Thursday 22 May [2008], Cape Town changed forever. The xenophobic violence that started 1,200 kilometres away in Gauteng spread to Du Noon township. On Friday the TAC offices began to get reports of violence on trains and Somali shops being looted. The details were scanty, but by Friday evening the consequences became visible even in the affluent city centre. About 150 people sought refuge outside Caledon Square, the city's main police station. Hundreds more gathered at the central train station so they could catch a train to Johannesburg in the morning and then leave the country.

A group of mainly Congolese men at Caledon Square explained that they had no trust in any South African government institution and demanded to see the UNHCR [United Nations High Commissioner for Refugees] so they could be repatriated. They said they would not move from Caledon Square until then even if it rained. One of them is a published writer and another lost his computer training school, worth tens of thousands of rands, in the violence. Angry young Burundians screamed at me that they wanted nothing more to do with my country. Malawian youths mournfully described how they felt they had no choice but to return home.

A Malawian husband and wife huddled with their child in the cold train station. The couple had been beaten and they were now returning home. Three men, who had not been beaten themselves were nevertheless terrified and determined to get back to Zimbabwe.

Soon we found out that thousands of immigrants, and some non-Xhosa speaking people from other South African provinces, had gathered into community centres in Khayelitsha, the metropolitan area's largest township, to escape the terror. . . .

Hundreds of volunteers, organisations and companies lent a hand. Jewish, Muslim and Christian organisations worked together. Habonim Dror made several thousand sandwiches in one day. The Bo Kaap [Malay district of Cape Town] mosques helped out many of the women and children staying at Caledon Square. His People sheltered up to 800 people at their N1 City church. The Methodist churches all opened their doors to refugees. St Georges [Anglican] Cathedral, the long serving bastion of struggle politics, was the venue for a large anti-xenophobic rally addressed by the Chief Justice. An enormous, urgent and co-operative civil society effort ensured that thousands of people, who have turned Cape Town into a fledgling cosmopolitan city, were reasonably fed and warm after the worst pogrom in our country's post-freedom history. . . .

South Africa's official opposition Democratic Alliance runs the city. The ruling ANC runs the province and national government. For the first few

days, there was hardly any response by the provincial and national government. So our media statements were more favourable toward the city.
But what shocked us was that the mayor, Helen Zille, and the provincial
premier, Ebrahim Rasool, would not meet or work with each other in the
face of Cape Town's biggest disaster. Every time we spoke to either party,
we would be given long, frankly boring and childish excuses with the one
blaming the other for non-co-operation.

The city's response, albeit better than the province at first, was also
awful. The inefficiencies can be forgiven—perhaps; the city is simply not
prepared for a disaster of this size. However, the decision by the mayor to
establish what are essentially refugee camps in damp, cold conditions on the
outskirts of the metropole, unserviced by adequate transport or health-care
is wrong for many reasons. . . .

The Caledon Square group is steadfastly refusing to go to one of these
camps. At one point they went on hunger strike with the simple demand
that they wanted a lawyer. Several lawyers offered services free to them the
next day. We have since gained their trust and as I write this they are staying
in a Jewish school hall in the mainly white suburb of Sea Point not far from
the city centre. The people who run the school have been overwhelmed by
their dignity and political acuity. . . .

Two weeks ago most people in South Africa and many people throughout the world believed we were the so-called rainbow nation, a country that
valued its diversity. Despite hiccups left over from the apartheid era and a
high crime-rate, this was apparently a society working hard to be tolerant of
difference. On Thursday 22 May I believed I lived in a city that was becoming urbane and sophisticated. These myths have now been shattered—and
they were never true. It is shameful that a terror so awful has been unleashed that some people would rather return to failed states like Zimbabwe
and Somalia than stay in Africa's richest and, at least so we thought, most
successful country.

The decade of racial politics by President Thabo Mbeki who has fostered
corruption, paid lip service to accountability and service delivery, denied
the science of HIV, prevaricated on crime and helped keep the Mugabe government in power [in Zimbabwe], has been sharply exposed. Government,
at every level, failed to respond appropriately to the xenophobes' pogrom.
And we all failed to realise how the inequalities in our society would rupture it so hideously so quickly.

The state's political failure over the last two weeks in South Africa has
been comprehensive. President Mbeki has been accurately and justifiably
denounced in the [Johannesburg] *Sunday Times*, *New York Times* and *Wall*

Street Journal and there is nothing further that need be said about this failed leader; he must simply be removed from power.

It is the leaders of the Western Cape and in particular Cape Town whose deplorable leadership needs to be exposed.

Ebrahim Rasool, the Western Cape premier[,] is embattled. His faction no longer controls the ANC in this province and he is plagued with accusations of improper conduct. He also appears to spend far too much of his time trying to remove the mayor from office. I was asked on radio last week what in particular I wished to criticise about his government's response to the mass displacement of people in Cape Town that started on 22 May. The answer was that there is nothing in particular to criticise because the Western Cape government did absolutely nothing useful for three critical days.

But it is Mayor Helen Zille, the leader of the opposition Democratic Alliance (DA), on whom I wish to focus most of this blog. I did not vote for her but before this disaster I was respectful of her and had some positive interactions with her. She has a deserved reputation for efficiency and financial incorruptibility, two attributes sorely needed in South African politics.

She has also been the main political beneficiary of the xenophobic violence and her behaviour indicates that she knows it and will exploit it.

For one thing, many people perceive her to have been the one political party leader to have responded to the displaced people. She can of course thank civil society for doing the bulk of the work that she and Premier Rasool should have worked together to do.

More importantly she undoubtedly realises that the Coloured vote upon whom she depends for power looks very secure. Many Coloured ANC voters or fence-sitters will have been frightened by the xenophobic attacks. If this happened to immigrants, could we be next, they will wonder. They will be concerned about a predominantly African party controlling the Western Cape and therefore be more likely to vote for the DA. Next year's elections, in which her party hopes to capture the Western Cape Province, look promising for Zille.

But Zille has been concerned that by keeping displaced people in community halls where weddings and other events are due to take place she would anger her potential voters. Therefore she has established refugee camps—which she euphemistically calls safe zones—far from communities and far from the city. Out of sight, out of mind.

These camps are a bad idea for a number of reasons that the UN and other expert relief agencies like Medecins Sans Frontieres have explained. The South African government has no expertise to run them. Containing health epidemics in such crowded unhealthy conditions is extremely difficult. They have the potential to become permanent or at least long-term and they make reintegration even more difficult.

Zille has refused to open community halls, such as the Sea Point Civic Centre for the Caledon Square group, to house displaced people. Many of the Soetwater camp displaced were originally in Ocean View's community hall but she gave in to the community's anger about having them there. Despite her claims to the contrary, we are aware of at least some displaced people being forcibly moved to these camps. The city continues to put pressure on displaced people, especially at smaller refuges, to move there. The Department of Home Affairs has been insisting on immigration status information from the people in the camps, further fuelling distrust. Also listen to the angry complaints of the displaced people in Youngsfield camp, a military facility incidentally. The Caledon Square refugees refuse to go to the camps because many of them have experienced the horrors of camps like these before in places like Rwanda and the DRC [Democratic Republic of the Congo]. They also need to get to work and their children to school, a Herculean task if one is based in most of these camps.

There is however an even more important reason why these camps are a bad idea. They signify victory for the xenophobes. The message Zille has sent out is that if you purge your community of people different to you, you can get away with it. The purged will lose and the purgers will win. So much for upholding the rule of law.

Then there have been her spate of thoughtless, even xenophobic, comments. I have been sceptical in the past of accusations against her that she uses race conflict as a political tool. But I have seen first-hand how she did it this past week.

"I have just witnessed a very disturbing incident where migrants behaved extremely abusively and perfectly good food was being thrown around. Some of the food may have been past its sell-by date, but it was good to eat. Local residents are understandably becoming very angry and an explosion will follow unless a serious security force deployment takes place," she told Disaster Management in front of TAC people. "We must all remember that not only refugees, or whatever they are [said dismissively], have rights. Other people have rights too," she said at the same meeting and in similar words to my colleagues and me at least twice.

"Community Halls were expressly intended from the outset, to be temporary measures during the height of the violence," she said in email correspondence justifying the camps, with the implication that the camps are not temporary.

"I cannot expect people to cancel a wedding in a community hall at a day's notice," she told us as an example of some of the people whose rights competed with the victims of last week's pogrom.

In another meeting she pointed out that those who booked community halls are tax-paying South Africans, forgetting it seems that every person who buys something in the country pays VAT and that the Bill of Rights does not differentiate taxpayers from non-taxpayers.

One thought has shaped Helen Zille's response to this crisis: If she plays her cards right, tomorrow the Western Cape belongs to her. . . .

There is no need to introduce conspiracy to understand what has happened over the past couple of weeks.

The outbreak of xenophobic violence can be explained by an unfavourable combination of a few factors: an already violent society, the acceptance—even encouragement—of xenophobia, massive inequality, the increased threat of poverty exacerbated by consistent service delivery failure and demographics.

South Africa's gini co-efficient (the standard measure of inequality) is about 58, making us one of the ten most unequal countries in the world and we are by far the most ethnically diverse of these. There is competition among poor people for basic materials like food and shelter but also commodities that allow people to be more included in our society: televisions, DVD players, cell phones, better clothes and computers for example.

All suburbs across the world's major cities are composed of communities whose members assist each other to obtain wealth. These communities are usually strongly centred around ethnic identity. Xhosas, Zulus, Afrikaners, English, Jews, Muslims, Somalis, Indians, Congolese, Nigerians, Zimbabweans and so on often assist people of their own language, religion or origin with business deals, favourable job applications and the like. In poor suburbs, criminal gangs often form in every group to use muscle to help compete for resources.

Immigrants are usually a more enterprising subset of the population from which they come. They generally realise they have to work extremely hard to thrive in their new country and their community networks are usually very strong. Majority local communities often do not do as well as immigrant or minority ones; they are seldom as organised or close-knit. When competition for resources is extreme, as in South Africa, jealousy builds up and xenophobic and racist ideas becomes common, even though the enterprise of many immigrants helps create jobs and services. Gangs in the local community, especially in a society like ours which is already very violent, target immigrant communities. Low-level xenophobic violence becomes a chronic problem. This has been the situation in South Africa for some time.

For example Somali immigrants have been frequently the victims of xeno-phobic attacks, often murderous ones, in Cape Town in the last few years. The Caledon Square group refugees have told me how they have been tar-geted by youths in Phillipi township for years. The situation is exacerbated by politicians, particularly local councillors, and journalists making com-ments which exacerbate xenophobia and racism, as well as the *systematic oppression of immigrants by the state*.

Soaring food and basic commodity prices have worsened poverty and the perceived competition within townships for resources in recent months. This could have increased the level of xenophobic violence.

At some point in the last two weeks, the number of xenophobic inci-dents reached a critical point, probably in Alexandra township in Johan-nesburg. When this happened, the visibility of the violence gave a green light to more and more gangs and individuals who had been considering xenophobic attacks, were prone to it, believed they could get away with it or occasionally took part in them. A domino effect ensued, first in one township and then across townships in Johannesburg and Pretoria and then across cities to Durban and Cape Town.

The above is surely not the full story and some commentators will pick holes in my argument, but it is a far better approximation of what happened than the Pahad brothers' one [Minister in the Presidency Essop Pahad and Deputy Minister of Foreign Affairs Aziz Pahad]. Though now there is cer-tainly the possibility of opportunistic politicians capitalising on hatred of immigrants to gain support and substantially worsen the situation.

Intergroup hatred and violence in a diverse society like South Africa has to be consciously confronted. Political leaders have to assume that by doing nothing each time a xenophobic or other hate-crime is committed, the situ-ation can deteriorate into what we've seen in the last two weeks. The Presi-dent, other political leaders, churches, mosques, synagogues, trade unions and civil society organisations have to speak out continuously against hate-crimes, day-to-day xenophobia and racism.

Yet many political leaders frequently make comments about immigrants being involved in crime, as *Helen Zille did a week ago*. President Mbeki's fail-ure to recognise the crisis of governance in Zimbabwe means that instead of receiving Zimbabwean immigrants with empathy, they are too often greeted with hatred in townships. His racial invective also worsens matters by creating a consciousness that encourages race-based beliefs instead of rejecting them.

We also need policies that alleviate the burdens of immigration from the poor. Many of Cape Town's poor have migrated here, and continue to do so, from the Eastern Cape over several decades. They compete with newly arrived poor people from other countries. Unfettered competition breeds hate in these conditions; state intervention to help all these communities is critical. We need policies that encourage settlement of new migrants in middle-class suburbs. And as at least one newspaper editor has opined, the Basic Income Grant, or similar, must be seriously considered. So should a large public works programme, not the Mickey Mouse one we currently have. None of this is easy.

Massacres frequently occurred under apartheid. A few were worse than the last two weeks. But what is different is that those massacres were a function of an almost universally reviled racist system. We could comfort ourselves in the knowledge that a better society lay ahead one day. The massacre and terror of the last two weeks is a step back, because that better society, our Constitutional Democracy, had arrived. . . .

The disillusionment with our failed politicians must be accompanied by active and sustained engagement by ordinary people to demand better political accountability and leadership. Most importantly we must demand policies that reduce the inequality and poverty that are the foundation of what has just happened. That is the only way we can improve South Africa's tragic politics.

Welcome to Our Hillbrow

Phaswane Mpe

Hillbrow, a densely packed Johannesburg neighborhood near the city center, has long been a neighborhood of immigrants, from Italians and Greeks in the mid-twentieth century to Congolese and others in the postapartheid years. In the last decade of apartheid, Hillbrow was also known as a racially mixed "gray area," where the official designation as a white group area had broken down as blacks moved into the city from the more remote townships. In the two decades since the introduction of democracy, many South Africans have associated the neighborhood with the presence of foreigners, known as makwerekwere, *often unfairly blaming them for broader South African problems, including crime and AIDS.*

In 2001 Phaswane Mpe (1970–2004) published Welcome to Our Hillbrow *as his first novel. The short novel deftly depicts many of the social ills afflicting post-apartheid society, from anomie and jealousy to AIDS and xenophobia. The selection draws a parallel between immigrants from other African countries who had alighted in Hillbrow and migrants from rural South African villages who had also settled there to pursue new opportunities. Like President Thabo Mbeki's "I Am an African" speech at the beginning of this part, the novel tries to connect all South Africans to a broader sense of belonging to Africa and to humanity at large.*

Like most Hillbrowans, Cousin took his soccer seriously. You and he had had many disagreements on the subject of support for foreign teams—especially those from elsewhere in Africa. You often accused him of being a hypocrite, because his vocal support for black non-South African teams, whenever they played against European clubs, contrasted so glaringly with his prejudice towards black foreigners the rest of the time. Cousin would always take the opportunity during these arguments to complain about the crime and grime in Hillbrow, for which he held such foreigners responsible; not just for the physical decay of the place, but the moral decay. His words were echoed by many others—among them, the white superintendent at your place in Van der Merwe Street, who told you when you moved in that Hillbrow had been just fine until those Nigerians came in here with all their drug dealing.

You, Refentse, child of Tiragalong (and, as you insisted in the days just before your death, also of Hillbrow), had never shared such sentiments. It was your opinion that the moral decay of Hillbrow, so often talked about, was in fact no worse than that of Tiragalong.

Think about it, Cousin, you would challenge. How many people are here in Hillbrow? How many of them are criminals? If you consider that the concentration of people in Hillbrow is dense, and work out the number of crimes in relation to the number of people, I tell you, you will find Tiragalong to be just as bad.

Anyway, there are very few Hillbrowans, if you think about it, who were not originally wanderers from Tiragalong and other rural villages, who have come here, as we have, in search of education and work. Many of the *Makwerekwere* you accuse of this and that are no different to us—sojourners, here in search of green pastures. They are lecturers and students of Wits, Rand Afrikaans University and Technikons around Jo'burg; professionals taking up posts that locals are hardly qualified to fill. A number of them can be found selling fruit and vegetables in the streets, along with many locals—so how can they take our jobs? Of course there are some who do drug trafficking. But when the locals are prepared to lap at them like starved dogs, what do you expect the struggling immigrants to do?

And while we're so busy blaming them for all our sins, hadn't we better also admit that quite a large percentage of our home relatives who get killed in Hillbrow, are in fact killed by other relatives and friends—people who bring their home grudges with them to Jo'burg. *That's* what makes Hillbrow so corrupt. . . .

You would want to add that some Makwerekwere were fleeing their war-torn countries to seek sanctuary here in our country, in the same way that many South Africans were forced into exile in Zambia, Zaire, Nigeria and other African and non-African countries during the Apartheid era. You would be reminded of the many writers, politicians, social workers and lecturers, and the endless string of South Africans hanging and jumping from their ninth floor prison cells because the agents of the Apartheid government wanted them to do so. The latter was called *Learning to Fly*. You would also remember the grisly details, draped in tears, from the testimonies of the Truth and Reconciliation Commission hearings, of South African policemen enjoying their beer and braai [barbeque] while black dissenters roasted alongside their roasted meat in the heat of a summer day—stuff that would be called surrealism or magic realism or some other strange realism were it simply told or written as a piece of fiction. And of course you could not forget all those black agents of the Apartheid State, playing their

Hillbrow street scene, 2007. Photograph by Thomas McClendon.

various roles with a mastery that confounded the minds of even the State itself. Black police officers contorting bribes from fellow blacks accused of political and other dissents. Black police and security forces hitting fellow blacks mercilessly for crimes that were often not committed. . . . *Teaching the kaffir a lesson or two,* as they said.

You would usually, however, spare Cousin these historical details, since he knew them just as well as you did; or rather, much better than you did, since he himself was part of the interrogating police force that knew only one reliable way of accessing truth from suspects: *torture.* Cousin would interrupt your thoughtful silence, by reminding you that you were ignoring more pressing concerns. Like the AIDS that *they* transport into the country.

Ah! This AIDS nonsense! I wish those girls and boys in our villages had more respect for their genitalia and did not leave them to do careless business in Hillbrow, only so that we can attribute the source of our dirges to Nigeria and Zaire and . . .

Cousin would not agree with you, of course. He never agreed with you where black foreigners from African countries, vulgarly referred to as *Makwerekwere,* were concerned. *Makwerekwere* was a word derived from *kwere kwere,* a sound that their unintelligible foreign languages were supposed to make, according to the locals. Cousin insisted that people should remain in their own countries and try to sort out the problems of these respective countries, rather than fleeing them; South Africa had too many problems of its own.

Surely we cannot be expected to solve all the problems of Africa? he would insist.

You agreed that we could not, even if we tried. But then, that was no excuse for ostracising the innocent, you also said.

The difference between you and Cousin was that he was a policeman. If *you* had no problems with *Makwerekwere*, then that was fine. What could you do anyway, even if you despised them with every drop of the river of blood and other juices that flowed in your body? On the other hand, being a policeman, there were many things that Cousin could do. And he did them. . . .

It was true that the beer you enjoyed was often bought by Cousin. And the food. You were, despite your disapproval of his actions, a beneficiary of his activities. Like so many people were beneficiaries. Including the close relatives and friends of his colleagues. Together with his colleagues, he would arrest *Makwerekwere*. Drive them around Hillbrow for infinite periods of time.

See it for the last time, bastards, they would tell the poor souls.

When the poor souls pleaded, the uniformed men would ask if they could make their pleas more visible. They did. Cousin and his colleagues received oceans of rands and cents from these unfortunates, who found very little to motivate them to agree to be sent back home. Some of the womenfolk bought their temporary freedom to roam the Hillbrow streets by dispensing under-waist bliss. They preferred to eke out a living here. Yes, they were ostracized, they agreed; but when the police left them in place, they could gather a thing or two to send back to their families at home. The foreign exchange rate really did favour them.

The *Makwerekwere* had also learned a trick or two of their own. Get a member of the police, or a sympathetic South African companion, to help you organise a false identity document—for a nominal fee. Or, set up a love relationship of sorts with someone from the city. It was better, so the word went around, to be so related to one who worked in the kitchens, as white suburbs are often referred to—the reason being that most black people eking out a living there were women doing kitchen and other household work (if, that is, one discounted the lovers and prostitutes engaged in bedroom work with the wealthy masters and madams). Police bothered you less often in the suburbs, because those were not regarded as high crime zones. And the security personnel who guarded those kitchens were often more preoccupied with chasing real criminals than people who simply came there to visit their friends and loved ones.

Which is not to say that these kitchens were absolutely safe. As you, Refentse, know so well!

The first time someone took out a knife on you, it was at Hyde Park Village, near Sandton, where you accidentally disturbed thieves stripping cars of their radio sets in the parking lot; Hyde Park, with its lily-white reputation for safety and serenity. You were not stabbed but only because you made it just in time into the courtyard of your aunt's employer's house, and the butcher knife pursuing you hit the door to the courtyard just as you turned the key to lock it.

You also liked to quote the story of how you and your University mates were held at gunpoint at Parktown Village in June of 1995, while a Wits University car that one of the students had borrowed was successfully redistributed. All the time that you and your friends were lying there, flat on your stomachs, people were jubilantly singing *Amabokoboko ayaphumelela* . . . in the streets, because the South African rugby team, the Springboks, had just won the Rugby World Cup.

There were other chilling stories of what happened in the kitchens. Of white madams raped and gagged by their South African garden boys—that is, black men to whom they could not afford to show any respect; of white men found hanging like washing waiting to dry, because they refused their so-called boys and girls permission to go home to bury a close relative; of whites killed simply because they were wealthy and tried to protect their wealth when robbers came to redistribute it; of whites hacked to death simply because they were white, an embodiment of racial segregation and black impoverishment, irrespective of their political allegiances and economic affiliations.

These are examples of the many cases of crime not caused by *Makwerekwere*, who were at any rate too much in need of sanctuary, even if it was sometimes a cold one, to risk attracting the attention of police and security services. *Makwerekwere* knew they had no recourse to legal defence if they were caught. The police could detain or deport them without allowing them any trial at all. Even the Department of Home Affairs was not sympathetic to their cause. No one seemed to care that the treatment of *Makwerekwere* by the police, and the lack of sympathy from the influential Department of Home Affairs ran contrary to the human rights clauses detailed in the new constitution of the country. Ambiguities, paradoxes, ironies . . . the stuff of our South African and *Makwerekwere* lives.

The World Cup

Christopher Merrett

South Africa's pariah status during the apartheid era curtailed the ability of individuals and, particularly, national teams to participate in international sporting events. International organizations and fans protested South Africa's sports policies, including the formation of racially exclusive national teams. Beginning in 1960 the Olympic organizing committee banned South Africa from competition. Everywhere South Africans competed, protests followed. A rugby match in 1969 between Swansea and the South African Springboks led to riots in England. The sports boycott became especially severe in the 1970s and 1980s. In Auckland a plane dropped smoke bombs and sacks of flour during a match in 1981 with the New Zealand All Blacks. In 1991 and early 1992, however, international sporting organizations lifted the boycotts following the rescission of apartheid legislation. In 1995 the Springboks hosted and won, in a thrilling final, the Rugby World Cup, cheered on by President Nelson Mandela.

In 2004 South Africa won the bid to host the FIFA (Fédération Internationale de Football Association) World Cup in 2010. Preparing for the event entailed the construction of numerous stadiums across the country and various infrastructure improvements. As the following piece, written by a freelance journalist, discusses, despite the excitement, hosting the tournament was not without controversy, including delays with building the stadiums, labor disputes, allegations of corruption, security concerns, and the evictions of poor people living in informal settlements. The tournament mainly proceeded smoothly from an international point of view, however, though the South African team was eliminated in the early rounds to the raucous sounds of the ubiquitous vuvuzela (plastic horn). In the final, Spain defeated the Netherlands 1–0.

This week, with the end of the Football World Cup, South Africa will cease to be FIFAland and regain its sovereignty. According to most South Africans with a media voice it has been a great triumph, although the successful teams hadn't read the script carefully enough. This was meant to be an African cup, or failing that a triumph for the global South. Nevertheless, it is hard to find an influential voice that is not waxing lyrical about rebranding the country, a new unity among South Africans and proof that an African nation can match the rest of the world.

There was always a very good chance that South Africa could host a successful World Cup. The money was there and the main challenge involved civil engineering and the construction of stadiums and roads. The politicians were on side and effectively nationalized football in their search for popularity, while lurking in the background was the heavy hand of FIFA. And there was never any doubt that South Africans could provide a good party.

The more responsible commentators are talking about legacy. There are high hopes, particularly of the tourist industry, but also foreign investment based on an improved national image. Then there is the expectation that the practical experience and psychological impact of organizing a successful mega-event will filter into other areas of South African life. Special World Cup courts, for example, operated with swiftness and efficiency unknown in ordinary experience.

But underneath the glossy façade of the World Cup, there were regular reminders of reality. Police fired stun grenades and rubber bullets at striking stadium security guards reportedly earning a pittance of 20 rand ($2.30) an hour. Two people died and 2000 were displaced when 500 shacks were destroyed by fire at Kennedy Road informal settlement in Durban (this was just three days before the Germany versus Spain semi-final). The country's former national police commissioner (and ex-head of Interpol), Jackie Selebi, was convicted of corruption. Government departments were found to have bought millions of rands' worth of World Cup tickets. This was illegal, but no one expects the culprits to be brought to book as they are ANC [African National Congress] loyalists. In the Eastern Cape, forensic scientists conducting autopsies were reported to be adapting their own tools bought from a hardware store to dissect bodies. And in the same province more than 30 young men died, and many more were maimed, by botched circumcisions conducted by unqualified traditionalists at initiation schools.

These are all symptoms of systemic failure. Most visiting football fans were probably entirely unaware of them. South Africans simply take them for granted, together with public education and health systems that have steadily deteriorated in the past 20 years. The country's electricity supply teeters on the brink of disaster and there are worrying indications of pollution, particularly from mines, that threaten water resources and agriculture. The capital city of KwaZulu-Natal, Pietermaritzburg, was recently put under administration after it was declared effectively bankrupt, its basic ser-

Cape Town residents blow vuvuzela trumpets in support of the South Africa soccer team, 2010. Photograph by Yves Herman. Used with permission from Thomson Reuters, JMIE66A168G0I.

vices near collapse. The appointed administrator described it as "run like a spaza shop [small store]." These are all indications of an inability to manage, plan and exercise the basic professional and technical standards common to all successful and democratic societies.

Football supporters, visitors and South Africans alike, have benefited from a new form of apartheid. Their interests have been carefully nurtured and protected[,] giving an impression of efficiency, progress and modernity. Elsewhere life has carried on as normal, characterized above all by pervasive indifference and a lack of competence. Recently in Mpumalanga, a man admitted to hospital with a fracture suffered such nursing neglect that his leg rotted and had to be amputated. Many teachers regularly abandon their classrooms to attend union meetings or look after their own affairs.

It is hard to see how running a successful World Cup will provide transferable skills to rectify these and myriad of other problems. And, since the mega-event has been six years in the making, why have lessons not been learned and applied? Improvements should already be evident.

The number of South Africans on welfare grants vastly exceeds the dwindling number of taxpayers. Yet politicians are already talking about a bid for the 2020 Olympic Games. This highlights a tragic South African tendency to depend on myth. The end of apartheid was labeled, and still widely believed to be, a miracle.

It was, in fact, based on a long process of negotiation by opposing nationalist forces led by realistic and able politicians such as Nelson Mandela and F.W. de Klerk who realized that they needed one another. The 1995 Rugby World Cup victory was widely hailed, but proved no more than a transient moment of euphoria. Hopes of a non-racial rainbow nation quickly evaporated under aggressive government policies of racial nationalism.

There is no particular reason to believe that the optimism built up around the World Cup will not go the same way. Public sector unions are gearing up for strikes, encouraged by settlements well above the inflation rate secured by transport and electricity supply workers who threatened to disrupt the World Cup.

Behind challenging wage demands there is fermenting anger at the bonus-fed lifestyles of top managers in parastatal organizations and frustration at incompetent management; as well as opposition to pervasive corruption known as tenderpreneurship that rewards the politically well-connected. Above all is the worry that after the international media has gone home, there will be renewed xenophobic violence directed at refugees from other African countries who show greater energy and enterprise than their township and informal settlement neighbors.

It may seem churlish to question what many see as an outstanding success. In some ways it has been. But ultimately it can only be justified by a demonstrable connection with improvements to fragile aspects of South African public life. A party that lingers happily in the memory is simply not good enough. Cliché it might be, but ultimately the people need bread, not circuses.

Glossary

amadhlozi Ancestors

ban Legal restriction imposed on person or organization under apartheid legislation

Bantu Language group to which most South African languages belong; used under apartheid to refer to Africans (now derogatory in reference to people)

Bantustan African "Homelands," formerly Native Reserves, under apartheid, referring to their purported self-ruled or independent status

bioscope Cinema; movie theater

black People of African, Asian, or mixed descent

boekevat Prayers

boer, Boer Farmer; as an ethnic term, refers to people of Dutch descent

Bushman Derogatory term for San-speaking foragers

Caffre, Caffrees Deeply derogatory word for Africans; before the late nineteenth century, simply a term to refer to particular groups of Africans (see also *kaffir*)

commando Boer citizen-soldiers organized for raiding and defense against Khoesan communities; adapted for guerrilla warfare in South African War

compound Family homestead, including dwellings, storage huts, and cattle enclosure, in African farming communities; also known as kraal

dagga Marijuana

heemraden Magistracy councilors

herrenvolkism Master-race ideology

Homeland African "Homelands," formerly Native Reserves, under apartheid, referring to their purported self-ruled or independent status

hostel Dormitory for migrant workers in urban areas and mines

Hottentot Colonial-era derogatory term for Khoekhoe people

inboek Peonage; bonded labor

induna Advisor; headman

inkosi Chief; lord

izinyanga (izinnyanga) Doctors; diviners

583

ja Yes

kaffir (kafir) Deeply derogatory word for Africans; before the late nineteenth century, simply a term to refer to particular groups of Africans

Khoekhoe, Khoena Herding and foraging peoples of the south-western Cape

Khoesan Group of click languages spoken by Khoekhoe and San

kholwa (kolwa) African Christian

kraal Family homestead in African farming communities (see *compound*); cattle enclosure within homestead

laager Boer defensive formation made by circling ox wagons

landdrost Magistrate

location Area reserved or designated for blacks

makwerekwere Derogatory term for African foreigners

mealies Corn (maize)

mfecane Disputed term for African upheavals of the early nineteenth century

Oumiesies Old missus

pass Document from the government or a white employer permitting a black person to be in particular area or to engage in particular activity

San Hunter-gatherer; often derogatory

sangoma Diviner

shebeen Illegal bar; common in black townships

sjambok Ox-hide whip

township Segregated black urban area under apartheid; post-apartheid, primarily black urban areas

trekboer, *pl.* **trekboere** Migratory cattle rancher

tsotsi Gangster

veld Grassland; countryside; open area

Voortrekkers Boers who migrated into the interior in the nineteenth century, during what was later called the Great Trek

witmens White men

Suggestions for Further Reading

There is a great deal of writing on South Africa. Our goal here is to suggest some of the most important works that speak to the themes covered in this volume. In addition to academic studies, we have included works from South Africa's rich literary traditions. In a few instances, works included here pertain to multiple headings. We also have included a section on some of the websites that offer readers an excellent way of further exploring South Africa's history, culture, and politics.

Part I. African Worlds, African Voices

Hamilton, Carolyn. *Terrific Majesty: The Powers of Shaka Zulu and the Limits of Historical Invention.* Cambridge: Harvard University Press, 1998.

Hofmeyr, Isobel. *"We Spend Our Years as a Tale That Is Told": Oral Historical Narrative in a South African Chiefdom.* Portsmouth, N.H.: Heinemann Press, 1993.

Landau, Paul S. *Popular Politics in the History of South Africa, 1400–1948.* New York: Cambridge University Press, 2010.

Peires, Jeffrey. *The House of Phalo: A History of the Xhosa People in the Days of Their Independence.* Johannesburg: Ravan Press, 1981.

Scheub, Harold. *The Tongue Is Fire: South African Storytellers and Apartheid.* Madison: University of Wisconsin Press, 1996.

Part II. Colonial Settlement, Slavery, and Peonage

Brink, André. *A Chain of Voices.* New York: William Morrow, 1982.

Elbourne, Elizabeth. *Blood Ground: Colonialism, Missions, and the Contest for Christianity in the Cape Colony and Britain, 1799–1853.* Montreal: McGill-Queens University Press, 2002.

Elphick, Richard, and Hermann Giliomee, eds. *The Shaping of South African Society, 1652–1840.* Middletown, Conn.: Wesleyan University Press, 1989.

Fredrickson, George. *White Supremacy: A Comparative Study in American and South African History.* New York: Oxford University Press, 1982.

Newton-King, Susan. *Masters and Servants on the Cape Eastern Frontier, 1760–1803.* Cambridge: Cambridge University Press, 1999.

Penn, Nigel. *The Forgotten Frontier: Colonist and Khoisan on the Cape's Northern Frontier in the Eighteenth Century.* Athens: Ohio University Press, 2005.

Ross, Robert. *Status and Respectability in the Cape Colony: 1750–1870*. Cambridge: Cambridge University Press, 1999.

Scully, Pamela. *Liberating the Family? Gender and British Slave Emancipation in the Rural Western Cape, South Africa, 1823–1853*. Portsmouth, N.H.: Heinemann Press, 1997.

Worden, Nigel. *Slavery in Dutch South Africa*. Cambridge: Cambridge University Press, 1985.

Part III. Frontiers

Comaroff Jean, and John L. Comaroff. *Of Revelation and Revolution: Volume 1; Christianity, Colonialism, and Consciousness in South Africa*. Chicago: University of Chicago Press, 1991.

Crais, Clifton C. *White Supremacy and Black Resistance in Pre-industrial South Africa: The Making of the Colonial Order in the Eastern Cape, 1770–1865*. Cambridge: Cambridge University Press, 1992.

Delius, Peter. *The Land Belongs to Us: The Pedi Polity, the Boers, and the British in the Nineteenth-Century Transvaal*. Berkeley: University of California Press, 1984.

Etherington, Norman. *The Great Treks: The Transformation of Southern Africa, 1815–1854*. London: Longman, 2001.

Lamar, Howard, and Leonard Thompson, eds. *The Frontier in History: North America and Southern Africa Compared*. New Haven: Yale University Press, 1981.

Landau, Paul. *The Realm of the Word: Language, Gender, and Christianity in a Southern African Kingdom*. Portsmouth, N.H.: Heinemann Press, 1995.

Marks, Shula, and Anthony Atmore, eds. *Economy and Society in Pre-industrial South Africa*. New York: Longman, 1980.

McClendon, Thomas V. *White Chief, Black Lords: Shepstone and the Colonial State in Natal, South Africa, 1845–1878*. Rochester, N.Y.: University of Rochester Press, 2010.

Mostert, Noël. *Frontiers: The Epic of South Africa's Creation and the Tragedy of the Xhosa People*. New York: Knopf, 1992.

Peires, Jeffrey. *The Dead Will Arise: Nongqawuse and the Great Xhosa Cattle-Killing Movement of 1856–7*. Johannesburg: Ravan Press, 1989.

Part IV. All That Glitters

Beinart, William. *The Political Economy of Pondoland 1860 to 1930*. Johannesburg: Ravan Press, 1982.

Beinart, William, and Colin Bundy. *Hidden Struggles in Rural South Africa: Politics and Popular Movements in the Transkei and Eastern Cape, 1890–1930*. London: J. Currey, 1987.

Bundy, Colin. *The Rise and Fall of the South African Peasantry*. London: Heinemann, 1979.

Callinicos, Luli. *Gold and Workers: 1886–1924*. Johannesburg: Ravan Press, 1981.

Carton, Benedict. *Blood from Your Children: The Colonial Origins of Generational Conflict in South Africa*. Charlottesville: University of Virginia Press, 2000.

Coplan, David B. *In the Time of Cannibals: The Word Music of South Africa's Basotho Migrants*. Chicago: University of Chicago Press, 1994.

Guy, Jeff. *The Destruction of the Zulu Kingdom: The Civil War in Zululand, 1879–1884*. London: Addison-Wesley Longman, 1979.

Harries, Patrick. *Work, Culture and Identity: Migrant Laborers in Mozambique and South Africa*. Portsmouth, N.H.: Heinemann Press, 1994.

Marks, Shula, and Richard Rathbone, eds. *Industrialisation and Social Change in South Africa: African Class Formation, Culture, and Consciousness, 1870–1930*. London: Longman, 1982.

Nasson, Bill. *The South African War: 1899–1902*. London: Arnold, 1999.

Packard, Randall M. *White Plague, Black Labor: Tuberculosis and the Political Economy of Health and Disease in South Africa*. Berkeley: University of California Press, 1989.

Redding, Sean. *Sorcery and Sovereignty: Taxation, Power, and Rebellion in South Africa, 1880–1963*. Athens: Ohio University Press, 2006.

Van Onselen, Charles. *Studies in the Social and Economic History of the Witwatersrand*. 2 vols. London: Longman, 1982.

Worger, William. *South Africa's City of Diamonds: Mine Workers and Monopoly Capitalism, 1867–1895*. New Haven: Yale University Press, 1987.

Part V. United and Divided

Abrahams, Peter. *Tell Freedom: Memories of Africa*. New York: Knopf, 1954.

Bosman, Henry Charles. *Mafeking Road: And Other Stories*. New York: Archipelago Books, 2008.

Bozzoli, Belinda, and Mmantho Nkotsoe. *Women of Phokeng: Consciousness, Life Strategy, and Migrancy in South Africa, 1900–1983*. Portsmouth, N.H.: Heinemann, 1991.

Bradford, Helen. *A Taste of Freedom: The ICU in Rural South Africa*. New Haven: Yale University Press, 1987.

Campbell, James. *Songs of Zion: The African Methodist Episcopal Church in the USA and South Africa*. New York: Oxford University Press, 1995.

Coplan, David B. *In Township Tonight: South Africa's Black City Music and Theatre*. 2nd ed. Chicago: University of Chicago Press, 2008.

Crais, Clifton C. *The Politics of Evil: Magic, State Power, and the Political Imagination in South Africa*. Cambridge: Cambridge University Press, 2002.

Dubow, Saul. *Racial Segregation and the Origins of Apartheid in South Africa, 1919–1936*. Oxford: Oxford University Press, 1989.

Giliomee, Hermann. *The Afrikaners: Biography of a People*. London: Hurst, 2003.

Krikler, Jeremy. *White Rising: The 1922 Insurrection and Racial Killing in South Africa*. Manchester, U.K.: University of Manchester Press, 2005.

La Guma, Alex. *A Walk in the Night and Other Stories*. Evanston, Ill.: Northwestern University Press, 1968.

Mamdani, Mahmood. *Citizen and Subject: Contemporary Africa and the Legacy of Late Colonialism*. Princeton: Princeton University Press, 1996.

Marks, Shula. *The Ambiguities of Dependence in South Africa: Class, Nationalism and the State in Twentieth-Century Natal*. Johannesburg: Ravan Press, 1986.

Marks, Shula, and Stanley Trapido, eds. *The Politics of Race, Class, and Nationalism in Twentieth-Century South Africa*. London: Longman, 1987.

McClendon, Thomas V. *Genders and Generations Apart: Labor Tenants and Customary Law in Segregation-Era South Africa, 1920s to 1940s*. Portsmouth, N.H.: Heinemann, 2002.

Moodie, T. Dunbar. *The Rise of Afrikanerdom: Power, Apartheid, and the Afrikaner Civil Religion*. Berkeley: University of California Press, 1975.

Moodie, Dunbar, and Vivienne Ndatshe. *Going for Gold: Men, Mines, and Migration*. Berkeley: University of California Press, 1994.

Vail, Leroy, ed. *The Creation of Tribalism in Southern Africa*. Berkeley: University of California Press, 1991.

Van Onselen, Charles. *The Seed Is Mine: The Life of Kas Maine, A South African Sharecropper*. New York: Hill and Wang, 1997.

Walker, Cherryl, ed. *Women and Gender in Southern Africa to 1945*. Cape Town: David Philip, 1990.

Willan, Brian. *Sol Plaatje: South African Nationalist, 1876–1932*. Berkeley: University of California Press, 1984.

Part VI. Apartheid and the Struggle for Freedom

Attridge, David, and Rosemary Jolly. *Writing South Africa: Literature, Apartheid, and Democracy, 1970–1995*. Cambridge: Cambridge University Press, 1998.

Brink, André. *A Dry White Season*. New York: Penguin Books, 1984.

Clark, Nancy. *Manufacturing Apartheid: State Corporations in South Africa*. New Haven: Yale University Press, 1994.

Evans, Ivan. *Bureaucracy and Race: Native Administration in South Africa*. Berkeley: University of California Press, 1997.

Fugard, Athol. *Selected Plays*. Oxford: Oxford University Press, 1987.

Gerhart, Gail. *Black Power in South Africa: The Evolution of an Ideology*. Berkeley: University of California Press, 1978.

Lee, Rebekah. *African Women and Apartheid: Migration and Settlement in Urban South Africa*. New York: Palgrave, 2009.

Lelyveld, Joseph. *Move Your Shadow: South Africa Black and White*. New York: Times Books, 1985.

Lodge, Tom. *Black Politics in South Africa since 1945*. London: Longman, 1983.

Mandela, Nelson. *Long Walk to Freedom: The Autobiography of Nelson Mandela*. Boston: Little Brown, 1994.

Marx, Anthony W. *Lessons of Struggle: South African Internal Opposition, 1960–1990*. New York: Oxford University Press, 1992.

Meli, Francis. *South Africa Belongs to Us: A History of the ANC*. London: James Currey, 1989.

Paton, Alan. *Cry, the Beloved Country*. New York: C. Scribner's Sons, 1948.

Posel, Deborah. *The Making of Apartheid*. Oxford: Oxford University Press, 1991.

Part VII. From Soweto to Liberation

Bozzoli, Belinda. *Theatres of Struggle and the End of Apartheid*. Johannesburg: Witwatersrand University Press, 2004.

Breytenbach, Breyten. *True Confessions of an Albino Terrorist*. London: Faber and Faber, 1984.

Davis, Stephen M. *Apartheid's Rebels: Inside South Africa's Hidden War*. New Haven: Yale University Press, 1987.

Gordimer, Nadine. *Burger's Daughter*. New York: Penguin Books, 1980.

Greenberg, Stanley B. *Legitimating the Illegitimate: State, Markets, and Resistance in South Africa*. Berkeley: University of California Press, 1987.

Magaziner, Daniel R. *The Law and the Prophets: Black Consciousness in South Africa, 1968–1977*. Athens: Ohio University Press, 2010.

Mandela, Winnie. *Part of My Soul Went with Him*. New York: W. W. Norton, 1985.

Mathabane, Mark. *Kaffir Boy: The True Story of a Black Youth's Coming of Age in Apartheid South Africa*. New York: MacMillan Press, 1986.

Murray, Martin. *South Africa: Time of Agony, Time of Destiny*. London: Verso, 1987.

Platzky, Laurine, and Cherryl Walker. *The Surplus People: Forced Removals in South Africa*. Johannesburg: Ravan Press, 1985.

Sachs, Albie. *The Soft Vengeance of a Freedom Fighter*. Berkeley: University of California Press, 2000.

Seekings, Jeremy. *The UDF: A History of the United Democratic Front*. Cape Town: David Philip, 2000.

Serote, Mongane Wally. *To Every Birth Its Blood*. Johannesburg: Witwatersrand University Press, 1981.

Sparks, Allister. *Tomorrow Is a Different Country: The Inside Story of South Africa's Road to Change*. New York: Hill and Wang, 1995.

Suttner, Raymond, and Jeremy Cronin. *30 Years of the Freedom Charter*. Johannesburg: Ravan Press, 1986.

Part VIII. Transitions and Reconciliations

Ashforth, Adam. *Witchcraft, Violence, and Democracy in South Africa*. Chicago: University of Chicago Press, 2005.

Coetzee, J. M. *Disgrace*. New York: Penguin Books, 1999.

Cole, Catherine M. *Performing South Africa's Truth Commission*. Bloomington: Indiana University Press, 2010.

Coombes, Annie. *History after Apartheid: Visual Culture and Public Memory in a Democratic South Africa*. Durham, N.C.: Duke University Press, 2003.

Donham, Donald L. *Violence in a Time of Liberation: Murder and Ethnicity at a South African Gold Mine, 1994*. Durham, N.C.: Duke University Press, 2011.

Krog, Antjie. *Country of My Skull: Guilt, Sorrow, and the Limits of Forgiveness in the New South Africa*. New York: Random House, 1998.

Mhlongo, Niq. *Dog Eat Dog*. Athens: Ohio University Press, 2012.

Murray, Martin. *The Revolution Deferred: The Painful Birth of Post-apartheid South Africa*. London: Verso, 1994.

Ntsebeza, Lungisile. *Democracy Compromised: Chiefs and the Politics of Land in South Africa*. Leiden, the Netherlands: Brill, 2005.

Nuttall, Sarah, and Carli Coetzee, eds. *Negotiating the Past: The Making of Memory in South Africa*. Cape Town: Oxford University Press, 1998.

Steinberg, Jonny. *Sizwe's Test: A Young Man's Journey through Africa's AIDS Epidemic.* New York: Simon and Schuster, 2008.

Wilson, Frances, and Mamphela Ramphele. *Uprooting Poverty: The South African Challenge.* New York: W. W. Norton, 1989.

Wilson, Richard A. *The Politics of Truth and Reconciliation in South Africa: Legitimizing the Post-apartheid State.* Cambridge: Cambridge University Press, 2001

South Africa Websites

The current ruling party has a website that also provides background information on the African National Congress: http://www.anc.org.za/.

The Government of South Africa's website: http://www.gov.za/.

The Parliament of the Republic of South Africa's website: www.parliament.gov.za.

Two of the most helpful sites on South African history and politics are the South Arica History Archive, http://www.saha.org.za/, and South African History Online, http://www.sahistory.org.za/.

A list of South African newspapers online: http://www.onlinenewspapers.com/sa.htm.

StatsOnline provides up-to-date information on the country's economy: http://www.statssa.gov.za/.

The Human Sciences Research Council (South Africa) website provides access to research on topics ranging from HIV/AIDS to governance: http://www.hsrc.ac.za/.

Acknowledgment of Copyrights and Sources

Part I. African Worlds, African Voices

"A Story Is Like the Wind," by //Kabbo, from *Specimens of Bushman Folklore*, by W. H. I. Bleek and Lucy C. Lloyd, translated by W. H. I. Bleek and L. C. Lloyd c. 1886 (London: G. Allen & Co., 1911), 290–316.

"The Sun Is Thrown into the Sky," by //Kabbo, from *Specimens of Bushman Folklore*, by W. H. I. Bleek and Lucy C. Lloyd, translated by W. H. I. Bleek and L. C. Lloyd c. 1886 (London: G. Allen & Co., 1911), 44–56.

"On God and Ancestors," by Ndukwana ka Mbenwana, from *The James Stuart Archive of Recorded Oral Evidence Relating to the History of the Zulu and Neighboring Peoples*, vol. 4, part 3, edited and translated by C. de B. Webb and J. B. Wright (Pietermaritzburg: University of Natal Press, 1979), 302–4. Used by permission of UKZN Press.

"The Black People and Whence They Came," by Magema M. Fuze, from *The Black People and Whence They Came: A Zulu View*, translated by H. C. Lugg, edited by A. T. Cope (Pietermaritzburg: University of Natal Press, 1979), 42–59. Used by permission of UKZN Press.

"Mhudi," by Solomon T. Plaatje, from *Mhudi: An Epic of South African Life a Hundred Years Ago* (Lovedale: Lovedale Press, 1930), 1–37.

Part II. Colonial Settlement, Slavery, and Peonage

"An African Woman at the Cape: Krotoa (c. 1642–74)," by Julia C. Wells, from "Eva's Men: Gender and Power in the Establishment of the Cape of Good Hope, 1652–74," *Journal of African History* 39: 3 (1998): 417–37. Copyright © 1998 Cambridge University Press. Reprinted with the permission of Cambridge University Press.

"The Necessity of Slavery," from "The Necessity of Slavery: The Replies of W. S. van Ryneveld to Governor Macartney's Questionnaire, 29 November 1797," in *Afrikaner Political Thought: Analysis and Documents, v.1: 1780–1850*, edited by André du Toit and Hermann Giliomee (Berkeley: University of California Press, 1983), 46–49 (abridged). © 1983 by André du Toit and Hermann Giliomee. Used by permission of University of California Press.

"A Rebel Slave," from "The Trial of Galant and Others," in *Records of the Cape Colony from February 1793 to April 1831* (London: Printed for the Government of Cape Colony, 1897–1905), 188–341.

"Unconfessed," by Yvette Christiansë, from *Unconfessed* (New York: Other Press, 2006), 155–65. Reprinted by permission of Other Press, LLC.

"Bobotie Recipe," adapted from traditional South African recipes by Clifton Crais. © 2013.

"The Subjugation of the Eastern Cape Khoekhoe," by John Barrow, from *An Account of Travels into the Interior of Southern Africa in the Years 1797 and 1798* (London, 1801), 110, 143–47.

"The Treatment of Indentured Laborers," by R. J. van der Riet, from "Letter from Landdrost R. J. van der Riet of Stellenbosch to Fiscal J. A. Truter, 1 April 1810," Cape Archives, St. 1129.

"Protesting the Vagrancy Ordinance," from "From a Public Meeting Held at Philipton, Kat River, 5 August 1834," Cape Archives ACC 50.

"Manifesto," by Piet Retief, *The Grahamstown Journal*, 2 February 1837.

"The History of the Afrikaans People," by C. P. Bezuidenhout, from *The History of the Afrikaans Speaking People*, translated by Maureen Rall (Bloemfontein: The Orange Free State Newspaper Company, 1883), 1–44.

"Biltong Recipe," adapted from traditional South African recipes by Clifton Crais. © 2013.

Part III. Frontiers

"Among the Xhosa in 1800," by Johannes Theodorus van der Kemp, from the London Missionary Society, *Transactions of the Missionary Society, Vol. 1, 2nd Edition* (London: Bye and Law, 1804), 421–27.

"The Problem of God," by Robert Moffat, from *Missionary Labours and Scenes in Southern Africa, 6th Edition* (New York: Robert Carter, 1844), 176–83.

"Visit to a Mission Community in Natal," by John William Colenso, from *Ten Weeks in Natal* (Cambridge: MacMillan & Co., 1855), 50–62.

"Nkosi Sikelel' iAfrika (God Bless Africa)," from "Nkosi Sikelel' iAfrica," composition by Enoch Sontonga (Johannesburg, 1897), lyrics by Samuel E. Mqhayi (1927).

"Dingane's Killing of Retief," by Rev. F. Owen, from *The Annals of Natal: 1495–1845. Vol. 1.*, edited by John Bird (Cape Town: C. Struik, 1965 [1888]), 346–47.

"Mpande Seeks an Alliance with the Boers in Natal," from *The Annals of Natal: 1495–1845. Vol. 1*, edited by John Bird (Cape Town: C. Struik, 1965 [1888]), 536–39.

"Statement of the Prophetess Nonkosi, 23rd October 1857," from Cape Archives, BK 81, 23 October 1857.

"Heart of Redness," by Zakes Mda, from *The Heart of Redness* (New York: Farrar, Straus and Giroux, 2000), 14–24. Excerpt from *The Heart of Redness* by Zakes Mda. Copyright © 2000 by Zakes Mda. Reprinted by permission of Farrar, Straus and Giroux, LLC and Oxford University Press.

Part IV. All That Glitters

"The Story of the Diamond Fields," from Anthony Trollope, *South Africa: Volume II* (London: Chapman and Hall, 1878), 353–78.

Part V. United and Divided

by permission of University of Chicago Press, Wits University Press, and David Coplan.

"Women's Labour," by Olive Schreiner, from *Woman and Labour* (Cape of Good Hope, South Africa: De Aar, 1911).

"Workers of the World, Unite and Fight for a White South Africa," by William Urquhart, from *The Outbreak on the Witwatersrand* (Cape Town: Hortors Limited, 1922), 16–38.

"The Persecution of Indians," by Mohandas K. Gandhi, from *An Autobiography: The Story of My Experiments with Truth* (Boston: Beacon Press, 1957), 111–17, 128–31, 148–58. Reprinted with permission of Navajivan Trust.

"The Journey to Pretoria," by Naboth Mokgatle, from *The Autobiography of an Unknown South African* (Berkeley: University of California Press, 1971), 171–81. Republished with permission of University of California Press; permission conveyed through Copyright Clearance Center, Inc.

"Township Life, Marabastad, Pretoria," by Es'kia Mphahlele, excerpted from *Down Second Avenue* (London: Faber and Faber, 1959), 34–40, 88–101. © Ezekiel Mphahlele, 1959. Reprinted by permission of the Es'kia Institute.

"Everyday Life in Soweto: The Photography of Santu Mofokeng," by Patricia Hayes. Written exclusively for *The South Africa Reader*. © 2013.

Part VI. Apartheid and the Struggle for Freedom

"Requiem for Sophiatown," by Can Themba, excerpted from "The Suit," in *Requiem for Sophiatown* (London: Penguin Books, 2006), 49–51. © The Estate of Can Themba. Reproduced by permission of Penguin Books (South Africa) (Pty) Ltd.

"Mr. Drum Goes to Jail," by Henry Nxumalo, from Michael Chapman, ed., *The "Drum" Decade: Stories from the 1950s* (Pietermaritzburg: University of Natal Press, 1989), 39–47. Used by permission of UKZN Press.

"Repeal the Pass Laws!," by ANC Women's League and the Federation of South African Women, from "The Demand of the Women of South Africa for the Withdrawal of Passes for Women and the Repeal of the Pass Laws," August 9, 1956, accessed May 23, 2012, http://www.anc.org.za/show.php?id=2583&t=ES.

"Programme of Action," by ANC Youth League, from "Programme of Action: Statement of Policy Adopted at the ANC Annual Conference," December 17, 1949, accessed May 23, 2012, http://anc.org.za/show.php?id=4472.

"Women's Charter," by the Federation of South African Women, from "Women's Charter," Johannesburg, April 17, 1954, accessed May 23, 2012, http://www.anc.org .za/show.php?id=4666.

"My Spirit Is Not Banned," by Frances Baard and Barbie Schreiner, from *My Spirit Is Not Banned* (Harare: African Publishing Group, 1986), 22–49. Reprinted by permission of the African Publishing Group.

"Freedom Charter," by the Congress of the People, from "The Freedom Charter," Kliptown, June 26, 1955, accessed May 23, 2012, http://www.anc.org.za/show .php?id=72.

"The Manifesto of Paramount Chief K. D. Matanzima, 1963," by K. D. Matanzima, from "The Independent Transkei: The Manifesto of Paramount Chief K. D. Matanzima," 1963, 385–87.

"The Peasants' Revolt," by Govan Mbeki, from *South Africa: The Peasants' Revolt* (Baltimore, MD: Penguin Books, 1964), 15–18. Used by permission of Dumisani S. Kumalo on behalf of the heirs.

"The Discarded People," by Father Cosmas Desmond, from *The Discarded People: An Account of African Resettlement in South Africa* (New York: Penguin Books, 1971), 172–73. © Cosmas Desmond, 1971. Used by permission of Penguin Books.

"The Pan Africanist Congress," by Robert Sobukwe, excerpted from "Opening Address" at the Launch of the Pan-Africanist Congress, April 6, 1959, accessed June 5, 2012, http://www.africaspeaks.com/reasoning/index.php?topic=7130.0.

"Statement from the Dock," by Nelson Mandela, from "Nelson Mandela's Statement from the Dock at the Opening of the Defence Case in the Rivonia Trial," April 20, 1964, accessed May 23, 2012, http://www.anc.org.za/show.php?id=3430.

Part VII. From Soweto to Liberation

"White Racism and Black Consciousness," by Steve Biko, from *Student Perspectives on South Africa*, edited by Henrik W. van der Merwe and David Welsh (Cape Town: David Philip, 1972). Reprinted by permission of David Philip Publishers, an imprint of New Africa Books.

"Reporting from Soweto, 17 June 1976," from "Police Fired—Then I Saw Four Children Fall," by Nat Serache, and "I Saw Death at the Hands of Child Power," by Derrick Thema, *Rand Daily Mail*, June 17, 1976. Reprinted by permission of AVUSA.

"Students and the Soweto Uprising," press release by Khotso Seatlholo, chairman of the Soweto Students Representative Council, October 15, 1976, in Thomas G. Karis and Gail M. Gerhart, *From Protest to Challenge: A Documentary History of African Politics in South Africa, 1882–1990. Volume 5: Nadir and Resurgence, 1964–1979* (Bloomington and Indianapolis: Indiana University Press, 1997), 585–91. © 1997 Thomas G. Karis and Gail M. Gerhart. Reprinted with permission of Indiana University Press.

"The United Democratic Front," by Allan Boesak, from *If This Is Treason, I Am Guilty*, Allan Boesak (Grand Rapids, MI: W. B. Eerdmans Pub. Co., 1987), 36–43. Reprinted by permission of the author.

"Sanctions and the Armed Struggle," by Oliver Tambo, from "Victory Is within Our Grasp," June 16, 1986, accessed May 22, 2012, http://www.anc.org.za/show.php?id=4484.

"The Church and the Struggle," by Archbishop Desmond Tutu, from "A Nobel Prize," December 11, 1984, accessed March 10, 2012, www.nobelprize.org/nobel_prizes/peace/laureates/1984/tutu-lecture.html. © The Nobel Foundation 1984. Used by permission of The Nobel Foundation.

"Crossing the Rubicon," by P. W. Botha, August 15, 1985, accessed March 10, 2012, http://www.nelsonmandela.org/omalley/index.php/site/q/03lv01538/04lv01600/05lv01638/06lv01639.htm.

"Never Give In," by Andries Treurnicht, from "It's Time for a Change," from *Treurnicht Praat*, translated by P. Van der Kooi (Pretoria: The Conservative Party of South Africa, 1992), 73–75.

"The Future of South Africa," by Mangosuthu G. Buthelezi, previously published as "The Future of South Africa: Violent Radicalism or Negotiated Settlement," in *Vital Speeches of the Day*, LIII, no. 7, January 15, 1987 (City News Publishing Co.), 194–96. Used by permission of The Heritage Foundation.

"Violent Times," from Emma Mashinini, *Strikes Have Followed Me All My Life: A South African Autobiography* (London: Women's Press, 1989), 119–26.

"The Funeral of ANC Guerrilla Thanduxolo Mbethe," from "Funeral of ANC Guerrilla Thanduxolo Mbethe, Uitenhage, March 14, 1986," in *From Protest to Challenge: A Documentary History of African Politics in South Africa, 1882–1990, Vol. 6*, edited by Gail Gerhart and Clive Glaser (Bloomington: Indiana University Press, 2010), 422–29. Copyright © 2010 Gail Gerhart and Clive Glaser. Reprinted with permission of Indiana University Press.

"Struggle Songs," by Alton B. Pollard III, from "Rhythms of Resistance: The Role of Freedom Song in South Africa," in *This Is How We Flow: Rhythm in Black Cultures*, edited by Angela M. S. Nelson (Columbia: University of South Carolina Press, 1999), 98–124. Reprinted by permission of University of South Carolina Press.

"'Reforms' and Revolution in South Africa," from Joe Slovo, "'Reforms' and Revolution in South Africa," August 24, 1984, accessed March 10, 2012, http://www.sacp.org.za/people/slovo/ruth.html.

"Politics and Violence," by Rian Malan, from *My Traitor's Heart: A South African Exile Returns to Face His Country, His Tribe, and His Conscience* (New York: Grove Press, 1990), 268–76. Also published as *My Traitor's Heart: Blood and Bad Dreams: A South African Explores the Madness in His Country, His Tribe and Himself* (New York: Vintage Books, 1991). Copyright © 1990 Rian Malan. Reprinted by permission of Grove / Atlantic, Inc., and The Random House Group, Ltd.

"Preparing Ourselves for Freedom," by Albie Sachs, from "Preparing Ourselves for Freedom: Culture and the ANC Constitutional Guidelines," in *TDR* 35: 1 (Spring 1991): 187–93. Reprinted by permission of the author.

"Release from Prison," from "Nelson Mandela's Address to a Rally in Cape Town on His Release from Prison," by Nelson Mandela, February 11, 1990, accessed August 1, 2011, http://www.anc.org.za/show.php?id=4520.

"White Referendum," from "The Result of the Referendum," by F. W. de Klerk, March 18, 1992, accessed May 22, 2012, http://www.givengain.com/cgi-bin/giga.cgi?cmd=cause_dir_news_item&cause_id=2137&news_id=73753&cat_id=1595.

"Record of Understanding," by F. W. de Klerk and Nelson Mandela, September 26, 1992, accessed March 10, 2012, http://www.nelsonmandela.org/omalley/index.php/site/q/03lv02039/04lv02046/05lv02092/06lv02096.htm.

"Inaugural Address," by Nelson Mandela, May 10, 1994, accessed June 5, 2012, http://www.info.gov.za/speeches/1994/990319514p1007.htm.

Part VIII. Transitions and Reconciliations

"I Am an African," by Thabo Mbeki, May 8, 1996, accessed March 10, 2012, http://www.info.gov.za/speeches/1996/960819_23196.htm.

"Mass Struggle, Negotiations, and the 1994 Elections," from Alex Callinicos, "South Africa after Apartheid," *International Socialism* 70 (1996): 3–46. Reprinted by permission of the author.

"The Rape of Women," by Antjie Krog, from *Country of My Skull: Guilt, Sorrow, and the Limits of Forgiveness in the New South Africa* (New York: Times Books, 1998), 238–42. Copyright © 1998 by Antjie Samuel; introduction copyright © 1999 by Charlayne Hunter-Gault. Used by permission of Times Books, a division of Random House, Inc., and The Marsh Agency Ltd.

"The Cradock Four," from the South African Truth and Reconciliation Commission, Human Rights Violations Submissions—Questions and Answers, Nomonde Calata, April 16, 1996, accessed March 2, 2012, http://www.justice.gov.za/trc/hrvtrans/hrvel1/calata.htm.

"Amnesty or Impunity?," by Mahmood Mamdani, originally published as "Amnesty or Impunity? A Preliminary Critique of the Report of the Truth and Reconciliation Commission of South Africa (TRC)," *Diacritics* 32: 3–4 (2002): 33–34, 57–58. © 2005 The Johns Hopkins University Press. Reprinted with permission of The Johns Hopkins University Press.

"Repeal the Black Authorities Act," from "Submission of the Rural People's Movement to Parliament: Repeal of the Black Authorities Act," July 2010, accessed May 23, 2012, http://d2zmx6mlqh7g3a.cloudfront.net/cdn/farfuture/DRez4ovobf-cyP5rmjBZ9UjsXtCaeqhuQMKkvVKUL9A/mtime:1279797204/files/docs/100720rpm_0.pdf.

"The Myth of Timeless Africa in the Game Parks," by Shirley Brooks, from "Rereading the Hluhluwe-Umfolozi Game Reserve: Constructions of a 'Natural' Space," *Transformation* 44 (2000): 63–79. Reprinted by permission of the author.

"AIDS and Poverty," speech of the president of South Africa at the opening session of the 13th International AIDS Conference, Durban, South Africa, Office of the Presidency, 9 July 2000, accessed 10 March 2012, http://www.virusmyth.com/aids/news/durbspmbeki.htm.

"Global Day of Action," from Treatment Action Campaign, "TAC Calls for a Global Day of Action," 24 August 2006, accessed 10 March 2012, www.tac.org.za/GDOA%20Docs/Leaflet.pdf.

"Zuma's Rape Trial," by Steven Robins, originally published as "Sexual Politics and the Zuma Rape Trial," *Journal of Southern African Studies* 34, no. 2 (June 2008): 411–27. Reprinted by permission of Taylor & Francis Ltd, http://www.tandfonline.com.

"Lessons Learned," by Bafana Khumalo and Dean Peacock, codirectors, Sonke Gender Justice Project, originally published as "Zuma Won but the Nation Lost," *The Johannesburg Star*, May 10, 2006. Reprinted by permission of the authors.

"Murder of Noxola Nogwaza," by Sokari, Ekurhuleni Pride Organizing Committee (EPOC), originally published as "24 Yr Old Lesbian, Noxola Nogwaza Found Raped and Murdered in Gauteng," April 27, 2011, accessed July 30, 2011, http://

Index

abolition, 34, 46, 49, 71, 75. *See also* peonage; slavery

Act of Union (1910). 197. *See also* Union of South Africa

African National Congress (ANC): early history of, 26, 100, 199, 201, 204, 211, 244, 281; elections and, 540; Freedom Charter and, 320–24; Nelson Mandela and, 345–55, 460–64, 470–72; negotiations ending apartheid and, 465, 467–69, 481–89; Pan Africanist Congress and, 339; Programme of Action and, 301–4. *See also* African National Congress Women's League; African National Congress Youth League; armed struggle; Mandela, Nelson; Umkhonto we Sizwe (Spear of the Nation, MK)

African National Congress Women's League, 298, 300, 314. *See also* African National Congress (ANC)

African National Congress Youth League, 282, 301–4, 320, 339, 443, 526, 561, 563. *See also* African National Congress (ANC)

Afrikaans, 5, 7, 26, 33, 55, 78, 83, 160–68, 207, 296, 371–74, 379, 382, 498

Afrikaner Bond, 160, 162, 169

Afrikaners, 5, 34, 78–83, 160–95, 198, 226, 291, 407, 540, 559, 570. *See also* Afrikaans

Afrikaner Weerstandsbeweging (AWB), 486–87

amalaita gangs, 248

ancestors, 10, 17, 19, 88, 98, 111, 114, 119, 557–58

Anglo-American Corporation, 124

Anglo-Boer War. *See* South African War (1899–1902)

Anglo-Zulu War (1879), 141, 510

apartheid: final years of, 357–59, 384–98, 401, 407, 410–15, 417–18, 420–24, 436–41, 465–67; history of, 2–6, 10, 34; policies of, 289, 293, 298; segregation and, 199–200, 240, 248; separate development and, 329–35; Soweto Uprising and, 371, 376, 379–81. *See also individual acts*; grand apartheid; National Party (NP); petty apartheid; segregation

armed struggle, 283, 345, 358, 391, 393–96, 410, 413, 424, 433, 436, 442, 460–62. *See also* Umkhonto we Sizwe (Spear of the Nation, MK)

Azanian People's Organization (AZAPO), 446–48

banning, 283, 298, 320, 325, 339, 348, 367, 385, 398–99, 430

Bantu Authorities Act (1951), 280, 327, 329, 505

Bantu Education Act (1953), 331–33, 343, 348, 387, 395–96, 413, 443

Bantu Self Government Act (1959), 325

Bantustans, 3–5, 197, 261, 279–80, 329, 331, 335, 359, 401, 403, 438–40, 486, 505. *See also* apartheid; Bophuthatswana; Ciskei; grand apartheid; KwaZulu-Natal; Transkei

Bapedi, 29

Barolong, 26–27, 29, 31, 82, 192–94

Basotho (Sotho), 83, 87, 122. *See also* Lesotho

Basutoland. *See* Lesotho

Bechuana (Tswana), 5, 27, 29, 92, 94, 96, 202, 324. *See also* Botswana

Bechuanaland. *See* Botswana